Marketing research

Sixth edition

Marketing research

Sixth edition

PETER CHISNALL

THE McGRAW-HILL COMPANIES

LONDON • BURR RIDGE IL • NEW YORK • ST LOUIS • SAN FRANCISCO • AUCKLAND
BOGOTÁ • CARACAS • LISBON • MADRID • MEXICO • MILAN • MONTREAL • NEW DELHI
PANAMA • PARIS • SAN JUAN • SÃO PAULO • SINGAPORE • SYDNEY • TOKYO • TORONTO

Published by
McGraw-Hill Publishing Company
Shoppenhangers Road, Maidenhead, Berkshire, SL6 2QL, England
Telephone +44 (0)01628 502500
Facsimile +44 (0)01628 770224
Website: www.mcgraw-hill.co.uk/textbooks/chisnall

British Library Cataloguing in Publication Data
A catalogue record for this book is available from the British Library

Library of Congress Cataloging-in-publication Data
The LOC data for this book has been applied for and may be obtained from
the Library of Congress, Wasshington, DC.

ISBN 007709751 3

Publisher	Andy Goss
Sponsoring Editor	Tim Page
Editorial Assistant	Nicola Wimpory
Marketing Manager	Petra Skytte
Production Editorial Manager	Penny Grose
Desk Editor	Alastair Lindsay

McGraw-Hill

A Division of The *McGraw-Hill* Companies

Designed by Claire Brodman Book Designs, Lichfield
Cover by opta design consultants
Printed and bound by Mateu Cromo Artes Graficas, Madrid

Sixth edition 2001

1 2 3 4 5 MC 5 4 3 2 1

BRIEF TABLE OF CONTENTS

Each chapter ends with a summary and review and discussion questions

CONTENTS

Now in its sixth edition, this classic Marketing Research text has been fundamentally redesigned and updated, continuing to meet the needs of undergraduate, postgraduate and professional students, as well as practitioners seeking a comprehensive knowledge of and insight into the theories and applications of marketing research.

The text is organized in four parts, covering firstly the evolution of marketing research, followed by the basic methodologies and finally the specific applications:

(i) General introduction

(ii) Basic techniques

(iii) Specific research applications

(iv) Data handling and interpretation

Taking a more student-friendly qualitative approach to marketing research, much of the heavy statistical data from the previous edition has been removed and replaced with further details of statistical software packages.

Pedagogically strengthened, this sixth edition now includes opening chapter learning objectives, integrated 'key points' boxes, chapter summaries, and chapter-end review and discussion questions. To further highlight the practical aspects of marketing research, six new cameo case studies have been integrated into the text. To assist you in working through this text, we have developed a number of distinctive study and design features. To familiarize yourself with the features, please turn to the Guided Tour on pages xiv–xv.

Six longer case studies have been placed at the end of the text. These look at marketing research within service industries, communities, and companies and highlight a diverse range of marketing research problems and solutions.

New to this edition

In addition to the enhanced pedagogical features, and the integrated and text-end case material, outlined above, this edition also includes the following new or revised coverage:

- Details of the Office of National Statistics (ONS) new category of socio-economic classification
- The latest developments of telephone research methodologies
- The meteoric growth of the Internet and its relevance to marketing research
- Current trends of qualitative research, panel research and store audits
- Life-style research and its developments in the UK and elsewhere within advertising research
- The latest geo-demographic methodologies are presented, and detailed examples of leading systems such as ACORN and MOSAIC are given.

- The chapter on test marketing has been augmented by considering the role of innovation in successful business development – simulated test marketing techniques are identified and assessed.

- The business to business research chapter subsumes former chapters dealing with industrial and also service marketing research, and provides a comprehensive and integrated examination of the research needs of modern economies.

- Extended coverage has been given to the many facets of international marketing research, including the vital need to study cultural influences on consumption.

- The topics of data fusion, database marketing and ethical constraints in marketing research have all been brought together in the last chapter covering the final stages of marketing research.

Finally to make this text more visually appealing a new two-colour open text design has been added.

PETER CHISNALL

TEACHING AND LEARNING RESOURCES

For this new edition we have provided a new range of on-line resources including: Teaching Notes and PowerPoint Slides to support lecturers in their teaching of Marketing Research. Please visit the text's website at **www.mcgraw-hill.co.uk/textbooks/chisnall** to gain access to these resources.

GUIDED TOUR

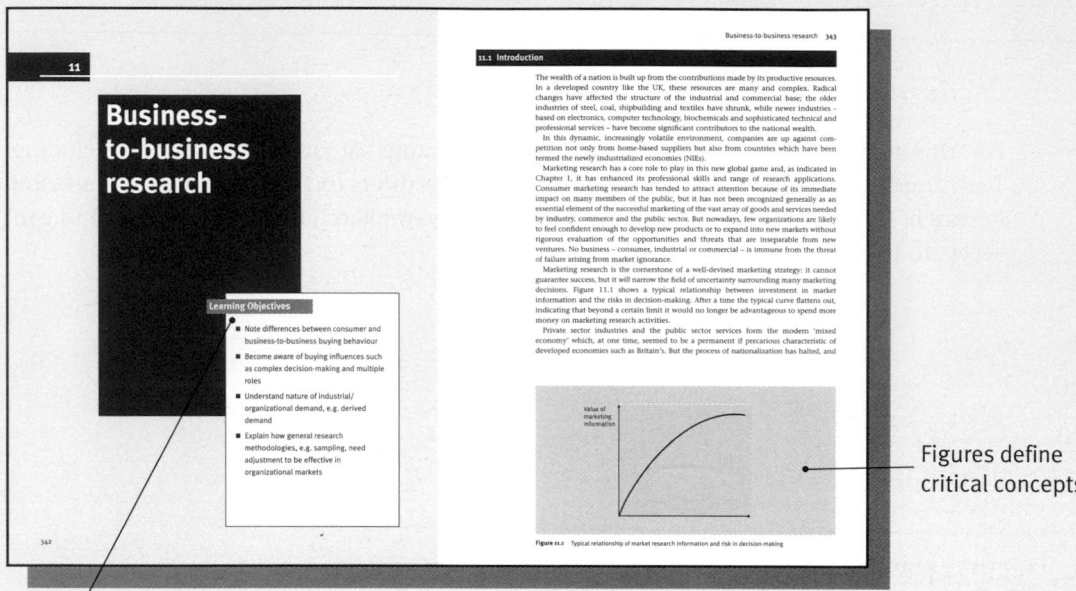

Figures define
critical concepts

Learning objectives identify the key topics
in terms of the learning outcomes you
should acquire after studying each chapter.

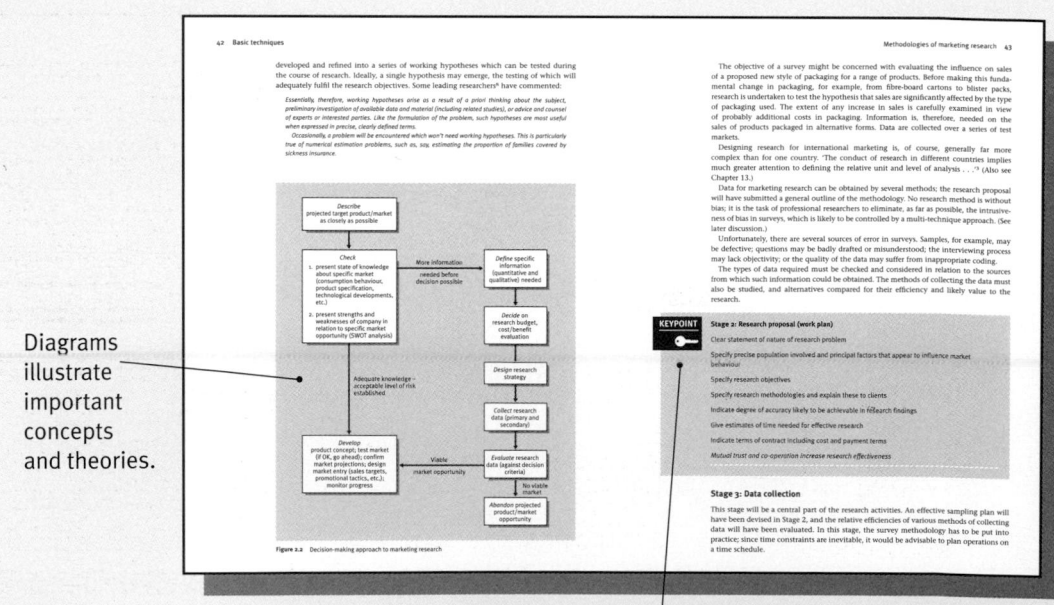

Diagrams
illustrate
important
concepts
and theories.

Key points boxes effectively summarize
critical aspects of the text, offering a
readily accessible method of revision.

Tables are colour highlighted
to show key statistical data.

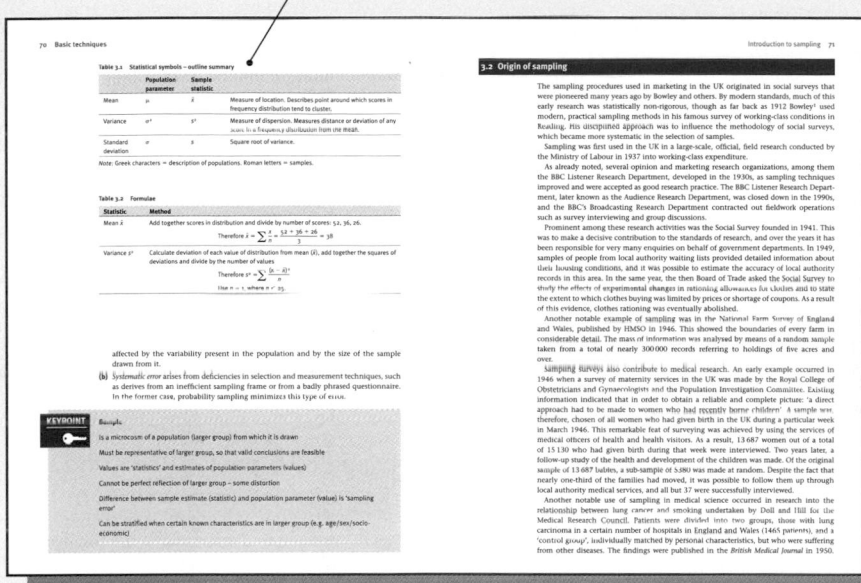

Review and discussion questions
help to check and reinforce
understanding of the chapter.

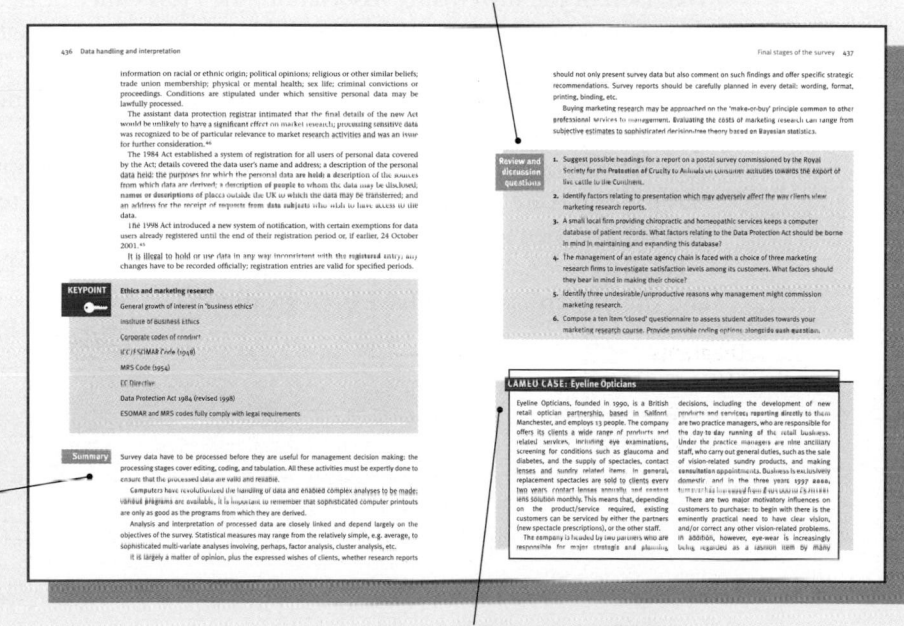

Summaries briefly
review the main
topics covered in
each chapter.

Cameo case studies
highlight the practical
aspects of marketing
research.

ACKNOWLEDGEMENTS

We would like to thank the following university experts who took the time and effort to take part in the market research. They have added enormously to the development of this text.

Geraldine Clarke – London Guildhall
Chris Vaughan-Jones – De Montfort
Bob McClelland – Liverpool John Moores
Teresa Smallbone – Oxford Brookes
Lyndon Simkin – Warwick

I would also like to thank the Market Research Society and NTC publications who have generously given permissions for the use of case material generated from articles in their publications.

In addition, I am again grateful to all of those leading market researchers who have provided extensive and up-to-date information about their specialized services. In particular I list, in random order, the following: Moira Bagnall and Colin Brown of AC Nielsen, Chris Goard of TNS, Daniel Jarrold of BMRB International, Michael Roe of Research International, Simon McDonald of IPSOS-RSL, Roger Pratt of NRS, Mike Waterson of the Advertising Association, the Press Office of ONS, John Rae of CACI, Sara Pearce of Experian (MOSAIC), Camilla Lister of Granada Media Sales, Boris Jacquin of TSMS Group, and Peter Jenkins of RAJAR.

The revision questions at the end of each chapter were kindly devised by Dr Darach Turley, and for which I warmly thank him.

Dr Jonathan Swift has contributed the cameo cases which appear throughout this new edition; these are particularly valuable because they feature real-life business situations which have been researched by him.

Finally I must also thank Tim Page and his colleagues at McGraw-Hill, whose expertise and friendly co-operation have been greatly valued by me.

1

General introduction

Nature and scope of marketing research

Learning Objectives

- Gain knowledge of critical facets of marketing management
- Understand role and responsibilities of marketing research
- Gain insights into sources of marketing research theory and practice
- Understand need for all managerial specialisms to work closely together

1.1 Introduction

At one time, businesses were small, customers were few, and markets were mostly local. Suppliers and customers were in almost daily, close personal contact; bargaining was done face-to-face; the market place was the hub of economic and social life.

Businesses were run not by corporate executives but by people who were similar to those whose custom they sought to attract. They shared the same culture – often they were kinsfolk – and communication was direct and resonant with cultural values.

With large-scale industrialization and vastly improved methods of transport and communication, entrepreneurs looked further afield for customers to buy their products. Today, technologies are dispersed over the world; new centres of production have been set up for motor cars, electronic equipment, and many other products that were once viewed as the prerogative of the Western developed countries.

Inevitably, the gap between producer and final consumer has widened: some firms are in danger of losing touch with the actual needs of their customers, particularly if they are thousands of miles away.

KEYPOINT

Traditionally, small firms have close links with their customers

Large-scale operations have widened gap between producers and consumers of their products

Modern communities are knowledgeable, experienced and critical

The management of the commercial, industrial, and many other kinds of organization which make up the mixed and advanced economies of countries like Britain seems to grow increasingly difficult as each year passes. Without valid and reliable information, management decision making would soon degenerate into some crazy game of chance. Hence, a systematic approach to the task of management is increasingly important in today's complex environment. One of the prime functions of management is to make decisions; marketing decisions are peculiarly difficult to make and their effects are felt throughout a business and, indeed, entire industries, as in the case of the British motor cycle industry whose products were once world-famous and are now no more.

Good information is the raw material used by management in deciding a company's policy and day-to-day operations. As the widely read text[1] *In Search of Excellence* showed, keeping 'close to customers', one of the critical factors identified during research, helped to make the American companies surveyed outstandingly successful over many years.

Marketing as a separate business, identifiable, management function evolved from the business philosophy that recognized the importance of the customer; to be successful in the new competitive atmosphere, the needs of the customer had to be satisfied. This re-orientation of business activities demanded a more analytical and systematic approach, founded on an assessment of customer requirements, with the objective of maximizing net profits by providing customers with products and services that really fulfilled their particular needs.

As already observed, marketing problems tend to become more complex with the growth of sophisticated business organizations, whose customers are becoming increasingly demanding of their suppliers.

It is sound business practice that marketing policies should be founded on carefully planned research; this is possible only by applying the systematic approach of research methodology used in other areas of investigation.

Today management decisions frequently carry considerable risks, and it is clearly prudent for management to do everything possible to minimize these. To survive, every organization has to be able to offer acceptable goods and services which satisfy the identified needs of specific kinds of people, industries, and firms. As Drucker[2] observed 40 years ago: 'Whatever a manager does he does through making decisions . . . management is always a decision-making process. . . . The important and difficult job is never to find the right answer, it is to find the right question.' He goes on to say that management is essentially concerned with performance, not with accumulating knowledge for its own sake.

KEYPOINT

Marketing is a necessary but not sufficient condition for success in competitive environments

Management decisions necessarily involve risk

Knowledge about customers and their needs is essential for successful decision making

Systematic, objective information confers competitive advantage

1.2 Critical facets of marketing management

In common with their colleagues in other functional areas of management, marketing managers have four specific responsibilities. These tend to overlap in real life but are distinguished here for purposes of discussion.

1. Analysis
2. Planning
3. Control
4. Implementation

Analysis

The first function of marketing management relates to finding out about markets in which a company operates at present or which it is planning to enter. Without valid and reliable data, marketing cannot be successful. Through systematic marketing research, present and emergent needs will be identified, analysed and evaluated. This evaluation will cover both quantitative and qualitative assessments related to specific markets and special segments judged to be of value to the business. The interpretation of market needs carries heavy responsibility; it demands, among other managerial qualities, the ability to assess risk and to cope with uncertainty.

Marketing decisions are peculiarly difficult to make; there are so many factors in the environment, such as the level of competitive activity or the effect of fiscal policies, which are almost entirely outside the control of the marketer. The marketing manager is expected to possess entrepreneurial flair and judgement without which he or she is unlikely to be successful. To rely solely on inspiration would, of course, be totally inadequate;

professional marketing calls for a blend of analytical and creative skills, especially in the highly competitive conditions which characterize most markets today.

Planning

The second facet of marketing management – planning – follows logically from the analytical approach which, in particular, characterizes professional marketing. Strategic planning involves choosing markets, developing products and services, devising attractive and effective marketing strategies, organizing marketing resources and forecasting levels of demand. These are certainly far-reaching responsibilities which demand expertise of a high order.

The success of many industrial firms rests in the ingenuity of their design and marketing staff in offering feasible solutions to the problems of their customers. By collaborating closely with customers in solving, for example, production bottle-necks, suppliers can build up a store of goodwill which will stand them in good stead in competitive markets.

Technological change and planned obsolescence have intruded into industrial markets. It is no longer safe for industrial product manufacturers to assume that the environment in which they seek business is immune from the instability and dynamic activity which often characterize consumer markets. Sometimes management fall so much in love with the technological beauty of their product that they fail to observe what is happening in the world outside the market. Steam locomotive manufacturers, convinced that steam would never lose its prime position, were dismayed to find their 'unchallengeable' market suddenly taken over by diesel-electric engines. They had failed to recognize that technological developments had resulted in a more efficient method of rail traction, and that the traditional solution of steam power was no longer acceptable to their customers.

The natural law dictates that organisms which fail to adjust to a changing environment eventually perish. If organizations do not modify their products or their methods of marketing, they run the risk of market extinction. In general, there is no shortage of production capacity in modern economies; there is still plenty of scope for industrial and service organizations to adopt a realistic approach to their markets, based on the principles of marketing which have been proved successful in other product fields.

Strategic planning is vital: it sets the direction and pace for the whole business – not just for the marketing staff. Decisions about products and services will be formalized in a marketing plan and this can be really successful only if all the other departments of a company are consulted and made aware of the projected market objectives.

Control

The third facet of marketing management – control – is essential to marketing productivity. Standards of performance such as territory sales quotas, market share ratios, cost/sales ratios, advertising/sales ratios, new product budgets, etc. provide critical measures of performance. An efficient feedback system should be devised in collaboration with financial colleagues. The entire span of marketing activities must be monitored and made cost-effective. As with production, standards should be drawn up in marketing operations so that corporate objectives are achieved within given constraints of time and cost.

Other useful marketing control tools will be customer profitability analysis; orders stratified by industry and customer size; the ratio of standard to specially manufactured products, etc.

The discipline of cost-effectiveness can be applied to marketing management with notable success. Large volume orders may be very seductive to sales staff, but to the professional marketing executive their effects on profits could be disastrous. No company can continue to operate for long without a reasonable level of profits; orders of dramatic size may help to fill production lines in the short term and it will be a matter of policy whether or not to accept them, but in the long term, only profitable business will ensure that the business continues to exist.

Implementation

This final facet of marketing management entails implementation of the overall marketing strategy and direction of the supporting tactics, ensuring, for example, that selling activities are efficiently targeted and fully co-ordinated; that pricing policies are reflected realistically across ranges and types of products and services; and that promotional plans are fully developed in terms of specific media, advertising appeals, target audiences, frequency of appearance, etc. (See Chapter 5 for further discussion.)

Detailed attention must be given to every aspect of implementing marketing efforts. Nothing should be left to chance, although, of course, environmental changes, such as competitors' behaviour, will occur and demand rapid evaluation.

KEYPOINT

Marketing research is the foundation of effective marketing management

1. Analysis: identify market trends, competitors' activities, customer preferences, etc. in (a) existing markets (b) potential markets

2. Planning: decide on range of products, and services likely to satisfy specific identified needs, present and emergent

3. Control and implementation: organize development, production and distribution of specific products/services; check that standards of performance (e.g. cost/sales ratio, market share, sales quotas, etc.) are maintained

Continuous monitoring of market behaviour provides an early-warning system for management

1.3 Definition of marketing research

There have been several attempts to define marketing research, and some confusion has been caused by the term 'market research' being rather freely used to describe the full range of activities properly covered by marketing research.

Although the term 'market research' is now largely used as a synonym for 'marketing research', there was originally a distinct difference between the scope of the activities they covered. The responsibilities of market research, as noted later, extend comprehensively, whereas marketing research is limited to finding out information about the market for a particular product. It is this rather narrow view of research that has inhibited management from taking full advantage of the opportunities which the systematic study of the market can offer. To restrict market investigation merely to surveying deprives management of vital contributions which can be made by researchers studying the marketing problems of an organization as a whole.

Marketing, as a specialized function of management, is generally interpreted today as including all those activities concerned with the development, production, and distribution of products to identifiable markets, where they will provide satisfaction to those who buy them. Marketing research is, therefore, far ranging in its enquiries; it covers product development, identifying the market, and suitable methods of selling, distribution, promotion, and sales/service facilities. In fact, every aspect of business activity from the 'idea stage' to eventual consumer satisfaction. As indicated in Chapter 12, marketing research is by no means restricted to profit-motivated business activities. It has very useful applications in, for example, the development of charities, public sector leisure, and cultural services, etc. The wide responsibilities of marketing research are reflected in the definition given years ago by the American Marketing Association:[3] 'The systematic gathering, recording, and analysing of data about problems relating to the marketing of goods and services'.

The above definition was echoed in the (British) Institute of Management's definition[4] which was published in 1962: 'The objective gathering, recording, and analysing of all facts about problems relating to the transfer and sales of goods and services from producer to consumer'.

A further definition of marketing research has been offered by the Market Research Society, the leading British professional body for those using survey techniques for market, social, and economic research: 'Market research is the means used by those who provide goods and services to keep themselves in touch with the needs and wants of those who buy and use those goods and services.'

Another definition of marketing research, specifically related to industrial products, was made by the Industrial Marketing Research Association (IMRA) – now subsumed into the Business and Industrial Group of the Market Research Society – as follows: 'The systematic objective, and exhaustive search for and study of facts relevant to any problem in the field of industrial marketing.'[5]

These definitions have much in common: market or marketing research is essentially about the disciplined collection and evaluation of specific data in order to help suppliers to understand their customers' needs better. From this fuller appreciation, which is likely to include economic, psychological, sociological, and cultural information, marketers are able to develop raw products and services, and also improve existing ones. Decision making necessarily involves some element of risk: market research data should be used to reduce, and control to some degree, the parameters of risk surrounding particular marketing proposals. (See Chapter 13 for Bayesian's approach in evaluation of marketing research.)

Buzzell,[6] writing in the *Harvard Business Review*, has expressed concern that the term 'research' had ever been adopted to describe the activities of data collection and evaluation for marketing decisions. He felt that this term was inappropriate for what essentially is some distance removed from pure academic research such as that conducted in a research laboratory under controlled conditions. Instead, he suggested that the function of marketing research was more analogous to military intelligence which had the duty of obtaining 'complete, accurate, and current information' for the development of strategic plans.

Marketing research should be viewed as a form of applied research that, while imposing on its practitioners the rigours and discipline of scientific enquiry, has a pragmatic purpose. Without this scientific orientation, marketing research would have little validity; it would deteriorate into subjective and biased assessments of market behaviour. Hence, an objective posture and systematic methods of enquiry are vital constituents of marketing research. It has been observed that marketing research is scientific in the sense that 'science may be at least partly defined in terms of the attitude of disinterest and impersonality one must take toward the outcomes of scientific investigation . . . science deals with the unembroidered fact rather than with opinion and belief'.[7]

KEYPOINT

Marketing research is a specialized function of marketing; it is by no means restricted to profit-motivated business activities

Large-scale operations have widened gap between producers and consumers of their products

Modern communities are knowledgeable, experienced and critical

1.4 Sources of marketing research theory and practice

It will be evident from earlier discussion that marketing research has borrowed liberally from other disciplines; this is not surprising because research methodologies and techniques have application over many fields of study. Like other emerging disciplines, marketing research theory has been developed by creative adaptation rather than blind adoption.

The extent to which marketing theory has been built on borrowed concepts was noted some years ago by the Marketing Science Institute of America. 'Historically, most sciences started by borrowing their conceptual approach and general theoretical ideas from other sciences. Our current state of marketing theory is no different.' However, the MSIA warned against the wholesale importation of methodologies from other areas of study.

Marketing investigations should be undertaken with 'scientific care and conceptual honesty'.[8] Discrimination, as noted earlier, had not always been practised in the development of marketing research. While it is true that most sciences often use techniques that originated outside their particular province, indiscriminate adoption tends to impede progress. Joyce[9] has observed that:

> Market research is not a practice or study isolated from other practices or studies. It has drawn freely from certain expert academic fields and will no doubt continue to do so. Further, market research organisations make use of people with expert, specialist training – especially from those fields known broadly as 'the social sciences' both as staff members and consultants.

As a discipline matures, the standards of its research should rise; these will depend significantly on the research methodologies and instruments that are in use.

Marketing research focuses on human and organizational behaviour and consumption habits. Buying behaviour is merely one element of human behaviour, and so it may be postulated that some of the theories and findings from the behavioural sciences make a relevant contribution towards understanding patterns of consumption. That curious, rational abstraction, economic man, which early classical economic theory projected, is now discarded and is regarded as an inadequate model of consumption. Rationality, even in industrial purchasing situations, is by no means the sole or dominant influence.

Because buying behaviour is complex and is affected by many variables – economic, psychological, sociological, cultural, and demographic – the approach by marketing researchers should be subtle and well designed. The interaction, for example, of economic and social factors may produce degrees of conflict. Cultural inhibitions may frustrate the introduction or diffusion of new products, such as dehydrated foods or contraceptives.

KEYPOINT

Marketing research is concerned with buying behaviour

Buying behaviour is merely one element of human behaviour

Buying behaviour is complex and influenced by many factors

Motivations may be a mix of economic, psychological, sociological, cultural and demographic variables

Behavioural sciences give insights into consumption

People seek what may be termed syntheses of benefits from the goods and services they consume. Benefits are often more than physical; even relatively fundamental needs such as food or clothing have become complex and sophisticated in modern advanced communities. On the simple foundation of nourishment, basically provided by food, people have built a highly elaborate edifice of needs that have been termed 'psychogenic' and are derived from psychology, sociology, aesthetics, etc. Choice has proliferated in response to the sophisticated behaviour of relatively affluent consumers. Those at the lowest level of subsistence in an undeveloped country eat eagerly and whenever they can; they do not have to be cajoled by advertising to try new experiences in foods. Their expectations and horizons are limited.

Psychology made its impact increasingly felt in marketing research during the period 1945–73.[10] Psychological theories have enabled market researchers to develop hypotheses about buying behaviour, and to apply some of the techniques of psychological investigation to obtain a deeper understanding of marketing problems. Learning theory, for example, has been utilized in studies of advertising effectiveness.[12,13] Psychological techniques have been linked with mathematical models and applied to learning behaviour related to the phenomenon of brand switching.[11,14,15]

The emphasis on building comprehensive models of buying behaviour has increased; qualitative assessments are now acknowledged to be vital components of marketing research designs. At the same time, the exaggerated claims of some psychological applications in research practice have been discredited, particularly those introduced from clinical psychology involving various kinds of projective techniques. Motivation research, based on Freudian psychology, has attracted particularly strong criticism. The subjectivity of such research methods, the selection and size of the samples involved, lack of quantitative analyses, and the generalizations that have been delivered, have caused considerable controversy about the validity of the resultant findings.

Over recent years, there has been a swing away from relying solely on these clinical methods of psychological enquiry into buying behaviour. Market researchers tend to make more use of methods like group discussions to guide in the development of new product concepts, advertising copy, etc. The use of groups, particularly during the exploratory stages of marketing research, will probably become a permanent feature of research methodology, since they offer a speedy and economical method of obtaining qualitative information 'which is often substantiated when quantification is carried out', using multi-variate statistical techniques.

Sociology has been influential in marketing research strategies. Social class gradings have been widely adopted by marketing researchers, particularly in advanced economies such as the US and the UK.

Apart from social classifications, sociology has also introduced into marketing research studies concepts such as social mobility, life cycle, opinion leadership, diffusion of innovations, household behaviour, etc.[16–30] These concepts have added immense depth and value to marketing research enquiries.

Cultural anthropology has also contributed to the development of marketing research, by focusing enquiries on environmental influences which affect patterns of consumption. The cultural values of a society are not abstract notions; they find expression in the products and services that are demanded; the acceptance of new products may be very dependent on cultural norms.

Cultural values have particular impact on export marketing strategies. Within national cultures, sub-cultures are often present with distinctive needs. The status of women in society tends to vary over cultures; these differences are particularly marked between advanced industrial communities and less developed countries. Such cultural differences have accounted for the difficulties in selling, for example, labour-saving domestic equipment

Cultural studies have been founded on work by Horney,[29] Riesman,[30] and Mead.[31]

Horne *et al.*[32] have observed that the 'fundamental discipline' of marketing research is statistics, in particular the law of probability. The sampling procedures used in marketing research were developed, therefore, from the concept of probability which is the core of sampling theory.

From statistics, marketing research has taken the theory of sampling; without sampling methodology, marketing research could never have originated. But the process has not been one-way, for marketing research practitioners have developed sophisticated sampling techniques, as in the case of multi-stage sampling, where 'clustering' techniques have resulted from demands for controlling the costs of commercial surveys.

Statistical theory has also contributed to the practice of marketing research through the application of techniques concerned with the acceptance or rejection of specific hypotheses. As seen earlier, the period 1945–73 had witnessed a refinement of techniques which had become more widely applied in order to improve the standards of research practice. Complex statistical computations became feasible with the introduction of computer packages such as Statistical Package for the Social Sciences (SPSS).

Another aspect of statistics, which has been helpful in developing marketing research as a science, emanates from the design of experiments towards which Fisher made a notable contribution. Green and Tull[33] noted that R. G. Fisher is to be 'credited with formulating rigorous statements regarding inferences to be drawn from sample observations. He defined the "null" hypothesis as an assertion about the real world whose validity was to be tested'.

Experimental techniques have been used in marketing research to test, for example, the relative efficiencies of advertising copy, packaging, pricing, etc.

Economics has also played a part in establishing marketing research as a management technique. Many of the early practitioners of marketing research were economists. It might be expected, therefore, that during the developmental stages of marketing research, economic analyses received substantial attention. 'Descriptive' economics related, for example, to the structure of industries, general background economic data, and the identification of trends in business and industry provided the essential framework of market research reports. These were valuable contributions which enabled marketing researchers to guide clients on the formulation of business policy. But Joyce[9] has observed critically that in the field of 'theoretical' economics, the contributions have been disappointing. 'If we take the study of the simplest, most basic economic relationships and occurrences – the theory of consumer choice – we find that the traditional theory is of little use or relevance to us.' The chief reason, as observed earlier, is the naïve assumption by earlier classical economic theorists that man is a rational or economic being who maximizes his utility or expected utility in all purchase considerations. The weakness in earlier versions of the principle of utility lay in a misunderstanding of basic human behaviour. These misconceptions have been largely corrected through the influence of the behavioural sciences like sociology and psychology; consumer choice studies would now be considered inadequate if the parameters were perceived to be solely economic.

The theory and practice of marketing research have drawn freely, therefore, from diverse academic disciplines. They have enriched the emerging discipline of marketing, of which marketing research is a core element. This process of selective borrowing, adaptation, and synthesis has transformed the entire nature and scope of marketing research investigations. Marketing research can never be a pure scientific activity; it 'is an applied field rather like engineering – which involves knowledge of metallurgy, electronics, mathematics, etc., but which has a technique and methodology of its own'.[9]

KEYPOINT

Marketing research has borrowed liberally from other disciplines

Economics: general background economic data; identification of business/industry trends; structure of industries, etc.

Statistical theory: sampling theory and methodologies; hypothesis testing and market experiments; mathematical modelling

Sociology: social class gradings; theories of social mobility; life-style, household behaviour, opinion leadership, and diffusion of innovations

Cultural anthropology: environmental influences on consumption; cultural norms and values; subcultural factors; diffusion of products/services

Psychology: perception and learning theories; qualitative influences on buying; group influences; reference group theory

Marketing research has effectively developed and applied these borrowed concepts in its own methodologies

1.5 Scope of marketing research

The area of marketing decisions is wide; it covers product design, pricing, distribution, and promotion. It acknowledges the fact that there are many variables affecting marketing activities which cannot be controlled by suppliers to a market. These environmental variables, such as the demographic structure of the population, economic conditions, legal restrictions, competitors' activities, and the shifting tastes dictated by fashion, cause marketing decisions to be complex and difficult to make.

Marketing management should, for instance, obtain a fundamental understanding of the structure of the market in which it operates or plans to enter; management should be aware whether it is relatively simple – where only a few producers and buyers are involved

– or complex where many buyers and sellers are active and the product has diverse applications, as with some industrial supplies. Analysis of market structure should be pursued into its constituent sectors and subsectors, so that the characteristics of specific types of demand are fully grasped. Undeveloped projections of macro demand are insufficient guides to effective marketing strategies.

Every organization must make marketing decisions of some kind. Frequently these involve large capital expenditure on the building and equipping of a new plant. Marketing decisions may result in the redirection of the resources of a business into entirely new markets, or in exploiting new technologies which have been developed by research laboratories. Also, as noted earlier, decisions may relate to the provision of specific cultural and leisure services by public sector authorities; or, perhaps, to the development of new types of firms offering comprehensive house buying/selling services and legal services.

Market research can help policy makers in both central and local government to design their programmes, 'in a way that takes into account the views of the consumers'. For example, social security beneficiaries might be surveyed to find out whether they would prefer cash payments to assistance in kind, as with subsidized travel or housing.

Statistical information can be gathered on the market in general, and also on particular segments that may be important, which will reveal the market standing of manufacturers relative to their competitors. Analysis indicates the general trend in that market, to be compared with the movement in specialized areas of the market, and to the sales trends of individual suppliers. The trend, evident in certain market segments, may be markedly different from the overall market movement. Market research attempts to isolate these phenomena and to explain the causes underlying them.

Information for marketing decision making may be broadly classified as: (i) strategic; (ii) tactical; and (iii) 'data bank'. The first type refers to information needed for strategic decisions, e.g. whether to enter a specific overseas market or to diversify into new markets; the second type relates to information for tactical decisions such as the planning of sales territories; the third type provides essential background knowledge about, for example, competitors' activities, market trends, VAT requirements, etc. Such information needs regular updating.

In practice, of course, these categories of information tend to become blurred, and companies often require a 'mix' of information.

KEYPOINT

Good information is the raw material of profitable business decisions

Buying behaviour is merely one element of human behaviour

3 types of management function: 1. strategic; 2. tactical; 3. data bank

In practice, these types tend to merge and companies require a 'mix' of information

Objective up-to-date knowledge is superior to 'hunch': marketing research is a key factor

Marketing management information has a two-way flow; from the organization to the environment (i.e. market), and from the environment to the organization; the principle of feedback is an essential element (see Fig. 1.1). In rapidly changing market conditions, it is imperative for management to have an up-to-date knowledge, to be aware of the entry of new, competitive products and services, and to be able to plan ahead for emerging trends in taste. Systematic enquiry is far preferable to hunch.

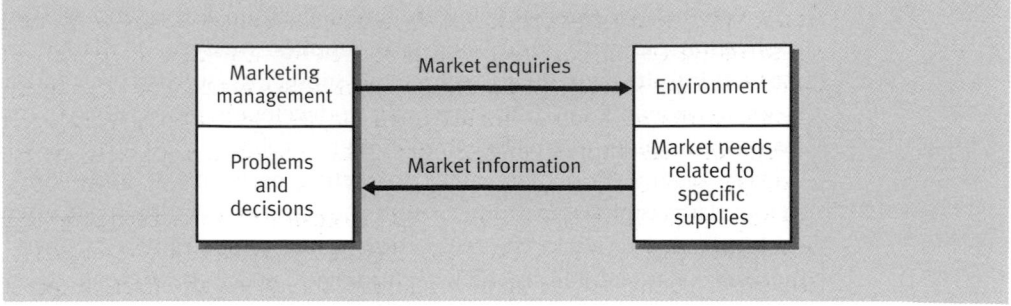

Figure 1.1   Two-way flow of marketing information systems

1.6 Main divisions of marketing research

Marketing research, as noted when discussing formal definitions of this activity, should result in thorough and detailed knowledge about all aspects of the marketing of goods and services. The various subjects covered in a typical marketing research programme will now be outlined separately, although, of course, in actual surveys these rather arbitrary distinctions will tend to be subsumed in the overall research design. (Further consideration of specific topics, such as promotion, socio-economic and geodemographic segmentation, occurs later in this text.)

KEYPOINT

Marketing Research should result in thorough and detailed knowledge about all factors likely to influence demand for specific products/services

The above 'boxes' cover research into specific aspects of market behaviour, but in actual surveys these rather arbitrary distinctions tend to be subsumed into the overall research design. It is important to integrate these various sectors of research activities, so that a balanced view can be taken of actual market conditions and opportunities. Entry into new markets may, for instance, require extended attention to feasible methods of sales and distribution to avoid head-on collision with existing suppliers.

Product research

This is concerned with the design, development, and testing of new products, the improvement of existing products, and the forecasting of likely trends in consumers' preferences related to styling, product performance, quality of materials, etc. Comparative testing with competitive products should be undertaken to assess realistically the values of comparative goods, particularly as perceived by customers. Included in these evaluations will be pricing studies. Strengths and weaknesses need to be objectively identified across specific attributes, such as quality, shelf-life, ease of handling, pack acceptability, etc. The essence of marketing research is objectivity, so any attempt to fudge enquiries should be strongly resisted.

The product line should be examined to ensure that it is adequate to attract custom, but also it must be economic, so that marketing efforts are not being wastefully dispersed over too wide a range, some of which may not be making an effective contribution to overall profitability. The product mix should also be analysed, particularly with reference to competitive products, as mentioned earlier. With some products – both consumer and industrial – efficient after-sales servicing is influential in attracting sales; this function should be carefully assessed, particularly where technical products or durable consumer goods such as television sets or washing machines are concerned.

Over past years, product design has become an increasingly important influence in the buying of many types of goods. Research is needed to evaluate what customers expect in terms of product performance, visual appeal, comfort, etc. Expectations are dynamic; what pleased people a few years ago is unlikely to satisfy them today. Manufacturers and distributors cannot expect to compete successfully against global competition unless the products they make and stock perform at least equally and also look as attractive as those, for instance, which may be marketed by new suppliers from distant lands.

The concept of the augmented or extended product or service is not just another attractive theory: it acknowledges that buying often involves complex motivations and satisfactions. Buyers, whether purchasing for their own consumption or for the needs of their organizations, seek more than just the simple or basic satisfactions of use or owner-ship. Around the core benefit expected of a product or service, shrewd marketers build in additional motivations to purchase; these added attributes may be based on psychological, social or other benefits, including, for example, a trusted brand image, efficient pre- or after-sales service, distinctive styling, etc. Marketing research can provide insights into buying expectations and motivations of a diverse range of products and services.

A leading air-conditioning equipment manufacturer puts particular emphasis on its ability to design whole systems to satisfy the specific needs of customers. It applies VA (value analysis) throughout its business, so that customers' problems are regarded as the concern of every department, beginning with design engineers, production management, installation staff and after-sales service.

James Pilditch,[33] who made a major contribution to the quality of British design, observed that 'it is not uncommon for a manufacturer to be genuinely surprised and disappointed when something he has designed, and about which he is expert fails to sell'. He cites a manufacturer of high-powered engines used in military vehicles who developed an engine half the size of any other available in the market. Although an example of brilliant engineering, it failed to win customers, who continued to prefer competitors' bulkier products. It was then discovered that competing engines were easier to maintain, and this was more important than compact size.

Design adds value to products and contributes to the rising sales graph of a very wide range of products: cars, washing machines, machine tools, textile machinery, spin driers, home computers, etc. Electronics has had a profound effect on product design; equipment has been 'miniaturized' and generally made much more reliable, e.g. telephone exchange equipment. In some cases, design has been largely cosmetic and limited to restyling. Products should not only function well, they should also look good. As technological differences between products become smaller and more difficult to discern, design (in its total sense) becomes more important.

The increased volume of spending power today is largely controlled by women, or heavily influenced by them. By their nature, they are generally more sensitive to colour and fashion, and they have become accustomed to a wide choice of well-designed clothing. In the area of household products, kitchen equipment, and cars, women are now successfully demonstrating their desire for products that will satisfy them aesthetically as well as practically.

The growing importance of packaging as a buying influence necessitates research; packaging protects products but it can also be a powerful promotion tool. With many types of products sold in supermarkets, the appeal of the packaging is of immense importance. Unless research is undertaken before packaging is developed for specific kinds of products, serious problems may arise. If, for example, packs are not capable of standing firmly on shelves or of being stacked without difficulty, sales of such products are likely to be severely curtailed. Shelf-life, possible contamination, and ease of handling by consumers are other aspects to be researched. Labels should be well designed so that brands can readily be recognized; sudden, radical changes in typeface or general layout may annoy buyers or cause suspicion about the quality of the contents.

Psychological segmentation, as Peter Sampson notes,[34] focuses on specific issues relating to consumer behaviour in specific product markets; in that way it is productive and provides a better understanding of such markets. 'By its very construction, psychological segmentation is bound to show discriminant behaviour between segments.'[34] As a result, its findings are 'more actionable and able to address a wide range of real marketing problems';[34] these may relate to the introduction of new products or to the development of existing products and brands.

Product testing entails a whole sequence of related events, from the idea stage, screening of concepts, development of potential new products, production viability, and organization of consumer evaluative tests (including 'blind' testing), test marketing, etc. (see Chapter 9). New product development demands close working relationships between specialists in many areas of activity within businesses, all of whom should be encouraged to contribute fully their respective skills. Companies such as Research International have long experience in new product testing; its MicroTest service is dedicated to the simulated test marketing of FMCG products (see Chapter 9 for full details).

Innovation is vital to corporate development, but it is, inherently, risky, and products fail for many reasons; sometimes they are 'before their time', or their diffusion is slowed down because they require radical changes in traditional patterns of consumption, or they may be rejected outright – as the Seven-Up Company in the US experienced when it developed another soda drink under the name of 7-Up Gold. Despite $10 million spent on network television advertising, the product was a fiasco (see Chapter 9).

Companies need to have information not just about specific products and trends in market performance, but also reliable indicators of likely patterns of consumption over the middle and long term. This type of strategic information is crucial in building a profitable product portfolio. Successful innovative companies make full use of all available resources, including the professional expertise of marketing researchers.

Profitable market segmentation strategies may be developed from product and packaging research, as was found with spray-on household polishes and traditional wax polishes. The tea market, for example, can be differentiated broadly by the intrinsic nature of the product (high-quality specialist blends versus relatively low-priced popular blends) and also by the style of packaging and product type (leaf tea versus 'bag' tea).

A creative product strategy which is a key input into the overall marketing strategy should aim to build a portfolio of products which will result in satisfactory development of a business.

KEYPOINT

Product service research covers:

1. Existing products/services

2. New product opportunities

3. Competitive products

4. Augmented product opportunities

Products that do not live up to buyers' expectations will fail

Products that cannot readily be distinguished from competitors' offerings, become commodity products, which sell chiefly on price

Products should provide buyers with a 'bundle of satisfactions'

Customer research

This covers investigations into buyer behaviour – studying the social, economic, and psychological influences affecting purchase decisions, whether these are taken at the consumer level, the trade distribution level, or in the industrial field (see specialist text).[35]

Reasons for preferences for certain brands, pack sizes, etc., of the products in a particular market will be examined. Attitudinal studies are valuable in distinguishing the appeals of competitive brands to certain types of users. The impact of the company's selling activities should be studied from the dealer and consumer angle; 'rationalization' of product lines can be interpreted unfavourably by customers and they may react by switching their purchases from other products made by the company to competitors. Consumer and dealer research is frequently planned jointly so that a useful cross-check can be made of the attitudes towards the company and its products. Unfavourable trade attitudes may be based on the failure of the company in the past to offer acceptable terms of trading, although the retailer may have no quarrel with the product range. Unfortunately, this may lead the retailer either to boycott those brands, or to give them merely nominal display in the stores. Deliveries may be another cause of dissatisfaction. Whatever complaints or prejudices exist, customer research is particularly useful in clearing them by pinpointing the causes which underlie them. Manufacturers depend heavily for the success of their marketing operations on the goodwill and cooperation of distributors, and it is nothing more than sound common sense to make objective enquiries into the trading relationships that exist between producers and channels of distribution. It is useful to management to know how its particular company compared with other suppliers in that product field. This can be done by some form of rating applied to critical aspects, such as design, packaging, price, delivery, accounting procedure, sales representation, adequacy of product range, etc.

Consumer research, as far as retail products are concerned, includes consumer surveys to study the opinions and behaviour of ultimate users of the products. This may involve national enquiries using formal questionnaires with a sample carefully selected to be representative of the total population in that consumer class. It may also cover a series of 'depth interviews' to analyse the motivations of people in certain buying situations. A variety of techniques can be used, which are discussed later in this text. Over the years, a great deal of expertise has been accumulated in consumer marketing research, which has tended to attract attention because of its direct impact on members of the public.

Following the successful path of enquiry which led to the publication of the American text *In Search of Excellence*, which was noted at the outset of this chapter, two British authors produced *The Winning Streak*.[36] Like the US book, this text examined companies which had impressive corporate behaviour over several years. The British companies surveyed included Sainsbury's, the giant supermarket chain, and it was observed that Sir John Sainsbury 'had no doubt that keeping a close ear to the ground on changes of consumer taste and needs is a major reason why his company has survived healthily into the 1980s while virtually every other big name in the grocery business before World War Two has disappeared or been taken over'. Sainsbury's is dedicated to the collection and evaluation of market data covering general aspects of the economy, trends in food consumption, and socio-economic environmental changes. Trends are monitored and new sectors explored. Competitors' developments in terms of new stores, marketing strategies and prices are examined closely.

In general, fast-moving consumer goods (FMCG) companies are more likely than industrial product companies to conduct marketing research, partly because of the dynamic nature of retailing which has been serviced by long-established market research organizations, such as Nielsen, AGB, Millward Brown, and Harris (see Chapters 8–10). In fact, it was found, in 1984,[37] that while 80 per cent of the former undertook research, only about 60 per cent of the latter did so; the principal reasons for not using marketing research were either that they felt that there was no need to assess their industrial markets, or that they already knew enough from first-hand experience. It was also found that a major obstacle to expansion into new markets was a 'genuine fear of the costs of marketing research' and a lack of belief in the benefits to be gained against the costs involved.

In 1986, the (British) Institute of Management[38] surveyed 12 leaders of British industry and 40 manufacturing companies. All said that good liaison with their customers was regarded as important; however, only a minority carried out thorough research to find out what their customers wanted. Only about one-quarter of respondent companies had actually researched product features that were regarded by them as vitally important and competitive.

While there are indications that business-to-business market research is now more actively pursued, and specialist research agencies have been developed to serve the distinctive needs of industry and commerce, this important sector still lags behind in its attitudes to and use of systematic market research.

Customer research should take note of people's media habits, and their attitudes to and likely responses towards promotional campaigns on television or elsewhere (see Chapter 11 for detailed discussion of this topic). In addition, manufacturers and retailers should extract full value from specialized research services, such as BMRB's well-recognized Target Group Index (TGI), and Research Service's SAGACITY segmentation – described in Chapter 11. Life-style and Life-cycle research are concepts of direct benefit to virtually every kind of consumer product and service. The increasing preoccupation with health, diet, and exercise offer many opportunities to alert marketers; these are being exploited successfully by the leading food producers and distributors like Kellogg's, Heinz, Sainsbury's, Tesco and Safeway. New ventures such as privately run health and exercise centres are popular with those keen to retain and improve their well-being. All these participatory sporting and leisure activities require various types of specialized equipment, and patrons willingly spend substantial sums in buying, for instance, squash rackets, golf clubs, exercise machines, tennis kit, etc. Perhaps largely because the nature of work – particularly in the service industries – demands less physical exertion and muscle power than in the older manufacturing industries, people's dietary habits and recreational interests have tended to change; calorie-controlled food products are now favoured and are generally available in supermarkets as well as in specialized outlets.

Associated with the trend towards healthy eating, is the emergence of the 'Green Consumer' – not referring to a naïve buyer, but to one who is sensitive to and well informed and concerned about the so-called green issues. This has triggered highly critical views of, for example, aerosols, phosphate-based washing powders or suspect food additives. Mintel, MORI, and Gallup conduct regular surveys on British consumers' views on the environment and related issues. 'Eco-shopping' is now an established feature of US shopping behaviour.[39] In the UK, this trend is apparent, but consumers seem less inclined, perhaps for reasons of economy or of wariness, to switch over quickly to products described as 'environmentally friendly'. More research may be advisable into people's underlying attitudes and perceptions which, of course, are likely to be subjective.

Since the early 1970s, the dietary habits of UK households have changed, sometimes fairly radically. Concern about the nutritional and health values of some foods, and, more recently, the BSE cattle crisis, have influenced consumers' perceptions, attitudes and buying preferences. Consumption of red meat has declined while that of poultry has increased significantly. Increased consumption of food outside the home is also a marked trend, particularly among younger age groups in fast-food catering outlets (77 per cent: 16–24: 1996).[40]

Family life cycle – a concept borrowed from sociology – has been applied in researching consumer markets. Various formulations of the typical family life cycle have been generated by researchers, but the fact is that the stages at which families find themselves during the course of their lives affect the nature of the goods and services they demand, and there are likely to be significant changes in the patterns of consumption.[36] Related to this concept, are the roles assigned to specific members of a family in connection with the duties of providing goods and services of many kinds: food, clothing, holidays, life assurance, housing, etc. Here again, market and social research can give penetrating insights into the patterns of family consumption and the decision-making processes involved; the role of women deserves particular attention when considering these matters (see Chapter 11).

Older people, many of whom continue to be active to advanced ages, represent an important sector of consumers in terms of both actual numbers and specific buying power. Many are articulate, knowledgeable and experienced buyers who enjoy relatively good health, live in comfortable accommodation with central heating, telephone, and modern kitchen facilities. They are particularly interested in travel and other leisure pursuits: firms like SAGA have been built up by specializing for the travel needs of the over-50s. But chronological age itself is, of course, an imperfect measure of people's interests, abilities and propensity to consume specific products and services. Socio-economic, educational and psycho-cultural variables all tend to affect the ways in which people of any age perceive themselves, and also influence their reactions to other people and events, as well as influencing their buying habits and preferences. The boundaries of middle age and old age are certainly elastic, and it is a fact that disposable income is often greater in the 55 plus age group than in younger age groups, preoccupied with bringing up children, paying mortgages, education bills and the myriad other costs which seem endless with young families.

In the US, 'OPALS' (older people with active life styles) are acknowledged to be important spenders and businesses are increasingly appealing to this relatively affluent, healthy and leisured sector of the community. Other jaunty descriptions of this 'third age' group have been 'WOOPIE' (well-off older people), and JOLLIES (jet-setting oldies with lots of loot) – which seem to fit well the groups of prosperous tourists in many airports.

In the UK, the 60 plus population accounted for over 20 per cent of adults in 1993; it is projected to increase to 23 per cent by 2010 and to reach 29 per cent by 2030. Life expectancy is still growing, and official figures record that it was 74 for men and over 79 for women in 1997.[40] Together with the general decline in birth rates, this so-called 'grey market' or 'third age' population is becoming a critically important market sector for cultivation by firms marketing a wide range of consumer goods and services. These demographic trends are also observable across Europe, the USA and other developed countries.

At the other end of the age spectrum, following the effects of the declining birth rate in Britain in the 1970s, there were falling school rolls in the 1980s. Population projections indicate that the 15–29 age range will be virtually static during the first quarter of the 21st century and may then decline slightly. It would seem, therefore, that this important market sector is likely to experience increasing competition to win the custom of young consumers. However, the affluence of young buyers will still make them attractive targets for suppliers of entertainment, sports goods and stylish cars.

Customer research is particularly important in export marketing, which is assuming far greater significance in the overall marketing operations of companies manufacturing a wide range of products. Successful exporting is built on reliable and up-to-date information about the specific needs of customers. With competition on an international scale increasing in intensity, manufacturers need to be more aware than ever before of the factors that influence customers in their choice of products and of brands. The characteristic behaviour of buyers in the home market will generally be more familiar to manufacturers than that of buyers in overseas markets, especially where these are being entered for the first time (see Chapter 12).

Lack of market knowledge can have disastrous effects; Douglas and Craig[41] refer to the 'total failure' of the Renault Dauphine car in the United States, which was ill-suited to the demands of American highway driving.

International marketing has necessarily to be undertaken in a complex, heterogeneous environment: there are many opportunities for management to make mistakes, perhaps in the formulation of food products, design of equipment incorporating acceptable safety standards, methods of distribution, etc. Alternative strategies may include licensing arrangements, joint venture operations, establishment of subsidiary overseas companies, or some mix of these methods of extending sales overseas. Political and other cultural factors may, as discussed in Chapter 12, be significant influences in the selection of suitable marketing opportunities.

KEYPOINT   **Customer research covers:**

1. Finding out what kinds of people (age group, socio-economic status, family background, etc.) buy certain products and brands

2. Evaluating their preferences related to specific brands

▶

3. Studying degree of brand/store loyalty for types of products/services

4. Evaluating the influence on consumers' preferences of 'Green Consumerism', and other issues such as food additives

Buying habits and preferences are influenced by many factors – economic, social, cultural, psychological

Buying motivations are often complex: 'rationalisation' may occur when buying preferences are discussed

Customer loyalty should never be taken for granted

Pricing research

All businesses have to make decisions about the pricing of their goods and services. Pricing is one of the critical factors affecting business success. It is also one of the variables in the 'marketing mix' – those fundamental inputs into a business deal that have been termed the four Ps (Product, Price, Place and Promotion). These inputs are necessarily interrelated and an effective blend is at the heart of successful marketing.

Pricing can (and should) be approached both analytically and creatively. Costs form the platform on which price is built and these must be known. But equally important is knowledge about the nature of demand, the level of competition, technological developments that may lead to substitute materials, etc.

Pricing can be used effectively to position a product relative to competitors' offerings. This suggests that some reliable information should be collected about competitive products specifically related to market segments. Price is an indicator of quality as well as an economic fact; products (and services) should be analysed for the benefits which they offer buyers, and, ideally, these should have been developed from objective knowledge of the expectations of certain types of buyers or users.

The sales of some products are highly sensitive to changes in price: as price falls, demand *tends* to rise, and vice versa, the extent of this movement is known as the elasticity of demand. The alternative, viz. inelastic demand, occurs when only small changes in demand follow from price alterations. Economists have developed sophisticated models of the relationships between price and demand; while theoretically impressive they often lack pragmatic value.

Market researchers may use various kinds of experimental designs to test price sensitivities (see Chapter 2: Causal studies and also Primary data – experimentation). Most markets have price ranges for specific products; the skill lies in knowing, with a fair degree of certainty, the price (including trade discounts) that will attract favourable buying decisions. Too low a price will arouse suspicions about quality, continuity of supply, etc.; while too high a price (unless it is deliberately designed to 'skim' the market) may well result in insufficient levels of sales. It may be feasible to organize market tests involving price differentiation as well as other variations to the marketing mix (see Chapter 10).

Pioneer research into price sensitivities was undertaken by Gabor and Granger[42] who, extending from earlier work by Jean Stoetzel of the Sorbonne, developed 'buy-response' curves related to specific types of products. Their research approach has since been adopted by the Nottingham University Consumer Study Group, based on analyses of consumers' propensity to purchase new products.

Another pricing research methodology is practised by Research International[43] whose 'brand-price trade-off approach' involves groups of typical buyers who are asked to make a series of selections from a proposed new product (at different prices) presented in company with several competing brands. The results of these simulated shopping sessions are subject to conjoint analysis.

Simulated market testing (see Chapter 9), involving consumer panels and 'laboratory' tests covering new product evaluation and also advertising copy testing and pricing sensitivities, are now well-established techniques used by leading market research agencies; as mentioned earlier, the MicroTest model has been extensively employed in market testing many major products in over 25 countries. Special pricing research packages are offered by the leading market research firms.

KEYPOINT

Pricing research covers:

1. Identifying the degree of price sensitivity for specific products/services in different market sectors

2. Estimating the relative effectiveness of price in the marketing mix

3. Identifying the degree of price competition in specific markets

4. Evaluating the impact of trade discounts and other trading incentives needed to secure market entry and expansion

Price is an indicator of quality as well as an economic fact

Product variations allow for price differentials

Too high a price may encourage product substitution

Costs form the platform on which price is built, but effective pricing is a policy decision which is helped by up-to-date market knowledge

Sales and distribution research

Selling activities and distribution arrangements are clearly closely linked, so research is, almost inevitably, likely to embrace both functions in which some degree of overlap occurs. However, for purposes of discussion, they will be considered separately.

Sales research involves a thorough examination of the selling activities of the company. This is usually made by sales outlets and/or sales territories, and preferably analysed so that direct comparisons can be made with published data. Information existing within the company should be fully utilized and matched with external data referring to the particular industry and its products. As observed already, the position of a company in its market should be checked in relation to its competitors; these should be identified and ranked in order of importance. If company sales are falling, the overall trend in the market should be checked, particular attention being given to those segments of the total market which may account for the company's main sales. Where it can be established that the total market is steady or improving in these significant areas, some urgent enquiries should be made to find out why company sales are not sharing this general trend. Research should aim to discover where these extra sales are being made – perhaps in outlets not adequately covered by the company sales plan. The effectiveness of the sales force should be examined; the distribution of territories, method of operation, system of remuneration, field supervision and training, all require careful analysis and assessment. Distribution plans should be compared for selling efficiency; if complete national coverage is desirable has this been accomplished at reasonable cost, or would alternative arrangements, e.g. through wholesalers, be more economical in certain areas? Is the sales force selling to those outlets that handle the majority share of the market? As an aid to realistic sales forecasting, research is recommended to ensure that estimates are based on sound knowledge of the factors likely to affect consumption in that market. This must take account of economic, political, and social developments and legislation in markets, whether in the UK or overseas.

Distribution research involves not only evaluating a company's selling arrangements in relation to its competitive opportunities, but also thoroughly identifying and appraising alternative methods of distribution. It is virtually a cliché – but nevertheless axiomatic – to say that there has been a revolution in the high streets of Britain. Retailing practices have undergone unparalleled changes in the lifetime of those who are still in their middle years.

Long-term trends of the UK retailing sector indicate that people still want to shop and buy not just the necessities of life – the term itself has undergone some redefinition – but also many of the 'luxuries' as well.

Further, changes in shopping facilities and retailing strategies are regularly projected. The widespread ownership of cars in Britain has encouraged the development of out-of-town shopping centres which offer customers easy car-parking and a bewildering array of keenly priced goods for their homes and gardens. These shopping centres, such as the Trafford Centre in Greater Manchester, offer not only comprehensive ranges of fashion clothing, household equipment and other merchandise, but also facilities for family outings, such as a wide variety of catering outlets, multi-screen cinemas, etc.

Location has always been recognized as critical to retailing success; customers favour stores that are conveniently sited – this, as noted already, includes worry-free car parking (over 70 per cent of UK households owned at least one car in 1997, and two-car households rose from 2 per cent in 1967 to 25 per cent in 1997; the size of households is another important factor affecting retailing strategies: the market trend is towards more households (7 million more in Britain in 1998 than in 1961, but fewer occupants (one-person households: 14 per cent in 1961, and 28 per cent in 1998). One-person households are particularly evident in the older age groups.[40]

Concentration is a marked characteristic of the UK retailing sector, such as grocery, where five major multiples account for an increasingly major part of the total turnover in the UK. In 1997, the top 20 per cent of grocery stores (ranked by turnover) accounted for just over 90 per cent of all grocery turnover. Between these large store groups, competition is intensive and further rationalization may occur. Of the superstores (sales area of 25 000 square feet or more), Tesco and Sainsbury's account for nearly 50 per cent of total grocery sales. The traditional 'corner shop' seemed, at one time, destined to disappear entirely, but in many towns the small 'neighbourhood store' has reappeared, often run by industrious Asian families. In the United States it has been predicted[44] that in ten years' time, interactive home-based shopping will achieve sales of $300 billion a year. In Britain, teleshopping is still a largely speculative innovation, although telebanking and telephone-based car and household insurance services are growing rapidly. The Internet, still in its early days of popular use, offers consumers novel opportunities for comparative shopping.

Technology cannot guarantee that innovations in products or services will be acceptable and diffuse at a uniform rate. Shopping, for instance, is a socio-cultural as well as an economic activity, and for many people it provides opportunities for self-expression, satisfying their curiosity, gathering news and views from friends and acquaintances, etc. Further, products can be assessed visually and also tactilely; food may be sampled, garments tried on, and competing products assessed side-by-side.

Bar-coding and electronic scanning at the point-of-sale (EPOS) have revolutionized the management of retail information – see Chapter 8 – and stock-control systems. The effects are felt throughout the daily activities of modern retailing, including research-based feedback on promotional campaigns, offered by leading market research agencies like Nielsen, Taylor Nelson AGB, and BMRB.

Electronic data interchange (EDI) – the transmission and exchange of business documents – for example, orders and invoices, over the telecommunication network is widely used by the large retail store groups and their suppliers, resulting in significant economies.

Research organizations, such as CACI ACORN and Experian MOSAIC have developed geodemographic research systems which are valuable in store location, consumer profiling, etc. (see Chapter 10).

Vending machines are no longer, of course, innovations, but their principle of easy access to a (limited) range of consumer products has been applied most successfully by the UK banks, whose clients increasingly avail themselves of the cash-point systems now widely installed outside bank premises.

Retailing innovations may be radical, as with hypermarkets and shopping malls, or they may be adaptations of existing methods to meet the dynamic needs of customers, as bakers discovered in recent years. Distribution research must be constantly alert to the many changes that, in a few years, have made shopping more of a family expedition than it has ever been: children's play areas, changing rooms, snack bars, and even recreational facilities, have added to the motivation to 'go shopping'. Many years ago, a highly successful stores chief told his staff never to forget that retailing had much to learn from 'show' business – people visited stores to be entertained as well as to buy goods, and if they were made to feel good, then they were more likely to become customers.

KEYPOINT

Sales and distribution research covers:

1. Existing selling and distribution arrangements

2. Evaluation of comparative performance in specific market sectors

3. Sales force organization relative to market opportunities

4. Evaluation of alternative methods of distribution

Concentrated buying power is present in several sectors of UK retailing, e.g. grocery, DIY, and floor coverings

Out-of-town shopping centres, hypermarkets and shopping malls are widespread in the UK and other developed economies

Shopping is a socio-cultural activity as well as an economic activity

---

Promotion research

This is concerned with testing and evaluating the effectiveness of the various methods used in promoting a company's products or services. These activities include exhibitions, public relations campaigns, merchandising aids such as show cards and point-of-sale stands, consumer and trade advertising, special promotional offers, etc. The variety of media available in most developed communities – television, press and magazine, cinema, radio, poster, exhibitions, etc. – and the wide choice of media within each of these classifications, make the task of selecting the most suitable media difficult in practice. So many variables affect purchasing decisions that only in very few cases can the real sales effectiveness of advertising be known with certainty.

In Chapter 10, the principal techniques used in audience research and evaluation in television and the press media are described in some detail. In Britain, the mass media are highly organized, sophisticated and diverse, and cater for most tastes and interests. Technological advances, such as satellite television and cable transmission, have enabled home-viewers to summon up, at the touch of a button, an amazing variety of programmes, some available free, others paid by subscription, while others are offered on a 'pay-as-you-view' basis.

Audience measurement of the specialized media – ranging from television, press, radio, poster and cinema – is generally the responsibility of bodies jointly organized by the media owners, advertisers and advertising agencies (see BARB, JICNARS, etc., in Chapter 10). Electronic systems of audience monitoring, like the Peoplemeter, are highly developed and standard practice in the US and in the major European countries.

Tracking studies – continuous measurement of the effects of specific promotional campaigns over certain time periods – are offered by many of the leading research companies, such as BJM, Nielsen (SCANPRO), Taylor Nelson, Millward Brown, and TSMS (who have an extensive portfolio of promotional testing and evaluation services covering 40 per cent of the UK television coverage).

In overseas markets, the availability of specific mass radio or television, should be carefully researched. The pattern of the mass media in the UK is by no means the same in other countries. Apart from technical considerations, cultural factors also influence the medium that is suitable for effective promotional purposes. Printed communications, for instance, are relevant to communities with high levels of literacy, but are ineffective in countries like Nigeria or Algeria (see Chapter 12) for widespread promotions.

Alternative and complementary forms of product promotion can be researched during the course of trade and consumer surveys. Many such surveys include questions on media habits, such as television viewing; magazine and newspaper readership; types of store at which purchases of particular products are made; brand recognition; and attitudes towards merchandising practices, e.g. 'special offers', 'banded packs', 'free gift vouchers', and trading stamps.

The most suitable methods of promoting products should be studied in detail. Present practice needs to be assessed for its effectiveness, and alternatives should be objectively considered. Where a company operates in more than one market, e.g. selling in bulk to the hotel and catering industries, and also in retail packs to the consumer through a network of stockists, separate promotional policies will be drawn up as the result of information collected through marketing research in these specialized sectors of the market.

Market research[45] by Elida Gibbs revealed that although Proctor and Gamble's 'Head and Shoulders' dominated the entire shampoo market in both the United States and Britain, there was need for a range of anti-dandruff shampoos – a special sector not yet exploited by the market leaders.

Elida Gibbs developed the 'All Clear' shampoo, test-marketed it, and launched it nationally in July 1979. The strategy included national TV advertising. Unfortunately, a strike by ITV staff soon after the initial launch forced a switch into press and radio. Despite this problem, an evaluation was made of the different media used in the 'All Clear' campaign, and the conclusion of the researchers was that the TV advertising campaign was the single most important factor in the successful launch of this product. It was noted that the television expenditure of £116000 in late July was reflected in the 6 per cent brand share recorded in August, whereas this dropped immediately to 4 per cent when it became impossible to use television advertising. It was not until the resumption of this medium in January 1980 that 'All Clear' regained its 6 per cent brand share.

Mass communication inevitably involves mass media, of which there are many types in developed economies. Advertising tends to be a contentious subject, both to those who pay for and to those who are opposed to it. But surveys have found that advertising remains extremely low on people's lists of concerns: it is not a vital topic of general conversation, and does not appear to inflame opinions in the way, for example, that political issues or environmental concerns tend to. What people in general find objectionable in advertising is not easily determined because different people give various reasons. Very few said that it was misleading; it was regarded as offensive in a very few specific cases; virtually no one saw it as harmful or wasteful; and intrusiveness did not appear to concern them.

KEYPOINT

Promotion research covers:

1. Identifying relevant methods of promoting specific goods/services

2. Identifying present methods of promoting specific goods/services marketed by likely competitors

3. Evaluating costs and effectiveness of media judged to be most suitable for promotional tasks

4. Developing 'communications mix' based on research information

Separate promotion policies may be needed for special sectors of a market, e.g. consumer food products or hotel and catering supplies

Promotion does not necessarily involve media advertising; merchandising activities may supplement or even replace the former

Effective promotion plans require sophisticated market knowledge

Media availability varies overseas; cultural factors such as literacy need to be researched

---

1.7 Complexity of buying behaviour

The discussion so far reveals that marketing research has a vital role in providing reliable, detailed information about buying behaviour, expectations and consumption patterns related to specific market sectors, both at home and overseas. Over the years, marketing research has greatly improved its professional skills and range of research applications. New techniques are still being developed so that manufacturers and distributors of a vast range of consumer goods and services are able to keep closely in touch with their customers' needs and aspirations. With the growing fragmentation of markets based, perhaps, on cultural and sub-cultural life-styles, there is even more need for highly-specific market information.

Buying behaviour is often complex; for example, reasons for purchasing preferences may be subtle and not always easily determined, so marketing research techniques based on psycho-social approaches have been applied successfully. Several influences may motivate people to buy (or avoid) certain brands of products or types of outlets: personal value systems, cultural beliefs and practices, family and group influences, life-cycle, or economic considerations are probably present to some degree or other. In Fig. 1.2 some of these major determinants of consumer buying behaviour are indicated.

These multiple influences will be likely to apply in different 'mixes' and in varying strengths, according to whether a purchase is often made – like buying most of the family groceries at a supermarket – or involving, perhaps, purchase of relatively expensive household durables, like a deep-freezer, or the choice of a family holiday venue. The significance and interplay of all the factors shown in the diagram should be considered when devising research objectives. Some of these influences, although often covert, may, nevertheless, spell success or failure in the marketing of goods and services.

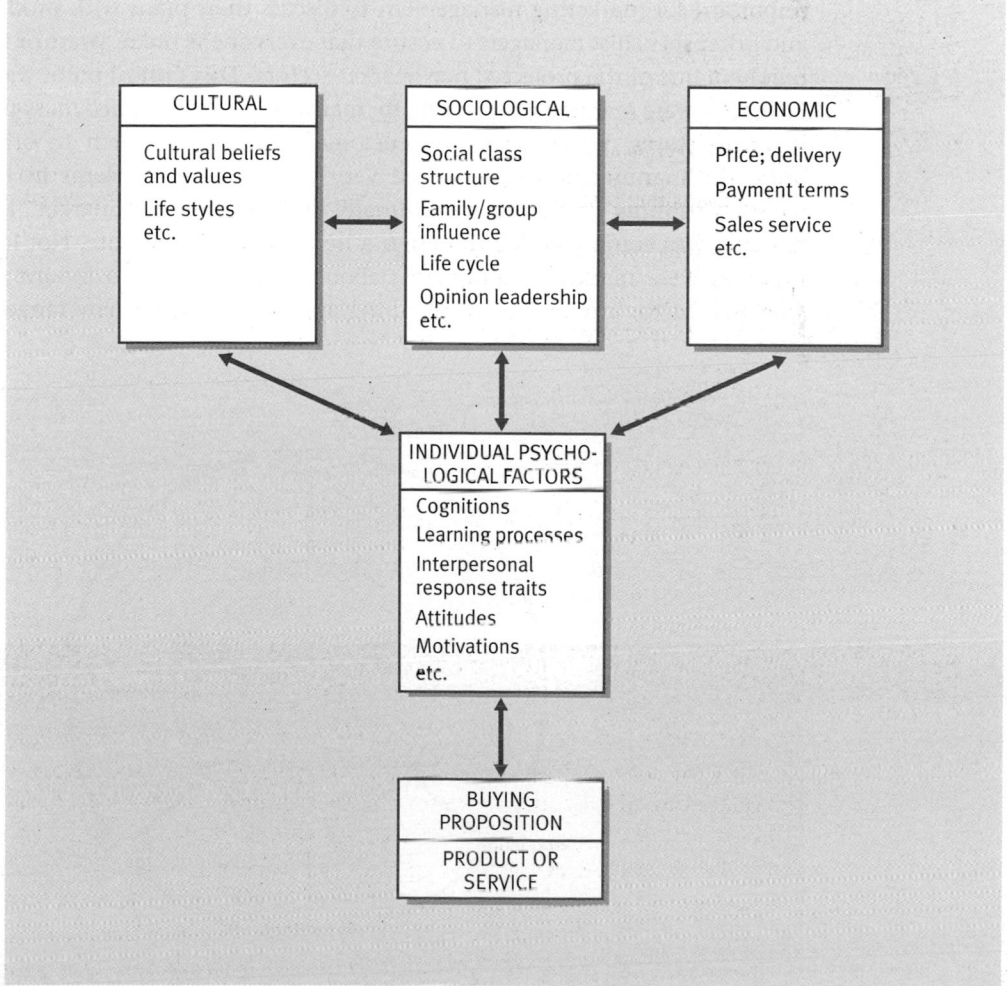

Figure 1.2   The complex pattern of buying influences (*Source:* Chisnall, 1994)[35]

1.8 Corporate performance: vital inputs and relationships

The various specialized functions of management should form a coherent and balanced set of professional skills: one weak performer in this 'circle of competences' can frustrate overall performance and even result in corporate disaster. Links between managerial specialisms should be actively forged and encouraged to strengthen. Every cog in a wheel contributes to the efficient running of the mechanism.

Information about markets, drawn from professional marketing research, should be discussed with designers, production engineers, purchasing officers, etc. Full value should be extracted from such important and often expensive data, so that, for example, product improvements and product innovations can be planned.

Marketing plans should never be drawn up in isolation from other functional areas of a business or organization. Information about market preferences and trends may signify the need for manufacturing resources to be expanded or fundamentally reorganized in time to be able to supply, perhaps, new types of products. Designers and buyers, likewise, should be made aware of the changing pattern of demand which could involve alternative kinds of raw materials, components, etc. If it is planned to enter new markets – perhaps those where consumers are sophisticated in their buying tastes – then it would be important for marketing management to discuss their plans with production, personnel and other specialist managers to ensure that everyone is made aware of the more exacting requirements of the projected new market sectors. This critical point was overlooked by a large tableware manufacturer which, for many years, had supplied mass-produced products to chain stores. When its largest customer decided to switch to other faster-moving lines, the manufacturer experienced very considerable problems in trying to keep its factories running profitably. It was finally decided to go 'up market', and a well known designer was commissioned to design a new range of tableware. Not long after the new products were marketed, complaints about quality started to mount up from the new stockists. In the excitement of planning and producing its new range of tableware, no

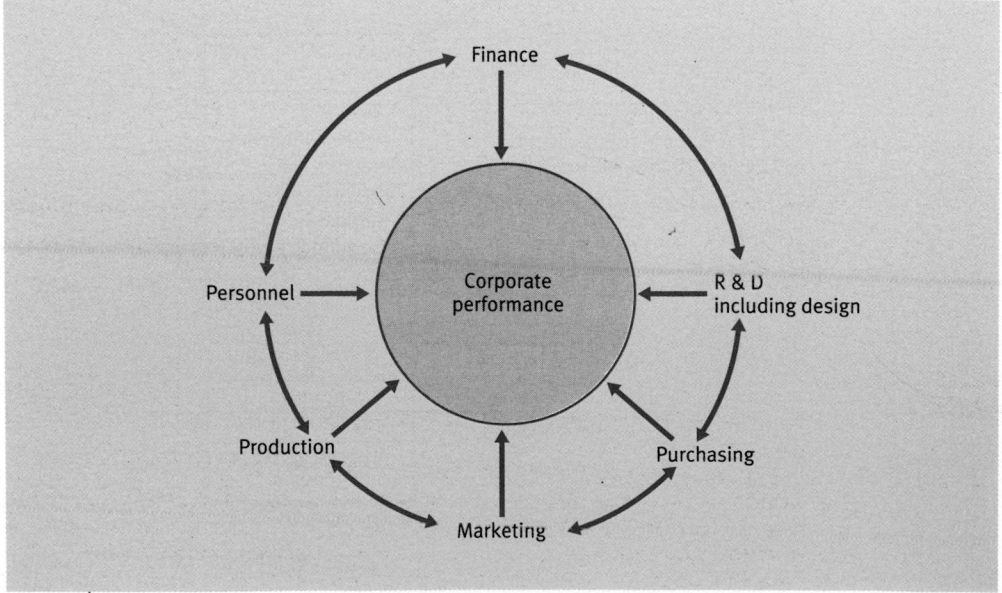

Figure 1.3 Vital corporate inputs to success

one had alerted the works staff to the far more critical market the company was entering, for the first time; there was need to retrain workers and also improve levels of inspection. These critical issues were completely overlooked. What should have been a successful and exciting new venture turned into a very painful and expensive learning experience. Corporate performance is essentially a team effort: professional specialisms should include co-operation across skill boundaries (see Fig. 1.3 showing that business success depends on teamwork).

Summary

Marketing research aids decision making by providing management with specific kinds of information useful for strategic and tactical planning. The terms 'market research' and 'marketing research' are now used interchangeably to infer systematic, objective research into all the factors, such as product pricing, promotion and distribution, which contribute to the successful marketing of goods and services. This systematic analysis covers both quantitative and qualitative assessments of existing and prospective markets.

Research should be the foundation of marketing strategy; unfortunately it tends to be used less in industrial and technical fields where the need is often critical.

Market research techniques have evolved from relatively rudimentary social enquiries; the methodologies of other disciplines have been creatively adapted. But market research can never be purely scientific – it has the quality of an applied science, and must seek to offer pragmatic solutions without destroying its essential core, i.e., objectivity.

Review and discussion questions

1. Identify the main developments in the world of business which led to the emergence of marketing research.

2. Distinguish between market research and marketing research.

3. What do you consider to be the more significant stages in the development of marketing research?

4. What are the principal disciplines from which marketing research has drawn? Summarize the contribution and relevance of each discipline.

5. Outline the main areas of customer research that a marketer of household exterior intruder alarms should investigate.

6. Locate a marketing/design magazine or newspaper that describes how any new product was developed. Summarize and evaluate the product research conducted prior to the launch of this product.

References

1. Peters, Thomas J., and Robert H. Waterman, Jnr, *In Search of Excellence: Lessons from America's Best-Run Companies*, Harper & Row, New York, 1982.
2. Drucker, Peter F., *The Practice of Management*, Heinemann, London, 1955.
3. American Marketing Association, 'Report of the Definitions Committee', Chicago, 1961.
4. British Institute of Management, 'Survey of marketing research in Britain', *Information Summary*, No. 97, London, January 1967.
5. Industrial Marketing Research Association, 'Regulations', Lichfield, 1969.
6. Buzzell, Robert D., 'Is marketing a science?', *Harvard Business Review*, January/February 1963.
7. Geldard, Frank A., *Fundamentals of Psychology*, Wiley, New York, 1961.

8. Halbert, Michael (Dir.), *The Meaning and Sources of Marketing Theory*, Marketing Science Institute, McGraw-Hill, New York, 1965.
9. Joyce, Timothy, 'The role of the expert in market research', MRS Summer School, July 1963.
10. Howard, John A., *Marketing Theory*, Allyn and Bacon, Boston, 1965.
11. Bayton, James A., 'Motivation, cognition, learning: Basic factors in consumer behaviour', *Journal of Marketing*, vol. 22, January 1958.
12. Estes, W. K., 'Individual behaviour in uncertain situations: An interpretation in terms of statistical association theory', in: *Decision Processes*, R. M. Thrall *et al.* (eds), Wiley, 1954.
13. Bush, Robert, and Frederick Mosteller, *Stochastic Models of Learning*, Wiley, 1955.
14. Kuehn, Alfred A., 'Consumer brand choice as a learning process', *Journal of Advertising Research*, vol. 2, December 1962.
15. Hyman, Herbert H., 'The psychology of status', *Archives of Psychology*, no. 269, 1942.
16. Hyman, Herbert H., 'Reflections on reference groups', *Public Opinion Quarterly*, autumn 1960.
17. Bourne, Francis S., 'Group influence in marketing and public relations', Rensis Likert and Samuel P. Hayes, Jnr (eds), UNESCO, 1959.
18. Lazarsfeld, Paul F., Bernard Berelson, and Hazel Gaudet, *The People's Choice*, Columbia, New York, 1948.
19. Rogers, E. M., *Diffusion of Innovations*, The Free Press, New York, 1948.
20. Merton, R. K., *Social Theory and Social Structure*, The Free Press, New York, 1957.
21. Sheth, Jagdish, N., 'A review of buyer behaviour', *Management Science*, vol. 13, no. 12, August 1967.
22. Menzel, H., and E. Katz, 'Social relations and innovation in the medical profession: The epidemiology of a new drug', *Public Opinion Quarterly*, winter 1955–56.
23. Asch, Solomon E., *Social Psychology*, Prentice-Hall, Englewood Cliffs, New Jersey, 1965.
24. Hill, Reuben, 'Patterns of decision-making and the accumulation of family assets', in: *Household Decision-Making*, Nelson N. Foote (ed.), New York University Press, 1961.
25. Wells, W. D., and G. Gubar, 'Life-cycle concept in marketing research', *Journal of Marketing Research*, November 1966.
26. Field, J. G., 'The influence of household members on housewife purchases', Thomas Gold Medals Awards for Advertising Research, 1968, Thomson Organisation, London, November 1968.
27. Sampson, P., 'An examination of the concepts evoked by the suggestion of "other members of the household" influence over housewife purchases', Thomson Gold Medals Awards for Advertising Research, 1968, Thomson Organisation, London, November 1968.
28. Horney, Karen, *Our Inner Conflicts*, W. W. Norton, New York, 1945.
29. Rieseman, David, *The Lonely Crowd*, Yale, New Haven, 1950.
30. Mead, Margaret, 'The application of anthropological techniques to cross-national communication', *Trans. New York Academy of Science, Series 11*, vol. 9, no. 4, February 1947.
31. Horne, Annette, Judith Morgan, and Joanna Page, 'Where do we go from here?', *Journal of the Market Research Society*, vol. 16, no. 3, 1974.
32. Green, Paul E., and Donald S. Tull, *Research for Marketing Decisions*, Prentice-Hall, Englewood Cliffs, New Jersey, 1975.
33. Pilditch, James, 'Reputation and reality in design', *Industrial Marketing Digest*, vol. 5, no. 1, 1979. 'The future of shopping', *The Economist*, vol. 332, no. 7877, August 1994.
34. Sampson, Peter, 'People are people the world over: the case for psychological segmentation', *Market and Research Today*, vol. 20, no. 4, November 1992.
35. Chisnall, Peter, *Consumer Behaviour*, McGraw-Hill, Maidenhead, 1994.
36. Goldsmith, Walter, and David Clutterbuck, *The Winning Streak*, Weidenfeld and Nicolson, London, 1984.
37. Hooley, Graham, J., and Christopher J. West, 'The untapped markets for marketing research', *Journal of the Market Research Society*, vol. 26, no. 4, October 1984.
38. Ovenden, Anthony, *Competitiveness in UK Manufacturing Industry*, BIM, Corby, Northants, 1986.
39. Simonian, Haig, 'Pitfalls of eco-shopping', *The Financial Times*, 5 January 1995.
40. Social Trends 29, Office for National Statistics, 1999.
41. Douglas, Susan P., and C. Samuel Craig, *International Marketing Research*, Prentice-Hall, Englewood Cliffs, New Jersey, 1983.
42. Gabor, A., and C. Granger, *The Attitude of the Consumer to Prices in Pricing Strategy*, Staple Press, London, 1969.
43. Greenhaugh, Colin, 'Research for new product development', ex *Consumer Market Research Handbook* (3rd edn), Robert Worcester and John Downham (eds), ESOMAR, Amsterdam, 1986.
44. *The Economist*, 'The Future of Shopping', vol. 332, no. 7877, August 1994.
45. McWilliams, Gil, 'The case for "All Clear" shampoo', in: *Advertising Works*, Simon Broadbent (ed.), Holt, Rinehart and Winston, Eastbourne, 1981.

2

Basic techniques

Methodologies of marketing research

Learning Objectives

- Obtain systematic knowledge of sequential stages of marketing research

- Understand nature of data and main classifications

- Understand desirability of combining research survey techniques

- Note significance of reliability and validity in research activities

In Chapter 1 it was observed that scientific research practice has influenced the development of marketing research and has encouraged high standards in surveys concerned with marketing activities in many spheres. To ensure the continued growth of marketing research as a valuable aid to management decision making, it is critical that the process of investigation is soundly based and organized in an efficient manner. This is helped by considering the marketing research process as a series of steps to be taken in gradually developing, planning, and executing research into specific problems.

2.1 Developing a research design

A central part of research activity is to develop an effective research strategy or design. This will detail the most suitable methods of investigation, the nature of the research instruments, the sampling plan, and the types of data, i.e. quantitative or qualitative (or, ideally, both). A research design forms the framework of the entire research process: 'If it is a good design, it will ensure that the information obtained is relevant to the research problem and that it was collected by objective and economic procedures.[1]

The critical significance of the research design is further emphasized by Oppenheim:[2] 'It is the research design which must hold all the parts and phases of the enquiry together. The design must aim at precision, logic-tightness and efficient use of resources. A poorly designed survey will fail to provide accurate answers to the questions under investigation.' Essentially, an effective research design should be a comprehensive plan, developed after intensive study of the problem to be researched, that will guide and control the entire research programme. Its foundations are firmly based on scientific rigour and objectivity, without which the entire research processes are seriously flawed. The principles of a sound research design apply to all research activities, irrespective of the discipline or subject of an enquiry. At this preliminary stage of the research activities, it is worth taking time and trouble to ensure that the research programme starts off from a well-constructed base. Impetuosity must be controlled; the urge to 'start doing something', i.e. devising some questions and finding people willing to answer these hastily formulated enquiries, should be resisted – such impatient behaviour can only result in a biased and inadequate survey.

KEYPOINT

Effective research is based on a sound research design

A productive research design is developed after intensive study of the problem to be researched

A well-devised research design guides the research programme

A research design details:

1. Types of data to be collected (quantitative and/or qualitative)

2. Most suitable methods of investigation

3. Sampling plan

2.2 Three types of research design

Research designs can be classified in various ways; a widely used method identifies them broadly as: exploratory, descriptive, and causal.

Exploratory designs

Exploratory designs are concerned with identifying the real nature of research problems and, perhaps, of formulating relevant hypotheses for later tests. These initial steps should not be dismissed as of little consequence; the opposite, in fact, is nearer to reality, for exploratory research gives valuable insight, results in a firm grasp of the essential character and purpose of specific research surveys, and encourages the development of creative, alternative research strategies.

Craig and Douglas[3] emphasize that the design of an international marketing research project is frequently more complex than domestic marketing research

In some cases, exploratory research based on published data (see later discussion of secondary data) may give adequate knowledge for particular marketing decisions to be made.

Oppenheim[2] recommends that these early exploratory interviews should be tape-recorded and listened to later by the research team, so that all involved in the programme are able to derive full value from the views expressed by respondents, including noting any limitations to the scope of specific enquiries related, perhaps, to sensitive topics, such as personal hygiene or honesty. Again, this early stage of research should not be undertaken flippantly; it warrants serious attention and, as experienced researchers know, can add significantly to the quality and usefulness of the ensuing enquiries.

KEYPOINT

Exploratory research

Often a first step in research and provides insights into research problem

Enables research problem to be more closely defined

Gives relatively speedy and economic way of acquiring overview of problem and its relevant factors

Useful in developing hypotheses about specific markets; tends to use qualitative assessments rather than detailed quantitative data

Makes full use of published data

Particularly valuable as a 'research filter' before further commitments made to more extensive – and expensive – research activities

Descriptive studies

Descriptive studies, in contrast to exploratory research, stem from substantial prior knowledge of marketing variables. For this type of research to be productive, questions should be designed to secure specific kinds of information, related, perhaps, to product performance, market share, competitive strategies, distribution, etc.

Other types of descriptive studies are censuses, public-opinion polls and various industrial, commercial, and public-sector surveys; the objectives of such surveys are diverse but they share the same basic functions of counting and describing specific features or characteristics of certain kinds of people or other subjects – they do not aspire to identifying or explaining relationships that may exist between kinds of people or types of activities. Nevertheless, such surveys are useful and frequently attempt to give insights into behaviour as well as measuring particular attributes and habits. Many enquiries, as

Moser and Kalton[4] note, aim to explain rather than describe: the problems of causality tend to be serious and these are considered in the next section.

Marketing research reports are largely descriptive; market demand, customer profile, economic and industrial phenomena, and other factors which characterize market behaviour are generally covered in quantitative and qualitative terms.

KEYPOINT

Descriptive research

Generally developed from exploratory research findings; describes specific market phenomena, such as product usage, frequency of store visits, etc.

Collects statistical data utilized in testing hypotheses developed in exploratory research

Provides data for comparative analyses of competitive products

Evaluates new product performance

Develops profiles of types of customers and their preferences

Causal studies

These attempt to identify factors which underlie market behaviour and to evaluate their relationships and interactions. For example, the extent, if any, of price elasticity of demand, or the degree to which advertising campaigns may influence sales.

The concept of causation needs to be approached with caution, and some understanding of the nature of causation would, no doubt, be helpful. Cause and effect relationships are notoriously difficult to deal with realistically and objectively; there is always the temptation to jump to conclusions, usually in support of a preconceived notion of how, for instance, the market behaves in specific situations.

The topic of causal relationships should, therefore, be approached cautiously, bearing in mind that scientific scepticism has much to commend it, particularly where human behaviour is concerned. Simplistic correlation between two variables, for example, has been found to be misleading, as shown by Ferber's[5] example of a high correlation between the birth rate in the US population and the price of pigs. Neither caused the other, the fluctuations in both variables being largely caused by the same factor, i.e. national prosperity.

Associations or correlations are certainly not to be accepted at first sight – if at all; far more subtlety and sophistication should obviously be used when studying research data. Oppenheim[2] also warns against the dangers of the *monocausal* model (A causes B), which suggests that a single cause can have a specific effect, because it often gives an incomplete account of events. Instead, he suggests a *multi-causal* model, whose factors may be independent or interrelated, as with poor dietary habits, low levels of hygiene, and bad housing leading to chronic health problems in communities.

Causation has two important aspects: (i) necessary condition and (ii) sufficient condition. It is accepted that an event can be regarded as the cause of another event if its occurrence is both the necessary and sufficient condition for the latter event to take place. 'A *necessary* condition means that the caused event cannot occur in the absence of the causative event. A *sufficient* condition means that the causative event is all that is needed to bring about the caused event. In other words, in a simple causative relationship, the two events *never* occur in isolation.'[6] This theory of basic and simple causative relationship does not, however, have much relevance to marketing problems which may, for example, be concerned with price reductions resulting in either increases, decreases or no effect at all upon sales, which themselves may change even if prices are unvaried. Environmental factors, such as fashion or consumer tastes, may contribute significantly to the perceived trend of sales.

Contributory cause has been defined as 'the occurrence of one event increasing the likelihood or probability of the occurrence of a second event'.[6]

A price reduction may attract business, i.e. increase the probability of buying, but if the lower price suggests to the buyer that the quality of the product has been debased, the probability of purchase will be likely to decrease instead of increase. In industrial markets, research[7] revealed that price reductions less than 1 per cent of competitors' prices caused virtually no changes in sources of supply, but cuts of 1–9 per cent resulted in about 40 per cent of buyers indicating that they would probably be prepared to change suppliers. However, where prices were reduced by over 10 per cent, only 14 per cent of buyers said they would be willing to switch to new sources; if prices are reduced too much, suspicions about quality tend to be aroused and fewer sales may result.

This probabilistic approach leads to experimentation in which, for instance, the results of two test markets are evaluated statistically. (See later section on experimentation.)

Three factors are likely to be useful in inferring causation: (i) *concomitant variation*; (ii) *time sequence of occurrence*; and (iii) *absence of other possible causal factors*.

Concomitant variation may be inferred where a marketing resource, such as advertising expenditure, is raised simultaneously across a number of market areas and sales in each are measured. If sales are high where extensive advertising occurs, but low sales are experienced where advertising expenditures are limited, it could be inferred (but not proved) that advertising causes sales to rise. Other tests might involve different elements of the marketing mix, e.g. packaging might be varied and sales measured in different territories or markets.

Time sequence of occurrence may also produce evidence of causation of some kind; one event must necessarily precede the other, otherwise it clearly cannot be said to cause the latter. If, for example, sales increases in specific test markets were not apparent until an improved discount structure was offered to distributors, then a causal relationship may be inferred.

Absence of other possible causal factors is most unlikely to happen in real-life business conditions; there is always the likelihood of some extraneous and hitherto unexpected factor to intrude into even the most carefully laid marketing plans. Simplistic interpretations of correlations are well-known hazards in forecasting. In theory, if every possible causative factor other than the particular one under focus was eliminated, then that factor could be accepted as the causative one. However desirable this may be, realism dictates that marketers have to exercise their skills in imperfect conditions and take every care in devising and interpreting market test operations. (See Section 2.8: Experimentation.)

KEYPOINT

Causal research

Attempts to identify cause-and-effect relationships between specific market behaviour, such as variations in pricing, packaging, advertising of products/brands

But correlations among variables need to be evaluated cautiously – association is not necessarily causation

Also, experiments and long-term measurement (panel research) are often adopted, but the former tend to be both involved and expensive (see later discussion)

KEYPOINT

3 types of research design:

1. Exploratory – investigating and identifying real nature of research problems.

2. Descriptive – concerned with counting and describing specific features (e.g. market demand, economic data) of markets, people, etc.

3. Causal – attempts to identify and evaluate factors underlying market behaviour: cautious approach vital.

Reliability and validity factors

Reliability and validity are crucial aspects of research practice and the importance of these criteria should be fully recognized by all who are engaged in survey work of any kind. These terms are not always readily distinguished; some degree of overlap seems almost inevitable and they are, in any case, interconnected.

Reliability refers to the stability and consistency of the results derived from research: to the probability that the same results could be obtained if the measures used in the research were replicated. Perfect coincidence of such measures would not be likely, however, and acceptability could range over specified limits, expressed in the form of correlation coefficients. Essentially, reliability is concerned with the consistency, accuracy and predictability of specific research findings.

Validity refers to how well a specific research method measures what it claims to measure. For example, a thermometer is designed to measure temperature, and a barometer to measure atmospheric pressure. It is generally more difficult to resolve validity than reliability.

Three main types of validity are: (i) *internal validity* which refers to the measures related to a specific survey rather than to the generalizability of the findings; (ii) *face validity* which refers to the results from a specific survey that appear generally plausible in the lack of supporting evidence – perhaps the appeal is to so-called common sense; and (iii) *external validity* which, as distinct from internal validity, refers to the degree to which specific research results could be generalizable to other, dissimilar, research situations. For instance, findings from a survey among students to discover attitudes and patterns of consumption related to some particular food may have high internal validity but would not necessarily reflect the food preferences of the general public, i.e. it would not be valid to generalize from such a survey.

For a research measure to be valid, it must also be reliable. But if it is reliable, it may or may not be valid. Hence, reliability is a necessary but not sufficient condition for validity. It may be known, for instance, that a certain clock consistently records the time as five minutes in advance of the actual time, so this instrument's performance may be regarded as having a degree of reliability or consistency, but it would certainly lack validity.

The main methods for estimating validity are briefly: *construct validity*; *content validity*; *concurrent validity*; and *predictive validity*.

Construct validity entails understanding the theoretical rationale which underlies the measurements derived from specific research. In practical marketing research, this type of validity is seldom given attention. Moser,[4] referring to scaling methods (see Chapter 7), notes that the essence of construct validity is its dependence on theory, and that the examination of the observed associations is as much a test of the theory as of the scale's validity. Content validity refers to the appropriateness of the research measure used; this logical approach assesses, for instance, whether the full range of attributes relevant to a specific product/service are included in a particular scaling technique, in a research survey aimed to discover people's attitudes and opinions about competing retail store groups.

Concurrent and predictive validity are viewed by Moser[4] as essentially the same, except that, as the terms suggest, the former relates to performance at about the same time as, for instance, when a scale is being administered, whereas the latter relates to future perform-ance. Hence, predictive validity is concerned with how well a research measure can predict something in the future, contrasted with concurrent validity which relates to the present time, and might be used to assess the appropriateness of a research measure designed to assess present buying intentions. Concurrent validity might involve comparing the results from two different types of survey methodologies (one existing and the other a proposed new approach using novel techniques); the objective might be to evaluate the quality of service offered to motorists at petrol stations in the UK. Provided the surveys were done under identical or similar conditions, the resultant measures could be compared and tested by correlation to establish the concurrent validity of the proposed new measures.

Principal methods of estimating the reliability of measurements are: (i) *test–retest*; (ii) *alterna tive forms*; and (iii) *split-half*. The first type involves repeating the same measure under, supposedly, identical conditions – examples are given in Section 2.8, ranging from simple to more sophisticated tests. However, this approach is seldom feasible in marketing research, because a second test cannot be considered as being quite independent of the first test. For example, asking people for their opinions about a new retail store in the locality would alert them to its presence, and similar enquiries on another occasion to the same sample would introduce bias into their responses.

The alternative forms method involves, as the name suggests, two forms of measuring instruments, which are assumed to be equivalent, being applied to the same sample, and the results correlated. For example, two versions of a survey questionnaire may be devised, both similar and basically covering the same topic, but the form of questions would be varied. The results would be correlated.

The third method – split-half – is really a variant of the alternative forms method, and is the most widely used; it entails dividing the sample into two matched halves, applying the alternative research techniques, and correlating the responses; a high correlation would indicate, for instance, that items on a scale (see Chapter 7) were measuring the same attribute of a product or service.

KEYPOINT

Reliability and validity are crucial aspects of research; some degree of overlap occurs; they are interconnected

Reliability refers to stability and consistency of results from research – that the same results could be obtained if the same methods of sampling, questioning and analytical measures were applied many times, i.e. replicated

Validity refers to the extent to which a specific research method measures (without bias) what it claims to measure

For a research method to be valid, it must also be reliable

But a research method may be reliable but not necessarily valid

Hence, reliability is a necessary but not sufficient condition for validity

2.3 Sequential stages of marketing research

Five logical steps can be identified in the survey process; these apply irrespective of the nature of the market – consumer, industrial, or public service (see Fig. 2.1).

KEYPOINT   5 sequential stages of marketing research are applicable to *all* enquiries: consumer, business-to-business, services or public sector

Stage 1: Research brief

This first stage is critical because it will decide the nature and direction of the entire research activity.

The marketing problem on which the survey is expected to focus should be clearly defined. Before this clear definition is possible, it may be necessary, as indicated earlier, to undertake some exploratory research into certain aspects of the client's business, e.g. the sales organization, methods of publicity, distribution arrangements, etc., in an attempt to pinpoint areas of significance to the enquiry. By consulting sales records, holding informal discussions with company executives and other staff, comparing published figures with company statistics, and generally checking through all those factors in the business that are likely to influence the situation as a whole, researchers gain a valuable insight into the client's business. Preparatory work of this nature, carried out conscientiously and objectively, is an essential element in the systematic study of marketing problems. After this preliminary study has been made researchers should be in a position to know whether it would be advisable for the clients to commission formal research into particular areas of their business activities, or if the present analysis provides adequate knowledge about their particular problem. The outcome will obviously depend on individual cases and their characteristics.

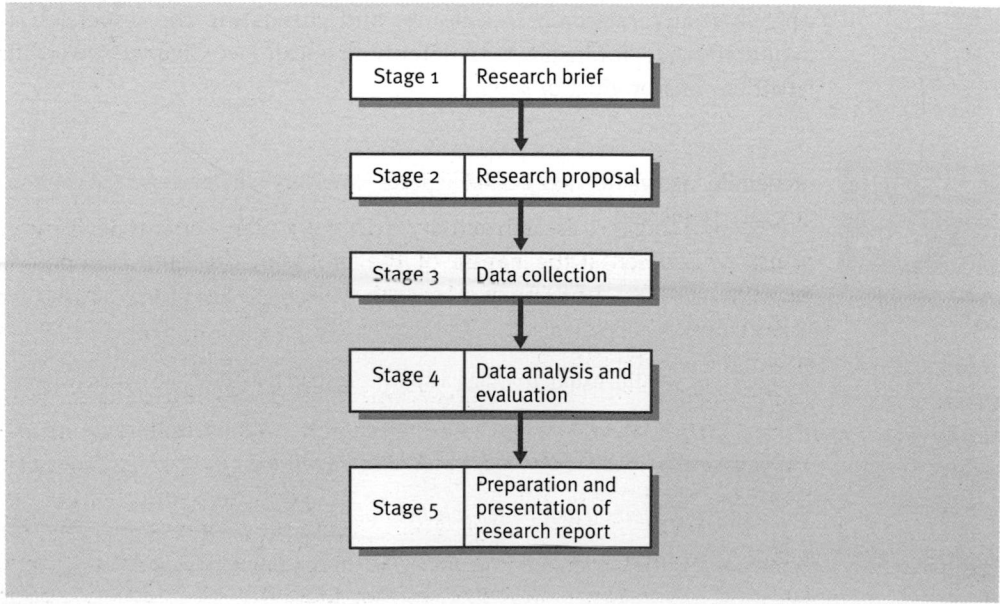

Figure 2.1   Five sequential stages of market research

Both management and researchers should work closely together in this crucial task of developing survey objectives. For example, it is extremely important to define clearly the actual population to be surveyed. Unless the briefing is thorough – and an unbiased account of the firm and its problems is given by management – the resultant research objectives may be irrelevant and even counter-productive. The researcher should indicate the limitations of survey methodology; both parties should agree on the degree of accuracy required, the date by which the report is to be submitted, and the appropriate costs involved.

Assuming that additional research is thought to be necessary, clients and researchers must now agree on the exact terms of reference, including a statement of the problems that is unambiguous and directly useful as a guide during the research operations. This statement will discipline the whole process of research, concentrating activities and integrating them effectively in an overall planned scheme of investigation.

At this stage it would be useful to refer to Fig. 2.2 which sets out a sequential approach to the decision processes involved in considering whether or not to commission marketing research. If knowledge about a particular market is judged to be adequate and the opportunities it promises have been carefully evaluated against demands on corporate resources (including assessment of the risks), it may be feasible to go ahead to product development and eventual launch without incurring the costs and inevitable delay of obtaining further market information. But nowadays, few companies are likely to feel confident enough to enter new markets or expand significantly their present activities, without rigorous and comprehensive evaluations of market trends, competitive strategies, etc.

KEYPOINT

Stage 1: Research brief

Clients and researchers should work closely in developing research objectives

Briefing by clients should be thorough and objective

Researchers should get to grips quickly with the specific problems facing their clients

Both clients and researchers should agree on the nature and scope of the research objectives

Stage 2: Research proposal

The second stage of research activity – the work plan – entails devising a research proposal which will describe the nature of the problem, the precise population involved, the principal factors affecting market behaviour, the methodologies to be adopted, and estimates of time and costs. This proposal should be agreed in detail before entering the next phase of research.

This stage of the research programme includes, for example, exploring and analysing relationships between variables that appear to be significant in the problem being surveyed. It may take some time before a satisfactory model can be built. Over a series of stages of development, through refining and clarifying the various factors in the problem, a useful model should emerge. The careful study involved in the search for facts and relationships will result in researchers having a thorough grasp and appreciation of all the facets of the research problem. This enables them to develop and select hypotheses that are appropriate to the research task. The objectives of the research have now been developed and refined into a series of working hypotheses which can be tested during the course of research. Ideally, a single hypothesis may emerge, the testing of which will adequately fulfil the research objectives. Some leading researchers[8] have commented:

Essentially, therefore, working hypotheses arise as a result of a priori thinking about the subject, preliminary investigation of available data and material (including related studies), or advice and counsel of experts or interested parties. Like the formulation of the problem, such hypotheses are most useful when expressed in precise, clearly defined terms.

Occasionally, a problem will be encountered which won't need working hypotheses. This is particularly true of numerical estimation problems, such as, say, estimating the proportion of families covered by sickness insurance.

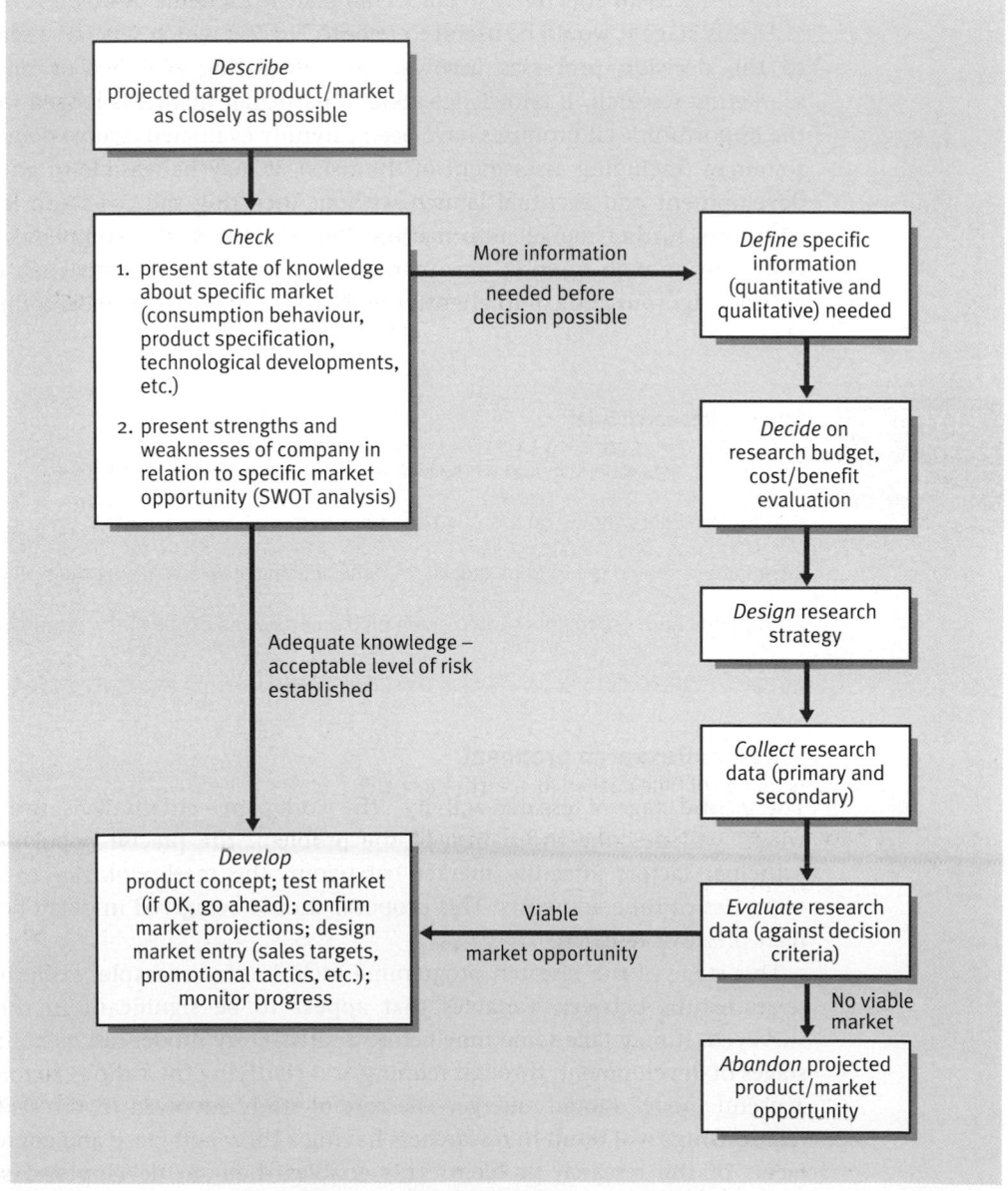

Figure 2.2 Decision-making approach to marketing research

The objective of a survey might be concerned with evaluating the influence on sales of a proposed new style of packaging for a range of products. Before making this fundamental change in packaging, for example, from fibre-board cartons to blister packs, research is undertaken to test the hypothesis that sales are significantly affected by the type of packaging used. The extent of any increase in sales is carefully examined in view of probably additional costs in packaging. Information is, therefore, needed on the sales of products packaged in alternative forms. Data are collected over a series of test markets.

Designing research for international marketing is, of course, generally far more complex than for one country. 'The conduct of research in different countries implies much greater attention to defining the relative unit and level of analysis . . .'[3] (Also see Chapter 13.)

Data for marketing research can be obtained by several methods; the research proposal will have submitted a general outline of the methodology. No research method is without bias; it is the task of professional researchers to eliminate, as far as possible, the intrusiveness of bias in surveys, which is likely to be controlled by a multi-technique approach. (See later discussion.)

Unfortunately, there are several sources of error in surveys. Samples, for example, may be defective; questions may be badly drafted or misunderstood; the interviewing process may lack objectivity; or the quality of the data may suffer from inappropriate coding.

The types of data required must be checked and considered in relation to the sources from which such information could be obtained. The methods of collecting the data must also be studied, and alternatives compared for their efficiency and likely value to the research.

KEYPOINT

Stage 2: Research proposal (work plan)

Clear statement of nature of research problem

Specify precise population involved and principal factors that appear to influence market behaviour

Specify research objectives

Specify research methodologies and explain these to clients

Indicate degree of accuracy likely to be achievable in research findings

Give estimates of time needed for effective research

Indicate terms of contract including cost and payment terms

Mutual trust and co-operation increase research effectiveness

Stage 3: Data collection

This stage will be a central part of the research activities. An effective sampling plan will have been devised in Stage 2, and the relative efficiencies of various methods of collecting data will have been evaluated. In this stage, the survey methodology has to be put into practice; since time constraints are inevitable, it would be advisable to plan operations on a time schedule.

Since so much of the efficiency of the complete research programme depends on reliable and valid data being gathered by researchers, activities during this stage of research should be carefully planned and executed, while control of field research should be in the hands of an experienced supervisor.

KEYPOINT

Stage 3: Data collection

Carefully check the following:

Sampling scheme

Data sources   (internal – desk research)
                (external – field research)

Time schedule of operations

Fieldwork organization

Stage 4: Data analysis and evaluation

The raw material of the research process, i.e. data, has to be processed by tabulation, analysis, and interpretation, so that the research findings can be communicated to clients and readily understood. This stage covers more than the mere mechanical handling of a mass of data. Significant relationships must be identified and discussed clearly and objectively in connection with the specific problems of the research. Data are expensive to collect and analyse; full value should be extracted from them.

According to the complexity and volume of the data collected, tabulations and analyses may range from hand processing through to sophisticated computer packages. But it is useless – if not decidedly dangerous – to apply sophisticated statistical tests to data that originate from an unsound research design. Unless care is taken at every stage of the survey process, the resultant information, masquerading as scientific, may be worth less than subjective opinion.

KEYPOINT

Stage 4: Data analysis and evaluation

Carefully check that:

Methods of analysis are appropriate for type of data (quantitative and/or qualitative)

Potentially important relationships between market variables are identified and discussed objectively

Relevant tabulations and analyses have been fully completed

Processed data are likely to fulfil research objectives

All statistical terms (such as 'significance') used are fully explained

Raw material ,i.e. data, has to be processed through tabulation, analysis and interpretation

Stage 5: Preparation and presentation of final report

This last stage in the research process should be done thoroughly. During the preceding stage, researchers will be planning how to present their findings. Tables, graphs, and other diagrams may be developed from the processed data to illustrate the principal findings of the research.

Writing a marketing survey report involves professional skills in communication. Both the content and style of the report should satisfy the needs of specific clients. The format, printing, and binding of the report deserve considerable care; they help to make a report intelligible and effective. Whether researchers should interpret the research findings is open to debate, and is discussed later in this text. Some clients are content with the facts being reported, while others seek for the researchers' interpretation because it is likely that they will have acquired special insight into the business and its markets. The scope of researchers' responsibilities should, of course, be clarified in the research proposal.

KEYPOINT

Stage 5: Preparation and presentation of survey report

Carefully check that:

Discussion of research findings develops in logical sequence

Report is clearly written and avoids jargon (explain technical terms and abbreviations)

Text is supported by well devised tables, graphs, etc.

Overall design of report – format, printing and binding – conveys professionalism

Summary of report is available for senior management to peruse quickly

This final stage of research activities should be done thoroughly: communication of research findings is an essential part of research responsibilities

2.4 Classification of data

In the preceding section, the main processes of research methodology were outlined; in this section more detailed attention will be given to the main sources of data and the research instruments used.

There are *two generic classifications* of data on which research designs depend:

1. *Primary data*: data that have to be collected for the first time by either one or a blend of
   (a) observation
   (b) experimentation
   (c) questionnaires

2. *Secondary data*: existing information that may be useful for the purposes of specific surveys. This may be available
   (a) internally
   (b) externally

KEYPOINT

Two generic classifications of survey data

1. Primary: collected for first time by either one or blend of:
    observation
    experimentation
    questionnaires

2. Secondary – existing information available:
    internally
    externally (official/commercial)

Check internal sources of relevant information

Proceed to identify specific external sources

Assess state of knowledge after thoroughly evaluating data from internal and external sources

Check research objectives, and decide whether present knowledge is adequate to provide client with required market information

If further information clearly necessary, proceed to primary data collection

Discrimination in data

During the late eighteenth century and the first half of the nineteenth century, the Industrial Revolution developed rapidly in Britain and led to the Industrial Age. In the latter half of the twentieth century, the service industries significantly replaced basic manufacturing industry, while the newer industries of, for example, electronics, biochemicals, computers and telecommunications have risen to prominence. The Information Age is the dynamic successor to the Industrial Age.

In many organizations often there is no shortage of information: the trouble is that it is frequently the wrong kind of information – excessive, irrelevant, incompatible, and also outdated. Relatively simple but up-to-date market information is more useful to management than sophisticated analyses which have lost most of their value because of excessive delay in collection and presentation. Discrimination should be exercised in the selection of data; sheer abundance leads merely to computerized confusion. Before seeking information, marketing management should discipline its search by defining with care the nature of the problem with which it is faced. Too frequently, managers appear to be trying to solve problems which they have not sufficiently identified and then blithely expect marketing researchers to pull the chestnuts out of the fire for them.

Although marketing research is indeed a valuable management tool, managers should not expect too much from it. For instance, the data collected may be of exceptional quality but the wrong decisions may be taken, perhaps because the data have been misinterpreted and/or wrong prognoses have been made. The fact that techniques such as marketing research may reduce the extent of risk in management decisions does not absolve managers from exercising skill, judgement, and initiative. The interpretation of the data in a marketing research report may give rise to different opinions which may be hotly argued. According to the requirements of the research brief, researchers may be asked to interpret as well as present the data collected from market surveys (see Chapter 13).

2.5 Main categories of research techniques

Both primary and secondary data will be discussed in some detail later in this chapter, but first of all, it would be worthwhile to reflect on the sad but true fact that the process of research is subject to many sources of bias. Every attempt should be made to reduce to the minimum, if not eradicate entirely, the intrusion of bias in research practice. With this point in mind it is advisable to note that two main categories of research techniques can be identified: *reactive* and *normative*. The former relates to survey situations where data originate from interaction between investigators and respondents as in interviews, questionnaires, or experiments. The latter techniques, also known as non-reactive measures, relate to surveys involving, for example, observation or library research, where there is no dependence on respondents directly to give information. It is recommended[9] that non-reactive measures, described as 'unobtrusive', should be more widely adopted by marketing researchers. Refer to Chapter 3 for further discussion on the nature and intrusion of bias in marketing research.

KEYPOINT

Research process is subject to many sources of bias

No research method is without bias

Professional researchers aim to eliminate, as far as possible, bias in surveys

A multi-technique approach uses several research tools in order to reduce bias arising from using a single technique

'Unobtrusive measures' help to reduce certain kinds of bias

(Specific biases are discussed in chapters on sampling, questionnaires, and interviewing)

2.6 Desirability of combining survey techniques

The multi-technique approach to research underlines the desirability of using several different methods, which together make up a sound research strategy. It is not so much a question of which *method* is best as which set of methods is likely to result in an objective research programme.

A strong plea for the 'triangulation' of research methods has been made by Webb *et al.*,[9] who are particularly concerned with the limitations of research, especially reactive measurement errors: 'So long as one has only a single class of data collection, and that class is the questionnaire or interview, one has inadequate knowledge of the rival hypotheses grouped under the term reactive measurement effects.'

These potential sources of error, some stemming from an individual's awareness of being tested, others from the nature of the investigator, must be accounted for by some other class of measurement than the verbal self-report.

The obtrusiveness of reactive measures occurs in the social sciences, and it is important for marketing researchers to realize that it is often extremely difficult to eradicate the biases which can arise. A series of linked research operations can be helpful in revealing errors in measurement, the weaknesses of one survey method being compensated for by the particular strengths of an alternative method of investigation.

As observed earlier, no research method is without bias; the specific problems of bias associated with interviewing, questionnaires, and sampling techniques are discussed in some detail later in this text, when it will be apparent that the whole process of research is fraught with many dangers. These can be minimized, however, by intelligent planning in the early stages of designing a research strategy. Admittedly, it is difficult to eliminate entirely the effects of measurement on the subjects of an enquiry.

> *The administration of IQ tests may alter an individual's future performance on tests of this type. Being subjected to socio-economic scales may alter respondents' behaviour by making them more conscious of their 'class' positions. The questions of election pollsters may stimulate a voter to take a stand on an issue.*[10]

Where observation is used, people are often aware that they are being studied and, as a result, may modify their behaviour in some way. In the opening scene of Shaw's play, *Pygmalion*, the behaviour of Eliza Doolittle is strongly influenced because she is aware of being observed by Professor Higgins.

Observation may also suffer from the observer's biases or expectations. The observer must be alert to the danger of seeing only those events which agree with his or her explicit or implicit hypotheses. Observation, to be of value to research, must be objective; observers should not allow themselves to become too involved, emotionally or socially, with those whom they are studying.

The selection and training of observers need to be undertaken with particular care. The reliability of individual observer's reports could be checked, of course, by comparing the reports of a series of identical events which have been observed by two or more observers. Bertrand Russell's witty comment on the study of animal behaviour well illustrates the problem of observer bias.

> *One may say broadly that all the animals that have been carefully observed have behaved so as to confirm the philosophy in which the observer believed before his observation began. Nay, more, they have all displayed the national characteristics of the observer. Animals studied by Americans rush about frantically, with an incredible display of hustle and pep, and at last achieve the desired result by chance. Animals observed by the Germans sit still and think, and at last evolve the solutions out of their inner consciousness.*[11]

The problem of maintaining objectivity arises particularly when participant observation takes place, i.e. the observer is disguised as a member of the society or group being studied, and must, to some extent, act out his or her role. While this type of hidden observation reduces considerably distorted behaviour by the group, it makes stringent demands on the observer, who needs special training for this work. Among the difficulties of operating this form of research is that of recording adequately what is being observed – obviously, overt note taking is out of the question. Participant observation may be particularly difficult in communities that are relatively 'closed', i.e. those which do not assimilate strangers easily, and the mere presence of a 'foreigner' may be sufficient reason for modifying the patterns of normal behaviour. In some cases, it may take a long time before the newcomer is accepted as a member of the group and is able to function usefully as an observer. In other cases, participant observation may have to be called off as impracticable. One of the best-known uses of participant observation in social studies was made by W. J. Whyte[12] in his study of American street-corner society. He lived for three-and-a-half years in a slum district in Boston as a member of various street-corner groups, though members of the group knew that he was studying their style of living.

The ethics of covert observation techniques were raised in a paper[13] published in the *Journal of the Market Research Society* in January 1993, and it was stated that 'many researchers question their use': deception may be present because: (i) the subjects studied are not informed of the research; and (ii) since they are unaware, subjects are not asked for the traditionally required 'informed consent'. However, some researchers are alleged to feel that such techniques are necessary in order to acquire 'truthful information'. On the other hand, the professional codes of the American Marketing Association (AMA) and the Market Research Society (MRS) strictly forbid researchers from engaging in research practices that are contrary to the interests of respondents (see Chapter 13). Noting the paper just quoted, the Chairman of the MRS Professional Standards Committee commented[14] that the concept of covert observation had many attractions both to social scientists and market researchers, but the MRS Code of Conduct was essentially concerned with 'protecting informants from unwelcome intrusion or harm, to respect their rights of privacy, not to reveal their identity without permission, and to ensure that they will be in no way adversely affected or embarrassed as a direct result of participation in a research project'. The topic of covert research appears to require informed and sensitive debate, and the specific issues that are arising will need clarification.

The problem of reactive measures is pervasive and it increases the complexity of research. To reduce this form of bias, researchers have developed techniques which have been classified by Eugene J. Webb and his co-authors[9] as 'unobtrusive measures' or non-reactive research.

Unobtrusive measures allow research to be conducted without the subjects being aware of the process of investigation. Unobtrusive methods include the study of records of births, marriages, and deaths, of official publications of various kinds, company records of purchases and sales, etc. Physical evidence may offer valuable information, e.g. wear and tear on carpets in display areas, fingerprints on museum exhibits, time spent by people in various departments of a store or exhibition. Advertising exposure in a magazine was measured by a 'glue-seal record'. A small spot of glue, which would not reseal once it was broken, was inconspicuously placed close to the binding of the magazine so that it lightly held together each pair of pages in a specially prepared issue. Advertising exposure was assessed by noting whether or not the gum seals had been broken following reading of the magazine. This method was useful in checking the answers to more conventional enquiries, particularly since there is a tendency among respondents to direct questioning to claim viewing or reading habits that do not, in fact, coincide with their actual behaviour.

An interesting account[9] is given of a Chicago automobile dealer, who:

> ... estimates the popularity of different radio stations by having mechanics record the position of the dial in all cars brought in for service. More than 50 000 dials a year are checked, with less than 20 per cent duplication of dials. These data are then used to select radio stations to carry the dealer's advertising.

Webb[9] comments that the generalization of these findings is sound, provided the radio audience is typically the same as those who have their car serviced at the dealership, and that a significant number of cars have radios. Apparently, the American car dealer finds high correlation exists between radio audiences and the 'dial research' findings.

Apart from direct observation, unobtrusive measures may adopt 'contrived observation' including the use of what has been termed 'hidden hardware' operated by the investigator. This method may use one-way mirrors, tape recordings (unknown to those being tested), cine and still photography, etc.

Webb and his associates review some applications of covert research techniques, which range from the videotaping of audiences to concealed recording by a microphone hidden in a mock hearing aid. 'It works extremely well in inducing the subject to lean over and shout directly into the recording apparatus. The presence of a dangling cord does not inhibit response.'

They also mention various studies which have been undertaken to measure eye movement and pupil dilation, indicating the degree of interest shown by subjects in particular advertisements or products. Instruments for testing eye reactions are used in 'laboratory' advertising tests, when, of course, the techniques are generally apparent to the subjects. Webb adds that earlier research reported that Chinese jade dealers were aware of the importance of pupil dilation in expressing a potential buyer's interest in various stones offered to him; apparently, astute buyers wore dark glasses to counter this communication.

Alfred Politz,[15] the veteran American researcher, studied advertising exposure to posters on the outside of buses by means of movie cameras, specially arranged to film people looking towards the buses as they travelled the routes. This pioneer photographic survey technique was used successfully by Politz in Philadelphia in 1959, and in Chicago in 1964–65. It was adapted for research on London Transport bus advertising during 1966.[15,16]

The objectives of the London Transport research project were to derive estimates of the total number of people who were in a position to see advertisements on the outside of London Transport buses. Two separate but complementary surveys were involved: a Greater London survey which recorded time spent on roads that were also bus routes; and a photographic study in which people present on the bus routes were filmed and counted. The results of the first survey were related to the frequency with which the buses travelled the routes, and estimates of the number of 'opportunities to see' advertisements on the outside of buses were made. These estimates were then refined by using the photographic survey to produce estimates of 'full-face' viewing of the buses.

Since the details of this research are interesting, they are reported briefly here. A randomly selected sample of adults in the Greater London area were interviewed during June and July 1966, and information was obtained from 986 persons. Details of the pattern of journeys (both regular and casual) made by informants during a particular period of time, i.e. the seven days preceding the day of interview, were sought. Travel outside the bus route areas was regarded as irrelevant to the study, which was concerned with potential exposure to bus advertising.

The photographic survey covered the period March to September 1966, and involved a random sample of garages from which two or three vehicles per day were equipped with specially mounted cine cameras. These operated for two or three days per week, and a total of 40 000 photographs were taken. In practice, the researchers found that there were certain limitations to this technique because of the effect of shadows and the difficulty of identifying whether or not people were actually looking at the bus. It was only possible to classify people as 'full face' or otherwise.

Filming was intermittent: 11 frames at one-second intervals every two minutes. The average resultant count was then multiplied up to account for the whole hour.

The researchers report that the photographic survey was valuable in providing a cross-check on the results from more conventional research, i.e. interviewing. Because people happen to be within the area of a bus route, it does not necessarily follow that they will see the advertisements displayed on a bus.

The overall results of these two survey methods showed a statistical difference, which was, however, expected because the photographic survey included all individuals on the streets at the time of filming, whereas interviewing covered only residents of the Greater London area. The researchers 'were encouraged to find that agreement between the two methods was as good as it was', and they noted that London Transport advertising data were 'based mainly on the results of the interview survey, which, in fact, was a significantly lower estimate of advertising exposure'.

This interesting example of a dual method of investigation underlines the value of combining techniques in order to check data from one particular source and to give it greater acceptability.

In 1934, La Piere[17] studied the relationship between written statements and overt acts (behaviour) in a research on prejudice. He travelled throughout the US in company with a Chinese couple and visited 250 catering establishments; they were refused service on only one occasion. Later, when questionnaires were sent to those same establishments, over 90 per cent said they would not accept Chinese customers. La Piere also sent identical questionnaires to a control group of 100 similar catering establishments, which had not been visited by his party, and the response was similar to his earlier finding. However, this particular research has attracted some criticisms, which are discussed elsewhere.[18]

There is need, therefore, for a more imaginative approach to research with a willingness to consider alternative and complementary methodological strategies. While 'questionnaires and interviews are probably the most flexible and generally useful devices we have for gathering information',[9] a more creative approach, using multi-measurement techniques, reduces the dangers of reactive effects. There is no standard strategy suitable for every research problem; researchers must examine scrupulously and sensitively the requirements of individual enquiries. Research strategies should be designed to meet the identified needs of specific studies, bearing in mind the earlier comment that a sound research strategy is concerned not so much with what method is best as to what set of methods is most likely to result in objective findings.

The value of combining survey methods was advocated by the well-known American researcher, Stanley L. Payne,[19] some years ago:

> Still, it is only recently that our eyes have been opened to the fruitful idea of using the basic survey methods in combination. We may have been too blind from looking upon them as exclusive alternatives to observe that they might be applied as complementary parts of a single investigation . . . sometimes a combination of all three methods (e.g. mail, telephone, personal interviews) may be used with the same respondents to produce results more efficiently than one method alone could do. What is wanted in survey design is an imaginative and flexible approach.

While contrived observation involving the use of 'hidden hardware' has methodological attractions, the increasing inventiveness of electronic apparatus in social research gives rise to the ethical implications involved in using them indiscriminately. In discussing such methods, Webb and associates, while recognizing the ethical issues which they raise: 'feel that this is a matter for separate consideration'. They do not feel able to pass judgement on the ethics of these complex issues, and invite 'thoughtful debate on these matters'.[9] The Market Research Society has specifically referred to this issue in its Code of Conduct to which members are expected to adhere.

Market research in countries where there are low levels of literacy, and where lists from which to draw samples are very unlikely to be available, demands considerable ingenuity in devising research instruments and tactics.

Observational and projective techniques avoid some of the problems associated with survey techniques since they do not impose on respondents any prestructured frame of reference, which may reflect the specific cultural referents of the researcher. On the other hand, the lack of structure implies that the onus of data interpretation lies on the researcher, and hence cultural bias may occur at the analysis stage.[3]

2.7 Primary data – observation

This non-reactive research technique, widely used in scientific studies and often termed the 'classical method of investigation', has several applications in marketing research. It can be used alone or in conjunction with other forms of research to supplement the data collected. It is particularly useful in checking the validity of answers given in a questionnaire. For many reasons, people may not give completely accurate accounts of their actual behaviour; what they say they buy, or where they actually shop may not necessarily coincide with the answers given to an interviewer. Experienced researchers know well the inclinations of respondents to protect their egos, to project favourable images of themselves, and, on occasions, to distort their reputed beliefs and behaviour in order to 'shock' those surveying them.

In Britain, as noted in Chapter 1, Tom Harrison popularized the use of observational techniques in social enquiries, and many of his studies have acquired the aura of pioneer investigations. However, it should be borne in mind that since those early days of market and social research, more elaborate and sophisticated alternative methods of collecting data have been developed and considerable expertise now exists in, for example, organizing non-directive discussion groups (see Chapter 8).

Observation, as indicated in the preceding section, may be either participative or non-participative. Participant observation would seem to have very limited application in marketing research.

In marketing research, *three methods of observation* are in general use: *audits*, *recording devices*, and *watching people's behaviour as buyers*.

Audits/recording devices

The audit technique is exemplified by shop audit research as practised by Nielsen's, by which physical checks of selected types of products are made every few weeks in order to estimate actual sales at certain outlets. Physical stock-auditing is now largely replaced by scanner auditing techniques (see Chapter 8). Traffic counts are often taken in shopping centres to note the intensity and flow of shoppers. This information is useful in locating display areas in strategic positions. Research on poster advertising is largely done by observing the volume and type of traffic that passes poster sites (see Chapter 10).

Recording devices used in observation include hidden movie cameras (see next section). In laboratory situations, devices like the psycho-galvanometer are used to check reactions to selected types of advertisements. This meter, by measuring changes in the electrical resistance in the palms of a subject's hands, registers perspiratory rates, which are increased by excitement. The impact of a series of advertisements is checked against meter readings.

Electronic recording equipment – bar coding, scanners and computer-based systems are now all integrated into retailing audits, panel research and advertising research; they have revolutionized data collection methodologies. Electronic Point-of-Sale Scanning (EPOS) facilitates check-out operations, stock control and sales analyses as well as being used for marketing research purposes (see Chapter 8). Scanner-based test marketing, using 'smart cards', which are presented by selected shoppers at check-out points, records purchases of specific products and brands (see Chapter 9). Both Nielsen and Taylor Nelson Sofres operate extensive home-based panels which use electronic scanners (see Chapter 8). BARB (Broadcasters' Audience Research Board) is responsible for BBC and commercial television research; electronic meters are fixed to a sample of television sets and record viewing habits. Television advertising research methods across the major European countries are based on similar electronic systems (see Chapter 10).

Watching people's behaviour as buyers

Observational techniques were adopted to evaluate the use of car seat belts in the UK. Observers were sited at a representative number of points to note the proportions of drivers and front seat passengers who were wearing their seat belts. The researchers[21] reported that this research technique was the principal one used by the Central Office of Information to monitor the effectiveness of the advertising campaign urging motorists to use their seat belts. If straight questioning had been employed, it was recognized that the usage of seat belts would be overstated.

It was reported[22] that Honda observed the ways in which people loaded the boots of their cars and, as a result, redesigned the Honda Civic hatchback. The manufacturers of Philips shavers identify customers' needs partly through observing, through a two-way mirror, a recruited sample's typical shaving techniques.

Surveillance cameras were introduced into stores in order to discourage shop-lifting which, apart from the crime involved, has grown to be a significant cost factor in retail operations. Banks, offices and other vulnerable establishments are now fitted with surveillance equipment.

Video cameras are now being used to study the ways in which people shop, and it was reported[23] that a new division of NOP is developing this observational methodology in retail stores in the UK. The cameras are placed either like standard monitoring devices or mini-versions are concealed inside display cabinets. It has been discovered, for instance, that shoppers in a supermarket take between 30 seconds and one minute before selecting each grocery item.

Shoppers' typical behaviour is recorded and analysed, for example, by body language and the degree to which couples appear to become involved in the processes of attention, selection and eventual purchase of certain types of products; researchers can discover how long prospective purchasers take before buying a particular product or brand; what attention they pay to the information on the labels of packaged foods, etc. As long ago as 1975, it was reported[1] that hidden movie cameras were used in research to evaluate the amount of information that should be given on packaging labels by a manufacturer of frozen juice concentrates. In a number of supermarkets, films were taken of shoppers selecting frozen juice concentrates. Analysis of these films revealed that far more time was spent in carefully examining and in selecting brands than had previously been believed.

Camera-based research is disciplined by the MRS's code of ethics, which states that consumers should not be filmed unless they are in a situation where they could reasonably expect to be seen or heard; this rules out, for example, the use of cameras in changing rooms.

Personal observation by trained observers can be useful in many situations. Rival stores frequently check the special displays, prices, and merchandising techniques adopted by competitors. Observers can watch people's behaviour when they enter a particular department of a store; how many walk round before settling down to consider specific styles or types of products; how important it is to shoppers to be able to handle goods, to feel their quality or weight; how many approach shop assistants for help, and how soon after entering the department; how carefully shoppers read labels, packaging, or 'guarantee cards' attached to products. All these (and more) can be checked and assessed for their importance as buying influences, and compared with answers received using questionnaires.

Observation of behaviour is rarely sufficient by itself; it yields information at a certain level, but it does not reveal hidden buying motives. When the technique is practised by skilled observers, it can be an economical method of acquiring additional knowledge about buying behaviour which may be unobtainable by other methods. Few people, for example, could accurately describe their customary shopping behaviour in detail, and the peculiarities of their behaviour may strongly influence their selection of products or brands of products.

Observers must be given clear instructions on the nature of the action or event which they are to observe. Detailed instructions should cover the time, place, and conditions involved to ensure that observations are likely to take place in representative situations. Traffic flow will obviously be affected by time; weather conditions may radically alter the normal pattern of buying behaviour. Observational data should be recorded on a specifically designed schedule to help in analysis and classification.

Apart from shoppers, the behaviour of shop assistants, for example, can be usefully observed. Do they appear biased towards a particular brand of product? Are they unwilling to demonstrate some item of domestic equipment? Do they appear to argue strongly with customers? This type of observational research has been developed further into so-called 'mystery shopping'.

Mystery shopping

Mystery shopping or mystery-customer research has developed markedly in the UK since the 1980s, and several market research companies offer this service. NOP, for instance, employs teams of professional 'mystery shoppers', who are fitted with unobtrusive micro-cameras to record the performance of sales staff. The 1998/99 Research Buyers Guide, published by the Market Research Society, listed 116 agencies offering mystery-shopping services; in 1994, there were 28 firms listed. The relatively rapid growth of this form of participant observation has obviously resulted from its increasing acceptance by leading clients such as Peugeot, Selfridges and Jaeger, who have wanted to evaluate the service received by their customers. Market research interviewers, posing as shoppers, are trained to observe closely all the aspects of customer service during a typical shopping trip. This type of research activity has also been extended from a client's own outlets to those of competitors. Competitor mystery shopping has aroused some concern, although research 'shoppers' are instructed that their activities should not involve staff in giving unduly extended time to these 'shopping enquiries'.

Mystery shopping is also used in the hotel and catering industries, travel organizations and financial services. It was valuable, for instance, as an input into London Underground's plans for the improvement of their public transport network in and around London. Each quarter, teams of trained 'service auditors' act as anonymous travelling customers and evaluate – on 10-point rating scales – specific aspects of the London Underground, including the appearance of stations and staff, and assessment of product knowledge and helpfulness. In order to check that the results from this 'mystery shopping' are a reliable and reasonable accurate measure of service performance, about 2400 face-to-face interviews are conducted every four weeks. The results of these customer satisfaction enquiries are subjected to regression analysis with the mystery-shopping scores, and it has been shown that there is statistical proof that changes in mystery-shopping scores feed through to changes in customer satisfaction.[24]

However, mystery shopping has attracted some criticism largely on account of the sample sizes., the quantitative measures used and issues of privacy, as well as professional ethics. The codes of conduct of the Market Research Society and also ESOMAR were said to leave some aspects of mystery-shopping, such as 'competitor mystery-shopping', 'open to interpretation and manipulation'. So the MRS Professional Standards Committee conducted a survey of client and agency views of this particular research activity. The findings 'highlighted a need for clearer guidelines regarding competitor mystery shopping to avoid the disruption of an organization's business'. It also recommended that this technique should 'ideally be regulated' to uphold its usefulness and to avoid it being conducted in a 'free for all' environment. The committee's report included 'specific suggestions' to the MRS to help the research industry 'in conducting high quality and ethical mystery-shopping research'.[25]

In March 1997, *Best Practice in Mystery Customer Research* was published, as the result of joint discussions between certain research clients and a special interest group of the MRS.

Despite its attraction of being unobtrusive, mystery shopping, like qualitative research, is prone to subjective interpretation, and comparatively little is known about its accuracy – the reliability and validity of the technique.[26] Some of these problems arise from the demands made on the memories of the assessors (assuming that hardware such as cameras are not being used) to recall and record all the relevant aspects of the observations made during a particular mystery-shopping event. This problem may largely be overcome by expertly designed assessment forms which guide the researcher through the sequences of the shopping encounter. As with well-drafted questionnaires (see Chapter 5), assessment forms should avoid suggesting that one kind of behaviour or response is to be preferred to another.

If it is planned to use mystery shopping inside an organization, staff should be informed of the nature and objectives of the technique and of the typical coverage of such an event. Further, they should be assured of confidentiality and that their identities would not be revealed in the resultant research report. It would also be advisable to ensure that staff representatives and unions were fully informed of the research plans.

2.8 Primary data – experimentation

In most fields of scientific enquiry, research is primarily centred around controlled experiments in which efforts are made to hold conditions constant, thus enabling the effects of a particular factor or variable to be studied and measured. Any change observed to have taken place in the test situation is measured, statistically checked by tests of significance, and, according to the results of these tests, the change may be held to be attributable to the intervention of the independent variable.

The ideal experimental conditions of laboratory testing are virtually impossible in the real-life conditions experienced in marketing. The environment in which commercial transactions take place is highly complex and many factors affecting product sales, e.g. competitors' activities, economic conditions, climatic changes, dealers' resistance, etc., cannot be controlled by the marketer. Marketing is deeply involved with human behaviour and with the reactions of people as consumers of a very wide range of goods and services. This involvement makes marketing experiments difficult to plan and execute, yet some attempt should be made to apply the principles of experimentation, as this is the only research method available for verifying cause and effect relationships in marketing studies. The marketing researcher has to be realistic in accepting the inevitable limitations of the marketing environment, and design his or her experiments so that the influence of the uncontrolled variables intrudes as little as possible in the research design.

In overseas marketing, Douglas and Craig[3] emphasize that while, in theory, experimental techniques are applicable to all cultural and socio-economic backgrounds, in practice it is difficult to design an experiment that is comparable or equivalent in all respects in every country or socio-cultural environment. Differences in distributive arrangements or in the nature and level of competition tend to frustrate the strict comparability of such tests.

The object of marketing experiments is to compare the responses to several alternatives in the marketing mix and to evaluate this information as a guide to management in deciding the most effective method of marketing specific products. Variations of product (flavour, colour); packaging (large packs, various kinds of packs); advertising (whether to advertise or not, what media to use); distribution arrangements (direct, appointed stockists, wholesale); price (price differentiation); sales force efficiency (sales training – formal/informal): these are some of the factors affecting marketing efficiency that could be subjected to experimentation.

Advertising experiments can be planned by using 'split-runs'; changing the style of advertisement in alternative editions or runs of a publication and checking the response, for example, to a coupon offer. The location of departments in stores can be experimentally changed and a check kept on sales. Display units may be placed in some stores (and not in others, which will be carefully chosen to act as 'controls') and comparative sales can be audited over a period of time.

Marketing experiments are often focused on short-term studies and this may possibly lead to wrong assumptions. The 'carry-over' effects of advertising, for example, may be significant from one selling period to another; for example, the case of the Du Pont advertising tests with 'Teflon' (Chapter 11). The time-lag before an idea is accepted may be considerable and acceptance may only occur after the promotion has finished. Where panels are used to evaluate the effects of advertising, the likelihood of 'carry-over' effects should be assessed. It may be advisable to extend testing beyond the actual period of advertising to ensure that the long-term effects are adequately measured.

The most popular use of experiments in marketing occurs with test marketing, which is discussed in some detail later. The techniques used in test marketing have improved considerably, although, of course, the environmental conditions of testing are still liable to be affected by unexpected interference, such as widespread labour redundancies in a test area. The experimental approach of test marketing is valuable in providing management with data collected in real-life conditions; the conclusions drawn from this research can be formally established as statistically significant or otherwise.

A model of the experimental method applied to marketing behaviour is shown in Fig. 2.3.

It will be seen that the model in Fig. 2.3 includes 'variation' which may be any of three types: (i) primary, (ii) secondary, or (iii) error. Primary variation refers to variation in the output caused by changes in the inputs, e.g. sales increasing because of price reductions. Secondary variation refers to variation in output resulting from changes in unidentified or exogenous variables, such as weather conditions. Error variation relates to variation in output caused by imperfect experimental conditions, e.g. measurement errors.

Figure 2.3 relates to a simplified market experiment; controls would be introduced to render the experiment more effective. Experimental designs vary considerably and may involve considerable complexity, e.g. before and after measurements, controls, multivariate analysis, etc.

For example, 'control' areas are frequently introduced when checking the effect of marketing stimuli such as comparative promotion campaigns for a consumer product. The effects on sales in different areas of alternative forms of promotion (e.g. press advertising versus local radio) can be compared and contrasted with sales in a control area where no kind of promotion took place. It may be found that some common factor, such as the temperature, may be influential in sales trends, and, in fact, the effects of promotion could be minimal.

A more detailed account of nine principal types of errors which can affect experimental results will be found in Green and Tull[1] and also in Aaker, Kumar and Day.[6] These are, briefly: premeasurement; maturation; history; instrumentation; selection; mortality; interaction; reactive error; and measurement timing.

Over recent years, greater emphasis has been placed on quantifying marketing problems, and this has encouraged the development of an analytical approach, based on variables which are considered within the framework of a decision model.

Sophisticated experimental designs in marketing may be tested by the statistical techniques of analysis of variance or, perhaps, Latin square designs.[28–30]

Experimental designs can range from the simple to the complex; there are four main types as shown below.

Time series analysis

This could involve just one treatment and subsequent measurement, or, alternatively, several intermittent treatments over a period of time with individual measurements after each treatment. This type of experiment could cover measuring the effect of special displays staged with selected stores. In the first example, sales at these selected stores would be audited for a period before the displays, and also after the displays have been made. Designs can be formed with or without control groups, and with measurements both before and after the intervention of the variable, e.g. advertising, or merely after its introduction. These types can be summarized as follows:

1. *After-only design without control group*

       X0   X = non-random group subject to variable.
             0 = measurement after intervention of variable.

   This is a generally unsatisfactory experimental design as there is no measurement made *before* the variable intervened, and no basis exists for comparison. Also, extraneous variables that could affect the results are not controlled. These shortcomings render this simplistic test inadequate as a basis for management decision making.

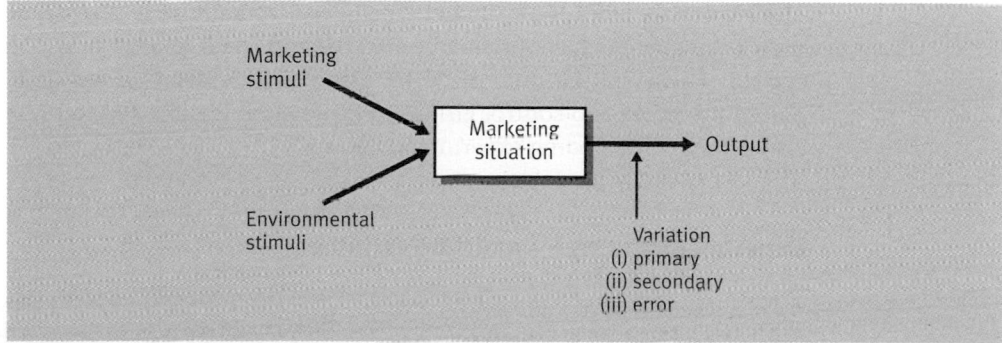

Figure 2.3   Simplified model of experimental method in marketing

2. *Before–after design without control group*

$$0_1X0_2$$

or   (multiple testing)

$$0_10_2X0_30_4$$

The difference between 0_2 and 0_1 indicates the influence of the variable tested.

This is the method applied in consumer panel testing. This is an improvement on 'after-only' designs, particularly when several measurements are taken. The absence of control groups reduces the general validity of this design.

3. *After-only design with control group*

(R) $X0_1$

(R) 0_2 (control group)

Both the test group and control group are randomly selected; the former is subjected to the effect of the variable being tested and the result is compared with the control group. No prior testing is undertaken, so comparisons with earlier situations cannot be made. In some cases, it may not be possible to measure before the test variable is applied, e.g. where a product had not been previously offered for sale. The design is suitable for testing the effectiveness of direct mail advertising, when mailing is directed only to the experimental group and the effectiveness is measured by the equation (0_1-0_2; as above).

4. *Before–after design with control group*

(R) 0_1X0_2

(R) 0_30_4 (control group)

Randomly selected groups control systematic errors. The experimental group and control group should possess similar characteristics in order to allow valid comparisons to be made.

The design can be extended to include several groups. It is useful for testing the effect of advertising in selected areas, although, of course, interpretation of the findings needs to be done with care. The control group is valuable because it is measured before and after the test applied to the other group, and, therefore, the likely effect of other factors during the time of the experiment will be reflected in the final measurement of the control group. This allows the effect of the test variable to be isolated more accurately in the test group comparison.

This type of experimental design is useful when sales data are being studied or in observational studies of consumers. If people are actually interviewed before an experiment, their subsequent behaviour may be affected and result in after measurements being non-typical. This could be minimized by using a more complicated (and more expensive) design involving two control groups, one of which is subjected to prior measurements as also is the corresponding experimental group.

Experimental design – multiple variables

The simple experiments considered so far have been concerned with single variables, such as the effect of advertising or point-of-sale display aids on sales. To restrict testing to only one experimental variable may be difficult in practice and also inefficient.

Factorial designs

These designs permit experiments involving combinations of observations of at least two variables to be tested simultaneously. This type of experiment could refer to a product offered for sale, at the same price, in several selected stores, and supported by varying combinations of display aids, special trade incentives, and display positions. The objective of the experiment is to identify the most profitable marketing mix.

Sophisticated experimental designs can be tested by the technique of analysis of variance, as in the case of Du Pont which used a factorial experiment on two different advertising media that were varied from very low to very high for each of the media. Twenty-seven markets, representing all possible combinations of the intensity test levels of the two media, were used.

Latin square designs

These are modified multi-variable designs, in that the interaction effects are usually assumed not to be significant. This simplifies the analysis, and reduces both time and cost.

These more complicated experimental techniques are fairly popular in studying marketing problems. At the same time, it should be remembered that it is good design practice to select the simplest possible experimental design for the particular problem being studied. Statistical textbooks deal with multi-variable tests in detail.

Davis[28] has stressed that where the relative merits of two or more different 'treatments' are to be assessed (as with comparative tests), a control area is necessary to avoid wrong conclusions. This was illustrated when two experimental methods of promotion in separate areas resulted in sales increases of about 10 per cent. However, a control area in which no advertising took place, showed the same sales increase over the time of the experiment. Apparently, some other factor, perhaps climatic, was affecting sales. Without the control area, the wrong deductions might have been made.

A study[29] conducted in the supermarket section of a large discount store chain in Israel indicated how experimentation can help in designing efficient shelf display. A 4 × 4 Latin square design was used to examine the effect of the four types of display equipment on sales in four stores in successive time periods. Sales from this experiment were subject to analysis of variance and covariance. The results enabled the researchers to suggest specific locations for effective displays in these stores.

James Rothman[30] has helpfully given an illustration of a relatively simple Latin square design related to a store test on a product with a very high rate of sales over four stores during a one-week period. The labels A, B, C, and D represent the different stimuli, and these are arranged (see Fig. 2.4) so that each test stimulus is used once in every week and once in each store.

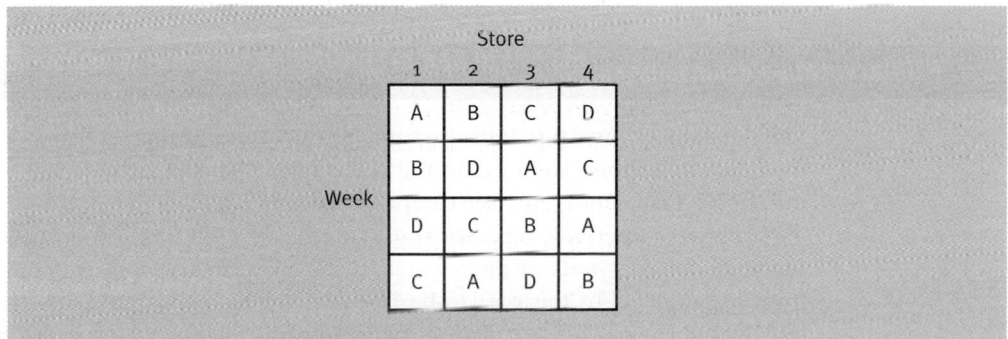

Figure 2.4   Simple Latin square design for promotion

Rothman observes that more advanced versions of this basic experimental design can be used to control the sample across three or more dimensions.

Factorial design experiments can contribute to the development of a new product in which the formulation can be varied.[31] For example, a new hair dressing for men could be varied in terms of colour, perfume, and consistency. It would be both uneconomical and unwise to separate these elements for the purposes of product testing because of the possible interactions of these attributes. A factorial design could be devised that would allow, for example, two variations of each of the three elements (colour, perfume, and consistency) to be evaluated thus:

Colour	Perfume	Consistency
a	a	a
a	a	b
a	b	a
a	b	b
b	a	a
b	a	b
b	b	a
b	b	b

In this design, these three elements are considered over eight different products; the results of the test would be subject to analysis of variance to indicate which, if any, of the three variables significantly affected consumers' reactions to the product and whether any two or all three of the variables revealed an interaction effect.

The economy of adopting this type of experiment is typified by the fact that if a sample of 100 informants was taken and the three variables were tested separately, the total number of interviewees would need to be 300. By using a factorial design, 16 of the 28 possible pairings of test products would entail comparisons of the two variations of each of the three variables. Hence, to obtain 100 reactions to each of these direct comparisons would require a total sample of fewer than 200 informants.

However, marketing experiments remain fairly expensive and their potential value should be estimated against the cost involved, and only proceeded with if it can be shown that the benefits they will bring to the business outweigh the costs incurred. This elementary principle tends to be overlooked at times, and it is as well to bear in mind that research in marketing entails management time and expense. The use of company resources in any area carries with it the responsibility of accounting for the profitable exploitation of them. Marketing researchers will find that the sound principle of accountability disciplines their efforts to advantage.

2.9 Primary data – questionnaires

Most marketing investigations use some form of questionnaire, either postal, face-to-face, including telephone surveys, and also electronic-based methods, such as fax, internet/intranet, e-mail, DBM, etc. (see Chapters 5 and 6).

Face-to-face interviewing is the most commonly used method of survey in the UK, and accounts for over half of all research turnover; primary data can be collected directly from respondents in business-to-business as well as consumer markets. Since the 1980s, however, there has been a distinct trend towards telephone interviewing. Technological developments, e.g. computer-assisted systems have accelerated this trend (see Chapter 5).

In the USA, personal interviewing, once the predominant method, has been largely replaced by telephone interviewing and other methods because of increasing costs and declining response rates.[32]

In 1993, comparative data on UK/USA data collection methods by value indicated[33] that personal interviewing in the UK accounted for 52 per cent against 12 per cent in the USA; telephone interviews represented 16 per cent of UK but 47 per cent of US data collection methods; group discussions were 11 per cent of UK methods against 9 per cent in the USA; self-completion/mail questionnaires 9 per cent in the UK compared with 13 per cent in the USA; and 'hall-tests' 12 per cent in the UK compared with 19 per cent in the USA. (These value data excluded audits and panels.)

The amount of information obtainable from observation and experimentation is limited, whereas interviewing is flexible and capable of yielding a very wide range of valuable new data.

Questionnaires are the backbone of most surveys and require careful planning and execution. The objectives of the survey should always be carefully borne in mind when compiling questionnaires. (The detailed structure of questionnaires is considered in Chapter 6.)

Methods of enquiry

Personal interviewing

This involves trained interviewers working with a carefully selected sample of the population that is under survey. This method is widely used in marketing research. Interviewers must be specially selected, trained, and motivated; they are frequently the weak link in the chain of research. (The problems of interviewing and interviewers are studied in some detail later.)

Face-to-face interviewing may take place in households, industrial, commercial, or public sector organizations, or, increasingly, in shopping malls. In the USA, shopping mall interviewing started in the late 1960s and has grown significantly, so that by 1979 it became the most popular venue for face-to-face interviewing in marketing research.[34] Clearly, it would be unwise to generalize freely from the data obtained from such methodology.

In 1989, it was stated[32] that in the USA there were over 600 permanent mall interviewing facilities in addition to over 1600 other malls or shopping centres which permit interviewing but have no permanent facilities. While mall interviewing is quick and low-cost, problems of sampling clearly arise – see Chapter 3 for discussion on the principles of sample selection. It is particularly important to note that 'mall intercepts' do not 'sample' shoppers, they sample 'shopper-visits'; hence, the frequency of visits will be likely to bias the research findings, even though some system of weighting may be used.

Postal or mail surveys

Questionnaires are mailed to a sample of the population to be surveyed. This method is superficially attractive on account of its cheapness, but this should be related to the relatively low response rate unless the subject of research is of particular interest to the recipients of the questionnaire. Further, non-response is not a random process and those who do respond may not be representative of the population. The adequacy of the sample rests largely on the quality of the sampling list available, this may be incomplete or out of date. Observational data cannot be gathered by postal questionnaires, and this type of information frequently adds to the quality of the responses given in personal interviewing. There is no opportunity to probe or clarify answers that must be accepted as written.

Telephone enquiries

These are increasingly used in consumer surveys, and also popular in the industrial field. They are valuable in pilot-stage research and in forming sampling lists. Problems of using this method of research and new developments based on computer links will be discussed later.

Panel research

This is particularly useful in tracing movements in buying behaviour over a period of time. Several research bodies have regular panels which are concerned with providing information on family budgets, buying, entertainment habits, etc. Some danger exists from 'conditioning', i.e. that panel members, after a while, begin to behave in a non-typical fashion by becoming more self-conscious in their buying behaviour. Considerable expertise has been built up in the recruitment and management of consumer panels. (A general appreciation of this methodology occurs in Chapter 9.)

Group interview technique

This involves using psychological methods of enquiry by which free discussion of certain marketing problems is encouraged. (This area of investigation is considered in Chapter 8.)

Focus groups

These are scaled-down versions of group discussions which are growing in popularity (see Chapter 7).

Special survey techniques

These include shop audits, television measurement, shop laboratories, etc., which are discussed in some detail in Part 3 of this text.

KEYPOINT

Methods of survey enquiries

1. Personal (face-to-face) interviewing

2. Postal/mail surveys

3. Telephone interviews

4. Panel research; audits, diaries etc.

5. Group discussions/focus groups

6. Special techniques: electronic equipment (meters, scanners, bar-coding; computer-based interview techniques, Internet)

A multi-technique approach to research may be used: it is a sound research strategy

---

Developments in survey methodologies

Over the past two decades or so, there have been notable advances in survey techniques based on computer technology and electronic-based systems of data capture. Computer-assisted data collection (CADAC) using sophisticated software packages have resulted in conspicuous developments in telephone interviewing: the computer-assisted telephone interview (CATI), and in face-to-face interviewing the computer-assisted personal interview (CAPI). Electronic mail survey (e-mail), internet/intranet survey, and computer-assisted panel research (CAPAR). Another innovation is Disk-by-Mail (DBM). These dynamic methods of data collection will be explored in the chapters dealing with questionnaires and interviewing.[35] It is clear that the impact of electronics and computer technology will continue to be felt in survey technologies. Interactive systems will be increasingly developed; these will use the videophone, fax and electronic mailing, particularly in business to-business markets.

These impressive technological developments have been a shot-in-the-arm for the market research industry and have greatly increased its productivity. Conventional systems of market research will not disappear; they are likely to be used in tandem with these newer methodologies. Some of the problems investigated by market and social researchers e.g. health care or financial matters, need to be handled with sensitivity and the assurance of privacy. Such enquiries will probably remain the province of skilled personal interviewers.

2.10 Secondary data – internal

The answers to many problems often lie within the files of an organization or in published material. But in many cases the only way of getting at the required facts is through a sample survey of a part or the whole population.[34]

Library or desk research, which has the attractive attribute of being non-reactive or unobtrusive, is an established method of collecting secondary data; it is economical, comparatively speedy, and can be undertaken with complete confidentiality. Only rarely is there no relevant information about a particular research problem; internal records or published records are often capable of giving remarkably useful information, and this may even be sufficient for the decisions that have to be made. This preliminary stage of research will help in developing the overall research strategy; it should always be undertaken before any further research is contemplated.

Many companies do not make full enough use of the information that is routinely collected. Internal records – production, costing, sales, and distribution – may be designed so that the information they contain is in a form useful for marketing research. Sales analysis should be designed to give information by markets, products, types of distributive outlet or industry, geographic area (home and overseas), characteristics of customers, such as heavy/medium/light buyers. Advertising expenditure should be carefully recorded and analysed by media, product type, and market. Other promotional expenses should also be available for market researchers to study. Some internal data may not be readily available and considerable checking of invoices may be necessary to establish product sales. If this is likely to be an extremely difficult task, some estimates may have to be made based on factory production figures for particular periods.

2.11 Secondary data – external

External sources of data include statistics and reports issued by governments, trade associations, and other reputable organizations. Research companies and advertising agencies frequently circulate useful information. Further information is obtainable from trade directories.

In the UK, the Government Statistical Service offers detailed data of great value to marketing researchers. Two very useful official publications are *Guide to Official Statistics* (ONS) and *Regional Statistics*. It should be noted that, in April 1996, the CSO merged with the Office of Population Censuses and Surveys (OPCS) to form the Office for National Statistics (ONS). This new organization serves both government and other users of statistical data, so developing further the 'user-friendly' approach adopted over recent years by the CSO.

In a unique partnership with Taylor Nelson Sofres in December 1994 the CSO announced a new report series: *UK Markets*. The 91 Annual and 34 Quarterly Reports are produced by TNAGB from data collected by the CSO from 28 500 manufacturers, covering 90 per cent of UK manufacturers' sales and some 4800 types of product. In response to EU PRODCOM (PRODucts of the European COMmunity), the data definitions are harmonized with the other EU countries. This enables UK manufacturing statistics to be directly comparable with UK Export/Import trade data and also with the same data published in other EU countries.

This innovative publication is available in three formats: hard copy (from HMSO); CD ROM (from TNAGB Publications); and, Intelligent FAX (I-FAX), giving interactive retrieval of *UK Markets* from any fax machine, anywhere in the world, 24 hours a day, 365 days a year.

PRODCOM replaces the PAS series of *Business Monitors*, but the other series are still active.

For details of principal sources of secondary data refer to Appendix I.

Summary

A central part of research activity is to develop an effective research strategy or design which details the most suitable methodology, sampling plan, and types of data to be collected. Five logical stages make up the survey process: brief, proposal, data collection, analysis and evaluation, and preparation and presentation of survey report. At every stage, professionalism is vital.

Two main types of data – primary and secondary. The former type could involve observation, experimentation, or questionnaires in order to collect new information about specific market problems; the latter type, known as desk or library research, involves collection of data that already exist – there are many sources of published information, from official or trade and industry sources. Every effort should be made to identify suitable secondary data which, in some cases, may provide adequate information for management.

A multi-technique approach stresses the desirability of combining survey techniques in order to reduce the bias inherent in one particular method, e.g. questionnaires. No research method is without bias of some kind, so a sound research strategy makes use of more than one technique in an effort to minimize bias: objectivity is the guiding principle of research. Electronic access to data has revolutionized secondary marketing research since the early 1980s. On-line services and CD-ROM have given virtually instant access to sophisticated information from across the world. Use of such highly developed systems entails costs which need to be carefully evaluated.

Review and discussion questions

1. State whether each of the following research projects is exploratory, descriptive, or causal.
   (a) A project to determine which factors make viewers zap during television advertisements.
   (b) An in-house sales audit based on returns for each sales territory.
   (c) Informal discussions with hospital patients to ascertain the broad criteria they use in evaluating the quality of nursing care.

2. Compose a research proposal for a survey to examine the cause(s) of an annual drop in sales of 20 per cent for an industrial cleaning product in the Greater Manchester area. Be specific in terms of possible objectives and hypotheses.

3. The management of a UK DIY chain is anxious to discover consumer preferences for barcoding as opposed to traditional price labelling on products. Suggest a triangular research design and highlight potential sources of error.

4. Give examples of exogenous variables which could affect an in-store experiment in two supermarkets to examine the impact of promotional taste-testing on sales of yoghurt.

5. What secondary data sources would you consult to determine the following?
   (a) The number, location and size of UK companies manufacturing surgical instruments.
   (b) An estimate of the amount of rape seed oil produced by British farmers.
   (c) The extent to which sales of kitchen tissue rolls in UK have increased/decreased in the past 5 years.

6. What would you consider to be the main shortcomings of using secondary data in answering marketing research problems?

References

1. Green, Paul E., and Donald S. Tull, and Gerald Albaum, *Research for Marketing Decisions* (5th edn), Prentice-Hall, Englewood Cliffs, New Jersey, 1988.
2. Oppenheim, A. N., *Questionnaire Design, Interviewing and Attitude Measurement*, Pinter Publishers, London, 1992.
3. Craig, C. Samuel and Susan P. Douglas, *International Marketing Research*, John Wiley, Chichester, 1999.
4. Ferber, Robert, *Market Research*, McGraw-Hill, New York, 1971.
5. Moser, C. A., and G. Kalton, *Survey Methods in Social Investigation*, Heinemann, London, 1971.
6. Aaker, Davis, V. Kumar and George S. Day, *Marketing Research* (6th edn), John Wiley, New York, 1998.
7. Buckner, Hugh, *How British Industry Buys*, Hutchinson, London, 1967.
8. Ferber, Robert, and P. J. Verdoorn, *Research Methods in Economics and Business*, The Macmillan Company, Toronto, 1969.
9. Webb, Eugene J., Donald T. Cambell, Richard D. Schwartz, and Lee Sechrest, *Unobtrusive Measures – Nonreactive Research in the Social Sciences*, Rand McNally and Company, Chicago, 1966.
10. Burgess, Robert L., *Behavioural Sociology*, Don Bushell, Jnr (ed.), Columbia University Press, 1966.
11. Russell, Bertrand, *Philosophy*, Norton, New York, 1927.
12. Whyte, W. J., *Street-Corner Society: the Social Structure of an Italian Slum*, University of Chicago Press, 1943.
13. Stafford, Maria Royne, and Thomas F. Stafford, 'Participant observation and the pursuit of truth: methodological and ethical considerations', *Journal of the Market Research Society*, vol. 35, no. 1, January 1993.
14. Reynolds, Joy, 'Note on "Participant observation and the pursuit of truth"', *Journal of the Market Research Society*, vol. 35, no. 1, January 1993.
15. Politz, Alfred, 'A study of outside transit poster exposure', National Association of Transportation Advertising, 1959.
16. Day, D. J., and Jeniffer E. Dunn, 'Estimating the audience for advertising on the outside of London buses', *Applied Statistics*, vol. 18, no. 3, 1969.

17. La Piere, R. T., 'Attitudes vs. actions', *Social Forces*, vol. 13, 1934.
18. Chisnall, Peter M., *Consumer Behaviour*, McGraw-Hill, Maidenhead, Berks, 1994.
19. Payne, Stanley L., 'Combination of survey methods', *Journal of Marketing Research*, vol. 1, no. 2, May 1964.
20. Horne, Annette, Judith Morgan and Joanna Page, 'Where do we go from here?', *Journal of Market Research Society*, vol. 3, 1974.
21. Meneer, Peter, 'Retrospective data in survey research', *Journal of Market Research Society*, vol. 20, no. 3, July 1978.
22. Skapinker, Michael, 'Why people-watching is essential for product development', *The Financial Times*, 2 February 1989.
23. Langton, James, 'The unseen eye keeping watch over shop flaws', *Sunday Telegraph*, 22 January 1995.
24. Wilson, Alan, and Justin Gutmann, 'Public transport: the role of mystery shopping in investment decisions', *Journal of the Market Research Society*, vol. 40, no. 4, October 1998.
25. Dawson, Janet, and Jill Hillier, 'Competitor mystery shopping: methodological considerations and implications for the MRS Code of Conduct', *Journal of the Market Research Society*, vol. 37, no. 4, October 1995.
26. Morrison, Lisa J., Andrew M. Coleman, and Carolyn C. Preston, 'Mystery customer research: cognitive processes affecting accuracy', *Journal of the Market Research Society*, vol. 39, no. 2, April 1997.
27. Elliott, Ken, and Martin Christopher, *Research Methods in Marketing*, Holt, Rinehart and Winston, London, 1973.
28. Davis, John, 'Marketing, testing and experimentation', in: *Consumer Market Research Handbook*, Robert Worcester and John Downham (eds), Van Nostrand, Wokingham, 1978.
29. Wind, Yoram, Susan P. Douglas, and Aaron Ascoli, 'Experimentation as a tool for the retailer', *Market Research Society Journal*, vol. 13, no. 3, July 1971.
30. Rothman, James, and John Downham, 'Experimental designs and models', in: *Consumer Market Research Handbook*, Robert Worcester and John Downham (eds), ESOMAR/Elsevier, 1986.
31. Collins, M., 'Product testing', in: *The Effective Use of Market Research*, Johan Aucamp (ed.), Staples Press, London, 1971.
32. Lysaker, Richard L., 'Data collection methods in the US', *Journal of the Market Research Society*, vol. 31, no. 4, October 1989.
33. Banks, Roger, 'Oh, say, can you see . . . the client runs free', *Researchplus*, June 1994.
34. Frankel, Martin R., 'Current research practices: general population surveying including geo-demographics', *Journal of Market Research Society*, vol. 31, no. 4, October 1989.
35. *ESOMAR Handbook of Market and Opinion Research* (4th edn), Colin McDonald and Phyllis Vangelder (eds), ESOMAR, Amsterdam, 1998.

Introduction to sampling

3

Learning Objectives

- Become aware of nature of sampling and its relationship to marketing research

- Obtain basic understanding of sampling theory

- Note significance of normal distribution in sampling theory and practice

- Become familiar with nature and role of sampling frames

Sampling is one of the major tools of marketing research, which is concerned with collecting, analysing, and interpreting market data. It involves the study, in considerable detail, of relatively small numbers of informants taken from a larger group.

A good appreciation of the function and principal methods of sampling is particularly useful to market researchers, who need also to have a clear understanding of their reliability and limitations. It is helpful, therefore, to define some of the terms used in sampling.

3.1 Definitions

1. *Population (universe)* is used in the statistical sense and refers to any group of people or objects which are similar in one or more ways, and which form the subject of study in a particular survey. Populations can consist of groups of inanimate objects, e.g. machine tools, as well as human populations, which may, in certain cases, refer to special sections of the general population of a country, such as those over the age of 18 and under 65. Before research is possible, the population to be surveyed must be clearly defined.

   Populations can be finite or infinite, e.g. the population of babies born in a year is finite, whereas all the possible outcomes of the tosses of a coin or rolls of a six-sided die form infinite populations, which are also known as theoretical or statistical populations.

   Populations have characteristics which can be estimated and classified according to the requirements of individual surveys. Attributes refer to particular characteristics that each sampling unit either does or does not possess, e.g. ownership of a colour television set; height six feet or over; left-handed; or blue-eyed. Measurement involves counting, or estimating, those members of the population having these attributes, so that this qualitative information is, in fact, quantified. It is then referred to as a variate or variable value. It can also involve calculating the extent or magnitude of some variable characteristic possessed by sample units, e.g. the average income of families in a certain area or the average weekly sales of canned soups in the Birmingham district.

2. *Census* occurs when a universe is examined in its entirety. This is unusual in commercial research, except where the universe is quite small and easily located, e.g. in some specialized industrial research. Most censuses are directed by governments and are designed to provide vital information of trends in population, trade, and industry. Censuses are expensive, relatively slow, and comparatively rare.

3. *Sample* occurs when a number of sampling units (fewer than the aggregate) is drawn from a population and examined in some detail. This information is then considered as applying to the whole universe. It may, of course, be biased if the sample includes a high proportion of abnormal members of the population. A sample is a microcosm of the population from which it is drawn. However, it cannot reflect a perfect image of that population; there will be some distortion, although attention to sound principles of sampling can keep this largely under control. Samples must, therefore, be representative of the populations from which they are drawn, so that valid conclusions about populations can be inferred.

4. *Elementary sampling unit (ESU)* refers to an individual element of the population to be sampled, e.g. a certain kind of person (socio-economic/age), or a particular type of retail store (a supermarket).

5. *Sampling frame* refers to lists, indexes, maps, or other records of a population from which a sample can be selected. In the UK, the Register of Electors is a convenient official frame for consumer surveys. The Postcode Address File (PAF) is increasingly used as a sampling frame in the UK.

6. *Statistic* also known as 'estimator' refers to any quantity calculated from a sample to estimate a population parameter.

7. *Parameter* refers to the value of a variable (or attribute) calculated in the population, e.g. the average or mean (μ).

8. *Sampling variability (experimental error)* refers to the fact that different samples drawn from a fixed population generally have different statistics, whereas population parameters for a given population do not change.

9. *Sampling distribution* refers to a frequency distribution based on a number of samples, e.g. 12 samples examined, their means calculated, and the 12 averages listed in a frequency distribution.

10. *Stratified sample* occurs when a sample is specially designed so that certain known characteristics in the population under survey are represented in certain proportions.

11. *Two broad types of sample:*
    (a) *Random* – 'probability': occurs where each element of a population from which the sample is chosen has a known (and non-zero) chance of being selected
    (b) *Quota* – 'non probability'; judgement; purposive: type of stratified sampling in which selection of sampling units within strata, e.g. age, sex, social group, is done by interviewers on a non-random basis, controlled to some extent by quotas allocated to the different strata.

12. *Sampling error* refers to the difference between a sample estimate and the value of the population parameter obtained by a complete count or census.

13. *Sample cells* are formed when the strata of a sample are further divided, resulting in two or more subdivisions of the sample with common characteristics, e.g. population divided into two main strata by sex, further subdivided into specific age groups, 21 and over, and under 21. Four sample cells are thus formed. It is obvious that the number of cells increases rapidly as control bases are added.

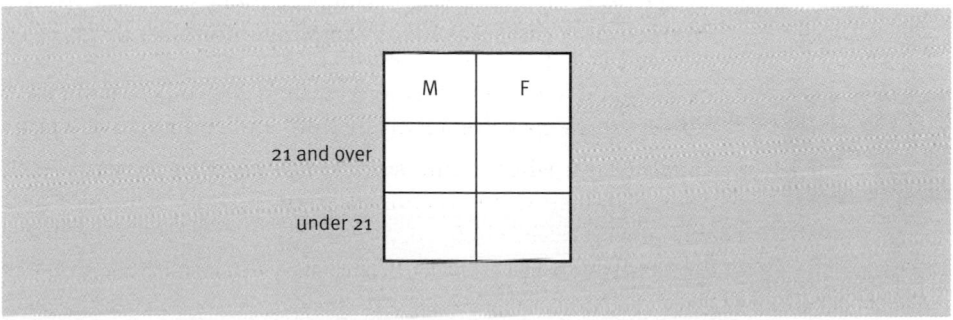

14. *Statistical symbols and formulae* are most easily shown diagrammatically as Tables 3.1 and 3.2.

It will be noted in these definitions that there are two types of error which may bias sample estimates:

(a) *Experimental error* arising from the differences in estimates that occur if repeated samples are taken from the same population. The degree of experimental error will be

Table 3.1   Statistical symbols – outline summary

	Population parameter	Sample statistic	
Mean	μ	$\bar{x}$	Measure of location. Describes point around which scores in frequency distribution tend to cluster.
Variance	σ^2	s^2	Measure of dispersion. Measures distance or deviation of any score in a frequency distribution from the mean.
Standard deviation	σ	s	Square root of variance.

Note: Greek characters = description of populations. Roman letters = samples.

Table 3.2   Formulae

Statistic	Method
Mean $\bar{x}$	Add together scores in distribution and divide by number of scores: 52, 36, 26. $$\text{Therefore } \bar{x} = \sum \frac{x}{n} = \frac{52 + 36 + 26}{3} = 38$$
Variance s^2	Calculate deviation of each value of distribution from mean ($\bar{x}$), add together the squares of deviations and divide by the number of values $$\text{Therefore } s^2 = \sum \frac{(x - \bar{x})^2}{n}$$ Use $n - 1$, where $n < 25$.

affected by the variability present in the population and by the size of the sample drawn from it.

(b) *Systematic error* arises from deficiencies in selection and measurement techniques, such as derives from an inefficient sampling frame or from a badly phrased questionnaire. In the former case, probability sampling minimizes this type of error.

KEYPOINT

Sample

Is a microcosm of a population (larger group) from which it is drawn

Must be representative of larger group, so that valid conclusions are feasible

Values are 'statistics' and estimates of population parameters (values)

Cannot be perfect reflection of larger group – some distortion

Difference between sample estimate (statistic) and population parameter (value) is 'sampling error'

Can be stratified when certain known characteristics are in larger group (e.g. age/sex/socio-economic)

3.2 Origin of sampling

The sampling procedures used in marketing in the UK originated in social surveys that were pioneered many years ago by Bowley and others. By modern standards, much of this early research was statistically non-rigorous, though as far back as 1912 Bowley[1] used modern, practical sampling methods in his famous survey of working-class conditions in Reading. His disciplined approach was to influence the methodology of social surveys, which became more systematic in the selection of samples.

Sampling was first used in the UK in a large-scale, official, field research conducted by the Ministry of Labour in 1937 into working-class expenditure.

As already noted, several opinion and marketing research organizations, among them the BBC Listener Research Department, developed in the 1930s, as sampling techniques improved and were accepted as good research practice. The BBC Listener Research Department, later known as the Audience Research Department, was closed down in the 1990s, and the BBC's Broadcasting Research Department contracted out fieldwork operations such as survey interviewing and group discussions.

Prominent among these research activities was the Social Survey founded in 1941. This was to make a decisive contribution to the standards of research, and over the years it has been responsible for very many enquiries on behalf of government departments. In 1949, samples of people from local authority waiting lists provided detailed information about their housing conditions, and it was possible to estimate the accuracy of local authority records in this area. In the same year, the then Board of Trade asked the Social Survey to study the effects of experimental changes in rationing allowances for clothes and to state the extent to which clothes buying was limited by prices or shortage of coupons. As a result of this evidence, clothes rationing was eventually abolished.

Another notable example of sampling was in the National Farm Survey of England and Wales, published by HMSO in 1946. This showed the boundaries of every farm in considerable detail. The mass of information was analysed by means of a random sample taken from a total of nearly 300 000 records referring to holdings of five acres and over.

Sampling surveys also contribute to medical research. An early example occurred in 1946 when a survey of maternity services in the UK was made by the Royal College of Obstetricians and Gynaecologists and the Population Investigation Committee. Existing information indicated that in order to obtain a reliable and complete picture: 'a direct approach had to be made to women who had recently borne children'. A sample was, therefore, chosen of all women who had given birth in the UK during a particular week in March 1946. This remarkable feat of surveying was achieved by using the services of medical officers of health and health visitors. As a result, 13 687 women out of a total of 15 130 who had given birth during that week were interviewed. Two years later, a follow-up study of the health and development of the children was made. Of the original sample of 13 687 babies, a sub-sample of 5380 was made at random. Despite the fact that nearly one-third of the families had moved, it was possible to follow them up through local authority medical services, and all but 37 were successfully interviewed.

Another notable use of sampling in medical science occurred in research into the relationship between lung cancer and smoking undertaken by Doll and Hill for the Medical Research Council. Patients were divided into two groups, those with lung carcinoma in a certain number of hospitals in England and Wales (1465 patients), and a 'control group', individually matched by personal characteristics, but who were suffering from other diseases. The findings were published in the *British Medical Journal* in 1950.

They are a source of interest to statisticians studying the statistical significance of sample data. This research did not, in fact, provide statistical evidence of a relationship between smoking and lung cancer. The researchers, noting this rather inconclusive evidence, commented on the relatively small sample and also that the data were sufficiently reliable to show general trends.

The 1966 Population Census of the UK was, in fact, a 10 per cent sample enumeration based on the 1961 Census record as a main sampling frame. By means of a computer program, a qualified sample of 1 in 10 private dwellings was selected in England and Wales. In Scotland, the main sampling frame was the 1964–65 Valuation Roll for each of the cities and counties, supplemented by a list of dwellings coming into occupation for the first time between May 1964 and March 1966; a sample of 1 in 10 was again drawn.

In the US the Bureau of the Census selected a 5 per cent sample from the 1940 Population Census, and additional questions were asked of these respondents. This innovation led to the development of a 'Master Sample' by the Bureau of Agricultural Economics. In 1945, these two American bureaux cooperated in producing a 'Master Sample' covering the entire population.

Research studies of all kinds now make use of sampling, the techniques and applications of which have greatly improved. There is little doubt that a great deal of the acceptability that sampling now enjoys in academic and commercial research operations stems from the early pioneer work done by official survey organizations in both the USA and the UK. Standards of research have greatly improved over the years, and it is interesting to note the strong development that took place during the Second World War when government enquiries were made, by means of sample surveys, into many different areas affecting the welfare of the community.

The fiasco of the *Literary Digest* poll in 1936 alerted researchers to the importance of sound methods of sampling, and today no reputable organization would be likely to select a sample with such a distinct bias (see later discussion).

Apart from national sampling surveys, the techniques of sampling extend internationally through the United Nations Statistical Office, which publishes survey reports on many topics.

Sampling has many advantages; it saves money, time, and labour; it frequently enables data of high quality to be collected; and it provides data that could not be assembled by other means.

The overall cost of samples is lower than a complete investigation (census), though the cost per unit of study may be higher because of the need to employ skilled interviewers, administrative expenses incurred in sample design, etc.

Samples mean substantial savings in time and labour. Censuses take many years to prepare for publication, whereas surveys can be published in a few months. In 1951, 1 per cent of schedules in the Census of Population were sampled for preliminary analysis, and summary findings were available in just over a year, which is considerably shorter than the time taken for the analysis of a complete census. Obviously, fewer staff are engaged in sample surveys than when complete censuses are taken. Labour economies also take place in the tabulation and processing of data.

Most censuses are directed by governments for purposes of estimating demographic trends, trade and industry developments, etc. They are expensive, relatively slow, and comparatively rare.

Because sample surveys investigate fewer cases, it is possible for them to provide more data, both quantitatively and qualitatively. In some instances, moreover, sampling may be the only possible method of collecting information. Blood counts are widely used and regarded as reliable in medical spheres; some industrial products are assessed by testing small samples of them to their utmost limits.

3.3 The theory of sampling

Sampling theory is concerned with the study of the relationships existing between a population and the samples drawn from it. Through the process of statistical inference, using probability theory, certain conclusions can be drawn about a population from a study of samples taken from it.

Ferber[2] has succinctly commented on the core of probability in sampling theory as follows. Probability is at the heart of all sampling theories. The very concept of sampling is based on the *probability* that one member will represent a group; on the *probability* that a number of members selected at random from a population will be so distributed as to provide a miniature representation of that population; on the *probability* that estimates drawn from this miniature will differ from the true population values only by a certain (measurable) amount attributable to the vagaries of sample selection.

Statistical sampling theory, based on the mathematics of probability, is particularly valuable in two ways:

1. *Estimation* allows estimates of population parameters, such as the population mean (μ) and variance (σ^2) to be made from sample statistics such as sample mean ($\bar{x}$), variance (s^2), etc.

2. *Hypothesis testing* enables certain probability statements, based on samples, about the characteristics of a population to be tested statistically. It involves the use of tests of significance that are important in the theory of decisions; for example, in determining whether the differences noted between two samples are the result of a chance variation or whether they are actually significant.

Estimation and hypothesis testing are distinct branches of statistical sampling theory, but they are related in that they both utilize the statistical measure known as the standard error. It will be seen later that the standard error is based on probability sampling techniques, and the conclusions drawn about populations studied by sample surveys are necessarily probability statements. The whole concept of sampling theory rests, therefore, on the fact that a sample has been chosen randomly, which implies that every member of the population from which the sample has been drawn has the same probability of being chosen for the sample.

Samples must be representative so that valid conclusions can be drawn about the populations they represent. Inevitably, some degree of distortion is likely, but this can largely be controlled through applying sound principles of sampling.

Estimates are continually being made of the distribution of age groups in a national population by studying a relatively small number of representative members, i.e. a sample. Production testing, traffic counts, etc., are all commonly used methods of estimating. Sampling estimates have been accepted practice in many areas for a long time; for example, tea tasting, wine tasting, handful of grain tests, and blood tests. The quality of the whole is judged by careful examination and testing of some small part. Often there is no alternative but to sample, as in the case of very large populations.

KEYPOINT

Sampling

Based on probability

Allows estimates to be made of population parameters

Enables hypotheses to be tested statistically

Saves time and money

Investigates fewer cases than complete count (census), so more detailed data can be collected

Since sampling is basically concerned with providing reliable estimates of population parameters (or values), those who wish to get a good grasp of the fundamental statistical concepts which underlie the processes of estimation should read sections 3.4 and 3.5. Fully worked examples will, it is hoped, help in understanding the principles of sound sampling.

3.4 Essentials for sound estimators

Estimation is concerned with finding good estimates of population parameters. There are certain criteria that determine good estimates:

1. *Lack of bias* occurs when the expected value of an estimate is equal to the population parameter. Otherwise, the estimate is 'biased', and the difference between the expected value and the population value is called the 'bias' or 'systematic error'. It is, of course, difficult to establish the value of the population parameter in actual practice and so it may not be possible to assess bias. Let (θ) = the expected value of the estimate and θ = value of parameter. Then $E(\theta) = \theta$ (where E = mathematical expectation). Bias in sample selection should be avoided in so far as it is possible, while particular care is needed in selecting the sample design. Random (or probability) sampling reduces the likelihood of bias.

   Bias can also result from sampling units being selected from a sampling frame or list that is incomplete, inaccurate, or inadequate. To select a sample of the general population from a telephone directory would obviously lead to bias.

   Bias also arises from non-response, either because some sampling units cannot be traced, or because, when contacted, they refuse to co-operate in the survey.

   The systematic errors or biases which may arise from any of these directions are not affected by increases in the size of samples. One of the cardinal concepts of sampling is representativeness, which means that a sample should adequately reflect, in the types of units it contains, the population it represents.

   It should be noted that the present discussion of bias is restricted to sample selection. Unfortunately there are many other sources of bias in survey work, and these are considered in later chapters. Researchers must be constantly alert to the possibilities of bias at all stages of research operations. Everything possible must be done to avoid distortion. Sound techniques must be vigorously applied throughout the surveys.

2. *Consistency* means that a sample estimate, such as $\bar{x}$, approaches the population parameter (μ) that is to be estimated, as the sample size increases. This has been formally defined as:

$$P(\bar{x} \to (\mu) \to 1 \text{ as } n \to \infty \text{ (or } N)$$

Table 3.3   Analysis of comparative properties of estimators

Parameter	Estimator	Unbiased	Consistent	Efficient
μ	$\bar{x}$	✓	✓	✓
μ	median	✓	✓	✗
μ	mode	✓	✓	✗
σ^2	$s^2 = \frac{1}{n}\sum(x_1 - \bar{x})^2$	✗	✓	✓
σ^2	$s^2 = \frac{1}{n-1}\sum(x_1 - \bar{x})^2$	✓	✓	✓

Table 3.3 shows $\bar{x}$ and s^2 are most suitable for estimating population values

i.e. the probability that the sample average approaches the population average as n becomes larger and larger is 1. Hence, consistent estimators tend to approach the value of population parameters more exactly as sample size approaches infinity.

3. *Efficiency* involves the comparison between estimators and is stated in relative terms. Estimator θ_1 is more efficient than estimator θ_2 if the variance of the first expression is smaller than that of the second.

For example, it is known that the sample mean is an efficient estimate of the population mean, whereas the sample median is an inefficient estimate of it. It can further be said that of all statistics used to estimate the population mean, the sample mean gives the best or most efficient estimate.

$$\text{Var. } (\bar{x}) < \text{Var. (median)} < \text{Var. (mode)}$$

The measure of efficiency can be expressed by the ratio of the variances.

Table 3.3 shows $\bar{x}$ and s^2 are most suitable for estimating population values.

3.5 Confidence intervals

When sample values are used as estimates of population values, it is important to know how reliable these estimates are. How near, for example, is the sample mean $\bar{x}$ to the population mean μ, of which it is an estimate. The usefulness of a sample estimate will be increased if some indication can be given of the degree of reliability.

By using confidence limits, also known as fiducial limits, a sample estimate of a population parameter can be given which is likely to occur within a given interval. It is important to remember that confidence limits can be ascertained only if the sample has been randomly selected. Confidence intervals or limits are used with the sampling distribution known as the normal distribution.

Normal distribution*

Further discussion of the concept of the standard error will be helped by some consideration of the mathematical function known as the normal curve or distribution. This is one of several sampling distributions relating to sampling theory and is widely used in studying statistical data.

The properties of the normal curve were first identified by scientists in the eighteenth century, when it was observed that repeated samplings of the same population showed

* Also known as Gaussian distribution, after Carl Gauss (1777–1855)

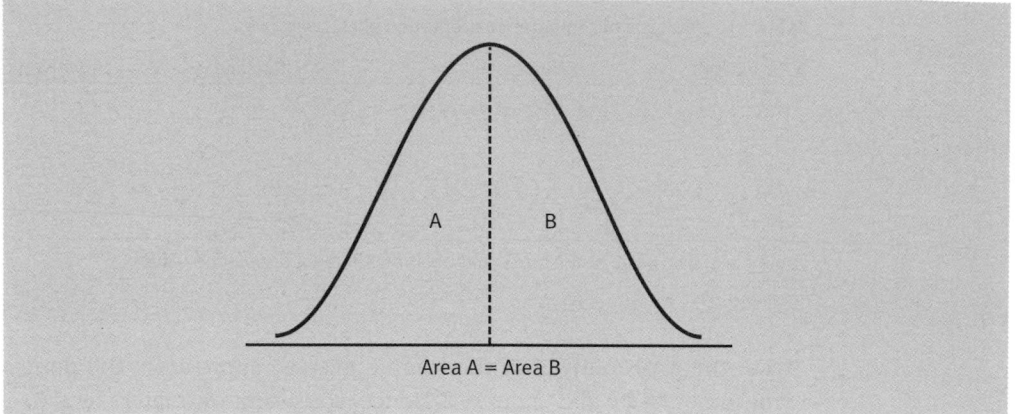

Figure 3.1   Normal distribution graph

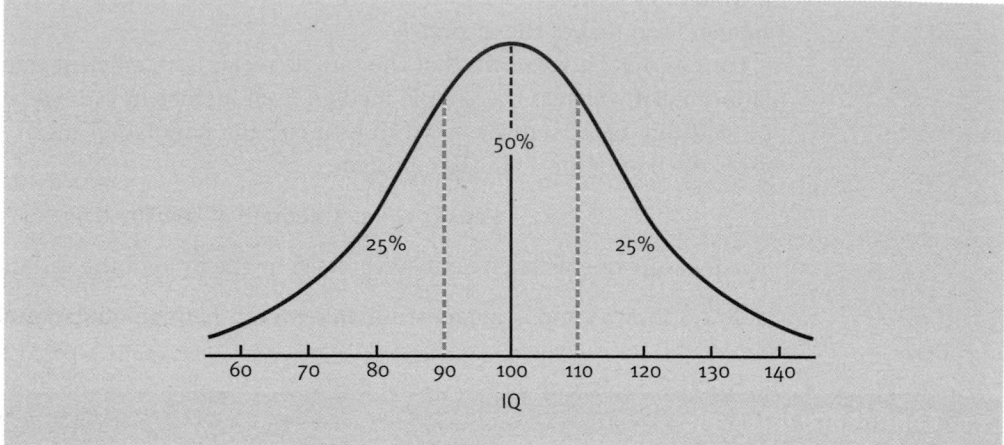

Figure 3.2   Basic technique graph

remarkable regularity in their distributions. The sampling measurements formed a bell-shaped distribution, which was symmetrical and extending indefinitely in both directions. The curve comes closer and closer to the horizontal axis without ever touching it, no matter how far it is extended. In actual fact, there is no point in extending the curve very far, because the value of the measurements obtained would be negligible.

Since there are equal frequencies in each half of a normal distribution (see Fig. 3.1), the mode, median, and mean are virtually the same for a frequency distribution which is approximately normal.

Many sampling distributions approximate to a normal curve, particularly, those involving measurement of human characteristics, such as height, weight, personality, intelligence, or muscular coordination. The symmetrical distribution of sampling characteristics allows researchers to make certain statements about the population under survey.

As shown in Fig. 3.2, 50 per cent of IQ scores are within a narrow band; the other half is evenly distributed as indicated. If the middle range is divided at IQ 100, the population is divided into four groups of equal size.

The normal distribution curves may differ in extent according to the distribution of particular attributes in the population. In simple occupations, there is less spread of

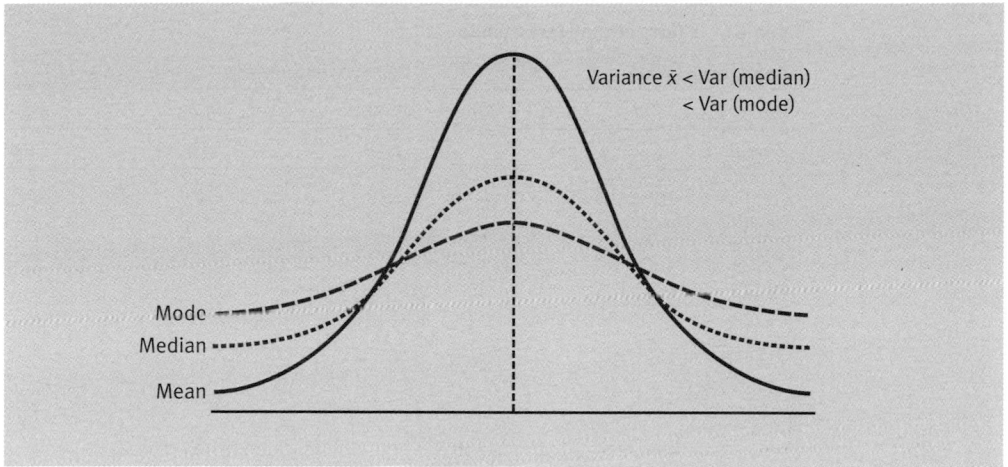

Figure 3.3   Variance graph

ability than in complex occupations. For example, experienced production-line workers vary only comparatively slightly in their production figures, though random samples will reveal that certain individuals tend to be superior in performance. Where complex skills are applicable, the tendency is for the spread of ability to be greater as improvement in performance is evident over a longer period of time.

The wider the spread of the distribution, the greater the variation between frequencies (see Fig. 3.3). The normal curve is always bell-shaped with a single peak, on either side of which there are equal frequencies. Normal frequency distributions are generally described numerically in two ways: central tendency and dispersion. The arithmetic mean or average is still the most widely used measure of central tendency, while the standard deviation is almost universally accepted as the measure of absolute dispersion of a distribution. It is important to note that because standard deviation measures dispersion in terms of the units sampled, it has limited use for comparative purposes. Because of this limitation, standard error, which is expressed as a percentage, is valuable.

The actual shape of the 'bell' of a normal curve is determined by the standard deviation of its distribution, and once the average and the standard deviation are known the complete distribution can be plotted. The sample average is not necessarily the same as the average for the population. The standard deviation is, therefore, useful in calculating the limits within which the population average occurs. Hence, the reliability of the sample average (or mean) of a frequency distribution depends upon the degree of dispersion about the average. Figure 3.4 illustrates the importance of the standard deviation in normal distributions.

Figure 3.4 shows that if standard deviations (σ) are drawn at intervals of one standard deviation from the mean, the proportion of the area under the curve will be as follows:

Approximately 68 per cent of the units sampled will be within $\pm$ 1 SD of mean.
Approximately 95 per cent of the units sampled will be within $\pm$ 2 SD of mean.
Approximately 99 per cent of the units sampled will be within $\pm$ 3 SD of mean.

The areas contained by normal distributions are to be found in special Z scale tables in most statistical textbooks. Table 3.4 lists several values, of which the 95 per cent and 99 per cent confidence limits are the most frequently used in surveys.

Table 3.4   Values of confidence limits

Confidence level					
x/σ	99.73	99	95.45	95	68.27
Z value	3.0	2.58	2.0	1.96	1.0

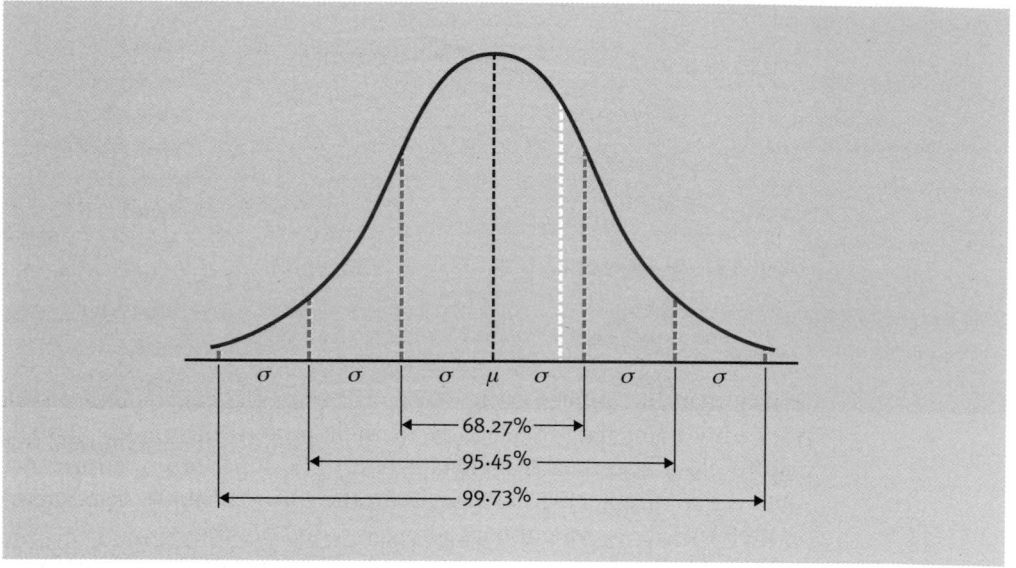

Figure 3.4   Standard deviation graph

Hence 95 per cent confidence interval for μ:

$$\bar{x} \pm 1.96 \frac{s}{\sqrt{n}}$$

99 per cent confidence interval for μ:

$$\bar{x} \pm 2.58 \frac{s}{\sqrt{n}}$$

(The figures 1.96 and 2.58 are often approximated to 2.0 and 3.0 respectively.)

Therefore, $\bar{x} \pm \dfrac{\sigma}{\sqrt{n}}$ covers 68 per cent of area under curve

$\bar{x} \pm \dfrac{2\sigma}{\sqrt{n}}$ covers 95 per cent of area under curve

$\bar{x} \pm \dfrac{3\sigma}{\sqrt{n}}$ covers 99 per cent of area under curve

Confidence intervals or limits for the mean of a normal distribution are useful in indicating the degree of accuracy to which μ has been estimated by $\bar{x}$.

Example   95 per cent confidence: from a sample of 100, the sample mean was found to be 40. If the population variation is 9, what is the confidence interval for this estimate, assuming the population to be normally distributed?

$$\bar{x} = 40, \sigma = \sqrt{9} = 3, n = 100, \mu = \bar{x} \pm 1.96\sigma/\sqrt{n} = 40 \pm 1.96 \cdot \tfrac{3}{10}$$

Hence,

$$\mu = 40 \pm 0.59; \text{ therefore } (39.41 < \mu < 40.59).$$

Example Let the data be the same as in the preceding example, but increase the sample size to 144

$$\mu = \bar{x} \pm 1.96\sigma/\sqrt{n} = 40 \pm 1.96 \cdot \tfrac{3}{12}$$

Hence,

$$\mu = 40 \pm 0.49; \text{ therefore } (39.51 < \mu < 40.49).$$

Comparing these two examples, it is evident that as the sample size is increased, the sampling error is decreased, and the confidence limits become narrower. This indicates that the precision of sample estimates improves as the size of samples for given populations increases.

The *concept of a sampling error* refers to the difference between a given sample estimate and the relevant population parameter. The concept of precision relates to the confidence interval for repeated samplings from a normal distribution, and is entirely a function of the size of the sample. The impact of precision on the sample size is discussed at some length in the section dealing with this factor.

The level of confidence with which a researcher wishes to give a population parameter will affect the limits of the confidence interval. If he or she wishes to state an estimate with high probability (99 per cent confidence), then the confidence interval will be wider than if he or she were content to give a lower probability (95 per cent confidence). A choice must be made between having a very narrow range within which the parameter will fall with lower probability, and a wider range but with higher probability.

Example 95 per cent confidence:

$$\bar{x} = 60 \quad n = 225 \quad \sigma^2 = 16$$

$$\mu = \bar{x} \pm 1.96\sigma/\sqrt{n}$$
$$= 60 + 1.96 \cdot \tfrac{4}{15}$$
$$= 60 \pm 0.52$$

Therefore,

$$(59.48 < \mu < 60.52)$$

Example 99 per cent confidence:

$$\bar{x} = 60 \quad n = 225 \quad \sigma^2 = 16$$

$$\mu = \bar{x} \pm 2.58\sigma/\sqrt{n}$$
$$= 60 \pm 2.58 \cdot \tfrac{4}{15}$$
$$= 60 \pm 0.69$$

Therefore,

$$(59.31 \sqrt{\mu} < 60.69)$$

These two examples, using similar data, indicate that higher probability is associated with greater tolerance in the estimated parameter limits.

The Central Limit Theorem states that if n is large ($\geqslant 30$ observations), the theoretical sampling distribution of $\bar{x}$ can be approximated very closely with a normal curve, and it is in order to use confidence intervals and tests of significance, and to regard $s/\sqrt{n}$ as a good estimate of σ/n.

Hence, 95 per cent confidence interval for

$$\bar{x} - 1.96\,\frac{s}{\sqrt{n}} < \mu < \bar{x} + 1.96\,\frac{s}{\sqrt{n}}$$

99 per cent confidence level for μ

$$\bar{x} - 2.58\,\frac{s}{\sqrt{n}} < \mu < \bar{x} + 2.58\,\frac{s}{n}$$

Example   A population has a mean of 50 and a standard deviation of 20. State both the 95 per cent and 99 per cent confidence limits of the sample mean for a sample of 25.

$$SE_{\bar{x}} = \frac{s}{\sqrt{n}} = \frac{20}{\sqrt{25}} = 4$$

At 95 per cent confidence levels: $\bar{x} \pm 2\,\dfrac{s}{\sqrt{n}} = 50 \pm 2 \times 4$

Therefore, $\bar{x}$ will lie between 42 and 58

At 95 per cent confidence levels: $\bar{x} \pm 3\,\dfrac{s}{\sqrt{n}} = 50 \pm 3 \times 4$

Therefore, $\bar{x}$ will lie between 38 and 62

Example   A population mean (σ) is 100 and $SE_{\bar{x}}$ is 20. Assuming that distribution is normal, what will be the 95 per cent confidence limits of sample means drawn from this population?

$\bar{x}$ is a good estimate of μ; 95 per cent confidence limit = 1.96 (or approx. 2)

Therefore, $100 \pm 2SE_{\bar{x}} = 100 \pm 40$

Therefore, $\bar{x}$ will lie between 60 and 140, at 95 per cent confidence level.

Example   What size of sample, taken by random method, would be necessary to give a 0.95 probability that a sample mean of the productive output of a workshop group (> 30) would be within 2.0 points of the true mean? Assume $\sigma = 14$.

Since $0.95 = 95$ per cent confidence level $= 1.96$

$$\text{Therefore, } 1.96\,\frac{s}{\sqrt{n}} = 2.0$$

$$1.96 \times \frac{14}{\sqrt{n}} = 2.0$$

$$\frac{1.96 \times 14}{2} = \sqrt{n}$$

$$n = 188$$

An alternative formula which is often used for calculating the sample size of a simple random sample is:

$$n = \left(\frac{Z\sigma}{E}\right)^2$$

Where: n = sample size

Z = Z-statistic corresponding to the desired confidence level (1.96 in above sample)

σ = the estimated value of the standard deviation of the population parameter (usually estimated from a pilot study/survey (14 in above example)

E = the maximum acceptable magnitude of error (2 in above example)

Example   The average weight of 500 students is to be estimated to within a 4 kg tolerance, and the estimate is required to be 95 per cent reliable. Assume σ = 12. How large does the sample need to be?

$$\text{Therefore, } 1.96\frac{\sigma}{\sqrt{n}} = 4.0$$

$$\frac{1.96 \times 12}{4} = \sqrt{n}$$

$$5.88 = \sqrt{n}$$

$$n = 34.57, \text{ say, } 35.$$

Example   What proportion of 4000 families in a certain suburban area of a large city own motorized lawnmowers? From a sample of 500 families, it appears that 50 had this gardening aid.

Hence, $p = 0.1$; $n = 500$.

$$SE_p = \sqrt{\frac{pq}{n}} = \sqrt{\frac{0.1 \times 0.09}{500}} = 0.0135$$

At a 95 per cent confidence level, i.e. taking two standard deviations, a sample probability of 10 per cent would be subject to $\pm$ 2.7 per cent, i.e. 0.0135 × 2.

Therefore, between 7.3 per cent and 12.7 per cent of the population would be owners of motorized lawnmowers (95 per cent confidence level) or between 292 and 508 families.

Example   A sample survey of 1000 motorists found that 248 or 24.8 per cent had taken their cars overseas on holiday. What is the standard error of this percentage?

$$SE_p = \sqrt{\frac{pq}{n}} = \sqrt{\frac{24.8 \times 75.2}{500}} = 1.37$$

At a 68 per cent confidence level, sample value would lie in area 24.8 $\pm$ 1.37 per cent, or between 23.4 and 26.2 per cent.

At 95 per cent confidence level, sample value would lie in area 24.8 $\pm$ 2 × 1.37 per cent, or between 22.1 and 27.5 per cent.

At 99 per cent confidence level, sample value would lie in area 24.8 $\pm$ 3 × 1.37 per cent, or between 20.7 and 28.9 per cent.

From examination of the data now obtained, it may be thought that the range is far too wide and more precise measures are needed. By increasing the sample size the standard error will be reduced and, as a result, the range within which the sample value falls will be narrowed.

However, as indicated earlier in this text, the reduced error does not correspond directly to the size of the sample because the standard error is a square root. If the sample size is doubled, the standard error is not cut in half. As Table 3.5 shows, the sample size would have to be increased *four* times to reduce the standard error by half.

Table 3.5 Relation between sample size and standard error

Sample size	σ% (based on example)
1000	1.37
2000	0.97
4000	0.68
8000	0.48

Table 3.5 clearly indicates that substantial increases are necessary in sample size in order significantly to reduce sample standard errors. Field costs, of course, increase directly with larger samples, though other costs, e.g. tabulation, are not likely to increase proportionally. Practical researchers must carefully assess the needs of the survey against the costs of achieving specific precision in the sample results.

These calculations refer to samples chosen by random methods; non-probability sampling techniques cannot legitimately use these precision measures.

Finite population correction

Before leaving the subject of standard errors, some mention should be made of the factor known as the finite population correction (f.p.c.). This is shown as $\sqrt{(N - n/N - 1)}$, where N = number of units in population and n = number of units in sample.

Where the population is very large relative to the sample, the f.p.c. approximates to unity and it can be omitted. As a general rule, the f.p.c. can be ignored in calculating the standard error if the sample does not exceed about 10 per cent of the population.

Hence, the formula $\text{SE}_{\bar{x}} = \sqrt{(\sigma^2/n)}(N - n/N - 1)$ will be acceptable as $\text{SE}_{\bar{x}} = \sqrt{\sigma^2/n}$, which is generally used.

The adjustment factor contained in the expression $\sqrt{(N - n/N - 1)}$ is never greater than one, and it is, therefore, practicable to ignore it and use the simpler formula $\sqrt{(\sigma^2/n)}$ assuming that sampling is being done from a very large population.

The following example illustrates that the f.p.c. can be omitted on these occasions:

Let sample $= 100(n)$ and population $= 10\,000$ (N)

$$\text{Therefore } \sqrt{\frac{N - n}{N - 1}} = \sqrt{\frac{10\,000 - 100}{10\,000 - 1}} = 0.995$$

It is evident that this result is so near to one as to make an adjustment for population size serve no useful purpose.

Sample size

So far the underlying concepts of probability theory, normal distribution, confidence limits and the standard error have been seen to be salient factors in sampling theory. Further, it has been noted that by increasing sample size, standard error is reduced. However, because the standard error is a square root, the reduced error does not correspond directly to the size of the sample. It is, as Table 3.5 shows, necessary to double the sample size in order to cut the standard error by half, i.e. to make the sample estimate closer to the population parameter.

Bearing in mind these theoretical constraints and the importance of sampling to professional competency in marketing research practice, extended discussion of sample size related to research activities now follows. It should be added that references to types of random sampling occur at this stage, and fuller treatment is given in Chapter 4.

It is sometimes presumed that a sample should be based on some agreed percentage of the population from which it is taken. The view that there is a constant percentage, often thought to be around 10 per cent, which can be applied when sampling populations of all kinds and sizes, is quite wrong.

The size of a sample depends on the basic characteristics of the population, the type of information required from the survey, and, of course, the cost involved. Hence, samples may vary in size for several reasons. The application of an arbitrary percentage to populations in calculating size fails to acknowledge the individual requirements of different surveys.

If, in fact, a population had certain characteristics that were completely homogeneous throughout, a sample of one would be adequate to measure those particular attributes. On the other hand, where certain characteristics in a population display considerable heterogeneity, a large sample is needed in order to assess these attributes accurately.

Since surveys have different objectives, it is necessary, first of all, to distinguish clearly the aims of a particular survey so that the sample (including size) can be designed specifically to obtain the right quality and quantity of information. This means calculating beforehand the degree of accuracy required in the results of the survey. Some attributes may be more critical than others and the degree of precision over these should be known to the researcher. In some cases, it may be difficult for sponsors to state these critical limits, but they must be able to make some reasonable assessment to enable researchers to form a sampling design.

The sub-groups, or strata, into which the sample is to be broken down, should be relevant to the objectives of the survey, and researchers must then, working backwards from the smallest sub-group, gradually build up the size of the sample. The smallest sub-group must contain sufficient sampling units so that accurate and reliable estimates can be found of the population stratum. The significant characteristics of a population should be represented in the various strata of a sample in quantities large enough to allow valid interpretation.

It is accepted that the larger the size of the sample, the greater its precision or reliability, but there are constraints which practical researchers must acknowledge. These can be listed as time, staff, and cost. Increases in the size of a sample contribute some measure of greater precision, but, inevitably, increase the cost of the survey.

Careful thought should be given to the time constraint: urgency may not allow an extended survey, though the validity of research should not be sacrificed to expediency. Sponsors should be told what accuracy they can expect from a hastily done, fairly small, sample survey. It is then their responsibility whether or not to commission research. Cost and accuracy are closely linked with the time taken to complete a survey, and to some extent there is bound to be conflict. Fieldwork is relatively slow and expensive: it must be done thoroughly for there is no point in processing a lot of very doubtful material. Researchers may occasionally have to advise clients that the constraints placed on the survey are unreasonable, and would prevent them from undertaking valid research.

When the size of samples is being considered, it is well to bear in mind the non-response factor, some measure of which will be unavoidable. If a final sample of 3000 is planned, and non-response is estimated at 25 per cent, it would be prudent to inflate the original sample figure to 4000. While this preserves the number in the final sample – thus helping its precision – it does, not, of course, mitigate bias arising from non-response itself.

As noted, the error of the sample is inversely proportional to the square root of the sample size. For example, a sample of 8000 is only *twice* as accurate as a sample of 2000 (sample size is increased fourfold; the square root of 4 is 2). Therefore, to double the accuracy of a sample, it is necessary to increase its size four times.

Where distribution of a significant attribute in a population under survey is fairly even, i.e. about 50/50, a larger sample is necessary in order to evaluate that attribute with reasonable accuracy, than in a population with an uneven distribution of the critical characteristic.

Computing the size of a sample is, therefore, a complex process; the adequacy of a sample depends on its own numerical size rather than on its direct relationship to the size of the population being surveyed. Each survey should be carefully assessed, on the lines of this discussion, for its individual requirements.

Samples in the USA range from 1500 to 2000 for national surveys, unless minority subsampling is involved when larger samples would be used. In the UK, national surveys of housewives' buying habits are frequently about 2000, and this figure is also relevant for Europe.

When random sampling techniques are to be used in a survey, it is possible to calculate mathematically the size of a sample designed to give a stated degree of precision in the survey findings. This is one of the most attractive features of probability sampling. It gives the findings of surveys sampled by this method a unique acceptance among professional researchers. Survey findings resulting from quota sampling cannot legitimately be interpreted with the same statistical precision.

To calculate the size of a sample to be taken by random selection, researchers must determine with what accuracy the results of the survey are needed. As seen earlier, this can be stated as a confidence coefficient, i.e. it can be stated with a specified degree of certainty that the sample design will result in measurements within the tolerance which has been selected of the true value. Alternatively, it can be quoted as a level of significance.

For example, a level of confidence of 95 per cent (which implies a probability of 0.95) would result in a 5 per cent level of significance, while a 99 per cent confidence level (0.99 probability) would result in a 1 per cent level of significance. These levels, incidentally, are most commonly used in practical research.

Sample values are estimators of the true population values, and it follows, for instance, that average values obtained from sampling procedures inevitably contain some measure of sampling error. The degree to which numerical data tend to be distributed about an average value (i.e. the mean, $\bar{x}$), is known as the dispersion or variation. A well-known and widely used measure of the variation of any distribution is termed the standard deviation (or its square, the variance).

The standard deviation of a sampling distribution is known as the standard error of the mean, sometimes referred to as $SE_{\bar{x}}$ (also shown as $s_{\bar{x}}$). From an examination of this statistic, an opinion can be formed of the precision and reliability of the sample estimate. As the number in the sample is increased, the standard error ($SE_{\bar{x}}$) becomes smaller. Hence, the larger the sample, the closer becomes the estimate of the population by the sample mean. This can be shown as

$$n \to N : \bar{x} \to \mu$$

where n = number in sample

N = number in population

$\bar{x}$ = sample average

μ = population average

If $SE_{\bar{x}}$ is very large, then the sample estimate of the population mean will vary greatly. Conversely, if $SE_{\bar{x}}$ is very small, then it can reasonably be assumed that the sample is a good estimate of the population mean.

Some statistical texts tend to use 'sampling error' and 'standard error' as meaning the same statistic, but the general tendency is to use the former to describe the class of errors arising from sampling, and the latter (or sampling variance, as the case may be) from the actual measures.

It may be useful to recall some statistical notation at this stage:

	Population	*Sample*
Average or mean	μ	$\bar{x}$
Standard deviation	σ	s
Variances	σ^2	s^2

Note: Greek characters = population parameters; italic = sample statistics.

Now, variance = σ^2, and the variance of a sampling distribution of $\bar{x}$ is σ^2/n. Standard deviation = $\sqrt{\sigma^2}$ or σ.

$$\text{Therefore, } SE_{\bar{x}} = \sqrt{\frac{\sigma^2}{n}} = \frac{\sigma}{\sqrt{n}}$$

By inverting the last formula ($SE_{\bar{x}} = \sigma/\sqrt{n}$), the value of n can be found, provided the standard deviation in the population is available, or, failing that, it is possible to use the standard deviation in the sample as a reasonable estimate of it. In addition, the size of the standard error tolerated must be known. Hence:

$$\text{Taking} \qquad SE_{\bar{x}} = \frac{\sigma}{\sqrt{n}}$$

$$\text{Inverting it} \quad \sqrt{n} = \frac{\sigma}{SE_{\bar{x}}}$$

$$\text{Therefore,} \qquad n = \frac{\sigma^2}{SE^2_{\bar{x}}}$$

In marketing research, an estimate of the population proportion (or percentage) using a product or service is frequently made. The standard error of the proportion in a population can be obtained by the formula

$$\sqrt{\pi(1 - \pi)/n}$$

which can be estimated from the sample proportion p. The equation then becomes:

$$\sqrt{[p(1 - p)/n]}$$

$$\text{Therefore, } SE_p = \sqrt{\frac{p(1 - p)}{n}} \text{ or } \sqrt{\frac{pq}{n}}$$

Where: p = percentage of sample who have attribute under study
q = percentage of sample who do not have attribute under study
Sum of p and q is always 100 per cent
By inverting the formula

$$SE_p = \sqrt{pq/n}$$

$$\text{Therefore, } \sqrt{n} = \frac{\sqrt{pq}}{SE_p}$$

$$\text{Hence,} \ = \frac{pq}{SE^2{}_p}$$

Both in calculating the standard error of the mean ($SE_{\bar{x}}$) and also in the standard error of the proportion (or percentage) (SE_p), it is necessary to have some estimate of σ and n respectively.

The formulae so far given relate, however, to simple random samples, but it has already been shown that practical marketing research usually involves more complicated random sampling techniques. Where, for example, stratification is used, these simple formulae are not strictly applicable. The alternatives are shown below:

Simple random sample

$$SE_{p(ran)} = \sqrt{\frac{p(1 - p)}{n}}$$

Stratified random sample (with uniform sampling fraction)

$$SE_{p(st/uni)} = \sqrt{\frac{\Sigma n_i p_i (1 - p)}{n^2}}$$

Where Σ = summation over all strata
$\quad n_i$ = sample number in ith stratum
$\quad p_i$ = proportion of sample in ith stratum possessing attribute in survey objectives
$\quad n$ = total sample size

Simple random sample

$$SE_{\bar{x}(ran)} = \frac{\sigma}{\sqrt{n}}$$

Stratified random sample (with uniform sampling fraction)

$$SE_{\bar{x}(st/uni)} = \sqrt{\frac{\Sigma n_i \sigma_i^2}{n^2}}$$

Example   A stratified random sample was taken to ascertain people's attitudes to metrication. The sample consisted of 1000 people stratified by socio-economic groups, A–B, C, D–E, and a uniform sampling fraction was used.

Procedure:
1. Work out the proportion in favour of metrication for each social group.
2. Combine these proportions in a weighted average sum. Because a uniform sampling fraction is used, i.e. a constant percentage is taken from the population, the population numbers can be used as weights.

A town with an adult population of 10 000 was studied and a uniform sampling fraction of 10 per cent was applied to known social groups. The results are shown in Table 3.6.

Table 3.6   Stratified random sample

Population group	n_i	p_i	$n_i p_i$	q_i	$n_i p_i q_i$
A–B	150	0.8	120	0.2	24
C	650	0.7	455	0.3	136.5
D–E	200	0.3	60	0.7	42
	1000		635		202.5

$$\text{Estimate } \pi = p = \frac{\Sigma n_i p_i}{n} = \frac{635}{1000} = 0.635 \text{ or } 63.5 \text{ per cent}$$

$$\text{Estimate } SE_p(\text{ran}) = \sqrt{\frac{p(1-p)}{n}} = \sqrt{\frac{0.635 \times 0.365}{1000}} = 0.0152$$

$$\text{Estimate } SE_p(\text{st/uni}) = \sqrt{\frac{\Sigma n_i p_i (1-p)}{n^2}} = \sqrt{\frac{202.5}{1000^2}} = \frac{\sqrt{202.5}}{1000}$$

$$= 0.0142$$

It will be seen that stratification has resulted in some reduction in the standard error, therefore, the precision of the sample is improved.

Example A manufacturer is interested in the average sales values of a new line of merchandise which, it is believed, will be more acceptable to some types of customers than others. Sales to the public are made through three types of outlet: A, B, and C. The total number of outlets is 5000, made up as shown in Table 3.7.

The mean turnover in population from the stratified random sample with variable sampling fraction, as shown in Table 3.8, is obtained by weighting means of different strata by strata populations.

$$\text{Estimate } \mu = \frac{\Sigma N_i \bar{x}_i}{N} = \frac{93\,000}{5000} = 18.6$$

$$\text{Estimate } SE_{\bar{x}(\text{st/var})} = \sqrt{\frac{\Sigma N^2_i s^2_i n_i}{N^2}} = \sqrt{\frac{5\,755\,000}{5000^2}}$$

$$= \frac{\sqrt{5\,755\,000}}{5000} = 0.4797$$

This example is considered with a uniform sampling fraction in Table 3.9.

$$\text{Estimate } \mu = \frac{\Sigma n_i \bar{x}_i}{n} = \frac{1860}{5000} = 18.6$$

Table 3.7 Types of outlet

Number of outlets		Average sales per period (£)	Sample	Standard deviation (£)
A	3000	20	75	6
B	1500	16	50	4
C	500	18	35	10

Table 3.8 Stratified random sample with variable sampling fraction

Type of outlet	Population N_i	Sample average $\bar{x}_i(£)$	SD of sample s_i	$N_i \bar{x}_i$	Variable sampling fraction		
					Sample size n_i	$\dfrac{s^2_i}{n_i}$	$N^2_i s^2_i$
A	3000	20	6	60 000	75	0.48	4 320 000
B	1500	16	4	24 000	50	0.32	720 000
C	500	18	10	9 000	35	2.86	715 000
	5000			93 000	160		5 755 000

Table 3.9   Stratified random sample with uniform sampling fraction

Type of outlet	Population N_i	Sample $\bar{x}_i(£)$	SD s_i	Uniform sampling fraction Sample size n_i	$n_i\bar{x}_i$	$n_i s_i^2$
A	3000	20	6	60	1200	2160
B	1500	16	4	30	480	480
C	500	18	10	10	180	1000
	5000			100	1860	3640

Mean turnover obtained for population:

$$\text{Estimate } SE_{\bar{x}(st/uni)} = \sqrt{\frac{\Sigma n_i s_i^2}{n^2}} = \frac{\sqrt{3640}}{100} = 0.6034$$

On comparing the computed SE's, it will be seen that by using a variable fraction the sampling variance has been significantly reduced.

In these examples, the standard deviations of the strata have been quoted and so it has been possible to use the formulae. It has also been assumed that the proportion is quite well known and division into outlets has been possible.

Since the SE is now known, it is possible to calculate confidence intervals for the mean in the usual manner. To simplify operations, the finite population correction (f.p.c.) has been ignored in these examples (see p. 82).

Examination of the formulae for the standard errors of stratified random samples shows that they involve far greater mathematical effort than simple random samples. The standard error for each stratum must be worked out individually, and the results for the strata combined into a weighted sum for the whole sample. This presupposes that the researcher knows a great deal about the population, or that he or she is able to form some reliable judgements.

In actual practice, researchers tend to avoid such complicated formulae in assessing standard errors by arguing that stratification of a random sample reduces the standard error, i.e. for a given sample size, the SE of a stratified random sample is less than the SE of a simple random sample. But a stratified sample is, often, also a clustered sample, and clustering tends to increase the SE. In view of all this, it is often assumed that these two tendencies roughly cancel each other out, and, therefore, it would be in order to calculate standard errors by the simple random sampling formulae. This view is not shared, however, better to keep to SE by some leading authorities, who have commented that available evidence suggests that stratification frequently results in little advantage, whilst clustering tends to increase considerably the size of standard errors.

Computing the desired size of sample is possible, within certain limitations, by mathematical processes, but, as noted earlier, other influences play an important part in deciding the eventual size and nature of the sample. In fact, for normal designs the proper estimation of a sample size may be quite complex and demand considerable knowledge or shrewd guesswork covering the population under survey.

Design factor

Most surveys entail more complicated sampling methods than simple random sampling, and the overall effects of these complex sampling designs are expressed by the design factor (√Deff). This is 'the multiplier used to convert standard errors calculated by methods appropriate to simple random sampling into the true standard errors appropriate to the complex survey sample design being used'.[3] Hence, if the basic standard error is given as, say, 3 per cent, and the design factor is 2, the true standard error is $3 \times 2 = 6$ per cent.

In actual practice, knowing what the design factor is for a specific sampling scheme is not at all easy, so some simple and arbitrary guidelines have been proposed; for example, that *any* standard error should be multiplied by a factor of 1.5 when the sample is drawn by other than simple random method.

As already discussed, the quality of sample methodology profoundly influences the accuracy of sample statistics, and the design factor is important in evaluating survey data. For instance, a sample survey of 1500 indicated an estimate of 5 per cent for some proportion, with a simple standard error of about 1.8 per cent. A well-formulated sample, with a design factor of 1.4, has a real standard error of approximately 2 per cent, whereas a less efficient sample scheme with a design factor of 2 would have a real standard error of over 3.5 per cent.

When surveys are not based on random samples, significant problems arise in applying the design factor, and it has been suggested[4] that a well-devised quota sample could be taken as having the same accuracy as a simple random sample of half its size.

Design effect

Associated with the design factor is the design effect (Deff) which is defined as 'the ratio of the actual variance of a complex sample to the variance of a simple random sample of the same size'.[5] The latter type of sample, as noted earlier, generally serves as a useful basis for comparing the various versions of random sampling.

The following equations result:

$$\text{Design effect (Deff)} = \frac{\text{Variance of complex sample}}{\text{Variance of equivalent-sized simple random sample}}$$

$$\text{Design factor (√Deff)} = \frac{\text{Standard error (SE) of complex sample}}{\text{Standard error (SE) of equivalent sized simple random sample}}$$

Applying the design effect to the two estimates of SE given in Table 5.1, the following equation results:

$$\text{Deff} = \frac{(0.0142)^2}{(0.0152)^2} = 0.873$$

Hence, the variance of the stratified random sample is seen to be about 13 per cent smaller than that of a simple random sample of the same size. To achieve the same precision, the size of the simple random sample (for the given example) would have to be $\frac{1000}{0.873} = 1145$.

Sample size does not guarantee accuracy

The American weekly magazine, *Literary Digest*, was accustomed to conduct an extensive mail poll of voters before national elections. In the last pre-election issue of the magazine, the state of the poll was reported according to the research.

In 1936, more than 10 million ballots were mailed, of which 2 350 176 were returned and included in the summary published on 31 October 1936. Of these, 55 per cent favoured Landon, and 41 per cent favoured Roosevelt.

In the actual election, Roosevelt polled 60 per cent of the votes cast. The difference between Roosevelt's proportion of the *Digest* poll votes and the actual percentage he obtained represented a 'sampling variation' of about 50 per cent.

Yet Gallup, using a sample of only a few thousand, had accurately predicted the election results.

The *Digest* sample was not proportional; it included too many upper-economic voters (telephone subscribers, car owners) and an inadequate representation of lower-level voters. The sampling lists used were telephone directories and similar lists biased towards upper-economic voters.

Non-response bias also existed, as only 20 per cent of mail ballots were returned, probably mostly from the more educated members of the sample.

The *Digest* sample was, therefore, biased in two ways: from an unsatisfactory sampling frame and also from non-response. One bias accentuated the other.

Although *Digest* forecasts had never been wrong for over 25 years, the 1936 predictions were hopelessly inaccurate. Unsound sampling methods may sometimes produce reasonably accurate data, but eventually they fail.

3.6 Sampling frames

Before a sample survey can be undertaken, it is vitally important to define closely the population that is to be sampled. This definition should be clearly understood and agreed by all those taking part in implementing the survey. Populations may be widespread and fairly general; for example, men and women in the age group 21 to 65, over the whole country. On the other hand, populations may be highly specific, as in the case of medical practitioners in the National Health Service, with surgeries within a 50-mile radius of Birmingham Town Hall.

Surveys may, therefore, cover many different subjects ranging from professional and technical enquiries to those concerned with social and commercial matters. If random sampling methods are to be used in these enquiries, the sample design, i.e. the method and planning of the sample, will be largely controlled by the types of sampling frames that are available. Where these are not available at once, the feasibility of constructing suitable frames should be considered. The quality of random sampling techniques rests largely on the selection of suitable sampling frames, and on their availability at the time of research.

There are five criteria[6] that are useful in evaluating sampling frames:

1. *Adequacy:* this means that a sample frame should cover the population to be surveyed and that it should do this adequately related to the purposes of the survey. If a random sample of people over pensionable age has to be drawn, it would be misleading to take as a sampling frame a list of those receiving retirement pensions.

2. *Completeness:* if the sampling frame does not include all those units of a population that should be included, the missing units will not have the opportunity of being selected and the resultant sample will be biased to this extent. This may be serious if those excluded happen to possess particular characteristics. It is frequently difficult to assess the completeness of a particular sampling frame, though some valuable research has been done by Gray and Corlett[7] on the Register of Electors.

3. *No duplication:* with some frames, it is possible for a unit to be entered more than once. If there is multiple entry, for example, as with some firms listed in telephone

directories, and where the sampling frame is the directory, some weighting system may have to be applied to avoid bias.

4. *Accuracy:* many sampling lists, such as those covering dwellings or people, contain 'non-existent' units, owing to the dynamic nature of these populations. It is difficult to obtain an absolutely accurate, up-to-date frame in these circumstances, particularly when current lists are several months out of date, as in the case of the Register of Electors.

5. *Convenience:* this refers both to the accessibility of the list, and to the suitability of its arrangement for the purpose of sampling. Numbering of entries will obviously help when selecting sampling units. Lists should also be studied to see whether stratification of units is feasible.

No sampling frame is likely to satisfy all these exacting requirements, but they are useful standards by which to judge individual sampling frames. Existing frames should be identified and assessed for their suitability for particular kinds of research. In some cases, it may be necessary to build a sampling frame because existing lists are not suitable, though this rather tedious task should not be undertaken before carefully examining available frames. Compiling a special frame will, inevitably, delay the survey to some extent, but the delay may well be justified by the quality of the research findings.

Sampling frames are available covering general population characteristics in most advanced countries, but in some overseas countries it may not be possible to obtain reliable frames, and some quota system of sampling may have to be considered (see Chapter 13).

The particular problems of industrial marketing research are considered in some detail in Chapter 11.

Sources of national sampling frames in the UK

In the UK, there are two national address lists suitable for use as sampling frames: the Register of Electors, and the Postcode Address File (PAF). The former, as the title suggests, is a list of *individuals*, whereas the latter is a list of addresses – several individuals may, of course, reside at one address.

Register of Electors

For samples of individuals, the Register of Electors is generally a useful frame. It is the duty of Electoral Registration Officers to compile a new register every October (qualifying date 10 October) that is published the following 15 February, by which time it is already four months out of date. By the time it is due for replacement, it is 16 months old; this is a serious disadvantage in a dynamic population.

The register records electors for both Parliamentary and local government elections. Four categories of electors are entered: civilian Parliamentary electors; civilian local government electors; service voters; and persons who will attain the age of 18 years between the 17 February and the 15 February of the following year. To qualify for registration as a civilian Parliamentary elector, a person must be a British subject (Commonwealth citizens are British subjects) or citizen of the Irish Republic resident at the given address; must have reached the age of 18 years (except as qualified above), and must have been resident on the qualifying date in the area covered by that particular register.

Registered electors' names frequently appear in alphabetical order at their recorded addresses, but, apparently, this sequence is not always followed. It is usually possible to determine sex by the registered forename, but there is no clue to an individual's age. This could be a serious handicap if a particular age group is significant in the survey.

In rural areas, electors are generally listed in alphabetical order of surnames, further qualified by alphabetical forename where surnames are the same. This means that electors' names are not in address order, and where people of different names are living at the same address, they are recorded in different places in the register. It will be seen that this could cause problems if a sample of addresses was being extracted.

Registers are fairly easily available, both locally or centrally. The British Museum has a complete set, and copies of the entire register or part of it can be purchased from Electoral Registration Officers.

Experimental studies by Gray, Corlett, and Frankland in 1950,[7] found it to be 'fairly reassuring as to its completeness and accuracy'. Deaths and removals are factors that influence the register's validity as a sampling frame. It has been estimated that about 12 per cent of electors are no longer at their registered address by the time that the register comes up for renewal. However, it has also been shown that about 70 per cent of these electors will be found to be living near their original address, and some effort to trace them will improve sampling.

It also appears that about 4 per cent of electors do not register, but it is considered that this relatively small loss is spread over all groups in the population and no bias is, therefore, likely. On the other hand, 'movers', estimated at about 5 per cent loss per month, contain a high proportion of under 30s, which results in some slight bias in the age distribution of the population remaining in the sample frame.

A survey was conducted by the Office of Population and Censuses and Surveys (OPCS) soon after the 1991 Census as part of the Census Validation Survey, and it was found[8] that 7.1 per cent of eligible voters, who were in the 1991 Census at private households in Great Britain, were not on the Electoral Register; in 1981 the figure was 6.5 per cent. Not surprisingly, perhaps, Inner London had the highest proportion (20.4 per cent) of non-registration, followed by Outer London (10.3 per cent); there was also a distinct age bias: those under 30 were disproportionately represented; also recent movers, New Commonwealth citizens, non-white ethnic groups and private renters.

In addition, between 6.0 and 7.9 per cent of the names listed at addresses occupied when the Census was taken, did not correspond with people actually living there at the time. However, these statistics compare favourably with the previous census (1981: 7.1–10.4 per cent).

To use the register for sampling individuals, the sampling interval must be calculated; this is done by finding the ratio of the population and the sample. In a population of N size, with sample size n, the sampling interval will be N/n. Therefore, let $N = 500$ and $n = 50$, then the sampling interval is $500/50 = 10$. Any random number between 1 and 10 is chosen, say 3, and the series will then be 3, 13, 23, 33, etc. It is important that the population list should be randomly arranged.

It is more difficult to obtain a sample of households from the register, as the probability of selection is affected by the number of registered electors at any one address. Some system of weighting has to be devised to equalize probabilities. For example, addresses with four registered electors could be weighted $\frac{1}{4}$, and single-person addresses could receive a weighting of one. This method tends to be a bit troublesome in practice.

An alternative approach is to make a random selection of every nth individual, as outlined earlier, taking note of the address and the number of resident registered electors. This establishes the probability of selection of each household. A final sample is then drawn by selecting *every* address with one registered elector, every *second* address with two electors, every *third* address with three electors, and so on. The resulting sample of addresses will have equal probabilities.

Where it is not possible to construct sampling frames, some alternative method of sampling, such as quota, may have to be used. But it is often practicable to devise special frames, provided a reasonable amount of careful thought is given to the problems of particular surveys. Existing lists may have to be rearranged before they can be used for specific research purposes. It is advisable for researchers to acquire a good knowledge of the many specialist directories that could prove useful in constructing sampling frames. This applies particularly in the area of industrial and technical marketing research.

Researchers should, therefore, study the objectives of the survey, the population to be surveyed, the methods of sampling proposed, and relate these factors to the records available. Lists should be assessed for reliability, completeness, and adequacy, as already noted, and before using them as sampling frames, researchers should be satisfied that they will provide a sound foundation on which to construct the research project.

Postcode Address File (PAF)

Every address in the UK is post-coded; the system enables the Post Office to use mechanized sorting of mail.

The post code is a combination of up to seven alphabetical and numerical characters that define, in a unique way, four different levels of geographic unit, e.g. WA15 9AE.

The largest geographical unit, of which there are 120, is termed a post code area, e.g. WA, referring to Warrington. In turn, each area is subdivided into carefully chosen smaller geographical units known as districts (represented by 15 in the code quoted). These 2700 post code districts are next subdivided into post code sectors, of which there are 8900 in total (9 in quoted post code). Finally, the complete post code identifies one street, or part of a street, with the last two alpha characters (AE in above example, referring to an address in Hale, Altrincham) (see Fig. 3.5).

In the UK there are 1.5 million post codes covering 22 million addresses. Some very large users of mail (about 170 000) have their own unique post code, but, generally, there are approximately 15 addresses per post code.

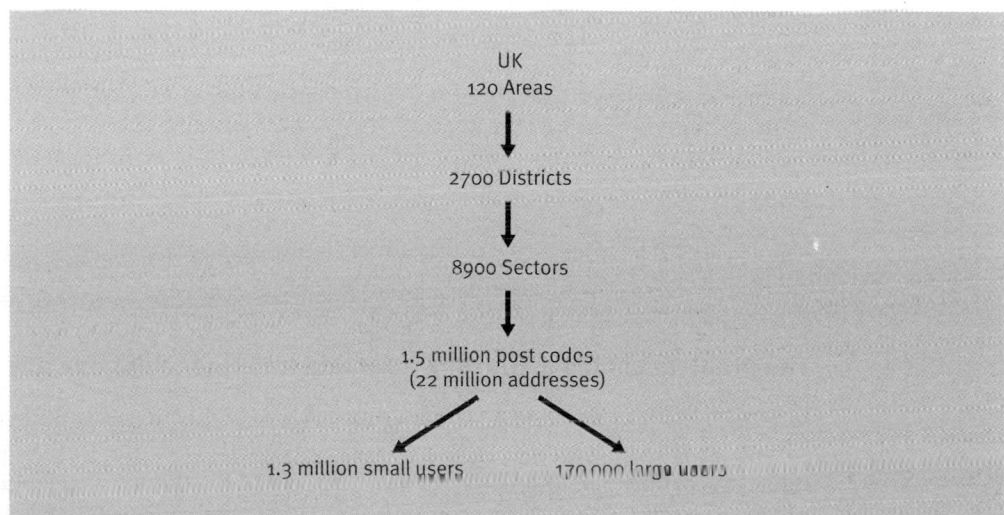

Figure 3.5   Structure of the UK post code

Post codes can be used commercially in many ways, e.g. constructing sales territories and defining sales staff responsibilities; locating distribution depots; sales analyses; advertising responses, etc. The Marketing Department of the Post Office can supply details of specific services such as post coding address lists by computer, post code maps, and post code directories.

For the purposes of marketing research, the post code system offers an attractive sampling frame; it is a complete listing of UK locations that is developed through three stages, viz. post code area, district, sector, and final street location. (Stratification of samples is discussed in the next chapter.)

Datamaps Ltd of Wembley publishes a series of coordinated business planning maps with overlays specifically related to the post code areas, as well as motorways, counties and regions.

The Postcode Address File has been adopted by the Office of Population and Census, and by leading market research organizations, such as Taylor Nelson Sofres for its home audit surveys (see Chapter 8).

Specific applications of the PAF to marketing research may involve, for example, interviewing adults at selected post code addresses, or, perhaps, taking at random a number of post codes and proceeding to interview an agreed number and type of respondents. However, PAF does not, as noted earlier, indicate the number of people living at a specific listed address, so some further process of selection would be necessary for individual respondents. For example, individuals at any one selected address would be numbered and then a final selection made by a random process.

The PAF is now widely adopted in official surveys, such as the British Crime Survey, the Family Expenditure Survey, the General Household Survey, the Labour Force Survey and the National Food Survey.

KEYPOINT

Sampling frames: lists, indexes, maps or other records of a population from which a sample can be selected

First criteria useful in evaluating sample frames: 1. adequacy, 2. completeness, 3. no duplication, 4. accuracy, 5. convenience.

No sampling frame likely to fully satisfy all of these exacting requirements

Existing frames should be assessed for suitability

Sometimes necessary to build a sampling frame – but this is tedious task

In most developed countries, sampling frames available

In some overseas countries, reliable frames are problematic

Two UK national sampling frames: 1. Register of Electors, 2. Postcode Address File (PAF)

The problem of bias in drawing a sample from the telephone directory

Bias may result in drawing a sample from telephone directories from two sources: (a) the extent to which domestic telephones are installed, and, (b) the completeness of the directory listings. At one time in the UK, rental of domestic telephones was largely restricted to the higher socio-economic classes, so that any attempt to sample the general population from telephone directories could lead to serious bias. In 1972, about 42 per cent of British households had a telephone: by 1981, this figure had jumped to 75 per cent, and in 1998/99, domestic telephones had reached 96 per cent – virtually complete coverage.[9]

Unlisted telephone numbers are estimated to be up to 40 per cent (50 per cent plus in major cities), either because people have asked to be 'ex-directory', or because of removals or new installations since the last reprint of directories.

In the United States, the incidence of unlisted numbers is high. There are significant area variations, and nationally nearly 30 per cent of telephones were unlisted in 1996. Of these, about 20 per cent represented people who were in the process of moving their residences. The remaining 80 per cent were subscribers who requested to be unlisted for a variety of reasons, e.g. to avoid crank calls, telemarketers, etc. Unlisted telephone subscribers (by choice) tend to be younger, urban and with above-average incomes.[10]

It is conceded that 'comparatively little is known' about ex-directory telephone owners (XDs) in the UK, 'and the effects their exclusion from telephone surveys using directory based samples might have'.[11] Hence, the Market Research Development Fund – an autonomous working party of the Market Research Society commissioned Wendy Sykes and Martin Collins to investigate the characteristics of XDs. An exhaustive study was made of 3100 respondents to the 1986 British Social Attitudes Survey. The major results were: 87 per cent of respondents were, or claimed to be telephone owners; 9 per cent of these were identified as ex-directory and 'little difference' was evident across socio-economic and age classifications, but there were 'noticeably higher' differences for London and some minority (generally *less* well off) groups. The findings of this report, 'Telephone Availability 1987', are instructive and emphasize the need for caution in using telephone surveys; the unlisted percentage is certainly markedly different from earlier estimates.

Random digit dialling

To overcome the problem of deficient sampling frames based on domestic telephone lists, the technique of random-digit dialling (RDD) was developed in the United States and is now widely used. From information supplied by the telephone company, researchers can generate telephone numbers by using a table of random numbers, so that any telephone number, whether listed in a directory or not, may then be dialled. This basic approach is costly and relatively unproductive, so RDD has been modified by two-stage sampling, and computer-based variants, to increase effective domestic contacts. In countries such as the UK where, as noted earlier, virtually all households have a telephone, RDD can be a very cost-effective method of sampling, especially in metropolitan areas, where unlisted telephones are likely to be disproportionately high. However, it could cause irritation to some unlisted telephone householders and might attract restrictive legislation. In the UK it appears to be in growing use by tele-marketing companies.

Research by Foreman and Collins[12] into the viability of random digit dialling (RDD) sampling procedures in the UK revealed 'considerable difficulties, both in drawing a sample within the irregular UK numbering system and in using the RDD approach within the quota sampling "culture" of UK market research companies'. Of the 25 research agencies contacted, 20 regarded ex-directory numbers as a problem, 12 had attempted some sort of solution, but all had doubts about the validity of using 'true' RDD in the UK.

An alternative tried by four of the twelve companies who had tried to tackle the problem, was 'Directory Plus 1' dialling; this entails 'selecting a sample of numbers from telephone directories and adding the integer one to those numbers to generate a sample of both listed and unlisted numbers'.[12] The researchers admit that while response rates for both methods 'were not good', the rate for RDD was not worse than that achieved for 'Directory Plus 1' dialling, and neither method produced a satisfactory demographic profile.

While it is felt that further experimentation with RDD may be worth while, many practical problems, in particular the high incidence of refusals, have to be overcome before agencies can be expected to adopt it. Further discussion of telephone survey methodology occurs in Chapter 6.

Summary

Sampling is one of the major techniques underlying marketing research, of which the sampling procedures originated in social surveys. Sampling theory is concerned with studying the relationships between a population and the samples drawn from it: probability is its heart, and it is particularly useful in (a) estimation, and (b) hypothesis testing.

Sampling frames are necessary for probability or random sampling; five criteria can be applied to evaluate the suitability of sampling frames: adequacy, completeness, no duplication, accuracy, and convenience. These exacting requirements are unlikely to be fully met, but they are useful standards. Two well-known national sampling frames are the Register of Electors and the Postcode Address File.

Sample size depends on the basic characteristics of the population, the type of information needed and, of course, the cost. It does not depend on the application of some arbitrary percentage.

The larger the sample, the greater its precision or reliability, but practical constraints such as time, staff, and cost affect marketing research in practice.

Sample values are estimators of true population values, and so the former inevitably contain some measure of sampling error; the degree to which numerical data are distributed about an average value is known as the dispersion or variation; a well-known and widely used measure is the standard deviation (or its square, the variance). The standard deviation, known as the standard error of the mean, indicates the precision and reliability of a sample estimate.

The design factor is important in evaluating the effect of sample design survey statistics.

The normal curve or distribution is one of several sampling distributions related to sampling theory and is widely used in studying statistical data.

Sampling frames are necessary for probability or random sampling; five criteria can be applied to evaluate the suitability of sampling frames: adequacy, completeness, no duplication, accuracy, and convenience. These exacting requirements are unlikely to be fully met, but they are useful standards. Two well-known national sampling frames are the Register of Electors and the Postcode Address File.

Review and discussion questions

1. The manager of a multiplex cinema is anxious to know how it is perceived, i.e. the image people have of the cinema. Identify three possible populations that may be surveyed to obtain this information.

2. The CBI would like to discover the views of managers in medium/large indigenous British companies on how electronic mail affects their relationships with clients. How might they identify possible sampling frames? Discuss the possible bias attaching to each frame.

▶

3. The chamber of commerce in a large British town wishes to conduct a random sample of retail outlets in the town. It is proposing to use a local commercial directory as a sampling frame. To what extent could this sampling frame lead to bias? How might such bias be minimized?

4. A large Scottish town has a population of 50 000 households divided into three social class groups as follows: 10 000 are upper class, 15 000 are middle class and 25 000 are working class. A uniform sampling fraction of 1000 households from this population yielded the following amounts spent annually on groceries. The upper class had a mean expenditure of £2000 with a standard deviation of £150; the middle class had a mean expenditure of £1000 with a standard deviation of £120; the working class had a mean expenditure of £800 with a standard deviation of £100. What is the 95 per cent confidence interval for the mean annual expenditure on groceries for all households in the town?

5. A British airline carrier has decided to conduct an in-flight survey of its customers using a random sample of passengers. It wishes to know the mean number of flights taken by each passenger annually and the proportion of these landing at Stansted. It estimates the standard deviation of flights per year to be 2.0 and will allow a confidence interval of ± 1 per cent flight. It estimates the proportion landing at Stansted to be 10 per cent and will allow a confidence interval of ± 2 per cent. It has decided that it needs a 95 per cent confidence level for both questions. If the airline intends to ask both questions in the same survey, what sample size should it take?

4. A Students' Union survey of undergraduate attitudes towards legalizing cannabis revealed that 65 per cent of a sample of 400 students were in favour. If the total undergraduate population is 10 000, calculate the confidence interval for the population of students who favour legalizing cannabis at the 95 per cent confidence level. What effect would doubling the sample size have on the confidence interval?

References

1. Bowley, A. L., and A. R. Burnett-Hurst, *Livelihood and Poverty: A Study in the Economic Conditions of Working-class Households in Northamptom, Warrington, Stanley and Reading*, Bell, London, 1915.
2. Ferber, Robert, *Market Research*, McGraw-Hill, New York, 1949.
3. Harris, P., 'The effects of clustering on costs and sampling errors of random samples', *Journal of the Market Research Society*, vol. 19, no. 3, 1977.
4. Koerner, Roy E., 'The design factor — an underutilised concept', *European Research*, vol. 8, no. 6, November 1980.
5. Kish, L., *Sampling*, John Wiley, New York, 1965.
6. Yates, F., *Sampling Methods for Censuses and Surveys* (2nd edn), Griffin, London, 1953.
7. Gray, P. G., and T. Corlett, 'Sampling for the Social Survey', *Journal of the Royal Statistical Society*, vol. 113, 1950.
8. Leventhal, Barry, 'Mastering the rolls', *Research*, no. 327, August 1993, Market Research Society.
9. Social Trends 30, Office for National Statistics (ONS), 2000.
10. Aaker, David, V. Kumar, and George S. Day, *Marketing Research*, John Wiley, New York, 1998.
11. McKenzie, John, 'Study of characteristics of ex-directory telephone owners', *MRS Newsletter*, December 1988.
12. Foreman, Jane, and Martin Collins, 'The viability of random digit dialling in the UK', *Journal of the Market Research Society*, vol. 33, no. 3, July 1991.

4

Types of sampling

Learning Objectives

- Obtain basic understanding of probability (random) and non-probability sampling techniques and their relative attributes

- Become conversant with limitations of sampling methodologies

- Note importance of efficient sampling design

- Understand how sample sizes are calculated (a) theoretically; (b) in practice, and that sample size itself is not sufficient

4.1 Probability sampling (random sampling)

Probability sampling, also known as random sampling, results in every sampling unit in a finite population having a calculable and non-zero probability of being selected in the sample. This means that the chance of a unit being included in a sample can be calculated. For example, if a sample of 500 people is to be chosen at random from a population of 50 000, each member of the population will have 1 chance in 100 of being selected in the sampling process.

Probability sampling has been widely adopted by leading research bodies because of its sound theoretical basis, which allows the legitimate use of the mathematics of probability. It is the only completely objective method of sampling populations. It is used almost exclusively by the Government Social Survey, and by the American Bureau of the Census. The results of random sampling are, therefore, statistically sounder; it is possible to calculate the standard error of the mean. Another advantage is that, because of the mechanical selection of those who are to be interviewed, the bias arising from interviewers interviewing only the most easily available informants is avoided.

The difficulties of random sampling should also be noted. In commercial practice, there are very few complete lists of a universe or population which are really satisfactory. National lists, such as the Register of Electors, quickly become out of date, and professional and trade directories vary greatly in their reliability. All are subject to printing delays.

Calls to obtain randomly selected informants may be widely scattered, causing considerable cost in time and money. The whole sample may suffer severe delay which will affect the usefulness of its findings. To overcome this delay, a larger interviewing staff could conceivably be employed, increasing costs yet again.

One of the principal drawbacks is the necessity of making 'call-backs', where the original call was not successful. It is important that randomly selected informants should be interviewed in order to maintain the statistical validity of the sample. Non-response is a serious source of bias (which is dealt with in Chapter 6) and every endeavour must be made to secure as many successful interviews as possible. Call-backs add to survey costs, but some proportion is inevitable in random sampling. Standard practice is to instruct interviewers to make up to three calls before abandoning the prospect of an interview. When this happens in rural areas, it increases travelling costs very considerably, apart from the probable physical difficulties of tracing some randomly chosen country dweller. Some system of substitution is often used after the third unsuccessful journey. Interviewers may well begin to lose interest in a survey which entails a great deal of repeat calling. Even after repeated calls have been made and the informant is eventually contacted, the interview may be refused.

As a result of these various drawbacks, random sampling tends to be fairly expensive, but like many other products and services, price by itself is no measure of comparison. The overwhelming view of experts is that the value of random sampling cannot be matched by other methods.

There are several forms of random sampling in general use which, to some considerable extent, overcome many of the disadvantages just discussed. These alternative forms are listed below and dealt with in some detail later.

1. Simple random
2. Systematic or quasi-random
3. Stratified random

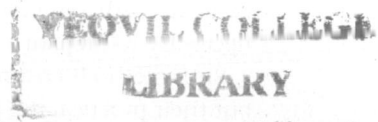

4. Cluster (including area)

5. Multi-stage

6. Replicated (interpenetrating)

7. Master

8. Multi-phase

There are other types which may occasionally be encountered, but the above cover most of the types of random sample commonly used. The section on sampling frames will be usefully referred to during the study of systematic (quasi-random) sampling.

KEYPOINT

Probability sampling (random sampling)

Every sampling unit in finite populations has calculable probability of being selected

Widely adopted by leading research bodies

Only completely objective method of sampling

Avoids problems of interviewer-bias in selection

Problems: very few complete sampling frames, e.g. Register of Electors quickly out-of-date; possibility of informants being widely scattered; considerable delays in completing surveys; 'call-backs' increase costs and cause delay

Overall, fairly expensive method

Part-solution: variations of random sampling, e.g. quasi-random, stratified random, cluster random

---

Simple random sampling

This can be done either by the 'lottery method' or by using random tables. The essential purpose of random selection is to avoid subjective bias arising from a personal choice of sampling units.

In the lottery method, every unit of the population is identified by a numbered disc or slip. These are placed in an urn, well mixed, and then by chance selection, a quantity is withdrawn until the required sample size is achieved. After each selection, the disc is usually replaced in the urn to maintain the same probability of selection for all discs. But even this simple method can be subject to bias. An interesting study revealed that in one case a particular colour of counter was apparently more slippery than counters of other colours, resulting in biased selection.

The other method is to use a table of random numbers specially designed for sampling purposes. There are several well-known tables: Kendall and Babington Smith[1] (Table 4.1), for instance: Fisher and Yates; and the Rand Corporation's *A Million Random Digits*. Statistical textbooks generally include some random tables in their appendices. Every unit in the population must be numbered. Digits are selected from the random numbers table in any systematic way (horizontal, vertical, diagonal, etc.), and those units whose numbers coincide with the random digits are included in the sample population. Obviously, it is necessary to prepare a list of sampling frames beforehand.

Both methods ensure random selection because they do not rely on human judgement, but their practical use is largely restricted to small populations. If a national survey of the

Table 4.1   Random sampling numbers

Fifteenth thousand

	1–4	5–8	9–12	13–16	17–20	21–24	25–28	29–32	33–36	37–40
1	12 67	73 29	44 54	12 73	97 48	79 91	20 20	17 31	83 20	85 66
2	06 24	89 57	11 27	43 03	14 29	84 52	86 13	51 70	65 88	60 88
3	29 15	84 77	17 86	64 87	06 55	36 44	92 58	64 91	94 48	64 65
4	49 56	97 93	91 59	41 21	98 03	70 85	31 99	74 45	67 94	47 79
5	50 77	60 28	58 75	70 96	70 07	60 66	05 95	58 39	20 25	96 89
6	00 31	32 48	23 12	31 08	51 06	23 44	26 43	56 34	78 65	50 80
7	01 67	45 57	55 98	93 69	07 81	62 35	22 03	89 22	54 94	83 31
8	24 00	48 34	15 45	34 50	02 37	43 57	36 13	76 71	95 40	34 10
9	77 52	60 27	64 16	06 83	38 73	51 32	62 85	24 58	54 29	64 56
10	36 29	93 93	10 00	51 34	81 26	13 53	26 29	16 94	19 01	40 45
11	94 82	03 96	49 78	32 61	17 78	70 12	91 69	69 99	62 75	16 50
12	23 12	21 19	67 27	86 47	43 25	25 05	76 17	50 55	70 32	83 36
13	77 58	90 38	66 53	45 85	13 93	00 65	30 59	39 44	86 75	90 73
14	92 37	51 97	83 78	12 70	41 42	01 72	10 48	88 95	05 24	44 21
15	28 93	48 44	13 02	49 32	07 95	26 47	67 70	72 71	08 47	26 18
16	09 68	01 98	80 27	49 78	56 67	49 22	13 66	61 33	53 18	36 03
17	61 73	92 33	89 48	20 42	32 33	79 37	68 88	44 59	35 17	97 61
18	82 35	37 33	53 42	52 04	16 54	08 25	48 89	57 87	59 89	96 76
19	39 20	77 72	55 19	66 58	57 91	38 43	67 97	52 66	45 29	74 67
20	51 90	71 05	82 38	37 40	94 52	24 09	35 44	37 33	35 29	65 89
21	97 49	53 79	17 25	02 65	77 70	88 45	53 51	63 30	89 66	42 03
22	73 18	91 38	25 82	29 71	56 89	86 74	68 58	75 36	93 13	33 31
23	17 79	34 97	25 89	01 17	67 92	62 25	54 70	52 88	28 05	61 17
24	97 27	26 86	17 67	59 56	95 07	49 05	70 06	70 35	21 35	26 18
25	56 06	63 00	07 40	65 87	09 49	70 34	67 02	33 39	04 40	01 51

Sixteenth thousand

	1–4	5–8	9–12	13–16	17–20	21–24	25–28	29–32	33–36	37–40
1	43 83	39 24	50 74	10 05	38 11	25 80	44 14	98 31	87 41	02 74
2	63 19	91 27	08 59	02 28	47 13	05 53	02 28	81 96	46 90	95 52
3	23 87	60 31	98 97	76 57	82 47	64 87	50 45	73 54	26 47	62 10
4	07 04	47 34	36 03	87 67	03 28	72 19	98 99	32 98	78 76	85 40
5	98 61	67 62	09 89	73 50	06 81	29 09	43 43	30 21	32 69	82 19
6	36 86	50 21	42 18	20 55	00 90	01 96	42 12	68 18	45 93	32 99
7	70 64	92 95	09 09	79 63	09 29	69 99	98 26	19 83	94 88	95 37
8	41 71	91 61	31 86	38 01	71 79	44 75	67 69	35 31	69 47	81 64
9	23 48	32 36	88 50	29 07	27 32	21 28	73 41	77 39	00 78	92 65
10	13 32	99 81	00 28	87 13	00 86	56 16	81 20	63 29	37 45	08 91
11	70 55	85 27	24 96	91 83	89 17	89 98	51 31	17 29	05 77	72 95
12	12 50	84 01	63 40	74 86	88 90	63 76	97 74	08 70	88 88	98 96
13	97 00	24 63	47 63	47 66	21 79	28 66	67 24	33 20	01 52	09 59
14	16 99	63 29	67 89	14 55	70 31	45 56	05 71	84 30	48 32	90 94
15	57 95	93 54	30 74	11 18	31 26	75 39	81 28	63 34	31 23	77 67
16	01 32	91 11	23 65	44 58	69 77	58 86	35 20	92 12	48 15	56 67
17	00 30	26 68	89 38	38 13	99 47	06 82	49 47	40 33	23 72	01 50
18	48 15	27 13	97 70	18 48	14 28	26 30	74 16	13 07	36 21	94 84
19	58 86	65 76	67 05	99 53	33 56	92 61	63 98	55 39	15 77	61 67
20	85 07	14 81	41 16	12 21	79 82	16 42	70 43	73 33	78 22	63 25

Table 4.1   Random sampling numbers (*cont.*)

	1–4	5–8	9–12	13–16	17–20	21–24	25–28	29–32	33–36	37–40
21	86 19	97 09	64 04	21 26	65 11	20 32	82 38	52 94	79 21	85 07
22	66 17	52 10	35 14	21 89	54 32	61 49	63 06	36 25	63 84	78 24
23	56 70	95 77	25 19	21 15	29 88	57 75	51 19	31 06	48 50	09 65
24	14 43	67 32	81 78	19 72	32 70	34 86	11 90	37 02	54 39	45 87
25	04 17	91 71	96 90	85 68	32 35	77 20	71 43	55 95	28 90	51 69

Seventeenth thousand

	1–4	5–8	9–12	13–16	17–20	21–24	25–28	29–32	33–36	37–40
1	34 51	16 59	02 45	39 71	72 53	96 32	81 60	47 92	90 09	27 20
2	20 23	36 13	23 12	60 71	99 12	65 55	07 97	09 60	52 61	88 14
3	76 68	10 33	58 10	16 70	54 96	94 81	99 37	12 66	99 93	88 34
4	80 82	10 98	00 30	85 07	67 55	92 50	59 19	75 25	71 38	54 26
5	42 25	41 73	49 19	52 51	57 28	37 83	26 76	88 64	78 20	15 67
6	26 46	28 74	47 63	13 67	03 78	71 82	02 10	39 66	92 35	62 25
7	68 99	45 26	07 70	50 41	79 30	29 91	54 35	27 54	85 51	81 24
8	87 31	65 32	41 62	04 03	22 04	51 76	64 73	39 26	29 39	81 71
9	06 14	44 15	83 78	99 51	20 01	30 27	97 05	62 64	35 74	06 00
10	38 47	56 59	19 55	74 36	52 90	49 97	05 57	70 89	40 26	11 91
11	89 13	92 60	35 31	05 13	64 38	43 52	24 87	06 54	87 66	67 47
12	15 51	88 78	45 84	46 06	67 48	21 82	94 35	63 00	67 03	67 10
13	70 02	74 26	04 86	41 76	11 84	98 33	32 35	39 41	39 51	84 00
14	57 77	07 06	55 97	19 69	53 37	37 39	70 87	73 75	28 96	25 75
15	51 07	68 68	36 99	06 42	23 74	15 56	86 28	30 87	48 08	53 48
16	89 21	03 65	84 88	85 72	22 08	63 78	95 56	69 91	69 67	21 43
17	24 31	92 71	55 69	02 45	14 91	48 47	34 58	54 12	00 70	22 82
18	00 33	45 41	03 23	97 65	49 67	75 63	74 02	13 24	92 66	69 21
19	59 56	56 08	10 14	68 21	06 51	25 66	16 28	01 07	87 11	51 42
20	57 34	54 02	75 26	66 35	52 72	19 95	20 38	98 40	37 26	20 36
21	72 97	03 22	47 61	64 15	99 32	89 71	31 92	41 63	24 36	76 75
22	08 94	07 60	27 12	26 06	60 20	37 87	56 54	59 88	44 11	38 06
23	00 78	97 34	17 57	07 84	19 25	27 56	11 92	26 76	99 52	97 52
24	89 38	07 16	20 25	37 78	52 85	90 75	35 07	97 12	39 78	37 47
25	52 58	28 43	32 38	41 74	88 13	90 58	05 47	50 21	95 25	42 01

Eighteenth thousand

	1–4	5–8	9–12	13–16	17–20	21–24	25–28	29–32	33–36	37–40
1	08 59	51 65	98 29	69 66	90 49	07 24	67 63	41 47	04 75	17 90
2	87 83	22 19	76 36	00 58	48 47	41 20	74 44	06 69	75 60	74 31
3	76 89	40 65	98 22	77 21	24 25	03 15	62 68	60 45	66 70	85 39
4	08 97	75 59	41 94	91 31	92 00	52 29	50 32	25 20	98 89	19 38
5	38 09	07 26	10 92	70 39	83 78	76 63	26 17	32 17	40 29	12 33
6	31 55	17 02	22 85	47 84	93 41	03 11	71 61	23 06	21 60	45 09
7	30 93	44 60	80 21	76 28	37 21	31 80	78 96	85 56	56 05	27 28
8	38 43	62 41	58 86	98 44	78 52	51 75	31 84	79 08	05 97	35 93
9	96 67	86 95	74 39	21 90	80 20	42 32	70 88	75 35	10 30	99 99
10	26 62	19 26	28 16	13 24	02 43	16 65	41 34	03 80	81 87	98 29
11	57 08	15 37	74 85	65 21	72 98	53 20	53 33	32 72	51 48	26 60
12	92 05	77 55	70 51	49 69	50 16	26 70	96 28	46 51	42 99	90 78
13	88 33	50 35	10 80	97 89	87 38	31 20	19 74	25 26	12 24	03 49
14	38 46	01 13	05 58	27 15	82 72	62 21	28 60	30 60	59 69	22 03
15	26 81	24 78	49 14	80 47	70 34	11 86	60 59	31 40	02 42	83 23

Table 4.1   Random sampling numbers (cont.)

16	83 90	62 31	22 49	82 42	16 53	60 29	52 33	06 50	41 27	09 41
17	25 77	95 10	09 71	25 90	63 05	29 87	11 24	29 23	31 22	86 42
18	46 40	99 89	30 12	15 22	89 32	27 54	73 30	67 19	32 48	82 83
19	42 74	95 44	01 16	25 94	44 34	06 67	87 33	16 98	83 60	41 63
20	84 59	72 14	30 36	29 74	19 68	76 88	09 74	51 29	98 89	02 04
21	27 86	32 94	70 15	16 43	12 34	68 71	55 21	92 09	31 34	79 40
22	97 94	92 04	28 78	99 60	87 02	88 51	88 58	20 78	20 75	45 82
23	39 24	29 44	32 10	89 26	80 43	45 83	01 06	23 14	44 84	85 30
24	57 24	53 05	16 41	38 58	97 95	51 45	89 15	15 93	87 30	74 49
25	04 00	60 69	08 96	35 88	82 58	24 22	39 72	04 89	32 20	37 17

Source: Reproduced from *Tracts for Computers*, no. xxiv, edited by E. S. Pearson.

general population were to be planned, the difficulties inherent in either of these techniques would be apparent. Apart from the mechanics of selection, the resultant sample might well be so widely spread geographically that it would make interviewing difficult and expensive.

Systematic or quasi-random sampling

This differs from simple random sampling in not giving equal probability of selection to all possible samples which could be taken from a population. The method is widely used in the UK and offers the most practical approximation to random sampling.

It depends on the existence of some sampling list or frame of the population under investigation. Polling records are frequently used; other lists, depending on the nature of the population, could include customer record cards, telephone directories, trade association lists, etc. It is argued that lists can be considered as being arranged more or less at random, and that they are usually compiled independently of the subject of the survey.

Quasi-random sampling involves calculating the sample interval, obtained by finding the ratio of the population to the sample, i.e. N/n, and rounding the result to the nearest integer. A random number is then chosen between one and the sampling interval. From this starting point, successive random points are chosen by adding the sampling interval to each succeeding number. Hence, the selection of one sample number is dependent on the selection of the previous one, and so strictly speaking they are not chosen by a truly random process. The initial number is, of course, randomly selected, but successive numbers are not independently chosen because the sampling interval predetermines them.

For example, in a survey covering a population of 10 000 people, it may be decided to take a sample of 250. The sampling interval will be 10 000/250 = 40, and the population list will be used as a sampling frame. A randomly selected number between 1 and 40 is chosen, say 4, and the series then becomes 4, 44, 84, etc., until the sample of 250 is achieved. Persons whose names coincide with these positions in the list are selected for interview.

The Social Survey used a card index as the sampling frame, when an investigation was made into the incidence of pneumoconiosis among ex-miners. This method has been used in other official surveys and is generally considered to be satisfactory except in those cases where population lists may be subject to some periodic arrangement. Before using lists, it is advisable to check on how they were compiled.

Stratified random sampling

This means that the population to be surveyed is divided into groups with similar attributes. In each group or stratum, the population is more nearly homogeneous than in the total population, and this contributes to the accuracy of the sampling process.

The population to be surveyed is carefully studied. This analysis may reveal bases for stratification which will help substantially in increasing the precision of the sample survey. The population of the UK, for example, is made up of men, women, and children of different age groups, social groups, and occupations. Individuals may well be influenced by these characteristics in their views on the subject of a survey, and it may, therefore, be possible to form strata which contain individuals of similar characteristics so that their opinions can be more accurately assessed. The number that should appear in each stratum should be based upon its proportion in the population.

Within these defined strata, random selection takes place, and provided this is done correctly, stratified random sampling tends to be more accurate than simple random sampling. Significant characteristics of the total population are represented adequately in the different strata of the sample population. A simple random sample *may*, in fact, result in the correct composition of sampling units from the various strata of a population, but this cannot be assumed in every case. Sampling errors resulting from simple random samples will be greater than from stratified random samples of the same size. This arises because, when a population is sampled by simple random methods, two sets of sampling errors have to be considered: those *within* each stratum and those *between* the various strata. For example, people in one particular socio-economic group may well have different views from those in another. In addition, there is likely to be some difference of opinion *within* each socio-economic group.

When stratified random sampling is used, the variation between strata is taken care of because the sample has already been divided into strata of suitable attributes corresponding to those significant in the total population. As noted earlier, the process of random selection only takes place after stratification, and, therefore, sampling errors can arise from only one source, i.e. from within strata. It follows that stratification is more effective where there is a high proportion of the total variation in a population accounted for by between strata variation. Strata should, therefore, be designed so that they differ significantly from each other, and the population within each stratum should be as homogeneous as possible. In this way, the benefits of stratification are fully exploited.

Stratification factors should be distinctly relevant to the survey, and this means that the population under survey should be closely examined relative to the objectives of the investigation. Factors eventually selected must be significant and useful. In many consumer surveys, stratification by age, sex, and socio-economic group is fairly routine practice, particularly when using quota sampling methods. Other special strata may be introduced to cover the particular needs of surveys, perhaps qualifying the ownership of product types.

Too many strata complicate the survey and make preparation and tabulation more difficult. Little is to be gained from adding strata that are not significant to the survey as a whole. Pilot surveys can help to identify population characteristics which may be suitable for stratifying samples.

There are two methods used to stratify samples: with uniform sampling fraction (proportionate) or with variable sampling fraction (optimal or disproportionate):

1. *Uniform sampling fraction* (proportionate) occurs when equal proportions are sampled from each stratum. This may be necessary where there is little reliable information

available about the population, and a researcher may assume that variation within individual groups of the population is relatively equal, though the strata may differ markedly in average values. For example, a researcher may assume that the average consumption of bread varies substantially by family size, although the variance about the individual averages of the family strata would tend to be similar. By applying proportionate or uniform sampling fraction, the number of observations in the total sample is distributed among strata (family size) in proportion to the importance of each stratum in the population. This results in a rather more accurate sample than a simple random sample, because stratification has ensured that the various family sizes are already present in the sample.

2. *Variable sampling fraction* (disproportionate or optimal), in which it is more likely that both the mean and variance will differ significantly among strata in a population, and in these cases a variable sampling fraction is used in preparing a stratified sample. Larger proportions are taken from one stratum than from another according to the variability existing within strata. The more mixed or variable the population within particular strata, the more difficult it is to represent those strata by merely taking a uniform sample from them.

For example, if a survey of chemists in the UK were planned to investigate selling prices of a range of toiletries or drugs, a sample population of 1000 might be considered, and it might be known that of these outlets, 40 per cent were owned by Boots. Within the stratum represented by Boots' stores, price variation is strictly limited, but in the remaining 60 per cent of the population there may be significant price variations among independent chemists. In such instances, disproportionate stratification would be suitable, because fewer examples of Boots' stores need to be sampled in order to give the overall picture of their stratum, while independents, on the other hand, require greater representation in the sample owing to the greater degree of variance existing within the different strata to which they belong. If it could be established beforehand that all Boots' stores observed the same selling prices for the products under survey, it would be feasible to represent this particular stratum by just one sampling unit. The vast majority of enquiries could be profitably concentrated on the 'independents' where it is believed that prices are subject to some fluctuation. Stratification by this method results in greater precision in the investigation of heterogeneous populations, and acknowledges the fact that some types of sampling units are more important than others in order to obtain valid survey findings.

Some years ago, an American advertiser who used television extensively was particularly interested in the media habits of inhabitants of rural areas and in other areas with relatively low television coverage. In these areas, the size of the sample was increased so that a detailed analysis could be made of these relatively minor sections of the national sample. The other case was of a major market beer study for a regional brewer where it was particularly important to obtain the preferences and attitudes of African-American beer drinkers. The size of the sample in those blocks in which more than half of the household heads were African-American was, therefore, doubled so that the views of an adequate number of African-American respondents could be obtained.

The results for each stratum must be weighted by the size of that stratum to achieve a valid population mean or other measurement. This entails extra work, of course, and researchers need to assess whether the additional precision which results from using variable sampling fractions is worth while. Apart from the additional work entailed by weighting, it should be borne in mind that sampling errors may be increased.

Table 4.2   Disproportionate sampling

Number of stores	Per cent of total grocery sales	Allocation of 100 sample stores
1000 cooperatives	15	15 shops
1000 multiples	50	50 shops
8000 independents	35	35 shops
Total 10 000	100	100

Source: Nielsen.

Frequently, researchers lack sufficient knowledge of the relative variability in strata when surveys are being planned. Some guidance may possibly be forthcoming from earlier surveys covering similar populations. Failing this, a pilot survey is valuable in indicating the general structure of the population it is proposed to stratify. The approximate figures obtained will not, of course, be precise, but they serve to act as reasonable bases for stratification.

Neyman[2] has shown that for a sample of a given size, optimum distribution among strata is given by sampling each stratum with a sampling fraction proportional to the standard deviations of the variable within the strata. Obviously this depends on knowing the standard deviations beforehand, and, as already observed, this is not generally the experience of survey planners. Disproportionate sampling is adopted by the AC Nielsen organization to cover enquiries involving, for example, 10 000 grocery outlets. In round figures, Nielsen estimates that 100 stores provide basic data to give an overall picture of the market.

Note that in Table 4.2 multiples account for 50 per cent of total sales, although they represent only 10 per cent of the total number of stores. Nielsen selects, therefore, 50 multiple stores (50 per cent of the total sample) for the audit. In the case of independents, only 35 are included in the sample because their proportion of total sales is 35 per cent, despite the fact that, in the example, given, they total 8000 outlets. These examples illustrate the general principles which, in practice, are modified to take into account variations in turnover in each of the categories.

Cluster sampling

This form of probability sampling occurs when interviews are concentrated in a relatively small number of groups or clusters which are selected at random. Within these randomly selected areas of clusters, every unit is sampled. (Refer to discussion on post codes as sampling frames in Chapter 3.) For example, in a national survey of salesmen in a company, sales areas could be identified and a random selection taken of these. Of the areas chosen, every salesman would be interviewed.

This method of sampling is particularly useful where the populations under survey are widely dispersed, and it would be impracticable to take a simple random sample. Systematic sampling may not be possible because of the absence of a suitable sampling frame, and it could be expensive and cause delay to construct one.

In the USA a method of cluster sampling known as area sampling is used in conjunction with maps. By map references, large areas can be divided into several small districts. Where, as frequently happens, census tracts or blocks are used, *all* the households in the selected areas would be surveyed, viz. one-stage sampling. However, if these areas are, first of all, sub-sampled and households are then surveyed, two-stage sampling occurs. This system has been used by the United States Bureau of the Census, when difficulties have been experienced with population listing.

Although cluster and area sampling are attractive in terms of time and cost, the draw-back is that they tend to increase the size of the sampling error of a given sample size. Cluster samples may possibly miss complete sections of human populations, because they are not thoroughly mixed. Basically, the problem is whether or not the sampling units within the clusters are homogeneous, because, unfortunately for the researcher who intends to use cluster sampling, it has been found that clusters often include people with similar characteristics. Studies have shown that inhabitants of a particular district of a town tend to be more like each other than like people in other districts (see Chapter 10 ACORN segmentation). The dangers are obvious to researchers seeking representative samples. Clustered sampling can, therefore, miss whole sections of the community under survey. If relatively few clusters are taken, it can readily be seen that the resultant sample might be biased or non-representative of the population that it is intended to survey.

If, however, clusters are heterogeneous, i.e. they contain a good mixed population, then the sample which they make up is more likely to be representative. With this point in mind, researchers who plan to use cluster sampling should consider building up proposed samples from large numbers of small clusters. If relatively few large clusters are used to form samples, the sampling errors will be considerably greater than with the former method. In practice, a national sample in the UK would generally cover 2000 to 3000 sampling units spread over 80 to 100 first-stage units.

Multi-stage sampling

To attempt a national survey using simple random or systematic sampling methods would be extremely costly in both time and money. Where populations are widely dispersed, interviewing will be difficult, and the time taken to complete a survey will be considerably extended. In a dynamic market situation, this delay may affect the usefulness of the information collected.

Some alternative method of sampling national populations is obviously desirable, so that interviews can be concentrated in convenient areas. This, in fact, is the essence of multi-stage sampling which, as its name suggests, involves the process of selection at two or more successive stages. At each stage a sample (stratified or otherwise) is taken until the final sampling units are achieved. An added advantage of multi-stage sampling is that there is no need to have a sample frame covering the entire population.

For example, the first stage of a national sample survey would divide the country by standard regions as classified by the Registrar General. Each region would be allocated interviews on the basis of population. The second stage would involve selecting a sample of towns and rural districts, and then, in the third stage, a sample of individual respondents would be taken from the electoral registers of the second-stage area.

This process of sub-sampling of successive groups could be further refined so that administrative areas would be divided into wards, and then polling districts.

A four-stage sampling design of adults 18 years and over in private households in Britain (south of the Caledonian Canal) would, for instance, be as follows:

Stage 1   Parliamentary constituencies stratified by standard region, population density and percentage owner occupation, and selected systematically with probability proportionate to size of electorate

↓

Stage 2   Polling districts
↓

Stage 3   Addresses chosen with probability proportionate to their number of listed electors
↓

Stage 4   Individuals – one at each address (or household) chosen by a random selection procedure.

Where towns are being sampled, a system of sampling with probability proportional to size is customarily used. This means that irrespective of the size of the town, every inhabitant in the towns being sampled has an equal chance of being selected for interview. If one town were to have five times as many inhabitants as another town, the individual members of the population have five times more chance of being included in the sample selected at random than those living in the smaller town. Hence, to overcome this bias, the *same* number of second-stage units is selected from both towns, which results in the same probability of selection for all the inhabitants. This can be seen from Table 4.3.

The overall chance of being selected in town x, y, or z has been made equal by sampling with probability proportionate to size as shown in Table 4.3.

In the case of post codes (see Chapter 3) used as a sampling frame, the first stage would involve post code areas, followed by districts, sectors, and eventually complete post code locations (clusters of around 15 homes). Within districts and sectors, selection would be more with probability proportionate to the number of addresses each contained.

Cluster sampling and multi-stage sampling are closely related, though they have distinctive characteristics. Multi-stage sampling occurs where there is sub-sampling within the clusters selected at the first stage; where these clusters are individually sampled, cluster sampling takes place. A useful example in marketing is where it is planned to investigate the efficiency of a national sales force. Assuming that the company's organization includes selling areas, a random selection of these is made and every salesperson in the chosen areas studied for sales efficiency. This is the clustered sample approach.

Alternatively, from the random sales areas, a random sample of salespeople within these areas could be selected for interview. This is a simple multi-stage technique which could, of course, be made more sophisticated by stratification. Sales areas, for example, could be included in the sample design.

Estimates based on these techniques are less reliable, on the whole, than those obtained from simple random samples of the same size. However, because of the economies inherent in their use – it is obviously much easier to complete interviews where respondents are clustered together than if they are widely scattered over the country – larger samples can be undertaken successfully, and this compensates to some extent for the relative reduction in their accuracy. Figure 4.1 shows comparative sample designs for a salesperson's efficiency survey.

Table 4.3   Probability of selection

Town	Population	Probability of selection	Size of sample for each town	Probability of selection for any individual within town	Overall probability of selection
x	50 000	5	200	200/50 000	(1/50)
y	25 000	2.5	200	200/25 000	(1/50)
z	10 000	1	200	200/10 000	(1/50)

Replicated sampling (interpenetrating sampling)

Instead of taking one large random sample from a universe, it is sometimes useful to divide the sample into a number of equal sub-samples, each being selected using the same method, at random from the population. Each of these sub-samples will be a self-contained miniature population. They are interpenetrating in that they are dispersed among each other as independently representing their common population. This sampling procedure has been developed by Professor E. W. Deming in his classic text, *Sample Designs in Business Research.*[3] He claims that one of the chief advantages of this method is the ease with which standard errors can be calculated.

Replicated sampling can be used with any basic sample design (including quota sampling) and is particularly valuable where the size of the sample is too large to permit survey results to be available quickly. The total sample can be split into representative sub-samples and one of these used to produce results ahead of the main survey.

Another major practical advantage lies in the valuable comparisons which can be made between different sub-samples, while some interesting controlled experimentation could be introduced. Possible sources of bias could be revealed as basically the sub-samples would be alike. Interviewer bias may be detected in some sub-samples, although, of course, systematic errors common to all interviewers would not be revealed.

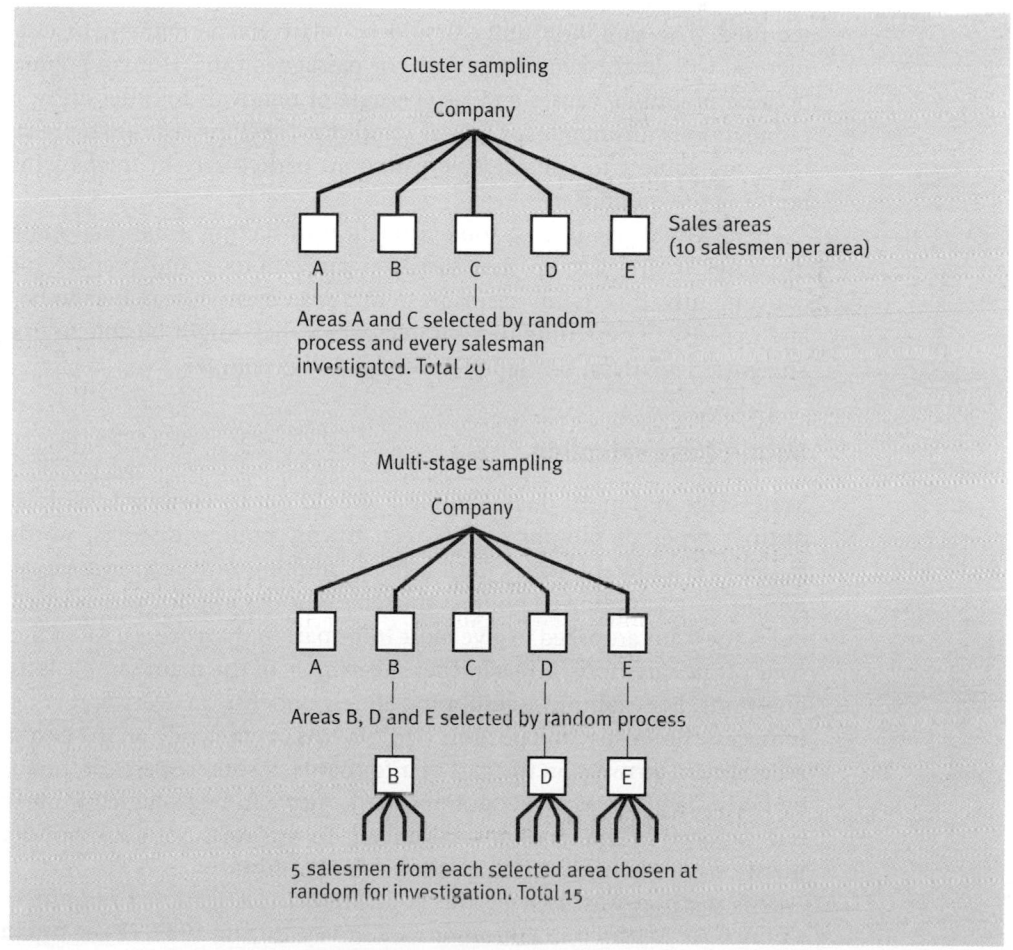

Figure 4.1 Cluster sampling and multi-stage sampling

In an investigation of 60 000 households a total sample of 1500 households might be planned. It is possible to take a systematic random sample at a sampling interval of 40, i.e. 60 000/1500 and select a starting random number between 1 and 40, successively choosing every fortieth household. By replicated sampling the total sample of 1500 households is divided into a number of sub-samples, chosen at random. The number of chosen sub-samples usually falls between 2 and 10, with higher numbers being more frequent. If, in this present example, 10 sub-samples are selected, each will contain 150 households. Each sub-sample must be a random sub-sample of the total sample, failing which the whole process is invalidated.

In the example just given, sub-samples contain a reasonable number of sampling units, i.e. 150 households, but there is a general tendency for sub-populations to be fairly small so that they are not really capable of being accurately examined in detail. Care should, therefore, be taken in using this sampling technique, for the whole purpose of sample surveys is to collect reliable information of a quality and quantity suitable for the agreed objectives.

Master samples

Where there is likely to be repeated sampling of a *static* population, it is useful to construct a master random sample from which sub-samples, chosen at random, can be taken as required. The sampling units should be relatively permanent or else the value of the method will decrease markedly with the passage of time. Human populations are dynamic because of natural causes and also because of removals to other areas, and so this type of population is unsuitable for master sampling. Dwelling lists are more stable, though even these are subject to considerable variation, particularly in towns where there is a large building programme.

There would seem to be some attraction in having a national master sample of, say, dwellings in the UK, so that survey organizations could prepare individual enquiries conveniently. It certainly seems wasteful for so many researchers to be put to the trouble and expense of designing new samples when they might be able to draw, on payment of an agreed fee, useful sub-samples from a master sample.

Multi-phase sampling

Multi-stage and multi-phase sampling should not be confused. With the former method, distinct types of sampling units, e.g. towns, polling districts, wards, individuals, are sampled at different stages until a final sampling unit, e.g. individual, is defined. With multi-phase sampling techniques the *same* type of sampling unit is involved at each phase, but some units are asked to give more information than others. All of the samples are asked *some* of the questions, and a further sub-sample of the main sample is asked more detailed questions. For example, questioning all respondents on every aspect of a survey could be unnecessarily costly, and possibly result in loss of efficiency on the part of interviewers and reliability of answers on the part of informants. If some aspects of the survey are known to be fairly stable or relatively unimportant, they can be excluded from the general sample but included in the random sub-samples. In this way, not all respondents answer all the questions on the questionnaire, thus reducing costs.

This method was used by the Population Investigation Committee and the Scottish Council for Research in Education in a survey, during 1947, of the intelligence of 11-year-old pupils in Scotland. Group intelligence tests were administered to about 71 000 children. A sub-sample of 1120 children was selected by taking all those whose birthdays were on the first day of even-numbered months, and these were given more detailed and extensive tests. As a result of studying the scores from both the main sample and the sub-sample, an estimate of the 'intelligence quotients' of the whole group of 71 000 children was formed. It was reported that this multi-phase sampling proved most satisfactory. It is important to note that the ages and intelligence scores of the pupils in the sub-sample were 'closely similar'[4] to those in the main sample.

Multi-phase sampling won official recognition in the US when it was used in the population censuses of 1940 and 1950.

In addition to reducing costs, this method often permits the main sample to be used as a sampling frame for subsequent sub-samples. It may additionally provide information useful for stratification which will serve as a guide for optimal sampling fractions.

4.2 Non-probability sampling

There are two basic methods of sampling, probability and non-probability. With probability sampling – an American term introduced by Professor E. W. Deming to describe what is generally better known in the UK as random sampling – each unit of the population has a known chance of being included in the sample.

With non-probability sampling, individual units in the population do not have a chance of selection. Non-probability sampling is a type of stratified sample, sometimes referred to as 'judgement or purposive sampling', or expert choice. It occurs when selection of the sample is dependent on human judgement, and not on the rigorous application of probability theory. As Kalton[5] points out for instance, an educational researcher may choose a selection of schools in a city to give a cross-section of school types. But in practice, different experts rarely agree on what makes a 'representative' sample. The representativeness of such a sample is open, therefore, to some doubt. Subjective judgement, though sincere, cannot be said to be based on objective criteria.

There are occasions, however, when judgement samples are regarded as indicators of the overall quality of a batch or consignment; for example, an expert may take a small amount of wheat from the top of a large batch to check its quality. It would be physically impossible to select a random sample from somewhere inside the heap. But the expert's approach is rendered acceptable because he/she may be presumed to have special knowledge about the general characteristics of the particular variety of wheat. Hence, a small judgement sample may be taken as a reliable indicator of its overall quality.

Other kinds of non-probability sampling have been variously described as haphazard, convenience, or accidental. These might refer to relatively indiscriminate methods of sampling such as street-corner interviewing, viewers responding to television programmes purporting to convey public opinion, etc. Clearly, it would be unacceptable to regard any such results as valid bases for making inferences about general populations.

Quota sampling

This is a form of judgement sampling in which the biases arising from the non-probability method of selection are controlled to some extent by stratification, weighting, and the setting of quotas for each stratum.

The population to be sampled is divided into sub-groups or strata according to the requirements of the survey, usually age, sex, and social class, though other classifications may be used. Too many sub-groups make survey work difficult and expensive. Quotas are set by researchers and interviewers are given allocations of specific types of informants. Selection of the actual informants is the responsibility of interviewers, and this can lead to bias, the degree of which 'cannot be objectively measured'.[6]

Quota sampling was widely used in the USA during the 1930s and 1940s for a variety of surveys, but statisticians disliked the method and encouraged the use of probability sampling. A significant turning point occurred when the Bureau of Census selected a 5 per cent random sample from the population in the 1940 Census. With the development of random sampling techniques, researchers have grown more critical of the drawbacks of quota sampling.

In the UK the Government Social Survey occasionally used quota sampling methods in its early days, though for many years it has been using random techniques exclusively. There is still considerable controversy about the merits of the two methods, and opinion is sharply divided among those who would reject quota sampling entirely and others who are prepared to give it qualified approval. Provided certain precautions are taken, such as the careful selection and training of interviewers, the method may be useful for certain types of survey.

Statisticians have tended to criticize the method for its theoretical weakness, while market researchers have defended it on grounds of cost, ease of administration and execution, and also because it appears to be quite adequate for many of the surveys which they are asked to undertake. In some cases, it may not be possible to draw a random sample, perhaps from lack of suitable sampling frames or because of the urgency with which information is needed in order to make some vital decision.

Further, it has been observed that as 'most market research is intended for decision-making and decisions are generally based upon comparisons rather than on absolute measurements, these comparisons seldom have to be very accurate. It is, in fact, usually difficult to find any reasonable system of weighting that would affect the decisions implied by a market research survey.'[7]

In establishing a quota sample, researchers must aim to achieve distribution over various subgroups in proportion to their importance in the total population. (See later discussion of quota controls.) This means that researchers must study the universe to be sampled and analyse it into classifications covering basic characteristics useful for the purposes of the survey. To assist this task, researchers need to refer to published data, such as official censuses covering population, distribution, and production; reference could also be made to surveys published by the IPA and other professional organizations. The larger publishing houses also provide useful data.

The characteristics of the population which are considered significant will then be expressed as percentages in the following manner:

Let p = population; p_1 = units in population of certain characteristics; s = sample to be taken. Then, $p_1/p \times s$ = required number in sample stratum.

For example, if p is a population of 100 000, also p_1 represents 800 sampling units (e.g. people of a certain age) and s is a sample of 2000 which it is proposed to take, the equation becomes: $800/100\,000 \times 2000 = 16$.

Other characteristics can be calculated in the same way, and quotas formed to cover the total sample. Interviewers are expected to obtain effective interviews within the controls set by the quota scheme.

Consumer surveys are frequently classified by geographical regions, urban/rural area, and size of town. Stratification is, therefore, used in both random and quota sampling, but in the former method the final sampling units are selected by random process, whereas in the latter instance, the selection of final sampling units is made by interviewers with variable success. In actual practice, it is difficult to stratify random samples on the bases of age, sex, and social groups, as available sampling lists are unlikely to include this type of information. Other stratifications may be made to meet the needs of special surveys, but it is unwise to increase strata too much, as interviewing will become more difficult; marital status, occupation, income, working wives, etc., are all frequently used. Care should be taken in deciding on strata, so that only those relevant to the problem being surveyed are included, though, of course, their relevance may not be apparent before the survey is done. In such cases, judgement and experience are valuable.

Classification by sex and age is not, on the whole, difficult in consumer surveys, and quota controls can be found from official sources. Social grouping, however, is notoriously difficult, both in setting the quotas and also in selecting suitable informants. (See later section on socioeconomic classifications.)

Random route or random walk

This is another type of non-probability sampling which is popular with some marketing research agencies. By this method, interviewers are instructed to start at specified points which are randomly chosen in each district and to call on households at set intervals. For example, clusters of streets could be chosen at random within the boundaries of selected wards; interviewers could be directed to approach the third house on the left side of a particular street, and then to continue their quota of calls according to the specific instructions given them. It has been observed by a leading British marketing researcher[8] that random routes or walks are open to even greater errors than a quota sample, tending to become virtually as expensive as a random sample.

Random location

This form of sampling is similar to random route sampling; interviewers are instructed to work in a highly specific, homogeneous area and to call at addresses until certain well-defined quotas are achieved, e.g. housewives of various age groups, numbers of dependent children, etc.

BMRB: GRID sampling

The British Market Research Bureau (BMRB) has developed a method of sampling, called GRID, in order to eliminate the more unsatisfactory features of quota sampling without the costs and other constraints attached to strict probability methods.

Respondents are drawn from a small set of homogeneous streets, selected with probability proportional to population after stratification by their ACORN characteristics (see Chapter 11). Quotas are set in terms of characteristics relevant to the needs of particular sample surveys. Interviewers are instructed as to distribution, spacing, and timing of interviews.

A GRID-based sample takes as its universe all enumeration districts (150 households) in Great Britain. Each enumeration district as contained in the Census Reports of the Registrar General is stratified as follows:

1. Standard region.

2. Within standard region-by-ITV area.

3. Within strata (1) and (2) by ascending area of ACORN neighbourhood types.

The required number of enumeration districts are then selected with probability proportional to population.

GRID sampling differs principally from BMRB's traditional random location sampling technique at the final selection of streets stage. Random location sampling used, as its first stage of design, wards and parishes listed within ascending order of ACORN neighbourhood types, and, within these selected wards and parishes, streets were selected at random.

However, GRID sampling is a one-stage sample design and, as already observed, the universe is enumeration districts (150 households) listed within ascending order of ACORN neighbourhood types. This results in increased sensitivity of this technique and is caused by: (i) the cluster analysis performed on enumeration districts to determine ACORN neighbourhood types, and, (ii) the increased scope and sophistication of modern computer equipment.

BMRB states that the published literature on ACORN has indicated how apparently similar areas in terms of standard socio-economic classifications of populations differ considerably in their behaviour and GRID sampling technique allows BMRB to control and measure these differences at street level.

Sequential sampling

Instead of starting a research survey with a predetermined size of sample, sequential sampling involves gradually building up to a size where, as the result of a sequence of sampling, an acceptable level of knowledge has been gained from the research, perhaps related to the critical level of ownership of some specific product, or the circulation of a particular publication, believed to be around a certain percentage of households in an area. A series of interviews could follow, and the resultant data analysed, either simultaneously or at specific intervals of time, after which a decision would be made as to whether additional research was necessary, or whether to accept the information so far collected as indicative of the pattern of ownership, readership, etc.

The advantage of this method of sampling lies in its economy[8] – a relatively small sample can yield a sufficiently accurate result and in conjunction with computerized technology, sequential sampling is likely to become increasingly popular (see Chapter 5).

KEYPOINT

Non-probability sampling

Also known as judgement, purposive, or quota sampling

Unlike probability sampling, individual units in populations do not have a known change of being selected

Selection of sample depends on human choice

It is type of stratified sample, e.g. age/sex/social class

Biases arising from interviewers' subjective choice of informants controlled to some extent by quota controls

▶

Interviewers allocated specific numbers of various types of informants, usually age/sex/socio-economic status

Quotas of types of informants devised in proportion to their importance related to survey objectives.

Variations of non-probability sampling: random route/walk/location; sequential

Specific problems of quota sampling

Pioneering research by Moser and Stuart[9] on the representativeness of quota sampling methods has shown them to be unrepresentative in two major factors, occupation and education. There was a definite tendency for interviewers to interview too high a proportion of better-educated people. This finding appears to confirm earlier views on the matter. In addition, there was some bias evident in the occupations of respondents obtained by quota methods, as a high proportion were 'in distribution, transport, the public service and building and road-making and a correspondingly small proportion of persons employed in manufacturing'. It is important to bear in mind that such bias is significant only if it is closely related to the subject of the study.

Another problem of quota sampling lies in the marked tendency for interviewers, even when experienced, to select distinctly different samples. This variability is not present in random sampling. It would seem that interviewers may, consciously or otherwise, avoid certain districts or types of people because of personal dislikes. Apparently, some serious bias could result as experiments have indicated that the composition of quota samples showed up to three times the variability of random samples of the same size. This point should be considered carefully when comparing the costs of the two forms of sampling; superficially the cost of quota sampling is between one-third and one-half that of random sampling.

Because quota sampling is frequently used in street interviewing, people who are out at the time of the survey are most likely to be sampled. Hence, the tendency noted earlier for a high proportion of non-factory workers to be interviewed. When home interviewing is conducted, only those women who are home at that particular time are available for interviews. Certain types of families, e.g. young mothers with babies, are more likely to be at home than 'working women', whose children are probably at school. If the survey was interested in young mothers, then there would be no cause for anxiety about a biased sample. Quota sampling is, therefore, easily frustrated by the interviewers' pattern of work; at different times of the day samples of the same size may be quite dissimilar. It may also suffer from the bad spacing of calls, when interviewers fill up their quotas as quickly as possible by calling at the nearest house in a street, or several people are interviewed in the same factory or office when the sample is supposed to be well spread.

Admittedly, some of these dangers can be minimized by sound methods of controlling field staff. Reputable survey organizations are constantly trying to ensure that these sources of bias are eradicated as far as possible.

Quota sampling is particularly deficient because it has been said to be impossible to estimate the sampling error in the estimates obtained, and so there is no way of evaluating the reliability of estimates based on samples constructed by arbitrary selection. This defect has caused statisticians to prefer the greater reliability of random techniques because the whole concept of sampling rests on the theory of probability. This principle is abandoned when quota sampling techniques are used. It is not legitimate, therefore, to apply the mathematics of probability to the results achieved by this process. Some researchers argue that quota sampling methods have so improved that it is in order to calculate the standard error on the same lines as for random sampling. This view, however, is not widely shared, and most survey organizations, particularly official ones, accept the statistical limitations of quota sampling. It is only fair to comment that Moser and Stuart,[9] after considerable research into the results of quota sampling, found this method gave fairly accurate results provided it was controlled by experts.

Advantages of quota sampling

Quota sampling has advantages as well as disadvantages. The former can be summarized as: speed, economy, and administrative simplicity.

First, the method allows investigators freedom to obtain interviews without unnecessary travelling. There is no need for call-backs, as in random sampling; this may be specially significant where information is urgently needed. Memories are not very reliable, in general, and quota sampling may be very effective in obtaining valid responses.

Second, quota sampling is substantially less expensive than random sampling. But, as noted earlier, superficial costs should be related to reliability. Field costs are lower because there are no call-backs or elaborate systems of substitution. It is sometimes claimed that the problem of non-response does not arise with quota sampling. Unlike random sampling, there are no pre-selected informants who can refuse to answer questions; interviewers in quota samples merely have to obtain interviews to complete certain set quotas and they do not have to seek successful interviews with specific informants. While this is perfectly true, it does not state the case accurately: there is non-response with quota sampling in the sense that some people will not agree to be interviewed. Unless interviewers note such refusals, preferably with some description of the people concerned, the extent and type of non-response cannot be assessed. In both random and quota sampling, refusals occur. An experiment by Moser and Stuart[9] indicated a refusal rate of about 3 per cent for the former, and 8 per cent for the latter method.

Although it is argued that quota sampling minimizes the problem of non-response, it may, in fact, merely substitute a replacement respondent for an unwilling or unavailable respondent. So, while a quota sample is completed, it does not take account of the beliefs and opinions of those who, for various reasons, did not participate in the survey. It is these people who are less likely to be under-represented in a random sample because, as noted earlier in this chapter, interviewers must make several call-backs in an attempt to secure interviews with those who have been specified by random selection.

Third, quota sampling is administratively simple because it is independent of sampling frames. These may not always be available, and so the delay and expense of preparing special lists are avoided. In some overseas markets, for example, there are very sparse data available from which to build sampling lists, and in cases like these, quota sampling may be the only possible method of investigation.

In general, quota sampling is much more flexible than random sampling, and its advantages make it attractive, under certain conditions, to commercial researchers. Practical considerations may often be strong influences in survey work.

KEYPOINT

Non-probability (quota) sampling

Problems:

Unrepresentativeness – occupation and education

Some interviewer-bias in selecting likely respondents

Bias also from street interviewing during·normal working hours of respondents (not available)

Bias also from 'working wives' unlikely to be at home

Impossible to calculate statistical reliability of quota samples

Advantages:

Speed – no need for call-backs

Cost – substantially less than random sampling

Simplicity – no need for sampling frames

Some support for view that quota sampling, *if expertly controlled*, gives fairly accurate results

In general, quota sampling much more flexible than random sampling, and particularly attractive to commercial researchers

Quota controls

These have been developed to improve the quality of quota sampling. The technique involves identifying stratification factors which are important to the subject of the survey. Sample proportions of these factors are then used to structure a sample for interviewing purposes.

Each interviewer is given an allocation of specific characteristics of informants to be interviewed; for example, age, sex, and social class. Proportions of the various types within the sample reflect their actual distribution in the population.

Stratification, as already observed, is usually done by region and town size, as well as demographically. Special controls may be introduced to meet the needs of particular surveys; for example, occupation and industry.

There are two broad types of quota controls: independent and interrelated.

With independent quota controls, interviewers have a simple task, merely to obtain a number of interviews in certain specified strata which are not connected to each other. These could be related to sex, age, and social class independently as shown in Tables 4.4 and 4.5.

Simple examination of Table 4.4 will reveal the unsatisfactory nature of the control exercised over interviewers. In Table 4.4 the interviewer could conceivably fulfil the quota of 12 males entirely from one age group or from one social class. Similarly, if social class only is controlled, informants might be chosen from disproportionate age groups, perhaps all over the age of 45. In general, this system of quota control is unlikely to ensure that a representative sample is obtained.

The other method, interrelated quota control, is far more reliable. Interviewers are allocated specified samples, distributed systematically over stratification factors such

Table 4.4   Independent quota control

Sex		Age		Social class	
Sample	Total	Sample	Total	Sample	Total
Males	12	16–24	4	AB	3
		25–34	5		
Females	15	35–44	5	C	7
		45–64	9		
		65+	4	DE	17
Total:	27	Total:	27	Total:	27

Table 4.5   Interrelated quota control

	Sample		
Age	M	F	Total
Socio-economic group AB			
16–24	1	1	2
25–34	—	—	—
35–44	—	1	1
45–64	—	—	—
65+	—	—	—
Socio-economic group C			
16–24	1	—	1
25–34	—	1	1
35–44	1	—	1
45–64	1	2	3
65+	—	1	1
Socio-economic group DE			
16–24	—	1	1
25–34	3	—	3
35–44	2	1	3
45–64	2	4	6
65+	1	3	4
Total	12	15	27

M = males, F = females

as age, sex, and social group. This system is more generally used, and is illustrated in Table 4.5.

In this case it will be seen that a far greater measure of control is exercised on interviewers, who are handed quota sheets for particular assignments. This avoids some of the biases which could arise from the indiscriminate selection of informants.

KEYPOINT

Quota controls:

Improve quality of quota sampling

Need to identify relevant quota factors (e.g. age/sex/class/region, etc.)

Allocate proportions of various types of informants according to actual distribution in population

2 broad types of quota controls:

'Independent' quota results in biased selection

'Interrelated' quota is far more reliable and controls types of respondents to be interviewed

Quota controls are usually demographic but other factors may be designed, e.g. size of firm (employees, turnover, etc.)

4.3 Socio-economic classifications

Apart from the NRS A–E socio-economic gradings (also see Chapter 10), other social classifications are in use for official surveys as well as for commercial analyses. Some of these principal classifications are now outlined

National Statistics Socio-economic Classification (ONS)

In 1998, a new social classification for use in government statistics was introduced and will replace the Registrar General's Social Class based on Occupation. This new categorization – the National Statistics Socio-economic Classification – was jointly sponsored by the Office for National Statistics (ONS) and the Economic and Social Research Council (ESRC).

The new classification (SEC) has seven major classes, based on occupation, plus an eighth into which people who wish to work but never have, are placed. There are certain differences between the official classification and the A–E socio-economic grades of the NRS, which was mentioned earlier in connection with quota sampling. Further discussion of the SEC classification and of the A–E NRS grades occurs in Chapter 10 under Advertising Research.

International Standard Classification of Occupations

The International Labour Office (ILO) in Geneva issued an International Standard Classification of Occupations in 1969 which was a revised version of the occupational information that originated in 1949. Its objectives were to provide a systematic basis for presenting occupational data related to different countries and to facilitate international comparisons. There are 10 major groups, plus the armed forces, as shown in Table 4.6. Of these groups, there are 4 levels: 8 major groups, 83 minor groups, 284 unit groups, and 1506 occupational categories. These give 1881 titles in total

EU Socio-economic Classifications

Socio-economic status groups in the EU contain 14 classifications (see Table 4.7). Most marketing research firms in Britain who undertake inquiries in EU countries tend to use the British National Readership Survey socio-economic groupings as a basis for consumer analysis. In some cases the analysis is reduced to the three main socio-economic groupings: upper class, middle class, and lower class, corresponding to AB, C1C2, and DE.

Table 4.6   International Standard Classification of Occupations

	Definitions of titles
Major group 0/1:	Professional, technical, and related workers
Major group 2:	Administrative and managerial workers
Major group 3:	Clerical and related workers
Major group 4:	Sales workers
Major group 5:	Service workers
Major group 6:	Agricultural, animal husbandry and forestry workers, fishermen and hunters
Major group 7/8/9:	Production and related workers, transport equipment operators and labourers
Major group X:	Workers not classifiable by occupation
Armed forces:	Members of the armed forces

Source: ILO

Table 4.7   Socio-economic status groups of EU

Community code	Socio-economic status
1	Farmers
2	Other agricultural workers
3	Employers in industry, construction, trade, transport, and services
4	Own-account workers in industry, construction, trade, transport, and services
5	Employees and own-account workers in liberal and related professions
6	Managers, legislative officials and government administrators
7	Employers with liberal and related professions
8	Foremen and supervisors of manual workers (employees)
9	Skilled and semi-skilled manual workers (employees)
10	Labourers (employees)
11	Supervisors of clerical workers, sales workers and service staff; government executive officials
12	Clerical, sales, and service workers
13	Armed forces (regular members and persons on compulsory military service)
14	Economically active persons not elsewhere classified

Source: OPCS

Euro-demographics: ESOMAR

As the result of a working party in 1988, ESOMAR developed a refined version of a social grading system. The resultant Social Grade Variable had been derived from data collected in seven European countries, and has six social grades which are aggregated to a more practical four categories: A, B–C1, C2, D–E. Full details of this system are given in Chapter 12 (International Marketing Research).

Most marketing research firms in Britain which undertake enquiries in the EU countries, tend to use the British National Readership Survey socio-economic groupings as a basis for

Table 4.8   Gallup classification by occupation

Code	
1	Farmer/trawler owner, etc. (own account only)
2	Farm worker
3	Businessman, top manager
4	Executive; professional
5	Skilled tradesman, artisan, craftsman
6	Salaries, white-collar; junior executive
7	Worker
8	Student
9	Housekeeper
10	Unemployed; retired

consumer analysis. In some cases the analysis is reduced to the three main socio-economic groupings: upper class, middle class, and lower class, corresponding to AB, C1–C2, and DE.

In a multi-country consumer survey in the EU, Social Surveys (Gallup) used the classification of the occupation of the head of household as shown in Table 4.8.

KEYPOINT

Socio-economic classifications widely used in survey analyses, often with other demographic analyses

1. *Official:* Socio-economic classification (Office for National Statistics: ONS). Introduced in 1998 for use in Government statistics related to UK population: based on occupation 'bands'

2. *Official:* International Standard Classification of Occupations (International Labour Office: ILO); 6 major groupings

3. *Professional:* National Readership Survey (Joint Industry Committee for National Readership Surveys: JICNAR). Established 1954 for research into readership; 6 demographic analyses: A–E

Pan-European Social Grading: ESOMAR; 6 social grades aggregated to more practical categories: AB, C1, C2, DE

4.4 Sample design

Sample design is an integral part of the total research design and contributes significantly to its integrity.

Survey designers must take account of all the factors that contribute to the overall productivity of the research process. Of these, an efficient sampling scheme or design is of paramount importance. A sample is essentially a means to an end: to provide a well constructed base on which survey techniques may be centred and put into practice. If the sample design is sound and the research methodologies appropriate, relevant data should be collected from a number of carefully selected sources which are representative of a specific population.

The success of research surveys rests largely on the quality of the sampling, and great care is needed at every stage in the development of suitable samples. Surveys are undertaken for many different reasons and they differ also in their complexity. Sampling on a national scale is particularly complex, and most national random samples are of sophisticated design, mostly multi-stage stratified.

An experienced researcher will have full knowledge of the research objectives and the degree of accuracy required of the findings. But the pragmatic constraints of time and cost must also be recognized when evaluating feasible research methodologies, including, of course, the nature of the sample that is likely to contribute significantly to the efficiency of the entire programme.

4.5 Facets of sampling surveys

The problems of sampling surveys can conveniently be considered under four headings: population, method, number of stages, and stratification of population.

Population

The first step in the design of a sample is to define as closely as possible the population to be covered by the enquiry. This is frequently done by demographic, geographic, and other characteristics such as professional or technical areas of interest. It is essential to define geographical areas so that there can be no misunderstanding, either during the course of the survey, or when the survey findings are being eventually studied. The importance of clear definitions can be appreciated by reference to a large metropolitan area such as London. To different authorities, this geographic description has particular significance, e.g. the City of London, Greater London, the Metropolitan London Police area, the Diocese of London, the London television area, etc. In the case of the term 'Birmingham area', this is sometimes intended to cover Coventry and also the Black Country, or to extend to include the residential towns of Sutton Coldfield and Solihull. It will be apparent, therefore, that the geographical boundaries of the survey should be closely defined and agreed by both researchers and their clients.

Age groups must also be well defined and relevant to the objectives of the survey. Other special characteristics must likewise be defined. If, for instance, the sample is to cover pensioners, it is important to define this class of persons. Is the receipt of a state old-age pension to be the criterion, or are people to be included who do not receive the old-age pension, or who may have retired from paid employment before the customary retirement age? If the sample is to take account specifically of young people's interests, is it important to include the armed forces in the survey?

Method

The next step is to decide whether a complete enumeration (census) is feasible or if a sample survey would be suitable. This decision will be affected by the constraints of time, finance, urgency, and staff availability.

Where random sampling techniques are to be used in selecting a sample, it is possible to calculate mathematically the size of sample required in order to give a desired level of precision in the results (see Chapter 3, Section 3.5, 'Sample size').

Number of stages

The third step in sample design is concerned with the number of sampling stages. Most national random samples necessarily adopt some form of multi-stage sampling because of the practical limitations of surveys, namely, cost, administration, time, etc. At two or more successive stages a sample is taken by random selection (stratified or otherwise) until the final sampling units are achieved.

A four-stage sampling design could be distributed as follows:

Stage I Administrative district
Stage II Polling district (or electoral ward)
Stage III Household
Stage IV Individual

A two-stage design could consist of:

Stage I Administrative district
Stage II Individual

Detailed consideration of multi-stage sampling is to be found in the section dealing with types of random sampling; it can briefly be said to consist of a series of sub-samples drawn from successive stages of the sampling process.

Stratification of population

The fourth step in sample design involves stratification or division of the population to be surveyed into groups with characteristics identified as relevant to the needs of the particular survey. Stratification, as noted, is widely used in both random and quota sampling methods; commonly used strata in consumer surveys cover age, sex, and socio-economic grouping. In some cases, it may be necessary to undertake a pilot survey in order to establish suitable bases for stratification of a survey population.

In the section on stratified random sampling, it was noted that the number of strata chosen must be carefully controlled, as too many will complicate the survey. Samples can be stratified either by uniform sampling fraction (proportionate), or by variable sampling fraction (optimal or disproportionate). With the former type of allocation, each stratum is represented *pro rata* in the sample, say, 10 per cent of each stratum, calculated thus:

n = sample size, 100, and N = population size, 1000

$$\text{therefore } \frac{n}{N} = \frac{100}{1000} = 10 \text{ per cent (or 0.1).}$$

The number of actual sampling units from each stratum is dependent upon the size of that group in the population.

With variable sampling fraction, different proportions are sampled from each stratum: the method is specially useful where considerable variation occurs between strata, or when some strata contain only a small number of sampling units.

The standard error of a stratified random sample using a variable sampling fraction is less than that resulting from the use of a uniform sampling fraction, and both of them are superior to the standard error of a simple random sample. This can be shown as:

$$\begin{array}{ccc} \text{SE} \geqslant & \text{SE} \geqslant & \text{SE} \\ \text{(RAN)} & \text{ST/UNI} & \text{ST/VAR} \end{array}$$

When random sampling is adopted on a particular sample design, it is usually necessary to develop a suitable sampling frame unless, fortunately, one is already in existence. (See Section 3.6: Sampling frames.)

Quota controls must be planned in the case of quota (non-probability) sampling, and these should be relevant to the nature of specific surveys. The matter of sample size is difficult; a general guide is that sufficient cases must be sampled from each stratum to allow the population stratum value to be reasonably estimated.

In designing samples, cost must also be borne in mind, and some assessment should be made of the value of research information. Researchers should be prepared to evaluate the cost of research, and it may well be that an 'ideal' sampling plan is just not economically feasible. The information which management is seeking may, in fact, be adequately obtained by a less sophisticated sample design.

The cost of obtaining additional information could outweigh the benefits to be derived from it, and some critical control of research is obviously desirable. What should always be remembered is that extra information can usually be obtained, but the cost (not just 'direct' costs) will, at some stage, fail to bring in proportionate returns. The 'perfect' sampling plan may not always be the best from the company's viewpoint. Basically, the apparent high cost of marketing research has to be set off against the benefits which should be experienced by clients from the acquisition of highly relevant information about their market opportunities, etc. If the survey yields information on which major policy decisions are to be made, then its cost is best viewed as a necessary investment which narrows the field of uncertainty. Some methods of evaluating research expenditure are given in Chapter 13, and it will be seen that these are based on decision theory. The discipline of cost-benefit analysis should clarify consideration of the contributions which professional marketing research could make to organizations of many kinds.

It will be recalled that random sampling tends to be fairly expensive and it is certainly more costly than quota methods. Alternative sampling plans should be considered not just from the cost aspect, but also from the quality of the information they may be expected to supply. Researchers should offer clients an objective evaluation of alternative methods which could be suitable for the particular objectives of the survey. Inevitably, the technical aspects of sampling plans will be affected by factors, such as time, cost, and available interviewing staff, and some reasonable compromise may be necessary if the survey is to be put in hand. This does not mean that researchers should be forced into accepting conditions which would vitiate good research; it means merely that they, like other skilled technicians, must practise their expertise in the conditions which exist in today's markets.

KEYPOINT   **Sample design**

Efficient sample scheme/design of paramount importance to overall success of research effort

Necessary to have full knowledge of research objectives and degree of accuracy required

Must note constraints of time and cost

Four important steps:

1. Define closely population to be surveyed (demographic, geographic, etc.)

2. Decide whether census feasible or sample survey suitable; if latter, decide on method of sampling (random or quota)

▶

3. Decide on number of sampling stages (multi-stage sampling often used)

4. Define stratification factors relevant to survey objectives

Summary

There are two main types of sampling: probability (random), and non-probability (quota). Of these there are several variations, e.g. stratified random sampling.

Simple random sampling is rarely undertaken – systematic or quasi-random sampling, usually involving stratification of some kind, is more likely to be used.

Stratification may use either a uniform sampling fraction (proportionate), or a variable sampling fraction (disproportionate, or optimal).

Random sampling has been widely adopted by leading research bodies, e.g. the Government Social Survey, because of its sound theoretical basis which allows the legitimate use of statistical tests.

Non-probability sampling occurs when selection of a sample is dependent on human judgement and not on the rigorous application of probability theory. With suitably devised controls, this method of sampling may be very useful for certain types of enquiries; it may also be used in combination with random sampling techniques.

Various methods of socio-economic classification have been applied for setting quota controls: a popular one in marketing research is the A–E grouping used in the National Readership Survey.

A new official social classification – the National Statistics Socio-economic Classification – with seven major classes was introduced by the Office for National Statistics (ONS) in 1998, and will be used for all government statistics.

ESOMAR has developed eight social grade categories, which can be aggregated into four main classes: AB, C1, C2, DE.

Review and discussion questions

1. In which circumstances would a cluster sample be more appropriate than other forms of random sample?

2. Suggest a multi-stage sampling procedure for the management of a large manufacturing firm (with ten regional plants) which wishes to discover employee views on job-sharing.

3. Outline the principal features of quota sampling and summarize the procedural differences between quota sampling and stratified random sampling.

4. A marketing research firm is about to conduct a survey on consumers' purchasing behaviour for high quality running shoes. It intends to use a quota sample. Suggest four quota controls or strata which the firm might profitably employ in selecting sample members.

5. Marketing surveys by UK research houses are increasingly using non-probability samples. What factors, in your opinion, might lie behind this development? Does this development involve possible implications for the manner in which survey results are interpreted?

6. Locate any recent newspaper or magazine in which survey results are reported. Try to ascertain whether this survey was based on a census, random sample, or a non random sample. Give your views on the efficiency of the method employed.

References

1. Kendall, M. G., and B. Babington Smith, *Tables of Random Numbers, Tracts for Computers*, no. 24, Cambridge University Press, Cambridge, 1939.
2. Neyman, J., 'On the two different aspects of the representative method; The method of stratified sampling and the method of purposive selection', *Journal of the Royal Statistical Society*, vol. 97, 1934.
3. Deming, E. W., *Sample Designs in Business Research*, Wiley, New York, 1960.
4. Political and Economic Planning, 'Sample surveys – Part Two', PEP Report, vol. 16, no. 314, Political and Economic Planning, London, June 1950.
5. Kalton, Graham, *Introduction to Survey Sampling*, Sage Publications, New York, 1984.
6. Yamane, Taro, *Elementary Sampling Theory*, Prentice-Hall, New York, 1967.
7. Rothman, James, and Dawn Mitchell, 'Statisticians can be creative too', *Journal of Market Research Society*, vol. 31, no. 4, October 1989.
8. Collins, Martin, 'Sampling', in: *Consumer Market Research Handbook 1*, Robert M. Worcester and John Downham (eds), Van Nostrand Reinhold, Wokingham, 1978.
9. Moser, C. A., and A. Stuart, 'An experimental study of quota sampling', *Journal of the Royal Statistical Society,* vol. 116, 1953.

5

Questionnaires

Learning Objectives

- Note nature and role of questionnaires in marketing research
- Understand critical need for expert planning of questionnaires
- Obtain insights into pitfalls of question phrasing, e.g. bias
- Note principal methods of questioning in practice: (CATI; CAPI; CASI; CAPAR; DBM; EMS; Internet)

5.1 Introduction

A questionnaire is a method of obtaining specific information about a defined problem so that the data, after analysis and interpretation, result in a better appreciation of the problem. It is an important element of the total research design, and its preparation and administration demand considerable professional expertise.

Questionnaires and interviewing are interrelated aspects of survey practice: there are several types of questionnaire and various methods of interviewing informants. Questionnaires may be structured, unstructured or a blend of these styles; they may be administered in face-to-face personal interviews, over the telephone, by means of computer-assisted interviews, and by e-mail (EMS), fax and the internet. Questionnaires may be mailed to selected informants. In this instance as well as in diary panels and some types of computer and electronic-based methodologies, informants complete self-administered questionnaires. In addition, qualitative investigations may be conducted in group discussions and focus groups by trained interviewers using checklists or interview guides (these are discussed in Chapter 6). There is, therefore, considerable diversity in methods of questioning and in styles of interviewing.

A questionnaire form which has to be completed by an interviewer is often referred to as a schedule. The type of questionnaire obviously depends on the method of survey, and this will be dependent on the nature of the problem being investigated, the kind of population sampled, and the sample size.

It is feasible, as Oppenheim notes,[1] to distinguish two general categories of survey: (i) the descriptive, enumerative, census-type; and, (ii) the analytic, relational type. These generic types are not necessarily exclusive and elements of each may be found in some surveys.

The general form of questionnaires lies between two extremes. At one end of the continuum lies a highly structured questionnaire consisting of a series of formal questions designed to attract answers of limited response. Standardized questions are administered in the same way to all respondents. At the other extreme is the unstructured questionnaire where formal questions are replaced by a freer style of investigation. The interviewer encourages conversation to develop, during which respondents are invited to answer in their own words a series of open-ended questions, often phrased by the interviewer to suit individual respondents. The interviewer will have as noted an 'interviewing guide', also known as a 'checklist', which outlines the sort of information to be collected, but the precise wording of questions is left to his or her discretion. This type of questioning calls for highly skilled interviewers.

In practice, surveys frequently mix the styles of questioning. However the questionnaire is formed, individual questions must be designed to attract respondents to give valid and reliable information about the subject of the enquiry, and to do this with the minimum distortion or bias.

Clearly, this cannot be done without a thorough background knowledge of the subject. Where the survey is to be undertaken by an outside organization, some preliminary study of the company and its products is necessary. It may then be possible to define the problems with which the survey has to deal and, therefore, the type and scope of questioning.

Some pilot survey work is advisable to assist in understanding the problems and difficulties of actual or potential users of the product or service. A series of informal discussions with selected individuals and groups should provide valuable background knowledge which could then be used in developing questions around certain subject areas, such as the extent and application of labour-saving appliances in the home. During the course of these unstructured interviews, ideas will emerge which may throw new light on the problems being surveyed, though the temptation to chase too many hares must be resisted.

The objectives of the survey should now be reviewed in the light of this additional information. It may be necessary to modify those originally projected so that they are feasible (see next section).

KEYPOINT

A questionnaire is a method of obtaining specific information about a defined problem

Type of questionnaire depends on: sample population, method of sampling, nature of problem, and sample size

Questionnaires may be highly structured with formal questions, unstructured with free-style questions, or a mix of these types

Questions must be designed to attract respondents to give valid and reliable information

5.2 Planning the questionnaire

In Chapter 2, the five stages of the marketing research survey process were described: the first stage, i.e. research brief, gives the essential guidance needed for development of the research proposal (second stage). At this stage, the overall plan of the research will be described, including an outline of the main areas of questioning. Researchers should discuss and agree with clients the proposed research strategy and satisfy them about, for example, the coverage of the questionnaire.

Five classes of information which are generally useful for marketing decisions have been identified[2] as follows:

1. *Facts and knowledge:* what are the present beliefs, perceptions, and depth of knowledge of the survey respondents about, for example, specific products, services, industries, or organizations?

2. *Opinions:* what are the existing attitudes towards products, etc., including an assessment of the strength with which these attitudes are held?

3. *Motives:* what underlies specific types of market behaviour, i.e. what motivates buyers of various kinds of products or services?

4. *Past behaviour:* what are the patterns of consumption of certain kinds or brands of products over specified time periods? Insight will be given into factors such as brand loyalty. Observational techniques, such as home audits, will help in verifying reported consumption behaviour.

5. *Future behaviour:* indications of possible future behaviour may be gleaned from sensitive questioning about, for instance, levels of satisfaction with existing products, nature of expectations, social habits, etc.

Included in this general approach would, of course, be an evaluation of the nature of buying behaviour which may be complex both in terms of the people involved (see Chapter 12 for discussion of industrial decision making) and also the sophisticated mix of motivations which could be influenced by economic, psychological, social, and cultural factors (see Chapter 1, Section 1.7: Complexity of buying behaviour).

KEYPOINT

5 classes of information needs:

1. Facts and knowledge

2. Opinions

3. Motives

4. Past behaviour

5. Likely future behaviour

Buying behaviour may be complex and influenced by many factors: economic, psychological, social and cultural. Specific information may be needed according to nature of product/service and buying habits

5.3 Question requirements

It has been seen that the questionnaire is a vital part of most surveys and great skill is needed to design an effective series of questions. Experts agree that there is no easy way to do this; it remains largely a matter of art rather than science. Fortunately, there are some general principles which can help in the design of questionnaires, though this essential tool of survey work can hardly be called a scientific instrument. At its best, it is a remarkably versatile method of gathering information about a wide variety of topics. Used with care and understanding, it can provide valuable data which, otherwise, would not be available.

Three conditions are necessary for ensuring a true response to a question: (i) respondents must be able to *understand* the question; (ii) they *must be able* to provide the information requested; and (iii) they *must be willing* to provide the information. If these simple but basic guidelines were observed, a great deal of the frustration experienced by researchers and respondents would be avoided.

Questions are the raw material of questionnaires, and on them depends the quality of the research. Some discussion of the factors which influence the construction of effective questions is, therefore, appropriate.

The frame of reference is important in determining what questions mean to respondents and how they will react to them. 'When drawing up a questionnaire we tend to forget how circumscribed our own experience is and we take for granted that whatever the word means to us it will mean to everyone else.'[1]

Questions should be phrased in simple language which can be easily understood by the particular respondents interviewed. There should be no attempt to impress respondents by the use of unusual words; the message in the question should be clearly understood in the meaning intended by the researcher. The language used should be within the common experience of all those who are being interviewed. Unilateral, for example, means one-sided, 'which for ordinary purposes is a more intelligible expression' and, the former word should 'be confined to the jargon of diplomacy and physiology, to which it belongs . . .'.[3]

Names of meals, for example, dinner or tea, may well mean different meal times for a sample taken from the general population of the country. For many topics, it has been discovered that the frame of reference is likely to be influenced by occupational groups, leading to professional or technical jargon which would not be understood in a general survey. The golden rule is to stay within the working vocabulary of the population which is being sampled, avoiding words which do not communicate the meaning of questions clearly and precisely.

Use simple words and avoid those with ambiguous meanings, such as normal, usually, average, regular, natural, family or neighbourhood – unless these are clearly defined. Research agencies list these types of 'dangerous' words which can, nevertheless, creep into some questionnaires and result in biased answers.

The use of unfamiliar words should be avoided. It was reported,[4] although with some reservations, that when members of a small community in South Wales were asked: 'Who or what is devolution?', 10 per cent said he was Jeremiah's brother, 10 per cent that it was an aria from Elijah, 10 per cent thought it referred to the last book of the Bible, and the remainder said that he was a French prop forward. An imaginative if rather ill-informed 12-year-old schoolboy at a Shrewsbury school when asked for a definition of 'nostalgia', wrote: 'It is Welsh for ' "Goodnight".'[5]

Research has shown that many words, though apparently in common use, are not properly understood by all who use them: 'incentive', 'proximity', and 'discrepancy' were known by half the population, while words like 'paradox' and 'chronological' were known by about one-fifth. Although, as Jean Morton-Williams[6] points out, context can aid understanding, often the reverse occurs and an unfamiliar word can make a whole sentence incomprehensible. Words should be selected carefully and used sparingly in questionnaire construction.

Questions should be specific; they should be related to particular aspects of the survey and ask for information in well-defined terms. Such enquiries as: 'Are you a regular user of product X?', or, 'Do you go to the pictures often?', can only produce a collection of very unreliable data. Researchers should take care to qualify questions so that respondents are quite clear in their minds about the nature of the information which is being sought. For example, questions about media habits should be carefully drafted. 'What newspapers have you read during this week?' might well include responses from:

1. Those who actually bought the papers in question
2. Those who read someone else's paper
3. Those who read the specified papers in depth
4. Those who just skimmed quickly through the newspapers

In addition, what time period is actually covered by 'this week'; is it intended to include, for example, the Sunday papers?

Questions should be economically worded; they should not ramble on as their length will merely confuse respondents. Complex questions should be broken down into a series of readily answerable short questions which focus attention on one specific, well-defined issue. For example, the following question: 'What do you think of the economic policies of this Government and how do you think they should be modified, if at all?', is likely to baffle most respondents who may decide to limit their response to the second part of the question. This type of question might well be split into two or more shorter enquiries confined to particular issues.

Third-party questions should be avoided if possible. It is better to ask people what they know from their own experience. Facts are to be preferred to opinions.

There is little use in taking uninformed opinion, or attitudes unrelated to experience, as firm guides to future action. Thus, the opinions of informants who have never lived in centrally heated houses, or have not used particular kinds of goods, are unlikely to be of use in deciding on long-term production plans. In such cases, firm information can be derived from sample surveys only by a process of observing the reaction of informants to changes which widen their experience in a particular direction, or which offer new opportunities.[1]

Writing about opinion polling, Harold Lind[7] remarked that a public sophisticated enough to recognize a pointless and frivolous question will be tempted to respond likewise. Market researchers should, therefore, be aware that respondents are also likely to give ill-considered answers to questions about consumption habits which they consider hypothetical or irrelevant.

It is often tempting to ask hypothetical questions, but the value of the responses they attract is small. Surveys should be concerned with collecting meaningful data, and prediction of likely behaviour is difficult enough without complicating it with information of dubious merit.

Questions should not place too much strain on the memories of respondents. Information should be sought within the ability of respondents to recall accurately. Where detailed information is required over a period of time, it is better to have some system by which respondents can actually record their expenditure or other behaviour, e.g. the diaries used by consumer panels.

The proximity to the event, the intensity of the stimulus, and the degree of association affect memory. Some events will be easily recalled over a long period of time; for example, the date of marriage, the birth of children, the purchase of the first car, or some personal accident. The memory of other events may soon fade, and a time limit should be written into questions about matters which have comparatively little personal significance; perhaps the price of some basic food like salt could be recalled soon after purchase, but it is doubtful if this could be done successfully in even a week's time.

Checklists to aid recall should be used with discretion, as they may introduce bias.

Association is frequently used in advertising research in order to assist recall of particular advertisements. A magazine cover might be shown to respondents who are then asked if they have seen the issue and, if so, what advertisements they recall. Further questioning follows when particular advertisements are named, to test the impact of campaigns.

Lists of publications are often shown to respondents who are invited to say which they have read over the past week or month. (These periods need to be clearly defined.) Prestige bias often intrudes in the answers given.

KEYPOINT

3 conditions for ensuring true response to question

1. Respondents must *understand* the question.

2. They *must be able* to provide information requested.

3. They *must be willing* to provide it.

Questions should be carefully designed: in language readily understandable by the people being interviewed

Use simple words; avoid unusual words

Questions should be short and specific

▶

Ask what people know from experience

Facts are preferable to opinions

Information sought should be within ability of people to recall accurately

Check lists may be useful, but use with care.

5.4 Bias in questions

Bias should be avoided in questions; this means that questions should be phrased carefully in order to avoid suggesting that certain answers are more acceptable than others. There is no generally agreed definition of a leading question.

Moser and Kalton[8] have defined it as one which by its content, structure, or wording, leads respondents in the direction of a certain kind of answer. Some American researchers[9] concluded, after studying many interviews, that in most uses of leading questions, the components or 'expectation' and 'premiss' were present. The expectation component of a question occurs when an interviewer indicates the response which it is anticipated the respondent will give (or, alternatively, not give). The answer is of the closed (YES/NO) type, for example: 'You are 30 years old, aren't you?' Expectation can also arise through the interviewer's intonation, for example: 'Did you *agree* with this decision?' or 'Did *you* agree with this decision?' It is almost impossible to formulate a question that does not depend on some kind of premiss or assumption. If the premiss is incorrect, it is suggested that it is easier for the respondent to correct an open than a closed question, since the former allows the respondent to make a freer answer which modifies the influence of the premiss.

There are 'leading' words and phrases, such as: 'You don't think . . . do you?' which researchers should carefully avoid; these are usually more influential in attitudinal questions than factual questions. For instance, 'Nowadays most people think that corporal punishment in schools is wrong, do you?' The apparently innocuous question: 'When did you last borrow a video tape?' assumes that (a) all respondents own or have access to a video-tape player; (b) that they generally borrow tapes; and (c) that someone else may borrow a tape on their behalf.[1]

Bias may operate particularly with checklists or multi-choice questions. Tests have shown that when respondents were asked directly whether they read a particular low-prestige magazine, a larger proportion admitted readership than when the magazine was included in a checklist with high-prestige magazines. It was further discovered that the data from direct interviewing coincided closely with published circulation figures.

Respondents should not feel social pressure to answer in some particularly acceptable manner. This influence was felt in a survey undertaken some years ago to investigate readership of *Gone with the Wind*. To the question: 'Have you read this book?', an excessively high proportion of respondents said 'Yes'. Obviously, those who had not read it were reluctant to say no. Rephrasing of the question to 'Do you intend to read *Gone with the Wind*?' produced a more valid finding, as even those who would never read it could pretend that they would do so. But the people who had already read it did not fail to stress this point.

With some topics, questions may be perceived by informants as having elements of social expectations or norms, and they may feel that their behaviour is being exposed to covert criticism. For instance, enquiries about drinking habits, gambling or smoking may be regarded as 'threatening'. Some respondents may deliberately 'trim' their consumption habits to what are regarded as acceptable limits. On the other hand, a few may exaggerate actual consumption, perhaps to assert their independence of conventional behaviour (see later discussion).

In that excellent primer, *The Art of Asking Questions*, Payne[10] illustrated the influence of leading questions by his story of the snack-bar waiter in America who increased spectacularly the sale of eggs in milk shakes. He asked customers not whether they wanted an egg or not, but whether, in fact, they wanted one or two. While this was a good sales technique, it would, of course, be quite unsuitable for research.

Another seemingly harmless question such as: 'Would you rather use Camay toilet soap than any other toilet soap?' would be likely to attract more favourable responses than if respondents were just asked 'What is your favourite toilet soap?'

Biased replies could also arise from the likelihood of respondents observing that earlier questions in a survey seemed to show interest in a particular brand, with the result that when later questions referred to products of that type, respondents may well be influenced to mention that particular brand.

Bias in questionnaires may arise from the order in which certain questions are placed, so particular attention should be given to question sequence. Every endeavour must be made to rid questionnaires of anything that might be perceived by respondents to be 'threatening', judgemental or unacceptable for reasons of race or religion. Every question should be vetted for possible bias, e.g. suggesting expectations of behaviour that would put respondents 'on their guard'.

KEYPOINT

Biased questions arise from

Leading questions; check lists; multi-choice questions; social expectations/norms; threatening or taboo subjects; brand sensitivity; question sequence

5.5 Questioning approach

Apart from government censuses, co-operation in surveys is voluntary and relies largely on the goodwill of informants. Some people, of course, will talk freely and at considerable length about any subject, particularly themselves, but willingness does not necessarily guarantee accuracy of observation. The purpose of survey questions is to obtain reliable data from as many members of the sample population as possible. There will, therefore, be respondents who are not always disposed to answer a series of questions, and special efforts must be made to encourage them to respond.

Some simple introduction should explain the nature of the survey and invite the respondent's cooperation. With personal interviewing, the interviewer may wish to reassure the respondent by showing a letter or card of authorization. There should be no attempt to coerce the respondent, as the quality of the responses will suffer in the unlikely event of an interview being granted. Tactful and courteous persuasion is far more likely to be successful, and this can be reinforced by quoting, perhaps, the first question in the survey.

This opening question should be as interesting as possible to the respondent and fairly easy to answer. Some researchers favour an opening question which builds up the respondent's confidence; it may not even be particularly significant to the survey. The value of the ensuing interview will depend largely on establishing effective *rapport* between respondent and interviewer, and so it is worthwhile to give the opening question some thought.

Succeeding questions should guide the respondent's thought in a logical progression from one topic to the next, each topic being explored before passing to its successor. This enables the respondent's mental processes to develop easily, and recall is facilitated. Past associations and memories are awakened by this steady, systematic approach.

Particular care is needed in planning the sequence of topics to avoid conditioning the respondent in his or her answers to later questions. To avoid this kind of bias, the 'funnel' technique is often used. This involves asking, first, the most general or unrestricted questions. In this way, the area of questioning is gradually restricted to precise objectives. The method is particularly useful for learning something about the respondent's frame of reference from earlier open questions. The smooth flow of questioning from the general to the more specific also builds up a good relationship between the interviewing parties (see Figure 5.1).

In a survey concerned with eczema treatment, respondents might be gradually 'funnelled' through a sequence of questions starting with health concerns, then on to skin complaints; from there to methods of relieving eczema, and finally to specific proprietary lotions for the relief and treatment of psoriasis and eczema.

An enquiry into housewives' attitudes towards a semi-prepared foodstuff (cake-mix, instant coffee, etc.) which might be affected by 'guilt' feelings, could be started with a general discussion of household tasks (including use of various labour-saving devices), narrowed down to cooking, further focused down to labour-saving foods (e.g. tinned or frozen foods), then on to semi-prepared foods, and finally, to the subject of the survey, which might be cake-mix.

Another example of the funnelling technique in survey questioning occurred in a study[11] of attitudes to the noise of aircraft around Heathrow. Informants were asked a series of questions, starting with those of a fairly general nature so as to avoid biasing responses, and aimed to discover eventually their experience of and attitudes towards aircraft noise, e.g. 'What do you dislike about living around here?' 'If you could change

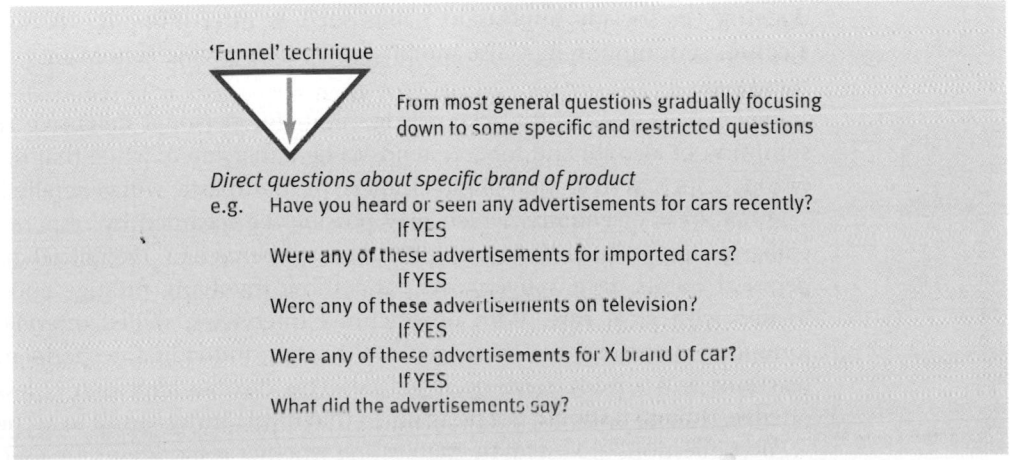

'Funnel' technique

From most general questions gradually focusing down to some specific and restricted questions

Direct questions about specific brand of product
e.g. Have you heard or seen any advertisements for cars recently?
        If YES
  Were any of these advertisements for imported cars?
        If YES
  Were any of these advertisements on television?
        If YES
  Were any of these advertisements for X brand of car?
        If YES
  What did the advertisements say?

Figure 5.1 Funnelling technique in survey questioning

'Inverted funnel' technique

From specific questions first and thence opening up to more general questions. Compared with 'funnelling', little-used.

Figure 5.2   Inverted funnelling technique in survey questioning

just one thing about living round here, what would it be?' 'Have you ever thought of moving away from here?' 'Why?' 'What are the main kinds of noise you hear round here?'

Only after these sequential questions had been answered, was the subject of aircraft or aircraft noise mentioned. (The possibility of bias exists, however, in the wording of the first question, and this would have been improved by inserting 'if anything' after the word 'dislike'.)

The opposite technique known as 'inverted funnel' sequence is sometimes used; specific questions are asked first of all and then successively more general questions widen the area of enquiry. This obviously lacks the advantage of 'funnelling', but it is occasionally applied where the topics surveyed do not evoke strong feelings (see Figure 5.2).

As noted already, it may be necessary to discuss topics which are 'threatening' or 'taboo', about which respondents feel reluctant to answer questions. These sensitive areas of enquiry need to be handled with delicacy and skill, if valid responses are to be attracted. Questions of this nature should be deferred until the middle or towards the end of a questionnaire when goodwill has been firmly established. There is no point in forcing people to give information which they are reluctant to disclose, perhaps for reasons of social embarrassment, as the answers they will give are likely to be self-defensive and will not reflect their true opinions. Another good reason for deferring these questions is the risk that some respondents may abruptly discontinue interviews which include questions which they consider personally embarrassing. If these questions are placed near the end of an interview, the majority of information will already have been collected.

Indirect methods of questioning are sometimes helpful in securing information about subjects which are considered by respondents to threaten their self-esteem. Such threatening or taboo subjects might include enquiries into personal honesty; for example, 'fare dodging', or socially unpleasant habits such as litter dropping. Personal smoking and alcohol consumption may also inhibit people from giving factual answers to questions in these areas.

Experienced researchers acknowledge that, for personal defensive reasons, the consumption of alcohol and tobacco tends to be understated, while that of more 'approved' products such as soap, household cleaners, or toothpaste, will generally be inflated.

Other areas of enquiry, which may possibly be regarded by respondents as taboo or embarrassing, include racial prejudice or sexual behaviour. Prejudicial questions covering personal habits, race, religion, etc., and those involving prestige and pride should be treated with great care. With unstructured interviews, skilled interviewers are able to formulate questions on these subjects to suit individual respondents, whose likely reactions will already have been judged. This flexible approach is less likely to cause offence, though it should not be assumed that it will always result in accurate information.

Filter questions are useful in establishing whether respondents are users or non-users of products or services being surveyed. If the answers are in the affirmative, further questions may cover particular aspects of the problem, for example: 'Do you smoke?' YES/NO. Those who replied YES would be asked whether they smoke cigars, pipes, or cigarettes, and perhaps how much per day/week. Non-smokers would skip these further questions and go to the next question sequence.

A survey, by personal interviewing of people's attitudes towards flying and a comparative evaluation of competitive carriers, might start as follows:

Q1. Have you ever travelled by air?

> YES
>
> NO
>
> If YES go to Q2
>
> If NO close interview

Q2. About how many journeys did you make by air in 1999?
    (Count return journeys as 2)

Note that since the survey is concerned with those who have had actual experience of air travel, the filter question at the start of the interview immediately ensures that respondents will be able to give information based on their actual experiences.

Classification questions, i.e. those asking about age, sex, marital status, income, education, family size, etc., should normally be left to the end of the interview unless quota sampling is being used. It is necessary in the latter case to check the suitability of respondents in order to complete a representative sampling survey. Questions asking for personal information should be prefaced by a few introductory remarks, as respondents may well feel that it is unnecessary for interviewers to know so much about their personal background. They should be assured that the information will be treated confidentially, and that it will not result in their names and addresses being entered on some list of sales prospects.

Precise ages of respondents need not be sought, as age groups will normally be quite adequate. Respondents could be handed a card and asked to indicate their age group. Occupational classification is often difficult, and descriptions by respondents (particularly wives) are frequently subject to prestige distortion. Such descriptions as clerk, engineer, secretary, civil servant, or businessman need fuller qualification to be useful to the researcher.

Payne[10] instances the man who described himself as a 'bank director'; his actual duties were to 'direct' customers to the correct bank official.

A job applicant in the West Country described his last position as 'room director'. Later enquiries translated this impressive title into 'bouncer at a London club'.

A supermarket employee in Yorkshire who described himself as 'transport manager' was actually in charge of the trolleys in the store.

This natural tendency of respondents to inflate the importance of their occupations can be checked by experienced interviewers who can tactfully probe and secure more accurate job descriptions.

Classification details supplied must be useful within the definitions of the survey. Housing, for example, should be defined precisely so that it can be correctly allocated in the survey analysis. Respondents should be guided, for example when they are counting the number of living rooms and bedrooms in their houses. Interviewers should qualify these descriptions so that the data collected during the survey are homogeneous. If a survey is interested in the number of bedrooms, it would confuse respondents to ask: 'How many rooms are there upstairs?' as they would probably include the bathroom and lavatory.

Researchers should understand that classification questions are not always welcomed by respondents. Unnecessary questions of a personal nature should not be asked; every question should be examined for its relevance to the objectives of the survey and excluded if there is no good reason for asking it.

At a seminar[12] organized by the Survey Control Unit of the Central Statistical Office, Peter Menneer criticized the use of questions involving meaningless concepts as, for instance, 'To what extent would you consider peanut butter as an alternative to jam?' Many people might not consider this in any way to be an alternative. He also warned against the use of double negatives like: 'Would you rather not use a non-medicated shampoo?' Ambiguity in questioning was also instanced by another researcher who quoted the question: 'How did you find your last job?', to which the statistician expected a response such as 'From the Job Centre', and who was disappointed to get the reply 'Very interesting and enjoyable'.

Oppenheim[1] has drawn attention to the problem of the double-barrelled question, such as: 'Have you suffered from headaches or sickness lately?' An informant might possibly answer YES to the 'headaches' or NO to both ailments. He also warns against the use of hypothetical questions, which ask people to make predictions about their future behaviour or likely reactions, for instance, about a new road development or new type of magazine. The predictive value of such responses has been found to be 'poor predictors', especially of things which are novel to respondents.

KEYPOINT

Questioning approach

1. Introduce nature of survey

2. Show letter-card of authorization

3. Invite respondent's co-operation

4. Don't coerce respondent: be tactful

5. Ensure that opening question is interesting and easy to answer

6. Succeeding questions should open up discussion pleasantly and logically

7. Use 'funnelling' technique

8. Don't adopt a judgemental attitude to any responses

9. Be polite and tactful but persistent

10. Thank respondent for co-operation and assure them of confidentiality

---

5.6 Types of question

There are two main types of question which are commonly used in surveys: open-ended questions and closed questions.

Open-ended questions

An open-ended question, known also as 'free answer' or 'free response', calls for a response of more than a few words. The topic is established for the respondent, who is left to structure a reply as he or she sees fit. The respondent has considerable freedom in phrasing an answer, which may be lengthy and detailed, and in his or her own words. For example, a housewife might be asked if she had bought any groceries yesterday, and if these purchases included tea. A probing question would ask if this item was leaf tea or tea-bags. This enquiry would be followed by an open question: 'Why did you choose to buy . . . type of tea?' A woman who had bought packeted leaf tea might respond that it was more economical or of better quality than the tea-bag variety. The interviewer might then invite her to expand a little on her preferences.

Interviewers are expected to record answers verbatim. There is the danger of interviewer bias intruding through inaccurate recording. An interviewer may, deliberately or otherwise, write down only part of the answer, and this selective recording may not adequately represent the full reply. Where answers are coded later, there is the real danger that some of the essential richness of the original responses will be lost. Frequently it is difficult to compress 'free answers' into a limited number of codings, though this handicap can be reduced by the experience gained during the piloting stage of the survey. This will have led to the drafting of principal classifications.

Open ended questions are most likely to be used in the early stages of a study, when the unrestricted responses they attract are of value in giving researchers a general map of the area of survey. This can lead to the identification of significant aspects affecting the subject under survey, so that later stages of research can be designed to cover these factors.

In order to build up goodwill with the respondent, it is often advantageous to start a survey questionnaire with an open question. This will allow the respondent considerable latitude in forming a reply. A typical question might be: 'What do you like to do in your spare time?' Most people like to talk about their hobbies and spare-time interests, and will not be reluctant to tell an interviewer something about these activities. In doing so, they are more likely to form a favourable attitude towards the interviewer, and be more willing to answer the remainder of the questions.

Open questions are interesting because of the spontaneity and individual flavour of the replies, but questionnaire designers should not use them indiscriminately. Payne[10] warns: 'remember that the coding of thousands of verbatim replies adds up to a lot of work'. It might, therefore, be wise to see whether it is possible to convert open questions to some form of alternative choice questions.

In unstructured interviews where informal methods of enquiry are customary, open questions predominate. Skilled interviewers are responsible for phrasing questions in a style suitable for their particular audience, and also, of course, in agreement with the objectives of the survey. However, it should be borne in mind that the extent to which interviewers may 'tailor' questions, so that they are readily understood by informants, must be carefully checked and be within the limits of their interviewing instructions. Otherwise, serious bias may result because different interviewers may introduce, for example, slight deviations to their questions, so that the results from a survey over, say, 100 sampling locations may not be compatible. Interviewers should be briefed as to the extent to which they can probe for further information, to expand or clarify some statement in the open answer. Additional information can be gathered by using either an 'extension' or an 'echo', related to preceding questions. An extension is a request for further information about something which the respondent has already said.

An echo is an exact or nearly exact repetition of the respondent's words by the interviewer.

Questioning techniques to improve the quality of earlier responses include the 'summary', which, as the name suggests, summarizes the information already given by the respondent and asks implicitly or explicitly for confirmation or correction.

Another technique is the 'confrontation', which consists of asking a question that underlines an earlier inconsistency in the respondent's answers. Kinsey tended to use this method in his social surveys.

Payne[10] has suggested that when seemingly inconsistent replies occur, it may be possible to 'discover something' by confronting such respondents with their apparent inconsistencies.

Also popular is the use of 'repetition', which occurs when earlier questions are repeated if they are answered incompletely. They may also be repeated as a check on the accuracy of earlier responses.

These various types of antecedent question cannot easily be incorporated into a questionnaire because they depend on the kinds of responses which informants give. These, of course, will not be known in advance, though interviewers are sometimes allowed to deviate from scheduled questionnaires in certain circumstances. The Government Social Survey classifies questions as factual, opinion, and knowledge. Interviewers are allowed to repeat or explain factual questions and to ask for clarification of answers thought to be vague or ambiguous. Probing can be risky, and it should be done with care and sensitivity. Interviewers should not cause confusion by their questioning techniques. There should be no attempt to force people into certain categories of replies; they may not really know sufficient about the subject under survey to be able to give a definite answer. 'Don't know' may reflect genuine ignorance of the subject, disinterest, or even failure to understand the question. Experienced interviewers should attempt to judge why a respondent is content to give a 'don't know' answer.

The Government Social Survey allows no deviation from printed questions or opinion matters. Probing is likewise forbidden, but interviewers are allowed to repeat the question, if the answer is not clear, by asking a respondent to 'explain a little more fully what he "meant by that"'.

With knowledge questions, respondents should not be pressurized into giving substantive answers. They may not know exactly, and the duty of interviewers is not to inhibit them from saying 'Don't know' in such cases. The interviewers' responsibility is to obtain valid and reliable responses, and these may well include 'Don't know' on some occasions.

Closed questions

Closed questions call for responses which are strictly limited. The respondent is offered a choice of alternative replies from which he or she is expected to select an answer corresponding to his or her personal views on a particular subject. Closed questions may be:

1. Simple alternative questions: these have only two choices of response. For example: YES/NO; GOOD/BAD.

   Respondents are divided into two sub-groups or categories affecting certain basic characteristics of the sample population, such as car ownership. Quantification is simple.

   These simple questions, sometimes referred to as dichotomous, are useful as filter questions, separating users from non-users, e.g. 'Did you buy product X last week?'

2. Multi-choice questions: these are an extension of simple alternative questions. Respondents are able to choose from a range of possible answers, which are designed to reflect different shades of opinion or variations in use of a product (see Figure 5.3).

Careful pilot work is necessary in order to ensure that the alternatives offered in multi-choice questions provide sufficient scope for respondents to make valid answers. Alternatives must be mutually exclusive, so that respondents are able to differentiate between them without difficulty. Respondents can be shown a list of possible answers or interviewers can read them aloud. As bias can arise from the positioning of entries – extremes attract most attention – some system of randomizing the alternative answers over the sample should be considered. This was done during the IPA National Readership Survey (1954), when the order of periodicals within any one group, e.g. weeklies, was randomized to prevent biased presentation. For example, after establishing by the response given to a simple alternative question, that a respondent has bought a certain product, an interviewer might then ask for further information, such as 'In what kind of shop did you buy it?'

	Coding
Department store	1
Furniture shop	2
Hardware shop	3
Grocery shop	4
Other (describe)	5

The appropriate code corresponding to the answer given by the respondent is ringed by the interviewer. Multiple answer lists generally include a coding ('Other') for unusual answers, which should be qualified by interviewers. Pre-coding of answers is very helpful when surveys reach the analysis stage.

Some researchers, as Oppenheim[1] notes, use the split-ballot technique in pilot work; the sample is divided into two or more equivalent parts with different answer sequences, so that it is possible to measure the ordinal bias and make allowances for it.

Checklists should be prepared from information gathered during piloting, and these should be as complete as possible. At the same time, respondents may well experience fatigue in reading carefully a lengthy list, and they may take the easy way out and select one or two entries just to close the interview.

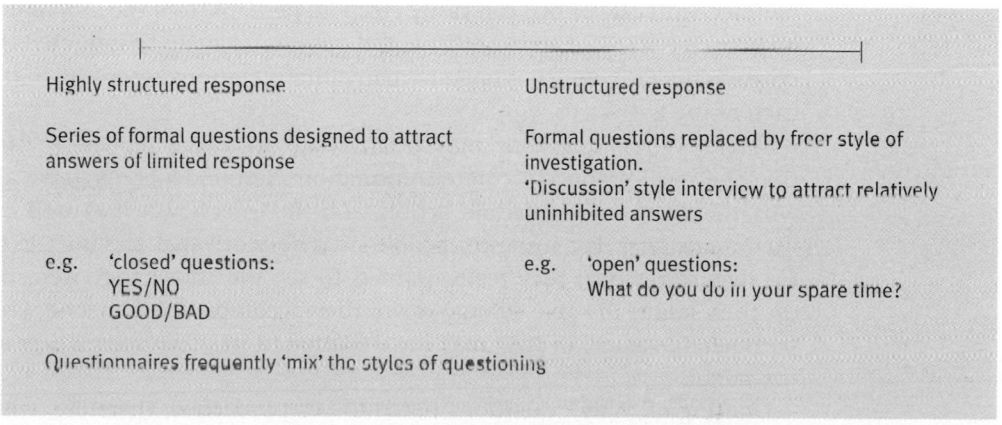

Highly structured response

Series of formal questions designed to attract answers of limited response

e.g.   'closed' questions:
        YES/NO
        GOOD/BAD

Unstructured response

Formal questions replaced by freer style of investigation.
'Discussion' style interview to attract relatively uninhibited answers

e.g.   'open' questions:
        What do you do in your spare time?

Questionnaires frequently 'mix' the styles of questioning

Figure 5.3   Questionnaire continuum

Another difficulty with checklists is that entries on them may, in fact, suggest alternatives of which respondents had not previously thought.

An element of bias, may, therefore, affect their choice, particularly in readership surveys. Some respondents may be more inclined to tell interviewers that they read *The Times* than to admit that they are actually regular readers of a newspaper of lower standing. Some checks on this tendency are possible, and 'dummy' features are sometimes mentioned in questions. But even then human memory is fallible and tests have shown that people will state quite positively they recognize advertisements which have never gone beyond the proof stage.

Closed questions could lead to bias by 'forcing' respondents to choose between certain alternatives, but provided the piloting stage has been thorough this risk can be minimized.

Respondents of low socio-economic status and education may prefer closed questions to open questions, since they can then answer questions which they do not fully understand without revealing their lack of understanding to interviewers. Survey planners should, therefore, take note of this potential source of bias, and design questionnaires which are likely to result in valid responses. This can depend on factors such as the respondent's degree of knowledge about the subject of the survey and the extent to which this can be established before formal interviewing takes place. Whether open or closed questions are appropriate is a matter to be judged in relation to the problems of specific surveys. In some situations, open questions may be preferable to closed questions; it is not possible to lay down general rules.

Some researchers have attempted to lay down guidelines on the effective use of open and closed questions. The general principle is to start the survey with open questions to encourage response and to obtain some background knowledge which will be useful in later stages of the survey. More specific questions (closed) follow, progressively narrowing down the field of enquiry.

This scheme is advocated by Gallup in his 'quintamensional plan of question design',[13] which outlines five steps in question formation. The first step is to find out whether the informant is either aware of or has thought about the issue under survey. This is followed by some open questions to attract his or her general feelings on the matter. The third step usually consists of multi-choice questions dealing with specific aspects; these, in turn, are followed by questions to discover the reasons for the particular views just given. The final stage is concerned with finding out how strongly these views are held.

Questions asking for further information – follow-up or 'Why?' questions – need to be handled with care or bias can easily creep in, perhaps from the different intonations given by interviewers to an apparently neutral question. Payne[10] has quoted the question: 'Why do you say that?', which is open to many interpretations according to the stress placed on each of the five words.

Single 'Why?' questions may often result in vague replies. It cannot be assumed that they will produce accurate information. Respondents may give all sorts of reasons why they performed a certain action, and the interviewer may well collect a bundle of useless material. For instance, people may be motivated to visit the theatre or cinema for diverse reasons: they really wanted to see the show; they were bored or had time on their hands in some strange town; they accompanied someone whose company was particularly valued; or they may have wanted to sit down somewhere and perhaps avoid the rain.

Drafting of 'Why?' questions needs to be approached, therefore, with care. For strong personal motives of self-esteem, prestige, or self-defence, respondents may not give reliable answers. They may rationalize their earlier behaviour, either consciously or otherwise, and so researchers may well question the validity of these types of question. Qualitative research methods, such as depth interviews, could be used to supplement the more formalized questioning techniques, and also to act as a useful means of checking the responses obtained from these formal methods. Qualitative research studies have shown that, in many cases, direct questioning is a fairly blunt tool to use in some delicate areas of investigation. Less direct methods may, through their more subtle and sensitive approach, reveal the true motivations of respondents.

KEYPOINT

Types of question

Open-ended: free response

Allow respondents to reply as they think fit

Interviewers must record answers verbatim

Often useful in opening up questioning

Special training needed to handle open questions

Closed: limited response

Simple alternative: YES/NO

Multi-choice (special care in drafting)

Always allow for 'don't know'

Follow-up questions like Why? must be carefully handled

Direct questioning is a fairly blunt tool; less direct methods (qualitative research) likely to be more productive

---

In addition to open, closed and multi-choice questions, and to give respondents opportunities to express their feelings, for instance, about types and brands of products, various kinds of scales are used in questionnaires. These are discussed in Chapter 7, and it will be seen that attitude scales frequently result in obtaining sensitive insights into people's feelings and opinions. Scales also add variety to a questionnaire, and help to keep respondents interested in the survey.

5.7 Pilot testing

It is vitally important to make sure that the questionnaire is pilot tested through all the stages of its development.

This may involve rewriting questions several times, changing their sequence or their style of composition, for example, constructing multi-choice questions from the answers received from earlier open-ended questions. This calls for patient attention to detail so that the questionnaire used in the final survey contains questions which are specific, clearly understandable, capable of being answered by the particular population sampled, and free from bias. Well-organized piloting reveals possible misinterpretations owing to ignorance or misunderstanding of questions, and indicates differences in the frames of reference between the researchers and respondents.

In one study, the question: 'Do you like tomato juice?', was changed to: 'Do you like the taste of tomato juice?' Pre-testing revealed that considerable ambiguity surrounded the first phrasing. Some housewives liked the amount of vitamin C their children received from drinking tomato juice, whereas others liked the tenderizing effect that tomato juice has in cooking meat dishes, etc.

Another survey, which was concerned with health care in America, also underlined the importance of testing carefully the phrasing of questions. Matched sets of respondents were given alternative forms of a question, resulting in significant differences in overall responses, as the following examples show:

1. 'Do you think anything should be done to make it easier for people to pay hospital or doctor bills?' — 82 per cent 'YES'
2. 'Should' replaced by 'could' — 77 per cent 'YES'
3. 'Should' replaced by 'might' — 63 per cent 'YES'

Only one word was changed, but the alternatives had different connotations for respondents.

In an international research survey[1] of various health problems, it was decided to include some factual questions about domestic facilities available to respondents: one of these items was 'running water'. Piloting the questionnaire revealed that people in developing countries often interpreted 'running water' as referring to a brook or river near their homes. The wording was changed to 'piped fresh water supply', which was also pilot tested to ensure that its meaning was clearly understood.

Perhaps one of the more amusing insights into the way in which questions are prone to subjective perception occurred in an investigation[14] concerned with respondents' interpretation of survey questions connected with the IPA National Readership Survey. An 82-year-old respondent who answered that 'young people' were not likely to be influenced by violence on television programmes, on subsequent questioning about the ages of the young people he had in mind, said: 'Oh, between 30 and 40'.

Pilot tests should be done under conditions which reflect in miniature the main survey. Respondents should be of the same socio-economic and age distribution as those in the main sample survey. They should be of similar educational achievement and possess any other characteristics which may be of significance in the specific sample, for example leisure-boat owners. It would also be advisable for those conducting the pilot interviews to be representative of the level of competence likely to be exercised by the subsequent interviewing team. 'Average' interviewing performance will affect the ability of respondents to answer a questionnaire. A wrong impression might be gathered of the efficiency of a questionnaire, if only very experienced interviewers were used at the testing stages.

The Office of Population Censuses and Surveys (OPCS) – now incorporated in the Office for National Statistics (ONS) – conducts hundreds of 'post-enumeration' personal interviews to check the information given on census forms. These quality checks have revealed that questions, despite extensive piloting, are sometimes misunderstood or the instructions misinterpreted.

The arbitrary size of a pilot survey is often taken at about 10 per cent of the main survey, though this would obviously be affected by such factors as time, cost, and practicability.

The value of pilot tests lies in other areas of survey practice, apart from questionnaire construction. They are useful, for example, in testing the accuracy and reliability of sampling frames before extending their use to the main sample survey. They also indicate if extreme differences occur in some measured characteristic, such as the weekly expenditure on food or housing. If the variability is excessive, the results of pilot studies enable researchers to plan the final sample size so that it adequately reflects the population characteristics. With highly variable characteristics, the sample will need to be of a larger size than if there were little variation over significant characteristics. Another important use is in calculating the probable non-response rate from estimates of the results achieved in the piloting process. It might be feasible to vary slightly the sequence of some of the questions in part of the pilot survey, and compare results for effectiveness. Interviewers can also be compared for relative efficiency; they should be asked to report in some detail on respondents' reactions to the pilot questionnaires, and also to give their own estimation of the fieldwork. In addition, the pilot survey will indicate the time and cost involved, and if these are likely to be excessive, modifications may be made before the main survey is put into operation.

The pilot testing of questionnaires brings with it, therefore, many associated benefits apart from those directly concerned with the phrasing of questions. In the case of mail questionnaires, it is advisable to test not only the questions themselves but also the physical presentation of the survey. This covers such details as the type of paper (colour and texture), the layout of the questions (important for readability), the letter of introduction, and reply-paid facilities. It is important to do everything possible to make mail questionnaires pleasant in appearance and easy to complete. Respondents are influenced by these detailed aspects of presentation and researchers should plan to make their co-operation easy to win.

The length of questionnaires must also be carefully checked, particularly where surveys of a general nature are being planned. Although some respondents will not object to questionnaires of some length, there is evidence that fatigue sets in after a while, and affects the quality of responses. Moser[8] has commented that the length of a questionnaire must be presumed to affect the morale of both parties to the interview and this inevitably results in deterioration in the quality of the data collected. The law of diminishing returns appears to operate with questionnaires after a certain amount of time and effort have been expended. Piloting helps to estimate the likely effects, but no general principles can be laid down. Hague,[15] a highly experienced industrial market researcher, strongly advocates the piloting of questionnaires; it can be, he says, 'a salutary lesson for whoever designs a questionnaire to hold a clipboard and carry out the first few interviews. There is no finer way of learning if the questionnaire works.'[15]

5.8 Mail questionnaires

An alternative method of collecting information by questionnaire is to mail it to a list of potential informants (see Chapter 2).

Because of the impersonal nature of mail enquiries, the drafting of effective questions is more important than ever. These must be clearly worded and easily understandable; only one interpretation should be possible. The language in which they are phrased should be suitable for the sample population. In a general level survey, questions may be informally worded. Colloquialisms may help to attract genuine responses.

Open-ended questions must be strictly limited, for they are inclined to cause respondents some anxiety which may well result in rejection of the whole questionnaire. In general, only simple, straightforward questions can be asked which are capable of being answered relatively easily. Apart from special surveys covering professional and technical enquiries, questions should be limited in their field of enquiry and in the depth of knowledge required to answer them.

Questionnaires have to be self-contained, and this means that instructions have to be printed on them to guide respondents. These instructions must be clearly worded and appear next to the questions involved. Simple guides such as: 'Check the answer you prefer', or: 'If No, please go to question 4', should be used.

Where respondents are asked to detail, for example, the number of bedrooms in their house, questionnaire forms should give some simple definitions to ensure that answers are similarly based: 'In counting bedrooms, exclude toilet and bathroom'. The Family Census questionnaire of the Royal Commission on Population has to be filled in personally, though enumerators are allowed to assist where difficulties are experienced. It is a good example of a detailed enquiry with simple, well-positioned instructions.

Particular care is also needed in qualifying time intervals, such as 'week' or 'month'. In verbal enquiries, interviewers can qualify these and so avoid inaccuracies in response. These time intervals should be closely defined in relation to the objectives of the survey, and the questionnaire should state clearly what is meant by 'a week' or 'a month'. If enquiries are concerned with trading results, it would be ambiguous to ask for 'last month's sales'. Many firms have accounting periods that do not precisely coincide with calendar months. In any case, what is meant by 'sales'? Is this meant to refer to orders booked (and received) at head office, invoiced sales, or sales invoiced and paid for? This analytical probing could continue, of course, but it illustrates the need to make mail questionnaires capable of being answered accurately and easily without the intervention of investigators. Respondents appreciate questionnaires with clear instructions and definitions, and are inclined to co-operate more willingly in such enquiries.

Layout and printing are particularly important in mail questionnaires. Enquiry forms should look attractive; a poorly duplicated set of sheets will not impress recipients. Respondents should be approached in the right manner, and this relates to mail surveys just as much as to more personal methods of enquiry, such as interviewing.

The quality of paper, envelopes, and printing, should all be carefully considered. Layout should assist respondents to reply easily by inserting a cross or tick in appropriate 'boxes' against multi-choice questions. Coding is also helpful, and respondents can be invited to circle or underline the chosen answer. Whatever method is chosen, it is important to ensure that the instructions given are definite, otherwise analysis may be difficult.

Wherever possible, mail questionnaires should be individually addressed with the correct title, initials, and name accurately spelt. (This point is also discussed in Chapter 11.)

It is sound practice to include a covering letter with a mail questionnaire. The letter should outline the objectives of the survey and invite informants to respond by completing and returning the enclosed questionnaire. The letter should stress that information provided by respondents will be treated confidentially, and their names will not be revealed in any subsequent publication. As people may well wonder why they have received a questionnaire on a particular subject, some simple explanation of the method of sampling should be given.

KEYPOINT

Mail questionnaires

Impersonal – so special care in drafting questions

Instructions should be clear, so that response made easy

Qualify terms like 'week, month' or 'rooms in house'

Layout, paper and printing influence response

Send covering letter giving objectives of survey and sampling method

Stress confidentiality

Supply pre-paid envelope

The publishers of *Reader's Digest* are consistent and large users of mail surveys; every year they send out over half-a-million questionnaires. In their view, an accompanying letter is critical for an acceptable response rate.

> *It must be constructed to induce the recipient to complete and return the questionnaire, and it has a lot of ground to cover in what should look like a short easy to read communication. It must seek to involve him, tell him why he has been selected, what's in it for him, and why it is important that everyone should reply. It should tell him that his information is either anonymous or confidential, strike a note of urgency and acknowledge that he is doing the sender a favour; tell him about the stamped reply envelope and thank him.*[16]

Mail questionnaires have certain limitations, apart from the type of questions which can be asked. Answers must be accepted as written, without the benefit of additional explanations which interviewers could obtain by probing questions. In rare cases, it may be possible to check written answers by personal interviewing, but this would obviously add to the cost of the survey.

In general, mail questionnaires are not a suitable method of enquiry where sample populations are of low intelligence or poorly educated.

Because mail questionnaires can be read through completely before being answered, bias can result from knowing the overall structure of questioning when answering individual questions. With personal interviewing, the pattern of questioning is not immediately apparent, though a different type of bias may arise, namely, interviewer bias.

Responses to mail questionnaires may frequently represent the views of more than one person; this would be undesirable where the survey wanted the views of individuals. Some questionnaires, particularly those dealing with technical matters, may profit, however, from being dealt with by specialists in functional areas. (This point is expanded in Chapter 11.)

Personal interviewing allows investigators to supplement the answers given by respondents by some qualitative assessment which adds to the value of the survey. These observational data are lacking in mail enquiries.

Mail questionnaires require some systematic follow-up to increase response to an acceptable level. Apart from official censuses, surveys are voluntary and researchers rely on the goodwill of informants. Follow-up reminders should be tactfully worded, bearing in mind the many quite valid reasons for non-response.

Good planning in the early stages of the survey is important in reducing likely non-response, but it would be unrealistic to expect a high response from a general mail questionnaire. Two reminder letters are often sent to non-respondents, usually at about 14-day intervals. It is advisable to include a copy of the questionnaire, as the original will probably have been mislaid. Research[17] on whether a questionnaire should be included in a follow-up to a mail survey indicated that, on balance, it was worth while to do so. In a mail survey[18] of the ethical perceptions held by advertising managers in the United States, a follow-up duplicate questionnaire increased the response rate from 22 per cent to 32 per cent: 218 effective responses were achieved from a stratified sample of 687 advertising agency executives and advertising managers.

Returns from reminders typically decrease over time, and it is necessary to call off the search after some reasonable time has elapsed or the survey will never be completed. Time and cost are factors to keep well in mind. Each reminder will delay the results by several weeks, though this may not be as critical as the quality of the survey findings.

Bearing in mind that respondents and non-respondents may well differ in significant characteristics; for example, age, sex, social group, or location, it is advisable to check the replies attracted by reminder letters against those received from initial respondents. Some valuable clues may be revealed which will lead towards a better appreciation of the subject under survey.

Non-response is a critical limitation of mail surveys, an aspect which is considered at some length in Chapter 11. In general, the response rate tends to be substantially lower than when investigators are employed in surveys.

Although the loss in sample size from non-response must be considered, the problem is really the probability that non-respondents are significantly different in their opinions from respondents. They differ, obviously, in their behaviour towards the survey, but this may not be the only significant difference. The reasons for their lack of response will remain unknown, unless some special effort is made to check these, perhaps by telephoning or personally interviewing a sub-sample of non-respondents. It may be possible to send non-respondents a simpler form of questionnaire and ask them to give some salient features which will act as a guide in assessing the characteristics of non-respondents.

Response rates are closely linked to the type of population sampled, the subject of the survey, and its presentation. Sponsorship, where it can be revealed, may also encourage response. Professional sponsorship of a survey to a population sample which has particular interest in the subject surveyed, generally attracts high response. A record 81 per cent response was reported by Gray and Corlett to a pilot survey of midwives sponsored by the Working Party on Midwives in 1950.

Controlled studies may be useful in indicating whether or not a particular method of mail enquiry improves response rates; in an experiment for the Bureau of Census, two types of covering letter were used. One was short and authoritarian; the other, polite and tactful. The former attracted a slightly better response.

A US study[19] examined the effects of 'address personalization' on the response quality of a mailed questionnaire sent to subscribers of a large health maintenance organization in a major metropolitan area in the Midwest. Of 2375 questionnaires mailed, 762 were returned, with four unusable, resulting in an overall response rate of 31.9 per cent. The hand-addressed group had a 32.6 per cent response, while the computer-generated label respondents had a 31.2 per cent response rate. However, statistical tests showed no significant difference existed, and the researchers suggested that computer-generated labels can continue to be used in mail surveys 'with little concern for negative effects'.

In the UK, valuable research on this matter has been done by Christopher Scott and reported in 'Research on mail surveys'.[20] He found that stamped, self-addressed envelopes produced a higher response rate than business reply envelopes. (Presumably, respondents felt that this reflected a more personal approach.) While the official sponsorship of the survey studied by Scott improved response rates, he reported that 'personalizing' the covering letter made no difference. He concluded that the more interested people are in the subject under survey, the better they will respond, even to quite lengthy questionnaires. A wave-like effect was noted in responses, and it was considered that informants who were particularly interested in the survey problem generally responded earlier. Scott's observations related to social surveys involving individuals, not organizations, so it is possible that responses to mail surveys to the latter may not be influenced in the same way. Delays may be caused, for example, by problems in deciding who would be the most appropriate person to deal with the enquiries, particularly if specific technical or other specialized data were requested.

Two experiments[21] to evaluate the effects of different postage combinations (first class, second class post, and business reply service) and speed of reply showed, for both national and regional samples of shoppers, that whereas the use of second instead of first class postage did not reduce levels of response, the use of business reply facilities resulted in a reduced number of returns compared with hand-stamped cards. Although second class post delayed the reception of the survey and the returns, the cost advantages were considered to outweigh these time-lags.

The findings of the research quoted above are related to a review by Linsky[22] of the research literature on stimulating response to mail questionnaires, who found that the following tactics were very effective:

1. Use of one or more follow-up postcards or letters, and especially reminders by telephone, registered mail, or special delivery letter

2. Contact with respondents *before* questionnaire is mailed to them

3. More 'high-powered' mailings, such as special delivery, are superior to ordinary mail, and hand-stamped envelopes are more effective than post-permit envelopes. (Note: compare Scott's report)[20]

4. Small cash rewards or types of premiums

5. Sponsoring organization and status of person signing letter accompanying questionnaire

The use of incentives to boost return of mail surveys should be approached cautiously, otherwise bias may be caused. In some cases, the enclosure of redeemable coupons or pen or pencil may create a feeling of obligation, but it may also generate irritation, leading to rejection of the research questionnaire.

Two studies[23] on the effects of including a non-monetary incentive in mail surveys were undertaken on a sample of the general public in The Netherlands and the results showed that an incentive, such as a ball-point pen, produced a higher initial response rate, but follow-ups reduced the effect of the incentive to a non-significant level.

An American study[24] investigated the effectiveness of two types of promised incentives in a mail survey: a personal cash payment ($1) versus a contribution to a charity of the respondent's choice. These two motivational appeals – egotistic and altruistic – were made to three groups (each of 150) of Denver area residents. The overall response rate was 30.2 per cent, of which 41 per cent opted for the charity incentive, 26 per cent for no incentive at all.

In 1973, *The Financial Times* launched the European Businessman Readership Survey, and achieved a 54 per cent response rate for this mail survey. This survey, carried out every two or three years, covers an estimated 250 000 senior business individuals across 17 West European countries, and includes establishments with 250 or more employees, head offices of companies employing 150 or more people, plus the head offices of bank and insurance companies, regardless of size.

The methodology of this very extensive survey illustrates the thorough approach adopted throughout the research. The main sources for industrial and commercial establishments are Kompass directories or their local equivalents, supplemented by an international source, *Duns Europa*. Details of financial institutions were derived from the Banker's Almanac, supplemented by the *Telerate Bank Register*, and the *Assecuranz Compass Yearbook of International Insurance Companies*, which was merged with the *World Insurance Yearbook*.

The next stage involved telephone enquiries to obtain the names of the heads of up to two job functions in each company. These were then sent a questionnaire and covering letter in their own language; countries covered were Austria, Belgium, Denmark, Finland, France, Germany, Greece, Italy, Luxembourg, The Netherlands, Norway, Portugal, Spain, Sweden, Switzerland and the UK. Altogether, 21 versions of the questionnaire were produced. The total sample was 9912, representing a response rate of 52.2 per cent to the mail survey, which was conducted by RSL – Research Services Ltd.

Higher response rates and lower costs are achieved by ensuring that questionnaires are designed so that they attract the interest of respondents; this may be effected by the content of the cover letter, the form of the questions (structured versus unstructured), the style of print, the use of cartoon characters or symbols in the margins of the questionnaire, or the features of the paper stock (e.g. colour, texture, weight, and scent). Clearly, a well-planned total scheme is necessary to make mail surveys productive, while the focus of the questionnaire on specific topics, for example professional or personal interest, is also of importance.[25]

A mail survey[26] of 3104 American marketing executives involved a two-page questionnaire, equally distributed over white, blue, pink and yellow coloured paper. The covering letter and envelope were white. An overall effective response rate of 25.34 per cent resulted: the only significant difference was found to be between the colours pink and yellow. The researchers suggested that: 'One possible explanation . . . is that the former is an action-oriented colour' compared with yellow. Apart from this observed significant difference, 'it appears that colour has little or no influence on response rates of mail questionnaires',[26] but the researchers also wisely suggested that because of the particular population surveyed 'who may have a level of sophistication not normally found with the general public',[26] additional research on more general population sectors would be advisable.

It is reasonable to assume that people tend to be influenced – favourably or otherwise – by the general appearance of mail questionnaires, even though some reactions may be largely subjective. Oppenheim[1] observes that while there have been many experiments with layout, type face, colour and quality of paper with mail questionnaires, no clear conclusions have been reached. He feels that it is best to project a relatively 'conservative' but pleasant appearance.

An unusual experiment[27] was conducted in the US to determine whether an 'envelope teaser' affected mail survey response. A 'teaser' was defined as a short question printed on the outer envelope to lure the recipient to examine its contents, as used by direct marketers, who claim, apparently, that it can significantly increase responses to mailing shots.

A systematic random sample of 200 US home-owners was drawn from a list of 13 000

Californian residents who were entitled to a refund of the unused portion of the prepaid premium held by the Federal Housing Administration, because they had not defaulted on their mortgage payments. A mail questionnaire enquired about respondents' awareness of, and attitudes towards, the refund to which they were entitled. Two groups were involved in the study: a control group, and a 'treatment' group which had the 'teaser' message: 'Did you know you are entitled to more money?' stamped in black ink on the outer envelope.

The envelope 'teaser' resulted in a response rate of 21 per cent against the control group's response rate of 8 per cent; it also dramatically increased the speed of the response: 47 per cent of the 'treatment' group replied within one week, compared with a nil response from the control group in the same period.

However, the researchers admit[27] that the main limitation of this technique is that it appeals primarily to young, low-income people, but it could, nevertheless, be very relevant in surveys among such populations. Older people may have more fixed and unfavourable attitudes towards envelope 'teasers', associating them with so-called junk mailing shots.

The effect of respondent identification on response rates of mail surveys has been the subject of much debate over a long period of time, and some degree of ambivalence exists. A study[28] of 1500 policyholders of a large property and casualty insurance company in the United States focused on two randomly selected groups of insured clients over 65 years of age. One group received an insert with their most recent premium notice discussing reducing premiums and lowering rates for clients over 65 years old. A control group did not receive this insert with their premium notices. Both groups were sent identical questionnaires, except that the experimental group were asked several questions specific to the insert. Respondents were asked to return the questionnaires in pre-addressed, post-paid envelopes, and although they were not asked to identify themselves and keying was not used, provisions for a return address were included on the envelope.

Of the total sample, 66 per cent returned completed questionnaires and names and addresses were included on 890 envelopes (90 per cent of returned questionnaires). In this particular population, it appears that respondents to a mail survey are quite willing to identify themselves, presumably because of their commitment to the insurance company and the degree of trust which they have in that organization.

However, another US-based mail survey[29] – of 500 industrial accountants who were asked questions covering sensitive topics such as role conflict, job tension, and job satisfaction – revealed that anonymity was a significant influence in increasing response rates, a deadline by itself increased response rates, but not at significant levels, whereas a combination of these incentives was significant. The researchers suggest that anonymity seems to be 'especially appropriate' with respondents who are professionally responsive to this factor, and where the survey covers sensitive issues. They also believe that the use of a same-day deadline might be recommended with groups, such as accountants, who have 'an inherent respect and appreciation for deadlines'.

The setting of a deadline in a mail survey[30] of dentists for the American Bureau of Community Health Services resulted in an initial response rate 24 per cent higher from the four groups given a specific date for response. The cost of the follow-up on the remaining sample, including those who did not receive a deadline, was thus reduced by about one-quarter. But this research was organized by a health authority and involved dentists who clearly had a close professional involvement with it, so the results of imposing a deadline cannot be generalized. In other circumstances, attempts to 'discipline' respondents might well be counter-productive.

Linsky's[22] finding related to the effectiveness of telephone reminders in securing responses to mail surveys was also experienced in research[31] undertaken for AT&T. Because the survey mailing was local, telephone costs compared favourably with those normally incurred in printing, addressing, and mailing reminder postcards.

A study[32] of the factors affecting the response rates of international mail surveys concerned two surveys in 1971 into radio listening habits in Kenya and the Ivory Coast. General conclusions were that while techniques such as registration, personalization, and sending advance postcards may effectively increase response rates in international mail surveys, using more than one of these techniques in a single survey is not likely to be more productive than if only one were used. Of these techniques, registration was consistently more effective and, in addition, provided researchers with data on undelivered letters. If overall registration was too costly, it is suggested that part of the survey could use registered mail, and this would help to provide an estimate of actual return rate.

Research into the impact of asking for race information on a mail survey[33] of domestic telephone subscribers in the United States was conducted in race regions for the AT&T Company. In each geographic sector, a random sample of 300 telephone customers was selected and divided into a control and test group. Both groups received the same questionnaire, except that the test groups were also asked to describe their ethnic background as well as their demographic profile.

The mailing and follow-up procedures were developed from an earlier study[31] for AT&T. An overall response rate of 75 per cent was achieved; the test and control groups displayed, however, some regional variations, but these were not substantial. Hence, it was concluded that 'asking for race information produced neither positive nor negative effects on the response rate'.

By cross-tabulating refusal responses to the race questions with those to other personal demographic questions, such as age, sex, relationship to head of household, and income, it was found that 80 per cent of those who refused to answer the sex question also refused to answer the race question; similarly, 86 per cent of those who refused to give information on relationship to head of household, also refused to provide ethnic data. The researchers suggest that those who refused to provide race information had 'a more general refusal syndrome', and only a very small minority who cooperate in a mail survey are unwilling to be identified in terms of sex, age, relationship to head of household, and race. But the researchers point out that these results may not be fully applicable to other surveys; local telephone services are close to communities, and other parts of the questionnaire covered 'rather well-known and familiar' topics.

To conclude, mail questionnaires are useful where the sample population is widely scattered, or difficult to meet because of professional or other commitments. They are often considered to be particularly attractive in cost terms, but this assessment needs to be more critical. Costs should be more accurately compared against the quality of information obtainable by alternative methods of investigation. Costing should also be comprehensive if it is to be validly used: it should cover all the preparatory work involved in the survey. This is particularly significant in the testing of questionnaires. Mail questionnaires need to be tested several times because their questions must be absolutely clear to all who read them. Also to be considered are the costs of physical presentation (paper, printing, envelopes, postage) and also those arising from preparing, posting, and analysing reminders.

The real cost will eventually be governed by the rate of response, and it would, therefore, be unrealistic to cost out the operation solely on the number of enquiries sent out. It is the number of effective replies which is of vital interest in assessing the comparative costs of mail surveys.

Apart from financial costs, some opinion should be formed as to the time factor involved in mail surveys. This factor is often critical in management decisions, and mail questionnaires 'in general, cannot be regarded as a speedy method of gathering information if by speedy is understood a matter of weeks'.

KEYPOINT

Aspects of mail questionnaires

Self-administered, so bias likely

In general, not suitable for survey among those of low intelligence or poorly educated

Questionnaire can be read through before answering, so degree of bias may result

May frequently represent views of more than one person: undesirable if individual views needed

Observational data cannot be gathered

Efficient follow-up needed to ensure adequate response rate

Response rates influenced by subject of survey and interests of informants

Incentives to reply need to be carefully planned to avoid biasing response

Costs of survey should be evaluated against net response rates and quality of information collected

Several reminders delay completion of survey; unsuitable for urgent enquiries

Self-administered questionnaires

Mail surveys are, inevitably, self-administered and have to be completed without the guidance of interviewers. As noted earlier the content and design of the questionnaire is important if a high response rate is to be achieved. Respondents should be helped by clear instructions on how their responses should be recorded and what they should do, for instance, if their answer is either YES or NO to specific guidelines. ('Go to Question X', or 'OMIT next question if you answered "NO" to this question.')

It is helpful to introduce some questions with a brief mention that, for instance, with a survey dealing with aspects of health, that people often feel anxious about many things and that the questions should be answered as honestly as possible and, of course, in confidence. Understandably, people sometimes feel very sensitive about giving information which may be thought to reflect adversely on their moral or social probity. They need to be assured that their experiences and views are important and relevant to the overall quality of the research findings.

Self-administered questionnaires may also be distributed to respondents by interviewers, health service workers, teachers and others in professional or official occupations. In these cases, respondents are told of the nature and purpose of a particular survey, and arrangements are made to collect the completed questionnaires within a certain time limit. A version of this type of survey may involve groups, such as students or invited audiences, but special care should be exercised to minimize bias arising from individual informants consulting with one another or copying responses.

Self-administered questionnaires are not a suitable method of research for heterogeneous populations which, as already observed, include those of low intelligence or poor education. Ognibene's[34] research involving a random sample of 176 men in the New York metropolitan area, confirmed that demographic differences tend to exist between respondents and non-respondents. The lower socio-economic groups responded least well. 'Education, occupation, and income levels of non-respondents are all significantly lower than those of respondents.' (The 117 non-respondents were followed up by telephone.) Ognibene concluded that 'education is probably the key demographic trait, because the other traits are derived from it to a large extent'. He suggested that with higher levels of education, people are more likely to be familiar with research and hence be more willing to co-operate in surveys.

As discussed earlier in this chapter, respondents of low socio-economic status and education have been observed by some researchers[9] to prefer, during personal interviews, closed questions to open questions, because they are then able to respond to questions which they do not fully understand and without revealing their ignorance. This potential source of bias should be borne in mind by researchers when designing self-administered questionnaires.

In some instances it may be possible to deliver questionnaires personally and invite co-operation in the survey, leaving respondents to complete questionnaires at a later time. This strategy would not be feasible with a very large and widely dispersed sample population, but it may be a practical and highly efficient method of attracting high response rates in clustered and relatively small samples which are homogeneous.

Some years ago, Sudman[35] provided empirical evidence that self-administered questionnaires which were left with household respondents for completion after a lengthy personal interview, attracted high rates of effective response. Rates of response which ranged from 64 per cent to 89 per cent varied according to the characteristics of respondents and the method of return adopted.

An effective response rate of 77 per cent was achieved by Manchester Business School in a household survey[36] in which self-administered questionnaires were left after briefly informing residents of the nature of the research and arranging to pick up the completed surveys in one or two hours' time.

A mail survey of 1000 UK adults, drawn by random sample from a database generated from previous consumer surveys by a market research company, was concerned with people's perceptions of UK zoos as desirable venues. An unusually high response rate of 75.2 per cent was achieved; this may have been influenced by the following factors: a brief notification letter, addressed personally and written in a friendly style, was sent one week prior to the survey questionnaire; both the pre-notification letter and that accompanying the questionnaire, were on university-headed paper; confidentiality and anonymity were assured; a deadline for returns was not specified, but responses were requested within 14 days of mailing (85 per cent of all responses were received within this time period); an incentive of a free prize draw for a nominal amount of gift vouchers for respondents who replied in the specified period was offered. It was not possible, however, to identify which of these factors was responsible, individually or in total, for the high response. There must have been some degree of interplay between the various influences.[37]

A newer type of self-administered questionnaire was reported in an article[38] in the *Journal of the Market Research Society* during 1978. Two matched samples of women were administered a questionnaire probing bathing habits; one set was interviewed by a conventional field interviewer, while the other group was faced with a computer-controlled television monitor which presented the questions, and a keyboard to be used for responses.

The two sets of resultant data were broadly similar, but there was a marginal tendency to give what might be construed as more 'frank' answers to the computer, and also a marginal tendency to adopt more extreme values of each scale in 'computer responses'. The researchers concluded that computer-administered questionnaires have a role to play in modern market research. [See section on computer-assisted telephone interviewing (CATI), and computer-assisted personal interviews (CAPI).]

5.9 Telephone questionnaires

In Chapter 3 some of the problems facing researchers drawing samples of households from telephone directories were considered, and the technique of random digit dialling (RDD) was discussed. Further attention will now be given to the techniques, and limitations, of the telephone as a survey technique, while in Chapter 11 its particular applications in industrial market research will be reviewed.

The rapidly growing use of telephone surveys in both consumer and business-to-business research is already evident in the UK. As seen in Chapter 2, survey techniques based on computer technology, such as computer-assisted data collection (discussed later) and other related methodologies, have spurred this advance. Also, the significant increase in domestic telephone installations in the UK has now resulted in virtually complete coverage. In Chapter 3 it was noted that by 1999, telephones were in 96 per cent of UK households. However, unlisted numbers are now around 40 per cent of total UK domestic installations, and probably are over 50 per cent in major cities, because of requests to be 'ex-directory', and also because of removals or new installations since the directories were last published. The problems of unlisted numbers was tackled in the USA by the development of random-digit dialling (see Chapter 3), and this was later introduced into the UK, where it was proved to be a cost-effective method of contacting unlisted domestic telephone subscribers, particularly in metropolitan areas.

Despite some sampling difficulties, the advantages of telephone surveys of consumers outweigh the disadvantages.

The advantages of the telephone, briefly, are as follows:

1. It is convenient
2. It is imperative
3. It confers anonymity
4. It attracts freer response
5. It can be used at precise times
6. It is easily controlled and supervised

The disadvantages could be termed either serious or just marginal. Of the former type, telephone interviews are limited to verbal communication, and until fairly recently, no 'visual aids' could be used to assist the process of questioning. (Later, consideration will be given to new developments which should reduce this drawback.) It is often argued that telephone enquiries are restricted in time and are largely confined to structured interviews. However, these objections are becoming marginal with the latest technological developments; they also tend to overlook the growing tendency towards more open discussions related to specific topics, particularly those of distinct professional concern. Interviewing, particularly over the telephone, is a critical function of successful survey operations, as discussed in the next chapter. In face-to-face interviewing, experienced interviewers quickly 'tune-in' to respondents, whose facial and body movements may give valuable clues to guide interviewers in developing good rapport and securing satisfactory interviews.

This vital link is missing in telephone interviewing, although, of course, well-trained interviewers may be able to judge from the tone and inflexions of respondents' voices whether they are likely to co-operate and provide valid and reliable information. Considerable patience and toleration may have to be exercised when conducting telephone interviews, and every effort made to avoid causing suspicions to arise about the nature of a telephone call. It is advisable for interviewers to have a prepared script so that they can readily introduce themselves, state clearly the objectives of the research being undertaken, and invite the co-operation of those who answer the telephone, ensuring, of course, that they are the persons most likely to be able to respond adequately to the survey enquiries.

Centralized telephone interviewing under supervision has increased the professional standards of this form of data collection, as discussed later.

As with 'traditional' methods of collecting research data, mixed-mode techniques may be used productively, as discussed in Chapter 2, where the desirability of using several different but complementary methods was recommended. For example, from an initial sample of telephone respondents, a sub-sample may be selected for extended face-to-face interviews, group discussions, or recruitment to a research panel (see Chapter 8). Telephone interviewing in the US is frequently part of an overall research effort that embraces mixed-mode data collection. In the UK, telephone research is now a well established methodology, as noted earlier and also in Chapters 11 and 12. With the significant decline in response rates to interviewing, particularly in face-to-face situations, flexibility and ingenuity are necessary inputs when developing research designs.

In 1986, the Market Research Society[39] set up a Telephone Research Working Party to develop a telephone survey version of the MRS Interviewer Identity Card Scheme for face-to-face interviewers, so that respondents could verify the authenticity of telephone enquiries. A Freephone Market Research Society facility enables telephone respondents to check the authenticity of a survey without cost to themselves.

Ford of Europe[40] tracks the acceptance of its products and ensures that its design and engineering staff know, almost immediately, exactly what new car buyers feel about their vehicles in the main European markets. This regular quality tracking study uses extensive and highly organized telephone surveys of new car buyers who had about 30 days' experience of their vehicles. Previously, mail surveys had been used, but it was found that, frequently, customers described faults inadequately, or their comments were too brief, vague, or over-generalized: telephone research led to more precise 'diagnosis'.

Telephone ownership of new (as distinct from used) cars is over 90 per cent in the principal European markets, so sample bias was clearly relatively small. The response rate was 'exceptionally good': if this is taken to mean the number of successfully completed interviews as a proportion of all eligible sample respondents, the achieved response rate is between 60 per cent and 80 per cent, according to the market segment and country surveyed. This 'strike rate' is particularly impressive, since average survey time has been 30 minutes.

It is important to note that Ford, working closely with a leading marketing research company, has developed effective telephone survey practice which, for instance, details how interviewers should approach respondents who are told how their names and addresses have been obtained, how the information will be used by Ford, what the expected time of the interview will be, and an assurance that there will be no sales follow-up of any kind.

A review of the methods used by 83 leading market research firms in 17 countries, including the UK and the USA, indicated that there were 'enormous differences' in how they designed and used telephone surveys of the public. The biggest differences occurred between countries, although there were also many differences within countries. In general, the 'most striking finding was the complete absence of consensus on almost all aspects of sampling and weighting'.[41] For instance, 40 per cent of firms described their methods as 'quota sampling', and 45 per cent as 'probability sampling with weighting'; only half had used random-digit dialling; call-back procedures to telephone numbers varied from none to over ten. About half the firms substituted numbers within geographic cells for non-response; the rest do not. Most research firms – including those describing their methods as 'probability sampling' – applied quotas to control sampling in the field; these controls varied greatly. Refusal rates were said to vary from under 10 per cent to over 60 per cent. Weighting of telephone-derived data is done consistently by less than one-third of firms; some do no weighting at all.

These marked deviations in research indicate a general lack of agreement on 'best practices', especially related to the conduct of telephone surveys. In view of the growing use of this method of data collection, it seems 'timely to conduct a more comprehensive and detailed study' of the ways in which telephone research is being developed.[41]

The marked advantages of using the telephone as a method of making personal interview appointments was noted in a health care survey[42] of the elderly in three survey sites in the USA. One random half sample in each site received a lead letter, followed by a telephone call to arrange a personal interview, while the other half sample were sent a lead letter, followed by a personal contact, but with no intervening telephone call. The first type of approach resulted in a 20 per cent saving in data collection costs with only a 1 per cent decrease in response rate. While this particular finding related to a specific sample, viz. 1260 Medicare eligible senior citizens, the researchers feel that, in general, telephone calls to make arrangements for personal interviewing hold 'great potential' in reducing data collection costs with little risk of increasing refusal rates.

An experiment was conducted[43] by the Center for Disease Control and the Opinion Research Corporation to determine the effectiveness of paying physicians monetary incentives to participate in a 20–30 minute telephone survey of influenza immunization. The research design included an introductory letter, guarantee of anonymity, promise of a copy of the report, and expressed willingness to interview the doctor by appointment either personally or by telephone. From a nationwide sample, 150 physicians from each of four main specialities were selected at random. These 600 doctors were then systematically distributed among three equal sub-samples, to which were allocated 'no incentive', $25, or $50, respectively.

Financial incentives appeared to be effective in increasing the response rate to a 25-minute telephone interview among private practice doctors from about 58 per cent ('no incentive') to nearly 70 per cent for the $25 incentive, and around 77 per cent for the higher incentive. How far such incentives could be offered before bias distorted survey findings would clearly be a matter for very careful consideration.

KEYPOINT

Aspects of telephone questionnaires

Rapidly growing in both consumer and business to-business research

Advantages: convenient; imperative; confers anonymity; attracts freer response; can be used at precise times; relatively easy to control and supervise

►

> *Disadvantages*: limited to verbal communication; tends to be restricted in time and confined to structured interviews; lack of opportunities for interviewers to see and assess impact of enquiries
>
> *Pre-planning of interview vital for success – use script for introduction*
>
> *Centralized telephone supervision has raised interviewing standards*
>
> *Virtual saturation of UK domestic telephone coverage, but problems of unlisted telephones*

5.10 Developments in telephone surveys

As observed already, the use of the telephone as an effective method of collecting marketing research data has been growing in the United Kingdom; this trend has been emphasized by the development of centralized telephone facilities, now operated by several market research companies and by the extension of electronic technology which has led to computer-assisted telephone interviewing (CATI), direct computer interviewing (DCI), and Viewdata.

Although a discussion of interviewing people in general takes place in Chapter 7, here we extend the present coverage of telephone surveying to include these developments.

Central location telephone interviewing

During the last quarter of the twentieth century, telephone research – as noted earlier – was generally regarded as a rather minor methodology. It was accepted to be useful, perhaps, in business-to-business research but was unsuited for general consumer research because domestic telephone rentals were mostly restricted to the higher socio-economic classes (ABC1). For instance, by the mid-1970s, only just over 40 per cent of UK households had a telephone. Today, as already noted, virtually every UK household has a telephone. In addition to this conspicuous dispersion which, in theory at least, has rendered telephone research more generally useful, considerable advances have been made in technology and in the organization of telephone surveying.

Telephone interviewing progressed rapidly from relatively elementary arrangements to central locations serviced by powerful PCs, with quick-response telephone researchers, and controlled by effective supervision.

CATI involves a number of interviewers who, from a central location, contact listed telephone subscribers or, perhaps, use random-digit dialling to contact unlisted numbers, as noted already, and administer a questionnaire. In the early days, this was read from a paper script, but nowadays the questions are most likely to be shown on a visual display unit (VDU). The results are then subject to the usual processes of editing, etc.

BMRB has 70 CATI stations, staffed by interviewers working under close, direct supervision. With telephone surveys, it is possible to have very high quality unclustered sample designs; survey time is reduced significantly; all interviewers can be personally briefed; and the time and cost of telephone recalls is minimal. Of the BMRB's Target Group Index (TGI: see Chapter 11), 93 per cent are on the telephone and only 12 per cent have indicated that they will not participate in future research projects.

Central telephone interviewing facilities are now offered by about 100 research companies in the UK. The Gallup Telephone Research Centre at Thame, Oxfordshire, operates 60 direct lines, and they view telephone surveying as one of the fastest growth areas in marketing research. It is seen to be a particularly ideal way of contacting opinion leaders and obtaining their views on a wide range of topics.

Taylor Nelson Sofres Telecoms provides, on a global basis, a comprehensive range of specialist telecom research services, and they work closely with most major telecommunication companies in North America, Western Europe and Asia Pacific.

The geographical spread of the sample and the time taken directly affect the costs of telephone surveying. Jean Morton-Williams has pointed out that whereas in face-to-face surveys, the costs of making contact means that it is more economical to have a relatively long interview, at least up to about 40 minutes; lengthy telephone interviews inhibit response although 'making contact is relatively cheap'.[44]

Central location telephone interviewing offers attractive opportunities for global business-to-business surveys. Obviously, the range of such enquiries is constrained by the effectiveness of some overseas telephone systems, as well as by the availability of interviewers with relevant language skills (see Chapter 12: International Market Research).

In the United States, with its different time zones, central location interviewing can be conducted virtually round the clock, with teams of interviewers working on a shift basis – which is customary with this methodology. Such operations clearly call for expert planning and control systems.

Computer-assisted telephone interviewing (CATI)

Central location telephone interviewing has, as seen, grown in sophistication and effectiveness with computer-based technologies. Of these, computer-assisted telephone interviewing (CATI) is a notable development. Paper questionnaires are eliminated entirely: questions are displayed on a monitor, and responses (pre-coded) are keyed by the interviewer directly into the computer. This direct method is termed 'simultaneous direct data entry' (SDDE).

Various CATI characteristics have been developed, but they all involve the same basic procedure: an interviewer is seated before a computer-terminal, reads the question on the screen to the telephoned respondent, and then records the response by means of the terminal's keyboard. CATI originated in the USA in the early 1970s, and developed from pioneer work undertaken by AT&T in the late 1960s. Since those early days, CATI systems have spread widely, aided also by concessionary rates of telephone lines in the US. CATI has been slower to diffuse in the UK because, as discussed, of general attitudes towards telephone surveying as well as – until fairly recently – the incomplete coverage of UK households by telephone. However, virtually all major telephone research suppliers have now invested in CATI systems.

British Telecom's Customer Attitude Research Survey (Telcare), costing an estimated £6 million, has significantly boosted CATI in the UK. Both business and residential customers are covered by this comprehensive survey; summarized results are readily available for BT's management.

Marplan, a medium-sized UK market research company, now part of Research International, has a 50-line central location telephone facility called Hotline! which covers about 250 different surveys a year, including a large number of foreign language surveys to all parts of continental Europe (Euro Hotline!). Marplan's mainframe computer and CATI are both available to these specific surveys. (Also see Chapter 8, Section 8.7: Telephone panels.)

NOP's telephone research facilities include 280 CATI stations at six centres, all within easy reach of central London. They also conduct, from the UK, international telephone interviewing using mother-tongue interviewers. Additionally, NOP have two units of specially trained interviewers who do depth interviews by telephone.

Telephone Surveys of Northampton also specializes in central location CATI surveys. On-Line Telephone Surveys of London, which has links with MORI, operates 80 CATI stations and undertakes telephone research covering a very wide range of activities, such as political research, public opinion polling, advertising awareness, corporate image, financial, international, social, and government and local authority surveys. International enquiries include telephone research enquiries to the Far East, the Pacific Basin, USA/Canada, and throughout Europe.

Distinct advantages associated with CATI are related to the measure of control exercised in the interviewing process: the computer is programmed so that the interview cannot proceed until a valid answer has been keyed in on the keyboard, so a question cannot be inadvertently omitted, or an answer given which is inconsistent with previous responses. Interviewer error is, therefore, eliminated, as also is the need (as with conventional interviewing) to write down replies on to a paper questionnaire which then has to be processed. CATI is also advantageous in that routings (sequence of questioning) are worked out automatically by the computer, and the next relevant question is automatically displayed on the VDU.

Although CATI can steer through quite complex sequences of questioning, it appears to be limited in its ability to handle open-ended questions.

The US Bureau of the Census[45] has studied the possible applications of CATI and concluded that the technology had great potential but, like other data collection methods, conferred specific benefits while also having certain disadvantages.

> Its advantages and cost-effectiveness should be greatest in repeated surveys, and in carefully planned and thoroughly pre-tested surveys and censuses with large samples, the types of data collection which constitute the greater part of the Census Bureau's work. Its use in smaller one-time surveys and special applications presents more operational problems and less confidence of cost-effectiveness, although the experience of CATI agencies in the private sector suggests that such applications can also be handled in a cost-effective and timely manner.

The Census Bureau is continuing to test and develop this new interviewing technique.

A specific advantage of CATI is the immediacy of research responses; by sequential sampling techniques interim results of surveys can be readily obtained.[46] (See Chapter 4.)

A significant step in the European development of CATI was taken in 1993, when a network of four independent European agencies launched a 'one-stop' telephone interviewing service with a 200-station CATI capacity. This harmonized networked service covers France, Germany, Italy, Spain and the UK — where FDS International is the constituent member agency.

Computer-assisted personal interviewing (CAPI)

This development of CATI has been pioneered in the UK by Research International. By means of laptop computers, researchers conduct personal interviews and input data down the telephone. This dramatically reduces the time of the research process: 'Using the CAPI system, a Research International multinational client obtained the data on 500 interviews with US retailers within a week. In the past it would have taken five weeks.'[47]

An innovative application of CAPI occurs with a consumer-based fragrance database operated by Sandpiper Fragrance Research International Ltd[48] across five countries (UK, USA, France, Germany, and Japan). Groups of consumers in these countries rate each fragrance on 70 attributes, such as 'strong, fruity, fresh, exotic, sharp, and clean', which are presented on computer screens set up in local houses. It is claimed that this method results 'in high quality data with low respondent fatigue; order effects are removed as attribute groups and individual attributes can be randomized'.[48] Stratified probability sampling is used to recruit women aged 16+; a minimum sample size per model is 500.

In 1993, Social and Community Planning Research (since 1999 known as the National Centre for Social Research), decided to test the suitability of CAPI for collecting the data needed for its annual surveys; its success led to the 1994 survey being conducted entirely by CAPI. The researchers concluded that in some respects CAPI clearly improved the survey data; it reduces the tendency to give 'extreme' responses.

The Social Survey Division of the OPCS stated that they had been using CAPI methods on the Labour Force Survey since September 1990; 'the only measurable change was a decrease in the number of NAs because interviewers could no longer be caught out by complex filtering instructions'.[49]

The NOP Group, which employs 2000 field interviewers and 650 telephone interviewers, has equipped many of its interviewers with hand-held computers, in line with its belief that CAPI provides higher quality data, and computerizing the questionnaire results in added flexibility and faster turnaround time.

In July 1992, the National Readership Survey (NRS – see Chapter 11) switched its media readership data collection method from traditional personal interviewing to CAPI.

Taylor Nelson Sofres run Omnimas, a weekly CAPI-based consumer omnibus survey of 200 adults across Great Britain (see Chapter 8).

IPSOS–RSL launched Capibus Europe in 1995, a single survey which is claimed to be capable of covering 84 per cent of the EU population and delivering the results much more speedily than existing non-electronic European surveys. In this continuous survey, based on CAPI technique, RSL works closely with the other constituent companies of the IPSOS group, which operate in France, Germany, Italy and Spain. These five research companies have combined resources of 800 staff and 5000 interviewers, and can organize 5000 weekly, face-to-face CAPI interviews (1000 in each country) of adults aged 15+, using random location sampling with demographic controls in more than 500 sampling points (see Chapter 4). Results are promised four weeks after the receipt of questions.

Jean Morton-Williams[44] has noted that CAPI is becoming firmly established as a mode of data collection, and that a high proportion of experienced interviewers adapt to using a computerized questionnaire after suitable training and apparently enjoy an increased sense of professionalism. Also, the public does not appear to be more resistant when being interviewed with the aid of a computer; 'indeed, it seems that response rates may even be a little higher, due partly, perhaps, to the effect of increased self-esteem on interviewer morale'.[44]

Computer-assisted self interviewing (CASI)

In this system of computer-based data collection – also referred to as computerized self-administered questionnaires (CSAQ), prepared data entry (PDE) or direct computer interviewing (DCI) – the respondent interacts directly with the computer instead of through the medium of an interviewer (see Section 5.8: Self-administered questionnaires).

Both CATI and the variously named CASI research methods share the same technology, but whereas professional interviewers are in charge of the former technique, in the latter case, respondents have to make inputs themselves. In theory at least, CASI offers informants some of the advantages of self-completion questionnaires, such as privacy and the opportunity to respond with openness to sensitive areas of questioning; it also avoids interviewer-bias. It has been suggested that interactive personal input may be successful in encouraging respondents to give information which they may be unwilling to disclose to an interviewer.[38] CASI methodology may therefore improve the quality of research data, although empirical evidence is still sparse, and there is a dearth of systematic cost-comparison information.[50]

CASI may sometimes be used in conjunction with CAPI; for instance, informants are asked to input responses directly from the screen for a short time, while the interviewer remains on hand to deal with any problems that may arise and to ensure that informants maintain their motivation to participate.

One of the distinct limitations of this type of data collection is that it necessarily involves informants having access to and familiarity with computerized systems of response. The younger generation, who are exposed to computers at an early age, and those whose occupations involve the use of computers, are likely to regard CASI as conventional as traditional printed questionnaires. An early experimental study by the English Tourist Board found that whilst most respondents considered DCI to be interesting and easy to use, older people and also women tended to find VDUs and keyboard inputs rather intimidating at first.[51] Since the time of that investigation, people generally have become more accustomed to keying-in processes, e.g. at cash withdrawal points, and other computer-linked systems, as well as the now rising development of internet shopping and interactive television. In addition, industry, commerce and the public sector services make extensive use of computerized systems, and staff will mostly be fully aware of and competent in handling such equipment. Further, official statistics state that 34 per cent of British households had a computer in 1999 – a rise of 62 per cent since 1992.[52]

Disk-by-mail (DBM)

Over recent years, experimental versions of CAPI have been tried out, and DBM integrates the mail survey with the personal computer (PC). Respondents are mailed a floppy disk containing a questionnaire, which they complete via their PCs. The disks are then returned to the researcher for processing. Important considerations would be computer compatability and the danger of viruses. A few years ago an experiment[53] compared DBM with a standard paper questionnaire, and although distinct reservations were made over the findings, the researchers felt that this comparatively novel method of collecting survey data may well follow the now acknowledged success of CATI.

Computer-assisted panel research (CAPAR)

Computer-assisted panel research, using computers in panel members' homes, was developed about the same time as CAPI, with technological advances and the availability of inexpensive modems.

The Sociometric Foundation developed an interview program for a home computer which was tested by a panel over six months, and is now used for a consumers' panel by the Dutch Gallup Institute, NIPO.[54]

Nielsen and other leading research agencies operate household panels in the UK and elsewhere which record details of specific purchases by means of a bar-code scanner which, via a medium, is linked to the telephone for transfer of the stored data to a host computer (see Chapter 8). Television audience measurement, under the aegis of the Broadcasters' Audience Research Board (BARB) has developed over the years from diaries and set meters to on-line meters capable of monitoring VCR activity as well as the direct TV viewing of a selected panel of households (see Chapter 10). Electronic point-of-sale screening (EPOS – see Chapter 8) also provides input data for retail audits, and is widely used in the USA, the UK and in many other European countries (see Chapter 9).

Electronic mail survey (EMS)

E-mail, bulletin boards and also fax offer relatively easy and rapid access to specific types of market sectors. It would be advisable to obtain the agreement of likely informants to participate in e-mail research before proceeding to download questionnaires on to their computers: modern communications should not be allowed to corrupt good research practice!

E-mail surveys have been noted[55] as having some distinct advantages over traditional research methodologies. For example, they cut out the costs of postage (and pre-paid facilities), printing, and stationery, while the laborious task of stuffing envelopes is eliminated. More positively, transmission is almost instantaneous, as, hopefully, is response; the method may project a sense of urgency and so motivate the interest of potential informants; it may also be perceived as an environmentally friendly system. However, certain disadvantages were also noted:[55] sample coverage is low and biased towards those who are responsive to technological advances; some countries lack e-mail directories; e-mail is restricted to textual matter with limited choice of font and layout. Research-based findings among a small group (500) of administrative and teaching staff from the Chinese University of Hong Kong showed that e-mail surveys resulted in faster but lower response rates than mail surveys. It was concluded that it was premature to regard e-mail 'as a practical method for collecting data from commercial organizations and consumer households', but because of its dynamic nature, it was projected to 'soon become a standard method in the near future'.[55] Perhaps, as an experienced marketing consultant has observed, e-mail 'will bring a renaissance of the self-completion questionnaire'.[56]

Fax has been used very successfully in researching the financial and banking services needed by small–medium sized enterprises; in one particular survey an effective response rate of 82 per cent was achieved, and the quality of information gathered was excellent. Sampling was greatly assisted by fax directories. The costs of response are, of course, born by respondents, but this factor did not seem to cause problems. The relative novelty of the research approach and its immediate interest to SMEs resulted in the high response; a sub-sample of respondents agreed to be personally interviewed, so that some specific topics, which seemed to be of salient significance, could be explored more fully. Opportunities for fax-based (or mixed-mode) research may exist in other sectors, although it is probable that just as fax replaced the telex, so e-mail will supplant fax in due course.

5.11 Internet survey

In only a few years, the exponential growth of the internet and e-commerce has had an unprecedented effect on economic and social behaviour across the globe. Almost effortlessly, the internet vaults over national boundaries and opens up the developed world to new concepts, products and services which can be accessed with relative ease. The world wide web (www) has rapidly become one of the most widely recognized acronyms, perhaps largely because of the daily invocations of it when radio and television announcements are made on a wide variety of topics.

In the late 1990s, the use of the internet for market research purposes was regarded with curiosity, cynicism as well as fairly unbridled speculation. But internet-based market research is no longer considered to be just 'a gimmick', and greater attention is now being given to its potential as another acceptable type of research methodology.[57]

Basically, web technology, applied for market research purposes, provides a low-cost and convenient means of quick feedback from certain market sectors. The biggest problem lies in securing representative samples of the general population, because at present sampling frames are limited to those who are linked to the internet. In the UK, penetration of the internet in 1999 was estimated by NOP to be about 20 per cent of the total population; it was 2 per cent two years earlier. Most internet users are male, 25–35 years old, and with above average income – a distinctly narrow market sector. Almost 40 per cent of the US population had a home computer, and over 15 million people were 'online' via the internet in 1998.

However, for research connected with specific population sectors, known to be users of the internet, it is likely to be a valid and reliable methodology.

Research shows that most users of the internet in the USA are white males, aged 18–59, of above average socio-economic and educational status, and either white collar or professional workers. A pilot study to measure response rates on the internet related to a large sports website in the USA, which offers patrons a variety of information on world-wide sporting events. Out of a possible 700 000 'hits' per month, 116 (98 men and 18 women) customers of the website completed a questionnaire, i.e. less than 1 per cent response rate. Participants had been offered sports-related incentives. The information requested covered detailed demographic data (full name and e-mail address, car ownership, hobbies, etc.). The resultant low-level response may, as the researchers admit, reflect the fact that many individuals may be unwilling to release on the Web so much personal information.[58]

A study[59] of private trading – buying, selling and exchange activities carried out by some people but not as a regular source of income – was conducted by using an online questionnaire with mostly open-ended questions; these produced qualitative data that were subsequently coded. 8300 invitations were drawn from a sampling frame plus a quota of 30 per cent of academic addresses; from all these resulted 240 completed, 'an apparent response rate of less than 3 per cent'. Subject to accepting that a very high per cent (perhaps 80 per cent) of the addresses 'were redundant', the researchers claimed a 'real response rate of 14.5 per cent'. But the outcome would seem to be unrepresentative of internet users targeted for the survey. The fact that those who did respond were self-selected adds to the biases in this type of research.

On-line focus groups are an interesting development in internet research, which involves participants attending a virtual group held at a website. Group members can type in their comments, and also see what the moderator and the other participants type; at the close of the session a transcript is available. Whilst this version of electronic focus group discussion allows participants – and clients – to remain in their environments – there is the problem, alluded to earlier, of the representativeness of online participants, and also that the 'non-verbal side of group behaviour is lost'.[60] The 'impersonal' nature of such electronic interchanges denies the moderator and participants the opportunity of gathering clues from body language or the tone of voices.

Opinions differ as to the seriousness of the lack of this immediate personal reaction:

some researchers believe that 'in most cases exactly the same conclusions were reached from the on-line groups as conventional ones' and promote their intrinsic attraction of being much more convenient for all those involved. On the other hand, other researchers feel strongly that 'something intangible is missing from the Internet groups',[60] and that it is better to use this methodology as an adjunct to, not a replacement for, face-to-face methods'.[60]

It is possible, however, to alleviate – if not overcome – the disadvantage of 'impersonal' participation by the use of a one-way mirror dividing focus group members from clients. Split-screen views enable the moderator and the clients to see the responses inputed by participants and also to communicate with one another on a hidden screen.[61]

The internet may also be useful in conducting 'live' depth interviews or on-line discussions, although further development may be less promising than earlier experimental exercises because participants need to have relatively good typing skills, possess compatible equipment, and arrangements would have to be made to reimburse their costs of 'air time'.[62] Several leading market research agencies in the UK are very active in internet-based research, including online panels. Among these are Nielsen, Taylor Nelson Sofres, Ipsos, and Millward Brown.

As noted, internet research has many applications and, in common with other research techniques, some distinct limitations. It is highly productive in gathering background information, i.e. desk research, although as in traditional desk research, discretion is needed when assessing such data. There are over 15 000 bulletin boards on the Web; these cover a very wide range of topics. In the UK, the Office for National Statistics (ONS) operates a statistical information website: www.statistics.gov.org. There are also many commercial online sources of specialized data, and as seen, several market research agencies offering online research services.

The internet can survey virtually unprecedented samples of people; it can also survey micro-samples of specific populations; it can show lists, diagrams and images; it can attract high levels of interaction and verbatim responses; its speed of operation is unparalleled; it is economic to use.

In the USA, the Harris Poll surveyed 103 000 people for their E-Commerce Pulse service and completed all the interviewing in 10 days. A survey of 10 000 people with specific medical conditions was gathered in one week. 'Only the internet enabled us to do this at an affordable cost'.[63]

The internet has been seen to be effective in researching specific segments, for example, business and professional workers, where reasonably reliable sampling frames may be available. It may be used to test website effectiveness or to track online advertising effectiveness; it may be used in panel research. It is particularly valuable where contacts are widely dispersed, perhaps over countries or even continents. Compared with traditional research methodologies, internet is inexpensive, rapid, does not suffer from interviewer bias (although it is prone to bias because of its self-completion basis), and attracts responses from young, highly skilled professionals, who can interact comparatively easily.

As already noted, internet has limitations, including sampling issues and relative technical complexity.[64] However, online data can be weighted by demographic variables such as age, sex, education, occupation, race and ethnicity, as the Harris Poll have done successfully in development of a system of 'propensity weighting'. The weights used are primarily drawn from Harris' 'parallel telephone and online surveys, based on the assumption that some large differences reflect biases in the online sample because of the greater or lesser propensity of different people' to be on their online surveys.[63]

Developing and maintaining databases demands significant investment in hardware, software and staff: these are the principal costs of online research, not the actual collection of data. Harris Poll have five million people in their data base and plan to add many more, in the United States, Europe, Japan, and elsewhere.[63]

Whilst expert opinion generally accepts that online research is now a vital constituent of professional research practice, and its methodologies are seen to be in tune with the dynamic pace of contemporary life, some tentative doubts have also been expressed. These are concerned, for instance, about whether 'natural growth in internet connections will be as high over the next five years as to provide nationally representative samples of the population.[65] It has already been seen that Harris Poll, and other leading market research organizations, are experimenting with weighting systems which will, it is hoped, largely overcome this problem. It is recognized that the data collected by internet research have to be capable of standing up to critical comparison with those derived from existing methodologies. It is unlikely that internet research will sweep away entirely established research practices, but it will certainly add vigour and pace to the market research industry, and – as noted – be accepted as a potentially valuable element of the research tool-kit.

Meanwhile, mobile telephone technology is now linking mobile phones with the internet, so that information from internet web sites can be displayed on the screen of a phone. Wireless Application Protocol (WAP) will enable the internet to be accessed by mobile phone users. *The Economist* describes the linking of the mobile telephone and the internet as 'a match made in heaven'. It adds that hardly a day passes in America and Europe without the announcement of 'a new alliance or "strategic partnership" between dotcoms, telecom firms and computer companies, all jostling for advantage in the brave new world around the corner'.[66]

In May 1998, the Market Research Society founded 'org.org', Europe's first internet research interest group. After consulting research bodies in five continents ESOMAR produced guidelines on internet research. These are aimed to protect the interests of internet respondents and also users of internet research findings. Internet research must also be conducted in ways that are acceptable to the general public and in accordance with national and international regulations. Among these requirements, researchers should always alert respondents to any costs, for example, online time, that they might incur in co-operating in internet surveys.

KEYPOINT

Developments in telephone surveys

Central Location Telephone Interviewing
increased in sophistication with random digit dialling (RDD) and

Computer-Assisted Telephone Interviewing (CATI)
precoded questions displayed on monitor and responses keyed in by interviewers(also known as Simultaneous Direct Entry: (SDDE)

Computer-Assisted Personal Interviewing (CAPI)
interviewers with laptop computers conduct personal interviews and input data down telephone

Computer-Assisted Self Interviewing (CASI)
respondents interact directly with computer making inputs themselves; sometimes used in conjunction with CAPI; requires informants to be familiar with computers and to have ready access.

▶

Disk-by-Mail (DBM)
respondents are mailed floppy disk with questionnaire which they complete via their computers. Important to have computer compatability and be aware of danger of viruses

Computer-Assisted Panel Research (CAPAR)
panel research in homes via home computers

Electronic Mail Survey (EMS)
e-mail, bulletin boards, also fax, cut costs of postage, pre-paid facilities, printing, etc.; virtually instant transmission; conveys urgency; lack of e-mail directories in some countries; self-completion style of questionnaire; mixed-mode research feasible; useful in specific market sectors and specialized sample populations

Internet Survey
fast growth because of exponential expansion of internet and e-commerce; internet research no longer just a gimmick; but it is impersonal; developments: on-line focus groups; 'live' depth discussions; panel research; ready access to dispersed and specialized market segments; inexpensive

Biggest problem: lack of general sampling frames

Leading market research firms active in internet surveying.

Summary

Questionnaires are a vital element of the total market research design; they demand skill in composition.

Various methods of applying questionnaires are used: personal interviewing, telephone, mail (including self-administered).

Questionnaires should be carefully planned to cover the needs of specific research objectives. In devising questions, care must be taken to avoid bias, e.g. leading questions. A favoured sequence of questioning is known as 'funnelling': from the general to the specific.

Two main types of question are commonly used: open-ended and closed; the latter may be dichotomous (simple alternative) or multi-choice.

Pilot testing of questionnaires is imperative: this should be done with representative sub-samples.

Mail questionnaires must be self-contained and clearly worded; no interviewer will be present to assist respondents. The real costs should be based on the number of effective replies received; response rates tend to be low. Every aspect of mail survey presentation deserves special attention in order to boost responses.

Computer-assisted self interviewing (CASI) involves respondents in direct interaction with the computer instead of through the medium of an interviewer. Both CATI and the various types of CASI research methods share the same technology, but with the former, professional interviewers are in charge, whereas with the latter, respondents have to make inputs themselves.

CASI and CAPI may sometimes be used in conjunction. Computer-assisted panel research (CAPAR) is another and specialized form of computer-based methodology.

Electronic mail surveys (e-mail) may also be useful with some specific market sector researches.

Internet survey technology is now becoming well established because of its ready access to widely dispersed and specialized sectors. While Web technology, applied to market research, is low-cost and convenient, the biggest problem is representative sampling.

Review and discussion questions

1. Identify six common terms which, in your opinion, might lead to confusion/misinterpretation on consumer questionnaires.

2. Evaluate the wording of the following statements for use in questionnaires. If you consider them unsuitable, indicate why and suggest an alternative version.

    (a) 'Do you know if smoking is allowed on London Transport buses?'

    (b) 'Do you think management at your workplace is too authoritarian?'

    (c) 'If you were buying a car tomorrow, what product features would you look for?'

    (d) 'Do you think school meals should be more nutritional?' (Q. for parents)

    (e) 'What is your age?'

    (f) 'The average adult reads 4.5 newspapers per week, how many do you read?'

3. A researcher, using a structured questionnaire, is anxious to find out how long it is since his female respondents purchased their last bottle of perfume. He is concerned about the accuracy of the recall responses he will receive. Can you offer him any advice on this matter?

4. Construct two questions in sequence on any topic of your choice to illustrate the order effect.

5. Describe the strengths and weaknesses of mail surveys. What strategies can researchers use to reduce non-response levels for mail questionnaires?

6. Identify three marketing research projects for which a telephone questionnaire rather than a mail questionnaire or personal interview would be more appropriate.

CAMEO CASE STUDY: MarketingNet Ltd

The area of e-business has developed at a phenomenal rate over the past five years, providing many opportunities for a whole new generation of specialist companies, among which MarketingNet is a key player. Founded in 1995, the company is an independent British internet consultancy service, based in Royal Leamington Spa, providing internet-based solutions to help clients achieve their marketing objectives. MarketingNet offers a comprehensive range of electronic-based business services for customers in a variety of industry sectors, such as the Chartered Institute of Marketing, PricewaterhouseCoopers, Motorola, The Army, Galileo, GKN, Little Chef, Dunlop Aviation, and Travelodge. To date all the company's clients have been UK based, but in 2000 a contract was secured with a large US client, which opens up the potential of international expansion.

Whilst the company has a wide range of customers, it has targeted the financial services and travel sectors in the past. Developing close relationships with customers is the preferred marketing strategy; existing customers are serviced by Account Directors, who encourage the purchase of enhanced and additional services. Potential new customers are identified by the Senior Management team, targeted through the Telesales team, and invited to any of 12 invitation-only events a year. Typically, the servicing of existing customers ('hosting' and 'maintenance' activities) occurs on a daily basis, whilst selling websites is more likely to be done on a weekly basis. Longer-term activities, such as consultancy, are generally undertaken every three or four months, whilst major projects tend to be commissioned on a yearly basis. The services provided to these and other customers include the design and construction of websites, the creation of electronic corporate identities, on-line promotion and marketing, and various aspects of 'e-strategy' consultancy. The competitive advantage enjoyed by MarketingNet lies in its combination of marketing and IT expertise.

At present MarketingNet employs 52 people in the UK across three offices. The company favours a

▶

'flat', non-hierarchical management structure, based around teams: the Production team is headed by a 25-year-old, and comprises Programmers, Designers and Production managers; the Client Services team acts autonomously and consists of Sales, Marketing, and Account Management. The Financial department comprises a team of Finance and Administration staff.

Financially, the company has gone from strength to strength – turnover has doubled each year since the company's formation, from £0.5 million in the financial year 1997–1998, to £1.20 million in 1998–1999, and £2.75 million in 1999–2000. There is a projected turnover of £4.2 million for the period 2000–2001.

The company views marketing research as an essential element of strategic business development, either for its own business development, or for specific client requirements. For desk research, MarketingNet buys significantly from Forrester (www.forrester.com), and for other projects, such as focus groups, it uses Millward Brown. There is a paucity of relevant secondary intelligence in this sector, which means that MarketingNet relies heavily on its own 'grass roots' primary research, in particular that based on focus groups or 'scenarios'. Whilst there is a growing 'macro level' body of data on internet usage and trends, there is relatively little available on more specific 'micro-level' trends such as pricing, private Extranets, Intranets, etc. The company is therefore forced to acquire data and turn this into useful knowledge as quickly as possible, as the shelf life of marketing research in internet marketing is very limited. One method of marketing research makes intelligent use of the very medium by which the company supplies its service; as the account director explains:

Clients and prestigious prospects are invited to join an exclusive online network. All members of the Internet Marketing Advisory Board (IMAB) are given password access to the IMAB internet site (www.imab.co.uk) which contains 'white paper' information on emergent thinking in internet marketing. We use sophisticated user-tracking software to build up a profile of users' needs and preferences when they visit the site. From this intelligence we maintain a database which is linked to our telesales activity. Appointments are made only when there is a specific need and budgets/project outlines are agreed. The Internet Marketing Advisory Board is a showcase for our intellectual property and is used as an intelligence gathering tool to generate leads. The Extranet is going to be rolled out as a fee-based subscription service.

In this dynamic sector, access to up-to-date information is the key ingredient in the success of the business: particular attention is paid to the changing environment and demands of customers. Other areas of importance are testing design concepts, the identification of specific market segments, scenario planning, the identification of market opportunities, environmental analysis for different industry sectors, the identification of distributors, and specific links and online promotional opportunities. Design issues are usually addressed through focus group research.

Whilst most of the client websites are produced for the UK market, MarketingNet recognizes that they are likely to be viewed globally; websites are therefore produced in more than one language, giving the client company a truly global coverage.

The company has identified three main competitors, including IXL.com, Agency.com, and Bluewave.com: the activities of these and other competitors are monitored on a weekly basis through their websites and the trade press, such as *New Media Age* and *Revolution*, to check on new products/services offered and new clients won.

Questions

1. In terms of the industry sector in which they operate, what are the major marketing research challenges likely to be faced by MarketingNet over the next 5–10 years?

2. In international markets, what aspects of their website production (other than language differences) might need to be altered? How could these aspects be identified?

3. The company generally tests design issues through focus group research. What other ways of testing design issues can you suggest, and what are the likely strengths and weaknesses of each?

Jonathan S. Swift

References

1. Oppenheim, A. N., *Questionnaire Design, Interviewing and Attitude Measurement*, Pinter Publishers, London, 1992.
2. Barker, R. T., and A. B. Blankenship, 'The manager's guide to survey questionnaire evaluation', *Journal of Market Research Society*, vol. 17, no. 4, October 1975.
3. Gowers, Sir Ernest, *Plain Words; A Guide to the Use of English*, HMSO, London, 1948.
4. 'Peterborough', *The Daily Telegraph*, 27 November 1978.
5. 'Peterborough', *The Daily Telegraph*, 18 December 1980.
6. Morton-Williams, Joan, 'Questionnaire Design', in: *Consumer Market Research Handbook* (3rd edn), ESOMAR/Elsevier, Amsterdam, 1986.
7. Lind, Harold, 'If you ask a silly question', *The Daily Telegraph*, 21 September 1988.
8. Moser, C. A., and G. Kalton, *Survey Methods in Social Investigation*, Heinemann, London, 1971.
9. Richardson, S. A., Dohrenwend, and Klein, *Interviewing – Its Forms and Functions*, Cornell University, Basic Books, 1965.
10. Payne, S. L., *The Art of Asking Questions*, Princeton University Press, 1957.
11. McKennell, A. C., 'Aircraft noise annoyance around London (Heathrow) Airport', Social Survey Report 337, Central Office of Information.
12. Brierley, P. W., 'Ask a silly question!', *Statistical News*, no. 30, August 1975.
13. Gallup, George, 'Qualitative measurement of public opinion. The quintamensional plan of question design', *Public Opinion Quarterly II*, American Institute of Public Opinion, 1947.
14. Belson, William A., 'Respondent misunderstanding of survey questions', Survey Research Centre, LSE, Reprint Series 40, in: Polls, vol. 3, no. 4, 1968.
15. Hague, Paul, *The Industrial Market Research Handbook*, Kogan Page, London, 1992.
16. Whitley, Edward W., 'The case for postal research', *Journal of Market Research Society*, vol. 27, no. 1, 1985.
17. Heberlein, Thomas A., and Robert Baumgartner, 'Is a questionnaire necessary for a second mailing?', *Public Opinion Quarterly*, vol. 45, no. 1, spring 1981.
18. Ferrell, O. C., and Dean Krugman, 'Response patterns and the importance of the follow-up duplicate questionnaire in a mail survey of advertising managers', *European Research*, vol. 11, no. 4, October 1983.
19. Wunder, Gene C., and George W. Wynn, 'The effects of address personalization on mailed questionnaires response rate, time and quality', *Journal of Market Research Society*, vol. 30, no. 1, January 1988.
20. Scott, Christopher, 'Research on mail surveys', *Journal of the Royal Statistical Society*, vol. 24, 1961.
21. Brook, Lindsay L., 'The effect of different postage combinations on response levels and speed of reply', *Journal of Market Research Society*, vol. 20, no. 4, 1978.
22. Linsky, Arnold S., 'Stimulating responses to mail questionnaires: A review', *Public Opinion Quarterly*, vol. 39, spring 1975.
23. Nederhof, Anton J., 'The effects of material incentives in mail surveys' (two studies), *Public Opinion Quarterly*, vol. 47, no. 1, spring 1983.
24. Robertson, Dan H., and Danny N. Bellenger, 'A new method of increasing mail survey responses: contributions to charity', *Journal of Marketing Research*, vol. 15, no. 4, November 1978.
25. Dommeyer, Curt J., 'Does response to an offer of mail survey results interact with questionnaire interest?', *Journal of Market Research*, vol. 27, no. 1, 1985.
26. Fullerton, Sam, and H. Robert Dodge, 'The impact of color on the response rates for mail questionnaires', in: *Developments in Marketing Science*, vol. 10, p. 413, 1988.
27. Dommeyer, Curt, J., Doris Elganayan, and Cliff Umans, 'Increasing mail survey response with an envelope teaser', *Journal of the Market Research Society*, vol. 33, no. 2, April 1991.
28. Skinner, Steven J., and Terry L. Childers, 'Respondent identification in mail surveys', *Journal of Advertising Research*, vol. 20, no. 6, December 1980.
29. Futrell, Charles, and Richard T. Hise, 'The effects of anonymity and a same-day deadline on the response rate to mail surveys', *European Research*, October 1982.
30. Roberts, Robert E., 'Further evidence on using a deadline to stimulate responses to a mail survey', *Public Opinion Quarterly*, vol. 42, no. 3, autumn 1978.
31. Roscoe, A. Martin, Dorothy Lang, and Jagdish N. Sheth, 'Follow-up methods, questionnaire length, and market differences in mail surveys', *Journal of Marketing*, vol. 39, no. 2, April 1975.
32. Eisinger, Richard A., W. Peter Janicki, Robert L. Stevenson, and Wendel L. Thompson, 'Increasing returns in international mail surveys', *Public Opinion Quarterly*, vol. 38, no. 1, spring 1974.
33. Sheth, Jagdish N., Arthur Le Claire, Jnr, and David Wachspress, 'Impact of asking for race information in mail surveys', *Journal of Marketing*, vol. 44, winter 1980.
34. Ognibene, Peter, 'Traits affecting questionnaire response', *Journal of Advertising Research*, vol. 10, no. 3, June 1970.

35. Sudman, Seymour, *The Cost of Surveys*, Aldine Company, Chicago, 1967.
36. Chisnall, Peter M., 'Effecting a high response rate to self-administered household questionnaires', *European Research*, vol. 3, no. 4, July 1976.
37. Turley, Sophie K., 'A case of response rate success', *Journal of the Market Research Society*, vol. 41, no. 3, July 1999.
38. O'Brien, Terry, and Valerie Dugdale, 'Questionnaire administration by computer', *Journal of Market Research Society*, vol. 20, no. 4, 1978.
39. Deacon, Ruth, 'Telephone research matters', *MRS Newsletter*, November 1987.
40. Smith, R. P., and A. F. K. Watson, 'Product excellence on a complex product through telephone interviewing', *European Research*, January 1983.
41. Taylor, Humphrey, 'The very different methods used to conduct telephone surveys of the public', *Journal of the Market Research Society*, vol. 39, no. 3, July 1997.
42. Bergsten, Jane Williams, Michael F. Weeks, and Fred A. Bryan, 'Effects of an advance telephone call in a personal interview survey', *Public Opinion Quarterly*, vol. 48, no. 4, 1984.
43. Gunn, Walter J., and Isabelle N. Rhodes, 'Physician response rates to a telephone survey: effects of monetary incentive level', *Public Opinion Quarterly*, vol. 45, no. 1, 1981.
44. Morton-Williams, Joan, *Interviewer Approaches*, Dartmouth Publishing, Aldershot, 1993.
45. Nicholls, William L. II, 'Development of CATI at the US Census Bureau', Proceedings of the *American Statistical Association Survey Methods Section*, Toronto, Canada, 1983.
46. Fry, Paul, 'The use of sequential sampling techniques (SST), in market research', *Market Research Society Conference Proceedings*, 1983.
47. Slingsby, Helen, 'A high street revolution', the *Financial Times*, 30 September 1990.
48. Bigham, Jane, 'A new approach to international fragrance research', in: *Comparability Across Borders. Seminar on International Marketing Research*, ESOMAR, Amsterdam, November 1988.
49. Knight, I. B., 'Smooth change to CAPI', letter to editor, *Research*, November 1992, Market Research Society.
50. de Leeuw, Edith D., Joop J. Hox, and Ger Snijkers, 'The effect of computer-assisted interviewing on data quality', in *Journal of the Market Research Society*, vol. 37, no. 4, October 1995.
51. Bartram, Mary M., and Antony E. C. Eastaugh, 'Let respondents speak for themselves!', Market Research Society Conference, 1981.
52. *Social Trends 30*, Office for National Statistics (ONS), 2000.
53. Higgins, C. A., T. P. Dimnik, and H. P. Greenwood, 'The DISKQ survey method', *Journal of Market Research Society*, vol. 29, no. 4, October 1987.
54. Saris, Willem E., and W. Marius de Pijper, 'Computer assisted interviewing using home computers', *European Research*, vol. 14, no. 3, July 1986.
55. Tse, Alan C. B., 'Computing the response rate, speed and response quality of two methods of sending questionnaires: e-mail vs mail', *Journal of the Market Research Society*, vol. 40, no. 4, October 1998.
56. Moseley, Dominic, 'Information needs for market entry', *Journal of the Market Research Society*, vol. 38, no. 1, January 1996.
57. Perrott, Nicky, guest editorial, *Journal of the Market Research Society*, vol. 41, no. 4, October 1999.
58. Basi, Ramit K., 'WWW response rates to socio-demographic items', *Journal of the Market Research Society*, vol. 41, no. 4, October 1999.
59. Kent, Ray and Matthew Lee, 'Using the internet for market research: a study of private trading on the internet', *Journal of the Market Research Society*, vol. 41, no. 4, October 1999.
60. Comley, Pete, 'Research hits the web site', *Research*, Market Research Society Special Report, 1998.
61. Kehoe, Louise, 'Hooked into the on-line market', a *Financial Times* Guide 'Doing Business on-line', *Financial Times*, December 1996.
62. Walker, David, 'But does the reality fit the theory?', *Research*, Market Research Society, June 1996.
63. Taylor, Humphrey, 'Does internet research work?', *International Journal of Market Research*, Winter 1999/2000, vol. 42, issue 1.
64. Johnston, Alex, 'Welcome to the wired world', *Research*, Market Research Society, November 1999.
65. Blyth, Bill, 'Current and future technology utilization in European market research', in: *Computer Assisted Survey Collection*, Mick Couper (ed.), Wiley, 1998.
66. 'i-modest success', *The Economist*, vol. 354, no. 8161, 11 March 2000.

Interviewing

Learning Objectives

- Understand nature and contributions of interviewing to effective market research practice

- Note need for flexibility in interviewing styles according to research tasks

- Recognize dangers of interviewer effect/bias in interviewing

- Note bias arising from non-response

6.1 Introduction

Questionnaires and interviewing are virtually inseparable topics: they are opposite sides of the same coin, so discussion in Chapter 5 has, inevitably, tended to flow from one to the other because of their interdependence. In this chapter, the specific nature of the research interview and the important role of the interviewer are explored.

In the early days of market and social research surveying, 'it was thought that any intelligent person could do a survey', as Jean Morton-Williams[1] alleged after a lifetime in survey organizations. For too long the interviewer had been the 'Cinderella of the survey industry', but fortunately there is now increased recognition of the vital role of the interviewer in successful surveys, although the 'status of the survey interviewer remains low'.[1] However, standards have improved and the Market Research Society has consistently championed good interviewing practices through the Interviewer Quality Control Scheme.

The growing sophistication of methods of interviewing resulting from computer technology and the internet have possibly tended to downgrade the significance of professional interviewing. But it is well to remember that with in-home research, face-to-face interviews are still important. The methodology is, of course, traditional and, perhaps, outmoded by the new generation of dynamic systems discussed in Chapter 5. It is, nevertheless, remarkably flexible and capable of collecting research data of impressive quality. In some cases, personal face-to-face interviewing would seem to be the only way to conduct sophisticated enquiries or those likely to give rise to feelings of social embarrassment or inhibitions. Qualitative research, discussed in the next chapter, uses to advantage the skills of professional moderators in group discussions and focus groups.

6.2 Definition of interview

An interview has been defined as: 'a conversation directed to a definite purpose other than satisfaction in the conversation itself'.[2] It is concerned with a purposeful exchange of meanings, and it is this interaction between the interviewer and the respondent which contributes so much to the success of the interview. The psychological atmosphere of an interview is at least as important as the mechanics of the interviewing process, for effective interviewing requires 'insight into the dynamics of interaction'.[3] If this interaction is treated with skill and sensitivity, the data collected during the interview will be accurate and, perhaps, unique. The quality of the interview depends largely on the interviewer developing a relationship with the respondent which will encourage good communication. This is a two-way process to which both interviewer and respondent subscribe in fulfilling their particular roles. The distinctive role of the interviewer is concerned with securing valid information about a particular problem which has been carefully defined in the objectives of the survey. But an interview is not, as Oppenheim[1] points out, an ordinary conversation, although he concedes that while the exploratory interview appears similar in some respects it is essentially a one-way process, and must be so or else 'it will lose much of its value because of the biases introduced by the interviewer'.[4]

The interview must, therefore, be directed and controlled by the interviewer if it is to fulfil its essential function of a conversation with a purpose.[2] The techniques used should be those that are most likely to result in data which will satisfy these objectives. Flexibility is, therefore, an important attribute of the interviewing process, and there is no one ideal method which can be applied generally. There are some techniques which are more appropriate than others in particular cases; the success of the survey rests on the skill with which the interviews have been devised.

Where the information to be gathered from each respondent is of a similar kind, e.g. consumer buying habits, and it is planned to submit identical questions to all respondents, some form of standardized questionnaire can generally be constructed to be administered in the same way to all those taking part in the survey. This materially assists in the analysis and processing of data.

An alternative form of the standardized (or structured) interview replaces the formal questionnaire by allowing interviewers to vary the wording or sequence of questions in order to attract maximum response from individual informants. This method is discussed in Chapter 5.

It is particularly suitable where respondents are likely to be heterogeneous and the subject matter of the survey includes topics which are not customarily discussed freely. The interviewer is free to choose the most suitable timing for certain questions, though this imposes greater personal responsibility, and also makes recording and analysis more difficult.

It is possible, of course, to combine 'schedule' and 'non-schedule' interviews effectively by treating simple factual details in a systematic manner and applying a more flexible approach to questions covering more sensitive areas of behaviour, or those which may be more vulnerable to language barriers.

The other general classification of interview, typified as non-standardized, does not attempt a systematic collection of the same classes of data from every respondent. There are many varieties of unstructured interviews, and they are often used as a preliminary to prepare the structure for more formalized techniques. In this way, the salient features of a problem can be identified, though valid comparisons of individual behaviour are not possible.

In Chapter 7, yet another type of interview, termed depth discussion or focus group, will be discussed. This kind of research, which calls for special skills, is concerned with survey topics for which direct questioning would not be likely to result in valid information being given by respondents, perhaps for reasons of self-defence, or because they may rationalize their behaviour when answering 'straight' questions. This indirect approach to gathering 'sensitive' information could not be undertaken by the general level of survey interviewers. The method is also expensive and is, therefore, limited in its application.

6.3 Forms of interview

Three forms of interview are commonly used:

1. *Limited response*: the informant is expected to respond to a series of questions, generally administered in a predetermined order. Closed questions tend to outnumber substantially open questions. As the description suggests, the scope of the informant's response is distinctly limited: the topic is closely defined and the respondent is expected to reply in a few words.

2. *Free response*: gives the respondent a great deal of freedom in answering questions arising from some general points of discussion made by the interviewer. Open questions are more general than closed questions, and the interviewer has the delicate

task of encouraging the respondent to take an active part in the interview while, at the same time, keeping irrelevant discussion to a minimum.

3. *Defensive response*: the interviewer attempts to exert some pressure on the respondent over a range of topics, and the latter is expected to defend himself or herself by refusing to be forced into any situation which is not really agreeable. There are few published examples of this type of interview, and it has been sharply criticized as being antithetical to well-established survey practice, namely, the establishment of a good relationship between respondent and interviewer. Kinsey, in his surveys of sexual behaviour, used the technique widely, and his respondents do not appear to have objected to his style of interviewing. Some of his informants apparently found the topic so absorbing that they were tempted to enlarge on their actual experiences.

It may well be possible to incorporate more than one of these techniques in a particular interview, so that the attention of the respondent is kept, especially through a long interview.

KEYPOINT

An interview involves:

A conversation with a defined intention

A purposeful exchange of meanings

A psychological experience

A process of interaction between interviewee and interviewer

Various methods of questioning and styles of interviewing

Limited response; free response; defensive response

6.4 Interviewing techniques adjusted to types of respondent

It has been noted that there are sensitive areas of enquiry which need skill and delicacy on the part of the interviewer in order to attract cooperation. These 'threatening' or 'taboo' subjects cover personal and intimate matters, which respondents may be reluctant to discuss openly, perhaps fearing that self-revelation *may* possibly disclose deviations from norms. To be successful in such cases, the interviewer must be able to adjust his technique to the needs of the respondent. He or she should, therefore, form some estimate of the personality of the person being interviewed. Admittedly, this is no easy task, for it is known that 'one of the most disconcerting sources of error in judging personality is the tendency for judgements on specific traits to be reflections of the interviewer's general impression of people'.[2]

This 'halo' effect, identified by Thorndike in 1920, was refined by Bingham (1939), who distinguished between the valid and invalid halo. The former refers to the tendency for ratings to reflect the actual correlation among themselves, e.g. there will probably be some relationship between 'emotional maturity' and 'dependability', since they are, in fact, correlated. 'Invalid halo refers to the excess of overlap beyond that to be expected due to correlation among the traits under consideration.'

Years ago, Walter Lippmann drew attention to the phenomenon termed 'stereotype'; that we frequently have 'pictures in our heads' of the supposed appearance of members of a given race, class, occupation, or social group. In 1926, Rice clearly showed the power of 'stereotypes' in affecting judgement, and Paterson (1930),[5] after careful study of this problem, stated that 'The impression that personality can be judged from physical appearance is a myth which stubbornly defies extinction'.

The classical study done by Sir Charles Goring, of the English prison service, at the beginning of the twentieth century, to disprove that there is a specific criminal type with recognizable physical stigmata, effectively disposed of this misleading assumption. However, Bingham and Moore suggest 'there may well be some connection between anatomy and physiology, with temperament and ability, but it is not obvious or readily observable'.[2]

It is as well for interviewers to bear in mind that this phenomenon may influence their relationship with respondents and, to some extent, bias the interview. Because of the interpersonal nature of interviews, respondents also may form a stereotyped judgement of interviewers, and refuse to cooperate or respond unwillingly. The subtle influence of stereotypes may, therefore, extend to both parties in an interview.

Motivation within an interview can be either extrinsic or intrinsic. Extrinsic motivation occurs when a communication is made in order to influence, in some way, the person addressed. For example, the communicator may feel it worth while to give certain information in the hope or belief that it will lead to some desired change or action taking place. There is some expectancy of a 'pay-off' of some personal benefit. Intrinsic motivation depends more directly on the personal relationship between interviewer and respondent, who may feel disposed to talk freely about matters of interest even though the interview will not benefit him or her directly. This intrinsic motivation is at the heart of a good interview, and it again underlines the importance of the interviewer, who must be able to establish sound social relationships of goodwill and trust with those being interviewed. He or she should not attempt to 'score off' the respondent, arousing suspicions and encouraging the use of defensive tactics, such as suppression, rationalization, and repression. Lack of trust or confidence merely buries the repressed material deeper: 'direct probing or clever subterfuges more often than not merely increase motivation to keep repressed material hidden'.[2]

The fact that certain needs are repressed does not prevent them from influencing behaviour. Interviews make certain demands on informants; they should be encouraged to respond with a natural flow of information, and helped to overcome fears and inhibitions which may frustrate the purpose of the interview.

KEYPOINT

Motivation within an interview:

either *extrinsic*
or   *intrinsic*

Extrinsic motivation e.g. expectation of 'pay-off'

Intrinsic motivation: heart of good interview and underlines importance of interviewer

Respondents should be encouraged, not coerced

6.5 Interviewers

The interaction between those taking part in an interview is vital to the success of this method of obtaining information. Relations between the parties are complex, and are coloured by both conscious and unconscious reactions which can distort or, happily, attract communication.

Interviewers are active in the area of marketing research which frequently involves submitting questionnaires to carefully selected samples of a defined population. They are an important and essential link in the chain of research and their efficiency and reliability influence the whole structure of research. It is unfortunately evident that interviewers are one of the main sources of error in field research. Although some research has been done on interviewer selection and training methods, there does not appear to have been a great improvement on the unsatisfactory situation which Boyd and Westfall[6] reported in 1955. They recommended then that there should be systematic research on the development of criteria for selecting, training, and supervising interviewers. More recently, Moser[7] has indicated that the selection, training, and supervision of interviewers are closely bound up with response errors.

Selection of marketing research interviewers is a difficult task because it is frequently hard to assess the suitability of candidates. It would seem that there is no such person as a good 'interviewer-type' with definable characteristics. Interviewing is such a personal matter that some types of people seem to be better for some kinds of survey than for others, and to be able to establish *rapport* more easily with some respondents than with others. There appears to be a strong argument in favour of fitting interviewers to interviewing situations, and selecting applicants for their likely aptitude for specific areas of research. This means that selectors must have intimate knowledge of the nature of the surveys for which they are recruiting staff. An interviewer profile should be drawn up as a guide to the selection of candidates.

The selection process will probably be based on the scrutiny of application forms, which should give a useful indication of the ability of candidates to complete, accurately and neatly, detailed information. These background data will give personal details of value in forming a shortlist for interview. At the interview, some clerical tests could be set to assess the general suitability of the applicant to undertake fairly routine work. There is no general agreement on the value of intelligence and aptitude tests in the selection of interviewers, for some applicants appear to be able to pass such tests without ever being able to conduct a satisfactory interview.

The 'dummy-interview' technique, normally applied after the candidate has been initially selected, can be extremely effective in isolating good interviewers from those less suitable. It involves exposing interviewers to a series of interview situations which have been 'rigged', and in which informants are in collusion with the sponsors. 'Difficult' situations can be simulated to test and evaluate interviewers' reactions. The information they are able to collect is assessed against already known data. While this type of test is valuable, it tends to be costly in time and money, but it may well be worthwhile where investigations cover areas of critical importance.

In practice, interviewers seem to be selected in various ways, some more systematic than others. Leading research organizations tend to have more rigorous methods of selection. These methods are particularly effective with the Government Social Survey which employs about 200 part-time interviewers throughout the UK. The British Market Research Bureau (BMRB) has paid particular attention to the recruitment and training of interviewers; only 1 in 10 of those who apply to join BMRB's field force is eventually employed.

A three and a half day general training programme involves market research theory and practice, including 'live' interviewing under supervision. BMRB's standard quality procedures entail regular field supervision of interviewers (twice a year; also a 10 per cent personal check of all surveys); the first day's work is done with a supervisor. The average interviewer has at least two years' BMRB interviewing experience; supervisors have an average of more than 10 years with the company.

Experienced researchers are concerned about the quality of interviewing in general. Selection processes often appear to be arbitrary and unrelated to the importance of the task. If marketing research is to develop improved techniques leading to greater validity and reliability, the role of the interviewer deserves serious consideration.

Sound methods of selection can contribute significantly to the reduction or even eradication of some of the biases that, unfortunately, are prone to distort interviewing.

A Working Party Report[8] of the Market Research Society gave guidance on factors such as age, personality type, speech, and education which were considered to be of primary importance for the selection of suitable interviewers.

A substantial proportion of market research interviewing is undertaken by women, mostly on a part-time basis. The Market Research Society Working Party Report[9] noted that women interviewers tend to be preferred for several reasons, among which are that: they are more suitable for interviewing housewives; they are available fairly readily; they have a natural aptitude for routine and repetitive work; they are equally acceptable to interviewees of both sexes; they are not so aggressive; and they are more likely to be invited into homes when fairly lengthy interviews are necessary. However, 50 per cent of BMRB's panel of interviewers are male. Joan MacFarlane-Smith[9] has observed that men who are available for part-time interviewing tend to be 'untypical and non-homogeneous', but that they are often preferred to women for industrial and technical interviewing and then usually on a full-time basis.

Effective selection needs to be followed by a systematic training. The character of this will vary according to the experience of the recruits and the nature of the work they are expected to do. Basically it should cover the general objectives of the survey, the survey methods, and the techniques of interviewing. Some practice sessions should be included, and it would be helpful to distribute a training handbook to new members of the research team. It is important that they have a clear understanding of the responsibility which interviewing bears to the success of the whole research operation.

As with selection methods, the techniques used in interviewer training vary considerably from formal short courses, which include supervised fieldwork and periodic assessment, down to virtually no actual training, survival being dependent on achieving an acceptable level of competence in the field. Again, the Government Social Survey has a well-organized training programme for interviewers; the BMRB's interview scheme has already been given in outline.

The value of experience to interviewers was the subject of research done by Durbin and Stuart[10] to assess the success of experienced professional and inexperienced student interviewers in *obtaining* interviews. The former were from the Government Social Survey and the British Institute of Public Opinion, and the latter from the London School of Economics. There was a striking difference in the 'success rates' (questionnaire wholly or partially completed) between the two classes of interviewers, though there was hardly any difference between GSS interviewers and BIPO interviewers. This is an interesting finding in view of the extra training undergone by GSS interviewers.

The effectiveness of short, intensive training courses against longer, more extensive courses, was studied by the American Bureau of the Census in 1951, and its findings were strongly qualified. It was conceded that shorter courses might, in fact, be adequate, provided they covered the essential features of interviewing.

Jean Morton-Williams has observed that it is sometimes said that effective interviewers are 'born not made'; this belies 'the fact that experienced interviewers tend to achieve higher response rates than new interviewers'.[11]

Some training is obviously necessary, but the small amount of research which has been published (some of which is now rather old) does not provide an adequate basis on which to form valid judgement. Further research is desirable, and meanwhile practitioners should at least give their staff a thorough briefing on the objectives of the survey, so that they are able to appreciate the value of their contribution as interviewers.

Some system of field supervision is necessary in order to maintain the quality of interviewing; the Government Social Survey operates well-organized systems of supervision on a regional basis. The local supervisor is a valuable link in communication between head office and interviewing staff. Some systematic check, often 10 per cent of calls made by interviewers, should be the responsibility of the supervisor. Completed questionnaires should be scrutinized for inaccuracies or inconsistencies, and results obtained by individual interviewers compared to detect possible biases. If response rates are found to vary substantially, the supervisor should investigate the work of those interviewers who fail to achieve certain accepted standards. As in other areas of management, acceptable standards of achievement are laid down and deviations from norms are subjected to special investigation to establish the causes. The supervisor should not be content with mere 'policing' of the activities of interviewers. A vital part of the supervisory task is to motivate field staff by positive training methods, encouraging them to achieve better response rates, advising them on the inevitable problems which will arise, and generally building up morale in an occupation which, at times, exposes people to considerable frustration.

Morale will tend to be affected by the interviewers' own evaluation of their role in the survey process; success in obtaining satisfactory interviews will contribute to their self-esteem. Also, acceptable response rates are partly dependent on interviewer morale; therefore, the quality of the research findings will be at risk.

Morale is affected by working conditions, which include the type and level of payment. Pay rates are generally low for interviewers, and no doubt this contributes to the high labour turnover. Some professional surveys operate differential rates and interviewers are graded, as in the Government Social Survey which has four grades determining remuneration and type of work involved. Survey interviewing can be arduous, both physically and mentally; it calls for painstaking and conscientious attention to detail with an ability to assess the character of the respondent. Where informal interviewing takes place, the responsibility of the interviewer is considerable and great skill and background knowledge are demanded. The success of interviews depends so much on the quality of interviewing, that it would seem prudent to recruit the right type of applicant by offering attractive terms of payment and reasonable types of assignment.

In order to protect professional standards and to allay any possible fears experienced by members of the public approached for interviewing purposes, the Market Research Society, in 1981, introduced the MRS Interviewer Identity Card system. This well-devised scheme has the full support of the leading survey firms, and it forms part of the MRS Code of Conduct. (See Chapters 12 and 13 for further discussion, and also refer to the MRS's initiative to protect the quality of telephone interviewing, as given in Chapter 5.) The MRS Interviewer Identity Card (MRS IID Card) enables an individual member of the public to check the genuineness of the intended interview.

Interviewer quality control scheme (IQCS)

This scheme is jointly run by the Market Research Society Quality Control, The Association of Market Survey Organizations, the Association of British Market Research Companies, the Association of Users of Research Agencies, and a number of companies in the UK. The 'basic philosophy of the IQCS is, firstly, that a properly trained and managed interviewer will do better work than one who is less well trained and managed . . . The second strand . . . is that clients have a right to know that certain standards of data validation are undertaken and documented'.[12] Survey organizations subscribing to this scheme are visited by quality control inspectors who audit their research operations with the common objective of maintaining and raising the standards of fieldwork. The IQCS has 'at its disposal a wide range of sanctions against those who do not "come up to scratch" '.[12]

KEYPOINT

Dynamics of interviewing

Effective interviewing depends on successful interaction

Interviewer is important link in chain of research

Selection, training and supervision important

Strong support for 'fitting' interviewers to interviewing situations

Advisable to draw up interviewer profile

Supervision should aim to motivate, to build morale

6.6 Duties of interviewers

Interviewers are responsible for collecting specific kinds of information that meet the objectives of particular surveys. Interviewers are a major influence on this process of communication which may relate to many different topics demanding, at times, expert knowledge as in highly technical enquiries. Aspects of this type of interviewing are discussed in Chapter 12. The majority of marketing research surveys, however, do not require interviewers to have knowledge in depth of the area of research. They should be given sufficient information about the subject of the survey and its objectives to enable them to do a worthwhile job of interviewing.

First duty of interviewers

The first duty of interviewers is to locate people who fulfil the requirements of the chosen method of sampling. With random samples respondents are pre-selected and interviewers are given lists of randomly selected persons who are to be interviewed. The responsibility of interviewers is limited to making effective contact with those listed. They will be given instructions on the problem of non-response, call-backs, etc. In quota sampling, interviewers have greater personal responsibility as they select respondents, within the limits of quota controls set by the researcher. This greater freedom is not without some danger to the quality of the survey findings, though it makes the task of interviewers rather less onerous.

Second duty of interviewers

The second responsibility of interviewers is to translate contacts into effective interviews. This may sometimes involve several call-backs in the case of random sampling, so interviewers need to be persistent and tactful. It is really quite surprising how willing people are to be interviewed, and after a preliminary warming-up period, how freely they are prepared to talk about a wide range of topics. Interviewers are frequently faced with the problem of limiting responses to the specific area of the survey. People's co-operation should not, however, be taken for granted. Interviewers should introduce themselves, briefly, perhaps by showing a card or letter of authorization, particularly when home interviews are planned. They should then outline the nature of the survey, the reasons why it is being done, and the method of sampling used. Very often people are curious to know why they, in particular, have been selected for interview, and interviewers should set aside any likely suspicions by giving a simple account of the technique used. In explaining the application of quota sampling methods, some tact is advisable as respondents may not necessarily agree with the interviewer's opinion of their social and economic grading; reference to specific personal details should, therefore, be avoided.

Interviewers should endeavour to build up empathy, which 'can cover a very broad spectrum of feeling'.[1] Essentially, it is the ability of an individual to respond sensitively and imaginatively to the feelings of another person. An interviewer may, through their approach, personality and behaviour 'project confidence, interest and warm friendliness'.[1] This may well evoke a similar response from an informant, which would make rejection difficult. Informants might feel guilty of unkindness and selfishness, and their own self-esteem would be lessened, unless there was a strong reason, such as a family crisis, why they felt unable to participate in a survey.[1]

Third duty of interviewers

The third duty of interviewers is to secure valid and reliable answers to questions, which may be formally presented in a structured interview or administered at the discretion of individual interviewers. The answers to questions provide the raw material which is processed into survey findings. It is, therefore, important that questions should be carefully worded and presented so that they lead to answers which give information useful to the objectives of the survey.

Some uniformity is obviously desirable in the course of a survey, and interviewers need to be trained to achieve comparable efficiency in handling questionnaires. Researchers have to remain alert to the dangers of interviewers changing the form of questions, even by just a word, or of elaborating standardized questions. In some cases interviewers are allowed to 'probe' and to follow up respondents' chance remarks, but these activities should be authorized before the survey takes place.

The wording, sequence, and presentation of questions fundamentally influence the responses given. Interviewers are human beings, subject to individual variations in behaviour, and they react in various ways to the circumstances of a particular interview. While researchers aim to achieve uniformity in the interviewing process, the risks of bias arising from interviewers' non-conformity cannot possibly be completely eradicated. The design of questionnaires should encourage positive reactions from interviewers rather than tempt them to change questions to satisfy their personal interpretations.

Fourth duty of interviewers

The fourth duty of interviewers concerns the recording of responses given during interviews. These must be accurately reflected in the opinions of those who were interviewed, and this calls for conscientious attention to detail with particular emphasis on objectivity. The sampling method chosen by the researchers must be faithfully adhered to, even if it results in some personal inconvenience, such as call-backs to secure interviews where random sampling is used. Interviewers experience fatigue, psychological as well as physical, and they need strong motivation to maintain consistently high standards of interviewing. Field supervision has an important role to play in the continued training and encouragement of interviewers to achieve these standards.

Interviewers also need to understand all the details of recording, such as the coding of answers and the use of some agreed pre-coding system. Coding should be consistent throughout the interviews, otherwise the survey findings will not be valid.

During their training, interviewers should be checked for their ability to record, in some detail, responses given to a series of set questions. Trainers should endeavour to identify individual biases which can be revealed by comparing data collected with known characteristics of the population.

In addition to completing question-and-answer sequences in questionnaires, interviewers should record useful observational data about respondents, such as their general reaction and behaviour during the interview. Comments like these add to the value of surveys.

KEYPOINT  **Duties of interviewers**

1. Responsible for collecting specific data from respondents (a) specified in random listing or (b) according to quota controls

2. Translate contacts into effective interviews (with random sampling, call-backs likely)

3. Secure valid and reliable answers to questions, and be alert to dangers of bias

4. Conscientiously record responses as given (ensure coding of answers used correctly), and record useful observational data about respondents

---

6.7 Characteristics of interviewers

The personality of the interviewer is crucial to the success of the interview. Interpersonal relationships are formed during the interviewing process and, as noted, the success of the interview depends so much on personal factors. These are difficult to isolate and apply indiscriminately in assessing the suitability or otherwise of individual interviewers.

However, Bingham and Moore,[2] as a result of their considerable studies in this area, have suggested that in order to be successful, an interviewer must be: 'fairly well put together himself '; capable of reacting empathically to the other person, unhampered by personal predispositions; and be widely read and extremely thoughtful about personality and its dynamics.

In fact, the successful interviewer appears to possess qualities which are not all that widely spread. People who are fortunate enough to have these endowments may not be able or willing to act as interviewers. Selection will have to be made from those who apply for this type of work. The successful applicants should be trained to become more aware of themselves, of the influence they have on others, and of the vital need for objectivity in all research activities.

High intelligence and education are not essential for general survey interviewing; the levels should be adequate for the specific tasks of individual surveys. As with other occupations of a repetitive nature, it would be unwise to employ people of too high a calibre on routine investigations, as they would soon experience boredom and probably leave the task uncompleted.

Research[13] at the Survey Methods Centre of City University Business School revealed that the following interviewer characteristics affected success in obtaining interviews: experience, training, and communication skills. The key to success was the flexibility of the interviewer, particularly when problems were encountered in interviewing.

6.8 Interviewer effect

The problem of bias in survey practice was referred to in Chapter 2 and also in subsequent discussion, and it will now be considered in connection with interviewing. Bias arises, unfortunately, from several causes: faulty sampling frames and non-representative samples, poorly designed questionnaires, low rates of response, false answers (deliberate or accidental), as well as errors at the stages of analysis and interpretation of data. Added to this woeful list is the bias which may occur because of the influence exerted on respondents by interviewers.

The phenomenon known as 'interviewer effect' or bias occurs when the influence of the interviewer on the respondent is such that it results in responses that do not accurately reflect the attitudes and opinions of the respondent. There are many sources of interviewer bias, some of which can be dealt with effectively by sound methods of selection, training, and supervision. Other biases may be more difficult to identify and may be largely covert. 'The possibility has long been recognized that two interviewers, asking questions of the same respondent, might obtain different answers.'[14] Despite the fact that features of a survey such as questionnaire design, common briefing of interviewees, or sampling arrangements may be identical, the interviewer effect persists.

Research on the influence of interviewers on survey information started when, as the result of careful scrutiny, unusual patterns in responses to survey questioning became evident. Classical research on the tendency for personality characteristics and attitudes to intrude in the interview was done by Stuart Rice.[15]

In 1914, the New York Commissioner of Public Charities ordered a study of the physical, mental, and social characteristics of 2000 destitute men, who applied for a night's rest at the municipal lodging house. They were interviewed systematically by trained social workers, each interview taking between 20 and 30 minutes and covering four pages of questions. When the results were carefully examined, it became apparent that there were consistent patterns in certain kinds of answers recorded by two of the interviewers, although these differed remarkably between the two investigators. One of the questions asked each man to give an explanation of his destitution, whereas the other interviewer attributed it more to social and economic conditions, such as hard times, lay-offs, etc.

What was even more interesting emerged when the explanations of the destitute men themselves were studied. They also attributed their miserable condition principally to excessive drinking on the one hand, and poor social environment on the other. In fact, they reflected the consistent biases of the interviewers.

It was subsequently discovered that the first interviewer was an ardent prohibitionist, and the other was a socialist. Both were well-trained, conscientious, and experienced investigators, probably unaware of how their attitudes were biasing results. Not only were *their* judgements biased, but the actual statements of the men interviewed appeared to have suffered contagion.

Personality factors, such as age, sex, social group, and attitudes, seem, however, to be less influential than interviewers' expectations of the responses to the survey. Bias of this nature arises where interviewers expect respondents to show consistent attitudes throughout their answers, and in cases where later responses are rather vague and interviewers interpret them in the light of attitudes revealed by earlier answers. Interviewers may also interpret marginal answers according to the typical answers which they would expect from the kinds of person being interviewed. This 'stereotype' influence has already been noted.

Kahn and Cannell[3] emphasize that each person comes to an interview with many firmly fixed attitudes, personality characteristics, motives, and goals. Each participant has a 'constellation of characteristics' reflecting group memberships and group loyalties; these may well be potential sources of bias in the interviewing process.

If the two parties to an interview differ widely in their personality characteristics and experience, their attitudes and motivations are likely to be substantially different from one another. This will tend to make mutual understanding more difficult to achieve and could lead to bias. It has been suggested that interviewers should be matched closely to respondents in vital personal characteristics.

Whether it is preferable to have either men or women interviewers is a matter on which opinions vary: the subject of the survey, the place and time of the interview and, in the case of multi-racial societies, ethnic conventions, may all be influencing factors. It is, of course, the perceptions of prospective respondents which are at issue: how these (and other factors) affect their willingness, or otherwise, to become involved in a process of interrogation, no matter how benign.

There is research evidence that people in some circumstances are more willing to help female than male interviewers, and that the latter 'tend to get significantly lower response rates than females'.[1] However, this differential declines when levels of experience are also considered. When surveys concern sensitive subjects – which generally tend to get relatively high refusal rates – it is advisable that mature and experienced interviewers should be used, as these have been proved able to attract significantly better response rates than those less experienced.

Face-to-face interviewing of particular sectors of the community, such as the elderly, the disabled, or young children needs to be handled with special consideration, and the agreement of parents and carers should be obtained beforehand. In family situations, it would appear that women interviewers are more likely to attract co-operation.

In a survey[16] to assess the demand for campaign medals after the Second World War, it was found that ex-servicemen when interviewed by elderly women interviewers, indicated more definite interest in decoration than when they were interviewed by young women.

In Western society, survey practitioners largely work within their own culture which for many years has accepted and understood the nature and purpose of surveys. In Europe, including some parts of Britain, there are now fairly high densities of ethnic communities with distinctive sub-cultural traditions. There are likely to be some differences in reactions when interviewers seek to conduct interviews in such environments, especially where language differences form a significant barrier to communication, particularly in older age-groups. Ethnic matching of interviewers and respondents has 'long been accepted as important in surveys dealing with matters concerning racial issues'.[1] With opportunities for education and professional training, a degree of acculturation is likely over the generations, so traditional inhibitions about being interviewed may be largely dissipated.

Several investigations, mostly in the United States, have been concerned with the effects of disparity in race between interviewer and interviewee in personal surveys. As Collins[14] has observed: 'The one interviewer characteristic that seems consistently to be important is that of race.' Most studies have focused on the effects on Black respondents of being interviewed by white interviewers who constitute the majority of professional interviewing staff.

Weeks and Moore[17] have investigated the effects of interviewer ethnic origins involving non-Black ethnic minorities; 1472 elementary school children from four districts: Miami (Cubans), El Paso (Chicanos), NE Arizona (native Americans), and San Francisco (Chinese), were surveyed by 101 interviewers (50 ethnics; 51 non-ethnics), who were carefully selected for their interviewing experience.

Twenty pairs of interviewers were randomly selected; each pair consisting of the interviewer who was not of the respondent's ethnic group and who did not speak the respondent's language and one interviewer who was of the same ethnic group and who did speak the respondent's language. From subsequent analysis, it was found that, as with black/white situations, a difference in ethnicity between interviewer and respondent did not appear to affect survey responses to non-sensitive questions. 'It should also be pointed out that in the survey as a whole the non-ethnic interviewers seemed to be at no disadvantage working with an ethnic sample *vis-à-vis* the ethnic interviewers, and actually outperformed the latter slightly on the basis of response rate and field costs.'

Another study[18] focused on the more unusual phenomenon of white respondents surveyed by Black interviewers in metropolitan Detroit. Results indicated that white respondents were 'at least as susceptible to race-of-interviewer effects as black respondents, and they thus call into question earlier interpretations which focused entirely on asymmetrical racial deference'. Respondents of both cases appear anxious to avoid responses that might offend interviewers of the 'opposing' race, and tend to be franker with interviewers of their own race. 'Tentative evidence' suggests that the more educated whites are likely to have the strongest urge to appear tolerant and are, therefore, more inclined to emphasize liberal views when interviewed by Blacks. Whether a comparable bias arises with educated Black respondents and white interviewers seems to be uncertain.

An investigation[19] into whether race-of-interviewer effect is also present in telephone interviews was undertaken with a random sample of Alabama residents 18 years of age and older: 590 individuals were contacted of whom 548 answered the question asking their race. The results of this study were 'consistent with previous findings concerning a race-of-interviewer effect in other forms of surveying', viz. race of interviewer has little or no effect on non-racial questions; race of interviewer does have some effect on some, but not all racial questions; and on racial questions, respondents interviewed by an interviewer of another race were more 'deferential' to that race than are respondents interviewed by a member of their own race. The researchers, however, draw attention to the nature of the research location in which race is specially salient. In other situations these particular findings may not be applicable.

In 1992, the Harris Research Group surveyed, on behalf of a London borough, unemployment among young West Indian males. In a pilot study, half of the sample were interviewed by white interviewers, the other half by interviewers from their own peer group. When asked about what efforts they had made to secure work, respondents told white interviewers that they consistently sought work by daily visits to Job Centres, applying for interviews, scouring local job advertisements, etc. However, the peer-group interviewers were told by their respondents that they did only what was necessary to continue to draw benefits. The truth, it was noted,[20] was probably somewhere between the extremes of reported behaviour, but it was said to illustrate clearly that bias can arise from using unsuitable research interviewers. However, with other research projects, such as haircare and make-up, it was reported that the interviewers' own origins had no effect at all on the responses.

But interviewing Asians can be problematic because of language and other cultural barriers; for example, conservative Muslims would be greatly offended if a woman attempted to interview a man – and vice versa. Language differences may impose special problems for interviewing, because of the diversity of several major Asian languages (Urdu, Punjabi, Hindi, Gujarati, Bengali or Chinese).[20] Fortunately, as Jean Morton-Williams[1] observes, many Asians speak more than one Asian language fluently.

In a review of the problem of interviewer variability, Collins[14] has noted that within the panels of interviewers recruited by professional interviewing organizations, there is no evidence to suggest that one type of interviewer tends to obtain different answers from another, and that there is no reason to recommend that recruitment should be concentrated among women rather than men, or among the middle-aged rather than the young or the old; the question of training is vitally important.

In another paper,[21] Collins reported a carefully planned experiment for the OPCS over 32 electoral wards to evaluate the effects of (i) interviewer variability in asking the questions or in interpreting and recording responses, and (ii) the geographical clustering of interviews into electoral wards – each ward was covered by two interviewers. Overall, the two effects were found to be of similar scale, but while interviewer effects tended to be stronger for attitudinal items, sample design effects tended to be stronger for factual items.

In approaching the problem of area and interviewer variance, it was observed that these are, of course, radically different aspects of research methodology. 'The former is inescapable: only its effects can be moderated by the avoidance of excessive sample clustering. The latter can – at least in principle – be tackled through questionnaire design, pre-testing and interviewer instruction.'[21]

An extensive study[22] of interviewer variability was connected with the purchasing and attitudinal patterns of adults who regularly travel abroad from the UK. Interviewers were subjectively graded according to relative ability on a scale 10 (best) to 1 (poor); in practice the actual scores ranged from 3 to 9. In addition, interviewers were set quotas running from 10, 20, 30, to 40. The main findings were that interviewer grading is related to interview quality, while the effects of quota size on response levels 'remained uncertain'. It was recommended by the researchers that monitoring and play-back of the performance of individual interviewers should be done in order to maintain field morale and reduce overall variability.

 **KEYPOINT** **Interviewer effect/bias occurs when**

Influence of interviewer biases responses of interviewee

Interviewers misinterpret 'marginal' responses to fit in with their own expectations

Interviewer and interviewee differ widely in personality, experience, etc.

6.9 Other sources of bias

The MRS Working Party report[9] regarded the attitude of interviewers to the concept of market research to be a very important factor. 'If the applicant is not wholeheartedly in favour of it, or regards interviewing as an imposition on members of the public, she cannot be expected to carry out her work conscientiously.' Other possible sources of bias may emanate from political beliefs, or, perhaps, attitudes of a husband.

Bias can also arise from respondents who may be unwilling to give correct answers, perhaps from ignorance of the subject or difficulty in self-expression. They may also, consciously or unconsciously, not wish to give accurate answers, for various reasons, such as embarrassment, privacy, or personal dislike of disclosing information about their behaviour. There may also be genuine misunderstanding of questions, as in the experience of an American researcher[2] who interviewed textile workers on strike. He found that 'arbitration' had come to mean in the workers' vocabulary the same as 'surrender'. 'Are you in favour of arbitration?' was interpreted as 'Are you in favour of giving in completely to the employers?'

Respondents often tend to give the answer which they think interviewers want. The 'accommodating answer' is frequently attracted by a 'leading question', which had not been spotted when the questionnaire was designed. A question, such as: 'Have you seen this advertisement?' in which an advertisement is shown, has been proved to inflate positive replies by as much as three times over responses obtained by a less biased approach. (See Chapter 5, Section 5.4: Bias in questions.)

Sponsorship of surveys is not normally revealed to respondents as identification tends to influence their answers and may inhibit critical comment. Respondents may well feel inclined to look for clues in questions which will enable them to identify the sponsors, so particular care should be taken in drafting questionnaires. Unexpected events may also bias answers as respondents may mistakenly relate the sponsor of a survey with some news event concerning another organization.

A proposed survey on attitudes towards major airlines was postponed when one airline had the misfortune to make headlines as a result of two dramatic and fatal crashes within a two-week period.

Interviewers may also be influenced by knowing the identity of sponsors, and it is generally considered unwise and unnecessary for names of brands of sponsors to be revealed. Bias could result from individual preferences for particular brands influencing interviewers. In cases where the survey is not handled by a research agency, it is advisable for the company involved to disguise its identity by some 'cover' name. In the case of mail surveys, 'cover' addresses also need to be used.

The place and time of interview may also bias response. Questions asked at an inconvenient time may well result in misunderstanding or attract a series of rapid replies designed to get rid of the interviewer as quickly as possible.

In such cases, it is better for the interviewer to ask for a more convenient appointment.

Sound practical advice[1] is that, if possible, interviewers should make their first visit to an area in daylight; and they should not fail to advise the local police station of their survey activities.

In planning[23] the 1986 Welsh Inter Censal Survey, it was established that there was a case for rationalization of call patterns to achieve maximum response and minimal costs. A consortium of five market research companies, led by Taylor Nelson, organized this research which was concerned with housing conditions in the Principality and the social aspects of residents. Interviewers were given a four-hour detailed briefing.

The day, date, and time of the attempts to interview were recorded and analysed, and the following significant factors emerged: (i) a fairly clear preference by interviewers for Monday–Thursday calling, and for working between 1 pm and 5 pm; (ii) higher than expected correlation between times for the first and second calls, particularly between 2 pm and 4 pm; (iii) interviewers' patterns of working were more related to their preferences than the working practices of any market research agency; (iv) greater probability of achieving successful interviews by controlling the *time* at which interviewers called on any particular day, than by controlling the *day* on which they called on respondents; (v) encouraging interviewers to make evening calls might lead to increased 'strike rates', while minimizing costs.

KEYPOINT

Other sources of bias in interviewing

Attitude of interviewers to concept of market research

Respondents unwilling to give correct answers, perhaps from ignorance or problems of self-expression

Respondents giving 'accommodating answers'

Sponsorship of survey not normally revealed, but respondents may suspect particular sponsor and give answers in support (or otherwise)

Interviewers may also be influenced by suspected sponsorship

Place and time of interview may frustrate co-operation (careful planning needed to avoid this bias)

6.10 Bias from non-response

Some degree of non-response is almost inevitable in surveys, and if this is large, survey findings are likely to be biased. The greater the proportion of non-respondents in the sample, the more serious the resulting bias. Research has shown that non-respondents often differ significantly in their opinions and behaviour from respondents; it would be unwise to assume that they do not.

Considerable consideration has been given to the problem of non-response. It is possible to keep it to a minimum by improving sample design and interviewing techniques.

A substantial proportion of non-respondents will obviously affect the size of the sample and, therefore, its precision or reliability. To reduce the effect of non-response bias, the final sample should be as near to the projected sample as possible. It is argued that if non-respondents are significantly different from respondents, merely substituting additional respondents will not solve the problem, although it will, of course, secure a final sample of adequate size.

In the case of random sampling, where fieldwork has shown a sampling frame to include units that do not, in fact, exist, e.g. demolished houses, deceased persons, etc., non-active units should be subtracted from the size of the sample before non-response rates are calculated. It would then be feasible to select substitutes for these non-existent units using a random technique.

With random samples, in particular, there will also be non-response owing to unsuitability, e.g. infirmity, language difficulties, etc., and interviewers must be instructed to substitute as appropriate.

Names selected randomly from the Electoral Register are bound to include some people who have moved. As already stated, the 1954 IPA Readership Survey of about 17 000 persons, found that 2400 had moved. Of these, 1400 had moved to an address covered by the survey and were traced successfully. Alternatively, it would be possible to substitute by sampling the new household in the place of the one that had moved. Earlier investigation by Durbin and Stuart[24] shows that 10 per cent of an initial sample taken from the Electoral Register had moved address, the Register being 10 months out of date at the time of study.

The 'not at homes' may represent a fairly high proportion if common sense is not used by interviewers. Married women who work outside the home and those without children are less likely to be at home than those who do not go out to work or who have small children. By spring 1999, 75 per cent of married or co-habiting women of working age in the UK were economically active, and of these, about one half worked full-time.[25] American research[26] has found that the not-at-home rate varies considerably according to size of city, with the lowest rates in rural areas. Durbin and Stuart[24] reported that experienced interviewers had less difficulty (10.4 per cent) with 'not at homes' than less experienced colleagues (15.9 per cent). The same researchers also showed that when appointments were made, 71 per cent of second calls resulted in interviews, as against 40 per cent when none was made.

Some recalling is obviously necessary to bring non-response down to a minimum. The Government Social Survey stipulates a minimum of three calls (initial plus two call-backs). Other organizations usually request interviewers to make three calls, but extra cost is inevitably incurred, apart from lengthening the time of the survey.

Regarding the pattern of calling, it has been noted[1] that it is customary research practice for interviewers to make at least four calls to obtain an interview, each call being on a different day and at a different time. At least two of these calls should be during the evening or at the weekend.

In the National Readership Survey (NRS – see Chapter 10), up to 1977, three calls were demanded before abandoning the prospect of an interview, but this figure was later increased to four in an attempt to offset the declining response rates.[1]

Attempts have been made by some American statisticians, e.g. Politz and Simmons, to overcome the problem of call-backs by 'weighting' responses which had been obtained, but there does not appear to be any published evidence on the validity of the theory.

Bias can also arise from refusals to take part in a survey. Survey Research Center (USA) interviewers,[6] who are highly trained, experience 2.4 per cent refusals on first calls, 4.1 per cent on second calls, steadily increasing to 10.6 per cent on sixth calls. Experienced interviewers were far more successful in securing interviews than those less experienced. In general, the refusal rate for surveys is remarkably low, and most interviewers experience difficulty in dissuading some people from talking at too great a length about the problem surveyed.

Non-response bias operates in many ways, and everything possible should be done to reduce it. Some knowledge, however slight, should be obtained about non-respondents. People who refuse to fill in a questionnaire may be persuaded to complete a postcard giving a few basic facts, which may help the survey planners to form some opinion of the nature of non-respondents.

It may be possible to compare the composition of the achieved sample with published data, in order to assess the extent and type of non-response bias.

Better training methods and increased motivation have been shown to improve the response rates achieved by interviewers. Respondents, also, have reacted favourably in an experiment reported by Ferber and Hauck.

A 90 per cent response was obtained from half of a sample receiving a long explanatory letter in advance, whereas only a 76 per cent response was obtained from those receiving a much shorter letter of explanation.[6]

Where interviewing takes place in factories, offices, colleges, and other institutions, some of the non-response factors which have been considered in some detail will not apply. Where quota sampling methods are used, non-response factors such as 'movers', 'not at homes', and 'refusals' can be modified by substitution.

KEYPOINT

Bias from non-response

Some degree of non-response almost inevitable

Non-respondents' views and behaviour often significantly different from respondents

Can be controlled by good sample design and interviewing techniques

Substantial non-response affects sample size, hence reliability of findings

With random sampling, interviewers given 'substitution rules'

Bias may arise from refusals, but refusal rates generally very low

Good planning and use of experienced interviewers keep response rates high, so reducing biases

Declining trends in survey response rates

Concern is being expressed by experienced researchers over the observable decline in long-term trends of survey response rates. Face-to-face interviews with the general public are more difficult to obtain. Response rates in the NRS have declined from just below 74 per cent in 1982 to 67 per cent in 1987, with a slight improvement recorded in 1988, but with the overall declining trend persisting.

Because the research design was altered in 1992, direct comparisons of trends in earlier response rates are not feasible. However, the 1994 fieldwork (based on CAPI technique – see Chapter 5) resulted in response rates of 86.8 per cent for households, and 70.2 per cent for 'selected persons', yielding an overall rate of 60.9 per cent. (See Chapter 10 for further discussion.)

These results are very similar to most of the major surveys for which long-term trends are available.' Problems of the inner cities have made their populations less inclined to be interviewed and have also affected the willingness of interviewers to work in these areas.

Leading research firms, such as Mintel, also feel concerned about the declining trend of survey response rates, particularly related to business and professional surveys, and suggest that the need for participation incentives will rise. GPs, for example, are already paid in some cases for interviews. Clearly to avoid further biases arising, it is critical that payments are not too generous.

Summary   Interviewing is a core function of marketing research, and types of interview range from formal, unstructured interviews to informal discussions. Response can be limited, free, or defensive, and a creative interviewing approach would probably contain a mix of these tactics.

Successful interviewing depends significantly on the establishment of an effective relationship between interviewer and interviewee. There is a strong case for fitting interviewers to interviewing situations ('horses for courses').

Selection training and motivation are essential elements for building up 'a productive interviewing team'. Interviewing tasks are as follows:

1. Locate respondents who fulfil requirements of specific samples
2. Translate these contacts into effective interviews
3. Secure valid and reliable responses
4. Record survey responses accurately

Interviewer effect occurs when the influence of the interviewer on the respondent results in responses that do not accurately reflect the respondent's attitudes and opinions. Research directors should pay special attention to the training and monitoring of interviewers in order to keep bias of this nature at a minimum level.

Review and discussion questions

1. Illustrate by any way of example how the invalid halo effect operates and show how it might bias interview results.

2. Outline the principal duties of the research supervisor.

3. A research company has been commissioned by a local health agency to investigate the views of the over 70s in its catchment area on home help for the elderly. A free response interview is proposed. What measures would you suggest to reduce interviewer effect?

4. Which of the two survey methods, telephone interview or personal interview, would, in your opinion, be more prone to interviewer effect? Justify your choice of survey method.

5. A multinational tobacco manufacturer has commissioned a survey on adult attitudes towards cigarette smoking. Discuss the impact of sponsorship disclosure on response bias.

6. The manufacturers of a national brand of toothpaste wish to discover consumer perceptions of their brand. A mall intercept interview has been proposed by their research department. Outline the possible forms of non-response bias that this interview method might generate.

References

1. Morton-Williams, Jean, *Interviewer Approaches*, Dartmouth Publishing, Aldershot, 1993.
2. Bingham, Walter Van Dyke, and Bruce Victor Moore, *How to Interview*, Harper, 1941.
3. Kahn, Robert L., and Charles F. Cannell, *The Dynamics of Interviewing*, Wiley, New York, 1957.
4. Oppenheim, A. N., *Questionnaire Design, Interviewing and Attitude Measurement*, Pinter Publishers, London, 1992.
5. Paterson, D. G., *Physique and Intellect*, Appleton Century, New York, 1930.
6. Boyd, Harper W., Jnr, and Ralph Westfall, 'Interviewers as a source of error in surveys', *Journal of Marketing*, April 1955.
7. Moser, C. A., and G. Kalton, *Survey Methods in Social Investigation*, Heinemann, London, 1971.
8. Market Research Society, 'Fieldwork methods in general use', Working Party in Interviewing Methods: First Report, Market Research Society, London, 1968.

9. MacFarlane-Smith, Joan, *Interviewing in Market and Social Research*, Routledge and Kegan Paul, London, 1972.
10. Durbin, J., and A. Stuart, 'Differences in response rates of experienced and inexperienced interviewers', *Journal of Royal Statistical Society*, part II, 1951.
11. Morton-Williams, Jean, *Interviewer Approaches*, Dartmouth Publishing, Aldershot, 1993.
12. Harvey, John, 'Aims of Interviewer Quality Scheme', *MRS Newsletter* (Supplement), January 1988.
13. Collins, Martin, 'Responding to surveys', *ERSC Newsletter*, no. 62, June 1988.
14. Collins, Martin, 'Interviewer variability: A review of the problem', *Journal of Market Research Society*, vol. 22, no. 2, 1980.
15. Rice, Stuart, 'Contagious bias in the interview', *American Journal of Sociology*, vol. 35, 1929.
16. Wilkins, L. T., 'Prediction of the demand for campaign medals', The Social Survey, no. 109, 1949.
17. Weeks, Michael, F., and R. Paul Moore, 'Ethnicity of interviewer effects on ethnic respondents', *Public Opinion Quarterly*, vol. 45, no. 2, 1981.
18. Hatchett, Shirley, and Howard Schuman, 'White respondents and race-of-interviewer effects', *Public Opinion Quarterly*, vol. 39, no. 4, winter 1975/76.
19. Cotter, Patrick R., Jeffrey Cohen, and Philip B. Coulter, 'Race of interviewer effects, in telephone interviews', *Public Opinion Quarterly*, vol. 46, no. 2, 1982.
20. Watson, Michael, 'Researching minorities', *Journal of the Market Research Society*, vol. 34, no. 4, October 1992.
21. Collins, Martin, 'Interviewer clustering and effects in an attitude survey', *Journal of Market Research Society*, vol. 25, no. 1, 1983.
22. Bound, John, John Freeman, and John Mumford, 'The effect of the quality and quantity of interviewers on quality and quantity of data', ESOMAR, Monte Carlo, September 1980.
23. Swires-Hennessy, E., 'The optimum time at which to conduct survey interviews', *Journal of the Market Research Society*, vol. 34, no. 1, January 1992.
24. Durbin, J., and A. Stuart, 'Callbacks and clustering in sample surveys: An experimental study', *Journal of the Royal Statistical Society*, vol. 117, 1954.
25. *Social Trends 30*, Office for National Statistics (ONS), 2000.
26. Mayer, Charles S., 'The interviewer and his environment', *Journal of Marketing Research*, November 1964.

Qualitative research and attitude research

7.1 Introduction

This chapter will deal first with qualitative research and then discuss attitude research, although, as observed later, distinctions are often blurred and some degree of overlap may be inevitable.

In Chapter 1, it was seen that marketing research theory and practice had borrowed liberally from various fields of study as, indeed, had other emerging disciplines. Since marketing research focuses on specific aspects of human and organizational behaviour, viz. consumption habits, it was found that several psychological concepts and methodologies, such as attitude scales, projective techniques and focus groups, were valuable in gaining insights into buying motivations, attitudes, etc. In the middle and late 1950s, there tended to be an over-enthusiastic and at times rather naïve adoption of behavioural research techniques. Motivation research, in particular, attracted many disciples who, fascinated by its flamboyant claims, failed to discern the preposterous nature of some of its concepts and findings.

The early excitement generated by the indiscriminate importation of behavioural methodologies has largely dissipated, and a more stable and realistic use is now made of these techniques in marketing research. This more mature approach has strengthened the theory and practice of marketing research, enabling it to develop creatively and make a significant contribution to marketing strategy.

This has led to a growing interest in improved methods of measuring the behaviour and attitudes of peoples as consumers of a wide range of goods and services. It became apparent that, when investigating people's feelings about some aspects of buying behaviour, a more subtle approach was needed than direct questioning. For many reasons, such as personal prestige or the pressures of social conformity, respondents may feel reluctant to express their true feelings when confronted with direct questions.

> In consumer research, it is rarely much use asking people why they bought a particular product or prefer one brand to another. They may not know. Even if they do, they are not always willing to say. Motives can be socially embarrassing. Moreover, people on the whole like to appear reasonable, both to themselves and to others, and direct questions are apt to elicit plausible but misleading answers.[1]

This greater awareness by marketing researchers of the importance of more subtle forms of investigation has encouraged experiments in the use of some of the techniques applied in psychology and sociology. Interest has centred particularly on the influence of attitudes on consumers' buying habits, and attempts have been made to measure more accurately the motivations, attitudes, and preferences of consumers.

The nature of attitudes and their effects on people's behaviour are fully discussed elsewhere,[2] and it has been noted in Chapter 1 that the variety and complexity of human behaviour, motivated by so many causes, many of which are not easy to identify, admittedly make the study of consumers difficult. In the process of satisfying their many needs, inherent and also acquired through learning and experience, people develop attitudes which influence their choice of products and brands. Cooper[3] has said 'we prefer to do things for their practical benefits and justify ourselves as rational and worthy, yet underlying this are deeper meanings . . . of which we may or may not be conscious'. The symbolic power of specific brands, for example, is often influential in buying decisions.

The particular experiences of individual consumers may include the satisfaction – or otherwise – which a brand of product gave them. These experiences will have contributed towards the attitudes which they hold, and it is likely that they will have discussed products with other consumers. In this way, attitudes tend to be acquired or modified. Personal influence is subtle, and studies have shown it to be very important in the purchase of foods, toiletries, clothing, and several other products. The diffusion of new products and the formation of favourable attitudes depend greatly on word-of-mouth recommendation. Opinion leadership has attracted considerable attention among marketing researchers; it is a subject which advertisers should not overlook. If products fail to live up to consumers' expectations, not only will repeat sales to those consumers be lost, but also the chances of selling to their friends and acquaintances will have been reduced.

Over 20 years ago, a special committee[4] of the Market Research Society observed that qualitative research has 'long since extended from its original function of uncovering consumers' motivations to that of providing the constant conceptual link between consumer and decision maker in marketing and advertising development'. It was also noted that qualitative research is not 'scientific' in the way that some quantitative research based on statistical sampling theory and formal methods of interviewing may claim to be. As in some areas of enquiry covered by the behavioural sciences, where observational data lack precise measurement and replication, qualitative research, in general, may be perceived as lacking 'theoretical bona fides derived from any existing philosophy of science'. But it has to be admitted that the indubitable usefulness of qualitative research justifies its existence. Data may be rather inappropriately described as 'hard' or 'soft'; this does not necessarily endorse numeric data as being superior to non-numeric data: they are essentially complementary.

A judicial blend of qualitative and quantitative research involving a combination of survey techniques was advocated in Chapter 2. Data of any type should result in *insight*; numeric data do not automatically result in that.

A report by the Qualitative Interest Group of the Market Research Society in 1992 stated qualitative research to be a 'wide-ranging craft encompassing many different approaches, and can range from large, time-consuming Government/social research contracts to pre-testing of consumer advertising'.[5] The particular value of the interpretative process rendered qualitative research 'such a useful tool for exploring markets, understanding consumers, solving problems, and so on . . . it is the *quality* of the ideas that counts . . .'.[5]

Cooper and Branthwaite[6] summarize the uses and rationales of qualitative research in a useful model given in Fig. 7.1.

The upper 'layers of response' are overt, communicable, deal with matters of which the respondent is aware, and can, though subject to the usual problems of bias, be elicited by structured interviews, e.g. brand awareness.

Further down the marked arrow, structured interviewing becomes increasingly difficult, and subject matter more likely to deal with 'private' feelings, irrationalities, 'illogical' behaviour, or repressed attitudes. Cooper and Branthwaite[6] observe that an essential feature of qualitative research is the level of trust developed between interviewer and respondents.

The essence of qualitative research is that it is diagnostic; it seeks to discover what may account for certain kinds of behaviour; for example, brand loyalty. It seeks deeper understanding of factors, sometimes covert, which influence buying decisions. It is impressionistic rather than conclusive; it probes rather than counts. It observes and reflects on the complexity of human activities in satisfying many needs. Intrinsically, it is subjective. For its findings it cannot produce statistical evidence based on probability sampling. But for all its limitations, qualitative research is able to provide unique insights to inspire and guide the development of marketing strategy and tactics.

Sometimes, as the MRS study group notes,[4] marketers seek information that is too subtle and sophisticated to be derived from the structured, standardized techniques of quantitative research. They then seek for methods of enquiry that are unstructured, flexible, and oblique, such as non-directive group discussions, non-directive individual interviews, and projective techniques. Moser[7] observed that the chief recommendation for informal methods of enquiry is that they can 'dig deeper' and get a richer understanding than the formal interview.

Qualitative research has been a term rather freely used to describe several specific kinds of marketing research; for example, exploratory research, unstructured research, motivation research, depth interviewing, attitude and opinion research, etc.

Some of the techniques originally used in qualitative research were generally termed 'motivation research', but this classification is misleading, because since those early days the techniques have been applied to a variety of studies apart from buying motivation. Also, they do not represent the entire repertory of techniques available for researching motivation.

Wendy Gordon[8] emphasizes that 'motivational research' and 'qualitative research' are not synonyms. The former is based on psychological interpretations of information gathered through conversations, etc., while the latter refers to the methodology (mostly focus groups and 'depth interviews') and a 'cognitive model of analysis based firmly on the "data" derived from the interviewing processes'. Qualitative research is projected[8] to

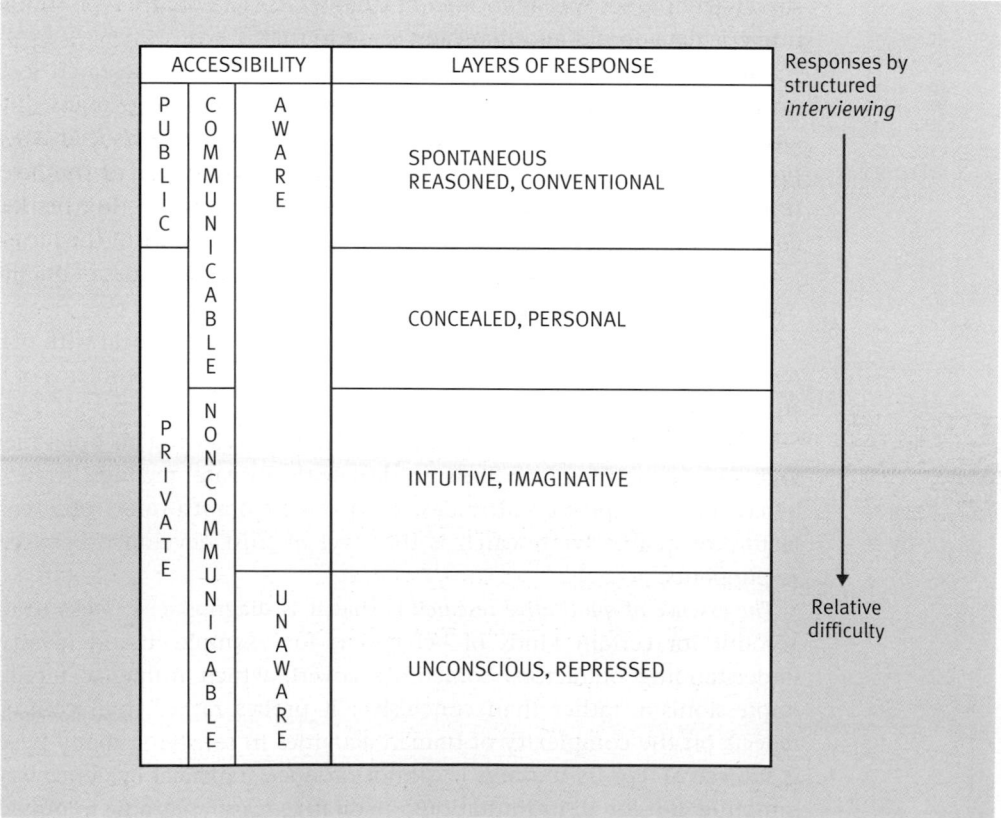

Figure 7.1　Responses to interviewing[6]

become even more specialized and eclectic in its concepts and methods, leading to further fragmentation of professional skills. Other influences are already apparent with the growth of electronic and video technologies, and interactive and collaborative software systems. The feasibilities of using the internet for qualitative research are being explored (see Chapter 6). New opportunities certainly exist, but Wendy Gordon[8] urges that qualitative researchers who wish to operate successfully in socio-cultural environments different from their own should be sensitive to the prevailing behavioural norms when interpreting the results of qualitative research overseas (also see Chapter 12).

Sampson[9] has warned that because qualitative research appears to be familiar to almost everybody, but really understood by relatively few, there is a danger that it could be presumed to lack subtlety and to require little skill. To the expert, however, the facts are just the reverse: it is a field of research calling for sophisticated and sensitive skills.

Qualitative research has grown significantly in Europe and in the United States. It is 'now more mature, robust and confident', and a 'significant contributor to the market research industry'.[10] It is prominent in new product development (NPD), concept research and advertising pre-testing.

In the US and also in the UK, several different kinds and functions of qualitative research have been classified:[11] (i) *exploratory research* – to generate language, and hypotheses for subsequent quantitative validation; (ii) *pre-testing research* – to check, sort and prioritize potential advertisement, pack, product concepts; (iii) *exploratory research*; and (iv) *everyday life research*.

The distinctive contributions of qualitative research are, therefore, both varied and valuable in marketing decision making. Modern information technologies have resulted in a veritable 'data deluge' on both sides of the Atlantic;[11] qualitative research in partnership with quantitative data, the warp and the weft, form the fabric of a creative research design.

Qualitative research is particularly valuable in the early stages of market studies, when concepts are being explored, insights into behaviour gained, and research ideas are generated. Quantitative research brings rigour and disciplined enquiry to the overall research activities; it is likely to benefit significantly from the more flexible and spontaneous approach of qualitative techniques in, for example, the design of effective questionnaires, the development of creative promotional ideas, the generation of new products and services, and understanding the many motivations that influence buying behaviour.

KEYPOINT

Qualitative research is

Essentially diagnostic

Concerned with deeper understanding of buying motivations

Impressionistic rather than conclusive

Concerned with probing rather than mere counting

Observant and reflective

Able to give insights to guide marketing actions

The partner of quantitative investigations

7.2 Techniques of qualitative research

Sampson[12] traces the origin of qualitative research to a meeting in the 1940s of refugee Freudians and neo-Freudians who sought to apply some of the principles of psychoanalysis in a marketing context, and the pollsters who also sought to extend the applications of their specific skills related to the measurement of behaviour and attitudes. He notes that two major approaches or 'styles' of qualitative research are emerging strongly: 'the more superficial approach of the cognitivists, and the deeper, psychoscopic one of the "new" qualitative researchers; the latter adopt a more intensive and diagnostic approach to questioning as opposed to simply asking people to describe their behaviour and then explain it, or, simply, to express verbally their beliefs, opinions, attitudes and feelings.'[12] The former approach tends to over-emphasize the reasoned, rational and socio-normative responses to questions, perhaps tempting respondents to give 'acceptable' answers.

The basic techniques of this type of research are 'varied and eclectic';[11] they include depth interviews – either as individual unstructured interviews or as group discussions, focus groups, synectic groups, extended creativity groups (ECGs), sensitivity groups, brainstorming, Delphi role-playing, various kinds of projective techniques, etc. This imposing battery of qualitative research approaches has, as discussed earlier, attracted some critical views: focus groups, in particular, have tended to be closely associated by the public with political policies, and have become the target of unfavourable comment by sections of the mass media, including television and radio commentators keen to stir up controversial issues. Focus group sniping seems to have developed into a type of open sport, in which all freely indulge. In the market research industry itself, critics like Gerald de Groot[13] feel distinctly unhappy about some of the assumptions and practices of qualitative research which, though fascinating, are thought to drift away from its main purpose, viz. as part of general market research which is concerned with providing reliable, valid and usable information.

KEYPOINT

Qualitative research techniques, varied and eclectic include

Depth interviews

Group discussions, focus groups

Conflict groups

Mini-depth interviews

Projective techniques

These are not exclusive: discrimination is needed

Techniques should be relevant to specific problems

Depth interviews

Basically, depth (or in-depth) interviews are non-directive interviews in which the respondent is encouraged to talk about the subject rather than to answer 'yes' or 'no' to specific questions. Like the group discussion technique – to which it is closely related – it endeavours to 'understand the nature and make-up of the area being researched, rather than to measure the size and shape of it.'[14] Characteristically, it is a flexible, encouraging approach which will vary to some degree according to the objectives of the research and the type of informant being interviewed. Responses are usually recorded on tape for later analysis and reflection. According to Peter Cooper, in-depth interviews 'were born out of a European fascination with the ultimate freedoms of the human mind to express and free-associate all aspects of thought and feeling'.[15] Although its present use is derived from the clinical interview, Cooper declares that it can be traced back to the 'searching enquiries of Socrates and Plato 2400 years ago'.[15]

The length of time to conduct an in-depth interview will vary according to the nature of the subject under discussion – its relative complexity, for example, involving, perhaps, technical aspects of product design, or of enquiries concerning intimate health and hygiene behaviour. In general, this type of informal, unstructured interview might last 45 minutes, but this is very dependent on the rapport developed as the interview progresses.

Group interviews/discussions

Because individual depth interviews are costly and time-consuming, qualitative enquiries tend to take place in groups; this is beneficial, as people are generally less inhibited in a group. The 'funnel' technique may be used – discussion at first on the broadest possible level, and gradually narrowed down through sequentially more restricted channels (see Chapter 5). The investigator, who is also known as a moderator or facilitator, has a list of points which should be covered during the interview. He or she guides conversation (without directly influencing it by formal questioning), so that all the principal points are covered adequately.

Whereas depth interviewing is concerned with the study of one individual, group depth interviewing, or group discussions, studies the interaction of group membership on individual behaviour. It is this interaction – this free exchange of ideas, beliefs and emotions – which helps to form the general opinion of people sharing common interests and responsibilities. In the atmosphere of a group, people react to one another and the ways in which they influence personal attitudes can be studied. Sharp criticism of individual beliefs is frequently aroused, and the discussion generated among the group by their shared interests, tends to become extremely frank. Professions such as physicians, accountants or engineers, who are not always easy to interview individually, seem to be far more open and willing to discuss when in a group of people with common professional interests.

Groups vary, not only in their constituents and in the subject matter, but also in their ability to grasp concepts and move forward to a constructive exchange of ideas, etc. Dichter, one of the pioneers of qualitative research, drew participants for his discussions from a panel of housewives recruited by his organization, the Institute for Motivational Research. Other types of groups have resulted from contacts among professional institutes. So the successful group moderator needs not only psychological training but also a considerable degree of personal flexibility in encouraging people of diverse backgrounds and experience to participate fully in this type of qualitative investigation.

Studies of group behaviour have indicated that group dynamics – the ways in which people interact – are influenced by the numbers of members. It appears that, generally, between five and seven people are able to participate constructively in group discussions, and that a period of no more than one and a half hours allows for topics to be adequately explored. A skilful moderator will be aware of any attempts by group members to dominate the discussion, and diplomatically intervene so that everyone in the group feels encouraged to contribute their own opinions on the matter under consideration.

The actual size of groups tends, as Gordon and Langmaid observe,[16] to be a compromise between the ideal and budgetary and/or time constraints. The complexity of the problem under investigation is another important determinant; also, decisions have to be taken about the geographical distribution of the interviews. As with sampling in general (see Chapters 3 and 4), care must be taken to avoid, as far as possible, bias, which, as noted earlier, intrudes so easily into research activities. It would obviously be unwise to organize a series of group interviews restricted to the London area, and then project the findings as representative of the UK as a whole. Oppenheim[17] states that there can be no 'definite answer' to the number of depth interviews to be conducted on a particular topic, but he feels that 30 or 40 interviews are probably typical, and that it generally becomes apparent when a series of interviews reaches the point when no new ideas are emerging.

The analysis and interpretation of qualitative research, such as group discussions, are demanding tasks: they require expert and objective attention. Content analysis – objective and systematic analysis of the actual content of taped records of group discussions – may be used. Critics of qualitative research have suggested that some of the 'findings' of this method of enquiry are too greatly influenced by the individual analyst's training and background, with resultant subjectivity, which may tend to bias analyses.

Focus groups

This scaled-down version of group discussions grows in popularity, and, as mentioned at the opening of this section, it has become the target of suspicion and unfavourable comment. Gordon and Langmaid[16] in their comprehensive guide to qualitative research have expressed misgivings: 'The syndrome of a "few groups" has spread like a rampant disease that undermines the qualitative product itself . . . Far more expertise is involved than merely organizing a "few groups" '. The uninhibited adoption of such techniques is seen as one of the problems facing professional researchers in both the UK and the US and, to a 'lesser extent', in Europe.

Wendy Gordon[8] admits that there is growing 'media suspicion of qualitative research', and she cites the growing cynicism about focus groups findings based on the views of 'eight ordinary people' who are deemed to be representative of the population at large. Such misgiving is honest, for this practice reflects badly on the research profession as well as on the use that clients make of such precariously-based data.

Perhaps like a swan gliding with apparent effortlessness across a lake, a well-run focus group 'seems to take place . . . like an informal chat . . . rather than a process that requires skill and experience to handle'.[8] The first stage in any form of research activity – quantitative or qualitative – is to define carefully the problem to be investigated and then to consider suitable methodologies. In some cases, a series of focus group studies may be valuable in giving insights that could guide in the development of, for example, new products or brands. Nestlé's research manager for beverages states: 'Historically we tended to use them (group discussions) more with a product or product focus'. They are also used 'not to look at any specific issues but to act as a sounding board on general issues from the public'.[18]

Focus group methodology has been used by Ciba-Geigy's agricultural division in the USA to augment 'traditional' market research methods in the evaluation of new products. For instance, small groups of avocado growers – who would be likely users of the company's agricultural pest control products – were encouraged to describe how they went about their work, the problems encountered, such as insect pests, and the kinds of products used to meet this problem. From these focused discussions, Ciba-Geigy obtained valuable clues for the development of new products.[19]

Variations on a theme

Although depth interviews, group discussions and focus groups form the solid centre of qualitative interviewing, there are several productive variations within these main methodologies. For instance, *re-convened group discussions*, which are in three stages:

1. group participants may be given, for example, key information about the retail distribution of household branded products;

2. they are then set a task which might entail visiting one or more stores and searching on the shelves for a specified brand. If they experience problems in locating the product, they would be expected to find out whether this was due to ineffective distribution, inadequate stock control, etc. They would also note the ways in which their enquiries were treated by the sales staff;

3. after this practical exercise, participants return for a further session of group discussions, during which they are able to speak from immediate experience about certain aspects of retailing, as seen from the shopper's viewpoint.

Extended creativity groups (ECGs)

Another special form of qualitative research combines depth interviews and projective techniques. ECGs have been used in a study of groups of medical practitioners (usually about eight in each group, representing high and low prescribers of drugs). Over an extended period of time, usually between 3–4 hours, a variety of releasing and projective techniques (see later discussion) was used. It was made clear to the GPs that the moderators (usually two per session) were not skilled in pharmacological matters, but wanted to know 'what really goes on'. They were, of course, skilled in handling these interviewing techniques.[20] As noted, ECGs may last up to four hours or even longer in order to allow members time to associate themselves fully with the objectives of the exercise, and to be able to take active participation in it.

The conflict group

Deliberately designed to stimulate controversy when exploring specific issues, this then attempts to negotiate how these differences may be settled satisfactorily. In the introductory session, the moderator will have told members that they have been selected *because* of their known different views and agendas; it is the task of the group to investigate fully the nature of their different viewpoints. Such a group might be faced with the task of reconciling strongly-held attitudes towards genetically modified food.

Mini-depth interviews

Possibly useful in exploring – over a short period of up to half-an-hour – a focused issue with a group of between four and six participants. This might be concerned with such topics as promotional literature, logos, or perceptions of comparative advertising themes. This type of depth interview is useful 'alongside conventional survey research . . . to provide "flesh to the bones" of quantitative data'.[8]

Observation

As discussed in Chapter 2, the non-reactive research technique of observation has several valid applications in marketing research. Skilled observation of shoppers' typical behaviour may lead to improved labelling, the design of shelving, etc. 'Mystery-shopping' – a form of observational research, discussed in Chapter 2 – has developed over the past 20 years or so, and has been applied not only in retail stores but also in the hotel, catering, travel and financial services. In addition to personal observation, video recorders are used, but as Wendy Gordon states:[8] 'The main disadvantage of simple observation is that we can find out how people behave in a particular context or situation but not why they do so'. She suggests that it may be feasible for retail outlets to co-operate in an extended period of research, during which the researcher is allowed, after observing for instance a shopper handling several packs and reading closely details of their contents and eventually selecting a particular brand, to intervene and ask what influenced the final decision.

The ethnographic method (participant observation) was used in a study of domestic toilet-cleaning attitudes and behaviour. The process of toilet-cleaning was videoed, combined with a commentary by the respondent while doing this task. Interviews before and after this household chore were also recorded. This mixed method research resulted in realistic insights into people's attitudes and behaviour, e.g. the types of cleaners and brands used and the perceived problems of this task.[8] It also demonstrated the value of combining research methodologies.

Researching ethnic tastes

Ethnic minorities represent about 5–6 per cent of the total population of Britain and, in general, they have a younger age structure than the white population; for example, 16 per cent of the latter were aged 65 and over in 1998/99 compared with 3 per cent of Pakistani and Bangladeshis (Social Trends, 2000).

Group discussions and depth interviews are used successfully in ethnic minorities research in the UK, and surveys have led, for instance, to the labelling of ethnic foods, so that prospective purchasers can reassure themselves that the contents conform to their dietary laws. However, group discussions are said to encounter potential problems when researching ethnically sensitive topics, and particular care is needed when recruiting participants to ensure that groups are representative of the populations being surveyed. 'There is no such thing as an "Asian group discussion". A group of three Hindus, two Sikhs, two Moslems and a Christian is asking for problems'.[21] Young West Indians in groups can also be difficult to research, as they 'try to keep their street credibility intact'.[21]

Qualitative research has a special role in developing countries, especially where there are no reliable sources of data available, and where cultural practices may significantly affect patterns of consumption.[22] In interpreting the findings from these research activities, it is, of course, important that researchers should always be aware of the 'constricting nature' of their own 'personal maps', and so avoid biases which may result from distorted perceptions of the beliefs, attitudes and actions (including brand preferences) of those being researched.[8]

Projective techniques

Projective techniques use indirect methods of investigation, borrowed from clinical psychology, in order to obtain data that cannot be secured through more overt methods, e.g. direct questioning. They are also concerned with testing the hypotheses which have been constructed as a probable explanation of the causes underlying people's behaviour as consumers. These techniques are useful in giving respondents opportunities to express their attitudes without personal embarrassment or incrimination.

The concept of projection has its roots in Freudian psychology with its emphasis on the influence of the subconscious on the human psyche. Instinctive theories of motivation were re-emphasized by Sigmund Freud (1856–1939) and his associates. His ideas have pervaded psychology, sociology, and medical science, and have also extended to the marketing, especially advertising, of products and services of many kinds. Although Freudian psychoanalytic theory has been subject to severe criticism by psychologists and other commentators, largely because many of its projections lack substantial empirical validation, Freudian theories of motivation are valuable in drawing attention to the existence and significance of unconscious influences in human behaviour. For instance, guilt, anxiety and other conflicting emotions and beliefs may influence patterns of consumption, including brand preferences.

Oppenheim[17] has listed the following benefits from using projective techniques:

1. They can help to penetrate the barrier of awareness – people are frequently unaware of their own motives and attitudes.

2. The barriers of irrationality can be breached – people feel they must have 'rational' motivations for all purchases.

3. The barrier of inadmissibility may be broken – people are loath to admit to some kinds of 'non-ideal' behaviour.

4. The barrier of self-incrimination is penetrated – this is related to (3) and concerns kinds of beliefs, feelings, and behaviour that might lower other people's opinions of the person involved.

5. They can breach the barrier of politeness – where convention and actual politeness inhibit the expression of real feelings.

Oppenheim's list of benefits cover, it will be seen, aspects of self-defence, rationality, self-incrimination and the suppression of real feelings, all of which are derived from Freudian psychological theory.

Projective techniques, according to Ernest Dichter,[23] one of the progenitors of motivation research in the US, provide verbal or visual stimuli which, through their indirection and concealed intent, encourage respondents to reveal their unconscious feelings and attitudes without being aware that they are doing so.

Dichter, who died in 1991 at the ripe age of 84, liked to regard himself as a 'cultural anthropologist' who, in depth interviews endeavoured to probe people's opinions, motives, etc., related to specific buying situations. He founded the Institute for Motivational Research in Croton-on-Hudson in the US.

Like several other talented researchers, such as Paul Lazarsfeld, Dichter left Vienna in the 1930s to avoid persecution on account of his Jewish origins.

Critics have felt that Dichter tended to exaggerate the claims he made for the success of motivational research, and have speculated on how much of his advice was based on sound common sense or ordinary intuition, and how much sprang from the Freudian clinical approach he adopted. Some of the more fanciful ideas of motivation research were revealed by Vance Packard in his popular text: *The Hidden Persuaders* which, in the late 1950s, shocked many by its exposé of methods of investigation into the covert motivations influencing consumers' purchasing habits.[2] Inevitably, a backlash against motivational and related qualitative research practices occurred, and it took some

20 years or so before qualitative research regained acceptability as a legitimate research methodology. Dichter's pioneering contributions were reassessed and, despite occasional lapses, were recognized as opening up the field of qualitative marketing research in the US and elsewhere.

A pioneer study involving projective methodology was connected with stereotyping of types of American housewives' grocery buying habits. In 1949, the Mason Haire instant coffee study[25] was undertaken to determine the motivations of consumers towards instant coffee in general and the Nescafé product in particular.

When housewives were asked the direct question whether they liked instant coffee or not, most of those who rejected it gave as the reason the taste of this type of coffee. However, there was a suspicion that this was not the real reason and that there were hidden motives. Two shopping lists were prepared, identical except that one had Nescafé instant coffee and the other Maxwell House (drip-grind) coffee. Details of these shopping lists are given below:

Shopping list 1	*Shopping list 2*
1½ lb hamburger	1½ lb hamburger
2 loaves of Wonderbread	2 loaves of Wonderbread
Bunch of carrots	Bunch of carrots
1 can Rumford's baking powder	1 can Rumford's baking powder
1 lb Nescafé instant coffee	1 lb Maxwell House coffee (drip-grind)
2 cans Del Monte peaches	2 cans Del Monte peaches
5 lb potatoes	5 lb potatoes

A group of 100 respondents was asked to project themselves into the buying situation and characterize the woman who bought the groceries. The two lists were distributed (only one list to each person), each respondent being unaware of the existence of an alternative list. The findings revealed that the buyer of instant coffee was seen as lazier, less well organized, more spendthrift, and not as good a wife as the housewife using the conventional type of coffee.

Haire's research has been subject to considerable scrutiny over the years. Arndt[26] undertook a similar survey among Norwegian housewives in 1971 with some slight modifications to product brands: the baking powder was changed to 'Freia', and Nescafé replaced by Friele coffee. Because pilot research revealed criticism of the Haire shopping list for alleged lack of proportion in the quantities specified for the various items, some modifications were also made to quantities, e.g. carrots were increased from one to two bunches. The results indicated that the 'instant coffee' housewife may have become associated with 'modernity and more intense involvement in the world around'.

In 1978, more fundamental evaluation of Mason Haire's research was made by James C. Anderson,[27] senior research psychologist of the marketing research division of Du Pont. He stated that most of the numerous studies had been content with replication and the question of the validity of Haire's research techniques was not adequately considered. What had not been evaluated before were the interactions of other products on the shopping lists with the two test products. Because this factor had been overlooked both by Mason Haire and by those who replicated his research, it was 'not possible to draw valid marketing conclusions about the perceived user characteristics [and] use of the technique for this purpose should be discouraged'.

This professional opinion reflects on the fragility of the research design underlying some projective techniques. In addition, changed attitudes towards the consumption of certain kinds of food have rendered Mason Haire's original findings out of date. Not only have social taboos against instant coffee almost entirely disappeared, but starchy foods like potatoes are less favoured.

Projective techniques can be viewed as release mechanisms which enable people to bring to the surface of consciousness, and to express, either individually or in groups, their thoughts and feelings about specific topics, products and brands. Through taking part in non-incriminating exercises, respondents are disposed to reveal emotions and beliefs which they may have suppressed for various reasons. These may relate to feelings of social inferiority (or superiority), or because of professional inhibitions.

Projective techniques may be used, it will have been noted, in groups or in individual sessions; they are of many kinds but, fundamentally, they should enable and encourage participants to involve themselves in a relatively unstructured task related, however, to aspects of consumption behaviour. The perceptions of competing brands of toilet soap, ice-cream or cars might be evaluated by these methodologies.

Types of projective techniques have been listed[24] as:

1. Association procedures
2. Completion procedures
3. Transformation procedures
4. Construction procedures

KEYPOINT

Projective techniques

Borrowed concepts and techniques from clinical psychology

Respondents given opportunities to express their attitudes without embarrassment or guilt

Penetrate barriers of awareness and self-defence

Breach barriers of irrationality

Release-mechanism for thoughts and feelings

4 main types of projective techniques

1. Association procedures
2. Completion procedures
3. Transformation procedures
4. Construction procedures

The first category – association procedures – includes *word association tests* (sometimes called *free word association*). This is probably the best known and oldest projective technique. The informant is given a single word and asked to say immediately what other words come into his or her mind. A series of words is fired at the respondent so that he or she is more likely to blurt out a meaningful response. For example, a spontaneous response to 'hot' is likely to be 'cold'; to 'library', 'books'.

Neutral words are mixed in a list of test words in order to overcome mental defensive tactics. Lists are carefully devised to reveal attitudes towards the subject under research.

Responses can be classified by the frequency with which a particular word is used as a response, the interval of time before response is made (hesitation), and by the total failure of some respondents to complete a sequence (blocking).

Hesitation occurs when a respondent takes more than three seconds to respond, and this indicates comparative emotional involvement in the particular word. Sometimes the stimulus word evokes such strong feelings that the respondent 'blocks' – i.e. is unable to give any response.

Obviously, a stimulus word which has both a high hesitation rate and also a high 'blockage' rate, would not be suitable for an advertising message, as use of these words would result either in distortion or complete non-reception by the audience concerned.

There are many variants to this test ranging from one-word response to 'controlled' response, when selection is made, for example, from a given list of products to which respondents are asked to give brand names.

Household products like disinfectants or soap and foods, such as 'prepared meals', could be researched by this method.

Successive word association involves the respondent in supplying a chain of associations with the stimulus word. These links can be centred round samples of actual products, illustrations, or complete advertisements.

Word association tests are useful in selecting brand names, and for obtaining consumers' assessments of the relative qualities of a range of competitive goods. Tests could be staged before and after advertising and other promotions to measure the effectiveness of these on a selected panel of consumers.

The Rorschach ink blot test consists of a series of 10 standardized ink blot shapes, named after the Swiss psychiatrist who developed them for the study of psychopathology. These ink blots are shown to informants, who are invited to say what they see in them. It is claimed that what they see guides manufacturers in developing brands of their products to appeal to specific personality types

The second category – completion procedures – is typified by *sentence completion* and *story completion* tests. With the former test, people are asked to complete a short sentence and an analysis is made of the response, which is usually tape-recorded. If the area of enquiry is sensitive, the series of sentences opens with a few innocuous sentences, gradually 'funnelling' down to more difficult ones (compare questionnaire wording techniques: Chapter 5). Typical sentences might be:

A mother who serves margarine to her family is . . .
The food value of margarine is . . .
The family using margarine instead of butter is . . .
or
Powdered coffee is popular because . . .
The best flavoured coffee is . . .
Coffee that is easy to make is . . .
People who drink coffee are . . .

The responses can be classified into approval (strong, general, qualified), neutral, disapproval (graded), thus revealing attitudes. Like word association tests, the respondent is subjected to some pressure in order to give spontaneous replies. It is possible for some individuals to 'rationalize' their replies, but, in general, the method is one of the most useful and reliable of the many projective techniques in use. This test was useful where people would not openly express their anxieties and annoyance about increased airport noise near their homes. The depth and type of their hidden fears were revealed by a combination of sentence completion and word association tests.

Story completion is a logical development of the sentence completion test. Respondents are given an opening sentence or sentences describing, for example, shopping for household supplies, and they are asked to continue the narrative. The ways in which individuals develop a featured situation is thought to give insights into their typical psychological reactions and likely behaviour. A marketing example could conceivably be concerned with shoppers' attitudes and behaviour related to 'special offers' in supermarkets.

Other versions of completion procedures are *cartoons* (blank balloons); these frequently depict in outline two people talking in a particular setting. The comments of one person are shown in a 'speech balloon'; the other person's 'balloon' is empty and the informant is asked to give the reply which he or she thinks fits the situation. Typical situations could cover conversations between husband and wife, mother and child, shop assistant and customer, garage mechanic and car owner, etc. This 'third party' test is particularly useful as it allows people to be less inhibited than they might be if asked to describe their own reactions.

Related to the 'blank balloon' approach is what is knows as the *Thematic Apperception Test* (TAT), in which a respondent is shown a series of pictures and asked to describe the situations shown, and also what led up to those situations. Additionally, they are asked to give their idea of the likely outcome. The resultant 'stories' are then analysed and interpreted by skilled qualitative researchers. The first cartoon, for example, might show a simple outline drawing of a woman shopper at a cosmetics counter, standing near to a display of low-priced cosmetics; the second cartoon shows her near a display of cosmetics clearly marked at much higher prices. Respondents are shown one of the cartoons (in random order) and asked to describe the person in the cartoon and also the quality of cosmetic involved. Again, respondents' reactions would be subjected to expert interpretation. This test has been used successfully in connection with male business travellers.[16]

Associated with completion tests is the *Rosenweig Picture Frustration Test*, originally developed for personality testing and later used for attitude studies. Cartoon characters are shown in frustrating circumstances in order to arouse the frustration–aggression aspects of the viewer's personality. The reactions of informants can be compared with those established in a set of 24 typical cartoon situations. Marketing issues might relate to store service: ('Sorry, we're out of stock until next Wednesday') or to attempts to secure the attention of a waiter in a busy restaurant.

The third category – *transformation procedures* (which are also known as 'expressive types') – involves, for instance, 'psychodrawing', when participants might be invited to express graphically their feelings about a specific product/brand or an event such as a family holiday. 'Before' and 'after' graphic illustrations might indicate the relief experienced as the result of taking a dose of branded analgesic for headaches or gastric disorders. This kind of technique is said to work 'particularly well for personal products . . . where the end user often has some fantasized end result that may guide or determine her purchasing, but which she dare not speak rationally'.[16]

The fourth category – construction procedures – might involve some form of role playing, when people are asked to act out, for example, a particular buying situation, so that their responses could be studied. A typical instance might relate to selecting a pair of shoes. It will be seen that this technique shares some of the characteristics of the third category.

7.3 Principal methods of researching consumer products

Some qualitative research techniques which could be used in developing ideas for new products include gap analysis, depth interviews, action studies, brainstorming and synectics.

Gap analysis is concerned with identifying potential opportunities for new products from analysis of the positions (as perceived by consumers) of existing products and brands. (See the discussion on perceptual mapping in Chapter 13.) A simple perceptual model of the market, as viewed by the consumer, is constructed and research is then aimed at discovering 'unoccupied territory'.

A representative sample of consumers would be interviewed and a series of attitudinal measurements relevant to particular products would be collected. By means of multivariate analysis techniques, the resultant data would be analysed and indications may be given of new product opportunities.

Depth interviews, as discussed earlier, may be used to discover people's covert feelings about, for example, day-to-day tasks such as housekeeping, cooking, laundry, etc. New product ideas may be sparked off during these interviews.

Action studies – case histories – in which very detailed studies of specific consumers' behaviour are made may provide useful guides to marketers. A panel of housewives may be asked to keep a detailed record ('diary') of their cooking habits – products bought, methods of usage, etc. These records may be used to assist recall in subsequent depth interviews. From these studies it may be possible to detect, for example, irritation with existing versions of products, and suggestions may be given about improved or wholly new product concepts.

Brainstorming is a method of group idea-generation which was developed by an advertising executive, Alex Osborn, in the late 1930s. In Osborn's[28] words the essence of brainstorming is 'to practise a conference technique by which a group attempts to find a solution for a specific problem by amassing all the ideas spontaneously contributed by its members'.

During the idea-generation stage, no judgement or evaluation is to be made; the process is intended to encourage *ideas*. Later, these will be subject to rigorous analysis; many are likely to be rejected, but some may well contain the elements of new product concepts.

Synectics 'is the study of processes leading to invention, with the end aim of solving practical problems, especially by a synectics group, a miscellaneous group of people of imagination and ability, but varied interests' (*Chambers, 20th Century Dictionary*).

This technique is attributable to W. J. J. Gordon[29] who, in 1961, summarized the results of over a decade of research into creativity. He suggested that individual creativity was associated with certain psychological states. If these could be induced, the incidence of creative breakthroughs might be increased. He collaborated with George Prince who developed this technique.

The synectics process aims to encourage people to view problems in a new light; to be willing to perceive how strange elements may be fitted into the framework of what is familiar or known. At the same time, people are stimulated to acquire a new way of looking at familiar objects or methods of operation; to break free from the limited perspectives imposed by familiarity.

As distinct from brainstorming, which Gordon felt was inclined to produce solutions before all aspects of a problem had been adequately developed, synectics was intended to give only a very broad indication of the problem so that creative thought would range freely.

One example of the application of this process involved designing a vapour-proof method of closing vapour-proof suits worn by workers who handled high-powered toxic fuels. Conventional devices such as zip, buttons, and snaps, were inadequate. Osborn would have described the problem in just this form to a brainstorming group. Gordon, on the other hand, would have kept the specific problem a secret and instead sparked off a discussion of the general notion 'closure'. This might lead to images of different closure mechanisms such as birds' nests, mouths, or thread. As the group exhausted the initial perspectives, Gordon would gradually interject facts that further defined the problem. The group then had new fields to discuss. Only when Gordon sensed that the group was close to a good solution would he describe the exact nature of the problem. Then the group would start to refine the solution. These sessions would last a minimum of three hours, and often longer, for Gordon believed that participants would become so weary that sheer fatigue would eventually liberate ideas.

Brainstorming and synectics are related techniques; both aim to solve problems by encouraging people to develop innovative, open-minded approaches when considering matters that are put before them.

These techniques seem closely related to the concept of *lateral thinking* which has been popularized by Edward de Bono[30] who, with zealous commitment, has advocated the superiority of lateral thinking over traditional vertical thinking in problem solving. In following the latter strategy, different approaches are pursued in a sequential, logical manner until a promising one is found at last. However, the former strategy involves continuing to generate as many approaches as possible even *after* a promising one has been found; no sequential discipline is exercised during these various steps. *Lateral thinking* encourages exploration in pursuing themes, stimulates creative imagination, and may lead to unexpected but highly useful discoveries, as well as improving the quality of decision making. Many successful innovations have been developed – inventions which have curious origins.[2]

KEYPOINT

Some principal methods of researching consumer products

Gap analysis

Depth interviews

Action studies (case studies)

Brainstorming

Synectics

Lateral thinking

7.4 Modified approach to qualitative research

Wendy Gordon[8] refers to the belief that 'most market research attempts to understand the past, and by so doing, predicts the future'. She feels that few would argue that the past does not influence the present, but that the linear relationship cannot be upheld; it is essentially non-linear and attempts by market researchers to forecast future patterns of behaviour 'are rarely accurate'. The reason, she says, is simple and should be known to all: 'people do not know what they will do until the reality of the product, service, new commercial or new identity makes them head on in the future'.[8] Their responses will then depend on their existing needs and circumstances. Sobering thoughts indeed from one of the leading qualitative researchers practising today. But organizations and individuals must prepare for the future as well as living – and hopefully – prospering in the present from decisions taken at some time in the past.

New products and services are the life-blood of organizations (see Chapters 1 and 9), and it is pertinent to ask what, if anything, qualitative research can do to aid the vital process of innovation. This problem has occupied Peter Sampson's attention for some years, and in a classic article[31] he stated that because traditional techniques used in a conventional way provide very little of value in obtaining new product ideas *direct* from consumers, he had developed variations in the hope that these would be more productive.

Sampson's researches involved a 'traditional group' (B, C1, C2 housewives, all with young children) whose group discussions were concerned with the use of existing children's products generally and products especially given to their children. They were asked to suggest new products. Sampson found them 'singularly lacking in imagination', and very little of value came from the group discussions.

A second group were of both men and women from teenagers upwards and ranging over B, C1, and C2 social classes. They were recruited on their ability to give 'divergent' answers to a certain problem: 'How many uses can you think of for a housebrick?' Only those able to give a minimum of six unusual answers to this question were selected to take part in the group discussions which had three stages.

In the first stage, group members were asked to imagine they were children in considering children's food and drinks. The next stage involved subdividing the group and presenting each sub-group with the task of inventing a viable new product specifically for children; the types of product to be considered were specified as: a drink, a breakfast food, a spread, a dessert, a savoury, and a biscuit. The nine group members were divided into three groups of three to invent the first product, and re-shuffled to consider the remaining products. Hence, each person contributed to two sub-groups which focused on two products. The third stage consisted of evaluation by the panel of each proposed new product. The panel was arbitrarily divided into 'parents' and 'children'.

This modified synectics approach to generating new product ideas resulted in much more imaginative results; six potentially good product concepts resulted.

Marketing research clearly plays, or should play, a central role in the identification and profitable exploitation of new product ideas. This means that firms should constantly monitor the markets in which they operate (or plan to operate), so that trends and market gaps related to resources are identified. Creative flair is not to be frustrated, of course, but the basic analytical approach should be applied to the productive ideas of 'brainstorming' and other creative sessions.

Of course, marketing research itself cannot guarantee successful innovation. Data need interpretation and business decisions have still to be taken. Risk is always present – otherwise managers would largely be superfluous.

7.5 Attitude research

The measurement of behavioural factors such as attitudes and motivation has been attempted by researchers using a variety of techniques.

None is fully satisfactory, the ones that are the most reliable and valid from a technical viewpoint generally being the most difficult, and expensive, to apply. The selection of the 'best' technique in a particular situation is still a highly controversial question.[32]

In practice, researchers endeavour to measure attitudes by means of attitude scales and related techniques such as semantic differential scales. In addition, disguised methods involving projective techniques may also be used for studying motivation.

Two important factors are fundamental to all research activities, including attitude scaling: *validity* and *reliability*. In Chapter 2 it was stated that these concepts are crucial and deserve full recognition by all who are engaged in research of any kind.

These concepts are interrelated; they are not readily distinguished and some degree of overlap seems almost inevitable.

The *validity* of an attitude scale refers to the extent to which it is free from both random and systematic error, and measures what it is supposed to measure – examples were given in Chapter 2 of a thermometer and a barometer.

To be valid, a research measure must also be reliable. But if it is reliable, it may or may not be valid. Hence, *reliability* is a necessary but not sufficient condition for *validity*. For example, a certain type of attitude scale may possess the quality of *reliability*, but it may not be *valid* to use it in a particular research project. Generally, it is easier to check the former than the latter.

Reliability, as noted earlier, refers to the stability and consistency of the results derived from research; to the probability that the same results would be obtained if the measure used in the research were replicated.

Reliability can be tested by the following methods:

1. By repeating a given test and comparing the two measurements (test–re-test). This is done by calculating the correlation between the results of the replicated and original tests.

2. By comparing measurements on two comparable forms of the same test (equivalent forms).

3. By the traditional method of comparing measurements on one-half of the test with those noted on the other half, the result being expressed as a coefficient of correlation (split-half).

Oppenheim[17] notes that reliability is always a matter of degree, which is expressed as a correlation coefficient, and it is rare to find reliabilities in the social and behavioural sciences much above 0.90.

Validity of a test rests on suitable external criteria being available, and it can be determined by any or all of the following methods:

1. *Content validity*: established by the personal judgements of experts in the particular field.

2. *Concurrent and predictive validity* involving matching test results against some external criterion; there appear to be few cases of this type of validation.

3. *Construct validity* by testing 'known' groups or types of respondents who could reasonably be expected to hold certain attitudes which differ towards some defined object.

An American handbook[32] gives a clear and comprehensive account of the most important scales used in marketing, consumer behaviour and social research – 124 scales are described and systematically evaluated against criteria such as construct, description, development, validity and statistical scores.

7.6 Types of scales

Before considering specific scaling techniques it will be helpful to review briefly the principal types of scales which are in use. These can be classified as: nominal, ordinal, interval, and ratio.

Nominal

Nominal scales are the least sophisticated; they involve nothing more than simple classification by certain attributes which are then quantified. These may refer to population characteristics based on age or sex, or ownership of a specific consumer durable such as an automatic washing machine.

Ordinal

Ordinal scales, also called ranking scales, rank the objects which are being studied according to certain characteristics. Ranking is a technique which has been widely used for many years in psychology and sociology. While the rank order of a group of items according to some characteristic is indicated, no measure of the differences between the ranks is given. The 'distance' between two ranks may be substantial and yet another pair of ranks may have only a very slight difference between them. For example, the distance between ranking one and ranking two may be substantially different from that between ranking two and ranking three. Ranking is very widely used in grading people, products, and events. It is important to define clearly the attribute which is being ranked; this could refer to competitive products in terms of taste or freshness, or in evaluating shoppers' reactions to various types of grocery outlets (independent shop, 'symbol' shop, large company supermarket, etc.). The method of 'paired comparisons' is sometimes used with ordinal scales. The objects to be ranked are considered two at a time, and all possible combinations of pairs are considered. This results in a steeply rising number of combinations as the number of objects increases, and because of this the method has rather limited usefulness. To illustrate this difficulty, paired comparison will be calculated for 5, 10, and 20 pairs, using the formula $\frac{1}{2}n(n-1)$ where n = number of objects to be ranked: A, B, C, D, E. This involves comparisons between:

A and B	B and C	C and D	D and E
A and C	B and D	C and E	
A and D	B and E		
A and E			

By formula $\frac{1}{2}n(n-1)$:

$$= \frac{5}{2} \times 4$$

$$= 10 \text{ (as shown independently in detail above)}$$

Taking 10 objects, by same formula:

$$= 5 \times 9$$
$$= 45$$

Taking 20 objects, by same formula

$$= 10 \times 19$$
$$= 190$$

Statistical techniques which can be applied to ranked data are limited to positional measures which deal with *order*, e.g. median, quartile, percentile. Ranking or ordinal scales are, therefore, limited in the quality of the information which they can provide. Mere ranking of a group of items with regard to some attribute held in common, does not imply that the 'steps' between ranks are equal.

Interval

Interval scales (also known as 'cardinal') use equal units of measurement. This makes it possible to state not only the order of scale scores but also the distances between individual scores. The zero point is fixed arbitrarily and measurements are taken from it, as in a temperature scale. This limits the arithmetical calculations, since no value on the scale is a multiple of another. While the differences between pairs of scale positions, e.g. 2 and 3 and 7 and 8, are identical, it is not correct to say that score 8 has four times the strength of score two. This can be checked readily against temperature readings of 80°F and 20°F, taking the formula for converting Fahrenheit to Centigrade:

$$T_c = \tfrac{5}{9}(T_f - 32)$$

$$\text{Therefore, } 80°F = 26.6°C \text{ and } 20°F = -6.6°C$$

If three competitive products were being assessed for buying preferences, the first might attain the highest score of, say, 8, the second score might be 4, and the lowest score 2. It cannot be said, however, that the first product is twice as much liked as the second one, because in an interval scale the zero point, as noted already, is fixed arbitrarily. But it is acceptable to report that the first product is clearly more favoured than the other two, and that the degree of buying preference between the first and second product is twice that existing between the second and third products.

Interval scales permit the use of statistical measures such as the arithmetic mean, standard deviation, correlation coefficient, and tests of significance.

Ratio

Ratio scales have fixed origin or zero points, which allow all arithmetical operations to be used. This means that, among other calculations, multiplication of scale points for comparison purposes is allowable. Ratio scales are found in the physical sciences, e.g. for measuring length or weight. Many marketing measurements, e.g. sales, market share, number of customers, etc., possess the properties of a ratio scale because in each instance a natural or absolute zero exists.

KEYPOINT

Attitude research

Attitude scales

Semantic differential scales

Projective techniques:

Two important factors: 1. validity and 2. reliability

> *Principal scaling techniques:*
>
> Nominal (simple classification)
>
> Ordinal (ranking)
>
> Interval (equal units of measurement)
>
> Ratio (fixed origin or zero points; used for marketing analyses)
>
> *Variety of techniques but none fully satisfactory*

7.7 Principal scaling methods

Rating scales are those which measure by means of ordinal, interval, or ratio scales; they may be verbal, diagrammatic, or numerical. They are, as Oppenheim observes,[17] relatively overt measuring instruments used in surveys. Too much should not be expected of them, because they are not designed to give subtle insights into individual cases – they divide into broad groups people who hold similar attitudes related to the subject of a survey. Respondents are put on a continuum in relative, not absolute, terms.

Several kinds of scaling methods exist and have been used widely in marketing research. The principal scaling methods are now considered in some detail.

Thurstone's equal-appearing intervals (differential scale)

This classic example of an interval scale entails elaborate preparation and involves sophisticated mathematical procedures. Because of these complications, the method tends to be little used in commercial practice.

In the late 1920s, Thurstone and Chave[33] published a series of scales relating specifically to measuring attitudes towards such matters as capital punishment, evolution, free trade, patriotism, war, censorship, etc. Thurstone scales can be adapted to measure attitudes towards any type of object, using the following procedure:

1. A large number of statements (favourable and unfavourable) relating to the survey subject is collected by the researcher.
2. These statements are independently assessed by a large* number of judges, who classify them in 11 groups, from 'most favourable' to 'least favourable'. The median values of each group are calculated.
3. Between 20 and 25 statements are finally selected, after discarding those which do not attract general support, as indicated by the interquartile range which measures the scatter of judgements.
4. These selected statements are presented, in random order, to respondents, who are asked to confirm all those statements with which they agree.
5. Respondents' total scores are calculated simply by taking the mean or median of the median values of all the statements which have been confirmed.

---

* This has varied considerably over reported studies. Between 100 and 150 statements and 40 and 60 judges have been involved, though with some tests as many as 300 judges have been used.

Critics of this method feel that the attitudes of those who judge the original collection of statements may bias the selection of those used in the test. Research into this problem does not appear to be conclusive, though Ballachey and colleagues[34] comment that 'the attitude of the judge will bias his judgements of items. However, in most cases this effect will be small. Only judges with extreme attitudes will show substantial distortion.'

It would seem that caution should be exercised in selecting judges who are most likely to be similar in their attitudes to the people eventually to be surveyed. Some researchers have speculated on whether ethnic judges would be likely to produce the same scale measurements as white judges on a subject such as colour prejudice. Obviously, it would be unwise deliberately to include judges with extreme views about the matter under survey.

Empirical evidence has indicated that reliable scale values for statements can be obtained from a relatively small number of judges. In some of Thurstone's early experiments as many as 300 judges were used; later researchers have obtained reliable scale values with fewer than 50. Clearly, this affects the time and work involved in the preparation of Thurstone scales.

Likert summated ratings

Rensis Likert published 'A technique for the measurement of attitudes'[35] in 1932, in which he described a new method of attitude scaling known as Likert scales – a type of verbal rating scale. The following procedure is used:

1. A large number of statements relating to the particular object being surveyed is collected by the researcher.

2. These statements are then administered to a group of people representative of those whose attitudes are being studied, and they are asked to respond to each statement by indicating whether they:
   (a) strongly agree
   (b) agree
   (c) are uncertain
   (d) disagree
   (e) strongly disagree

3. These five categories are then scored, usually using 5, 4, 3, 2, 1, respectively, for favourable statements, and the reverse order for unfavourable statements.

4. Individual scores are achieved by totalling the item scores of each statement. This total can be compared with the maximum possible score. For example, a set of 12 statements carries a maximum possible score of 60 (5×12), and a minimum score of 12 (1×12). If an individual's total score amounts to 50, it would indicate a decidedly positive attitude to the survey problem.

5. Item analysis is now done to select the most discriminating items by computing for each item the correlation between item scores and the total of all item scores. Those with the highest correlations are retained for inclusion in the survey questionnaire. The number of items in a scale is arbitrary and is sometimes quite small.

Likert does not produce an interval scale, and it would not be correct to reach any conclusions about the meaning of the distances between scale positions. Respondents are merely ranked along a continuum relating to the study of a particular attitude. Scores achieved by individual respondents are only relative to other respondents' total scores.

Table 7.1   Scoring of statements

Statements	Strongly agree	Agree	Uncertain	Disagree	Strongly disagree
'Positive' +	5	4	3	2	1
'Negative' −	1	2	3	4	5

Moreover, it cannot be assumed that the mid-point on a Likert scale is necessarily the precise middle between the two extreme scores.

Likert scales are popular because they have been shown to have good reliability, are simpler to construct than Thurstone scales (with which they correlate favourably), and give rather better information about the *degree* of respondents' feelings. This allows respondents rather more freedom in expressing their views than restricting them to simple 'agree/disagree' endorsements as used in Thurstone scaling.

Example   If Likert scaling is applied to advertising, the collected statements, ranging from positive to negative, could be scored as shown in Table 7.1. Statements which could be used are as follows (and other statements could be devised):

- − 'Advertising increases the prices we have to pay for products.'
- + 'Advertising is an important source of information for consumers.'
- + 'Advertising makes an important contribution to modern living standards.'
- − 'Advertising is socially undesirable and a wasteful use of resources.'

Respondents are asked to indicate their reaction to each statement. High total scores reflect strongly favourable attitudes to advertising; lower total scores indicate unfavourable attitudes. However, it is important to note that a given total score may have different meanings because individual scores may, of course, be differently distributed.

Used in connection with tracking studies (see Chapter 10), a typical Likert scale item might be: 'I like the commercial for brand X very much.'[37]

Another example of this type of scale might be concerned with an evaluation of a retail store's image. A sample of shoppers would be asked to respond to a series of statements such as

Statements	Strongly agree	Agree	Uncertain	Disagree	Strongly disagree
– is generally a friendly store		✖			
– is a well-laid out store		✖			
– is a store for good bargains	✖				

etc.

Values of 5 (strongly agree) down to 1 (strongly disagree) would be totalled to produce a summated score. So far, the example shows a markedly positive attitude towards the store.

Worcester[37] has observed that not only are Likert scales the most frequently used method of scaling, but they also tend to be most misused because of the relative ease with which they can be devised. While a Thurstone scale demands care in construction, a Likert scale can be constructed fairly easily. All the overworked research executive has to do is to 'think up a few contentious statements, add a Likert agree–disagree scale, and, hey presto, he has a ready-made questionnaire'.

Likert scales are easy for respondents to understand, but this strength is also a research weakness, for simple wording does not guarantee that perceptual differences will not arise. Is a scale position such as 'very dissatisfied' the precise negative of 'very satisfied'?

From a statistical appraisal of the relative precision of verbal scales, Worcester pleaded for care in the selection of words such as 'some', 'moderate', and 'considerable' to avoid misunderstandings.

A modifying adverb such as 'slightly' should be used to balance the side point statements, as follows:

agree strongly		agree strongly
agree *slightly*		agree
	preferred to:	
disagree *slightly*		disagree
disagree strongly		disagree strongly

In balanced 'agree–disagree' statements 'slightly' seems better than 'fairly' or 'quite', but in balanced 'satisfaction' scales, 'fairly' appears to be preferable. Another interesting insight from this research revealed that boxes indicating scale positions 'are not necessarily as "accurate" as some verbal tags'. (See also Chapter 13 for discussion of SERVQUAL scales to measure, as the title suggests, the perceived quality of service received by consumers.)

KEYPOINT

Likert summated ratings

popular rating scale;

series of statements rates over five evaluations: strongly agree . . . strongly disagree;

scored 5, 4, 3, 2, 1 (favourable); 1, 2, 3, 4, 5 (unfavourable)

individual scores totalled and compared with maximum possible score;

scores are merely relative to other respondents' scores

good reliability; easy to construct; respondent given freedom of expression; give information about *degree* of respondent's feelings

Care needed in drafting statements used in scale.

Guttman's scales (scalogram analysis)

Shortly before the Second World War, Louis Guttman and his associates[38] developed a method of cumulative scaling which attempted to define more accurately the neutral area of an attitude scale.

The method is rather complicated, but basically it is as follows:

1. Respondents are asked a series of attitude questions on the same subject and relating to the same dimension of that subject.

2. Intensity of feeling is registered by asking after each question: 'How strongly do you feel about this?'

    Answers are classified by such intensities as: strongly agree, agree, undecided, disagree, strongly disagree. 'Favourable' statements are scored 4 to 0.

3. Each individual respondent's content score is computed, e.g. the maximum will be the number of statements times the highest intensity score. (If there are 7 statements and 4 is the highest score, $7 \times 4 = 28$; the range of possible scores will lie between 0 and 28.)

4. Scores of individual respondents are entered on a 'scalogram' board, which is a device designed to simplify the process against content scores, and the resulting curves are termed 'intensity curves'. The shape of these curves is of considerable value in indicating the distribution of attitudes in a given population. A flat-bottomed, U-shaped curve indicates a wide area of neutral attitudes, whereas a sharply angled curve downward and then rising steeply indicates that attitudes are held by two strongly contrasted groups.

Critics of Guttman scales have commented on the method of selecting the initial set of attitude statements, and it does seem that this selection of suitable statements was a matter of intuition and experience.

The fact that Guttman's method of scaling tackles the problem of the neutral region of attitude measurement makes it worth serious consideration by marketing researchers. As has already been seen, the other scaling techniques fail to deal with this region satisfactorily.

Apart from classifying responses from 'strongly agree' to 'strongly disagree', intensity of feeling can be conveyed graphically by a scale with divisions printed in various type sizes:

YES	YES	yes	no	NO	**NO**
SLOW	SLOW	slow	fast	FAST	**FAST**

A Guttman scale is similar to a Likert scale in that respondents express their agreement or otherwise with a series of statements about a specific subject. However, the distinctive difference between these types of scale arises because the Guttman technique is a cumulative scale, which means that statements are selected so that the responses to succeeding statements can be reasonably inferred from the response given to an earlier one. For example, a set of statements concerning company sales might be drafted as follows:

1. Group sales next quarter year will be considerably higher than this quarter.

2. Group sales next quarter will be higher than this quarter.

3. Group sales will show an improvement next quarter.

4. Group sales in the next quarter will be about the same or better than this quarter.

These statements are termed 'scalable', because if a respondent agrees with statement 1 it can be assumed that he or she will also agree with the succeeding ones. It is evident that this respondent has a more optimistic view of future business than another respondent whose agreement is confined to statement 4.

The survey concerned with evaluating people's awareness and attitudes to aircraft noise in the vicinity of Heathrow Airport used a Guttman scale and this technique was also applied to investigate attitudes towards ball-point pens.[39] However, in this particular study, the researcher concluded that the complexity of the Guttman technique rendered it not particularly suitable for relatively simple problems in attitude research.

Oppenheim[17] describes Guttman's procedures as laborious and lacking the certainty that a usable scale will result. Also, problems of validation exist with scalogram analysis, although, as a rule, reliability is high, and many Guttman scales have been developed successfully in, for example, socio-political, psychiatric and consumer research.

Semantic differential

This popular, diagrammatic scaling procedure was developed by Osgood *et al.*[40] of the Institute of Communications Research of the University of Illinois, to measure the connotative meaning of concepts. It rests on the assumption that the meaning of an object for an individual includes both the more obvious denotative meaning, which can readily be given, and also the connotative meanings which are frequently more subtle and difficult to describe. The semantic differential has been shown to be an easy method of quantifying the intensity and also the content of attitudes towards certain concepts.

The procedure is flexible, reasonably reliable, and much simpler to use than either Thurstone or Guttman scales. Basically, it usually consists of a number of seven-point rating scales that are bipolar with each extreme defined by an adjective or adjectival phrase. It is important that the bipolar terms used define accurately the difference between two extreme feelings. The words should be carefully chosen so that respondents are not confused.

The antonyms should, of course, be relevant to the subject being surveyed. *Monopolar* scales, such as 'warm–not warm' may be used, and in this case, the mid-point merely signifies a step on the scale from 'not warm' to 'warm'. On the other hand, a *bipolar* scale would measure the quoted attributes as 'warm–cold', which means that the mid-point represents a neutral point meaning neither warm nor cold.[41]

Jean Morton-Williams[41] has commented that some researchers prefer five-point rather than seven-point semantic scales, because the former are easier for interviewers to explain and for informants to understand. From an inspection of answer patterns on seven-point scales, there appears to be a tendency for many respondents to restrict their answers to the extreme position and one other on each side of the mid-point.

However, research[17] has indicated that seven-point intervals are usually optional, although some researchers prefer to use five-point or even three-point scales for specific purposes:

Respondents are asked to rate each of a number of objects or concepts along a continuum. They should respond spontaneously as researchers seek first impressions, not studied answers.

As with Likert scales, the mid-point of a semantic differential may not coincide with the precise neutral region between two opposing attitudes. Further, it cannot be assumed that the seven points on the continuum are equally spaced.

Osgood developed 20 rating scales which have wide application:

active/passive	unsuccessful/successful
cruel/kind	important/unimportant
curved/straight	angular/rounded
masculine/feminine	calm/excitable

untimely/timely	false/true
savoury/tasteless	usual/unusual
hard/soft	colourless/colourful
new/old	slow/fast
good/bad	beautiful/ugly
weak/strong	wise/foolish

Scales have also been used successfully for marketing research investigations into consumer attitudes covering corporate image, product image, brand image, advertising image, etc. In these areas it is often difficult for consumers to articulate their feelings, and the semantic differential offers them a convenient and easily understood method of expressing themselves.

The mechanics of operating semantic differential scales are simple:

Fair	. X	Unfair
Active	. . X	Passive
Usual	. . . X . . .	Unusual
Modern	. . . . . X . . .	Old fashioned

Respondents are asked to describe some particular concept along a seven-point scale by placing a check mark (X) in the position which reflects their feelings. The seven positions could be shown as:

Extremely fair	Both	Slightly unfair
Very fair	fair and	Very unfair
Slightly fair	unfair	Extremely unfair

Weights are assigned to continuum positions, e.g. 3, 2, 1, 0, -1, -2, -3 (this assumes equal intervals). Total ratings of individual respondents on the same scale can be combined and group mean scores computed which will give profiles for subjects along certain dimensions. Interesting comparisons can be made over time of attitudinal changes towards a company, its products, servicing arrangements and other important areas of activity.

Descriptive phrases instead of bipolar adjectives can be particularly effective in measuring the acceptability of certain features of a product or service. The 'image' which products acquire can be analysed, and the contribution made by individual features can be quantified. Competing brands can be subjected to the same test, and their profiles compared. Figure 7.2 relates to a fruit-flavoured 'soft' drink of which there are three well-known brands in popular demand.

Types of consumer can also be scaled and profiles established for different brands of products. This gives rather more qualitative information about consumers than the usual demographic breakdown. For example, housewives could be classified along a scale:

Careful shopper	Free and easy shopper
'Working' housewife	'Non-working' housewife
Likes to entertain friend	Likes a quiet life

Cars could be profiled along some of the following dimensions:

Expense account car	Family man's car
Holds the road well	Does not hold the road well
Looks a successful man's car	Looks like anyone's car
Quiet running car	Noisy running car
Sturdy looking	Does not look well built

Supermarkets could be surveyed using semantic differential scales designed to give profiles of them as seen by consumers: the following bipolar scales would be relevant:

good/bad	large/small
friendly/unfriendly	fair/unfair
modern/old fashioned	reliable/unreliable
pleasing/annoying	active/passive
convenient/inconvenient	low prices/high prices
clean/dirty	roomy/crowded
neat/disorderly	

Semantic scaling has proved to be a popular methodology; it is convenient to use, lends itself well to graphical representation – particularly comparative evaluations, as seen in Figure 7.2; it is flexible and can be applied to many types of products/services. However, its intrinsic versatility is tempered to some degree by the following considerations: (1) the adjectives or phrases used at each end of the scales must be carefully chosen and be directly relevant to the particular issue being surveyed. This might, for instance, be concerned with the effectiveness of car servicing facilities at a nominated garage. Osgood originated – as seen earlier – 20 rating scales which resulted from his researches. Other adjectival scale points have been derived from discussion groups, etc. In all cases, researchers must be careful in their choice of antonyms; subjectivity is almost bound to influence responses to the pole extremes of 'fast' and 'slow': a BMW Series 3 driver's rating of speed is likely to be rather different from that given by the driver of a low-powered car; (2) there may be a tendency for the so-called 'halo effect' to be influential, viz. when a generally favourable (or unfavourable) impression of, for example, a retail store or a hairdressing salon, tends to spread and influence reactions to specific aspects of these establishments. To minimize

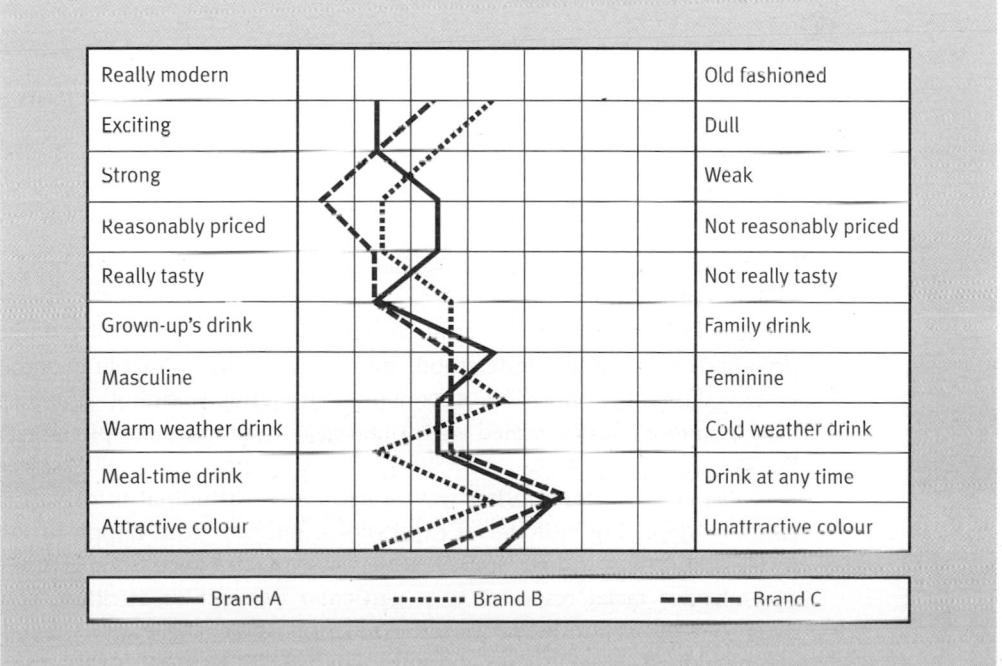

Figure 7.2 Brand profile – fruit-flavoured soft drink

this type of bias, the positive end of the bipolar scale should be randomized when constructing semantic differentials.

KEYPOINT

Semantic differential scaling (Osgood)

popular and easy method of quantifying intensity and also content of attitudes towards specific concepts;

flexible, reasonably reliable and easily usable system;

basically 7-point scale with bi-polar adjectives/phrases: active/passive; false/true; slow/fast.

scored 3, 2, 1, 0, −1, −2, −3;

many applications: people, products, events, etc.;

convenient, useful graphics, comparative evaluations, flexible and adaptable;

but danger of subjectivity and halo effect.

Stapel scale

This is a modified version of the semantic differential, and is a type of rating scale used with single adjectives/phrases instead of bipolar opposites. The scale is even-numbered and could range from +5 through to −5. It might be useful to evaluate the quality of car-servicing arrangements at competing garages. Respondents would be asked to place a circle around the score which corresponded with their perceptions; comparative scores from a sample of car drivers could be computed from the results obtained from this type of relatively simple enquiry:

Quality of car-servicing   +5   +4   +3   +2   +1   −1   −2   −3   −4   −5

(This evaluation could be made more useful by specifying certain aspects of the car-servicing arrangements.)

Diagrammatic scales

Various diagrammatic rating scales have been devised to meet the needs of certain types of research project.

Thermometer scales are sometimes used to simplify multi-choice questions. The graphic presentation is readily understood, and is particularly valuable in some overseas markets where difficulties may be experienced in understanding qualitative phrases. The 'thermometer' can be scaled with numerical values and simple adjectives, as shown in Fig. 7.3.

'Smiley' scales offer another way of gathering attitudinal information by using simple cartoons depicting basic facial expressions, ranging from happy to miserable, as shown in Fig. 7.4. The so-called 'smiley' scale can be very effective in juvenile research studies; the relevant facial response to a particular concept or attribute could be underlined or ringed by respondents. At the evaluation stage, the various facial images could be given values 1–5, and scores computed for specific elements of the product/service under survey.

7.8 Kelly's personal construct theory

Some leading marketing researchers have felt that traditional approaches to the study of attitudes are not entirely satisfactory and a more comprehensive method of appreciating consumers' needs is desirable.

It is desirable, for instance, that marketers should know more about how those who buy their products or use their services 'see' the world about them; how they interact with their families or their colleagues; how they deal with the various messages they receive, ranging from personal and professional correspondence to mass media communications like radio, television and the press as well as the non-stop flow of diverse kinds of promotional activities, such as brand advertising.

This more comprehensive approach rests on personal construct theory, which was a new theory of human behaviour, based on a 'repertory grid' technique of interviewing and classifying subjects, propounded by Professor George A. Kelly in his book *The Psychology of Personal Constructs*. Professor Kelly, who died in 1967, was Professor of Psychology at the

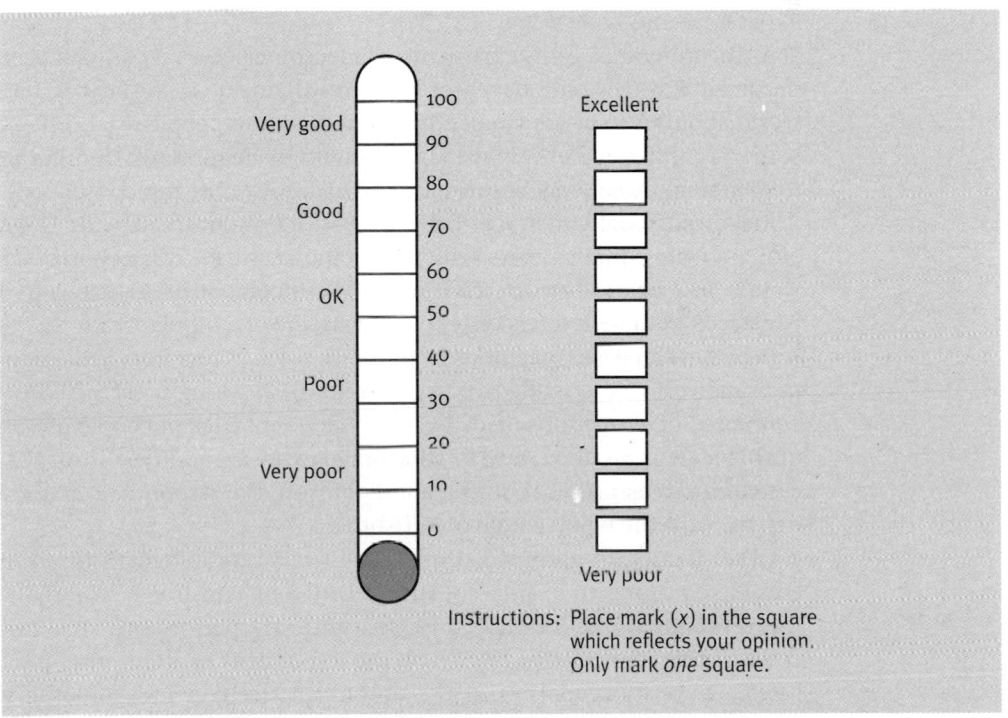

Figure 7.3   Presentation of questions – the thermometer

Figure 7.4   The 'smiley scale': basic facial reactions to specific aspects of product/service

Ohio State University, qualifying first as a mathematician and physicist before taking a psychology degree.

Kelly visualized all as scientists: '. . . each in [a] personal way assumed more of the structure of a scientist, ever seeking to predict and control . . . events in which he [or she] is involved'.[54]

Man is active and involved in determining his actions – not a mere pawn in the business game as Vance Packard and other popular writers have suggested. Attempts to understand what is happening and to predict the course of future events use certain criteria in evaluation. The criteria used will be personal to him or her, and these Kelly termed 'constructs'. Within the limitations of these constructs, an individual endeavours to bring some order into the perceptual world. Kelly held that since an individual's behaviour is governed by attempts to predict the future, a detailed study of these constructs will give insight into his or her whole personality and behaviour.

In the course of living, the individual develops a series of constructs to help in dealing with situations which arise. The terms of these constructs may limit, of course, the appreciation of particular situations, but they form, in general, an economical method of dealing with problems and allow the future to be considered within the limits of personal experience and knowledge.

As the individual gains experience of life, some personal constructs may be discarded or modified and new ones developed which will enable a satisfactory relationship with the world about us to be continued. It is conceded that people react differently to events and some, according to Kelly, may exhibit certain inadequacies stemming from deficiencies in their system of personal constructs, of which they may not consciously be aware.

Kelly's personal construct theory is basically concerned with classifying personality along a series of constructs which are bipolar, single dimensional scales. For example, weight is a true construct referring to the bipolar scale light/heavy. But light is not a construct, because it refers only to one extreme of a bipolar scale.

Kelly developed an ingenious technique known as repertory grid analysis which enabled personality to be classified on a scientific basis along a set of constructs. The grid is composed of evaluations made by a respondent of a list of people presented to him in sets of three. He is asked to state in what way any of them differs from the other two. In the case of three men, Smith, Jones, and Robinson, the respondent may use the construct of height, with the bipolar scale of tall/short.

Other names, in groups of three, are then taken systematically from the list and are considered along the same construct. Different constructs will then be developed by the respondent and similarly assessed until a repertory grid has been constructed of certain criteria or constructs used by the respondent in attempting to classify the persons listed. Correlation analysis of the entries on the grid indicates the way in which the respondent's constructs are related to each other.

Table 7.2 shows a possible repertory grid analysis.

Table 7.2   Repertory grid analysis

	Tall/Short	Good/Bad	Fat/Thin	Etc.
Smith	0	1	1	
Jones	1	0	0	
Robinson	0	1	0	

(Score 1 for left-hand pole; 0 for right-hand pole)

Bipolar constructs may be used in conjunction with scaling concepts, as Kelly indicated in developing his theory (see Figure 7.5). It will be noted from this diagram that a product would be rated favourably if it is perceived to be durable, pretty and cheap, whereas it would be regarded unfavourably if it were perceived to be non-durable, ugly and expensive.

The value of Kelly's construct theory to marketing analysis has been given relatively little attention. In the case of brand development, it is important to know what attributes are likely to be perceived as relevant to their needs by certain types of consumers. Conflict between projected attributes may arise: 'Should we include a "brand for young people" or a "brand that washes whiter", if it is not feasible to have both versions of this type of product? And what, if any, is the significance of either attribute?'[43] With such problems, Kelly's Grids may be useful in the preliminary stages of discriminating characteristics of brands which are likely to attract certain kinds of consumers.

That Kellian psychology can make a valuable contribution to advertising studies is also acknowledged by Francis Harmar-Brown,[44] who points out:

Advertisements are today quite an important part of the mass of data that a person has to organise and control in order to predict future events. It would be extremely interesting to know what constructs in this area, different sub-groups of people have in common; and in what way these sub-groups are related to existing media groups, for example. Repertory grid analyses on a group of respondents using as data a series of different advertisements in a related product field, would, I think, yield fascinating results. But as far as I know, this has not yet been done. Instead, the advertising business has ignored, almost completely, Kelly's theories of human behaviour and has rushed to apply repertory grid techniques in areas for which they are totally unsuitable, simply because the techniques are objective, scientific, and statistically respectable.

This carefully qualified approval of Kellian psychological techniques deserves further consideration. Harmar-Brown stresses that Kelly's techniques were designed:

not to classify the data available to a person but to reveal a person's inadequacies, or successes, in attempting the task for himself. As a marketing tool, all that repertory grid analyses tells us is that the mind of the average housewife is totally inadequate to the task of categorising a product market – not a very surprising result.

The application of Kellian methods is seen as having severe limitations as a tool of marketing analysis: 'I have been concerned with only four cases in which repertory grid analysis has been used to categorise a market. In every case the results were extremely limited, obvious to the point of banality; or downright incomprehensible.'

The valueless nature of some of the responses derived from repertory grid interviews is also noted by Sampson,[9] who categorizes two virtually useless responses:

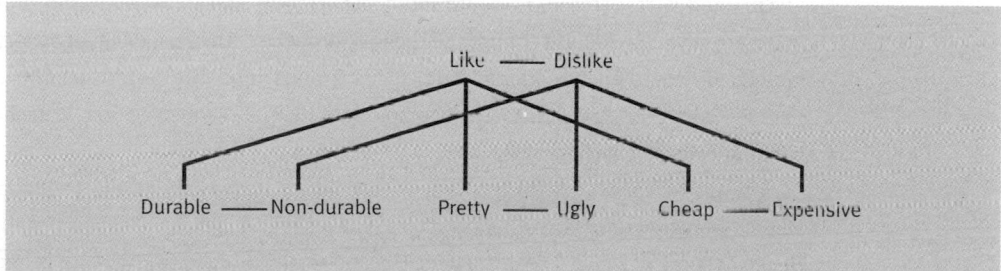

Figure 7.5   Examples of Kelly's Personal Construct Theory

1. Those which are too descriptive or irrelevant. ('Those two come in bottles; that one comes in a cardboard packet.')

2. Those which are too evaluative. ('I like those two; I don't like that one.')

Repertory grids have been used in developing new product concepts, and frequently to obtain attributes for semantic scales.

Further consideration of construct theory in the marketing sphere is called for; the intellectual attractions of Kellian techniques need to be tested at some length before they can be expected to win the support of practical researchers.

Gordon and Langmaid,[16] in fact, state that the repertory grid technique was 'all the rage in the 1960s but subsequently fell into disfavour', probably because respondents tended to express *rational* rather than *emotional* differences between brands, but these, they declare, were 'simply irrelevant to brand purchase motivations'.[18] As a result, procedures in applying the repertory grid technique have been modified, so that emotional as well as rational differences between competing brands are investigated. This is effected by giving respondents logos of three brands and asking them to divide these into a pair and a single brand, and state the reasons underlying the similarities and differences. These responses are explored in individual depth interviews.

Qualitative Research Guidelines

Both ESOMAR and the Market Research Society have issued guidelines for interviewing (see Chapter 6) and, in particular, for conducting qualitative research because it frequently entails enquiries into personal and sensitive facets of life. The MRS Qualitative Research Guidelines interpret and expand the existing Code of Conduct, and their 'main aim is to ensure that research is transparent to respondents in order to promote public support for market research. More generally, they seek to promote professionalism in the conduct of qualitative research'.[45] In addition, the Association of Qualitative Research Practitioners (AQRP), which is the UK's specialized professional body for those practising, or with interests in, qualitative research, issues *Best Practice Guidelines for Qualitative Research Recruitment.*

ESOMAR, the MRS and the AQRP are fully committed to upholding high professional standards of competence and ethical practice.

Summary

Qualitative research is essentially diagnostic; it seeks deeper understanding of factors, sometimes covert, which influence buying behaviour. Intrinsically it is subjective but for all its limitations it is able to provide unique insights which direct questioning is unable to obtain.

Qualitative research uses depth interviews (group and individual) and projective techniques; there are several variations of both of these approaches. The former cover synectics, brainstorming, indirect or non-directive interviewing, focus groups, etc. The latter include tests such as: third person, word association, sentence completion, thematic apperception, Rorschach ink blots, story completion, and psychodrama.

Attitude research uses various sealing techniques such as Thurstone's equal-appearing intervals, Likert summated ratings, Guttman's scales (scalogram analysis) and semantic ratings (Osgood *et al.*). Because some of these scales are versatile and relatively easy to use, care is needed to ensure that the resultant information is valid and reliable.

Kelly's personal construct theory provides a creative approach to understanding better how an individual deals with the many events in his perceptual world. Repertory grid analysis is a technique used to evaluate an individual's constructs, and has been useful in developing bipolar scales.

<table>
<tr>
<td>

Review and discussion questions

</td>
<td>

1. To what extent can qualitative research be considered scientific research?

2. In what circumstances might a group depth interview be more appropriate than an individual depth interview?

3. Why do you think projective techniques are so called?

4. State whether responses to the following questions will yield nominal, ordinal, interval, or ratio data:
   (a) How much money did you spend on petrol last month?
   (b) On a scale of 1 to 10, how would you rate your local supermarket for hygiene?
   (c) Did your formal education cease at primary, post primary, or third level?
   (d) What were your top ten British hits in descending order last year?

5. Outline the main differences between George A. Kelly's and Rensis Likert's approaches to measuring attitudes.

6. Many marketing research companies currently use the semantic differential as their preferred way of obtaining consumers' images of products and services. Can you suggest why this is the case?

</td>
</tr>
</table>

CAMEO CASE: Regatta Ltd

Regatta, an independent UK company, is one of the best known outdoor clothing manufacturers, specializing in the design, sourcing and supply of outdoor clothing and equipment. The company, which is based in Urmston, Manchester, was founded in 1960, and at present has 360 employees.

The company's major market segments consist of women's, men's and junior outdoor clothing, aimed at the walking/camping/boating markets; products include a range of breathables and non-breathables, such as anoraks, waterproof jackets, fleeces, walking trousers and shirts, and 'base layer' clothing (for quick drying). In addition to the wide variety of apparel, the company also makes a range of rucksacks and other accessories.

New product/design development is a key element in the company's success, and this work is generally done within the marketing department, and delivered through buying and design. This,

coupled with the ability to maintain a competitive pricing structure, means that, for customers, Regatta products represent good value for money; it is this, coupled with an extensive distribution network, that gives the company its competitive advantage in the UK.

Sales are split roughly 90 per cent–10 per cent between retail and wholesale markets, respectively, and exclusive sales agents are generally used when dealing with the retail market. Servicing existing business and generating new business is done via these sales agents and the company's own sales force. Due to the nature of the products, most sales tend to be on a seasonal basis, generally twice a year. Turnover has grown steadily, up 20 per cent in the period 1996–1997, 19.4 per cent in 1997–1998, and 16 per cent in 1998–1999. Regatta sells in three overseas markets: Benelux, Germany and France, and international sales represent some 10 per cent of turnover at present, but are growing rapidly year on year.

▶

The company uses marketing research in a number of ways, but generally to identify consumer profiles and to measure brand awareness. Most UK market research is carried out by UK research agencies, generally through the use of focus groups and/or questionnaires. International research is either done by UK-based companies or, more usually, sub-contracted to agencies based in the target country. Data generated is analysed and appropriate action is taken by Regatta's marketing department: for example, consumer and trade feedback alerted the company to the different colours and styles favoured by European consumers, and appropriate adaptations were made to some of the product ranges destined for export to these markets.

Marketing research is also used to monitor competitor activities in the UK: commercially produced reports detailing competitors' marketing spread are looked at twice a year, and the range of competitor products are examined on a seasonal basis, generally by looking at catalogues.

Questions

1. How would you measure brand awareness of the company's products in the UK? Would you adopt the same approach in the Benelux, German and French markets?

2. How would you select respondents for a focus group to identify ideas for new products? What are the main advantages and disadvantages of using the focus group as a market research tool for NPD (new product development) research?

3. Regatta has three distinct segments in its range of outdoor apparel: women, men, and junior. Using either a Likert scale or a Semantic Differential, show how you might identify to what extent and how the requirements of these segments may differ in relation to the purchase of (a) a rucksack, and (b) a fleece jacket.

Jonathan S. Swift

References

1. Lunn, J. A., 'Empirical techniques in consumer research', in: *Industrial Society*, Pelican, London, 1968.
2. Chisnall, Peter M., *Consumer Behaviour*, McGraw-Hill, Maidenhead, 1994.
3. Cooper, Peter, 'The new qualitative technology', in: *Qualitative Research: The 'New', the 'Old', and a Question Mark*, Peter Sampson (ed.), ESOMAR Marketing Research Monograph Series, vol. 2, ESOMAR, Amsterdam, 1987.
4. Market Research Society, 'Qualitative research – A summary of the concepts involved', R&D Sub-Committee on Qualitative Research, *Journal of Market Research Society*, vol. 21, no. 2, April 1979.
5. Robson, Sue, 'Analysis and interpretation of qualitative findings. Report of the Qualitative Interest Group', *Journal of the Market Research Society*, vol. 35, no. 1, January 1993.
6. Cooper, Peter, and Alan Branthwaite, 'Qualitative technology'; New perspectives on measurement and meaning through qualitative research. *Proceedings of the Market Research Society Conference*, 1977.
7. Moser, C. A., and G. Kalton, *Survey Methods in Social Investigation*, Heinemann, London, 1971.
8. Gordon, Wendy, *Goodthinking: a Guide to Qualitative Research*, Admap, Henley-on-Thames, 1999.
9. Sampson, Peter, 'Qualitative research and motivation research', in: *Consumer Market Research Handbook*, Robert Worcester and John Downham (eds), Elsevier Publishing, Amsterdam, on behalf of ESOMAR, 1986.
10. Cooper, Peter, 'Consumer understanding, change and qualitative research', *Journal of Market Research Society*, vol. 41, no. 1, January 1999.
11. Cooper, Peter, 'Comparison between the UK and US: The qualitative dimension', *Journal of Market Research Society*, vol. 31, no. 4, October 1989.
12. Sampson, Peter, 'Qualitative research in Europe: the state of the art and art of the state', in: *Qualitative research: the 'new' and the 'old' and a question mark*, Peter Sampson (ed.), ESOMAR Monograph Series, vol. 2, 1987.
13. de Groot, Gerald, 'Qualitative research: Deep, dangerous, or just plain dotty?', *European Research*, vol. 14, no. 3, July 1986.

14. Willis, Kate, 'In-depth interviews', in: *A Handbook of Market Research Techniques*, Robin Birn, Paul Hague and Phyllis Vangelder (eds), Kogan Page, London, 1990.
15. Cooper, Peter, 'market research and democracy', in: *ESOMAR Handbook of Market and Opinion Research*, Colin Donald and Phyllis Vangelder (eds), ESOMAR, Amsterdam, 1998.
16. Gordon, Wendy, and Roy Langmaid, *Qualitative Market Research: a Practitioner's and Buyer's Guide*, Gower, Aldershot, 1988.
17. Oppenheim, A. N., *Questionnaire Design, Interviewing and Attitude Measurement*, Pinter Publishers, London, 1992.
18. Savage, Mike, 'Soft focus', *Research*, Market Research Society, September 1999.
19. Sands, Saul, 'Can business afford the luxury of test marketing?', *University of Michigan Business Review*, vol. 30, no. 2, March 1978.
20. Cooper, Peter, and Giles Lenton, 'Doctor as drug', *Proceedings of BPMRG Symposium*, 1983.
21. Watson, Michael, 'Researching minorities', *Journal of the Market Research Society*, vol. 34, no. 4, October 1992.
22. Goodyear, Mary, 'Qualitative research in developing countries', *Journal of Market Research Society*, vol. 24, no. 2, April 1982.
23. Dichter, Ernest, *The Strategy of Desire*, Doubleday, New York, 1960.
24. Robson, Sue, 'Group discussions', in: *A Handbook of Market Research Techniques*, Robin Birn, Paul Hague and Phyllis Vangelder (eds), Kogan Page, London, 1990.
25. Haire, Mason, 'Projective techniques in marketing research', *Journal of Marketing*, April 1950.
26. Arndt, Johan, 'Haire's shopping list revisited', *Journal of Advertising Research*, vol. 13, no. 5, October 1973.
27. Anderson, James C., 'The validity of Haire's shopping list projective technique', *Journal of Marketing* Research, vol. 15, no. 4, November 1978.
28. Osborn, Alex F., *Applied Imagination* (3rd rev. edn), Charles Scribner's Sons, New York, 1963.
29. Gordon, W. J. J., *Synectics, The Development of Creative Capacity*, Harper & Row, New York, 1961.
30. Bono, Edward de, *Lateral Thinking*, Ward Lock, East Grinstead, 1970.
31. Sampson, Peter, 'Can consumers create new products?', *Journal of Market Research Society*, vol. 12, no. 1, 1970.
32. Bearden, William O., Richard G. Netemeyer, and Mary F. Mobley, *Handbook of Marketing Scales: multi-item measures for marketing and consumer behaviour research*, Sage Publications, Newbury Park, California, in association with the Association for Consumer Research, 1993.
33. Thurstone, L. L., and E. J. Chave, *The Measurement of Attitudes*, University of Chicago Press, 1929.
34. Krech, David, Richard S. Crutchfield, and Egerton L. Ballachey, *Individual in Society*, McGraw-Hill, New York, 1962.
35. Likert, Rensis, 'A technique for the measurement of attitudes', *Archives of Psychology*, no. 140, 1932.
36. Worcester, Robert M., and Timothy R. Burns, 'A statistical examination of the relative precision of verbal scales', *Journal of the Market Research Society*, vol. 17, no. 3, July 1975.
37. Franzen, Giep, *Brands and Advertising*, Admap Publications, Henley-on-Thames, 1999.
38. Guttman, Louis, 'The basis for scalogram analysis', in: *Measurement and Prediction*, Princeton University Press, 1950.
39. Richards, Elizabeth A., 'A commercial application of Guttman attitude scaling techniques', *Journal of Marketing*, vol. 22, no. 2, October 1957.
40. Osgood, Charles E., George J. Suci, and Percy H. Tannenbaum, *The Measurement of Meaning*, University of Illinois Press, Urbana, 1957.
41. Morton-Williams, Jean, 'Questionnaire design', in: *Consumer Market Research Handbook*, Robert Worcester and John Downham (eds), Elsevier Publishing, Amsterdam, on behalf of ESOMAR, 1986.
42. Kelly, G. A., *Psychology of Personal Constructs*, vol. 1, W. W. Horton, New York, 1955.
43. Feldwick, Paul, 'Brand research', in: *ESOMAR Handbook of Market and Opinion Research*, Colin McDonald and Phyllis Vangelder (eds), ESOMAR, Amsterdam, 1998.
44. Harmar-Brown, Francis, 'Constructing Kelly – The lure of classification', *Advertising Quarterly*, no. 18, winter 1968–69.
45. Market Research Society, *Qualitative Research Guidelines*, September 1998.

3

Specific research applications

8

Continuous marketing research

Learning Objectives

- Understand the nature and techniques of continuous marketing research

- Become familiar with the principal British and American panels and their methodologies

- Note how shop audit systems operate (bar coding; EPOS)

- Be aware of technological advances in stores audits and 'omnibus' surveys

8.1 Introduction

Broadly speaking, there are two types of market research data: ad hoc (specific, 'one-off' or 'ad hoc'), and continuous (monitoring) data which entails collection of similar data from the same sources over a period of time. This chapter discusses the nature and role of panel research, which has become a widely-used method of research in retail markets in particular. Its progress has been greatly aided by advances in data capture, such as electronic based methodologies.

8.2 Panels

A panel or longitudinal survey is a form of sample survey from which comparative data from the sampling units are taken on more than one occasion. Panels can be made up of individuals, households, or firms, and are a convenient method of obtaining continuous information over a period of time.

Regular monitoring of the market for specific products provides two levels of valuable information: (i) general, and (ii) specific.

The first type of data covers broad measurement of the trends in total market expenditure and gives, for example, indications of the impact of some popular news story about diet and health, as has happened in the case of cholesterol content of some foods and the risk of heart disease.

The second type of data provides continuous purchasing records of individual consumers; these enable changes in shopping preferences, such as brand switching, to be assessed against television viewing habits or some other factor, perhaps family size. Other important uses of continuous data relate to frequency of purchase, established repeat-buying, and repeat-buying pattern of a new brand.

Marketing takes place in a dynamic environment, where buying behaviour is frequently complex and affected by many variables, some of which may conflict with so-called rational decision making. The interaction of groups and personal behaviour, the inter-relationships between attitudes and behaviour, the challenge of authority and status, and the profound, and sometimes subtle, effects of culture, contribute to the intricate web of influences which surrounds patterns of consumption.[1] The impact of external events, perhaps governmental activities, influencing patterns of consumption and, hence, shopping habits can be checked relatively quickly by companies which subscribe to panel research services.

Manufacturers who subscribe to consumer panel surveys can obtain very valuable information about the types of consumer who buy their products, and their buying behaviour. A relatively small number of buyers frequently accounts for a large proportion of the sales of a product. Consumer panel research reveals the frequency of purchase as well as the extent of brand loyalty.

When matched but independent samples are used rather than the panel technique, the degree of sampling error is likely to result in the data being less reliable than those obtained by the latter technique. Because panels are inherently long-term research, data are collected which may reveal significant market segments for certain kinds of products as, for example, has been observed with consumer durables.

New homes, newly weds, and recently moved households are responsible for a disproportionate share of the sales of washing machines, refrigerators, cookers, and central heating installations. Since the early 1960s, the nature of the UK family and household has fundamentally changed. More people live alone; divorced and single-parent households have significantly affected patterns of consumption – in the UK, one-person households under pensionable age represented 4 per cent of all households in 1961; by 1998–99 this figure had increased to 14 per cent.[2]

Panels can be used to evaluate products, advertising viewing, consumer buying patterns, etc. Data are collected from the same sampling units at regular intervals either by mail or personal interview. Computer-assisted panel research (CAPAR) was developed about the same time as CAPI (see Chapter 5). The method is particularly valuable in studying behavioural and attitudinal changes – which is not possible with single interviews, unless a series of successive but independent samples is taken. The passage of time is always a problem with market investigation, particularly where variables outside the researcher's control may be subject to considerable change over a relatively short period.

Continuous research services demand considerable investment in back-up facilities such as specialized staff, computers, etc., and so retail audits and panels are dominated by the large research organizations – ACNielsen and Taylor Nelson Sofres. There are, however, several other research firms running highly successful continuous survey services.

Gerry Hahlo of BMRB International is of the opinion,[3] based on consideration of the technology now available and of American experience, that the future of quantitative research lies in panels. The evidence, he says, suggests that a properly balanced, well-maintained panel yields better quality data than a 'supposed fresh, ad hoc sample'. Further, switching to panel-based research also leads to new research opportunities, as BMRB has found with the development of *target samples*, enabling BMRB to locate, quickly and economically, co-operative minority samples.

Hahlo states that NFO Research – one of the dominant US research companies with a panel of over 425 000 households – operates specialist sub-panels: people with babies, recent home-movers, etc., as spin-offs from the main panel research activities.

KEYPOINT

Panel/longitudinal survey is

Form of sample survey from which comparative data taken on more than one occasion

Study of households, individuals or firms over period of time

Concerned with trend data

Useful in studying brand switching, purchasing frequency, advertising effects, 'price-offers', etc.

8.3 Consumer purchase panels

These are the most commonly used panels. Selection of the panel members follows the principles of random sampling used in single surveys. It is generally done by using either a systematic (quasi-random) technique or stratified random sampling. The aim is to achieve a representative membership of an adequately sized panel, which is not easy because people are being asked to supply information of a continuous nature.

The original Attwood Consumer Panel, which started in the UK in 1948, was based on a randomly selected panel of households and experienced some difficulties in recruitment. About 80 per cent of contacts agreed to be enrolled, but by the time the first reporting period arrived, 20 per cent of these failed to co-operate. The remaining 64 per cent of the initial sample did not all stay the course, and a further 16 per cent of the total were lost in the first six weeks, so that 48 per cent of the original sample was left. Those who refused to co-operate or who failed to do so, were replaced by households of similar demographic characteristics; but there remains the problem of bias. It is difficult to know how different those who do not respond are from actual panel members, and how non-response may affect representativeness of the panel.

Another problem of consumer panels is mortality, not just in the conventional sense of the phenomenon, but also because of the drop-out rate, as the Attwood example indicated. To some extent this can be overcome by inflating the size of the original sample, but, of course, this entails extra expense.

Less than one-third of a continuous panel operated by the Market Research Corporation of America were serving as members six months later. In addition, 40 per cent of those contacted had refused to co-operate.[4] The hidden biases, apart from heavy costs, are severe handicaps in developing panel research.

There is some evidence[4] that the stability of American panel membership is influenced by the range and types of products under survey. If only a few products are involved, interest in these products seems to be a prime factor: 40 per cent of cosmetic users withdrew from a panel concerned with cosmetic usage, compared with 59 per cent of non-users.

Other potential weaknesses of panel research may arise from atypical behaviour. New members may suddenly change; for example, their established patterns of television viewing or food buying. To overcome this bias, panel operators may exclude data from new members for a given period. Existing members of a panel may be subject to 'conditioning' and begin to behave in an untypical fashion. They may become self-conscious in their buying habits because they happen to be on a consumer panel, and there is a danger that their reactions in buying situations will become atypical. This danger can be reduced by limiting the time of panel membership and replacing members with others of similar demographic characteristics from a randomly selected 'reserve' list, though it is admittedly difficult to remove from the panel members who have been loyal and reliable. An additional safeguard lies in checking the panel against occasional random samples, taken independently of the population under study.

Yet another source of problems relating to panel research is the heavy costs involved in recruitment and maintenance. This tends to limit the size of a sample, and so affects the extent to which micro-market analyses are feasible.

One of the critical tasks of panel research is, therefore, that of maintenance, i.e. keeping up membership of a panel so that it retains its value as a continuous monitor over a long period of time. A continuity factor of at least 80 per cent should be aimed at. As noted already, panel members may show signs of 'conditioning', others move house, fall ill or even die, so there has to be a fairly regular effort made to recruit suitable replacements.

Further, it is difficult to investigate attitudes or motivations on a continuous or repetitive basis. The first questioning will have alerted respondents and caused them to develop radically different frames of reference which are likely to affect their later responses.

However, a distinct advantage of panel research is the fact that it *is* a long-term operation. This enables considerable investment to be made by research companies into designing high-quality samples and effective methods of ensuring that panels remain representative.

As with all sampling methodologies, representativeness is the principal requirement of a consumer panel. The objectives of a panel should be clearly defined, e.g. the nature of the population being surveyed and the geographical boundaries. The optimum size of a panel is the result of a compromise between the accuracy expected and the cost of subscription which subscribers are presumed willing to pay.[5] If information about specific brands or brand sizes of products is required, then very large sample sizes would be needed, and costs would shoot up; such a panel would only be feasible if these costs could be spread over many subscribers.

In line with general sampling theory, the larger the size of the sample, the greater its precision or reliability, but pragmatic constraints intervene. It would, in any case, be necessary to double the sample size just to increase its accuracy by half (see Chapter 3). Another factor to bear in mind when designing a panel relates to the segmentation analyses required, which may, for instance, refer to the usual demographic data of age, sex, household status, occupation, household size, etc. Stratification cells, as with quota sampling, should contain an adequate number of households.

In addition to sampling principles, panel research is influenced by other facets of sound ad hoc research, such as response rates and quality control. However, because of its nature, i.e. 'continuous measurement of the same data from essentially the same sample, panel design and conduct vary from ad hoc in a number of significant ways'.[6] Panel research is a very long-term commitment in terms of obligations to clients to provide valuable trend data, so the initial design of the panel must be very carefully planned to ensure that it will stand up to the test of time. Set-up and maintenance costs are high, so suppliers of continuous research services also have significant investment costs to keep in mind.

8.4 Panel methodology

Consumer panel data can be gathered at the point-of-sale using bar-coding and related electronic systems, or in the home by means of: (i) home audits; (ii) diaries; and, more recently, (iii) electronic scanners used in panel households [computer-assisted panel research (CAPAR)]. Home audits involve research staff visiting panel members' homes and, with their permission, physically checking household stocks of specific products surveyed by the panel. Used packaging is saved by the panel member and stored in a special container, so that these can also be checked ('dustbin check'). Respondents also answer a short questionnaire.

Most panels use some form of 'diary', which members fill in with details of purchases of a range of food and other frequently purchased products, and return to the controlling survey organization. Some organizations operate a weekly system of reporting, which is considered to result in more reliable data than if the time interval is extended. Costs obviously have to be borne in mind.

Diaries should be easy to complete: the layout and terminology should make the task of recording purchases as simple as possible. Completed diaries should be carefully checked by survey staff before processing the data, and any anomalies should be investigated.

It is customary to give panel members some relatively small financial reward for their co-operation. Where products are being tested, members are sometimes allowed to retain or purchase these at a nominal cost.

Useful market experiments can be undertaken with panels by studying the effects of some stimulus, e.g. advertising, to which half of the panel may be exposed. The other half, perhaps in a different part of the country, can be used as a control group. Brand-switching studies can be particularly applicable to panels as individual behaviour can be identified, which is obviously impossible using separate samples.

A major innovation in panel research methodology occurred with the introduction of EAN Coding (European Article Number or bar codes on products), and the greatly increased use of electronic point-of-sale scanning (EPOS) in retail stores (see later discussion of these technologies).

Information Resources Inc (IRI) of the USA first applied this new technology in the late 1970s and early 1980s, to consumer-based data collection. Consumer panel members are issued with a smart card – similar to a credit card – which is presented at the store check-out, where details of the household demographics and purchases are then downloaded from the retailer's computer. The success of the system depends on the full co-operation of all retailers in the master sample and, as happens in the USA, the existence of well-defined shopping catchment areas. In Britain, however, there is a high concentration of population in conurbations: about 32 per cent of the population lived in the seven metropolitan counties in 1991.[2] Development of this electronic data capture system in the UK will depend largely on the participation of the large grocery supermarket groups.

Associated with this scanning-based panel data, electronic data capture (EDC) has resulted from linking home computer systems with EAN coding. Panel members record their purchases using data terminals and bar code readers. The resultant data are then transmitted via a modem to a host computer, in the same way as with TV audience research panels' use of 'Peoplemeters' (see Chapter 10). How far and how soon the traditional diaries and 'dustbins' of home-based panel data will be entirely replaced by EDC will be determined chiefly by the investment costs and the co-operation of the people involved. A large panel operator in the US has already launched such a service with a target sample of 15 000 homes. In the UK, some of the major panel research suppliers are also planning to introduce similar services (see Scanner store consumer panels).

KEYPOINT

Panel methodology

Panel data gathered at point-of-sale:

Bar coding

EPOS

Scanning

Panel data gathered in households:

Home audits

Diaries, electronic scanning

Computer-assisted panel research (CAPAR)

Useful market experiments by split-panel stimulus, e.g. advertising or special offers.

8.5 American consumer panels

In the US, consumer panel research is well established and is used in many marketing enquiries covering official, professional, and trade activities. Large consumer panels are run by NPD Research, the Market Research Corporation of America (MRCA), Market Facts, and National Family Opinion (NFO). The NPD Panel covers 13 000 families nationwide; several local market panels are also organized. The MCRA Panel of about 10 000 households dispersed throughout the US operates weekly diaries recording, in detail, the purchases of a wide range of consumer products. Type of product, brand, weight or quantity, package size and style, price, place and time of purchase, also any special promotional offer, are all entered on these weekly sheets. Diaries are kept on a monthly basis for such items as clothing and photographic equipment, which are bought less frequently than food.

Another well-known American consumer panel with a membership of over 600 families in the metropolitan area of Chicago is operated by the *Chicago Tribune*. The information obtained from this research assists the advertising department of this famous newspaper in selling space.

J. Walter Thompson runs a consumer purchase panel using diary reporting on a monthly basis.

8.6 British consumer panels

Several of the larger research organizations offer continuous research services, and the following examples illustrate the types of panel research which are available. (See also Chapter 11 on advertising research.)

Taylor Nelson Sofres Superpanel

TNS, the leading UK-based marketing research organization, has offered continuous research services for many years. Of these, Attwood Statistics Ltd, which was eventually bought by AGB, was the first marketing research agency to operate a household consumer panel in Great Britain. It started operations in 1948 with a UK-based consumer panel, and extended later to a number of European countries.

TNS's Superpanel replaces its previous Television Consumer Audit (TCA) Toiletries and Cosmetic Purchasing Index (TCPI), and the long-established Attwood Consumer Panel services, and is claimed to be Europe's largest consumer panel.

The TNS Superpanel is similar to and in direct competition with Nielsen's Homescan (see later notes); it comprises 15 000 households – an estimated 45 000 individuals – who are equipped with electronic scanners, similar to those used at supermarket check-out desks, which record price, place of purchase, and selected brand. This enables rapid trend analyses to be supplied to TNS's clients.

Taylor Nelson Sofres Family Food Panel

This panel was established in 1974 to monitor family eating habits and behaviour. All food and drink, whether home-made or bought from stores, is covered by this continuous survey which operates by means of a two-weekly diary.

The data from this continuous panel of 4200 households containing 11 000 individuals, over the whole of Great Britain, are derived from a minimum of 2000 diaries which are completed each quarter. Stratification is by constituency/ward spread over 200 sampling points.

Data include types of food and drink consumed, brands, method of preparation, packaging, meal occasions, and demographic profiles of households. The National Dairy

Council has used the Family Food Panel to monitor trends in consumption, particularly of home-made foods. The Family Food Panel is now available in France and is being extended through Europe.

TNS Impulse is another TNS continuous panel with 4350 individuals aged 6–75 years, and designed to measure purchasing behaviour across a wide range of major, principally personal, purchases, such as confectionery, crisps, snacks, soft drinks, ice-cream, greetings cards, take-away beer, etc. This service replaces the long-standing PPI (Personal Purchasing Index) service, and is based on telephone data collection.

VIPer (Very Important Person exclusive research)

Taylor Nelson Sofres RSGB has been selected to run a new panel of 1000 AB1 adults in the UK. This exclusive panel is jointly owned by Channel 4, Classic FM and media planning agency Mediapolis, and it will cover both qualitative and quantitative research activities.

The highly specific coverage of this innovative panel research reflects the trend towards providing detailed information on the attitudes, perceptions and consumption patterns of lucrative market segments. Distinctive media habits, extensive travel commitments, sophisticated financial transactions, etc., characterize the life-styles of such significant market segments. (See life-style research, pp. 318–21, and geodemographic research systems, pp. 324–39).

Continental research: the Million Plus Panel

In October 1995, a new panel of over 1.5 million people, classified by more than 3000 criteria, and derived from the 4.5 million database developed by ICD, was launched. Minority samples down to the 2 per cent penetration level can be provided.

The British Household Panel Study (BHPS)

Although this panel-based research is not a market research programme, it is packed full of data and commentaries on the ways in which people's lives in Britain have changed in the 1990s. It covers, for instance, the impact of work on families; household and family changes; income, welfare and consumption; household and residential mobility; smoking habits, self-assessed health and subjective well-being; distribution of responsibilities and tasks within households; stability of voting intentions; and, 'reflections' on personal and family life.

The BHPS, launched in 1991 at the University of Essex's Centre for Micro-social Change under the auspices of the Economic and Social Research Council (ESRC), was initially developed from a two-stage stratified nationally representative sample of 5500 households and included over 10 000 individuals aged 16+, who will be reinterviewed each year by National Opinion Polls (NOP). As respondents change households, other members of their new households are also interviewed. From 1994, the panel included 11–15-year-olds from panel households.

So far, BHPS data have been generated from two 'waves': the first collected in the fourth quarter of 1992 and the second in the fourth quarter of 1993. As each 'wave' contains considerable information about events and conditions in the previous calendar year, the first report from these researchers is subtitled '1990 to 1992'. It is stated that the BHPS has been designed to improve understanding of the processes of micro-social change and the ways in which these are related to macro changes in society. The authors of the survey maintain that despite many, sometimes profound, changes, there are always some stable features in, for example, families, employment patterns, social structures and values, all of which are, of course, topics of interest to marketing researchers.

The BHPS is part of a Panel Comparability Programme (PACO), based in Luxembourg; a new 12-nation household panel – *The European Community Household Panel* – funded by the EU has recently been launched. The BHPS research venture should result in valuable insights into trends in the perceptions and behaviour of individuals and households in Great Britain.

The National Food Survey (NFS)

This official continuous survey of UK household food consumption and expenditure was introduced during the Second World War by the Ministry of Food to monitor the dietary habits of urban working class households. Later, it was extended to cover a representative sample of national households, and is a diary-based survey involving about 7000 randomly selected households who, over a period of one week, provide information about their domestic food consumption and expenditure.

The fieldwork is carried out by Social and Planning Research (SCPR, known as the National Centre for Social Research since May 1999) for the Ministry of Agriculture, Fisheries and Food (MAFF).

Research International

Formerly known as Research Bureau Ltd (RBL), the company has, since 1962, featured prominently among the leading UK agencies providing information for marketing and social planners. With offices in over 40 countries, RI is able to offer a comprehensive marketing research service throughout the world.

Within RI there are nine general *ad hoc* divisions handling a wide variety of client accounts. These include fast-moving consumer goods such as food, drink, and household products, together with more specific market sectors such as finance, retailing, travel, leisure, and consumer durables. RI Automotive offers both full-service, customized research and a continuous monitor – the Motorists' Diary Panel with data from 4000 motorists.

ACNielsen: Homescan

In June 1989, ACNielsen launched the Homescan panel, which was the first panel in Europe to use in-home scanning. This consumer panel, based on 10 500 households, covers the whole of Great Britain and Northern Ireland and was designed to reflect accurately household purchases of all grocery items, from fresh and pre-packaged food-stuffs to household products, petcare, toiletries, confectionery and liquor.

Each household on the Homescan panel is provided with a small, hand-held bar-code scanner or 'wand', and after each shopping trip purchased items are recorded by means of the 'wand'; inputs include the date, items bought, any promotional offers applicable, price, quantity and store used. When the programmed questions have been completed, the 'wand' is placed in a modem which is linked to the telephone for transfer of the stored data to Nielsen's host computer. To avoid bias arising from the exclusion of non-telephone households, Nielsen has installed equipment into panel homes which lacked a telephone. Non-bar-coded items are recorded by panellists in special books.

Electronic data capture and transfer allow daily collection of purchasing data, so Nielsen clients can be provided with up-to-the-minute information on consumers' responses to marketing initiatives. Core data can vary but standard analyses include: percentage of households purchasing; percentage of expenditure; average number of visits per buyer; average spend per buyer; average spend per visit; brand comparisons; level of trial of new products; brand loyalty/ brand shifting analyses; and demographic analyses. From Homescan data Nielsen discovered, for example, that a leading household brand was underperforming in one of the major national grocery chains; it was also found that this particular retailer had a lower than average share of that specific market. The manufacturer was able to make a strong case for the development of his brand, and offered assistance to the retailer to improve sales of that branded product. Analyses are available on the following options (or combinations) on 4, 12 or 52-weeks bases.

Figure 8.1 illustrates how Nielsen used a Markov process model (for details of this probabilistic technique refer to a statistical text) to examine the extent of consumers' switching between branded and own label products. Brand A's buyers were more likely to switch into Brand B than into own label. Brand B has slightly higher loyalty (58.1 per cent of all subsequent purchases was a repeat) than Brand A (54.9 per cent) and moreover, these buyers are more likely to switch to own label (20.2 per cent). Once switched to own label, the chances of buyers moving back are slim: 80 per cent loyalty.

Figure 8.2 shows how Nielsen analyses were applied to profile buyers of Brands X, Y and Z according to their preferences and degree of store loyalty. It will be seen that shoppers at

Share of transactions (per cent)		From				
		A	B	C	Own label	Others
	A	54.9	13.0	20.4	6.8	14.9
	B	18.8	58.1	15.6	8.2	15.6
To	C	7.8	3.9	50.4	1.7	2.4
	Own label	14.1	20.2	10.2	80.3	11.9
	Others	4.4	4.8	3.4	3.0	55.2

Figure 8.1 Consumers' pattern of switching between branded and own label products (*Source*: Nielsen)

this particular store group were heavy buyers of Brand X but their store loyalty was only 70 per cent of market average; it was apparent that there was considerable potential for additional sales.

Figure 8.3 shows that the results of a retailer focused analysis undertaken by Nielsen to determine the extent to which shoppers in a particular store group A buy Brand X from other retailers. It will be noted that Retailer B benefits most from purchases of Brand X switched from Retailer A. Linking the data shown in Figs 8.2 and 8.3, it is evident that Retailer A should carefully guard sales of Brand Y, which has reasonable loyalty and heavy buyers, whereas Brand Z would be vulnerable to brand rationalization.

The ICI Consumer Panel

For over 30 years, ICI Paints at Slough has tracked purchases of paint and decorating products on a regular basis. This service, originally called the HPR Consumer Panel, has been extended to cover a wide range of diverse products, and is available to other manufacturers. The ICI Consumer Panel is a household-based diary panel involving an average 5000 diary returns per month. These entries are usually made by the housewife who undertakes to record all relevant purchases made by all members of the household. This results in records covering the purchasing behaviour of approximately 10 000 individuals.

The sampling scheme, devised by the Office of Population Censuses and Surveys (OPCS) is a three-stage random sample; at the first stage, 52 local authority districts are selected; the second stage involves the selection of postal sectors within each of the chosen districts; and the third stage uses the Small Users Postcode Address File (see Chapter 3), from which 18 delivery points are selected from each postal sector. The annual coverage of the survey is derived from 32 periods of 10 days, during which interviewers follow up initial

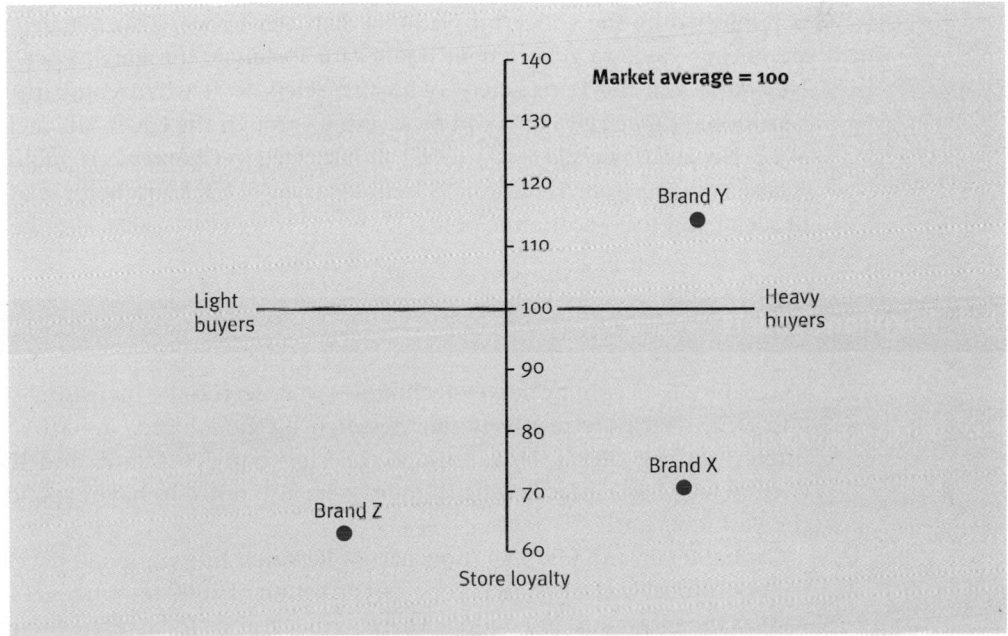

Figure 8.2   Retailer A's buyers of brands X, Y and Z profiled by brand preference and store loyalty
(*Source*: Nielsen)

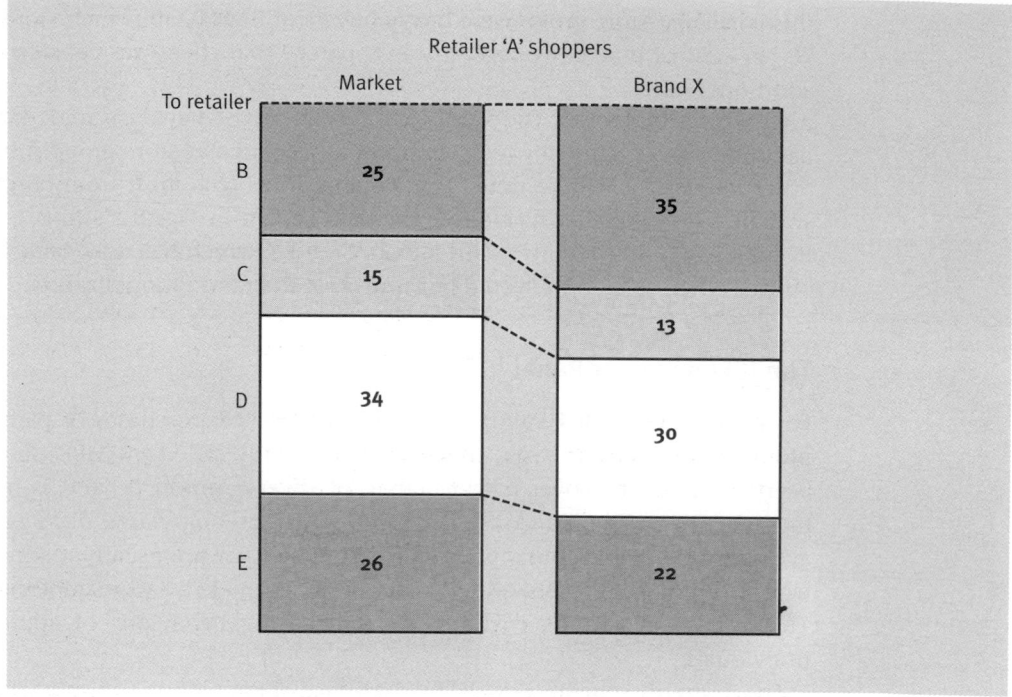

Figure 8.3 Extent to which Retailer A's shoppers buy Brand X from leading competitors (*Source*: Nielsen)

explanatory letters and assist participating households to complete the official diaries of their food habits. In 1993, an effective response rate of 65 per cent was achieved. Results are published quarterly by the MAFF, and an annual report – The National Food Survey – is published by the Office for National Statistics (ONS). This detailed information is of significant value to government bodies; for instance, the Retail Price Index is based on NFS data, and the Department of Health refers to it when comparing information on nutritional inputs. NFS data can be accessed through the ESCR data archive.

The General Household Survey (*GHS*), as indicated in Chapter 2, is published annually and is based on data from a continuous sample survey of UK households related to a wide range of social and socio-economic policies.

8.7 Telephone panels

In Chapter 6, telephone survey techniques were seen to be increasing significantly; CATI and DCI, which are relatively new research methodologies, are attracting considerable interest among survey organizations covering both consumer and industrial markets. Central telephone interviewing facilities were also noted to have expanded markedly over the past few years.

Capital Radio and Marplan (now part of Research International) developed a telephone panel – 'probably the first in Europe'[7] – consisting of 2000 respondents resident in Capital Radio's broadcast area in London. These were recruited to be representative of all adults in the area; all could be contacted at home or work by telephone, thus forming a 'direct access' telephone panel. This service no longer operates.

Capital Radio's direct access telephone panel was set up in 1978 for programme research, and following successful experience, it was decided to expand its scope to both advertising effectiveness and 'recognition' studies (see Chapter 11). In addition, the panel has been used frequently for public opinion polling on a range of topics, from housing to violence and vandalism.

Capital's Advertising Panel consists of 10000 individuals, representative by demographic profile and listening habits, and resident within Capital Radio's transmission area. This panel is used to evaluate leading advertising measures, and after the findings from each panel have been studied, a comprehensive report featuring key market data is compiled by the panel research company, Continental Research. While not strictly a telephone panel, Capital Radio use telephone-based research to monitor radio audiences in London.

Marplan[7] was convinced that direct access telephone panels would become the major tool of market and social research over the next decade, pointing out that in America the telephone interview is now the most widely used technique of survey. Marplan's prediction is certainly coming true.

Medical survey panels are operated by several marketing research firms, e.g. Facts International which telephones 500 GPs twice a month, and Martin Hamblin Research which operates a monthly telephone panel of 500 GPs.

8.8 Use of panels in forecasting

Panel research data are particularly useful in developing forecasts for the long-term sales of new products which have been subject to test marketing. The cumulative percentage of consumers who have bought a particular brand of product, and the percentage of those making repeat purchases, could be gathered from continuous panel research reports.

A typical set of figures of sales of a new brand of a product over a period of some weeks is shown in Fig. 8.4, while in Fig. 8.5 a typical pattern of repeat purchases is graphed.

From the examples displayed in Figs 8.4 and 8.5, the long-term market for the new product could be calculated thus:

$$\text{Market penetration} \times \text{Repeat purchase rate} = \text{Market share}$$
$$0.25 \times 0.10 = 2.5 \text{ per cent}$$

This forecast could be improved by incorporating a buying-rate index as follows:

Assume that buyers of this new brand represent 40 per cent of all buyers of that kind of product, but account for 45 per cent of the total market purchases. Hence, a buying-rate index would be $\frac{45}{40}$ or 1.125.

Applying this result to the early equation:

$$0.25 \times 0.10 \times 1.125 = 2.8 \text{ per cent}$$

It will be noted that the second method results in a slightly increased market share being extrapolated. Other refinements have been developed by researchers,[8,9] but it should be remembered that extrapolation assumes that market conditions remain relatively unchanged – which is problematical.

The prediction model has been further developed by Parfitt and Clay,[10] whose researchers enabled them to arrive at these important conclusions:

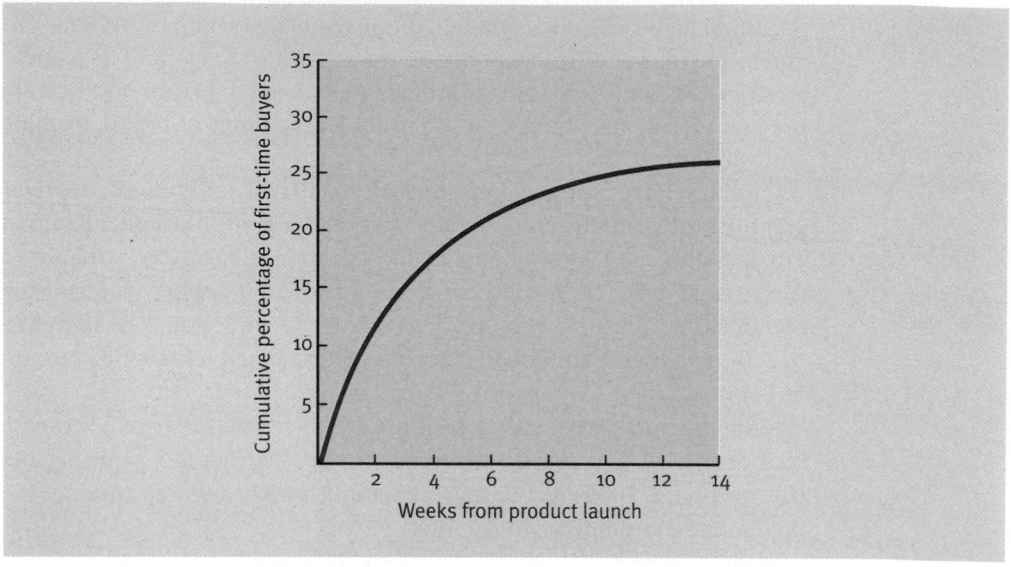

Figure 8.4   Typical cumulative sales of new product

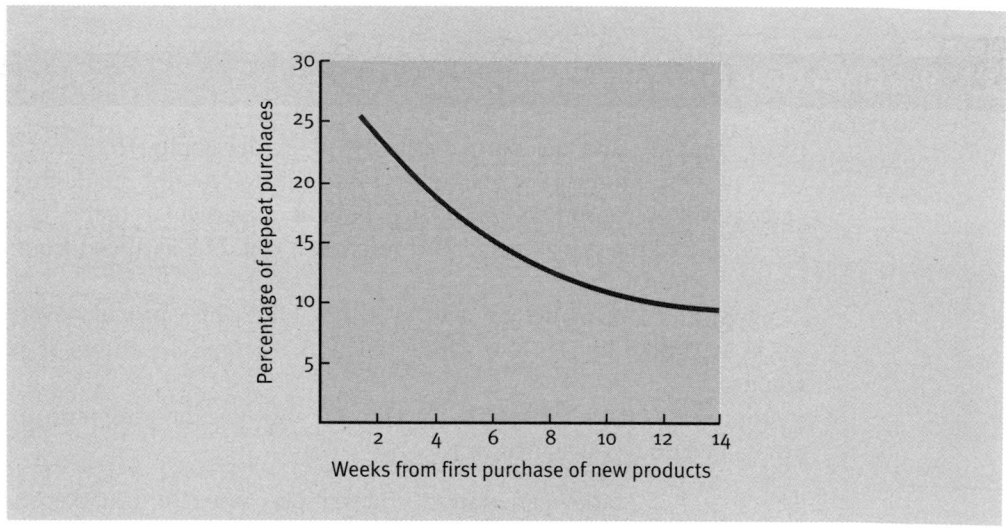

Figure 8.5   Typical repeat purchase pattern

1. Repeat buying is the most critical of the three factors which make up brand share (see above equation).

2. The later buyers enter a market the lower (on average) their repeat buying is likely to be.

8.9 Mail (access) panels

For more than 50 years in the USA, mail-based panels – also known as 'Access' or APs – have been run successfully by several research firms, including Market Facts, National

Family Opinion (NFO), and NPD Research. These panels contain between 130 000 and 600 000 people who are deemed to be a representative national sample of the population. Each quarter they are asked to complete sets of short questionnaires related, for example, to brand preferences of specific household durables. Response rates are said to be within the region of 75–85 per cent. Special sub-samples can be drawn covering particular occupations, age groups, etc., and also covering areas where test marketing is being conducted.

The US providers of APs have been encouraged by Procter and Gamble – 'the founding father of global access panels'[11] – to develop alliances overseas, and some approaches have been made to leading European agencies. In April 2000, the Aegis Group bought a 35 per cent stake in IPSOS Access Panels; this deal offers both firms the use of panels of 550 000 US households belonging to Aegis's subsidiary, Market Facts, and also to the 115 000 European households panel controlled by Ipsos.

Apart from any strategic issues, operational drawbacks may hinder progress of APs in Europe; the reliability of the US mail service has greatly assisted APs, whereas the level of postal service in, say, Italy, is problematic. Further, it is generally agreed that 'the internet is likely to prove the future to the APs in Europe'[11] (see Chapter 5 for discussion on internet panels).

8.10 Shop audit version of panel research

This was pioneered by ACNielsen in the early 1930s, and came to the UK in 1939. ACNielsen operates its retail index services across the globe. In the UK regular audits are operated to cover products sold through grocers, confectioners, tobacconists, newsagents, off-licences, pharmacies, drug stores, electrical and cash-and-carry wholesalers. This information provides a definitive source of retail sales to manufacturers.

ACNielsen Index Reports are based on both census and sample stores: this information is collated from tape delivery and using scanning auditing techniques in store on a regular weekly/four weekly basis. This information comprises purchases, sales promotions, forward stocks, pricing and sales over a range of products. The resultant data are projected to cover national sales so that manufacturers and retailers can understand vital movements of merchandise through retail channels. Market size, market share, geographic distribution of market, effectiveness of pricing, and promotional policies can then be evaluated at brand, subsector and category levels.

Ex-factory sales figures by themselves will not accurately reflect consumer demand for a product, and deliveries from the factory will have been at a high rate during the introductory stages in order to build up stocks in wholesalers' and retailers' stores in anticipation of demand. By the time consumer demand begins to climb to a peak, it is likely that deliveries from the factory will have fallen and this could lead to the wrong assumption, i.e. that consumer demand for the product is falling. Unless some research is undertaken, the real movement of the product in the stores will not be known.

The activities of competitors are likely to affect sales of an individual manufacturer who has launched a new product, and reliable information is needed to guide management. For instance, it could be critical to know whether the new product had expanded the total market for this type of product or if it had merely attracted sales from competing brands. If the total market has not expanded, the market shares of competitive manufacturers will have fallen, and their reactions will be noted by audit research.

Table 8.1   Trends in retail outlets (grocery) in the UK: 1971–99

Outlets	Number of outlets								Total turnover (%)			
	1971 No.	%	1988 No.	%	1993 No.	%	1999 No.	%	1977 %	1988 %	1993 %	1999 %
Co-operatives	7 745	7	2 704	5	2 395	6	2 241	7	13.2	10.9	9.3	6.7
Multiples	10 973	10	4 251	9	5 325	13	6 292	18	44.3	73.9	79.9	87.3
Independents	86 565	83	42 941	86	32 662	81	25 919	75	42.5	15.2	10.8	6.0
Total	105 283	100	49 896	100	40 382	100	34 452	100	100	100	100	100

Source: Nielsen

The distribution of the total volume of sales of a product type over various kinds of outlet, i.e. where consumers actually buy, is of concern to manufacturers in that market. A relatively small proportion of outlets frequently accounts for a large share of the volume of sales in a market. If a manufacturer plans to be in those outlets where the majority of consumer purchases are made, research is needed to identify these stores.

It is possible for a manufacturer to have high coverage of the distribution points in his or her market and for the product to be experiencing limited sales because it is largely distributed among small outlets. These may represent over 60 per cent of the stores retailing that product type, although their total volume of sales may be less than 20 per cent of the entire sales made in that market.

This point is reinforced by ACNielsen research in the grocery trade which indicated that 'top multiples' accounted for 71.9 per cent of grocery turnover in Great Britain in 1999. In 1950, 23 per cent of grocery turnover was handled by co-operatives, 20 per cent by multiples (10 or more branches), and 57 per cent by independents. By 1971, co-operatives accounted for 13.2 per cent of total grocery turnover, multiples had risen to 44.3 per cent and independents fallen to 42.5 per cent. These significant trends became even more marked as will be seen from Table 8.1 giving data for 1971, 1988, 1993 and 1999. Although independents represented 75 per cent of total outlets in 1999, they accounted for only 6.7 per cent of total turnover, whereas multiples, with 18 per cent of total outlets, claimed over 87 per cent of total turnover in 1999.

ACNielsen selects samples of stores for auditing purposes classifying them by type of organization (co-operatives, multiples, large independents, small independents) and by size, in terms of their volume of business. Auditing is concentrated on those stores which sell the most products, and the principle of disproportionate sampling is applied. Stated simply, this means auditing most where most of the sales are made and where variability in store characteristics is greatest (see Chapter 4). The store panel is continually checked to ensure that it is representative of the general pattern of distribution for the particular types of product audited.

From the large multiple chains Nielsen receives data on computer tape. The company also uses a field force of auditors to visit sample stores throughout Great Britain every month. Stocks of specific types of products are carefully checked and recorded by brand and size. This methodical approach also involves checking invoices and delivery notes which retailers have received covering the particular products audited. Note is also taken of selling prices, special offers, display material, and other factors affecting sales of audited lines.

From this systematic audit the sales to consumers of various brands (and sizes) of a product type can be accurately given:

Past stocks + Purchases − Present stocks = Sales facts

Nielsen indicates that an average audit takes about two man-days to complete. Every month Nielsen audits over 52 000 items. All the information recorded by the auditors and the computer tapes from the major multiple groups are received at Nielsen's Oxford headquarters. Here the data go through an intricate series of validation checks before processing. The heart of the operation is the IBM 30/84Q. In the computer, expansion factors are applied to the 'raw' data before the final chart and table masters are printed out by a laser scanner. Reports are then reproduced in the printing department.

Nielsen clients are given a formal presentation of the report's findings by experienced executives, who discuss market trends indicated by the research. Most Nielsen clients are 'online' to their Nielsen database and can obtain information at any time at the touch of a button.

A typical Nielsen report shows the following:

Consumer sales: value and volume.
Market shares: sales, stocks, deliveries.
Retail deliveries: total, direct or wholesale.
Retail stocks: shelf.
Distribution: shop, product category and turnover weighted.
Out of stock: total and shelf.
Average price: to the consumer.
Average sales and stocks: per store handling.
Average expenditure: manufacturer and brand.

Data are shown individually for trade sectors and regions.

This detailed analysis is given for Great Britain as a whole, and shown separately for the nine areas in which Nielsen operates, and by shop type and size. These regions are based on the major television areas, though they can be substituted by clients' own requirements such as sales areas.

Some large organizations do not co-operate with Nielsen, but this is adjusted by suitably weighting final survey figures. Critics in the past have commented on the method of sampling (quota) used, which can introduce bias, but Nielsen declares that its system of continuous checking and updating ensures that the samples it uses accurately reflect changing patterns of distribution in the trades covered. Inevitably, as with all research, there is a delay before the client receives the survey information, though modern systems of data processing have reduced this time-lag considerably.

Other ACNielsen specialized information services

ACNielsen's portfolio of continuous information services also covers catering outlets and cash-and-carry outlets. Key measurements of the latter include volume and price sales data, distribution by stores, product class value, stocks (average and weeks' supply), deliveries to retail stores, etc.

A specialized service, 'Pricing Optimization', is based on store-level data collected from ACNielsen's continuous retail measurement services. Clients are provided with up-to-date assessments of the impact of their pricing strategies at consumer level, and the effects of price changes on sales of specific brands. Price sensitivities can be evaluated against competitors' pricing levels. ACNielsen point out, for instance, that if a brand has a price elasticity of -2.12, i.e. for a 1 per cent increase in price, volume will decline by 2.12 per cent. That sensitivity is made up of two elements: 1. consumers' reactions to the price increase of the brand and 2. consumers' reactions to the relative deterioration in value versus competitive brands.

Pricing strategy should therefore bear in mind the likely responses to any pricing initiatives. If all competitors were to increase their brands by the same amount (projected as 1 per cent in this case), differentials would be maintained and sales of the company's brand would be likely to fall only slightly in volume terms. So assessments of the risks attached to pricing strategies could be aided by having ready access to ACNielsen data.

Retail Audits Ltd

Retail Audits Ltd was formed in 1966 through the merger of Test Marketing Services Ltd and the audit division of the British Market Research Bureau. In 1987 it became part of Nielsen and now specializes in surveys for the tobacco and automotive industries.

The tobacco research is carried out on a monthly basis through a sample representing all possible outlets where tobacco is sold. It comprises 100 vending operators and 1500 retail outlets representing:

Tobacconists
Grocers
Public houses
Off-licences
Clubs
Garages, etc.

Because of the coverage, the company is in the unique situation of providing total retail market research.

Automotive research is carried out on various product fields through garages and accessory shops. In addition, specialist research is provided on automotive spares and accessories within dealer franchises in the UK and this has now been extended into Europe.

8.11 Back-up services

Panel research is also associated with advertising media in order to give advertisers factual information about the effectiveness of campaigns (see Chapter 11). The increasing competition between media owners has resulted in the development of 'back-up' services for their clients.

Stats MR Ltd

This British company, founded in 1963 and bought by Nielsen in 1985, concentrates on providing a specialized range of retail research services, including continuous audits of grocers, chemists, CTNs, off-licences, free trade on-licences, and department stores. Regular distribution and pricing checks are also conducted over several retail sectors.

UK record industry music charts

In the UK, record industry music charts have been produced for over 40 years, over which time various publishing houses with music titles developed their own charts; but it was only in 1969 that a recognized industry chart, backed by the BBC and *Record Retailer*, was commissioned from BMRB. This depended on weekly diaries, manually entered, by an initial panel of 250 record retailers.

In 1983, Gallup was responsible for producing record sales data from a sample of 850 retailers, each of whom had an Epson computer linked to a light wand which read the bar codes on each item sold and registered it on disk. Because some items lacked bar codes, their sales had to be punched in by hand, and Gallup applied statistical methods to check errors in entry.

In 1990, Chart Information Network (CIN) – a joint venture between Spotlight Publications, publishers of *Music Week*, and the British Phonographic Industry (BPI) – was set up to run and administer the charts, which were still Gallup's responsibility. As a result of competitive tendering, Millward Brown won a four year contract from 1994 to collect relevant data and produce the UK music charts. This contract has been extended to June 2002. The charts are commissioned by MICS, a new joint venture between the record retailers' organization (BARD) and the record companies' trade association (BPI). Under the new ownership, Chart Information Service (CIN) was eliminated.

Electronically captured sales data are received at the research company's offices every night from a panel of over 4000 stores out of a population of 6000. These data are used to produce charts for 'Top of the Pops', Jazz FM, Classic FM and others. Once all the Saturday data are received and processed, the chart week ends its frenetic existence, and the following day, the singles, albums and video charts are produced and transmitted electronically to radio and TV stations, and also to the national and regional newspapers; an on-line service is also available. By early afternoon, 'product profiles' of every product in the charts, and analysed by non-overlapping ISBA regions, are available. The diffusion of EPOS among retailers ensures the accuracy and ready accessibility of music chart data.

8.12 Technological advances in store audits

Optical mark reading

Store auditing has traditionally relied on human observation linked to basic paper and pencil recording, a slow and often laborious task.

With optical mark reading (OMR), the auditor still uses a humble pencil or pen, but merely enters a simple mark against a selected response or a multi-choice printed form. Special scanning devices convert these marks into computer input; the presence or absence of a mark is detected by sensing reflected by infra-red light. OMR eliminates, therefore, punched cards and key entry, and also the possibility of errors in transcription.

However, OMR appears to be in rather limited use for retail audits, and data tend to be recorded on to computer printed forms which are subject to key punching. Smaller outlets will apparently still need to be audited by 'traditional' methods. Mintel reports[12] that OMR, used by BMRB in their massive TGI survey, has re-emerged as a cost-effective way of handling data entry.

Bar coding

Although bar codes originated in the US in the late 1940s, the development of this revolutionary invention was delayed for some 30 years until laser technology and reduced computer costs rendered it commercially viable.

Bar codes – a series of black lines of varying thicknesses with numbers beneath them – are now printed on many fast-moving packaged grocery products, and, to a very restricted degree, on some other types of consumer products.

Bar code scanners enable products to be identified by country of origin, manufacturer, brand, size, flavour and offer.

A bar code is unique to a product wherever it is sold within a country. There are two principal bar coding systems: 12 digit UPC (Universal Product Code) used in North America, and the 13 digit EAN (European Article Number) used within Europe, Asia and Australasia. The first two stripes identify the country of origin; the next five are allocated by the Article Numbering Association (ANA) to identify the manufacturer; the following five are used by the manufacturer to identify products; the last is a check digit allocated by computer. The ANA was formed in 1977 by European manufacturers and retailers. There are now 79 national product numbering associations over 86 countries.

Bar codes appear as a series of vertical black lines on a white background, which can be scanned readily at the point of purchase. Variants of a product, including 'special offers' packs are given individual bar codes. Linked to a hand-held computer, data from bar codes can be fed directly into a central computer via a telephone line, using modems (a device which couples a computer with a telephone). An auditor could use a light pen to identify bar codes on the packaging of goods on store shelves. ACNielsen has developed a special hand-held computer with a light pen auxiliary device with one megabyte of memory. This equipment – the Nielsen International Auditing Terminal (NIAT) – should overcome the disadvantage of limited capacity of other systems.

Bar codes do not appear on packing cases, so auditors still need to do some manual recording. Another problem refers to bar code standardization; this is being tackled by the Article Number Association (ANA). Nielsen has been appointed by ANA to provide manufacturers with sales data from a selected number of retail outlets with scanning installations.

While bar coding is a highly ingenious system for collecting and transmitting data, and it has radically transformed stock and retail sales auditing, one of its problems is overload of the machines involved in the daily processes, particularly because of the virtually never-ending flow of new products. 'Within FMCG markets some 3000 bar codes are recorded every week in the UK alone, and the need to keep item dictionaries up-to-date is absolutely paramount in the production of (marketing) information.[13]

Electronic point of sale scanning (EPOS)

Bar coding, scanning, and computerized information are all part of the new trend in retail auditing. An 'intelligent' terminal (the cash register) records the bar code on a product; this information is then fed to a central computer and used to compute the bill as well as recording the sale for stock-check purposes.

Mintel[12] has observed that an increasing proportion of input data for retail audits is now derived direct from retailers using output from EPOS scanning equipment. EPOS is diffusing rapidly, and about 80 per cent of UK multiples' retail outlets have this equipment. Mintel commented that the increasing penetration of EPOS will result in a rapid decline in traditional manual audits.

EPOS has also meant that stores can establish much closer, dynamic links with their suppliers and are able to hold lower levels of stocks. These can be replenished rapidly because of these electronic links, and so retailers can achieve economies by reducing the amount of working capital tied up in stocks. A retail group may also use EPOS systems to check readily the effectiveness of variations in the marketing mix across individual stores

In America and Canada, EPOS is widely used. Check-out scanners are now more competitively priced, bar coding is spreading, and the perceived benefits to retailers, such as better control of in-store 'shrinkage', faster check-out of customers, reduced labour costs, and immediate stock-checks, are helping the diffusion of this technology.

Scanner store consumer panels

The diffusion of scanning in the US has been significantly affected by the fact that retailers are traditionally very strong in their own region but have very limited national presence. This is in direct contrast with the retailing leverage exercised, for instance, in the UK grocery market by the major groups. The fragmentation of retailing in the US has, therefore, led to much freer exchange of information, and almost all US retailers use scanning data and permit the major research agencies to release this information with their identity revealed This level of co-operation contrasts sharply with the general UK trade policy (with the exceptions of Safeway, Tesco and Asda) of closely guarding specific details of retail performance.[14]

As noted, bar coding and EPOS have revolutionized panel research and also retail auditing because of the accuracy and speed with which data can be accessed. Research clients are able to have available, and in an unprecedented short time, precise and up-to-date information related, for instance, to the effects of in-store promotions, advertising campaigns, and test marketing operations. Such retail databases will be updated each reporting period (weekly, 4-weekly, monthly, etc.). Both Nielsen and IRI, the leading data suppliers, offer proprietary software for their clients to use with the data-base.[15]

In France, during 1970, A. C. Nielsen developed a range of electronic research services which it called ERIM (electronic research for insights into marketing). These services enable manufacturers to test new products and promotions; a major development occurred with the use of scanners. ERIM TESTSIGHT, for instance, involves the installation of television meters in a sample of panel households who receive individual commercials via a local relay station.

This particular service has been extended to the US; purchases of members of participating households, who use plastic cards to identify themselves, are recorded by store scanners, and their television viewing habits are measured by a Nielsen Telemeter attached to their TV sets.

The Telemeter enables A. C. Nielsen to broadcast TV commercials on a special frequency and insert them into regular programming. Software programs within the Telemeter can switch panel TV sets from the channel being watched to the TV commercial being tested and back again without the viewers being aware of this 'planned' intervention.

This sophisticated research methodology allows matched purchase panel testing of advertising copy over different market segments covering both cable, non-cable, and satellite reception of TV signals.

A. C. Nielsen has extended its electronic research services to other countries such as Germany, Great Britain, Italy, and The Netherlands.

ACNielsen: Scantrack

Scantrack is part of Nielsen's integrated data system which provides regular analyses of retail trends. Linked with Nielsen Retail Index and Homescan databases, Scantrack data are collected electronically from bar codings on packages and reports are delivered every four weeks.

The top UK multiple grocery retailers, which account for over 87 per cent of grocery trading (see Table 8.1), are covered.

KEYPOINT

Shop audits – pioneered by Nielsen

Past stocks + purchases − present stocks = sales facts

UK Record Industry Charts

Technical advances: bar coding, EPOS, scanner store consumer panels

8.13 Omnibus surveys

Several research agencies in the UK offer special facilities for clients to obtain data speedily. This is achieved by inserting questions in consumer survey questionnaires which are continuously in operation. This can be a quick and cheap method of collecting information at very short notice.

Basically, an 'omnibus' survey consists of a series of short questionnaires on behalf of different clients who share the cost of interviewing. Interviews may take up to 30 minutes. The method is economical to use provided an individual client's share of the interviewing time does not exceed about 10 minutes, after which diseconomies become evident and it might be cheaper to have an ad hoc survey done.

Questions can cover many areas of interest to individual manufacturers, e.g. brand awareness, price awareness, frequency of purchase, place of purchase, media exposure, etc. Advertising effectiveness could be checked by using 'omnibus' surveys before and after an advertising campaign has taken place.

The content of questions has to be kept simple so that they are easily understood and answered quickly. Open-ended questions are generally unsuitable for this type of survey because they usually take longer to answer and to record verbatim. Agencies charge a premium for including questions of this nature. Care is needed in formulating questions so that they are effective; this is customarily the responsibility of clients who are charged on a question basis plus an 'entry fee' to the survey.

Most omnibus surveys are based on national samples of adults or housewives, though there are a few specialist populations also covered, e.g. car owners. Where clients wish to investigate relatively limited markets the omnibus survey method may be expensive because charges per question are based on the number in the initial sample. This is likely to include a very large number of non-users of the product or service. Full value is obtained when questions are related to the general buying behaviour of the population covered.

Standard analyses offered by agencies operating 'omnibus' services cover the usual demographic breakdowns. Additional analyses are usually available at extra cost, and some clients may find it worthwhile to seek more refined data.

Speed is one of the principal attractions of 'omnibus' surveys. The time involved depends on the length of notice required by agencies to insert questions (some accept questions up to 10 working days before fieldwork starts), the time taken for interviewing, analysis, and preparation of data (up to four weeks), and the frequency of particular 'omnibus' surveys (this varies with individual agencies).

Omnibus surveys in the UK grew steadily and reached maturity by the mid-1980s, after which demand stagnated and the market became highly price sensitive. In 1992, RSL (now IPSOS-RSL) introduced CAPIBUS, the first personal interviewing omnibus to use lap-top computers (see Chapter 5: CAPI). This dramatically speeded up the availability of results from the usual 3–4 weeks for a paper-based survey to 7–8 days for a CAPI-based omnibus. But of even more importance, CAPI made it 'possible and cost efficient to hold complex batteries of questions which apply to a small minority group' to be triggered only when the informant is identified.[16] This innovation revitalized the omnibus survey market; it also led other major research suppliers to adopt CAPI for their surveys.

IPSOS-RSL have developed CAPIBUS-Europe as a weekly omnibus covering Britain, France, Germany, Italy and Spain. CAPI technology allows for questionnaires to be scripted in one location and transmitted electronically to other countries. Of course, accurate translation of question wording has to be done, but the benefits of standardized questionnaire formats and classification systems are significant.[16]

Other leading agencies offering 'omnibus' services include BMRB, who offer a range of ACCESS services for minority markets by telephone (CATI), face-to-face, internet, or multimedia. Since 1995, ACCESS omnibus surveys have been tracking the market size and profile of the internet. Other services include the Gallup Organization – which runs a weekly omnibus of 3000 individuals – and NOP. These professional research organizations advise clients on the suitability of this method of research for particular problems, and provide quotations. Unless specifically requested, charges normally cover presentation of the data in computer tables, which can then be processed and interpreted by clients' own research staff. NOP runs a random omnibus of 2000 adults weekly, and a fortnightly quota omnibus also of 2000 adults; these are all based on personal interviews using CAPI technology. The random sample is drawn from electoral registers and interviewing is in 180 Parliamentary constituencies. The quota sample is carried out at 180 sampling points among a representative quota sample of adults, 15+ years. In addition, NOP organizes TELEBUS, a telephone omnibus which covers 1000 adults each weekend; the sampling frame is derived from all the telephone directories in Britain, and a random sample of pages is selected each weekend. CATI facilities provide for rapid feedback of survey data to clients.

RSGB, part of the Taylor Nelson Sofres Group, also runs well-known omnibus surveys, including OMNIMAS, a weekly random face-to-face consumer survey of 2100 adults, 16+ years, across Great Britain. CAPI technology (see Chapter 5) enables results to be available within seven working days. A telephone omnibus survey focusing on small businesses is also organized by RSGB (BUSINESS LINE: 2000 small businesses surveyed every month); also a Baby Omnibus Survey which collects specific data each quarter from 700 mothers with a baby from 0–24 months, in Great Britain excluding Northern Ireland. Audience Selection, a division of Taylor Nelson Sofres, runs several specialist omnibus survey services; for example, PHONEBUS, based on a UK nationally representative sample of 1000 adults aged 15+ years. Carrick James Market Research offers specialized omnibus surveys covering children aged 5–15, mothers of children aged 0–15, and young people aged 16–24. These surveys are run at monthly intervals, and samples are flexibly designed according to the needs of clients. Topics covered include product awareness and usage, advertising and image measures, profiles of users, tracking studies, pre- and post-advertising tests, etc.; sampling points are distributed throughout England, Scotland and Wales, and interviewers are specially trained to deal sensitively with these enquiries which, in the case of young children, require the permission of parents or other responsible adults. This Child Omnibus service is planned for Germany, France, Spain and Italy. NOP International Omnibus offers multi-country coverage through a network of international contacts. Supporting this extensive system is a multi-lingual team of researchers, and full translation facilities are also available.

Omnibus survey services are also available in some European countries such as Germany, France, and Italy, and also in the US and Canada.

As with other market research services, the further development of omnibus surveys will be clearly connected to enhancements in software and hardware, as has happened with CATI and CAPI (see Chapter 5). As the internet expands, new market opportunities will doubtless occur; direct electronic links may virtually replace traditional interviewing.[16] In 1988, 18 per cent of UK households had a PC; by 1998/99, ownership of domestic PCs was 34 per cent, although only a small fraction of these households were linked to the internet.[2] But the marked trend in PC usage may be an indicator of the way in which research interviewing is likely to go in the foreseeable future.

KEYPOINT

Omnibus surveys

Short questionnaires incorporating questions by different clients

Questions can cover many areas of interest, e.g. purchasing frequency, media exposure, price awareness

Questions should be simple and easily answered

Several Omnibus surveys run by leading agencies

Most use CAPI

Results in 7–10 days

Weekly omnibus surveys across Europe

Developments on internet

Summary

Panel or longitudinal research provides data which enable trends to be identified; panels can be made up of individuals, households, or firms.

Consumer purchase panels use home audits and/or diaries. Several well-known research companies offer panel services; TNS, BMRB, Research International, etc. A new development is telephone panel research which could become a major tool of market research.

Panel research data are useful in developing long-term forecasts of new product sales.

Nielsen offers extensive shop-audit services and operates in 27 countries; another large organization in this specialized field is Retail Audits Ltd.

Technological advances in store audits are: optical mark reading, bar coding, and point of sale scanning. Scanner store consumer panels are now a significant factor in store audit in America; in

Great Britain, Nielsen's TOPS service, based on five large multiples, uses scanners to provide manufacturers with detailed analyses.

Smaller outlets will continue to be audited by 'traditional' methods.

Omnibus surveys consist of a series of short questionnaires on behalf of different clients who share the costs of interviewing, etc.: the type and scope of questioning are necessarily limited. Speed is one of the chief attractions of this service.

Review and discussion questions

1. Outline the principal problems involved in recruiting new members to consumer panels. How might the recruitment method for new members bias panel findings?

2. A marketing research company proposes to investigate food purchasing patterns among a sample of consumers. It intends using diaries as the research instrument. Which areas of food purchasing may the diaries possibly fail to uncover?

3. In your opinion, are there any advantages that technological store audits such as EPOS and scanners might enjoy compared to the more traditional consumer panel?

4. In addition to the examples cited in Section 9.6 identify product and service research areas for which telephone panels might be particularly appropriate.

5. A brand manager for a fast moving consumer product is anxious to monitor sales volumes, fluctuations, and reactions to promotions for her brand in the Greater London area. She is currently undecided as to whether a consumer panel or shop audit should be used. What factors should guide her deliberations?

6. A charitable organization is anxious to discover adult attitudes towards donating to Third World charities. The chairperson is currently in favour of doing so by means of an omnibus survey. How would you personally react to this proposal?

References

1. Chisnall, Peter M., *Consumer Behaviour*, McGraw-Hill, Maidenhead, 1994.
2. *Social Trends 30*, Office for National Statistics (ONS), 2000.
3. Hahlo, Gerry, 'The researcher who came in from the field', *Researchplus*, December 1994, Market Research Society.
4. Tull, Donald S., and Del I. Hawkins, *Marketing Research: Meaning, Measurement and Method*, Macmillan, New York, 1976.
5. Delmas, Denis, and Dominique Levy, 'Consumer panels', in: *ESOMAR Handbook of Market and Opinion Research*, Colin McDonald and Phyllis Vangelder (eds), ESOMAR, Amsterdam, 1998.
6. Blyth, W. G., 'Panels and diaries', in: *A Handbook of Market Research Techniques*, Robin Birn, Paul Hague and Phyllis Vangelder (eds), Kogan Page, London, 1990.
7. Clemens, John, Colin Day, and Debbie Walter, 'Direct access panel: The research mode for the eighties and beyond', in: ESOMAR, Monte Carlo, September 1980.
8. Parfitt, J. H., and B. J. K. Collins, 'Use of consumer panels for brand share prediction', *Journal of Marketing Research*, vol. 5, May 1968.
9. McCloughlin, I., and J. H. Parfitt, 'The use of consumer panels in the evaluation of promotion and advertising expenditure', ESOMAR Congress, Opatija, September 1968.
10. Parfitt, John, and Reg Clay, 'Panel prediction techniques – what we have learned and where we are going', in: ESOMAR, Monte Carlo, September 1980.
11. McElhaton, Noelle, 'Converting Europe to access panels', *Research*, Market Research Society, August 1999.
12. 'Market Research', Special report, Mintel, London, 1990.
13. Penfold, Mike, 'Continuous Research Art Nielsen to AD 2000', *Journal of Market Research Society*, vol. 36, no. 1, January 1994.

14. Penfold, Mike, 'Who is winning the scanning revolution?', *Researchplus*, Market Research Society, December 1994.
15. Mason, Neil, 'EPOS', in: *The Handbook of Market Research Techniques*, Robin Birn, Paul Hague and Phyllis Vangelder (eds), Kogan Page, London, 1990.
16. Denny, Mike, 'How the omnibus hit the fast track – and now, hold very tight', *Researchplus*, Market Research Society, February 1996.

Test marketing

- Understand the necessity of innovation for business success
- Realize the inherent dangers of product innovation
- Understand the role of test marketing and its sequential approach
- Gain insights into new methods, e.g. simulated test marketing (STM)

9.1 Introduction

Innovation is necessary for business development: no company can exist for long without new products and services; expectations rise and bring pressures on manufacturers and distributors to supply goods and services to satisfy, at least for a while, the needs of people and organizations. But the manufacturing and marketing of new products inevitably carry risks, particularly if the innovation is radical.

> *Though innovation is a necessity of business life, it is unnatural. It requires abandoning what's familiar and has been mastered for the unfamiliar and untried. Understandably, innovation does not happen automatically or easily. The only thing that's automatic is inertia – remaining with the accustomed and the comfortable.*[1]

Innovation is like a catalyst in industry and commerce; it invigorates efforts and brings new opportunities for profitable expansion. The need for innovation exists in all types of business and industry: the problem is that many companies do not recognize this by systematically developing a 'portfolio' of products across markets, both home and overseas.

The concept of product life cycle (PLC) and innovation strategy are directly associated. Products, in general, have limited lives during which they retain profit-earning capacity. The span of useful life varies considerably according to the nature of products, the rate of technological developments, the nature of demand and marketing management decisions. Basically, the PLC theory states that products tend to follow a pattern similar to biological development: from birth to growth to maturity and then eventual decline and death. Despite its many critics, the PLC concept has much to contribute towards sound marketing strategies.

The number of phases of the life cycle suggested by various researchers has ranged between four and six: a typical 5-phase model is depicted in Figure 9.1.

The pattern of growth and development reflected by the curve in Figure 9.1 is, of course, only a *general* tendency; individual products will tend to have characteristic market profiles over time. Considerable research, mostly with food products, supports the existence of the classic bell-shaped curve, although in some industrial markets, other types of PLC curve appear to exist.[2] The period of growth will vary; some products, particularly

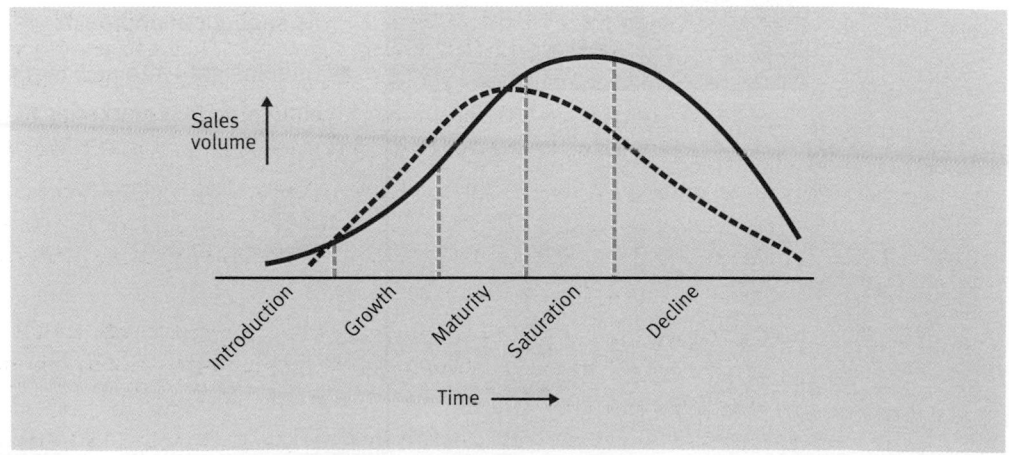

Figure 9.1 Generalized concept of product life cycle showing five sequential stages (dotted line refers to general trend of unit profits)

in fast-moving consumer markets such as 'pop' records or fashion clothing, will experience volatile patterns of demand. The length of profitable life, as well as the duration of each stage of the demand curve, will tend to vary significantly according to the types of products and services involved.

Closely linked to the PLC concept is that of the profit life cycle (see Figure 9.1, dotted line), but note that the profit cycle of a product does not follow the same curve as the sales volume trend.

Innovations may involve new inventions – for example, those based on the petro-chemicals and electronic industries – or it could refer to improvements in existing products, or to novel methods of promotion and distribution, as with e-commerce. All companies need to innovate; 3Ms corporate plans stipulate that 25 per cent of sales must be derived from products that did not exist five years before.[2] In his classic text[3] on corporate strategy, Ansoff characterized firms as either reactors, planners or entrepreneurs. 'Reactors' wait for problems to occur before trying to solve them; 'planners' attempt to anticipate problems; and 'entrepreneurs' deliberately anticipate both problems and opportunities. This latter and more enterprising type of management does not wait for a specific trigger but is constantly researching for strategic market opportunities so that profitable growth can be maintained.[2]

KEYPOINT

Innovation is

Necessary for business development

Inherently risky

Acts as a catalyst in business

Linked with product life-cycle (plc)

Of many kinds, e.g. inventions, improvements, new methods of distribution, etc.

Five important principles affect the acceptance of innovations in general, and these have been identified as follows:[4]

1. *Relative advantage* should be assessed from the *user's* viewpoint; hence the need to undertake systematic market research to establish customers' needs, levels of satisfaction with existing products/services, and expectations. Products should have attributes which give them competitive advantage: these may be a mix of techno-logical, economic, financial, or psychological benefits (see Chapter 1).

2. *Compatibility* concerns the need to understand the likely impact of new products/services on customers' beliefs, values, attitudes and experiences. At one time, dehydrated food products were perceived unfavourably by housewives, who regarded them as substitute, low-quality products.

3. *Complexity* relates to the extent to which an innovation can readily be understood by users and providers; for example, home computers, mobile phones, or microwave cooking.

4. *Divisibility* refers to the opportunities for prospective buyers to try out new products on a limited basis; for example, small trial packs of innovative food products, such as flavoured yoghurts or new varieties of cheese would be likely to attract first-time buyers.

5. *Communicability* refers to the success with which the results of an innovation are communicated and readily observable by adopters. In the case of pre-emergent weed-killers, difficulties were experienced in convincing farmers of the potential value of such products, so the rate of diffusion was slow.

These five factors are, of course, interdependent and significant influences in the diffusion of innovatory products and services. The spread of ideas and practices among diverse cultures has been studied by anthropologists for many years and it has been shown that the process of diffusion takes the shape of the normal curve.[5] A few people adopt the innovation at first; then the majority may follow suit, and finally the rest join in (see Figure 9.2).

KEYPOINT

5 important principles affecting acceptance of innovations

relative advantage

compatibility

complexity

divisibility

communicability

These 5 factors are inter-related

As noted, the communicability factor and the rate of diffusion of new products are closely associated, and the five stages of the diffusion process given in Figure 9.2 should be viewed as a continuum.[5] In general, 'innovators' appear to be well-educated, self-confident, well-informed and disposed to accept some degree of risk. They are also more willing to change their consumption habits – including switching brands – than later adopters. They may, in fact, act as 'opinion leaders' among their friends and contacts.[5] The 'late majority' and 'late adopters', sometimes referred to as 'laggards', represent around 50 per cent of a market, so it is important that the underlying reasons for their distinctive reluctance to buy earlier are thoroughly researched. Their delay in buying may be attributable to a mix of personality factors, such as aversion to risk which reinforces strong brand loyalty. Such shoppers

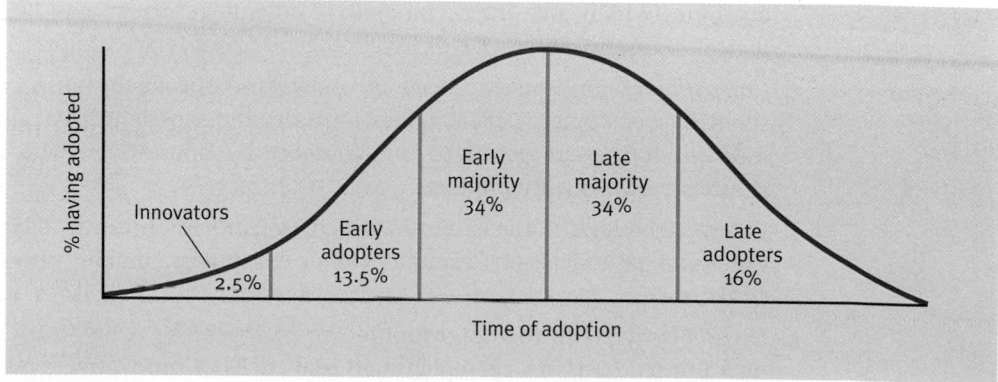

Figure 9.2   Five stages of the diffusion of innovations

might be attracted by 'money-back' offers, guarantees, small trial packs, after-sales service, etc.

KEYPOINT

Diffusion of innovations

Innovators: 2.5 per cent (opinion leaders)

Early adopters: 13.5 per cent

Early majority: 34 per cent

Late majority: 34 per cent ⎫
                                        ⎬ 'laggards'
Late adopters: 16 per cent ⎭

These 5 stages are a continuum

Necessary to research buying motivations of each type of prospective customers

'Laggards' should be encouraged by special promotional offers, etc.

Innovators and early adopters are critically important: their media habits should be known.

Product failures

Products may fail for many reasons, perhaps because they are 'before their time' (like Harry Ferguson's pioneering work on four-wheel drive vehicles, on which he spent a personal fortune but achieved no commercial success), because their adoption entailed too radical a change in traditional habits, or through neglect of marketing research and reliance on preconceived ideas about the needs of particular kinds of customers.

The Seven-Up Company in the United States had been tremendously successful with their first product to use the 7-Up name – Cherry 7-Up. This encouraged them to develop another soda drink, 7-Up Gold, but this product was a disastrous flop, despite $10 million spent on network television advertising. Among a variety of explanations was that the company's main product was promoted as the 'Un-Cola', but the new product was of a reddish-brown hue like a cola; it also had caffeine added, regardless of Seven-Up's earlier advertising theme: 'Never had it. Never will'. The advertising campaign for 7-Up Gold apparently failed not only to attract the targeted audience of teenagers, but also failed to reach an equally important market sector – mothers of young children. In addition, over-optimism had curtailed test-marketing operations; fuller tests might have revealed that consumers had confused perceptions, because 7-Up Gold clashed with the strongly developed image of Seven-Up's products: 'clear and crisp, and clean, and no caffeine'. Even experienced marketing management is prone to make mistakes from time to time.[5] Diffusion is a complex phenomenon involving both economic and psycho-social factors; the former may, in fact, be less important than the latter, as indicated by the confused perceptions of consumers of the 7-Up Gold product innovation.

In fact, American-owned companies seem to be as prone to marketing failures as British companies, and there is some evidence that traders are inclined to be rather more prejudiced when assessing the market performance of the products of American-owned companies. At one time, American-inspired products were launched in the UK with little or no modification to meet British tastes. Not surprisingly, many of them failed, and the hard lesson appears to have been learned that a shared language does not automatically mean similar preferences in consumer products. General Mills' experience with Betty Crocker cake mixes is now part of marketing folklore, and Campbell's soups have never been able to achieve the market position in the UK which they hold in the US. Campbell's type of soup – 'condensed' and, therefore, requiring the addition of water – was unfamiliar to British housewives, who compared its price and flavour to established favourites such as Heinz.

KEYPOINT

Product failures – many reasons

'Before their time'

Involve too radical change in habits

Neglect of market research

Preconceived ideas of what people want

Poor distribution

Product performance below expectations, etc.

Guides to market success

In the UK, only about 10 per cent of the top selling branded food products were launched in the 1990s; only two, Huggies and Sunny Delight, were introduced in the last five years. A new pan-European survey of almost 25 000 lines, conducted by ACNielsen – BASES and Ernst and Young revealed that 90 per cent of product launches in Europe fail within two years.[6] Distribution was found to be the 'single most consistent cross-market variable for defining the success of new product introductions'. If a new product in the survey achieved more than 50 per cent distribution after one year, it was rated a success; if it achieved more than 90 per cent, it was rated a star. The following 'golden rules for success' resulted from this extensive survey, which took place in the UK, France, Germany, Italy, Spain and Finland:

1. true innovation is more successful than 'me too' products or line extensions;
2. products must live up to the concept promise;
3. long-term support must be given;
4. 'major category players' are likely to have greater success;
5. 'first to market' tends to have lasting advantages; and
6. trial rates are key influences in achieving volume sales.

This last factor is 'perhaps the most interesting conclusion: without high trial rates no new product will succeed'.[6] This finding was confirmed by statistical tests which revealed a strong correlation (R22 = 0.84) between the trial rate achieved by a new brand in the first year and its ultimate sales. Distribution was 'identified as being ultimately more important than brand awareness in generating trial':[6] distribution drives trial and trial, in turn, drives brand volume.

Nielsen's New Product Barometer continuous consumer panel of 10 000 UK households identifies the different rates of trial needed for specific product categories; for instance, a confectionery brand should aim for a trial rate of at least 8.5 per cent penetration in the first year of launch. Weekly EPOS data can be used to track the progress of distribution (see Chapter 8).

KEYPOINT

Guides to market success – distribution is key factor

1. 'True' innovation' more successful than 'me too' products or line extensions

2. Products must fulfil expectations

3. Long-term support must be given

4. Prominent marketers have greater success

5. 'First to market' have greater success

6. Trial rates vitally important in securing volume sales

Nielsen research over 5 years in UK, France, Germany, Spain and Finland.

Markets change over time

Market inertia was experienced with some now well established durable products. Central heating, for example, is now generally thought to be an essential item of equipment in modern homes. But only a few years ago, central heating for 'popular' housing would have been dismissed as an unnecessary fad, and it would probably have been argued that the British climate is far more stable than America's, whose inhabitants needed complete heating systems far more urgently than in this temperate climate. Attitudes have again changed, incomes have risen, and consumers seek to satisfy their growing needs, which include greater comfort in their homes. Other household products are beginning to attract more general interest; deep freezers are following the pattern of refrigerators as 'necessary' household equipment. Refrigerators, including fridge/freezers, are now in virtually every British home (99 per cent in 1996). Central heating is enjoyed by almost nine out of ten households, showers are to be found in over 50 per cent, and double-glazed windows are fitted to nearly 60 per cent of British homes.

Diffusion of such products has been affected by many factors: greater awareness of the need for food hygiene (no larders in modern houses), expectations of comfort in homes, social contacts, small-bore central heating, automatic boilers, etc. The processes of adoption and diffusion involve both economic and non-economic factors and deserve the special attention of manufacturers and distributors of a very wide range of goods and services. Psychological, sociological and cultural influences are active as well as economic factors, such as price and delivery, and physical characteristics, like product design and performance.

Constant monitoring of markets is increasingly important and evaluations of product/ service concepts should be imaginatively, as well as pragmatically, designed. Cultural beliefs and values, social aspirations and inhibitions, and subjective perceptions all influence patterns of consumption in some way or other. For example, educational achievements tend to raise expectations, and success usually brings with it demands for better kinds of existing products and services, and the willingness, even eagerness, to try new types of food, travel and leisure pursuits.

One thing is certain: people are never completely satisfied for long; the apparent insatiability of human needs constantly challenges the ingenuity of designers, production development engineers and other specialists, and marketers, including, of course, marketing researchers.

This dynamic environment stimulated Taylor Nelson Sofres to develop a specialized service: 'Opti-test', which aims to give client companies' food technologists 'a clear, fundamental understanding of consumer preferences in their product area'.[7]

Taylor Nelson Sofres states that the 'Opti-test' approach is based on ideas developed by Fisher and other statisticians who were engrossed in agrarian research earlier this century. They had to contend with many variables that could not be controlled, such as the soil and its constituents, and external factors, like the climate; these problems could be considered comparable to those facing Taylor Nelson's researchers, who had to deal with people and also market forces.[12]

KEYPOINT

Markets change over time

Buying behaviour is dynamic, not static

Rising standards of living – new levels of demand (heating, holidays, health care, etc.)

Greater variety of products/services available

Increased expectations (product improvements, more exciting foods, etc.)

People never satisfied for very long (insatiability)

Marketers must monitor markets closely

Both economic and non-economic factors influence consumption

New product strategies

A *building strategy* is adopted by companies which seek to develop by planned innovation in design, production, marketing and distribution methods. They aim to be market leaders, and are willing and able to carry the risks associated with this aggressive strategy.

An *imitative strategy* adopts a 'wait-and-see' approach; it is essentially less adventurous than being a market leader. The performance of new products marketed by 'leaders' is monitored, and when it is judged to show symptoms of real growth, the 'market followers' prepare to enter the market. The time lapse may have been used to improve products and to avoid some of the mistakes made by market pioneers. Sometimes, the market initiative is taken by relatively small but dynamic firms which have developed highly innovative products, while large companies have been content to make and market traditional products. When Wilkinson Sword (then a small, specialized manufacturer), introduced stainless steel razor blades, Gillette's market share of conventional products was threatened. Eventually, they decided to introduce their own version of stainless steel razor blades, which they promoted heavily. Hoover and also Electrolux retaliated against Dyson's revolutionary, bagless, 'cyclonic' domestic carpet cleaner by developing their own versions of innovatory cleaner, again backed by mass advertising campaigns. Both cases illustrate that a sleeping giant, when finally aroused, has enormous muscle power in a market, and that an imitative strategy is not necessarily confined to 'second-rank' companies. IBM became involved with computers, and Texas Instruments with transistors, as the result of following imitative strategies.[2]

An *acquisitive strategy* may be followed by some companies which acquire firms which have specialized technical know-how, patent rights, etc., plus skills in exploiting innovations. This strategy of innovation may be productive, but there are often considerable personal and organizational problems, which tend to impede market progress.

KEYPOINT

New product strategies

Building: leaders

Imitative: followers

Risk assessment needed in competitive markets

Acquisitive: acquire firms with patent rights, specialist skills, strong brands

Decision-model approach to new products

The innovative strategy to be followed by an individual company cannot be quoted like a set of inflexible rules. As with market-share strategy (of which it is an intrinsic part), there are usually several alternative methods of innovation, which are open to careful evaluation. The most feasible solution may not necessarily be the ideal one, but at least it should have the virtues of realism.[2]

The viability of a new product could be analysed against the framework of a simple decision model, as shown in Figure 9.3. A checklist or logical decision model is often extremely useful in assessing potential marketing prospects for a new product or service. The basic model shown in Figure 9.3 may, of course, be further elaborated to meet specific corporate needs.

Figure 9.4 proposes six steps in new product development; these stages include preliminary and formal economic analyses, and also new product evaluation which, of course, should include marketing research.

The head of R&D at Sharp, the Japanese consumer electronics group, has declared: 'In the past, we could see market needs very clearly. But from now on, they will become more diversified. We must do more in-depth studies of what consumers really want. Research must be focused. We must explore potential needs hidden below the surface.'[9] Sony has also admitted that in the past its products were technology driven in the expectation that new ideas would catch on with consumers. 'Market research was often neglected on the grounds that consumers would not have a sensible opinion about an entirely new product.'[10] Now the company accepts that consumers' needs must be studied more, if innovations are to succeed. Peters, in fact, has asserted that, at one time, Sony 'proudly turned its back on market research and produced "user-friendly" designs by gut instinct'.[11]

9.2 Test marketing

The main purpose of a test market is to forecast the likely results of a planned national launch. It may also be used to check the relative effectiveness of different marketing mixes

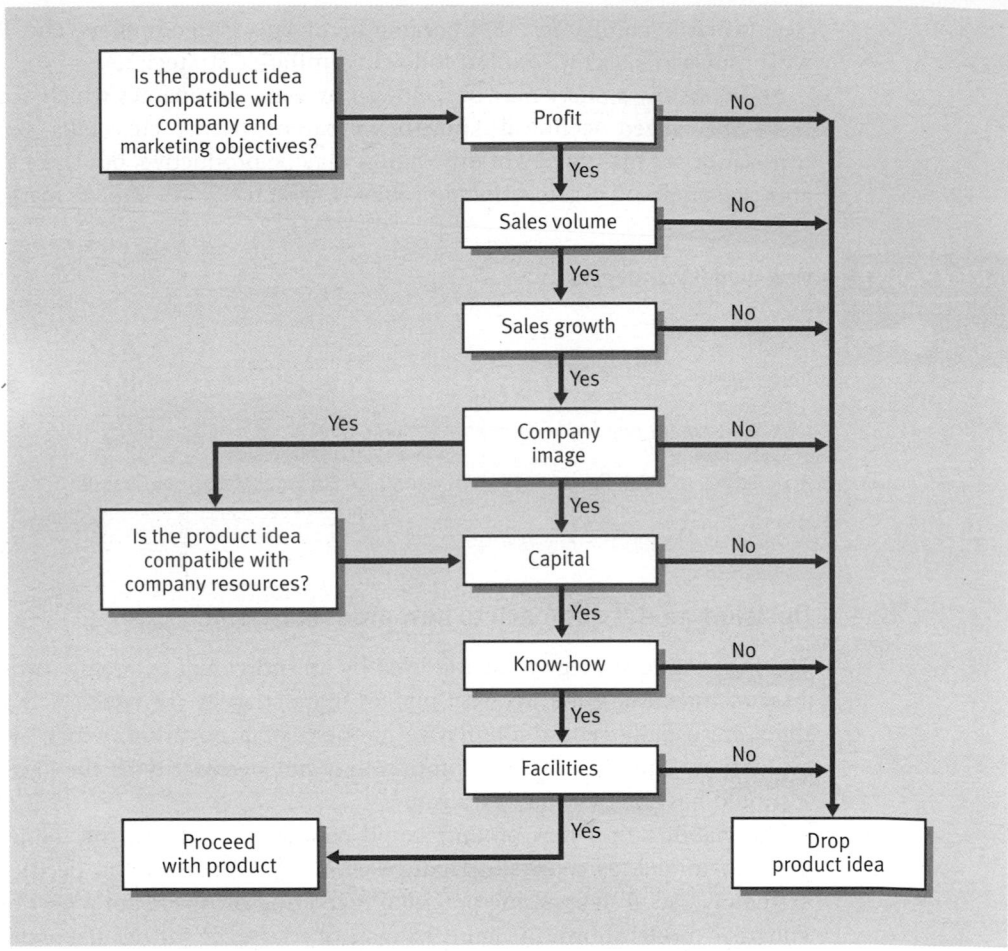

Figure 9.3   A simple decision model to assess the viability of a new product

in comparative areas. Additionally, it provides opportunities to test the operational efficiency of the marketing plan.

Basically, test marketing is a field experiment conducted under management discipline but, unlike laboratory experiments, not in a controlled environment. It was popularized with the advent of commercial television in the UK in the 1950s, and soon 'became a common feature of new consumer product development programmes'.[12] Local press groups were also quick to point out the advantages of combining their intensive local coverage with regionalized television campaigns.

For many years, test marketing has been used in the USA with considerable success, and Victor A. Bonomo, one of America's dynamic marketing men, warned against the dangers of unplanned marketing: 'Don't make a major capital excursion into the unknown without thorough test-marketing, for it is only through market test experience that any degree of certainty can be gained'.[13] This pragmatic advice indicates the critical role of test marketing, which is concerned with what happens in the real market place, as opposed to some theoretical concepts or projections of likely consumer behaviour towards a new product.

It is, of course, difficult to assess accurately people's likely behaviour. What they may, in good faith, have told an interviewer during a market research investigation could be

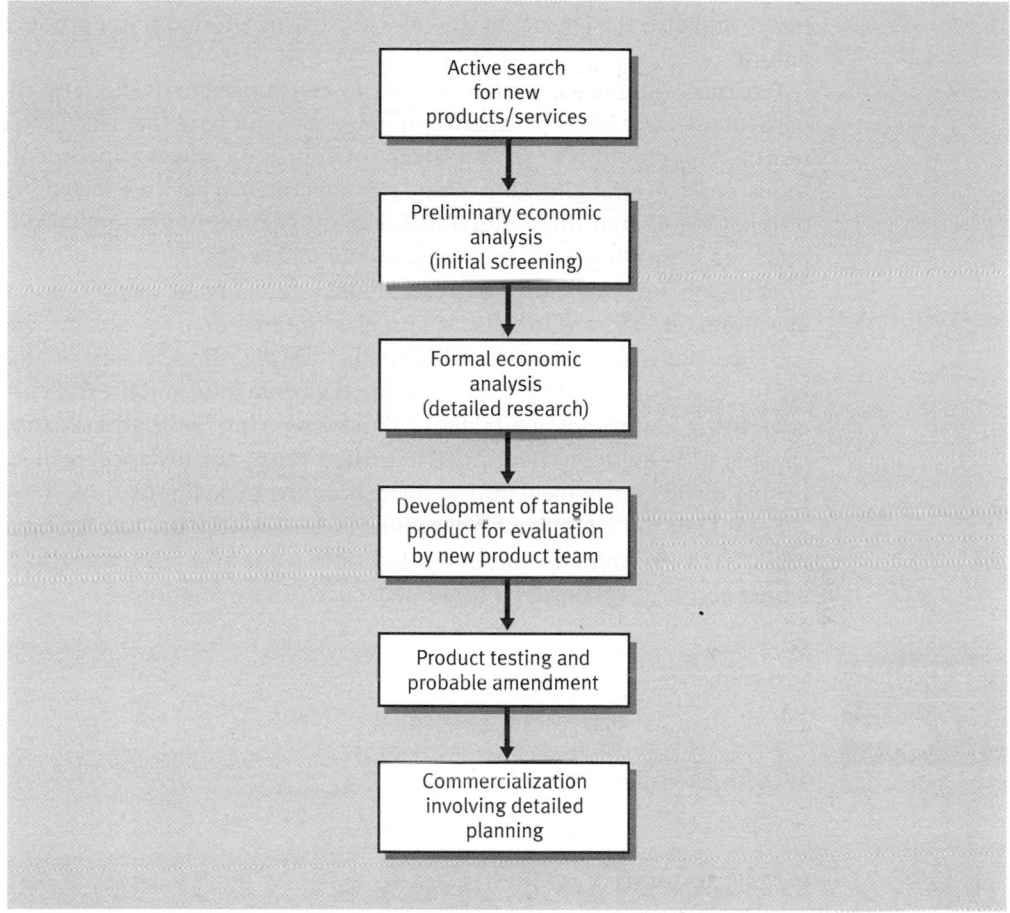

Figure 9.4   Outline steps in new product programme

contrasted with their behaviour at some later time when they are in the actual buying situation. The conditions of the market place are dynamic; there are many calls on people's disposable income, and there are many factors – political, social, psychological, etc. – which influence their final patterns of expenditure. In addition, the activities of competing suppliers to the market in the areas of pricing, packaging, advertising, special promotions, etc., will affect consumers' choice at the point of purchase. Test marketing is therefore concerned with finding out what people actually do when they are shopping for themselves and their families. The facts obtained from such exercises serve as guides to the development of future marketing plans.

In real-life conditions, a scaled-down version of the entire marketing programme can be tested in some carefully selected test areas, which should be representative of the eventual national market. New products and promotional back up are exposed to the acid test of consumer acceptance or rejection. This experimental marketing is a form of risk control. Test market proposals should be evaluated on a cost–benefit basis, i.e. by assessing the relationship between the costs involved and the estimated benefits which are likely to result. Where the financial risks of going ahead without test marketing are greater than the costs of conducting such research, it would be advisable to undertake test marketing. Apart from immediate financial risks, there may well be serious levels of risk related to corporate image and also the effects on the sales of existing products, if a product launch ended in failure.

Test marketing is generally confined to consumer goods, because industrial products, particularly large items of capital equipment, do not lend themselves to concentrated area testing. Some industrial products can, of course, be given experimental runs in certain industries, e.g. arranging with a food manufacturer to pack a selected line in a new type of film packaging, but these individual tests differ from highly organized test marketing as practised by leading consumer product manufacturers.

Although test marketing has contributed valuably to marketing knowledge and the development of strategic skills, it also encountered many problems, such as competitive activities designed to frustrate valid market testing, the selection of areas which could be regarded as representative of national buying behaviour, and the difficulty of ensuring that advertising campaigns, particularly those involving the national and local press, were capable of being replicated. Also, television areas, for instance, sometimes overlap, and people travel quite widely during their shopping expeditions.

Because of these problems, traditional test marketing has largely, but not entirely, been replaced by *simulated test marketing*. But since some area test marketing is still undertaken, a brief account will be given of the sequence of its operations.

KEYPOINT

Test marketing

To forecast likely results of national launch

To check different marketing mixes

To test operational efficiency of marketing plan

Basically, test marketing is field experiment.

Popularized with advent of commercial TV in 1950s

Used in USA for many years

Test area results indicate likelihood of national success

Generally confined to consumer products

Many problems encountered: competitive activities; selection of representative test areas; adequate media availability; cost and time involved

Largely, but not entirely, replaced by simulated test marketing (STM)

9.3 Sequential approach to test marketing

There are eight sequential steps in test marketing; these are outlined in the following sections.

1. Define the objectives

The first step involves defining and agreeing on the objectives of the exercise. As noted earlier, objectives will vary according to the specific products and market conditions, including the nature of competition. Statement of the objectives should be in writing, as this ensures that those who propose to undertake the test marketing have marshalled their thoughts in a disciplined manner. Decisions regarding the selection of test areas, control areas, sample sizes, audit frequency, etc., can then be rationally made. Whatever the objectives, care should be taken to ensure that there is complete understanding and agreement by all those taking part in the exercise, and, of course, ratification by top management. Ideally, one variable at a time would be tested in any one market. This could be, as in the case of Du Pont, the study of the effects of different levels of advertising. If too many variables are tested at the same time in one test area, it tends to be difficult to identify their specific influence, although sophisticated methods of statistical analyses have overcome this handicap to some degree.

2. Set criteria of success

Again, modern management techniques demand that performance should be assessed against agreed standards of success; this principle applies equally to test marketing procedures. The criteria set should be realistic and proportionate to the volume of sales, the level of distribution, or share of the market (some of several possible targets) which would be expected at national level. Where advertising·is being studied, it would be necessary for researchers to note the degree of increase in sales which would be regarded as significant.

Evaluation must be strictly objective – the enthusiasm of test marketing should not be allowed to influence cool, reasoned assessment of the opportunities which might exist for a new product on a national scale.

3. Integrate test marketing operations

It is vital to ensure that the test marketing campaign fits into the overall marketing plan. For example, the level of selling effort, or the amount spent on advertising, should be consistent with the general marketing policy of the company. Abnormal results are likely to occur if only 'crack' salespeople are used in test areas; likewise, excessive advertising will also distort the natural movements which test marketing is concerned to study. The assessment of an appropriate level of advertising raises special problems for marketing managers. These have been discussed by John Davis[14] in relation to a test area containing a hypothetical 5 per cent of the national population. One approach would be to place 5 per cent of the total advertising appropriation in a test area, but this would ignore the variations in cost per 1000 between, for example, regional television rates. The other approach involves projecting into the test area the schedule of advertising which would apply in the event of a national launch. However, this assumes that a national schedule as such can be compiled, whereas often the total advertising campaign tends to be made up from a series of area schedules. If a national schedule can be prepared (or an approximation to it is feasible), this still does not overcome the additional problem of quite strongly marked differences between television viewing habits over the country. These should, therefore, also be borne in mind when preparing a test campaign advertising schedule. But even then there may be differences in the weight of advertising of competitive brands nationally, and in a test area. The main point is that a very detailed approach to the establishment of the appropriate experimental conditions is needed in *all* test marketing activities.

4. Establish controls

Control areas should be set up in order to provide realistic evaluation of the influence of a particular variable in a test area. It is admittedly very difficult to ascribe to any single factor a causal relationship, and it may be considered desirable to check the effects of a single variable in more than one test market, and over the identical time period. These additional test areas should be comparable in those characteristics likely to affect sales of the product under test. It is good research practice to divide the period of testing into three phases so that valid comparisons can be made of market movements. Planned research is an essential element of market testing. First, it is necessary to know what the market situation is before the test campaign starts; this calls for some survey work to establish the level of competition, competitors' brands, consumer buying habits, attitudes to the product type, brand loyalty, price sensitivity, etc. Shopping habits will affect the types of outlets through which a product can be sold. Trade research is, therefore, advisable. This would cover attitudes to the product type, customary discount structure, quantity discount terms, merchandising practices by competitors, the degree of co-operation which may be expected from the trade, etc. During the test campaign further enquiries will be necessary to monitor market movements so that trends may be identified quickly and also to assess the likely outcome of the campaign. Consumer panels are often organized in test areas by leading research agencies. Auditing of stocks of specific products in stores is another tool of test marketing. This specialized form of research was introduced by Nielsen's in America, and it extended to Britain, where it has now been used by most of the leading food, drug, and related products' manufacturers for over 30 years. (See Chapter 8 for details.)

This systematic auditing of store stocks is also offered by some other research agencies, which have followed the very successful trail blazed by Nielsen's. Nielsen Shop Audits are usually on a monthly basis, though special arrangements can be made. Factory shipments by themselves will not give an accurate reflection of the present state of the market. There may, for instance, be a sudden fall in ex-factory sales because of the build-up of trade stocks. Auditing of trade stocks gives manufacturers a clear picture of the way in which their products are being bought by consumers. After the market test is over, a final survey should be done to confirm the experimental evidence gathered during the operation, and these findings should be compared with the initial survey. Before-and-after studies will assist researchers to obtain a deeper understanding of their markets, and should provide valuable guides for future action. This last phase of research should be extended to dealers, so that an overall appreciation of market influences is gathered. Dealers should be encouraged to give their frank assessments of the test operation – they will not usually suffer inhibitions – and manufacturers should be willing to listen carefully and evaluate these comments. Many valuable clues to guide future marketing activities can be gathered from objectively analysing the reports from trade sources.

5. Select representative areas

Test areas should reflect in miniature the national market, and careful selection is, there-fore, of great importance. At least two cities should be selected for each variable to be tested, and where it is intended to make sales projections on a national scale, at least four geographical areas should be used. Where marked regional differences are anticipated, it would be advisable to ensure that test markets cover adequately such regions.

In Britain there is also a marked tendency among researchers to concentrate tests in particular regions. It would be unwise, however, to select an area for a test marketing campaign which is too heavily dependent on one industry for its prosperity, because a setback in this industry during the time of test could affect buying habits radically. Areas with diversified industries are, therefore, less likely to be prone to sudden economic upset. Strong seasonal influences should also be borne in mind when choosing test areas; the possibility of prolonged major industrial strikes which would disrupt the normal economy of an area would be another factor to consider.

Test areas should have good publicity services. In Britain the major newspaper groups have newspapers in several provincial centres which can serve as test marketing areas. *Reader's Digest* and the colour supplements of the 'quality' Sunday papers offer special inducements for area advertising of products. Regional advertising facilities are available in some of the leading women's journals. They can be used for a wider range of media or market tests, as well as to give magazine advertising support to regional brands or to up-weight a television campaign in selected areas.

The commercial television companies have built up special facilities for test marketing of a wide range of products. Some companies are particularly active in this field, and many branded products have been tested first in the districts covered by them.

Some marketing people have expressed doubts on the typicality of test areas, but the fact that large national companies continue to use these districts suggests that critics may be generalizing too freely. 'Normally, the most that can be done is to ensure that the areas finally selected for an experiment are not too widely atypical, and then to cope with moderate degrees of atypicality through more sophisticated methods of interpretation and projection.'[14] The essential point is that it is vitally necessary to have a deep and full understanding of the test area it is proposed to use. Results can then be weighted to allow for known variations from national behaviour patterns, media availability, media costs, etc.

The dangers of 'over-testing' are also put forward as a decided disadvantage of using the same test areas, because, it is claimed, the reactions of consumers and the trade tend to become atypical. It is also thought that the sales force may become 'exhausted' by repeated efforts on new lines. These objections may contain some element of fact, but they tend to rather overstate the argument. After all, people are known to like variety and to seek new products; the number of new products on sale at any one time relative to the general run of merchandise offered is usually extremely small.

Another important aspect is the size of test markets; areas should be large enough to contain a reasonable proportion of the various socio-economic groupings of the general population. Areas should preferably have about 100 000–200 000 inhabitants. It may also be significant to note geographical factors. In America the influence of Nielsen on test marketing has resulted in all its test markets being in areas with populations ranging between 75 000 and 115 000. This size range occurs primarily because of the sample size required for Nielsen store audit procedure, and the company is quoted as saying that it prefers test cities of about 50 000–100 000 population. This allows them to maintain a high coverage with a sample of about 50 food stores and 15 to 20 drug stores.

A further factor is advertising economy: most Nielsen clients are relatively heavy advertisers and advertising costs less in terms of total dollar expenditure in small rather than in large cities. This point could be compared with television advertising in Britain, where the smaller television companies are able to offer attractively economic rates to test marketers. This should not, however, delude manufacturers into rather heavier use of advertising than they would be able to afford on a national basis. As already noted, the weight of advertising effort should be assessed so that the extent to which it is used in the marketing mix is in relation to that which could be undertaken in a national campaign.

6. Decide on number of test markets

It is advisable to consider using three rather than two test markets for each variable under test, because if tests are restricted to two markets and one of these is affected by some unexpected event, such as a large industrial upheaval or some natural catastrophe like a flood, there would still be two areas left to complete the market testing. These three areas should be selected so that they represent high, average, and low market penetration for the particular company. The combined results should be quite a good guide to average performance in national markets.

7. Establish duration of tests

The length of time allowed for tests will be largely affected by the nature of the product under survey, the buying frequency, the degree of competition in that particular product market, and the variable being tested. Enough time must be allowed for the test results to develop; this may entail waiting for consumers to use up the product and, if satisfied, to re-purchase, at least once. This period of time can stretch from a few months to a year or more.

The longer the duration of a test market, the more it will cost. Research activities need to be subjected to the sound management principle of accountability. Another important point affecting the time allowed for market tests is the degree of competition existing in that product market. The longer a test runs, the more likely are competitors to become aware of a company's intentions. Several cases have been noted where competitors have 'jumped the gun' and gone national at once, when they have discovered that a test campaign was under way in a market of interest to them. Procter and Gamble launched 'Ariel' bacteriological detergent on a national scale while Lever was still testing its product 'Radiant'. Similarly, Dawnay Foods beat Cadbury's to the national market with 'Dine' instant mashed potato, when it found out that Cadbury's was testing 'Smash'. Market testing is, therefore, subject to many hazards, both accidental and deliberately planned by interested parties.

It is vital to allow market tests to run their full course – this sometimes calls for steady nerves. If the tests are called off because early signs do not appear to be favourable, a good market opportunity may be lost. As already discussed, it may take some time for certain products to work their way into the shopping lists of housewives, and it is these long-term effects which are the real concern of test marketing. As tests progress, it may become evident that modifications may be necessary to the product or to the methods of presentation; these alterations should be made and the tests resumed, after carefully noting sales figures so far achieved.

Occasionally, companies 'go national' at once – and are successful. A notable example was the immediate national marketing by Weetabix of 'Alpen', a breakfast cereal based on the Swiss muesli, with nuts and fruits. After careful pre-testing of the product, Weetabix felt that it was on a winner, and marketed 'Alpen' on a national basis. Inevitably, its remarkable success attracted competition: marketers must accept the inevitable risks of launching new products. They have to evaluate the comparative risks of test marketing and a national launch.

When Rowntree originally launched its highly successful 'Yorkie' bar, it realized that it could be readily imitated. It was decided, therefore, to market at once throughout the London television area, and assess market reactions before launching nationally a year later.

8. Evaluate the results

This final stage in test marketing needs to be done thoroughly. On expert evaluation of the test results rest important business decisions, involving, perhaps, heavy capital investment and the setting up of volume production lines. Test market results may indicate that a certain percentage market success has been achieved, but merely to project this same percentage to the wider national market would be naïve and likely to be distinctly misleading. More sophisticated evaluation is called for; study should be made of significant factors, such as the demographic structure of the population, types of outlets available, strength of competing brands, and any particular variations among regions in competitors' activities, which may result in variations between the test area and the national market. After this more elaborate analysis, it should be possible to construct a forecast of future likely demand for the new product on a national basis, but always bearing in mind that the data collected are historic, whereas forecasts attempt to estimate the trends of future events.

Various approaches can be made to the projection of test market results; for example, direct market share, proportionate population, buying index, or sales ratio.

John Davis[14] has stressed the critical problem of converting the results observed in an experiment in a limited area into an assessment of what is likely to happen if the project is launched nationally. He differentiates between 'projections' and 'predictions', and between the results of these processes and forecasts.

Straight projection, as in direct market share (x per cent of test market = x per cent of national market) is obviously simple, but highly fallible. As discussed earlier, it ignores the inevitable differences in the multiple variables of market behaviour. It is very unlikely that test markets will be mirror images of national markets.

A prediction, on the other hand, derives from more complex calculations, in the process of which some attempts have been made to obtain a deeper understanding of market behaviour. A model is likely to have developed to act as a basic guide. The simple projection of market share, for example, could be improved by a prediction using a scale-up factor of which Fitzroy[15] gives two examples:

1. Buying index method:

$$I = \frac{\text{Product field national sales}}{\text{Product field test area sales}}$$

2. Per capita usage:

$$I = \frac{\text{National population}}{\text{Test area population}}$$
$$(I = \text{scale-up factor})$$

These formulae could be further elaborated by incorporating a 'correction factor' to allow for differences in distribution efficiency and other changes which may have taken place between the test marketing operation and the national launch.

It is unlikely that a new product will attract sales equally from existing brands in a test market; product positioning, strength of competition, brand loyalty, etc., will modify the extent of market share erosion. Taking these kinds of factors into account, test market results could be extrapolated if data were available on competitive brand shares before and after a market test.

Fitzroy[15] illustrates this approach with three competing brands and the impact of a new market entrant (see Table 9.1).

In the test market data shown in Table 9.1, product A retained 80 per cent of its market share, product B 66 per cent, and product C 80 per cent, while a new product achieved 25 per cent market share. National market shares are then subject to the percentage variations quoted above, and it will be seen that, after national launch of the new product, product A's market share will fall to 36 per cent, product B's to 10 per cent, and product C's to 33 per cent. The residual share of 21 per cent will fall to the new entrant.

These extrapolations assume, of course, that the conditions applying in the test market will be unchanged when national marketing is undertaken.

A forecast is, or should be, based on a comprehensive examination and evaluation of the data collected during test marketing, and an assessment of the resultant projections or predictions. Calculations are likely at different levels of probability and over short-, medium-, and long-term periods. This demanding task should be the joint responsibility of marketing researchers and marketing management, who would carefully check any changes that might have taken place in the market since the tests were undertaken.

If it is decided to launch the new product nationally, the marketing strategy must be planned to tie in with production facilities. Immediate large-scale production and distribution may not be feasible. Production lines often need a 'warming-up' time before they can cope with a large national demand; management may prefer to sell regionally for a short time to avoid the possibility of a national distribution problem. Furthermore, test market products are frequently made on special pilot plant, and there may be unplanned difficulties arising when production is switched to the regular plant. To avoid this type of trouble, marketing managers should discuss with factory management their test marketing plans and agreement should be reached on the practicability of producing such products on a regular and volume basis.

Regionally phased marketing has advantages, but speed and confidence often pull off prizes. This emphasizes the need for good planning well in advance of the start of test marketing, so that rising public interest may be exploited quickly and profitably.

KEYPOINT

Sequence of test marketing operations

1. Define objectives

2. Set criteria of success

3. Integrate test marketing operations

4. Establish controls

5. Select representative areas

6. Decide on number of test markets

7. Establish duration of tests

8. Evaluate results

Table 9.1   Test market extrapolation based on competitor market shares

Product	Test area market shares		National market shares	
	Prior to test	After test	Prior to launch	After launch
A	25	20	45	36
B	45	30	15	10
C	30	25	40	33
New product	—	25	—	21

Source: Fitzroy[15]

9.4 New approaches to test marketing

The conventional approach to test marketing, outlined in this chapter, has been seen to be slow, expensive, and prone to spying and sabotage, so alternative strategies were sought by mass-market suppliers. In some cases, and from about the late 1970s onwards, they abandoned test marketing altogether, as happened when Procter and Gamble marketed nationally 'Folgers' instant decaffeinated coffee, or when Pillsbury introduced 'Milk Break Bar'. But both products involved little risk, because Folgers had an established favourable brand image, and the snack bar market was booming.

Simulated test marketing (STM)

Simulated test marketing is now an attractive alternative to formal test marketing. STMs can be used for new product evaluation, relaunch of existing products, or for launching product line extensions, although the last-named require special consideration.[12] This inherent versatility has rendered STMs useful in several critical areas of marketing decision-making, although it has been conceded that 'the amount of data required for estimating is often considerable',[12] and complex mathematical formulae are involved. STMs use market research data to estimate sales volumes, and must therefore 'take account of marketing variables, such as distribution, advertising, promotions, etc. It is probably fair to say that this element of the (STM) model is more complex and problematic than the prediction of trial and repeat purchase'.[16] Clearly, it is very important to acquire and put into the model, realistic and reliable data about the various market variables.

Typically, a consumer recruited at a shopping centre reads an advertisement for a new product and gets a free sample to take home. Later she – most respondents are women – rates it in a telephone interview. The test-marketing firm plugs her responses and others into a computer to predict potential sales volume. Opinions are mixed about the effectiveness of this method: it is generally agreed, however, to be fine for weeding out failures but not so good at predicting the upside potentiality of products to achieve satisfactory sales.

Research International identifies three basic types of simulated test: (i) *mini-test markets* – involving a permanent consumer panel serviced by an exclusive retail system operated by the research agency; (ii) *laboratory test markets* – based on mock store or display units, with penetration/repeat buying factors being estimated by computer modelling; and (iii) *calibrated tests* – where responses to purchase-related questions are converted to trial, repeat and volume predictions using empirically derived weighting factors.

These three basic types of simulated test markets provide different solutions to different problems and at different points in the product development cycle; they are essentially complementary rather than competing alternatives for any particular problem, and their characteristics will now be discussed more fully.

Mini-test markets originally entailed setting up a consumer panel whose members were serviced for their weekly major grocery needs by a mobile retail facility operated by the research agency, such as the RBL Mini-test Market. However, these arrangements have now been replaced by *ad hoc* applications based upon the improved modelling techniques available. (See MicroTest marketing research service below.)

Laboratory test markets involve, at their simplest level, a sample of representative users of the type of product, into whose market the new product is being projected. At the first stage, respondents in a central hall location are shown advertising for the test product (placed among a reel of other products in the field) in order to generate awareness. They are then taken to a simulated store showing priced displays of the test product with other brands, given coupons typically covering the price of all the displayed items, and asked to make a purchase. If the test brand is chosen, it can be taken home; if not, respondents can be given it to simulate a sampling exercise. After the product is used at home for a specified time, respondents are recalled to another interview where they are given the opportunity to buy the test brand with their own money. They are also asked to allocate preference points between the test brand and other brands in their repertoire. Additional diagnostic questions are also asked.

The data generated are analysed using the Parfitt–Collins[17] model of market share assessment discussed in Chapter 8, viz.

$$\text{market share} = \text{penetration} \times \text{buying index} \times \text{repeat purchase rate}$$

To obtain the estimate of cumulative trial, the purchasing observed in the simulated shop has to be down-weighted using projected awareness and distribution figures supplied by the client company.

The preference question provides an estimate of the likely level of repeat purchasing. A pseudo *Markov* model can also be developed, taking the percentage of initial repeat purchase and calculating the level at which this will finally stabilize.

To arrive at the buying rate index, all respondents will have been asked to give their purchasing frequency in the product field. Those likely to take the test product into their repertoire can then be compared with the market as a whole to assess whether they are heavier or lighter users of that type of product. The result can be used to weight the share figure. Results can be available two or three months from set-up of the project.

The system obviously has strengths and weaknesses but, under the right circumstances, it offers a reliable measure of potential brand share, augmented by a range of diagnostic information giving reasons for the likely market place performance. A fair degree of realism is achieved from using simulated shops and actual repeat-purchase opportunities, which can offer some degree of reassurance to both researchers and clients. One of the main weaknesses is that the model is essentially a share-based system and so is not so suitable for products that do not operate in readily defined markets. Another weakness lies in the fact that research has to be conducted using finished packaging, advertising, etc., and so by the time a company is ready for such an exercise, a considerable amount of time and cost will already have been expended.

Calibrated tests involve recruiting respondents who are shown concept material for a new product, and questioned about the concept, purchase intentions, etc., as well as being asked more diagnostic enquiries. The resultant data are processed by the research agency's modelling system to provide predictions of trial, repeat purchase and volume. Research International's *MicroTest* is a fairly recent development of this system (see below).

As with laboratory tests, strengths and weaknesses influence *calibrated testing*; one of its main advantages is that it can be applied at a relatively early stage in the new product development cycle to isolate particular problems in the product mix before too much time and cost have been expended. It is also able to provide the greatest wealth of diagnostic information, and because it is volume based and does not involve simulated shop displays, it can be used across a very diverse range of product types. These may be impulse purchases and might not fit into any well-defined market category. On the other hand, principal advantages arise because the concept needs to be carefully chosen so that a genuine assessment of the final positioning is measured; further, all work of this sort needs considered interpretation, and because of the complex nature of calibrated techniques it is harder for client companies to appreciate, readily, the analysis procedures. Hence, the research agencies have to accept more responsibility to ensure that findings are adequately understood.

Research International's *MicroTest* marketing research service is based on a sophisticated computer micro-model that provides: (i) the probability that each respondent will *try* the new product; (ii) the probability that they will *adopt* it; (iii) the *frequency* of purchase; and (iv) the *volume* of sales involved.

KEYPOINT

Simulated Test Marketing (STM)

Attractive alternative to formal test marketing

Used for new product evaluation, re-launches of existing products, product line extensions, etc.

Requires considerable amounts of data, and involves complicated statistical treatments.

Research International: 3 basic types of STMs

1. Mini-test markets

2. Laboratory test markets

3. Calibrated tests

These three main types of STMs provide different solutions to different problems, and at different points in product development. Essentially complementary.

MicroTest was originally developed to be administered in the context of a conventional concept/product test. Hence, the core technique is positioned relatively early in a product development programme, although at or beyond the stage at which a product formulation is ready for testing and pricing relatively firmly. Even then, substantial development costs will have been incurred, and because of the need to predict potential sales at earlier and later points in the development programme, alternative applications of *MicroTest* technology have been developed. These are: *MicroTest Concept* – to predict the trial potential of a particular concept or of alternative concepts – and, *MicroTest Laboratory* – to relate the output of the *MicroTest Model* to the input of the conventional laboratory test market. These two developments of the basic *MicroTest Model* significantly increase its overall value to clients seeking reliable indications of the likely behaviour of their new products in real competitive conditions.

MicroTests have been carried out in more than 25 countries and over many major product fields. In many cases, the tested products were not marketed or only after modification, thus saving large investment costs, apart from consumer dissatisfaction and possible loss of goodwill.

Microscope is one of the range of consumer product analyses at retail level which is offered by Retail Marketing Services (RMS). It is specifically designed for regional television test marketing, and is based on the Border TV region, which is taken as a microcosm of the national market. It covers a population broadly made up of one-third Tyne Tees, one-third Lancashire, and one-third Scotland, and spans three Nielsen regions. Test-marketing facilities for new fast-moving consumer products sold in supermarkets include sales and distribution back-up, advertising and other forms of promotion, pricing, stock levels and merchandising, etc. These are evaluated before a client is committed to the further costs entailed in a roll-out or national launch. Border TV collaborates closely in the Microscope research programme, and 'control' stores can be provided to test, on a comparative basis, the effectiveness of particular advertising campaigns.

RMS also offer other specialized research services: *Brandscope* – a test programme which measures the effectiveness of brand development strategies in all types of retail market. Factors covered include product range extension, product reformulation, and packaging design changes. *Tradescope* enables suppliers and retailers to co-operate in experiments at the point-of-sale, evaluating, for instance, shelf profitability, optimum product mix, the relationship between stock cover and unit sales, etc. *Promoscope* tests and evaluates any type of product promotion; for example, added-value packs, couponing, sampling or in-store promotional displays.

RMS also undertake consumer research at the actual point-of-sale. This in-store research covers, for instance, brand perceptions, usage patterns, media awareness, etc. Other special research activities involve electronic traffic-flow measurement, observational research (see Chapter 2), and monitoring of the uptake of sales or promotional material.

American study of simulated test marketing

The American Advertising Research Foundation (ARF) published a study of simulated test marketing (STM) in June 1988, based on data from seven research companies, reported to account for 90 per cent of all STM business in the US and covering 42 major marketing companies that have used STMs extensively.

The trend in STM projects indicated a 1985 peak, followed by declines in the following two years. STM predictions 'tended to be correct on a more-or-less chance basis . . . with subsequent in-market results confirming the predictions in about 51 per cent of instances, and being either lower (41 per cent) or higher (8 per cent) in 49 per cent of cases (although it must be pointed out that the end result in 45 per cent of STMs was to discontinue the project)'.[18]

Further, the costs of STMs tended to rise significantly; an 'average' STM, as revealed by the ARF study, cost about $47 000. Goodyear takes a distinctly reserved view of the future for STMs in their present form but, nevertheless, is confident that they 'will be developed, modified, repackaged, re-launched and continue to satisfy a genuine – and increasingly complex – client need for some time to come'.[18]

Scanner-based test marketing

This sophisticated method has been outlined in Chapter 8 in the section headed 'Scanner store consumer panels'. Certain supermarket shoppers are given identification cards which they present at check-out points where scanners record their purchases. Consumers are not aware of which products are being tested; the results of the scanning process are fed to computers for analysis. Cable television (in the US) is also used to find out what kinds of advertising attract certain types of buyers.

Nielsen pointed out that, today, successful new grocery products tend to achieve peak market share in a matter of months rather than years; they achieve a 50 per cent distribution level within the first few months; they manage to gain distribution in at least a couple of the top five grocery retailers within two months of launch; and the growth of scanning stores means that a new product can be evaluated as a success or a failure within just a few weeks.

Summary

Innovation is a risky activity, but essential for business development. Test marketing aims to control risk through conducting area tests before national launch. Products fail for many reasons: bad timing; poor quality; ineffective advertising, etc.

Eight important steps in test marketing have been identified as: define objects; set criteria of success; integrate operations; establish controls; select representative areas; decide on number of test markets; establish duration of tests; evaluate results.

New approaches to test marketing have been introduced: (i) 'simulated test marketing', e.g. MICROTEST; and (ii) scanner-based test marketing. Test marketing is a remarkably versatile tool of marketing; by intelligently using it, a very wide range of information may be gathered. There is no real substitute for market experimentation: test marketing provides a disciplined approach to marketing many kinds of products. Like other research techniques used in marketing, it does not guarantee success; management must still make decisions, but these can be made with more complete knowledge of real-life reactions to products.

Review and discussion questions

1. How would you respond to a marketing manager who feels that simply asking consumers whether or not they would purchase some product innovation is just as effective as test marketing the product?

2. Suggest situations in which it might not be appropriate to engage in test marketing prior to a product/service launch.

3. An acquaintance of yours manufactures a limited line of confectionery at home and supplies the bakery departments of four local supermarkets. Currently she is considering launching a new product. What form of test marketing would you consider feasible for such an operation?

4. Outline a number of possible success criteria for test marketing a magazine advertisement designed to dissuade 18–24-year-old females from taking up smoking.

5. What problems are likely to arise in approximating market conditions at the national level to the specific areas in which test marketing is being conducted?

6. Differentiate between projection and prediction of test market results. What are the practical consequences of this distinction?

CAMEO CASE: Ecolatina

Ecolatina, an independent British tour operator based in Richmond, Surrey, specializes in providing the UK market with culture-based holidays in the South American Republic of Colombia. The company has a staff of two permanent employees (the Managing Director and the Financial Director), assisted by a small support team. Ecolatina was founded in 1998 by MD Luz Stella Osorio, in the firm belief that, despite the negative publicity surrounding her native Colombia, there is a small but wealthy segment of individuals interested in furthering their knowledge of the socio-cultural heritage of one of Latin America's most misunderstood countries. At present the company offers a range of ecological and cultural trips to various destinations in Colombia. As she herself puts it:

> Ecolatina, as a specialized independent tour operator, offers a unique range of exciting ecological and cultural tours to Colombia. Aware of Colombia's unique heritage, Ecolatina is committed to making an effective contribution in promoting the country's riches.

Her personal knowledge of the destinations and the numerous contacts that she has built up throughout the country give the company its competitive advantage, allowing it to compete with the larger operators in the market. In sharing this local knowledge with visitors, and giving them the opportunity to experience at first hand the land and people of Colombia, the company has an offering that is largely unmatched by other tour operators.

In the first financial year of operations (1998–1999), the company had a turnover of £30 000. Sales are not made on a regular basis, but depend on many factors, such as the time of year. The MD and her sales team are constantly looking for new ways to promote the company's offerings, and marketing research plays a key role in developing the customer base. Whether developing new destinations in Colombia, or looking for new market segments in the UK, most research is carried out by company personnel.

Cultural and business differences, coupled with the different requirements in each country, mean different approaches to research in the market (UK) and the destination (Colombia). Telephone contacts, trade publications, and brochures are the major means of gathering market data in the UK, whilst in Colombia, the personal approach is really the only way to do business. In common with most specialist operators who are concerned to develop a good reputation for quality, Luz Stella considers it essential to visit personally all the destinations offered by Ecolatina, in order to check on key elements such as hotels, transport providers, etc.

Whilst the unique positioning of Ecolatina means that the company faces very little direct competition, the activities of those competitors that do operate in Colombia and other Latin American destinations are monitored closely through their brochures. Of particular interest are price levels, and the range of products (destinations/tours) that competitors offer; new product development is a key issue in the highly competitive tourism industry, as destinations can very soon become 'old' and *passé*. As the business operates 12 months of the year, monitoring of competitors' activities is a constant process.

Questions

1. What is likely to be the biggest challenge (in terms of marketing research) facing the company over the next five years?

2. Whilst direct competitors may be relatively easy to identify, *indirect* competition may pose a greater long term threat as it is more difficult to identify. How would you go about analysing the level of *indirect* competition faced by the company?

3. How would you suggest that Luz Stella identifies new markets (either in the UK or in other European countries), and how can she most effectively identify new destinations?

Jonathan S. Swift

References

1. Levitt, Theodore, *Thinking about Management*, Free Press, New York, 1991.
2. Chisnall, Peter M., *Strategic Business Marketing*, Prentice-Hall, Hemel Hempstead, 1995.
3. Ansoff, H. Igor, *Corporate Strategy*, Penguin, Harmondsworth, 1968.
4. Rogers, Everett M., *The Diffusion of Innovation*, Free Press, New York, 1983.
5. Chisnall, Peter M., *Consumer Behaviour*, McGraw-Hill, Maidenhead, 1994.
6. Twyford, Craig, 'Sweet smell of success so often turns sour', *Researchplus*, Market Research Society, Autumn 1999.
7. Walker, Caroline, 'A spoonful of sugar sharpens your matrix', *Researchplus*, Market Research Society, September 1993.
8. Pessemier, Edgar A., *New Product Decisions*, McGraw-Hill, New York, 1966.
9. Jonquieres, Guy de, 'Industry has a cultural barrier', *Financial Times*, 5 December 1990.
10. Butler, Steven, 'Sony's lean manufacturing machine', *Financial Times*, 10 December 1992.
11. Peters, Tom, *Thriving on Chaos*, Macmillan, London, 1987.
12. Sampson, Peter, 'Modelling: simulated testing', in: *A Handbook of Market Research Techniques*, Robin Birn, Paul Hague and Phyllis Vangelder (eds), Kogan Page, London, 1990.
13. Bonomo, Victor A., 'The do's and don'ts of test marketing', *Nielsen Researcher*, vol. 2, no. 3, Nielsen, Oxford, 1968.
14. Davis, John, 'Market testing and experimentation', in: *Consumer Market Research Handbook*, Robert Worcester and John Downham (eds), Elsevier Publishing, Amsterdam, on behalf of ESOMAR, 1986.
15. Fitzroy, Peter T., *Analytical Methods for Marketing Management*, McGraw-Hill, Maidenhead, 1976.
16. Bond, Julian, and Joseph Debacq, 'Research in new product development', in: *ESOMAR Handbook of Market Opinion Research*, Colin McDonald and Phyllis Vangelder (eds), ESOMAR, Amsterdam, 1998.
17. Parfitt, J. H., and B. J. K. Collins, 'The use of consumer panels for brand share prediction', *Journal of Marketing Research*, vol. 5, May 1968.
18. Goodyear, John R., 'The future development of international research . . . the multi-lingual, multi-national, multi-variable', in: *Seminar on International Market Research*, ESOMAR, Amsterdam, November 1988.

10

Advertising research

Learning Objectives

- Gain introduction to principal theories of advertising influence

- Note specific aspects of advertising research, e.g. content and media (JICNARS, etc.; tracking studies)

- Obtain further knowledge of main British socio-economic grading used in advertising (NRS)

- Explain nature and value of geodemographic analyses, life-style research, SAGACITY; also SEC official classification

10.1 Introduction

Organizations of all types need to communicate effectively with those they seek to serve or influence. Their motives are varied: commercial gain, political advantage, altruistic activities, philosophical beliefs, etc.

There are five principal ways in which a company, for example, can communicate with its markets: (i) media advertising (commercial television, newspapers, periodicals, posters, cinema, commercial radio, and direct mail); (ii) public relations activities; (iii) selling; (iv) merchandising (point-of-purchase promotion); and (v) packaging. These various methods are not, of course, exclusive, and a 'mix' is usually used.

To be effective, communications strategies require the same degree of systematic planning and control as practised in other areas of management responsibility. Objectives, for instance, need to be fully discussed and defined; these should relate to the overall corporate strategy. They can be of many kinds, and range from attracting virtually instant sales, developing primary demand for a type of product or service, creating brand awareness and building brand loyalty, increasing the frequency of use of a product/service, promoting new uses for existing products, introducing new products/ services, announcing special offer, defending or increasing market share, encouraging distributors to stock and actively sell specific products, to appeals for charitable donations, etc.

The list is almost endless – frequently objectives are multiple, though one tends to be predominant.

Different promotional tactics make up the total communications strategy: advertising cannot be a solo performer, although it often plays a lead role. Colin McDonald[1] has commented that advertising does not often lead in creating overall demand for a product or service. It affects brands within markets, but 'at the market level, demand grows, stabilizes or declines for other reasons'. In many markets in developed economies, particularly packaged goods (FMCG) markets, saturation of total demand is now experienced. In such cases, advertising's power is distinctly limited. McDonald[1] sees the function of advertising as not so much to create demand but to build and propagate brand differentiation between competitive products. Markets, he declares, are at a stage of equilibrium, or moving towards it, and a few large suppliers use extensive advertising campaigns to increase their competitive advantages in markets experiencing what he terms 'dynamic tension'.[1]

Promotional activities are part of the 'marketing mix' (the 4 Ps). They are one of the interrelated variables (product, price, place, and promotion) which are at the heart of effective marketing strategies (see Chapter 1).

There are five principal ways in which a company can communicate with its markets:

1. Media advertising (commercial television and radio, the press, posters, cinema and direct mail/internet)
2. Public relations activities
3. Selling
4. Merchandising (point-of-purchase promotion)
5. Packaging

A creative promotional strategy requires systematic planning on similar lines to other areas of management activities. The first stage, therefore, is to define clearly the objectives;

the second is to design a promotional strategy that will be most likely to achieve these objectives which, as noted already, are likely to be several. In Figure 10.1, the sequential processes involved in this approach are set out.

Communication objectives, like corporate objectives, may be classified as (a) long term and (b) short term. Advertising is essentially persuasive communication, although it has, of course, other distinctive functions, such as 'awareness advertising' in preparing, for instance, a market for later entry in some countries. A leading advertising specialist formulated the 'familiarity principle': 'Something that is known inspires more confidence

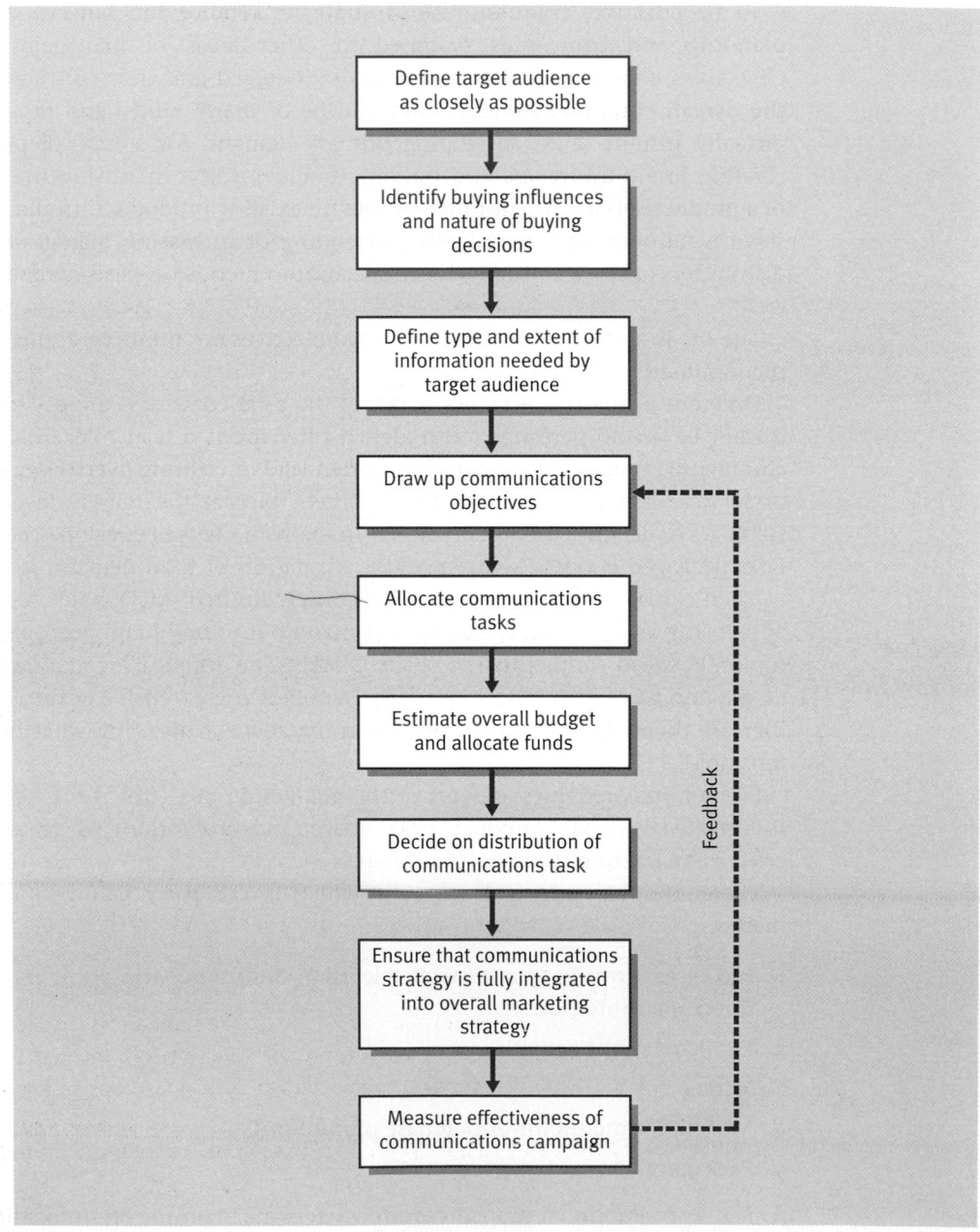

Figure 10.1 Planned sequence of communications strategy

than something that is unknown'.[2] Some advertising campaigns contain elements of 'reassurance advertising': the reduction of dissonance or post-purchase anxiety which, based on Festinger's theory of cognitive dissonance, often leads buyers of consumer products to seek confirmation of their purchasing decisions.[3] Car advertisements, for example, frequently include 'reassuring' messages to owners of their vehicles.

Being a market leader entails accepting the burden of high risk, particularly where markets are highly competitive and there is a regular flow of new products, as in the grocery trade. Innovation, as noted in Chapter 9, can sometimes lead to catastrophic losses, despite mammoth advertising expenditures. Development of attractive new products/services involves realistic assessment of the nature and extent of risk in entering new markets or extending existing ones. (The problems and opportunities associated with innovation are discussed at some length in a specialist text.)[3]

To design effective methods of communicating with their markets, organizations need to have access to objective data to guide their choice of media and the allocation of their overall promotional budgets. Target groups of consumers need to be defined and explored in depth, covering, for example, their perceptions, attitudes, motivations, patterns of consumption, brand awareness and loyalty, media habits, etc. As a prelude to a promotional campaign for the red wine Chianti, a survey was conducted in the UK to establish how the general public viewed this product compared with Beaujolais. An important finding was that it was clearly associated with eating, either at home or in a restaurant; this insight helped in developing suitable promotional plans.[4] The planning director of a leading advertising agency[5] has stated categorically that 'the really important research when developing advertising is that which helps us to understand the consumer, what is happening in the market, and why'. Without this fundamental knowledge, it is futile to start spending time and money on various kinds of advertising. As noted already, an effective communications strategy sets out clear objectives; these should never be overlooked, and should form an integral part of the advertising brief which a client gives to an advertising agency.

10.2 Theories of advertising influence

Many models and theories of the advertising process have been developed in efforts to explain how people are influenced by the various, and virtually unceasing, messages projected at them through the mass media.

Lannon and Cooper[6] have aptly characterized these diverse explanations as: (i) 'hammer and nail' theories; (ii) 'conversion' theories; and (iii) 'hierarchy of effects' theories. All are said to share a 'major oversight' – they make 'little allowance for the participation of the receiver of the communication in the process'.[5] These 'primitive but enduring linear sequential models' (which will be described later) have survived for several reasons: (i) they lend themselves readily to measurement; (ii) they tend to attract the support of 'the major US marketing companies in Europe'; (iii) the simple conditioning character of such advertising is so firmly associated with high quality cleansing products that it is effective; but, 'perhaps the simplest reason', is that the linear-sequential models are expressed in terms that are similar to the imperative language used by marketing strategists, for example, moving into markets, mapping out strategies, developing strategies, etc.

Colin McDonald[1] refers to a study by Hall and Mackay[7] among advertising professionals and marketing research practitioners of their perceptions of how advertising works. The following five 'conceptual models' resulted:

1. *Sales response model*: sales were regarded as the sole indicator of a campaign's effectiveness

2. *Persuasion model*: advertising influence and effectiveness can be measured through a linear sequence from awareness to understanding to choice

3. *Involvement model*: advertising's role is to build agreeable relationships with consumers

4. *Salience model*: advertising differentiates products and makes them highly visible

5. *Commodity model*: advertising is viewed as entirely functional – 'a narrow perception held mostly by small advertisers and non-users of agencies'.[7]

McDonald[1] observes that only the second, third and fourth models contain theories of how advertising may work, although even these are distinctly limited, as will be seen from later discussion. The two remaining models are incomplete projections; for instance, the *sales response model* evaluated advertising by its ability to cause short-term sales movements, and, in any case, this can only be useful with a fairly limited range of products/ services. Further, no account is taken of any psychological effects which advertising may have on the minds of those who view or listen to advertisements. The *involvement model* recognizes that viewers are not passive; advertisements are subject to many distractions, and filtering process include personal perceptions, interests, and values. 'Involvement advertising' is popular in beer marketing, and encourages people to identify closely with specific brands, and tends to be associated with the *salience model* of advertising which works on the assumption that advertising strongly differentiates a brand in competitive markets.[8]

Lannon and Cooper[6] see the emergence in Britain of the 'sophisticated consumer of advertising who is able to enjoy some advertisements for their creativity (but not necessarily being persuaded to buy the products in question), while rejecting other advertisements as patronising and/or conventional'. They propose a 'humanistic view' of advertising and branding; brands are held to have practical rational values, but it is their symbolic values that give them distinction and uniqueness. (This seems closely related to the salience model mentioned earlier, and also with theories of consumer-involvement buying behaviour, which appear to have particular relevance to promotional campaigns.)[3] Lannon and Cooper[6] feel that more appropriate theories of advertising are needed, based on language and concepts that are more in tune with the intuitive and mystical creative process, than with the rational, logical organizational process.

Alan Branthwaite,[9] in discussing ways of understanding the consumer, has proposed an 'eclectic perspective', which emphasizes that buying behaviour is influenced by a 'wide variety of motives, skills and experiences'.

This viewpoint is certainly supported by psychological research into cognitions, learning processes, attitudes and motivations, which shows that people discriminate, distort, and actively participate in their reception of advertising messages. Attention is selective, perception is subjective, while retention and recall are fallible and also selective.[3]

Consumption habits are formed in many ways: family tradition, social contagion, peer group influence, etc. – all play a part in the formation and restructuring of attitudes, related, perhaps, to smoking, processed foods or the use of credit, and also to the diffusion of products and services. Advertising cannot be productive unless the changing mood and interests of society are studied and interpreted skilfully.

The inadequacy of perceiving the advertising process as one of causality, that otherwise passive consumers are pushed into buying after exposure to advertisements featuring specific products and services is dismissed by McDonald.[10] People, he stresses, respond to advertising – they are not passively subject to it.

The viewer of advertisements is not, then, someone just waiting to be stimulated into buying: this simplistic and offensive view of the consumer lacks reality and credibility. In recent years, there has been a substantial cultural shift away from the 'passive' to the 'active' view of the consumer. This more enlightened approach recognizes the importance of perception and other behavioural phenomena which, as mentioned earlier, influence buying behaviour. However, it is conceded that the old sequential models may be appropriate in some cases, and the 'passive' consumer concept associated with them 'is by no means dead'.[9]

Joyce,[11] whose opinions on advertising have long commanded respect, has stated that, in most cases, advertising 'works by causing the brand to be added to the consumer's repertoire (or at least preventing it from being dropped); or causing it to be purchased more frequently (or at least preventing it from being purchased less frequently) . . . There is a continual tug-of-war between perception of advertising and brand attitudes, and between brand attitudes and behaviour. Further, advertising can evidently affect behaviour 'directly' without affecting attitudes as an intermediate variable in any measurable sense.[11]

Ehrenberg[12] propounds the ATR model (Awareness–Trial–Reinforcement) as an explicit and main alternative theory of advertising. It accounts, he says, for what seems to happen not only to established brands but also to new product launches. 'Advertising can first arouse awareness and interest towards a doubting first purchase . . . and then provide some reassurance and reinforcement after the first purchase.'[12]

The underlying model of consumer choice, Ehrenberg argues,[12] is that an individual has certain propensities to buy certain brands; these propensities are largely stable over a year or more, but differ from consumer to consumer. This is enough to account for the apparent degree of brand loyalty observable in aggregate buying behaviour for both fast-moving consumer goods and durables. He contends that, in the main, there are no strong brands and weak brands, but only big brands and small brands. It is in this context that advertising has to work.[12]

Linear sequential models

These have become so firmly entrenched in advertising theory and practice, that some further discussion of their theoretical origins and characteristics is called for.

Several variations of a basic sequential approach to the influence of advertising have been popularized by researchers and practitioners. The number of stages and the terminology tend to vary, but they share a common theme: the influence of advertising is a sequential process.

Daniel Starch,[13] one of the pioneers of advertising measurement, stipulated that, for an advertisement to be successful:

1. It must be seen
2. It must be read
3. It must be believed
4. It must be remembered
5. It must be acted upon

Later, he[14] outlined the behaviour of advertising thus: (i) using mass media to call attention to, and inform people about, products and services; (ii) to establish favourable associations between needs and brand names, so that these would be recalled when people sought to satisfy specific needs. Repeat advertising and satisfactory performance of the product would contribute to the establishment of favourable or preferential images; (iii) buying action would result from the processes described in (i) and (ii).

He admitted that this explanation of the sequence of advertising's influence was: 'to be sure . . . theory, but in the final analysis, it is likely to be the most accurate description of reality'.[14] It is certainly useful in acknowledging that product usage is a factor which affects the influence of advertising, and it attempts to be more comprehensive than his original rather simplistic approach.

Another popularity quoted model – AIDA – has been applied in analysing buying behaviour, including advertising influence, and also in sales training programmes. The various stages are:

> Attention
> Interest
> Desire
> Action

Lavidge and Steiner[15] postulated that people move up a series of steps impelled by the force of advertising. These steps are not necessarily equidistant. Some products are approached slowly; these are likely to have a greater psychological and/or economic commitment. Other products may be regarded as less serious, and it is likely that these will be bought with a relatively low level of conscious decision making. Once brand loyalty has been established, the threat from other brands is considerably less than with ego-involving products.

The six steps of advertising influence in Lavidge and Steiner's approach were related to three phases of psychological model based on the theory that an attitude has three elements, as follows:

Conative	Purchase ↑ Conviction ↑	Connected with action, viz. purchase of advertised product
Affective	Preference ↑ Liking ↑	Concerned with formation of favourable attitudes or feelings towards advertised product
Cognitive	Knowledge ↑ Awareness	Related to information or ideas

Another popular flow-model of advertising termed DAGMAR (Defining Advertising Goals for Measured Advertising Results) was developed by Colley,[16] who stated that the ultimate objective of a sale was to carry people through four levels of understanding: awareness → comprehension → conviction → action. Colley perceived the role of advertising as helping to move the consumer 'through one or more levels' to the final act of purchase and to do this with greater economy, speed, and volume than any other methods.

Colley's simple model – which he described as 'applied common sense' – viewed advertising as a persuasive process which took the consumer who had been exposed to some kind of advertising stimulus, by a series of 'logical and comprehensive steps' through to eventual purchase of the advertised products.

These linear sequential models have attracted considerable criticism because of their deficient assumptions. Kristian Palda[17] dismisses them as superficial and unconvincing, and describes them as 'sketchy views of the internal psychological process the typical consumer is supposed to go through on his way from the perception of an ad to purchase'.[17]

Professor Jack Haskins[18] of Indiana University made a spirited attack on what he termed the FIFO process (facts in, facts out) which characterizes so much advertising research. After carefully examining considerable evidence he stated that: 'Learning and recall of factual information does occur. However, recall and retention measures seem, at best, irrelevant to the ultimate effects desired, the changing of attitudes and behaviour.' He commented that it is relatively easy to write factual advertisements and to measure the recall of facts: this rote memorization is indeed encouraged by the prevailing system of education. 'As the products of that system, we consciously or unconsciously build that approach into our efforts at mass communication.'

Lavidge and Steiner's model assumes that attitude change precedes behavioural change, which ignores the complexity of the relationship between attitudes and behaviour (refer to specialized text[3] for further discussion of this contentious matter). Fishbein, Ehrenberg, Joyce and others have all stressed that the link between these two factors is by no means fully understood. As far back as 1964, Leon Festinger,[19] the well-known American psychologist, had declared that, after exhaustive research, he was unable to find any evidence in support of the theory that changes in attitude are necessarily followed by changes in behaviour.

Anne Wicks[20] has referred to the STARCH, AIDA, and DAGMAR 'classic models of the advertising process', and noted that while there are important differences of emphasis between them, 'they all share a rational, logical orientation and a linear sequential view of the way advertising affects consumers'. They are all, she observed, 'left-hand brain models which elevate the importance of the conscious, verbal, analytic and convergent processes of the human mind over the more intuitive, emotional, diffuse and impressionistic processes'.[20] Because of this, advertising effectiveness testing has tended 'to focus heavily on the measurement of transmission of the rational and functional messages'.[20] Hence, the importance placed on recall in advertising research. However, as already noted, the so-called rational, logical model lacks entire acceptability.

The learning processes were mentioned earlier among the factors affecting the influence of advertising and limiting the usefulness of the linear models of advertising. These suggest that people absorb a certain amount of information, which advertisers hope will move them along to the final stage of purchase. But classical learning theories, such as those based on simple S–R models, have been seen to be inadequate; a cognitive and organizing influence affects human behaviour, including the viewing of advertisements and the reactions to them. While learning from advertising messages may be mostly accidental compared with planned systematic learning (like formal study), it does not follow that viewers are gullible and easily manipulated.

That the various hierarchical models of advertising grossly oversimplify the influence of advertising is evident from this brief review; more detailed discussion is given elsewhere.[3] Subjective perception of advertising messages, and the fact that advertisements compete with other stimuli for the consumer's attention, are two of the many influences which affect their impact. Psychological, sociological, and cultural factors play important roles in buying behaviour; the complex interaction between attitudes and behaviour should be carefully studied.

Finally, Ehrenberg[12] feels it is time that some of the more exaggerated claims for the power of advertising should be set aside; they do not enhance the reputations of advertisers or their agencies and may well be counter-productive, particularly when expensive campaigns fail to increase sales significantly. He urges that there should be greater understanding of consumer buying behaviour (as advocated earlier in this section), which would lead advertising to adopt more responsible attitudes and become more accountable. Little is known, for example, about how advertising works for established brands, and 'advertising planning is often based on misconceptions about consumer behaviour'.[21]

In Chapter 7, the complementary contributions of qualitative and quantitative research were seen to be useful in, for example, the generation of new products/services and the development of imaginative promotional concepts. A creative advertising brief draws inspiration from the findings of a well-devised research programme that takes account, for instance, of the perceptions and motives underlying patterns of consumption.

10.3 Aspects of advertising research

Advertising research is concerned with the objective evaluation of advertising as a method of communication and persuasion. This study includes both qualitative and quantitative aspects, and can conveniently be considered under three main headings: advertising content research, advertising media research and advertising effectiveness research.

These aspects of advertising research will be discussed in relation to above-the-line media advertising, on which most advertising research focuses. This does not mean that other promotional activities should not be evaluated rigorously, although it seems that comparatively little systematic effort is made to test the effectiveness of such expenditure.

The advertising agencies commissioned by a client company to develop concepts for an advertising campaign should be fully briefed on its objectives, the nature of the product, the level of competition, the degree of brand loyalty, and the target market. Close collaboration between client and agency in these early stages is vital, so that creative ideas result in a series of mock advertisements to be researched with groups of representative consumers.

10.4 Advertising content research

This focuses on the ability of the advertisement to achieve impact and to project the desired message. Design and layout must be tested in detail, the basic theme – the copy platform – must be closely examined in a series of tests with representative audiences. The purpose of this research is to determine certain facts which will help copywriters and designers in producing effective advertisements. For example, in advertising a new model of car should the main appeal be that of safety, speed, economy, or prestige? Alternative appeals are evaluated during the course of the research.

Evaluative techniques adopted in 'content' research are used at two stages in advertising: pre-publication and *post-publication*. With pre-testing, the emphasis is on the development of ideas and methods of presentation, whereas post-testing is designed to measure how effectively these communication concepts were received by the intended audience.

In *pre-testing advertisements*, groups of individuals, representative of the intended audience, may be invited to view 'mock-up' advertisements (press or television). Afterwards they are asked a series of questions to test their degree of recall ('noting') of specific aspects of these advertisements, e.g. the advertising message, illustration, acceptability, etc. More elaborate techniques involve psychological methods of enquiry, such as depth interviewing and various projective tests. (These are discussed in Chapter 8.) Other tests may be devised to check the spontaneous emotional response to advertisements and include physiological measurements of different kinds, e.g. eye-blink rate, galvanic skin response (popularly called a 'lie detector'), muscle tension, pupil dilation, breathing rate, etc. Machines, such as the tachistoscope, can be used to expose advertisements to viewers for a very brief period. After this measured viewing time is over, the impact is assessed. Eye-blink rate indicates the intensity of interest and is measured on special equipment. These, and other measures of the autonomic nervous system, are costly and are, therefore, more likely to be confined to testing advertisements in relatively expensive media.

Hall tests ('central location tests') are also used to test the reactions of selected people to a product or concept, including, sometimes, advertising themes. These tests are held in conveniently sited public halls or other suitable accommodation, and respondents are recruited by interviewers who screen them for their suitability for the type of product under test. In the US, special facilities in shopping malls are available for hall tests, and similar facilities are now becoming available in the UK. A wide range of products – food, beverages, fragrances, household durables and tableware – can readily be tested by this method, but some products, such as soaps, and shampoos, are 'better tested in the home environment'.[22]

Hall tests are essentially quantitative, so questionnaires are usually structured or semi-structured, although some open questions may be used, and qualitative enquiries may be conducted with a sub-sample of respondents. Research results can be facilitated by direct data entry using PCs, or through a modem link (see Chapter 5).

Associated with hall tests, are theatre tests, but participants for these sessions are pre-recruited to view test commercials inserted in the test programme. These sessions are expensive; audiences fill out self-completion questionnaires.

An experienced English advertising practitioner has commented: 'Recall is such a complex process, involving perception, memory suppression and verbalization, that few psychologists feel happy when using it as a measure of attention, although the depth of their feeling is dependent upon the precise nature of the measurement.'[23]

Post-testing of advertisements devolves on the basic measurements of recall and recognition. Notable developments in this area were made by Dr George Gallup in the US during the early 1930s; another pioneer was Dr Daniel Starch who founded his advertising research service based on 'Starch Scores'. (Details of these surveys are given later.)

Tests to measure recall (verbal and pictorial) may be either 'aided' (prompted) or 'unaided' (spontaneous). Respondents in aided recall testing may be shown a series of advertisements (press or television). After these have been viewed for a specified period, the respondents are questioned to discover exactly how much of the advertising messages, product brands, etc., they can accurately recall. In unaided recall, respondents are asked if they have seen a particular advertisement and, if so, questioned about its impact on them.

Measuring advertising material by recall and recognition techniques rests on the theory that they are useful in predicting brand purchase. This view appears to be prompted by what might be termed the 'sequential approach' to influencing people to buy products, as discussed in the preceding section.

The issue of believability of advertisements has been subject to debate over the years, and it would appear that, in general, there is no clear relationship between belief and advertising effectiveness. Individual differences in perception, suggestibility, and even tolerance about what can be true or false, are bound to influence opinions. Present methods of testing believability tend to be unreliable.

Maloney has commented[24] on the value of 'curious non-belief', which may lead consumers to try the product being advertised. What is believable to some people will not be accepted by others, because advertisements are viewed by consumers against the background of their varying beliefs, experiences, and general attitudes towards promotional activities. Advertising messages, as planned by advertisers, may be unconsciously distorted by consumers so that they fit in with their attitudes and expectations. 'Levelling' may occur, when certain parts of the advertising message are ignored because they are considered disagreeable and likely to upset overall favourable expectations. Messages may also be 'sharpened'; in order to support existing beliefs, consumers may add subjective meanings to advertising messages, which advertisers had not intended should be read into their advertisements. Where existing attitudes are favourable towards a product, 'sharpening' of advertising messages by consumers may be advantageous to advertisers. What people believe from viewing advertisements is not, therefore, easily evaluated.

10.5 Advertising media research

This research attempts to eliminate waste in advertising by objectively analysing the media available for promoting products and services. It seeks to make valid comparisons so that advertising expenditure is distributed over media which are most likely to result in achieving the objectives of the advertising campaign. Over the past 40 or so years, a great deal of valuable research has been done by marketing research specialists and professional organizations to improve the standards of expert knowledge about the effectiveness of various advertising media. The development of television advertising has added to the competitiveness of the industry, and has encouraged media owners to produce research data of greater sophistication and reliability.

Over the past decade or so, retail auditing and advertising research in the UK has, as noted in Chapter 1, been radically changed by the introduction of electronic systems of data collection. Bar coding, electronic point-of-sale scanning (EPOS), and consumer panels based on in-home scanning have revolutionized the collection and availability of information about buying habits, including evaluation of targeted advertising campaigns. (Later in this chapter, tracking studies are discussed.) Computer-assisted personal interviewing (CAPI) has also contributed to the increased efficiency of readership, and other, surveys, as mentioned in Chapter 5.

In the UK, the advertising industry has highly organized systems of research into printed and visual media, and advertisers are offered a wealth of information about the suitability of particular media for specific market segments. The cost of advertising space or time is broadly related to the estimated number of readers or viewers; advertisers want to know the effectiveness of a particular medium in communicating with and influencing existing and potential users of their products.

The principal activities of media research will now be reviewed under the headings of the press, television, radio, cinema, and poster research.

Press research

Readership surveys have been of interest to advertisers, advertising agencies and publishers in the UK for many years. Pioneer research was done by the Hulton Readership surveys which were made annually between 1946 and 1955 inclusive.

In 1956 the NRS was taken over by the Institute of Incorporated Practitioners in Advertising (IIPA), which published the NRS until 1967. From 1968 until 1991 the NRS was administered by the Joint Industry Committee for Readership Surveys (JICNARS) under the aegis of a committee representing the Newspaper and Periodical Contributors Committee, the re-named Institute of Practitioners in Advertising (IPA) and the Incorporated Society of British Advertisers. In 1991 JICNARS was disbanded, and since 1992 the administration of the Survey has been conducted by NRS Ltd.

The Board of NRS Ltd, which governs all aspects of the Survey, currently consists (in the year 2000) of four members representing the Institute of Practitioners in Advertising (IPA), four members representing the Newspaper Publishers Association (NPA), and four members representing the Periodical Publishers Association (PPA), plus as non-voting members two representatives of the Incorporated Society of British Advertisers (ISBA), a chairman and a managing director. Between them the IPA, NPA and PPA cover the majority of the running costs of the Survey (£2.9 million in 1999). The Board is advised on technical aspects of the Survey by the NRS Development Advisory Group, which is similarly made up of representatives from the IPA, NPA and PPA, together with representatives from the research contractor appointed by NRS Ltd to conduct the fieldwork and process the data it publishes. The current research contractor is IPSOS-RSL Ltd (formerly Research Services Ltd), who have held the contract for many years.

Mechanics of social grading

Informants are placed in a socio-economic classification ranging from A to E, which indicates to buyers of press advertising media the types of consumers covered by certain publications. These socio-economic groupings are tabulated in Table 10.1. NRS provides their interviewers with detailed examples of the occupations that relate to the various groups involved in the survey.

Since its inception the NRS has classified informants into social grades and this method of socio-economic grouping has been widely adopted by marketing researchers (see

Table 10.1   Socio-economic groupings

Social grade	Social status	Head of household's occupation
A	Upper middle class	Higher managerial, administrative or professional
B	Middle class	Intermediate managerial, administrative or professional
C1	Lower middle class	Supervisory or clerical, and junior managerial, administrative or professional
C2	Skilled working class	Skilled manual workers
D	Working class	Semi and unskilled manual workers
E	Those at lowest subsistence levels	State pensioners or widows (no other earner), casual or lowest grade workers

Source: NRS Ltd

Chapter 4). 'A household' consists of either one person living alone or a group of persons, usually but not always, members of one family, who live together and whose food and other expenses are managed as one unit.

From July 1992, some changes took place affecting the significance of 'head of household' and 'chief wage-earner' in defining the socio-economic status of respondents. Briefly, the social grade of the informant's household was no longer based on the head of the household but on the 'chief income-earner' (CIE). Up to the time of this change, the head of household was a significant factor, except where this person was dependent solely on state benefit, in which case chief income-earner was used.

Under the current arrangement, the CIE is defined by the question: 'Which member of your household would you say is the Chief Income-Earner, that is the person with the largest income, whether from employment, pensions, state benefits, investments or any other sources?' If two persons claim to have equal income, interviewers classify the elder as CIE.

A pilot study by the Market Research Society in October 1991 revealed that about 15 per cent of women were classified as CIEs who, under the existing procedures based on 'head of household', would have been recorded as 'wife of head of household' rather than as 'Chief Income Earner' in their own right. The switch in 1992 to the procedures based on 'Chief Income Earner' removed this anomaly from the Survey's data.

Critical evaluation

From time to time, criticism of the NRS social gradings has been made on the grounds that socio-economic groupings based on the occupation of the head of the household were imperfect measures of the propensity of consumers to purchase certain types of products. This problem has dispersed with the more realistic classification of the chief income earner, discussed above.

The socio-economic groupings in Table 10.1 were certainly devised at a time when society appeared to be more stable and consumption patterns were largely class based. But the concept of life style behaviour does not necessarily coincide with social group membership. Disposable income will vary for several reasons, such as family traditions, middle class life styles with strong commitments to education, financial planning, etc. Family life cycle will be another modifying influence on expenditure.

The disposable income of the 'blue-collar' family may be as high as that of the professional, yet they will be classified quite differently. An established barrister is classified as an A together with a bishop of the Church of England; a teacher under 28 is a C1, but above that age becomes a B. A self-employed London taxi-driver or a plumber is a C2 type, whereas an articled clerk is classified as a C1, as are small shopkeepers.

Further anomalies arise from the growth of literacy, greater opportunities for university education, and the fact that social groups do not necessarily share consistent buying habits. The 'super-rich' – whose incomes are clearly 'super A', as well – tend to have conspicuous patterns of consumption, but the landed aristocrat living in his Queen Anne mansion may be struggling (a subjective term, of course) to meet the heavy costs associated with maintaining his elevated social position. He, also, is classified as an A; but his life style and patterns of expenditure are likely to be vastly different from the rock star. It is unwise to make generalizations, of course, but there is growing evidence that in many cases there are only tenuous relationships between social group membership and the consumption of specific products and services. Hobbies may attract disproportionate expenditure on equipment, materials, travel, etc., and attitudes towards such expenditure are likely to be indulgent.

At the request of JICNARS, Research Services Ltd[25] investigated the NRS social grading system. Among its comments it was stated:

> Although the historical development of social grading based on occupation is well established, the precise reasons for the choice in pre-war studies are not well documented. It would appear that occupations were first used because in the more rigid social order that existed the occupation of the head of the household was a simple and efficient method of deriving income categories. As the relationship between occupation and income has lessened, occupation has remained the background of social grading because no better methods have been found, and because it has still remained a powerful and useful stratification factor, even though the interpretation has become more complex. . . . Social grading analyses used in published tables of the NRS are to a large degree chosen because:
> (a) From a technical stand-point occupation is relatively stable and reliable at the data collection stage.
> (b) It is a reasonable 'general purpose' classification in that it is useful for most product fields without necessarily being the most ideal for particular product fields.

In 1981, the Market Research Society[26] published the findings of a joint industry working party (IPA; ISBA; ITCA; MRS; and NPA) on social grade validity. The report largely supported the continued use of the present A–E socio-economic grading which provided 'satisfactory discriminatory power' related to product and brand usage; none of the alternative systems studied was found 'to provide consistently better discriminatory power'. The existing method continued to keep its discriminatory power, but there was a need for guidelines to ensure greater consistency in its applications among research suppliers.

It was admitted that while there may be an 'ideal' variable superior to the A–E classification, the 'likely benefit derived would be out of proportion to the substantial expenditure required to investigate this point'. The report admits that the conclusions of the working party may lay them open to criticism of complacency, but it was felt that despite some of its specific shortcomings, the present system of measuring social grade is generally 'perfectly adequate'.

This view is challenged by two experienced marketing researchers[27] who observed that although social grading lacks a degree of reliability, this does not stop it from being a 'consistently powerful discriminator'. Its widespread use should not, however, be allowed to obscure its two distinct weaknesses: it imperfectly represents differences in people's tastes and interests based on cultural and educational dimensions, and it lacks measures of income and wealth. It is suggested that a combined scale which interlaced terminal education age with social grade discriminates more effectively in the consumption of certain products, such as hardback and paperback books. The other perceived drawback to social grading, viz. measures of income and wealth, could be tackled by developing variables known as Total Net Household Income (THI) and Disposable Net Household Income (DHI). It is concluded by these marketing researchers that: 'There are many markets and types of behaviour in which either income or socio-educational grade discriminates more strongly than social grade itself'.[27]

A sub-committee of the Technical and Development Committee of the Market Research Society published a report[28] in 1987 which stated that although the NRS social groupings were widely used, three main problems were encountered: classification by the occupation of head of household/chief wage earner was unpopular with respondents who objected to being classified by someone else's occupation; students and unemployed were variously classified; and certain new technological posts were hard to categorize.

A special tabulation of NRS data showed that about one-half of working women would be classified differently by their own occupation compared with that of the head of household, but the latter still seemed likely to be the best indicator of household life style, and so its continued use was recommended. It was also recommended that all students should be grouped as C1s, and people unemployed for up to six months should be classified according to their previous occupation.

The sub-committee recognized the arbitrary nature of these decisions, but it was felt that they met current needs.

In 1990, the Field Committee of the Market Research Society published *Occupations Groupings: a Job Dictionary*, which lists thousands of jobs in alphabetical order with relevant social gradings.

Readership surveys give information about what periodicals are looked at by certain kinds of people, but they do not offer explanations of behaviour: the 'what' is identified, the 'why' is omitted in these enquiries. [Later in this chapter, newer methods of consumer classification based on household and location (ACORN), and socio-economic groupings related to life cycle and occupational mobility (SAGACITY) will be examined; these, admittedly, are available to NRS subscribers.]

From July 1992 the NRS introduced, in addition to the concept of the chief income earner, a new 'shopper' question, aimed at discovering the extent of personal involvement in shopping for the household's food and groceries. The original 'housewives' question was: 'Who in your household would you say is mainly responsible for, or shares the household duties such as shopping and cooking?' It was recognized that the traditional image of a solo housewife was no longer appropriate, and that different members of a household can be involved to different degrees with various household duties, including shopping and/or cooking. All references to 'housewives' were therefore abandoned in both the questionnaire and the published data, and the concept of the 'main shopper' was introduced.

Main shoppers are identified as those individuals who personally select about half or more of the items bought for their household from supermarkets and food shops. The question now used is: 'Now I would like to ask some questions about your personal involvement in shopping for your household's food and groceries. Which of these best describes the extent to which you personally select the items when you are shopping at supermarkets and food shops?' The informant is then asked to choose one point in a four-point scale: (1) all or most items, (2) about half, (3) a few, (4) none or almost none. In addition, the informant is also asked to indicate how much they personally spend in an average week on food and stores. In 1999, the Survey found that within a total adult (15+) population of 46.5 million, 30.2 million individuals qualified as 'main shoppers', of whom 20.4 million were female and 9.8 million were male. (See end of this section for discussion of the new social classification published by the Office for National Statistics.)

KEYPOINT   **National Readership Surveys (JICNARS)**

Originated in 1946 – Hutton

NRS taken over by IPA in 1956

NRS jointly administered by media owners and users

Survey based on 'readership', but this subject to some criticism

6 social groups: A, B, C1, C2, D and E

▶

Various amendments and adjustments over years

Still some anomalies but widely used across all advertising media analyses

Use with discretion

Geodemographic systems and life-cycle analyses provide rather more sophisticated studies of consumption patterns

Methodology

Ipsos RSL (formerly Research Services Ltd) have held the NRS contract for several years; some details of this well-established and respected research design will now be given.

1. *Sampling*   The universe sample is all adults aged 15 and over living in mainland England, Scotland and Wales (approximately 46.5 million). Certain areas, particularly Scotland, have booster samples to allow reliable estimates to be made for certain regional daily and Sunday newspapers. The 1999 sample was 35 816.

   The sample design (see Chapters 3–5) is a multi-stage probability sample based on 2520 Enumeration Districts (EDs) as primary sampling units. Selection of addresses within each ED are derived from the Postcode Address File (see Chapter 6); one individual from each of these selected addresses completes the sampling sequence; modifications are made in multi-household, tenements and institutional addresses. Previously the Electoral Register had been used, but it was no longer considered reliable enough because of non-registration (see Chapter 3).

2. *Fieldwork*   This is continuous over 12 months and samples are weighted separately by month to make each month representatively balanced by sex, age, region and class.

   From July 1992, the survey data have been collected by computer-assisted personal interviewing (CAPI: see Chapter 6). This has led to fewer non-classified respondents, and also allows report results to be available within three weeks from the end of field-work. Interviewers make personal calls at specified addresses and attempt to interview one person according to a strict selection procedure, as noted earlier. Only the selected person may be interviewed for a household. A minimum of five calls have to be made before interviewers are allowed to abandon attempts to secure an interview at a selected address.

3. *Scope of readership enquiries*   Approximately 300 publications are measured; six titles are grouped together on 50 prompt cards, which are sorted into 'any publication seen in the last year' and 'no publication in the past year'. 'Not sure' cards are put on to the 'yes' pile; 'no' cards are rechecked by informants. 'Yes' cards are then dealt with individually, and highly specific questions are asked about the recency and frequency of readership of these particular publications. The order of presentation of the cards is rotated to avoid bias arising from the well-known tendency of respondents to be influenced by the sequence in which names appear. New titles are the subject of special questioning until such time as they become familiar.

4. *Analysis*   Results are weighted to produce estimates of the number of readers in the total universe of 46.5 million adults. Analyses include demographics, shopping behaviour, household composition, income, tenure, ownership/usage of video, teletext, computers, mobile telephones, etc., leisure pursuits, education, financial

arrangements, TV viewing habits and radio listening habits, access to the Internet, the Web and e-mail, and readership of any of the 300 titles covered by the survey.

NRS survey subscribers are provided with reports, published monthly and half-yearly, with 3-month, 6-month and 12-month bases as appropriate by type of journal. NRS present charts to help users to assess the statistical validity of any readership figure quoted, and they warn that small samples can lead to very unreliable data. The NRS invited the Office of Population Censuses and Surveys (OPCS) to check out the quality of the NRS data, and this highly respected official survey organization confirmed that NRS methodology is 'rigorous and designed to produce high-quality data'.[29] Although NRS response rates are already considered high in comparison with other commercial surveys, the OPCS was also asked to examine this important aspect of NRS's activities. The conclusion was that NRS 'is achieving a good first-contact rate – the point where contact is established with a selected family. Much of the second stage dropout, when making contact with the individual, randomly selected for interview, could be difficult to avoid.'[29] Bearing this in mind, the OPCS found the current overall response rate to be more reasonable. (See Chapter 6: section on 'Declining trends in survey response rates'.)

For some time, there has been general concern about refusal rates, which are rising steadily: 'more people are becoming refuseniks'.[30] This trend is noticeable 'even in flagship studies like the National Readership Survey,[30] where response rates are now around 60 per cent after eight or more calls on respondents.

Readership measurement by telephone surveys

After the launch of a new national newspaper and in order to get early estimates of readership, JICNARS has sometimes conducted telephone surveys. From a number of such studies, it was evident that there was a consistent bias: estimates of readerships of the upmarket 'quality' newspapers tended to be higher than those obtained from the main NRS, while readerships of the mass-market 'popular' journals were under-estimated.

An experimental telephone study was undertaken by Research Services Ltd[30] in 1988, and new questions were also added to the NRS itself, to try to identify the causes of these biases. Findings revealed that the prime reason lay in the considerable differences between the social grades attributed to respondents in personal and telephone interviews, even when both interviewing methods were conducted by the same research firm.

It was, apparently, 'often difficult to obtain on the telephone the extra information needed to classify a head of household with comparable accuracy to the face-to-face NRS interviewer'.[30] There was a 'net tendency' for some of the B social grade people to be classified in the telephone interview as C1s; at the other end of the socio-economic scale, it was easy to classify a pensioner with limited private resources incorrectly as an E from telephone data.

Interviewers make personal calls at specified addresses and attempt to interview one person according to a strict selection procedure, as noted earlier. Only the selected person may be interviewed for a household. A minimum of five calls have to be made before interviewers are allowed to abandon attempts to secure an interview at a selected address.

The cause of this bias is mainly that households that have acquired a telephone for the first time are excluded from published telephone directories, as are recent movers. ABs tend to be more completely recorded than C1s, and the bias gets worse further down the socio-economic scale.

NRS has developed a new telephone survey procedure which entails re-interviewing NRS informants who were interviewed a few months earlier. Since their social grade is known from the first interviews, as also their telephone numbers, the problems of using telephone directories are neatly avoided.

However, since 1988 NRS has not used telephone interviewing to produce any published readership estimates. All data published by the survey are generated by the face-to-face CAPI technique described in Chapter 6.

Regional press readership

In August 1990, the Joint Industry Committee for Regional Press Readership Research (JICREG) was launched so that Britain's regional newspapers could be evaluated in common with other media on readership and not just on circulation. JICREG resulted from extensive discussions between advertisers (ISBA), advertising agencies (IPA), and newspaper owners (The Newspaper Society and the Association of Free Newspapers). Initially, JICREG faced significant problems in designing effective research techniques for some 1600 newspapers and newspaper groupings. A pilot study by RSGB was followed by detailed planning of the research methodologies by Telmar. The modelled data are not intended to replace the existing readership research conducted by an increasing number of regional publishers; over 50 of these surveys have proved useful in establishing the parameter of the models.

All the JICREG data are held in the research database at The Newspaper Society.

Television advertising research

Since its introduction in the UK in September 1955, Independent Television has been dependent on advertising for its revenue. It became apparent that in order to sell advertising time effectively, the programme contractors needed to be able to describe their audiences. In 1957 the Joint Industry Committee for Television Advertising Research (JICTAR) was founded to represent three bodies: the Incorporated Society of British Advertisers Ltd (ISBA), the Institute of Practitioners in Advertising (IPA), and the Independent Television Companies' Association Ltd (ITCA). The first contract for measuring television audiences was held by Television Audience Measurement Ltd (TAM) in 1957. From 30 July 1968, JICTAR appointed Audits of Great Britain Ltd (AGB) to provide a research service based on a television panel of UK households. The costs of the service were borne by the three professional organizations in agreed percentages (programme companies 57.1 per cent, advertising agencies 28.6 per cent, advertisers 14.3 per cent).

Broadcasters' Audience Research Board (BARB)

To avoid difficulties arising from different research methods, a joint system for researching both BBC and commercial television audiences was implemented from August 1981.

This new television audience research organization was formed by the BBC and the ITCA which hold equal shares. Originally its company board consisted of directors exclusively from these two organizations. ITCA ownership is now shared between the BBC, ITVA, IPA, Channel 4, Channel 5 and BSkyB and the Company Board consists of directors exclusively from these organizations. Various committees report to the Board, many of which have representatives from the wider broadcasting industry.

These committees are responsible for taking strategic decisions about the data to be collected, the research methodology, and how the data should be deployed. They are supported by technical advisory committees which can give advice on issues of a technical nature; smaller working parties can be set up for specific issues (see Fig. 10.1).

BARB is responsible for commissioning television audience research, both quantitative (audience measurement) and qualitative (audience reaction). The existing system used by JICTAR was adopted for audience measurement, and, additionally, adapted to meet the needs of the BBC.

BARB is a provider of information to all elements of the television industry, broadcasters, advertising/media buying agencies and advertisers. It uses professional research suppliers to conduct and report on audience research. BARB is responsible for the specification and management of these contracts. As such, it retains a small number of staff for this purpose. The BARB office does not conduct audience analyses. Access to BARB data, other than that publicly available through the BARB website (www.barb.co.uk) is through data bureaux but is available only to subscribers.

BARB acts as an executive management body on behalf of the TV industry. It maintains regular contact with all subscribers through its Board of Directors and also through a management committee comprising representatives of all subscriber groups. A similar representative committee, the Technical Advisory Group, also meets regularly under BARB's chairmanship to examine all aspects of data quality and to consider any technical issues affecting the service. Through these two committees, any issues relevant to the service or changes that may be required, are discussed and agreed

Qualitative research is carried out by IPSOS-RSL. The rationalization of two competing audience measurement research methods was welcomed by the advertising professions.

As noted earlier, AGB was responsible for TV audience research on behalf of JICTAR and this arrangement continued until July 1984, BARB having taken over the contract in 1981. BARB awarded the next contract for TV audience research to Taylor Nelson Sofres (now TNS) by competitive tender. This contract ran for seven years from August 1984 (see below BARB research developments). From August 1991 a new enhanced service was started with a sample expanded to 4435 reporting homes, and a new contract was awarded to RSMB and TNS. This contract ends in December 2001. In May 2000, after receiving competitive tenders, BARB awarded a new contract, to run from 2002 to 2006, to the Swiss-based AGB group. BARB also awarded contracts to RSMB for survey design, methodology and quality control, and to IPSOS-RSL for the establishment surveys.

The organization of BARB is shown in Figure 10.2.

The collection of data: audience measurement

The system for measuring audiences is based on a development of the JICTAR system, i.e. electronic meters fixed to a sample of television sets. The first step in selecting the sample or panel of homes which will have these meters is the *Establishment Survey*. The Establishment Survey is based on a random sample of over 37 500 interviews conducted continuously throughout the year, and structured by post code areas within ITV areas. The questions are designed to determine patterns of television usage across the country and to ensure that the audience measurement panel is fully representative and up to date. The results of the survey, together with government census data, are used to select a fully representative sample of homes in terms of viewing habits, TV equipment ownership, family composition, demographics, etc., to take part in the audience measurement panel.

Television audience measurement developed from diaries and set meters in 1981 to on-line meters capable of monitoring VCR activity with individuals entering their viewing through a push-button handset in 1985. This system was further enhanced in August 1991 by improved metering equipment which identifies material played-back by the VCR following in-home recording and also allows guests to input limited personal demographics. As a result, reports on programme viewing now give consolidated audience figures for 'live' viewing plus video cassette recorder (VCR) play-back audiences. All television sets, including portables, as well as VCRs are monitored. Each set has its own handset for entering individuals and guests' viewing. Each person presses the appropriate button on when they start to view, and off when they stop, and the data are fed into the electronic meter. In case the panel members forget, a signal flashes on the meter if the television set is on but no buttons have been pressed.

Satellite broadcasting is monitored using the same equipment as a component within the panel. At TN Sofres a minicomputer automatically dials each panel home between 2 am and 5 am, retrieving the viewing data contained in the meter store. In this way, a detailed knowledge of viewing behaviour of the UK population is made available early on the following day, although reports are, in fact, completed weekly.

The use of video recorders has a significant effect upon the measurement of audiences. Some households use VCRs for 'live' viewing as the programme is transmitted, either because they get a better picture that way or because they have a remote control for the VCR but not for their television set. A separate VCR electronic meter is fitted to the VCR but the same button press for registering individual viewers is used for both the VCR and the television set.

Time shifting (i.e. viewing of a programme previously recorded at home) is complex to measure. If a programme is being recorded on a VCR, it will register on the meter, but

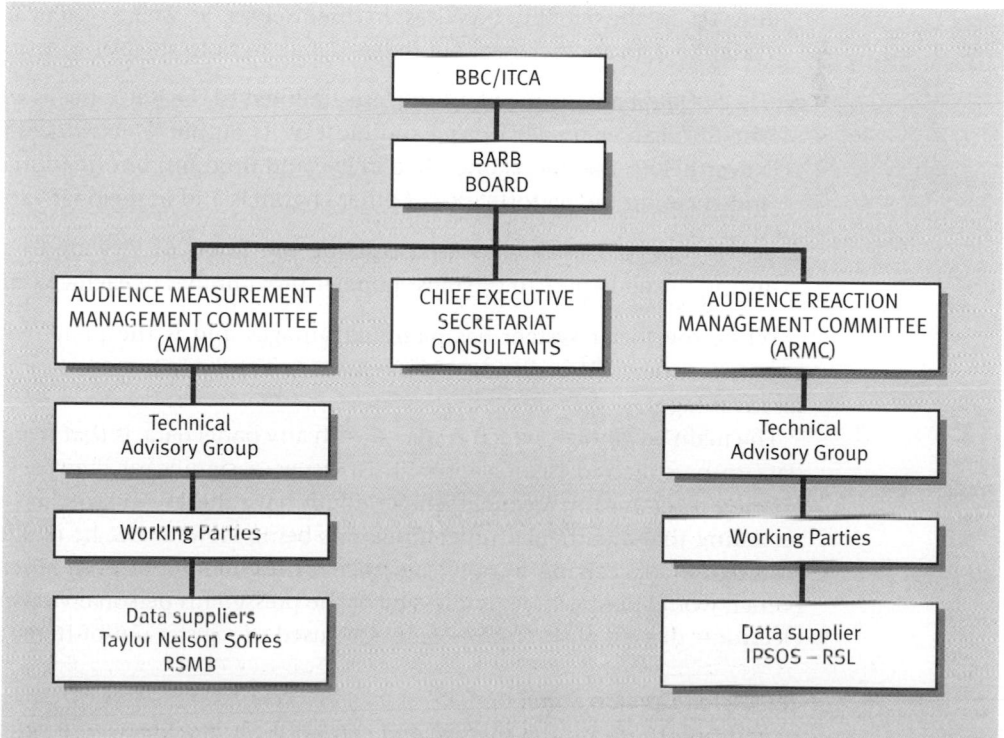

Figure 10.2   Organization of Broadcasters' Audience Research Board Limited

many recordings are never used and some are played back more than once, so recording information is therefore not very useful. The VCR meter imprints an electronic code (channel, date, time) on the video tape; when this is played back the TV meter 'reads' the code on the tape. In this way the amount of 'timeshift' viewing can be registered and reported separately or added to 'live' viewing information. The identity or contents of a pre-recorded tape (hired, or borrowed, or purchased) cannot be detected – viewing of these tapes is registered as 'other play-back'.

BARB estimates that the response rate from the panel is 98 to 99 per cent which ensures a very high degree of accuracy in the statistics.

After the meter records are collected, they are combined with details of programme and commercial broadcasts. The computer then makes a series of calculations to arrive at an estimate of audience size. The data collected are compiled into a form required by BARB's subscribers. The basic format is computer input data consisting of raw data from the meters (for those subscribers who wish to re-analyse it) or calculated audience statistics showing the number or percentage watching particular programmes or commercials.

In the past several bulky weekly reports were issued, but these have dwindled recently with the widespread use of more efficient computer facilities which BARB subscribers now have.

Three specialist reports are issued. The Network Report shows summary information for those primarily concerned with the advertising usage of the data, that is ITV, Channel 4, advertising agencies and advertisers. This summarizes the live and timeshift viewing figures for each of the main channels, looking at audiences to programmes and audiences to time segments.

1. *The Astra Report* summarizes the viewing statistics for those homes which can receive Astra channels, either by cable or by dish aerial. This information is of a special interest to the Satellite broadcasters themselves, as well as agencies and advertisers. (Satellite data are included, but in less detail, in both the Network and BBC Reports.)

2. *The BBC Report* is, as the name suggests, tailored to the BBC's needs which are different. The BBC carries no advertising and most of its output is networked (i.e. not regional). Nevertheless, the BBC is interested in live and timeshift information about programme audiences, in the performance of other channels and in regional variations.

3. *BARB issues a Weekly Press Release* giving the hours of viewing to each channel and listing the audiences to the most popular programmes of each channel.

While the meter system has many advantages and is the preferred method in most countries where TV audience measurement is conducted regularly, there are also some disadvantages.

The main advantage, which is shared with any panel data, is that it enables longitudinal data to be collected (see Chapter 9). However, a significant drawback is defining what viewing really means: a panel member might have the TV set switched on (and the meter recording that a particular programme was being viewed) but he or she could be asleep; reading a book; talking to other members of the family; or even absent from the room (which would not be known unless he or she pressed his personal viewing button). Unlike electronic diaries, push-buttons cannot be used to register out-of-home viewing.

Television Opinion Panel

In addition to measuring the size and composition of audiences, BARB also runs an *audience appreciation service* for the BBC and ITV. The national panel is now 6000 monthly, comprised of 2000 weekly panel members augmented with 4×1000 4-weekly respondents spread over a four week period, i.e.

	Week 1	Week 2	Week 3	Week 4	Separate Respondents Monthly
Weekly responders	2000	2000	2000	2000	2000
Monthly responders	A–1000	B–1000	C–1000	D–1000	4000

The basic operation requires panellists to complete weekly booklets. The programme diary requires respondents to rate on a scale from 0 to 10 each programme they watch. (The Children's panel only covers broadcasts up to 9 pm). These data are used to produce an Appreciation Index (AI) for each programme which is expressed as an average mark out of 100. Top-line data are also collected for viewing to the satellite channels (where appropriate). A second booklet consists of questions which can be asked by the broadcasters about any aspect of a particular programme on a particular day. They might wish to know, for example, what the public thinks about a presenter of a programme. More general questions about series or serials are also asked, usually at the end of the run. This information remains confidential to the broadcaster who asked the question. As noted earlier, RSL runs the current service which began in August 1994.

Television advertising measurement – overseas

In the 1990s television audience research methods across the major European countries have largely become standardized and based on the adoption of electronic (peoplemeter) systems.

With the growth of the EU, more attention is being given to the desirability of harmonizing research on audience measurement, so that comparable and compatible data are produced. ESOMAR's 1995 report on radio and television measurement in Europe[32] provides valuable information on the issues now facing the research industry across Europe.

In the US, the Schwerin research organization mails invitations to randomly selected households to see a theatrical presentation of films (general interest films, some commercials). Afterwards, a competitive preference test is organized, and viewers are offered a year's supply of a product, the brand of which they must choose. This test is said to encourage serious judgement, on the lines of everyday shopping, of the relative merits of competing brands. This form of advertising research was tried for a time in the UK, but eventually discontinued.

Television advertising measurement in the US also uses electronic meters (Nielsen 'Audiometer' for national ratings and Arbitron for local); diaries (Nielsen 'Recordometer' and Arbitron); telephone coincidental method (the Trendex service) which involves telephoning people whose names have been selected from the telephone directory, and asking them what television programme or radio programme, if any, they are watching or listening to, and what product or sponsor is being promoted. These enquiries enable researchers to give ratings on programmes within a few hours of transmission, against the inevitable delay of some weeks for a Nielsen rating. The dependence of this system on telephone directories as sampling frames means that bias is bound to occur in sampling. Another method of television research involves personal interviews in the homes of viewers. 'Aided recall' is used to assist respondents in recalling programmes viewed the day before; 7800 homes are visited each day. Inaccurate recall because of poor memory or deliberate falsification together with the relatively high costs of interviewing are significant problems of this methodology.

Radio audience measurement

Measuring radio listening is, in many ways, a more complex task than researching television audiences. Apart from national networks, there are regional and local services (both BBC and commercial stations), and also the BBC's World Service, and many foreign, as well as pirate stations.

Commercial radio broadcasts in the UK commenced in October 1973, when LBC and Capital Radio opened. Commercial radio stations in the UK have proliferated and there are 219 operating under licence from the Radio Authority, which took over responsibility from the Independent Broadcasting Authority in January 1991.

The BBC has been involved in audience research since 1936. However, the Audience Research Department was closed down in the early 1990s (see Chapter 3), and the BBC's Broadcasting Research Department contracted out fieldwork operations, such as survey and group discussions.

For radio research, the BBC has joined the Commercial Radio Companies Association (CRCA), formerly known as the Association of Radio Contractors (ARIC).

Radio Joint Audience Research (RAJAR) is, as noted, a company jointly owned by the BBC and CRCA – the trade association for commercial stations in the UK. RAJAR was established in February 1992, commenced operations in September, and replaced JICRAR (Joint Industry Committee for Radio Audience Research) and the BBC's Daily Survey. Its research covers both BBC and commercial radio stations, in total over 250 stations. With the BBC's national and local networks, there are now more than 600 segments to be sampled – each with its own unique repertoire of stations.

In 1996, in response to significant and rapid changes in radio transmissions, RAJAR commissioned the development of a new and improved system of gathering radio audience data, and in January 1999 a new method of measuring radio audiences was instituted. This is undertaken by IPSOS-RSL on behalf of RAJAR. Every week, more than 200 trained interviewers place radio listening diaries with over 3000 different and carefully selected respondents, aged 4+ living in private households. Each respondent is interviewed and shown how to record and complete a 7-day diary of his/her listening habits. These diaries are collected by the interviewers at the end of the week and returned to the research company, where they are electronically scanned and checked. After processing, the data are published, in print or electronically via the internet, for the 'latest three months' for the largest stations, and for the 'latest 12 months' for the smallest ones.

The new type of personal repertoire diary is more 'user friendly' than the previous system. An essential part of the new diary is made up of 'station cards', from which respondents select the stations which they might listen to during the week. In practice, the average number of stations tuned into during the diary week is usually in the range of 2–3.

RAJAR's new survey arrangements should improve the quality and reliability of the research findings, although the system remains complex. RAJAR constantly checks all available techniques for improving its research methods. One of these is the personal meter or 'radiometer', which monitors the listening habits of respondents in any location and at any time of the day or night, but such equipment would need to monitor the listener and not the set. Respondents would be obliged to carry or wear a metering device (whether a pager type or wrist watch). How willing they would be to do this and the cost-effectiveness of such a system have still to be determined.

As Michael Brown[33] points out, recall-based techniques may lead to severe under-estimation and to biases favouring relatively salient stations. 'Coincidental' measurement (as with electronic meters used in television research), largely eliminates recall problems, but this system is probably too expensive for radio audience research. Interestingly, radio metering 'long preceded the application of the techniques to television';[33] in the US with Nielsen Radio Index, from 1936 to 1964, used meters in association with diaries, but the service was discontinued because of the increasing numbers of car radios, small portable radios, and multi-set ownership.

The casual nature of much radio listening – particularly to 'pop' stations, and the fact that radio listening is not an exclusive activity but rather incidental to other pursuits, may also lead to some doubts about the accuracy of recall.

Over 90 per cent of radio listening is known to be secondary to activities such as driving a car, reading, preparing a meal, or doing homework, so radio listening is more difficult to define. However, Teer[34] suggests that panel members, knowing that they have to record their listening, may pay greater attention to the programme to which they are tuned.

BMRB's *Target Group Index* (*TGI*), discussed later in this chapter, is cross-tabulated with RAJAR, to provide life-style information about listeners.

The NRS also includes questions about radio listening, differentiating between BBC (national and local) stations and 'stations with advertising'. Respondents are asked which stations they have listened to 'in the past week – it need not be at home, it could have been in a car, in somebody else's home or outside'; 'how many days in the average week' they had 'listened at all to any radio stations with advertising'; and 'on an average day' for how long had they listened. The resultant data form part of the overall information supplied to NRS subscribers (see Press research above).

Cinema audience research

The NRS includes questions on the recency and frequency of cinema attendances, and data are also presented by the Target Group Index. The General Household Survey gives analyses of cinema attendances by income group for the UK population of 16 years of age and over. *Social Trends*, published by the Office for National Statistics, comments that recently cinema attendance in Britain 'has seen some resurgence . . . after nearly 40 years of decline'.[35] In 1987/88, 34 per cent of the population aged 15 and over attended the cinema; in 1997/98, 54 per cent did so, and admissions were 123 million.

In 1980, the Cinema Advertising Association (CAA) commissioned Carrick James Market Research to undertake an intensive study of cinema patrons; this research, known as *CAVIAR* (*Cinema and Video Industry Audience Research*), was repeated several times; it is now undertaken by BMRB. Interviews are with approximately 2800 individuals (7+), quota-sampled throughout Great Britain, and covers cinema-going habits, video viewership, and other media usage. The CAA has also commissioned several advertising recall studies. Carrick James monitors cinema attendance through its monthly omnibus surveys.

Poster research

Various attempts have been made over the past 30 or so years to research the advertising effectiveness of posters. The classification of poster sites has been one of several problems encountered in developing suitable methods of researching this medium.

The main problem of poster research 'lies in the nature of the medium itself'.[36] In the press and on television, advertising subsidizes news and feature articles and programmes, so 'it is possible to deduce the probability of someone being exposed to advertising on the basis of that person's claims about reading newspapers and magazines or watching television programmes'.[36] On the other hand, posters do not have editorial content and they are seldom studied closely. They tend to be encountered casually in the course of the day's events, so contact is hardly something memorable.

JICPAR (Joint Industry Committee for Poster Advertising Research) was established in 1983 as successor to JICPAS (Joint Industry Committee for Poster Audience Surveys). JICPAR comprises representatives of the Outdoor Advertising Association of Great Britain Ltd; the Incorporated Society of British Advertisers Ltd; the Institute of Practitioners in Advertising; and the Council of Outdoor Specialists.

In conjunction with JICPAR, the Outdoor Advertising Association (OAA) set up, in April 1985, the *Outdoor Site Classification and Audience Research* (*OSCAR*); this was funded by the UK's six major poster contractors. It was estimated[37] that 90 000 of the 125 000 UK poster panels were classified by *OSCAR*. In late 1992, the OAA was restructured to consist of the six full members, with smaller contractors (probably about 300) being allowed to join as associate members at much reduced cost. This arrangement was intended to result in significantly increased coverage of the *OSCAR* research database.

Initially, pedestrian and vehicular traffic counts were taken at a sample of poster sites in the UK; environmental factors were noted; these data were then subject to multi-variate analysis to establish the relationships between size of audience and the siting of posters related to types of ward, area, shopping facilities including proximity to named retailers, etc. A computerized model was developed which enabled detailed poster audiences to be estimated across the country.

NOP provides a range of research services to the poster industry, including the design and maintenance of an industry-wide database.

Research on poster advertising on London Transport buses involving special line-film techniques was described in Chapter 2. This ingenious approach to the measurement of 'opportunities to see' overcame some of the problems of researching the effectiveness of this advertising medium.

Cable television

In autumn 1982, the Hunt Committee Report opened the way for cable television networks in the UK and following the Cable Bill in 1984, the Cable Authority was set up and awarded franchises. Predictions on the future of cable television in the UK tend to be cautious. Much will depend, of course, on the attraction of programmes and the price charged to subscribers.

JICCAR (Joint Industry Committee for Cable Audience Research) another jointly-funded media research body, was set up to promote the development of audience measurement connected with cable television services. A pilot survey was completed in late 1984, and arrangements were made to issue pre-coded diaries to panel households using cable television. However, JICCAR no longer operates, and cable television contractors provide data on 'connections', but no systematic market research data collection is now organized.

10.6 Advertising effectiveness research

This research is concerned with analysing different media (and combinations of media) and evaluating the degree of success with which the advertising objectives have been achieved. It follows that certain criteria should be agreed by which success may be measured, e.g. the rate of growth of sales of a product brand, increase in market share, or, more qualitatively, greater awareness of the company. In some cases, the principal role of advertising may be defensive, i.e. maintaining the present market position of a specific brand of product. Whatever the objective, it should be clearly stated before the advertising plans are devised, so that every detail of the campaign can be carefully worked out to fulfil this.

It is admittedly difficult to make an accurate appraisal of an advertising campaign. Advertising rarely works in isolation – it is one element in the marketing mix, i.e. the amounts and kinds of marketing variables (price, promotion, packaging, distribution, etc.), which a firm may vary from time to time.

To measure the effectiveness of advertising, it is, first of all, necessary to know exactly what it is intended to achieve. This leads logically to the matter of communication objectives, which were discussed earlier. These may be multiple, so adding to the complexity of evaluating advertising's productivity. An experienced researcher and advertising director[38] has stated that in 1970, the systematic evaluation of advertising was relatively rare. Brand performances were monitored, but continuous monitoring of advertising and brand sales was not generally practised. Today, however, major advertisers now commonly conduct research with the development of econometric models and other sophisticated research techniques.

When Heinz faced aggressive pricing competition from other suppliers of baked beans, they deliberately chose to retaliate with a promotional theme that did not mention price. Instead, their 'Toast to Life' campaign, based on an 'involvement strategy', projected the distinctive, consistent values of their branded beans in an ever-changing world. Nothing was said about price, taste or quality; the promotion focused on the relationship which people had with the brand – it was virtually part of their everyday lives. The specific objective of the campaign was achieved, and the Heinz premier brand position was maintained.[39]

Since 1980, the Institute of Practitioners in Advertising (IPA) has run, biennially, an advertising effectiveness competition which has two-fold objectives:

1. to prove that advertising could add value and contribute to profits, and

2. to encourage 'best practice'.

When the IPA awards were first launched, it was conceded that many people doubted whether the effectiveness of advertising could be isolated or, indeed, proved. Nowadays, it is claimed that there are few who do not recognize that the value of advertising can be demonstrably measured. To back up their claims, the IPA has built up an Advertising Data Bank of 650 cases, which can be accessed via a new IPA computer system, with a more limited version located on the IPA internet site: http:/www.ipa.co.uk., or e-mail: lesley@ipa.co.uk.

Evaluation of advertising may, of course, be relatively straightforward, as happens with the direct-marketing campaigns of mail-order houses, 'special offer' promotions by retail stores, and internet marketing campaigns (see 'Coupon Research'). Test marketing research services may also provide information about the effects of specific promotional activities (see Chapter 8). At the same time, it should be remembered that these relatively basic measures do not take account of other market variables, such as competitors' marketing activities, including advertising or product improvements/innovations.

More complicated techniques used to check the effectiveness of advertising utilize elaborate statistical models. Classic research in this area was undertaken by Kristian

Palda[40] on the effects of advertising on the sales of Lydia Pinkham's Vegetable Compound during the period 1908 to 1960. Because of certain unique features, e.g. the product had no close substitutes and the company regularly spent between 40 per cent and 60 per cent of its sales revenue on advertising, Palda was able to indicate the usefulness of different equations in measuring the carry-over effects of Pinkham's advertising.

An interesting attempt to evaluate advertising effectiveness by applying statistical methodology and model building was published some years ago by the Advertising Association.[41] It covers research by Professor J. M. Samuels of the Graduate Centre for Management Studies, Birmingham, into the effects of advertising on sales and brand shares. No conclusive claims could be made and many of the studies showed no significant results, though within the limitations of the statistical techniques used some success was achieved. It was possible, for example, to see the influence of price and advertising on the level of brand shares in the household cleanser market.

There is still a great deal of work to be done in measuring advertising's contribution to the success of marketing operations. Controlled marketing experiments should be attempted, using the research techniques of the social sciences in order to acquire a better understanding of consumer behaviour, and implementing developments in statistical analysis.

Tracking studies

Leading advertisers and large business undertakings are concerned to keep up to date with the perceptions and attitudes of their customers and the public at large.

Tracking studies, as Peter Sampson[42] has observed, are 'methods of continuous measurement in which market research data are collected in a systematic way at intervals, accumulated and summarised periodically'. The time intervals may vary, according to the needs of the company involved. It is possible, for example, to track responses to specific bursts of advertising, related perhaps to the introduction of a re-formulated washing powder.

Tracking studies collect data from matched samples drawn from the same population over a specific period of time, in order to measure, for example, brand awareness, advertising awareness, attitudes to brands, brand preferences, brand usage, corporate image, etc.

Sampson[42] points out that, unlike the continuous panel (see Chapter 8), which collects data from the same sample of respondents over regular periods of time, a tracking study collects data from matched samples of the same population. Tracking studies can be used in conjunction with simulated test marketing (see Chapter 9), and they can be particularly helpful in developing marketing strategies.

General Foods, makers of Maxwell House coffee and other leading grocery products, have tracked the awareness of their brands and advertising campaigns for several years, particularly as the 'acid test for new commercials. Pretesting continues to minimize the investment risk behind production, but tracking is there to minimize the risk of deploying airtime funds against an ad that is failing to achieve the communication objectives in the real world of living rooms.[43]

Principal research organizations such as BJM Research, part of the MBL Group, provide advertising tracking services specifically designed to meet the needs of individual clients. BJM's *Stochastic© Reaction Monitor* is a continuous tracking system concerned primarily with brand positioning, advertising effectiveness, consumer attitudes and market behaviour, and covers both long-term strategic and short-term tactical issues. BJM's Monitor system operates in the UK, Australia, New Zealand and the Far East.

Millward Brown's *Link* tests are based on extensive monitoring of advertising campaigns in the UK and in many other European countries, as well as Canada, Latin America and Asia Pacific. *Link* programmes extend from pre-tests/copy tests through to continuous tracking to sales modelling. An 'awareness index', i.e. a relevant measure of increased awareness of a brand/product that is being advertised, has been developed. Print advertisements are always having to vie for attention from editorial content and other advertising; the successful advertisement has to win attention not only to the product type but also to the brand. Selected consumers are encouraged to talk about their typical shopping habits; about how they decide about brands and products in real life; about how they *feel* about the advertisements shown to them. Their responses are interpreted against the comprehensive databases held by Millward Brown.

TVLink, another Millward Brown research service, is concerned with pre-testing prospective versions of television advertisements, noting factors such as 'enjoyability', 'attention-getting', 'brand awareness', and 'ease of understanding'. Interviewers note carefully the perceptions of respondents, whose answers are subject to in-depth analysis and interpretation.

PrintLink researches either finished or rough advertisements via hall tests and the presentation of advertisements in a small folder which contains 'control' advertisements, and respondents are questioned on key points about individual advertisements. Through hall tests and parallel placement of advertisements in magazines, Millward Brown's experiments have shown that the most important rating scale is an 'interest' measure; the second rating is an 'eye-catching' scale. If print advertisements fail to score reasonably well on either of these factors, it is stated that they will not get much attention in real life.

It was also discovered that consumers, once they become involved, tend generally to look for a brand in a print advertisement; so a 'subjective branding' rating is applied. Other salient ratings are 'ease of understanding', particularly when evaluating advertisements in pre-test conditions, and 'how everything fits in', i.e. a 'comprehension' evaluation.

In addition to reactions to an advertisement as a whole, *elements* of it are also subject to detailed evaluation; such as eye-track – what respondents saw first, next and so on; *likelihood of reading copy*; *specific communication* properties; and *persuasiveness* – whether the advertisement has immediately increased interest in brand/product featured. Also, consumers' reactions are evaluated against newness, relevance, and credibility of the information presented in specific advertisements.

Millward Brown also offers *Link* tests concerned with evaluating cinema, radio and outdoor advertising.

ACNielsen: *Scan*Pro* is a new range of Nielsen services derived from the retail databases operated by this worldwide research organization, and is designed to give marketing management information about the precise impact of the promotional mix. It enables, for instance, sales and promotions to be tracked over time; evaluates the impact of promotions on brands and competitor sales; predicts the likely net effect of alternative promotional strategies; and guides the allocation of promotional funds to achieve maximum effectiveness on brand sales and share.

As with other forms of market research activities, tracking studies have become more sophisticated and far reaching in their coverage and tend to be fully integrated market studies. Tracking study data covering awareness, repeat purchase, etc., can be used for developing forecasting models, using regression analysis or econometric techniques.

Anne Wicks[38] points out that, 'strictly speaking' the term 'tracking studies' should be confined to data from continuous interviewing, although some companies 'track' four times a year or in bursts associated with their own advertising activity. Tracking questions are also used in usage studies and in syndicated surveys and omnibus studies.

Coupon research

The most direct way of evaluating an advertising campaign and checking the suitability of the media, occurs in mail-order trading, from which coupon research originated. Coupon research generally relates to printed media, although enquiries are now being invited in response to radio and television advertising. To attract enquiries, some interesting offer is made, e.g. to supply a colour chart or instruction booklet.

Replies are analysed on a cost-per-enquiry basis and the effectiveness of different publications evaluated. This is, of course, a fairly crude measure as the number of enquiries may not accurately reflect the degree of interest in the advertisement or its real effectiveness in winning sales.

Experiments can be made with the relative pulling power of various publications; the degree of variation over regions may be important. 'Split-run' tests, featuring different styles of advertisement for the same product, can be inserted in the same edition of a publication, and an evaluation made of their relative appeal. Several leading publishing houses offer 'split-run' facilities to advertisers. The alternative copies are distributed equally to ensure that the advertisements are viewed by comparable populations.

Many consumer and technical magazines run a 'reader service', which simplifies the task of their readers when asking for information from advertisers. Readers merely tick off manufacturers' names on a blanket enquiry form, printed usually at the back of the magazine. Advertisers then receive a list of enquirers from the magazine's advertising department. When computing the enquiry rate, it would be as well to bear in mind that some people appear to be compulsive coupon-fillers

Specific advertising research support

The various independent television programme contractors provide advertisers and agencies with specific market research data, offer ad hoc and continuous research services, and special test-marketing selling services.

The ITV companies

The UK is divided into 14 transmission areas, each with its own independent television company, with the exception of London, which has two TV companies. The London franchise is split weekday/weekend: Carlton Television broadcasts daily until 5.15 pm on Friday; London Weekend Television broadcasts from 5.15 pm on Friday until 6 am on Monday. In all areas, between 6 am and 9.25 am every day, there is a national Breakfast-time Service, run by the franchise holders, GMTV on a network basis.

TSMS Limited was set up in 1989 and is the leading airtime sales house. In 1994, it became a wholly owned subsidiary of MAI plc, and in April 1996, MAI merged with United News and Media plc; TSMS is now part of United's wholly owned subsidiary, United Broadcast and Entertainment Limited (UBE). TSMS sells airtime for: Anglia Television, HTV, UTV, Grampian Television, Meridian Television, and Scottish Television. Clients are offered a comprehensive range of promotional services, such as auxiliary sales teams, live in-store merchandising, store checks (through IRI INFOSCAN), brand assessment, TGI services (see later details), MediaSPAN (TN Sofres), ad-tracking and pre- and post-campaign awareness research.

Granada Mediasales, the sales arm of Granada Media and one of the largest ITV sales houses accounting for over one-third of the annual ITV Network revenue, handles airtime sales on behalf of London Weekend, Yorkshire, Tyne-Tees, Border, and Granada Television. These broadcasters cover nearly half of UK homes and over 22 million adults. Clients are offered a range of market research services, which are obtained from leading research agencies, including IRI grocery retail audit; TN Sofres Superpanel; BMRB TGT surveys, and financial data from NOP's FRS survey.

Granada Mediasales runs a monthly omnibus survey, now extended to include Yorkshire and Tyne-Tees, thus covering the whole of the north of England. Tracking surveys in the London area can also be arranged.

Carlton Television, through Carlton UK Sales, which is responsible for airtime sales for Carlton and Central Television contractors, also offers a wide range of marketing services to clients; these draw on TN Sofres, ACNielsen, BMRB (TGI), SRI INFOSCAN, etc. Comparative analyses, on a regional basis, are made of clients' advertising expenditures and those of their principal competitors. Readership and audience statistics are derived from NRS and BARB (refer to sections describing these specialist services).

Other media support services

Capital Radio offers advertisers cost-effective access to data from the *Capital Advertising Panel*, which consists of 10 000 individuals within the Capital Radio transmission area. Simple dipstick, pre- and post-study, full scale tracking, copy testing, and campaign evaluation services are offered according to clients' specific needs. The panel is updated/ replenished on a continuous basis, and the survey, using largely telephone interviewing, is undertaken by Continental Research, who prepare comprehensive reports in collaboration with Capital Radio (see also Chapter 8).

Taylor Nelson Sofres runs three syndicated industry research studies: Agridata is a farming readership study based on data from Agribus, a monthly omnibus survey of over 230 respondents; Hospital Media Survey measures readership of the major hospital publications and key specialist titles among all grades of hospital doctors, the data being derived from 1400 questionnaires sent monthly to a random sample of relevant doctors – a 40 per cent response is stated to be typical and reports are made every six months; Arcbuild is survey covering eight professional sectors from architecture, surveying, engineering, and building contracting – telephone screening is followed by face-to-face interviews with 2000 respondents on their reading habits and magazine preferences.

TNS Television Information Systems provide PC-based TV audience research analysis systems to the UK and other international markets. A range of UK on-line services enable full reporting of the BARB database.

The RSGB media division of Taylor Nelson Sofres offers customized research to the media industry covering the press sector and broadcast systems. They also run London Omnibus – a monthly survey of 1000 adults in the London ISBA area, providing cost-effective research among consumers of London media and advertising.

Readership studies are also conducted in the professional, trade and technical press covering doctors, agriculturists, pharmacists, architects, and a specialist service, introduced in 1994, which measures readership among the IT community.

Advertising research in practice

Starch Readership Service ('Starch Scores')

This was set up in the US in 1931 by Dr Daniel Starch to investigate magazine readership and the extent to which specific advertisements are read as well as being seen. Starch research is concerned with the 'recognition' of advertisements. Four degrees of readership are noted in Starch reports: *non-reader* (a person who cannot recall an advertisement in the issue); *noted* (percentage of readers who remember seeing the ad); *seen/associated* (percentage of readers who saw or read part of ad which indicated brand or advertiser); and *read most* (percentage of readers who read half or more of written material in ad).

Starch interviewers survey representative cross-sections of the population. Calls are made at homes and people are asked their reading habits. If they mention a specific magazine which Starch is researching, interviewers produce a recent copy and go through it page by page, noting the observations of respondents on articles and advertisements. Probing questions are asked about advertisement readership to establish the impact of various design and layout features.

Leading periodicals are studied by Starch, part of the cost being borne by the media owners who can use Starch readership measurements as a selling aid. Advertisers subscribe to receive an actual copy of the specific magazine in which they advertised, together with 'Starch Scores' shown on paper stickers attached to each advertisement. In addition, Starch supplies statistical summaries relating to the research findings and the cost of advertising.

While the Starch system of continuous research is extremely thorough, high Starch scores themselves do not guarantee that consumers will buy the product advertised. Advertisements may be remembered for many reasons; they may not be those which influence consumers to choose particular brands of products.

Gallup and Robinson

The American research firm of Gallup and Robinson was set up by George Gallup and Claude Robinson in the early 1930s, but neither of the founders has been involved with it for many years. When the company was eventually sold, George Gallup allowed the new owners to continue to use his name. However, the present firm is a separate, independent, totally non-associated company with the American Institute of Public Opinion.

American Gallup operates a research service into advertising readership which attempts to go rather deeper than the Starch enquiries. This system uses 'aided recall', and informants are rigorously questioned about specific magazines they claim to have read. Actual copies of advertisements are now shown, recall being aided by cards on which product brand names are entered. There are some deliberate 'plants'. Informants' remarks are taken down verbatim. The method, called 'Impact', is used also for television advertising research (see Gallup Impact Service below).

Gallup, famous for its Institute of Public Opinion, also has a company, Audience Research Inc., specializing in measuring the likely popularity of publications, films, and television shows not yet released for public viewing. This research centres round special theatrical presentations to invited audiences, who are tested for their reactions to commercials sandwiched between general interest films. The 'Mirror of America', as the theatre is described, is about 10 miles from Princeton. This pre-testing of advertisements also extends to print advertising. Gallup prepares a special magazine, called *Impact*, which has some feature articles plus advertisements for testing purposes. *Impact* is distributed to carefully selected homes, at which interviewers later call to obtain informants' reactions to the advertising features.

The rival attractions of the Starch rating system, based on recognition, and of the Gallup and Robinson recall ratings were the subject of a special investigation by the Printed Advertising Rating Committee (PARM) of the Advertising Research Foundation in 1955. Their findings were not conclusive; they agreed that both methods had controversial points, but that both contribute usefully, in their own distinctive ways, to print advertising research.

Gallup undertakes a large amount of research into advertising in the UK. (*The Gallup Organization, London*, is wholly owned by Gallup Poll of America.) A lot of this work is conducted using the Noting and Reading technique, the Evaluative Assessment technique, and the Impact 24-hour Recall technique. Each of these involves interviewing a cross-section of readers of a publication a few days after they have read it, asking them about advertising in the particular issue: Noting and Reading covering their readership of the whole publication; Evaluative Assessment covering their thoughts at the time they were looking at specific advertisements; and Impact covering their recall of a number of advertisements in the issue. In addition to these techniques there are placement pre-tests where specific pages are removed and replaced in specially prepared copies. These issues are then given to a representative sample of readers of the publication and a check is made subsequently on the way they read the publication. In this way advertisements can be tested in their natural environment without the reader being aware that the advertisement is under test.

Gallup also undertakes continuous tracking surveys, to measure public awareness and reactions to advertisements through its Omnibus service (through which *c.* 150 000 people are interviewed annually). In addition, the company also operates poster testing and advertisement pre-testing with audiences who are invited to attend special research sessions held in local centres (group discussions and hall tests).

Gallup Noting and Reading Service

This was developed by Dr George Gallup in the US as the Field Readership Index, and operates on an *ad hoc* basis in the UK. It measures audience noting and reading of editorial articles and advertisements. Checking over the years has built up a vast store of information relating to factors that influence the attention paid to advertising. Samples of between 200 and 250 people are selected to be representative of the publication readership, as noted in the National Readership Survey. Analysis of readership covers:

1. *Page traffic*: percentage looking at *any* item on each page.
2. *Noting*: percentage *noting* any part of the advertisement.
3. *Noting the name*: percentage noting advertiser's name.
4. *Reading*: percentage reading two or more sentences of advertisement copy.

Gallup Impact Service

This research service was also developed in the US and is now undertaken in the UK and major continental countries. Between 200 and 250 respondents at a time are shown a card listing the names of 20 advertisements which appear in the media they claim to have seen. If they then claim that some of the listed advertisements have been seen by them, they are asked to describe them in detail. The verbatim record is then analysed as follows:

1. *Claimed recall*: percentage who recall the advertising.
2. *Proved recall*: percentage who can prove they saw it by accurately describing it.
3. *Action*: percentage who are following up the advertising.
4. *Persuasion*: percentage who find the advertising persuasive.

Print advertisements, television commercials, cinema advertisements and posters can be checked by this technique. Gallup undertakes other special forms of research into the impact of advertising, particularly in specialized areas such as technical and farming publications.

BMRB International

The company uses its continuous consumer survey in order to check the effectiveness of advertising. In the belief that advertising works by helping to build in the consumer's mind a pattern of beliefs and attitudes relating to specific products, BMRB International seeks to identify, and measure over time, the beliefs and attitudes which affect brand choice.

BMRB International can also produce small-scale tests of advertising material, e.g. television commercials, to samples of between 20 and 30 people, representative of the target audience. Each respondent is the subject of a non-directive individual interview lasting for up to one hour. This pre-testing measures advertising communication and is also valuable in providing new creative ideas for copywriters.

Target Group Index (TGI)

This research service is also operated by BMRB and is available on subscription to advertisers, advertising agencies, and media owners. TGI is designed to increase the effectiveness of marketing operations by identifying and describing in detail specific target groups of consumers and their media exposure. TGI identifies heavy, medium, and light users, as well as non-users of a very wide range of product categories and sub-categories.

TGI provides particularly useful information about appliances and consumer durables by establishing who makes the decisions to buy and whether they had a major, or equal, say in purchase. By using TGI, the advertiser will know who uses his or her products and what they read, watch, and listen to; the advertiser will also have the same information regarding competitors.

TGI is based on a yearly sample of 24 000 adults who have been selected by a random location sampling procedure which incorporates ACORN. Respondents are personally interviewed in order to collect classification data, and those willing to participate are given a self-completion questionnaire; the effective response rate is consistently 60 per cent of those interviewed.

Fieldwork runs from April of one year to March of the next; the questionnaire is completely revamped every year. Volumes are issued annually in July/August; half-yearly data are available on computer tape.

BMRB International can also draw data for monitoring advertised brands of products from its 'omnibus' survey 'Access' (see Chapter 8). It also offers research to assist at any or all stages of planning and evaluating an advertising campaign, such as concept tests, attitude surveys, etc.

Publishing houses

The larger publishing houses and newspapers produce research data from time to time, frequently using the services of professional research organizations to ensure objectivity and acceptance by clients.

The BBC Magazines Group, which includes the *Radio Times* offers a range of services to advertisers and their agencies such as: computer analyses of NRS, TGI, Businessman Survey; market data from on-line text services (Profile, Harvest); ACORN or Town and City targeted inserts; pagination analyses of all major magazines (IMS Medialog data); noting and reading data on *Radio Times* (from Gallup).

Reader panel research is also conducted across the magazines. In addition, BBC Magazines have successfully applied cluster analysis techniques in order to target efficiently discrete groups of readers, e.g. the 'champagne and smoked salmon' set versus 'convenience cooks' versus 'pub grubbers'.

Sources of advertising data

British Rate and Data (BRAD)
This publication, published monthly by EMAP Media Ltd, gives detailed information on newspapers, magazines, television, radio, the cinema, outdoor advertising, and other media. This comprehensive guide to media facilities, including advertising rates, is valuable to researchers, as well as to advertising executives.

Advertisers' Annual
This is a comprehensive guide, published by Reed Information Services, to national and regional newspapers, consumer and business periodicals plus television and other mass media. It also contains information on promotional services, advertising agencies, and lists of principal advertisers.

Register/MEAL
Formerly Media Expenditure Analysis, the company publishes monthly analyses giving advertising expenditures by brand in press and television, with the name of the advertising agency responsible for the account.

The Newspaper Society
This society is a national organization which looks after the interests of morning, evening, and weekly papers published in England and Wales. In 1961, it published a comprehensive survey entitled 'Regional readership and markets survey', but this, of course, is no longer up to date. The Society does not now have a research department. JICREG data (see earlier section) are contained in the research database at the Newspaper Society.

The Audit Bureau of Circulations (ABC)
This is a professional body founded by advertisers, advertising agencies, and advertising media owners to secure, by standard and uniform methods of audit, accurate net sales, distribution, audience figures, etc., of advertising media. Audited figures listing average figures are issued at regular six-monthly intervals. ABC certificates give advertisers and agencies a quantitative and objective assessment of media, while media owners are given a 'hallmark' for their product. Rigorous standards of computing the published figures are observed. ABC circulation figures apply to the major part of the British press. Consideration is now being given to the problem of producing qualitative and geographical data, since ABC measurement has been solely quantitative so far.

Advertising statistics: IPA and AA

Statistical information on advertising is collected by both the Institute of Practitioners in Advertising (IPA) and the Advertising Association (AA). The AA has published statistics of the annual national total of advertising expenditure, analysed by main types of advertising and main types of media, for over 20 years. During the period 1948 to 1968, large-scale surveys were carried out every four years, estimates for the intervening years being projections based upon published material and selected unpublished information. From 1969, full detailed surveys have been carried out annually.

Life-style research

This was developed by the Leo Burnett Agency in Chicago and the University of Chicago. This type of psychographic research is designed to provide insights into attitudes and behaviour. It profiles people in terms of their patterns of work, leisure, living habits, interests, perceptions, etc. It adds qualitative values to the demographic profiles derived from consumer surveys.

This approach, typified as AIO (attitudes, interests and opinions) provides useful segmentation variables which, for example, have been applied to research into the consumption patterns of elderly consumers. By no means are these a homogeneous sector; apart from chronologically-based differences related to health, there are considerable differences connected to ranges of interests and levels of disposable income. In Britain, over the period 1997–98, about 75 per cent of couples over the age of 65 received occupational pensions in addition to the State retirement pension.[35] The 'relatively affluent' pensioners' segment has the time and income (and increasing life expectancy) to develop, for instance, new travelling tastes, or plan visits to concerts, etc.

Demographic trends in Europe, the USA and other developed regions and countries indicate that in these populations the proportion of elderly people continues to grow. In 1993, over 20 per cent of the UK population was aged 60 years or more; by 2010, this figure is to increase to 23 per cent, and by 2030 it is set to be 29 per cent.[35] Bearing in mind the general decline in birth rates, it is evident that the so-called 'grey market' or 'third age' population is becoming a critically important market sector.

When conducting qualitative research among Asian women in Britain it would be misleading to assume that the 'tenuous link of an Asian background will create the homogeneity that will make a group work'.[44] Differences between religions, ethnic origin, the degree of familiarity with the English language and age 'can create chasms between respondents'.[44] Among Asian women there is vast diversity of lifestyles. 'Sikh women are frequently highly educated, working, speak perfect English, and are very at home with the idea of discussing concepts, not fazed by going to a discussion group by themselves'.[44] Among the much larger and more diverse Muslim community, there are groups which are distinctly different, varying from older women who rarely move far outside their community to Muslim girl teenagers, born in the UK, who 'are often more independent than the community would like'.[44]

In modern society, life styles are dynamic: people are never completely satisfied for long, if ever, and seek new experiences, and their expectations tend to rise. Astute marketers recognize these fundamental influences and upgrade their products and services, adding acceptable new values in terms of taste, colour, overall performance, styling, availability, etc.

People of similar backgrounds and income groups tend to associate with each other and spend their money in characteristic ways. They form professional and recreational groups, and often live in fairly close proximity; their shared values, interests, and behaviour tend to develop into definable sub-cultures; these are attractive targets at which, through expertly selected media, manufacturers and distributors can project their goods and services. A typical example[45] is the relatively small family-owned clothing firm which produces the *Barbour* range of 'country casuals'. These premium-priced garments are sought eagerly by many who, like those whose *Range Rovers* seldom leave well-maintained urban avenues, delight in the dreams of country living. But the Barbour company spends little on advertising, preferring to sponsor outdoor events patronized by the gentry, and recognizes that it is in the field and rough moorland rather than in smart suburbia, that its core business lies.

In 1970, Daniel Yankelovich founded the *Monitor Survey* in the US; this tracks over 50 trends in people's attitudes towards time, money, family, self, institutions, the future and many other factors affecting their lifestyles. The Stanford Research Institute (SRI) developed *VALS* (Values and Life Styles), which characterized people as 'survivors' and 'sustainers' – the former were perceived as struggling for survival, and are typically elderly, distrustful, and with buying habits founded on basics; the latter were slightly better off, hoped that things would improve in time and so did not despair, and they were habitually price-conscious. *VALS* further segmented consumers into 'inner-directed' and 'outer-directed'; these were also analysed into sub-groups: 'belongers', 'emulators', and 'achievers'.

A 30 item *VALS* questionnaire resulted in data analysing markets in terms of VAL types for client companies.

Craig and Douglas have noted[46] that there has been particular interest among advertising agencies in identifying similar lifestyle segmentation on a regional or world-wide basis. European research, for instance, revealed 14 different lifestyle segments across 12 EU countries. But, it is pointed out, this type of approach requires identification of the link between the lifestyle segment and consumer preferences or buying behaviour related to a particular product category or life interest. If attitudinal or lifestyle characteristics are used to profile cross-national segments on, for instance, a demographic basis, the results seem more promising. Coca-Cola's global study of teenagers profiled differences and similarities of their attitudes, values and lifestyles in diverse regions of the world.

TGI Lifestyle measures the attitudes and values held by TGI respondents. Life-style data are gathered as part of the main TGI questionnaire and results are published in a separate volume. Respondents are presented with some 200 statements, each of which requires a response on a 5-point sliding scale from 'definitely agree' to 'definitely disagree'. Response to each statement can be analysed by all TGI variables, but even more advanced analysis is available as follows: (i) *correspondence analysis* – this links users of a certain type of product to particular groups of lifestyle statements. In this way the personalities of brands can be described, thus helping to differentiate between them. Correspondence analysis identifies which lifestyle statements most effectively discriminate within a market; and (ii) *cluster analysis* – segments a given population into discrete groups of like-minded people, based on their responses to lifestyle questions. It provides a powerful segmentation that is discriminatory within a given market.

Socio-cultural trend monitoring

The International Research Institute on Social Change (RISC)[47] was incorporated in Switzerland in 1978 to bring together researchers in Europe, South Africa and Japan who were interested in developing methodologies aimed at understanding socio-cultural trends. In 1980, their activities enlarged with the establishment of the first international programme – *ACE (Anticipating Change in Europe)*, which covered 8, then 12, western European countries. Seven years later, RISC expanded to US and Japan. *ACE EAST* commenced operations in 1989 'East Germany, Baltic countries and Russia', and now operates in 10 Eastern European countries.

Data are collected from an international common-core questionnaire, now administered in 29 countries, and including, originally, 45 questions which, in 1994, were expanded to 108. Sample sizes vary according to countries: 3000 in US and Japan; 2500 in France, Germany, Italy, Spain and the UK; 2000 in Belgium, Denmark, Finland, The Netherlands, Norway, Sweden, Switzerland, Belorussia, the Czech Republic, Estonia, Hungary, Latvia, Lithuania, Poland, Russia, Slovakia and Ukraine.

Surveys take place every year in the US, Japan and the five major European countries, and the 10 Eastern European countries; and every second year in the other countries.

From the answers to the 108 questions – which are intercorrelated to check patterns of responses over countries – trends are identified and from these 'maps' are constructed. For example, a pan-European map is derived from the aggregated results from the five major European countries, and individual maps for each of these countries are compared with the pan-European map.

Data from nearly 13 000 interviews conducted by the 1990 ACE European programme were plotted on a map with axes as shown in Fig. 10.3.

RISC comments[47] that the closer two individuals are, the more similar their values; the further away, the more different and sometimes antagonistic their values. Since 1992, RISC's research has indicated that young people have been moving towards 'openness to change' and 'ethics' and 'belonging' (social fairness, spirituality, environment, community, involvement in society).

RISC admits that 'many researchers' may feel that socio-cultural models are reductive and too systematic, but this can be said of any model, type of research, and any theory. To guard against such dangers, RISC regularly (1984, 1986, 1989, 1995) rebuilds its system, which is openly discussed within its network and also with clients.

Psychographic segmentation is closely linked with lifestyle analysis and was used successfully by Leo Burnett,[48] the Chicago advertising agency, with the help of IRI, a leading market research company specializing in EPOS-based data (see Chapter 9). After studying the influence of different kinds of advertising and promotion on shoppers' buying habits, they were able to challenge the simplistic belief that consumers could be characterized as buyers or non-buyers. Instead, four different behavioural groups were identified: (i) *Long loyals*: committed to one brand irrespective of price or competition; (ii) *rotators*: regularly switch among a few favoured brands – price is not important but

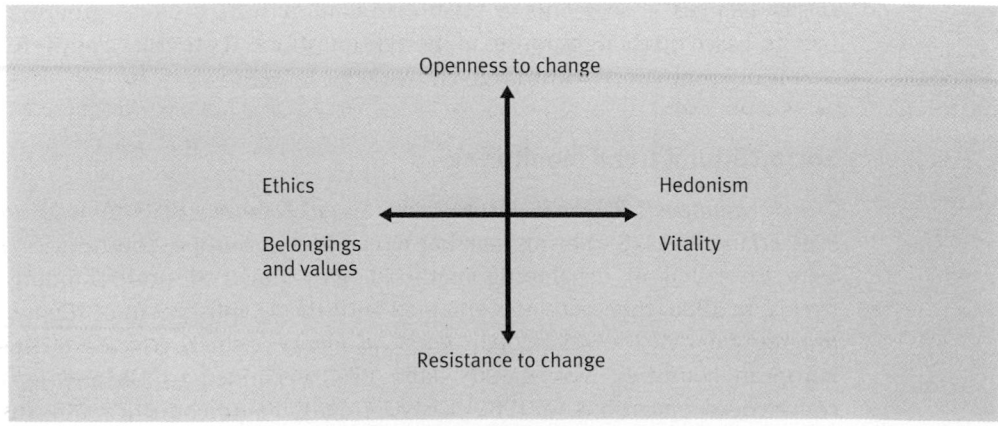

Figure 10.3 Socio-cultural space (*Source*: RISC)

variety is; (iii) *deal sensitives*: mostly buy the brand on special offer from their favoured few; and (iv) *price sensitive*: buy the cheapest product irrespective of brand.

These types varied across product categories; moreover, consumers generally lacked consistency in their motivations to buy different kinds of products, such as breakfast cereals, toilet tissues, etc. Leo Burnett emphasized that companies need to recognize that building up established brands depends on knowing more about their specific appeals to the types of consumers identified from their research.

Psychographics, according to Larry Hasson of RISC,[47] may be regarded as the ultimate phase of motivation research which developed in the 1950s (see Chapter 8). Since the early 1970s, he says, two major types of systems have developed: *life-style research* (based on typologies) and, *socio-cultural trend-monitoring systems* (as RISC's ACE programme).

Comment

While lifestyle may appear to some to be a rather nebulous concept that lacks the dependability of traditional demographic analyses, there are many occasions when its typologies have aptly projected the images of certain kinds of consumers. Admittedly, some of the labels attached to these groups have seemed to owe more to inventive copywriting than disciplined research. But value-systems cannot be ignored; they have been shown[3] to affect the acceptance and diffusion of new products and services, and are recognized to underlie food preferences, holiday habits, leisure pursuits and personal financial planning. Socio-cultural trend monitoring is now firmly established as a research approach based on three sets of dimensions: socio-cultural trends, demographics, and market dimensions. These salient aspects are integrated into what RISC has termed its *strategic cube*, and, responding to clients' wishes, RISC starts its research with analyses of specific market behaviour, identifying issues and evaluating options, before going on to examine socio-cultural trends. This modified approach has enabled it to provide clients with more comprehensive and relevant information.

National Statistics socio-economic classification (ONS)

Before proceeding to consider geodemographic analyses – which originated because of dissatisfaction with the NRS's A–E socio-economic classifications as used in media research – it is, perhaps, opportune to refer again to a new official social grading scheme which is now being adopted in Britain. In Chapter 4, brief reference was made to this system, which differs from the A–E classification in several ways.

In 1998, and as a result of a 3-year research programme jointly sponsored by the office for National Statistics (ONS) and the Economic and Social Research Council (ESRC) a new social classification was introduced for use in government statistics. It will replace the Registrar General's Social Class based on occupation, but it also is based on occupation.

This new classification – the National Statistics Socio-economic Classification (NS SEC) – has seven major classes plus an eighth into which are placed people who wish to work but never have. This seven-band scheme is shown in Table 10.2.

This occupation-based social classification has been designed to assist official statisticians to evaluate better the variations in, for example, health and social behaviour and attitudes in society. The new classification is based not on skill but employment conditions and relations which are considered important when describing the socio-economic structure of modern Britain.

Table 10.2 National Statistics Socio-economic Classification

1. Higher managerial and professional occupation (21 per cent)
1A Employers and managers in larger organizations (9 per cent)
  Company directors, senior police officers, senior local government officers, bank managers.
1B Higher professionals (12 per cent)
  Doctors, lawyers, dentists, higher civil servants, professors, professional engineers, teachers,
  airline pilots, social workers, librarians.

2. Lower managerial and associate professionals (17 per cent) Police sergeants and constables, prison service officers, firemen, journalists, nurses, physiotherapists, actors and musicians, professional sportsmen, lower ranking civil servants.
3. Intermediate occupations (14 per cent) Precision instrument makers, computer engineers, dental technicians, secretaries/PAs, airline flight attendants, driving instructors.
4. Small employers and own-account workers (9 per cent) Self-employed non-professionals
5. Lower supervisory, craft and related occupations (10 per cent) Electricians, TV engineers, car mechanics, railway engine and signal staff, printers.
6. Semi-routine occupations (21 per cent) Drivers, shop assistants, garage forecourt attendants, supermarket check-out operators, traffic wardens, caretakers, postal workers, gardeners, car assemblers, shelf fillers.
7. Routine occupations (8 per cent) Car park attendants, cleaners, road workers, refuse collectors, labourers, road sweepers.

Source: ONS

Although some of the classes in the NS SEC scheme seem similar to those of the social class-based system, the ONS points out that there are quite substantial changes because employment conditions are not necessarily related to skills. In fact, there are 'winners' and 'losers' in this new ordering of people: teachers and librarians, for instance, have 'moved up' from the old classification of social class II to class 1B of 'higher professionals'. Some employee occupations, such as check-out operators and sales assistants, however, have been down-graded from social class III non-manual to class 6 semi-routine occupations, which is said to reflect the relatively poor employment conditions of these jobs compared with those now described as 'intermediate occupations' in class 3 (see Table 10.2).

The new ONS classification was tested against health, employment and mortality statistics and revealed, for instance, that mortality rates for professional men in class 1 are 30 per cent lower than average, while male routine workers in class 7 (who formed part of the old 'working class' category) have 30 per cent higher than average rates. Although the ONS classification is based on detailed analyses of occupations, researchers can readily check the socio-economic class of specific occupations and employment by reference to available lists.

The ONS state that, although apparently similar to the official classification, the NRS A–E socio-economic grading, widely used in marketing research, is not used for official statistics. Edward Meier of IPSOS-RSL, who conduct the NRS survey, has acknowledged the value of the new ONS social classification for official statistics, but he considered that, for the time being, social grade was the preferred discriminator. But it was agreed that the latter also needed updating, and a working party would investigate what elements from the ONS system could be used to improve the present A–E grades.[49]

KEYPOINT

National Statistics Office Social Classification

1988 ONS introduced new social gradings for official reports: NS SEC presents 7 major classes based on occupation

Similar to NRS in some respects, but some occupations (e.g. teaching) up-graded, whilst others down-graded

NRS working party investigating how elements of SEC might improve A–E system

Geodemographic analyses

Dissatisfaction with the A–E socio-economic groupings, discussed earlier, inspired the development of a new method of identifying and targeting specific kinds of consumers. Geodemographic, as the name suggests, relates to analysis of the geographical dispersion of the population, as indicated by the Census of Population. Households are classified from multi-variate analysis of census data, and are grouped into several clusters or groups with distinctive types of housing and family behaviour.

The census operations are shared between the Office for National Statistics (ONS) covering England and Wales, the General Register Office for Scotland (GRO-S), and the Northern Ireland Statistical Research Agency (NISRA). Strict confidentiality is strictly enforced in all census outputs, so that individual persons or households cannot be identified. Small geographical areas or neighbourhoods may be identified; the smallest unit of census geography is the enumeration district (ED), which typically contains between 160 and 200 households (average 180), and is the territory covered by each enumerator. EDs were planned as sub-divisions of local government wards, so they do not match in with postcode geography. A directory linking EDs to postcodes is available.

In James Rothman's words:[50] 'Geodemographics is based on two simple principles: (i) that people who live in the same neighbourhood, such as a Census Enumeration District, are more likely to have similar characteristics than are two people chosen at random' and (ii) 'that neighbourhoods can be categorized in terms of the characteristics of the population which they contain, and that two neighbourhoods can be placed in the same category, i.e. they contain similar types of people, even though they are widely separated'. Put more simply perhaps: 'Birds of a feather flock together'.

Geodemographic systems have proved valuable in targeting customers for direct mail and mail order campaigns, etc.

Several geodemographic systems have been marketed in the UK over the past few years. They have much in common, for example databases are derived from population profiles at the enumeration district levels of the Census of Population; they are also closely linked with the post code system (see Chapter 3). They differ in some respects, mainly in the number and types of neighbourhood clusters which form their basic framework. The geodemographic analytical approach has existed as Census Tracking in the US for nearly 20 years. In the UK, the system, known as ACORN, was the first to offer this novel approach, and its success was followed by other research firms: some details of these competing systems are now given.

ACORN geodemographic system

ACORN, originated by a team of analysts led by Richard Webber at CACI Information Services, developed from work done in collaboration with the Centre for Environmental Studies in Liverpool during 1977.

ACORN classifies people and households according to the types of neighbourhood in which they live. It is based on the theme that neighbourhoods shown by the census to have similar social and demographic characteristics will share common life-style features and patterns of behaviour. At the invitation of Liverpool Council, Webber's earlier research focused on the incidence of urban deprivation in different sectors of the inner city. He discovered that provided that enough census counts were taken, 25 significantly different types of neighbourhood emerged. From an examination of local authority records of social problems associated with these areas, Webber found a significantly different mix of problems in each. There were not just rich and poor areas in general, but different sorts of poor areas requiring different social policies.

From this pioneering start, CACI, with the co-operation of the Census Office, then extended the methodology to classify each of the 17 000 wards and parishes throughout Great Britain. From multi-variate analysis related to 40 primary housing, demographic, social, and economic factors, as measured by the 1971 Census, 36 neighbourhood types were identified, each with its own clearly defined characteristics of age, structure, employment, joint income, family structure, type of housing, social status, and even car ownership. Where people live often influences significantly their life style.

British Market Research Bureau (BMRB) applied this 36 area classification to the 24 000 respondents covered in their annual Target Group Index (TGI) survey. ACORN segmentation was found to be an efficient discriminator for market targeting.

CACI's ACORN system of segmentation was then applied to the UK's 125 000 census enumeration districts, each of about 150 addresses which, because of their limited size, contain basically homogeneous households. The next stage was to match the 1.25 million post codes against the census enumeration districts, and so enable a list of customers' addresses (with post codes) to be readily analysed by ACORN criteria.

Experience indicated that 36 different types of neighbourhood sometimes resulted in unnecessarily fine analyses, and an effective 11 Family Group Classification was derived, originally based on 1971 Census data but later modified when 1981, and then 1991, Census information became available; the 36 Neighbourhood Types have now been increased to 54.

The 17 ACORN Family Group Classification is shown in Table 10.3. The 17 Main Groups are subdivided so that 54 Neighbourhood Types or sub-groups result. For example, Group A 'Thriving' represents 19.7 per cent of the population and is made up of wealthy, affluent and prosperous households. On the other hand, Group F 'Striving', representing 22.6 per cent of the population, consists of those who are less fortunate, who live in Council housing, or in crowded multi-ethnic areas. These and the other Types are described in quantitative and qualitative terms by ACORN analysts. Consumption profiles of specific neighbourhoods can be drawn, and areas of high consumption readily identified. For example, ACORN Type 1.2 'villages with wealthy commuters' represents 3.2 per cent of the (1991 Census) population; these very affluent commuter villages are to be found all over Britain, but are particularly evident in Somerset, Hereford and Worcester, and Wiltshire. They contain 20 per cent more than average 45–64-year-olds and 20 per cent fewer than average 0–4-year-olds; the ethnic profile is very homogeneous – 99 per cent white.

ACORN, as already indicated, is used by BMRB TGI analyses, and also by a widening range of retailers, mail-order houses, building societies and car manufacturers. It has particular use in direct marketing, leaflet distribution, and local media selection.

It would be naïve, of course, to conclude that *all* consumers whose residences fall within a specific ACORN Neighbourhood Group are likely to buy particular products or brands or read certain journals. By linking ACORN with TGI or with a company's own customer data, it is possible, however, to measure the varying probabilities of usage and to give guidelines for effective marketing strategies. As just mentioned, it is also feasible to focus mail shots on identified groups of households or businesses in any given television area, county, post town, or post code sector.

CACI offers a comprehensive range of data analysis services linked to ACORN segmentation: among these is a 'sample plan' which is a computerized system for sample point selection. The computer selects areas which will provide the most representative set of addresses (sampling frame) for interviewing. It then points out exact instructions to guide interviewers, either to specific addresses or to particular streets, with clear sampling instructions. 'Sample plan' can be used effectively for minority sampling as well as nationally representative samples. The system is widely used by survey organizations.

Another ACORN service is AreaData which, as its name suggests, is useful to retailers in planning the location of stores and also in deciding the range of merchandise to stock. AreaData reports show the demographic structure of area populations, say within five miles' radius of Solihull, as well as type of household (ACORN 54 Types and 17 Groups), and potential buying power for a range of products, including cars, household durables, central heating and travel. It is also available on-line at www.areadata.co.uk.

CACI provides a similar data service in the USA, using census data supplied by the American Bureau of the Census.

Household ACORN definitions are shown in Table 10.4.

In addition to the ACORN household composition groups in Table 10.4, analyses extend to 24 Life-style groups and 81 Life-style types which effectively integrate consumer demographic segments and geographic locations as Table 10.5 indicates.

As with ACORN, the Household ACORN analysis is linked to the major market research surveys such as TGI, as well as to CACI's full demographic database. For example, Area Data reports can give area breakdowns by Household*ACORN Group in addition to the features mentioned earlier (see ACORN) while the added precision of Household*ACORN is especially useful in direct mail operations. Prospective users can have their mailing lists or databases analysed across the 81 Types, and use the results to target mailing lists or other marketing or advertising activity with greater accuracy than before.

ACORN Lifestyles UK

Lifestyles UK is a new database of 44 million individuals who are rated 0–100 according to their propensity to have a product or service, e.g. a current account, credit card, types of holiday, listening to music, giving to charity, etc. In all, a total of 380 different lifestyle attributes can be selected from; each selection is bespoke. Existing customer files can be matched against the Lifestyles UK database, and clients can select the individuals who most closely resemble the existing customer base.

Lifestyles UK database can be linked to the full ACORN family classification system, census demographics, and electoral roll data.

Table 10.3   ACORN Family Group Classification

Acorn groups			Acorn types	
A Thriving (19.7%)				
1 Wealthy achievers, suburban areas areas	15.0%	1.1	Wealthy suburbs, large detached houses	2.5%
		1.2	Villages with wealthy commuters	3.2%
		1.3	Modern affluent home owners areas	2.7%
		1.4	Affluent suburbs, older families	3.7%
		1.5	Mature, well-off suburbs	3.0%
2 Affluent greys, rural communities	2.3%	2.6	Agricultural villages, home based workers	1.6%
		2.7	Holiday retreats, older people, home based workers	0.7%
3 Prosperous pensions, retirement areas	2.4%	3.8	Home owning areas, well-off older residents	1.4%
		3.9	Private hols, elderly people	0.9%
B Expanding (11.6%)				
4 Affluent executives, family areas	3.8%	4.10	Affluent working families with mortgages	2.1%
		4.11	Affluent working couples with mortgages, new homes	1.3%
		4.12	Transient workforces, living at their place of work	0.4%
5 Well-off workers, family areas	7.5%	5.13	Home owning family areas	2.6%
		5.14	Home owning family areas, older children	3.0%
		5.15	Families with mortgages, younger children	2.2%
C Rising (7.8%)				
6 Affluent urbanites, town and city areas	2.3%	6.16	Well-off town and city areas	1.1%
		6.17	Flats and mortgages, singles and young working couples	0.7%
		6.18	Furnished flats and bedsits, younger single people	0.4%
7 Prosperous professionals, metropolitan areas	2.1%	7.19	Apartments, young professional singles and couples	1.1%
		7.20	Gentrified multi-ethnic areas	1.0%
8 Better-off executives, inner city areas	3.4%	8.21	Prosperous enclaves, highly qualified executives	0.7%
		8.22	Academic centres, students and young professionals	0.7%
		8.23	Affluent city centre areas, tenements and flats	0.4%
		8.24	Partially gentrified multi-ethnic areas	0.7%
		8.25	Converted flats and bedsits, single people	0.9%

Acorn groups			Acorn types		
D	Settling (24.1%)				
	9 Comfortable middle agers, mature home owning areas	13.4%	9.26	Mature established home owning areas	3.3%
			9.27	Rural areas, mixed occupations	3.4%
			9.28	Established home owning areas	4.0%
			9.29	Home owning areas, council tenants, retired people	2.6%
	10 Skilled workers, home owning areas	10.7%	10.30	Established home owning areas, skilled workers	4.5%
			10.31	Home owners in older properties, younger workers	3.1%
			10.32	Home owning areas with skilled workers	3.1%
E	Aspiring (13.7%)				
	11 New home owners, mature communities	9.7%	11.33	Council areas, some new home owners	3.8%
			11.34	Mature home owning areas, skilled workers	3.1%
			11.35	Low rise estates, older workers, new home owners	2.8%
	12 White collar workers, better-off multi ethnic areas	4.0%	12.36	Home owning multi-ethnic areas, young families	1.1%
			12.37	Multi-occupied town centres, mixed occupations	1.8%
			12.38	Multi-ethnic areas, white collar workers	1.1%
F	Striving (22.6%)				
	13 Older people, less prosperous areas	3.6%	13.39	Home owners, small council flats, single pensioners	1.9%
			13.40	Council areas, older people, health problems	1.7%
	14 Council estate residents, better-off homes	11.5%	14.41	Better off council areas, new home owners	2.4%
			14.42	Council areas, young families, some new home owners	3.0%
			14.43	Council areas, young families, many lone parents	1.6%
			14.44	Multi-occupied terraces, multi-ethnic areas	0.9%
			14.45	Low-rise council housing, less well-off families	1.8%
			14.46	Council areas, residents with health problems	1.9%
	15 Council estate residents, high unemployment	2.7%	15.47	Estates with high unemployment	1.1%
			15.48	Council flats, elderly people, health problems	0.7%
			15.49	Council flats, very high unemployment, singles	0.9%

Table 10.3 *(cont.)*

Acorn groups		Acorn types	
16 Council estate residents, greatest hardship	2.8%	16.50 Council areas, high unemployment, lone parents	1.9%
		16.51 Council flats, greatest hardship, many lone parents	0.9%
17 People in multi-ethnic, low-income areas	2.1%	17.52 Multi-ethnic, large families, overcrowding	0.6%
		17.53 Multi-ethnic, severe unemployment, lone parents	1.0%
		17.54 Multi-ethnic, high unemployment, overcrowding	0.5%

Source: CACI.

Table 10.4　ACORN household composition

Singles	Adults living on their own, usually without young children
Couples	Two adults, almost certainly married, with or without young children
Family	Two adults, almost certainly married. They have at least one other relation living with them: child or other adult
Homesharers	Multiple adults living together but not a couple or family

Age structure	
Younger	Youngest – adults most often between 18 and 24 years of age
	Maturing – adults most often between 25 and 44 years of age
Older	Established – adults most often between 45 and 64 years of age
	Retired – adults most often over 65 years of age

Source: CACI.

Table 10.5　ACORN 24 lifestyle groups and 81 lifestyle types

Rural areas and villages

LA	*Rural singles*	2.7%
LA01	Younger men	
LA02	Younger women	
LA03	Older single men	
LA04	Older single women	
LA05	Affluent singles in commuter villages	
LA06	Affluent singles in agricultural villages	

LB	*Younger rural couples and families*	2.2%
LB07	Young couples	
LB08	Young couples with elderly person	
LB09	Maturing couples	
LB10	Maturing families	

LC	*Older rural couples and families*	1.8%
LC11	Established couples	
LC12	Established couples, older children	
LC13	Retired couples	
LC14	Retired families	

LD	*Affluent rural couples and families*	2.4%
LD15	Affluent couples and families in commuter villages	
LD16	Affluent couples and families in agricultural villages	

Suburbia

LE	*Younger suburban singles*	3.7%
LE17	Younger single males	
LE18	Younger single females	

LF	*Older suburban singles*	4.0%
LF19	Older single males	
LF20	Older single females	

LG	*Younger traditional suburban couples and families*	9.7%
LG21	Youngest couples	
LG22	Youngest couples with elderly person	
LG23	Maturing couples	
LG24	Maturing families	

LH	Older traditional suburban couples and families	5.3%
LH25	Established couples	
LH26	Established families with older children	
LH27	Retired couples	
LH28	Retired families	

LI	Younger very affluent suburban couples and families	4.2%
LI29	Youngest couples	
LI30	Youngest couples with elderly person	
LI31	Maturing couples	
LI32	Maturing families	

LJ	Older very affluent suburban couples and families	2.3%
LJ33	Established couples	
LJ34	Established families with older children	
LJ35	Retired couples	
LJ36	Retired families	

Council areas

LK	Younger singles in council areas	5.1%
LK37	Single men	
LK38	Single women	

LL	Older singles in council areas	5.0%
LL39	Single men	
LL40	Single women	

LM	Younger couples in council areas	6.8%
LM41	Youngest couples	
LM42	Maturing couples	

LN	Older couples in council areas	5.0%
LN43	Established couples	
LN44	Retired couples	

LO	Adult families in council areas	6.2%
LO45	Youngest couples and families with elderly person	
LO46	Maturing families	
LO47	Established families with older children	
LO48	Retired families	

Metropolitan and cosmopolitan city

LP	Affluent single metropolitan dwellers	3.1%
LP49	Younger men	
LP50	Younger women	
LP51	Older men	
LP52	Older women	

LQ	Affluent couples in metropolitan areas	4.0%
LQ53	Younger couples	
LQ54	Younger families	
LQ55	Older couples	
LQ56	Older families	

LR	Cosmopolitan inner city dwellers	2.4%
LR57	Younger singles	
LR58	Younger couples and families	
LR59	Older singles	
LR60	Older couples and families	

Traditional urban households

LS	Younger urban singles	2.8%
LS61	Men	
LS62	Women	

LT	Older urban singles	3.5%
LT63	Men	
LT64	Women	

LU	Younger traditional urban couples and families	6.8%
LU65	Youngest couples	
LU66	Youngest couples with elderly person	
LY67	Maturing couples	
LU68	Maturing families	

LV	Older traditional urban couples and families	4.3%
LV69	Established couples	
LV70	Established families with older children	
LV71	Retired couples	
LV72	Retired families	

Homesharers

LW	Homesharers in affluent areas	3.4%
LW73	Male homesharers in very affluent areas	
LW74	Female homesharers in very affluent areas	
LW75	Mixed homesharers in very affluent areas	
LW76	Male homesharers in traditional suburban	
LW77	Female homesharers in traditional suburban	
LW78	Mixed homesharers in traditional suburban	

LX	Homesharers in less affluent areas	3.3%
LX79	Male homesharers	
LX80	Female homesharers	
LX81	Mixed homesharers	

Source: CACI.

People*UK

People*UK is the first classification system of individual people in the UK; it is an individual level ACORN. Basically, it is a mix of geodemographics, lifestyle and life stage data condensed in an easy-to-use format. The system is arranged as eight life stages with 46 individual lifestyle types.

Irish*ACORN

This newest addition to CACI's ACORN segmentation covers the Republic of Ireland and is based on the 1991 and 1996 Census at District Electoral Divisions (DEDs) level. DEDs are classified into one of 21 types; in some cases census data are presented for subdivisions where DFDs are split into 'town' and 'out of town' areas.

Irish*ACORN is divided into five groups, which are then broken down into 21 detailed types as follows:

Group 1 – Private renting
  Type 1:   Younger city areas, bedsits and flats
  Type 2:   Restored working class flats
Group 2 – Affluent Executives
  Type 3:   Affluent areas
  Type 4:   Affluent couples with younger children
  Type 5:   Older affluent couples
  Type 6:   Out of town commuters
Group 3 – Rural areas
  Type 7:   Farms outside towns
  Type 8:   Rural family areas
  Type 9:   Irish speaking areas
  Type 10: Traditional farming areas
  Type 11: Remote farms/elderly people
Group 4 – Settled home owners
  Type 12: Older office workers
  Type 13: Home owning, older families
  Type 14: Younger families in new housing
  Type 15: Educated workers with mortgages
  Type 16: Mixed houses and flats
Group 5 – Low status and council areas
  Type 17: Young families, greatest hardship
  Type 18: Retired workers
  Type 19: Mixed flats and tenements
  Type 20: Postwar family housing council housing
  Type 21: Mature communities

As with the UK ACORN system, profiles are given of typical households and their educational background, employment, car ownership, etc.

Mosaic

This is another geodemographic system which was developed by Experian and, originally, particularly related to the needs of the large mail-order firm, Great Universal Stores, owners of Experian.

Like ACORN, it classifies every full post code in the UK which, as noted in Chapter 3, comprises 15 addresses, into one of 52 MOSAIC types, such as 'Corporate Careerists' or 'Chattering Classes', on the bases of housing, socio-economic grouping and population characteristics (see Table 10.6). These basic types of consumers are then organized into 12 MOSAIC lifestyle groupings, as shown in Table 10.7, from which it will be seen, for example, that 'High Income Families: A' represent 11 per cent of GB households and include MOSAIC types 1–5.

Although MOSAIC is based on data from the 1991 Census of Population, it also draws from a wide range of other data sources; these, in fact, represent over half of the data used in building up this demographic system. These additional data sources are updated annually and are available at full post code level. The full list of 196 variables is shown in Table 10.8.

MOSAIC enables marketers to understand their customers better and to develop their markets; among the many applications are: effective location of new outlets; closure of specific existing outlets; selection of merchandise suited to the needs of individual outlets; targeting local promotions and selection of local advertising media; and selection of addresses for effective mail-order marketing.

In addition to the Great Britain classification, Experian has developed regional classifications for London, Scotland and Northern Ireland; industry-specific classification Financial MOSAIC; individual classifications for 13 countries worldwide; and Global MOSAIC – a single classification system encompassing the entire world. A further development has been RISC which segments households by their values, beliefs and motivation, and places each Great Britain postcode into one of seven social value groups (see earlier reference in this chapter to 'socio-cultural monitoring').

Geographic Information Systems (GIS)

The data of a geodemographic study are enhanced by geographical maps of the output; these are invaluable in displaying spatial patterns, such as locations of supermarkets and their customer base, local media coverage, etc.[49] PC analysis/mapping systems provide geodemographic analysis and geographical mapping, and are offered by ACORN, MOSAIC, and other, geodemographic systems.

Geodemographics and survey research

The various geodemographic systems – of which two principal ones have been outlined – share much in common. 'The general conclusion', observes James Rothman is that their differences seem to be 'small and the choice between systems varies according to the subject matter and the judgment and other needs of the user'.[50]

Geodemographics can be applied in various research processes, such as survey design, sampling, weighting processes and analysis of final results. As indicated in Chapter 4, stratification improves the accuracy of samples, and geodemographics can be used for stratifying areas; the system may also be helpful in disproportionate sampling, where it may be desirable to over-sample some areas of greatest product potential.

As noted earlier, TGI has made a significant contribution to the development of ACORN in the 1970s, has retained its notable value and is in regular use by ACORN as well as other leading geodemographic systems. Other important syndicated surveys are also geodemographically coded and can be used to obtain cross-tabs. These include NOP's Financial Research Survey (FRS), MORI Financial Services (MPS), the National Readership

Table 10.6   The 52 MOSAIC types and their national penetration

Type	Description	GB households (%)
A1	Clever capitalists	1.4
A2	Rising materialists	2.3
A3	Corporate careerists	2.7
A4	Ageing professionals	1.7
A5	Small town business	2.9
B6	Green belt expansion	3.3
B7	Suburban mock tudor	3.0
B8	Pebble dash subtopia	4.2
C9	Affluent blue collar	3.1
C10	30s industrial spec	3.7
C11	Lo-rise right to buy	3.0
C12	Smokestack shiftwork	3.0
D13	Coalfield legacy	3.2
D14	Better off council	2.0
D15	Low rise pensioners	2.9
D16	Low rise subsistence	3.2
D17	Peripheral poverty	2.0
E18	Families in the sky	1.1
E19	Victims of clearance	0.3
E20	Small town industry	1.3
E21	Mid rise overspill	0.7
E22	Flats for the aged	1.4
E23	Inner city towers	1.6
F24	Bohemian melting pot	2.3
F25	Smartened tenements	0.1
F26	Rootless renters	1.4
F27	Asian heartlands	1.1
F28	Depopulated terraces	0.7
F29	Rejuvenated terraces	3.5
G30	Bijou homemakers	3.5
G31	Market town mixture	3.9
G32	Town centre single	2.3
H33	Bedsits and shop flats	1.1
H34	Studio singles	1.9
H35	College and communal	0.5
H36	Chattering classes	1.9
I37	Solo pensioners	1.9
I38	High spending greys	1.3
I39	Aged owner occupiers	2.8
I40	Elderly in own flats	1.4
J41	Brand new areas	0.8
J42	Pre-nuptial owners	2.1
J43	Nestmaking families	2.0
J44	Maturing mortgagees	2.6
K45	Gentrified villages	1.3
K46	Rural retirement mix	0.6
K47	Lowland agribusiness	1.8
K48	Rural disadvantage	1.1
K49	Tied/tenant farmers	0.6
K50	Upland and small farms	1.3
L51	Military bases	0.3
L52	Non private housing	0.05

Source: Experian.

Table 10.7   The 12 MOSAIC lifestyle groupings

Group	GB households Description	Percentage	Types
A	High income families	11.0	1–5
B	Suburban semis	10.4	6–8
C	Blue collar owners	12.8	9–12
D	Low rise council	13.3	13–17
E	Council flats	6.4	18–23
F	Victorian low status	9.1	24–29
G	Town houses and flats	9.7	30–32
H	Stylish singles	5.4	33–36
I	Independent elders	7.4	37–40
J	Mortgaged families	7.5	41–44
K	Country dwellers	6.7	45–50
L	Institutional areas	0.3	51–52

Source: Experian.

Survey (NRS), panel research services – TN Sofres Superpanel, and ACNielsen's Homescan.

Richard Webber, the founding father of geodemographics, believes that there will be a greater use of psychographic information: until now, geodemographic users have concentrated on who to communicate with', but, increasingly, he says, systems will be used 'to modify the message, proposition or incentive to different customer segments'.[51]

KEYPOINT

Geodemographic analyses

Based on geographical dispersion of population

Derived from Census data – households classified and grouped into clusters or groups of distinctive housing and family behaviour

Census tracking in USA existed for many years

Two principal systems in UK: ACORN and MOSAIC

Proved valuable for targeting specific types of households and people

Utilizes post code framework

Able to pinpoint areas of high consumption of particular goods and services

Widely used in mail-order selling, store location, etc.

'Sagacity' segmentation

In an endeavour to improve the discriminating power of income and demographic classifications, IPSOS-RSL developed 'Sagacity' in 1981. This consumer classification combines life cycle, income, and socio-economic groups. Using data from JICNARS/NRS, IPSOS-RSL grouped people into 12 easily described and identifiable classifications with markedly different characteristics in terms of media habits and product usage.

Table 10.8   Full list of 196 variables used in MOSAIC classifications

Person and household level data

Demographics

Gender
- Male
- Female

Marital status
- Single
- Married
- Head of household

Age
- Aged 18–25
- Aged 26–35
- Aged 36–45
- Aged 46–55
- Aged 56–65
- Aged 66+

Life stage
- Male – young
- Male – middle
- Male – old
- Female – young
- Female – middle
- Female – old
- Couple – young
- Couple – middle
- Couple – old
- Sharers – young
- Sharers – middle
- Sharers – old

Household composition
- Families
- Extended family
- Extended household
- Pseudo family
- Single male
- Single female
- Male homesharers
- Female homesharers
- Mixed homesharers
- Abbreviated male families
- Abbreviated female families
- Multi-occupancy dwelling

Length of residency
- Up to 1 year
- 1 to 3 years
- 4 to 10 years
- 11+ years

Property type
- Purpose built flats
- Converted flats
- Farm
- Named building
- Numbered house
- Other type

Socio-economic

County Court judgements/credit risk
- CCJs per elector
- CCJs > 3 years old
- CCJs < 3 years old
- Average value of CCJs
- Average value of CCJ per adult
- Average Delphi-for-mailing score

Company directors
- Director of small company (< 50 employees)
- Director of large company (> 50 employees)

Shareholdings/shareholding values
- Have government shares
- Have non-government shares
- Have blue chip shares
- Have investment trust shares
- Have building society shares
- Low value (< £5000)
- High value (> £5000)

Neighbourhood level (postcode level or above) data

Building stock

Property age
- Build pre 1920
- Built 1920–1945
- Built 1946–1979
- Built post 1980

Property type
- Detached
- Semi-detached
- Terraced
- Purpose built flats
- Converted flats
- Bungalow

Property size (average metres square)
- Households with garden
- Households with garage

Census of population statistics – 1991 ONS census

Demographics
- Aged 0–4
- Aged 5–14
- Aged 15–24
- Aged 25–34
- Aged 35–44
- Aged 45–54
- Aged 55–64
- Aged 65+

Ethnic origin
- Born Indian sub-continent
- Born Caribbean
- Born New Commonwealth
- Born rest of world
- Ethnic group – white
- Ethnic group – black
- Ethnic group – Indian
- Ethnic group – Chinese and others

Household size
- Rooms/person
- Rooms/household
- Cars per household

Household structure
- Married persons
- Cohabitee
- Single parents
- Students at term time
- Students 20–24
- Students 16–19
- Permanently sick
- Single non-pensioner households
- Single pensioner households
- Households with > 1.5 persons/room
- Households with 1–1.5 persons/room
- Three adult households
- Age 65+ and renting
- Age 65+ and owning
- Households with 6+ rooms
- Households with children
- Households with children and without car
- Two or more earners

Property type
- Converted flat or flatlet
- Bedsit
- Detached
- Semi-detached
- Terraced
- Purpose built flat

Tenure
- Outright owner
- Mortgage
- Furnished
- Unfurnished
- Renting from housing association
- LA or council tenant
- Moved last year
- Owners sharing pensioners in homes
- Residents in detention, defence and education

Amenities
- Central heating
- Share inside WC
- No inside WC
- No bath/shower

Employment
- Mining/manufacturing
- Services
- Unskilled
- Semi-skilled
- Skilled manual
- Non-manual
- Professional/managerial
- Agriculture
- Mining/manufacturing (ward level)
- Services (ward level)
- Women in manufacturing
- Work 41+ hours
- Unemployed
- Self-employed

Transport
- Walk to work
- Public transport to work
- Car to work
- 2+ car households

Residential property transactions
- Standardized average house price
- Number of sales in same period/household

Unemployment
- Unemployment rate

Motor vehicle ownership
- 2 door saloon
- 4 door saloon
- Convertible
- Coupe
- Estate
- 3 door saloon
- 5 door saloon

Table 10.8   (*cont.*)

Neighbourhood level (postcode level or above) data

Census of population statistics – 1991 ONS census

- Sports
- Four-wheel drive
- Vehicle age 0–1 year old
- Vehicle age 1–2 years old
- Vehicle age 2–3 years old
- Vehicle age 3–5 years old
- Vehicle age 5–8 years old
- Vehicle age 8–10 years old
- Vehicle age 10+ years old
- New cars
- Old cars
- Basic
- Small
- Lower medium
- Upper medium
- Executive
- Luxury
- Sports
- Minivans
- Sports utility
- Cars per household

Residential density
- Dead-end of street within 50 metres of postcode
- Persons per area (km square)
- Area per person (km square)
- Household per area (km square)
- Area per household (km square)
- Households per area for 1 mile radius
- Households per area for 2 mile radius
- Households per area for 3 mile radius
- Area per household for 1 mile radius
- Area per household for 2 mile radius
- Area per household for 3 mile radius

Retail accessibility
- Number of grocery stores within 1 km
- Number of grocery stores within 5 km
- Accessibility measure – 1 km radius
- Accessibility measure – 5 km radius
- Accessibility to major centre
- Accessibility to regional centre

Source: Experian.

The underlying theme of 'Sagacity' is that, as people pass through the various stages of their lives they have different aspirations and patterns of behaviour, including consumption of goods and services.

Four separate types are identified:

Dependant: adults 15–34 who are *not* heads of household or housewives, unless they are childless students in full-time education.

Pre-family: adults 15–34 who *are* heads of households or housewives, but are childless.

Family: adults under 65 who are heads of households or housewives in households with one or more children under 21 years of age.

Late: all other adults whose children have already left home or who are 35 or over and childless.

Cornish states that the cut-off point of 35 between the Pre-family and Late stages is arbitrary, and was chosen in preference to 45, which can be taken as the end of a woman's fertile period, on the grounds that the Pre-family stage should only include households in the relatively early years of household formation.[53]

After life cycle, SAGACITY then considers income and occupational characteristics of the individual or couple forming the household.

Income is defined as 'the net income of the head of the household at constant prices on a 10 point exponential scale, adjusted by the working status of the spouse of the head of the household'.

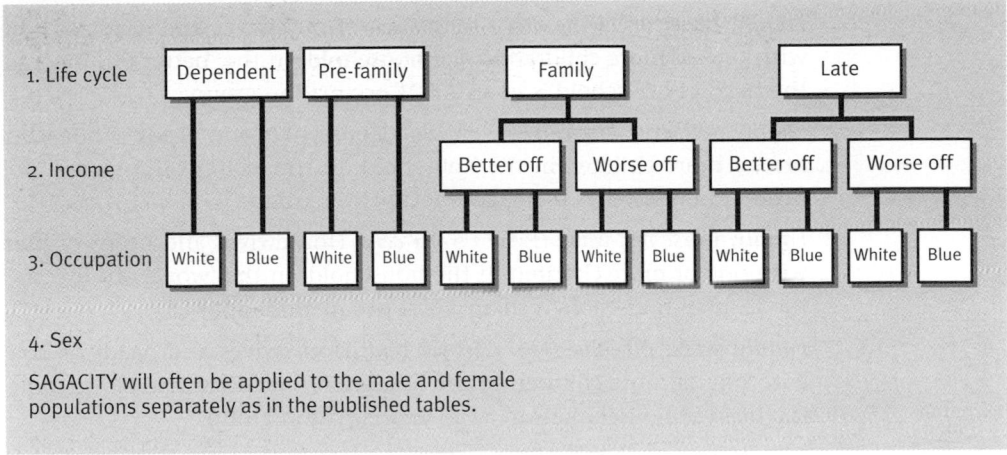

Figure 10.4   SAGACITY consumer segmentation model (*Source:* Research Services)

Income breakdown is applied only to the Family and Late stages, and households are characterized as 'better off' or 'worse off'. For instance, a white-collar adult in the Family stage could be classified as 'better off' if the head of the household's claimed or estimated net income falls within the two highest of 10 income brackets, provided he or she has no working spouse. Adjustments are made to cut-off points where the spouse works full- or part-time.

Dependant and Pre-family stages are not classified into 'better off/worse off' income groups on account of the relatively small sample sizes and also because differences in disposable income are considered to be less marked and therefore less important than in later stages.

Division by income rather than economic activity is stated to be particularly important at the Late stage, since there is a significant minority of retired people who qualify for the 'better off' income grouping, and who might well have consumption habits similar to those who are still working. (See earlier reference to the affluent middle-aged.)

The last element of the SAGACITY groupings refers to the occupation of the head of the household. Individuals are classified as non-manual (white collar) occupations (ABC1s) and manual (blue collar) occupations (C2DEs).

From combination of the three elements (life cycle, income, and occupation) with stages in the family life cycle, the paradigm shown in Fig. 10.4 emerges.

To assist understanding of the SAGACITY system, descriptive notations have been given for each of the 12 groups, together with an indication of their size relative to the total adult population.[54]

Dependant, white (DW) 7 per cent: Mainly under 24s, living at home or full-time student, where head of household is an ABC1 occupation group.

Dependant, blue (DB) 9 per cent: Mainly under 24s, living at home or full-time student, where head of household is in a C2DE occupation group.

Pre-family, white (PFW) 4 per cent: Under 35s who have established their own household but have no children and where the head of household is in an ABC1 occupation group.

Pre-family, blue (PFB) 5 per cent: Under 35s who have established their own household but have no children and where the head of household is in a C2DE occupation group.

Family, better off, white (FW+) 9 per cent: Housewives and heads of household, under 65, with one or more children in the household, in the 'better off' income group and where the head of household is in an ABC1 occupation group.

Family, better off, blue (FB+) 9 per cent: Housewives and heads of household, under 65, with one or more children in the household, in the 'better off' income group and where the head of household is in a C2DE occupation group.

Family, worse off, white (FW−) 5 per cent: Housewives and heads of household, under 65, with one or more children in the household, in the 'worse off' income group and where the head of household is in an ABC1 occupation group.

Family, worse off, blue (FB−) 10 per cent: Housewives and heads of household, under 65, with one or more children in the household, in the 'worse off' income group and where the head of household is in a C2DE occupation group.

Late, better off, white (LW+) 6 per cent: Includes all adults whose children have left home or who are over 35 and childless, are in the 'better off' income group and where the head of household is in an ABC1 occupation group.

Late, better off, blue (LB+) 7 per cent: Includes all adults whose children have left home or who are over 35 and childless, are in the 'better off' income group and where the head of household is in a C2DE occupation group.

Late, worse off, white (LW−) 10 per cent: Includes all adults whose children have left home or who are over 35 and childless, are in the 'worse off' income group and where the head of household is in an ABC1 occupation group.

Late, worse off, blue (LB−) 19 per cent: Includes all adults whose children have left home or who are over 35 and childless, are in the 'worse off' income group and where the head of household is in a C2DE occupation group.

The power of SAGACITY is to discriminate in relation both to markets and to media has been demonstrated by IPSOS-RSL. For example, package holidays abroad peak in the Pre-family and Late stages; even among the better off, demand is very much lower in the Family stage. The lower per capita disposable incomes of families with children and the problems associated with taking children abroad contribute to this trend. If NRS data showed that 20 per cent of all adults took a package holiday abroad, compared with 30 per cent in one SAGACITY group and 15 per cent in another, indices for these groups would be calculated thus:

$\frac{30}{20} \times 100 = 150$ and $\frac{15}{20} \times 100 = 75$ (The total population index will always be 100.)

Clearly, the type of package holiday will influence the target market definition. Media can also be selected to cover the SAGACITY groups shown to be the most likely prospects.

Ownership of cheque books contrasts with the pattern of distribution of overseas package holidays in that it is a function of age and social grade rather than income. Joint-stock bank accounts are held by virtually all white-collar workers in the Pre-family and Family stages, but fall off in the Late stage. The index for holding a bank current account by blue-collar workers is below 100 for Dependant, Late, and 'worse-off' groups. However, the Pre-family and 'better off' blue-collar groups have indices of 115 and 111 respectively. These figures may reflect a certain degree of success by the banks in attracting these groups of consumers who, as they enter succeeding life cycle stages, may maintain usage and so change the blue-collar indices.

SAGACITY segmentation is clearly a creative and realistic approach which has generally been 'welcomed by marketing and advertising professionals, although the caveat has been expressed that since it . . . does, however, presuppose the collection of class and income data . . . it would therefore benefit from any improvements to class and income classifications'.[55]

KEYPOINT

Sagacity segmentation

Combines life-cycle, income and socio-economic groups

Widely used in media analyses

Basic theme: as people pass through life, their aspirations and behaviour patterns (including consumption of goods and services) also change

4 separate types: dependant; pre-family; family; late.

Summary

Advertising research covers content, media, and effectiveness. Content research focuses on the ability of the advertisement to achieve impact and project the desired message.

Media research attempts to eliminate wasteful expenditure by objectively analysing various media. Joint research bodies have been set up to deal with specific media. BARB has direction of TV research in the UK; research is undertaken by research agencies and also by the BBC. JICNAR/NRS developed the well-known A–E socio-economic classification. Radio audiences are measured by the BBC, and also by JICRAR.

Effectiveness research is concerned with analysing different media (and combinations of media) and evaluating the degree of success with which specific advertising objectives have been achieved.

Sources of advertising data are: publishing houses, ABC, BRAD, independent TV companies, IPA and AA. Starch and Gallup have been active for years in reading and noting studies. Target Group Index (TGI) operated by BMRB offers comprehensive research data on patterns of consumption of wide ranges of goods and services.

Geodemographic systems of consumer segmentation based on census data, neighbourhood types, and life styles, are offered by several research organizations, such as ACORN (CACI) and MOSAIC.

SAGACITY segmentation on life cycle, income, and occupation.

Review and discussion questions

1. How would you respond to a manager who feels that advertising recall and recognition measures are a waste of resources and that the only reliable means of testing advertising copy is sales returns?

2. To what extent do sequential flow models of how advertising works fit in with the views of practitioners in Section 11.2 of this chapter?

3. How justified is the prominence accorded to social grading as a segmentation variable in consumer research?

4. A number of methods for measuring advertising effectiveness were outlined in this chapter. Which of these measures appeals most to you? State reasons for your preference.

5. Outline the advantages to marketers of geodemographic segmentation compared to socio-economic segmentation.

6. Identify three products or services that, in your opinion, would prove sensitive to segmentation by SAGACITY.

References

1. McDonald, Colin, *How Advertising Works: A Review of Current Thinking*, Advertising Association in association with NTC Publications, Henley on Thames, 1992.
2. Politz, Alfred, 'The dilemma of creative advertising', vol. 25, no. 2, 1960.
3. Chisnall, Peter M., *Consumer Behaviour*, McGraw-Hill, Maidenhead, 1994.
4. Hutton, Peter F., *Survey Research for Managers: How To Use Surveys in Management Decision-making*, Macmillan, Basingstoke, 1988.
5. Feldwick, Paul, 'Advertising as an act of faith is not enough', *Researchplus*, Market Research Society, February 1993.
6. Lannon, Judie, and Peter Cooper, 'Humanistic advertising: a holistic cultural perspective', in: *Effective Advertising: Can Research Help?*, ESOMAR, Monte Carlo, 26/28 January, 1983.
7. Hall, M., and D. Mackay, 'Science and Art: how does research practice match advertising theory?', Market Research Society Conference, 1991.
8. Hall, Mike, 'The tracking questions recall will not answer', *Researchplus*, Market Research Society, February 1993.
9. Branthwaite, Alan, 'Complex consumers and dynamic brands', *Researchplus*, Market Research Society, July 1993.
10. McDonald, Colin, 'Myths, evidence and evaluation', *Admap*, November 1980.
11. Joyce, Timothy, 'Models of the advertising process', *Marketing and Research Today*, vol. 19, no. 4, November 1991.
12. Ehrenberg, A. S. C., 'Comment on how advertising works', *Marketing and Research Today*, vol. 20, no. 3, August 1992.
13. Starch, Daniel, *Principles of Advertising*, AW Shaw, Chicago, 1923.
14. Starch, Daniel, *Measuring Advertising Readership and Results*, McGraw-Hill, New York, 1966.
15. Lavidge, Robert J., and Gary A. Steiner, 'A model for predictive measurement of advertising effectiveness', *Journal of Marketing*, vol. 25, no. 6, October 1961.
16. Colley, Russell H., 'Defining advertising goals for measured advertising results', Association of National Advertisers, New York, 1961.
17. Palda, Kristian S., 'The hypothesis of a hierarchy of effects: A partial evaluation', *Journal of Marketing Research*, February 1966.
18. Haskins, Jack B., 'Factual recall as a measure of advertising effectiveness', *Journal of Advertising Research*, March 1964.
19. Festinger, Leon, 'Behavioural support for opinion change', *Public Opinion Quarterly*, autumn 1964.
20. Wicks, Anne, 'Advertising research: an eclectic view from the UK', *Journal of Market Research Society*, vol. 31, no. 4, October 1989.
21. Summers, Diane, 'The truth of the matter', *The Financial Times*, 6 October 1994.
22. Dunning, Bill, 'Hall Tests', in: *A Handbook of Market Research Techniques*, Robin Birn, Paul Hague, and Phyllis Vangelder (eds), Kogan Page, London, 1990.
23. Burdus, A., 'Advertising research', in: *The Effective Use of Market Research*, Staples Press, London, 1971.
24. Maloney, J. C., 'Is advertising believability really important?', *Journal of Marketing*, vol. 27, no. 5, 1963.
25. Monk, Donald, 'Social grading on the National Readership Survey', Research Services Ltd, Joint Industry Committee for National Readership Surveys (JICNARS), London, July 1970.
26. Market Research Society, 'An evaluation of social grade validity', January 1981.
27. Cornish, Pym, and Mike Denny, 'Demographics are dead – long live demographics', *Journal of Market Research Society*, vol. 31, no. 3, July 1989.
28. Bound, John, 'The use of socio-economic grading', *MRS Newsletter*, December 1987.
29. Chidoub, Linda, 'OPCS endorses NRS data', *NRS Review*, No. 4, December 1994.
30. Fletcher, Winston, 'Why researchers are so jittery', *Financial Times*, 3 March 1997.
31. Consterdine, Guy, 'Directory and social grading biases', *MRS Newsletter*, November 1989.
32. Syfret, Toby, 'TV audience measurement in Europe', in: *The 1995 Report on Radio and Television Audience Measurement in Europe,* ESOMAR, Amsterdam, February 1995.

33. Brown, Michael, 'Diary measurement of radio listening', *Journal of the Market Research Society*, vol. 34, no. 3, July 1992.
34. Teer, Frank, 'Radio, outdoor and cinema research', in: *Consumer Market Research Handbook*, Robert Worcester, and John Downham (eds), Elsevier Publishing, Amsterdam, on behalf of ESOMAR, 1986.
35. *Social Trends 30*, Office for National Statistics (ONS), 2000.
36. Stocker, Ivor, 'Poster research', in: *A Handbook of Market Research Techniques*, Robin Birn, Paul Hague, and Phyllis Valgelder (eds), Kogan Page, London, 1990.
37. McEvoy, David, 'How OSCAR is pinning down a moving target', *Researchplus*, Market Research Society, May 1993.
38. Wicks, Anne, 'Advertising research', in: *A Handbook of Market Research Techniques*, Robin Birn, Paul Hague, and Phyllis Valgelder (eds), Kogan Page, London, 1990.
39. Bethel, Frank, 'Standing out on the crowded food shelf', *Researchplus*, Market Research Society, Autumn 1999.
40. Palda, Kristian S., *The Measurement of Cumulative Advertising Effect*, Prentice-Hall, New Jersey, 1964.
41. Samuels, J. M., *The Effect of Advertising on Sales and Brand Shares*, Advertising Association, 1971.
42. Sampson, Peter, 'The tracking study in market research', in: *Applied Marketing and Social Research* (2nd Edn), Ute Bradley (ed.), Wiley, Chichester, 1987.
43. Freeman, Paul, 'Continuous surveys and tracking in the UK', *Journal of the Market Research Society*, vol. 31, no. 4, October 1989.
44. Robertson, Pru, 'The rich interests of ethnic differences', *Researchplus*, Market Research Society, July 1994.
45. 'Family values', *The Economist*, vol. 329, no. 7843, 25 December 1994.
46. Craig, C. Samuel, and Susan P. Douglas, *International Marketing Research*, John Wiley, Chichester, 1999.
47. Hasson, Larry, 'Monitoring social change', *Journal of the Market Research Society*, vol. 37, no. 1, January 1995.
48. 'Consumer behaviour: strategic shopping', *The Economist*, 26 September 1992.
49. McElhatton, Noelle, 'Class war goes to conciliation', *Research*, Market Research Society, April 1999.
50. Rothman, James, Editorial, special issue on geodemographics, *Journal of Market Research Society*, vol. 31, no. 1, January 1989.
51. Leventhal, Barry, and Jonathan Reynolds, 'Site location studies and geodemographics', in: *ESOMAR Handbook of Market and Opinion Research*, Colin McDonald, and Phyllis Valgelder (eds), ESOMAR, Amsterdam, 1998.
52. Webber, Richard, 'Today, the nation; tomorrow, the globe', *Researchplus*, Market Research Society, May 1997.
53. Cornish, Pym, 'Life cycle and income segmentation – SAGACITY', *Admap*, London, October 1981.
54. Research Services Ltd, 'SAGACITY: A Special Analysis of JICNARS', NRS 1980 Data, London, 1981.
55. Twyman, Tony, 'Re-classifying people', the ADMAP Seminar, Admap, November 1981.

11

Business-to-business research

Learning Objectives

- Note differences between consumer and business-to-business buying behaviour
- Become aware of buying influences such as complex decision-making and multiple roles
- Understand nature of industrial/organizational demand, e.g. derived demand
- Explain how general research methodologies, e.g. sampling, need adjustment to be effective in organizational markets

11.1 Introduction

The wealth of a nation is built up from the contributions made by its productive resources. In a developed country like the UK, these resources are many and complex. Radical changes have affected the structure of the industrial and commercial base; the older industries of steel, coal, shipbuilding and textiles have shrunk, while newer industries – based on electronics, computer technology, biochemicals and sophisticated technical and professional services – have become significant contributors to the national wealth.

In this dynamic, increasingly volatile environment, companies are up against competition not only from home-based suppliers but also from countries which have been termed the newly industrialized economies (NIEs).

Marketing research has a core role to play in this new global game and, as indicated in Chapter 1, it has enhanced its professional skills and range of research applications. Consumer marketing research has tended to attract attention because of its immediate impact on many members of the public, but it has not been recognized generally as an essential element of the successful marketing of the vast array of goods and services needed by industry, commerce and the public sector. But nowadays, few organizations are likely to feel confident enough to develop new products or to expand into new markets without rigorous evaluation of the opportunities and threats that are inseparable from new ventures. No business – consumer, industrial or commercial – is immune from the threat of failure arising from market ignorance.

Marketing research is the cornerstone of a well-devised marketing strategy: it cannot guarantee success, but it *will* narrow the field of uncertainty surrounding many marketing decisions. Figure 11.1 shows a typical relationship between investment in market information and the risks in decision-making. After a time the typical curve flattens out, indicating that beyond a certain limit it would no longer be advantageous to spend more money on marketing research activities.

Private sector industries and the public sector services form the modern 'mixed economy' which, at one time, seemed to be a permanent if precarious characteristic of developed economies such as Britain's. But the process of nationalization has halted, and

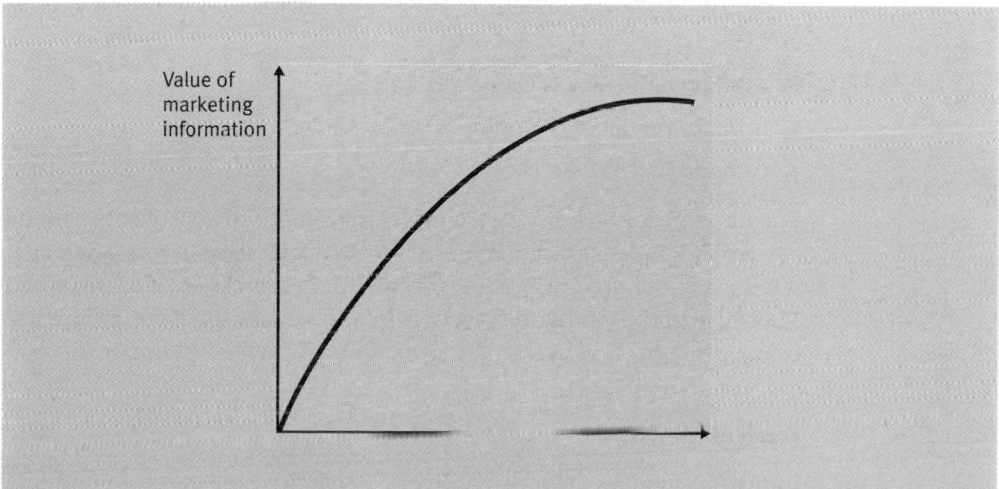

Figure 11.1 Typical relationship of market research information and risk in decision-making

the energy and water industries, and the railways have returned to the private sector. However, government departments and local authorities still exert very considerable market influence, either by directly placed contracts, for example, for motorway construction, bridge-building, defence systems, and the maintenance and expansion of schools and hospitals. Some industries are still virtually dependent for their viability on contracts placed by the public sector.

Before discussing marketing research applications in the business-to-business sector of the economy, a brief look will be taken at some of the fundamental characteristics which underlie its distinctive buying behaviour.

KEYPOINT

Business-to-business marketing research

Covers vast range of economic and social activities, products and services supplies to or bought by firms and organizations in:

Industrial, commercial, technical, professional enterprises and the public sector

11.2 Characteristics of business-to-business markets

Nature of supplies

In many cases, the products and services demanded by industry, commerce and the service industries will be similar to those bought by consumers, but the *reasons* for their purchase will be different: for example, paint, stationery, fuel, insurance and banking are supplied to both sets of customers. But business-to-business transactions are expected to contribute, directly or indirectly, to the progress (or profit) of an organization. Although corporate buyers in the public sector and those in profit-motivated businesses may differ in the nature of their primary motivation, they both, however, share the same responsibilities, namely to procure goods and services for use in their organizations as distinct from personal consumption.

Various ways of classifying business-to-business supplies have been attempted; a typical one is:

1. capital goods;
2. primary products;
3. intermediate products.

The first category covers, for example, equipment to assist further production. The second category includes, for example, steel or chemicals used in processes; and the third category relates, for example, to castings, cement and bricks used in making finished products. These categories cannot be precisely qualified, and the three groups are merely indicators of the principal types of what may be termed corporate supplies.

Derived demand

Industrial supplies are mostly directly dependent on trends in end-use markets. Demand for capital equipment is largely subject to prospective demand for goods which such plant can produce (see Figure 11.2). Industrial marketers of food processing equipment, for example, should be aware of patterns of consumption of the products manufactured on their types of machinery. Fluctuations in demand at consumer level inevitably affect, perhaps radically, the suppliers of raw materials, machinery, packaging, etc., involved in the chain of production.

If car sales fell off because of lower consumer demand, the effects would reverberate through many industries; for example, steel, tyres, electronic and electrical components, upholstery fabrics, etc. The prosperity of brick manufacturers and cement producers is clearly influenced by trends in the building and construction industries which, in turn, are highly sensitive to the general level of economic activity, government policies, interest rates, etc.

Vertical demand

Some products have many applications; others experience 'vertical demand' and have distinctly limited market opportunities, such as specific equipment for the nuclear fuel industry. Being a specialist supplier to such a vertical-demand market obviously entails significant parameters of corporate risk.

Horizontal demand

On the other hand, some products have uses across a wide range of industries, and so experience 'horizontal demand'; for example, surface coatings, polyester and cotton tapes, packaging, electrical components, etc. Such suppliers have many opportunities for developing sales and off-setting depressed demand in some market sectors. *Substitution* is another factor affecting industrial demand; for instance, synthetic fibres largely replaced natural fibres until the textile industry successfully developed various mixed fibres for use in carpets, clothing, etc.

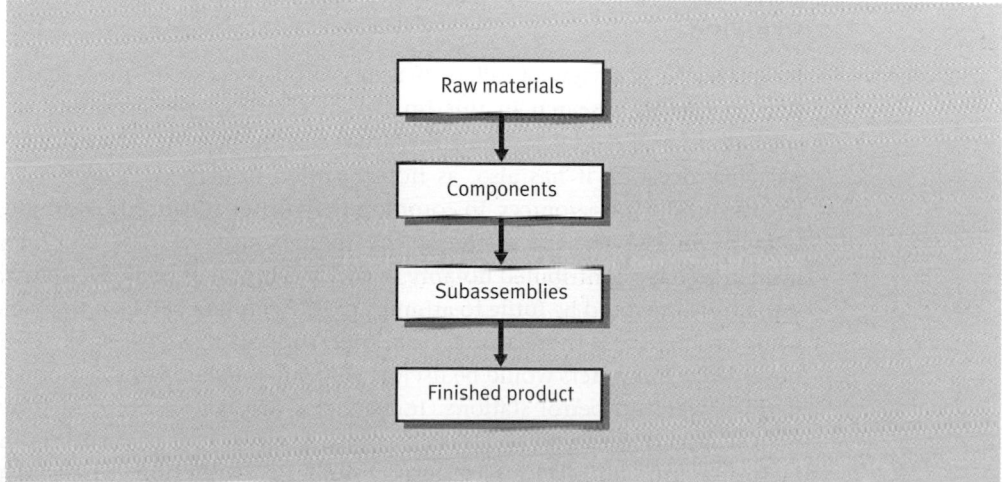

Figure 11.2   Pattern of derived demand for industrial raw materials

Complex decision-making

Business-to-business decision-making is generally more complex than consumers' buying decisions. The term 'decision-making unit' (DMU) was introduced into British marketing in the 1960s. Five roles have been noted:[1] gatekeeper, user, influencer, buyer, and decider – these make up the *buying centre*. The same person may sometimes fulfil all these functions but, more frequently, different persons are active in their various roles in particular buying situations. The degree of their influence is obviously related to their specialist knowledge and to their status in the management hierarchy.

Advanced technology-based industries, for example, electronic equipment, tend to have buying procedures quite different from those in firms having a narrow range of fairly standard, low-tech products, for which standards of quality, price and service are all well established.

An organization may be viewed as a complex series of interlocking patterns of human relationships, work-flow patterns and control systems, all of which give ample scope for individuals to exercise their professional skills and also to enhance their career prospects. Corporate executives are involved in making decisions under varying degrees of uncertainty, so while they aim to satisfy the objectives of their organization, they will also be influenced by instincts of self-preservation, particularly when high levels of inter-departmental competitiveness are evident. In some cases, the authority of the officially-termed buyer has been eroded because of the increasing complexity of certain corporate supplies, such as those subject to extended performance tests, as in aeronautical engineering, computer installations, etc.

Concentrated buying power

With industrial mergers over recent years, the 80/20 rule is increasingly evident in many corporate business markets; for instance, 'high street' banks, electronic capital equipment, and chemical and pharmaceuticals, where a handful of large organizations dominate the UK sectors. In such cases, buyers exercise strong leverage and suppliers' businesses may be at risk if one or two powerful customers represent a high proportion of their overall sales.

Overview

From this basic review of salient features of business-to-business markets, it will be seen that marketing research in this important sector of the economy is itself likely to be specialized and complex. The UK manufacturing base has shrunk significantly over the past few decades; it has also, as noted earlier, undergone radical transformation of its wealth-producing resources. In common with other advanced economies, Britain depends heavily on the tertiary sector as the main source of new employment; the service industries have contributed notably to the development of a new industrial society. At the same time, it would be futile to attempt to differentiate between the benefits derived from some products and those arising from their supporting services. As *The Economist*[2] acutely observed: 'Computers would be useless without software writers. Nobody would buy a car if there were no petrol stations. Indeed, the distinction between industry and services is now largely meaningless. In rich countries, over half the workers in a typical manufacturing firm do service-type jobs – design, distribution, financial planning; only a minority makes things on the factory floor.'

Characteristics of business-to-business markets

Nature of supplies: in many cases similar goods/services as in consumer markets but *reasons* for purchase are different

Derived demand: industrial demand largely dependent on trends in end-use markets

Vertical demand: some products have distinctly limited market opportunities

Horizontal demand: some products have wide range of customers, across many industries

Complex decision-making: generally more complex than consumers' buying decisions; 5 roles: gatekeeper; user; influencer; buyer; decider

Concentrated buying power: 80/20 rule applies in several sectors

11.3 Business-to-business marketing research

In Chapter 1, it was emphasized that, basically, marketing research is concerned with studying and evaluating buying behaviour, and that its usefulness extended beyond consumer products and services to industrial, technical, commercial and public sector investigations. Business-to-business research covers, therefore, an exceptionally wide range of economic and social activities. So, bearing in mind the problems of definition and the 'overflow' between goods and services, and also certain non-commercial activities pursued by central and local governments, it would appear that business-to-business marketing research is now a mainstream activity. It has a very wide range of opportunities to offer specific professional advice to decision-makers in technical, scientific, and other advanced economic activities.

The distinctive characteristics of business-to-business markets, which have been noted, indicate that marketing researchers should, in the early stages of an assignment, study the background and structure of the trading (or other) environment in which a client operates. This introductory work will result in a better understanding of the problems facing the client, and it may also suggest suitable ways of researching their market. It would also be helpful to researchers to familiarize themselves with the production and distribution strategies, the nature of competition, the type of demand for specific products/services and the related motivations to buy, as well as the extent of innovation and other critical factors in corporate performance.

Five sequential stages of marketing research were given in Chapter 2: these are generally applicable, so the first step is to obtain agreement on the nature of the problem to be investigated. This process of clarification and definition should not be shirked; unless the matters on which the research will focus are fully understood and agreed little productive research is likely later on.

Business-to-business marketing research

As usual, 5 sequential stages:

1. Research brief

2. Research proposal

3. Data collection

4. Data analysis and evaluation

5. Preparation and presentation of survey report

For a client to say: 'We want you to look at our market', is a totally inadequate research brief. Many firms operate in several markets which share, perhaps, general characteristics but which also tend to have distinct features. Also, there are usually particular features of a market which may affect the likelihood of success, and investigation may be needed in some depth in these areas. There may be times when a client is so unwilling to give adequate insight into her problem that no worthwhile marketing research would be feasible. Usually, however, experienced researchers are able to generate an atmosphere of trust and confidence which attracts even hesitant clients to co-operate in delineating their business problems.

Assessing market demand by consumption factors

The dependent nature of industrial demand has been noted to be an intrinsic feature of industrial markets. The influence of derived demand is felt through the various stages of production – from raw materials to finished products. At these several stages of economic activity, consumption of specific supplies of energy, steel, cement, sulphuric acid, petrol and oxygen occurs. These basic indicators of industrial activity could be studied in relation to particular regions, sectors of industry of specialized segments of an industry, and assessments made of specific consumption behaviour. The demand for fhp motors is related to sales of washing machines and other household equipment. Lead/lag indicators may be effective in some market sectors such as cars, sales of which affect the demand for steel, but this demand is lagged by about 18 months, hence providing an indicator of future activity in the steel industry. In some industrial markets, gross domestic fixed capital formation (GDFCF) could be a useful indicator in forecasting demand, for instance, for air-conditioning equipment.

This relatively sophisticated approach, involving statistical demand analyses and model-building is probably too complicated for most marketing research purposes, but it is briefly mentioned to illustrate how ingenious approaches may be used in assessing specific market behaviour.

KEYPOINT

Secondary data: starting point

Desk research: as with consumer research, start with secondary data

Official: business monitor standard industrial classification (SIC)

Commercial: trade directories, trade associations, research reports, on-line databases

Search thoroughly for relevant data

Desk research (secondary data)

As with consumer research, data collection should start at the secondary level, and full advantage should be taken of available information, both within companies and that published externally, to give a sound base to the whole research programme. There are many sources of published data to which researchers instinctively turn but, usually, there are valuable data to be gathered also from production, accounting, and sales records. Marketing research data may be culled from these internal sources at very low cost and, with a little ingenuity, a regular flow of specific information from the various areas of functional management could be of great value to developing and guiding marketing strategies.

Externally published sources of data include many of those already listed in Appendix 1. Principal sources are:

Census of Production
    Business Monitors
    Trade Associations
    Trade Directories

Stock Exchange Yearbook
    Exhibition Catalogues
    Research Associations

Business monitors

As noted in Chapter 2, business monitors provide detailed information about British industrial production. These series are regularly published so the information is more up to date than that in the Census of Production.

Trade Associations and Chambers of Commerce, as also noted in Chapter 2, should be contacted in the rigorous search for market data. In general, however, the search will not be very fruitful, for apart from a handful of such organizations, they are limited to giving an overall view of particular industries or trades, and economic data are unlikely to be available.

It would be as well to bear in mind that membership is voluntary and some firms, for reasons of policy, may not be members. The collection of information within associations depends largely on goodwill. The complete reliability of the data supplied is a factor to be carefully considered.

Some of the leading trade directories and yearbooks have been listed in Chapter 2; there are others which could be consulted in academic libraries and in the commercial libraries in the cities and larger towns of the UK and many overseas countries.

Trade directories are of variable quality; it is useful to check accuracy and reliability by scrutinizing entries relating to companies which are well known personally. In addition to these publications, there are very many specialist journals, and researchers should acquaint themselves with those covering the markets under survey.

Entries in exhibition catalogues can be used to build up a good general knowledge of particular industries, though it should not be assumed that these necessarily include all companies. Some may have individual methods of promotion which exclude trade exhibitions in some areas.

Some industries have research associations which publish market data; for example, the Furniture Industry Research Association (FIRA).

From this brief review of possible sources of externally published information, it will readily be appreciated that an effective market researcher, particularly when industrial marketing problems are being surveyed, needs to have some of the talents of the sleuth in tracking down relevant and useful data.

11.4 Primary research

Sampling frames

One of the salient problems of industrial marketing research is the availability of suitable lists of firms on which a survey could be based. Desk research enquiries, as just outlined, could be instrumental in developing sampling frames.

The UK Directory of Manufacturing Businesses 1993 replaces the *Classified List of Manufacturing Businesses*, which originated from the Business Statistics Office as the result of the co-operation of firms which, from 1970, contributed to the *Census of Production* (see Chapter 2).

The *Directory* contains about 20 000 business units (about 14 per cent of manufacturing units on the CSO register), in alphabetical order with *Activity Heading*; it also accounts for about 67 per cent of the employment in the manufacturing sector. Incomplete coverage results from the exclusion of smaller businesses from the *Census of Production*, and because some contributors refuse to agree to participate in the directory. The *Directory* is also available on micro floppy disk; special analyses can also be provided by the ONS website: www.ons.gov.uk (see Appendix 1).

Expert informants

In most industries there are usually people known to be well informed and to possess sound knowledge of its structure, technical development and commercial activities; they are not necessarily in the largest firms. Researchers should try to identify and contact these experts, who may be recommended by trade associations and other helpful sources. From a series of free-discussion interviews, an extremely good insight may be obtained on the structure and problems of a particular industry. One approach that was used involved subdividing a specific market into homogeneous sectors and then to commence enquiries in each sector with the best informed sources known. The sample size was not predetermined; successive firms were interviewed until a stable answer pattern emerged.

The editors and professional journalists attached to the trade and industrial press may also be willing to discuss the market being surveyed, and about which they may have specially relevant knowledge.

Sampling

In Chapters 3 and 4 the basic principles of techniques of sampling were discussed in some detail, particularly with reference to consumer markets. Industrial markets differ considerably from mass consumer product markets in many ways, and so some aspects of the sampling methodologies already covered may not be directly applicable, although, of course, the underlying concepts of representativeness and objectivity remain unchanged. Sometimes, industrial markets, for example, are very limited, and it may be possible to measure consumption, etc., through a complete census. In other cases, the market is widespread, with many different structures and patterns of consumption behaviour, and sampling has to be devised which is both feasible and, of course, valid.

In forming an effective sample design, it is desirable – even imperative – to know the structure of the market or market sector on which the research will focus. This preliminary knowledge is indispensable, hence the value of consulting knowledgeable people connected with specific markets. Intensive desk research will augment these discussions. All this preparatory work should be undertaken thoroughly, so that the market research project is firmly based.

Industrial products are often used in a variety of industries, and where a general survey is required it may be necessary to undertake a series of sample surveys into individual user-industries. Alternatively, it may be possible to apply some method of weighting to the data of a general survey. The problem for the researcher is obtaining reliable information about a well-defined area of investigation. Enquiries should, therefore, be directed specifically to those industries (complete or segmented) which are significant for this purpose.

Constructing a sample for industrial marketing research demands some general knowledge of the particular industry concerned. The more perfect this knowledge, the better the researcher will be able to form a sample which adequately represents the population under survey.

Facts about the structure of a particular industry can be obtained from some of the published sources given in Appendix 1.

As already observed, the total universe to be studied is usually small, from a mere handful of companies to a few hundred and, occasionally, a few thousand. Industrial marketing research typically requires far fewer interviews compared with consumer enquiries.

Industries are often dominated by a small number of companies, whose total output represents a significant share of the market, perhaps as high as 90 per cent. This residual output may be contributed by many comparatively small firms, whose individual market share is relatively unimportant although, of course, they may have a strong position in a specific market sector or niche (see section on concentrated buying power).

Some companies deal with a very restricted number of customers and, sometimes, two or three of these take almost the entire production.

In cases like these, it would obviously be incorrect to use a random sampling technique, as the survey findings would be unreliable if one of the major companies were not included in the sample taken. To avoid errors of this nature, the whole population would have to be surveyed, i.e. a census would be necessary. In some instances, it may be possible to avoid taking a complete census by carefully weighting a sample.

When some establishments are very much more important than others, the problem is to identify them, either in advance or by means of a sample design which increases the probability of reaching these important firms without incurring heavy expenses in non-productive interviews.

It may be possible to have access to a previous survey into a particular, or related, field of enquiry, which could help in developing an effective sampling scheme. While this 'short-cut' may be appealing, some effort should be made to evaluate the efficiency of the sampling plan that was used earlier, and the overall quality of the research findings would need to be carefully assessed.

A useful example of research methodology relates to a survey of the UK market for fork-lift trucks, which were known to have many applications. From previous surveys and various official statistics, a matrix of 13 business sectors (SIC groupings) and seven size (employee) classifications were developed. Extra inputs came from Dun and Bradstreet, Market Location, and the survey organization's own files.

Truck ownership was known to be comparatively low generally, and to vary widely across and within market sectors. Some type of disproportionate sampling was therefore considered.

From previous studies of this market, it was feasible to compute an estimated percentage penetration for each cell in the matrix, and by applying these figures to the number of establishments, an estimate was derived of the 'truck-equipped establishments'. Sample quotas were allocated to each cell in proportion to its relative importance in the total truck-owning market. Each of the 10 standard regions of Great Britain was allocated separate quotas.

To safeguard the efficiency of the quota sampling scheme, lists of contacts were pre-selected and issues to interviewers on a controlled basis: replacement addresses were issued only when the initial set had been fully accounted for.

Finally, this fairly sophisticated sampling procedure was followed by structured interviews by a team of 21 telephone interviewers, who were mostly home-based; but in the case of very large establishments with many trucks, face-to-face interviewing took place, which enabled qualitative assessments to be made.

To build up a satisfactory sampling frame for industrial marketing research, considerable patience and ingenuity are necessary, as the example just quoted illustrates. Comprehensive combing and integration of published data will help in filling in the gaps which are usually to be found in any one source of knowledge. It is obviously important to check such data for their validity and reliability.

The importance of knowing the impact of derived demand in specific markets and the application of end-use analysis have already been discussed. These approaches can be extremely useful in constructing effective sampling methodologies.

Interviewing and questionnaires

From the extended discussion in Chapter 6, it will be recognized that interviewing is a critical function of marketing research which, unfortunately, is subject to bias of many kinds. Good research practice aims to eradicate sources of error, and to control, as far as possible, the conditions under which the enquiries are made. Industrial research interviewing should not be regarded as an alternative occupation for members of the sales force; they may be able to produce some information which, at a superficial level, appears satisfactory. There remains, however, the risk of subjectivity, but despite this some organizations tend to rely on their sales staff to provide market information. It is argued that surveys are better undertaken by people who have an intimate knowledge of the product and the industry, but unless they are trained in market research, including interviewing skills, many are likely to find it difficult to set aside their business loyalties when attempting to find out more about the problems of an industry and its suppliers, as seen from the viewpoint of customers.

Interviewing in industrial marketing research tends to be largely unstructured, i.e. a formal questionnaire is not used and is sometimes replaced by an 'interviewing guide', which lists the main areas of research to be covered by the interviewer. It is more a guide to conversation. Since good 'timing' may sometimes attract the right response, the interviewer is left free to use discretion in the sequence of questioning.

Where questionnaires are used, it is important to ensure that technical terms are correctly handled and that the area of scientific or technical enquiry is clearly understood by both parties. This calls for considerable skill in drafting questions covering specialized fields of knowledge. It also demands interviewers capable of obtaining information, often of a highly technical nature, from management over a representative range of companies. Such interviewers need to have expert knowledge of the industries which are being covered by the survey, or they should have the intellectual ability to acquire sufficient information in a short period of intensive training. They should also possess the type of personality which will help them to be accepted by senior management with whom they must necessarily establish confidence, if the interviews are to be successful.

The considerable debate about whether or not industrial marketing research interviewers need to be highly qualified technically in the specific industries they are surveying is not easily determined. Even in technical markets, factors other than those directly related to product design and manufacture may frequently be involved; for example, delivery time, prices, credit policy, attitudes, or advertising effectiveness. To restrict interviewing to those who are highly trained specialists in engineering and so on, may well affect the findings of specific research surveys because they lack vital business orientation and experience.

Of course, researchers, including interviewers, need to be adequately briefed: this may entail intensive study *before* field research starts. In a comparatively short time, intelligent field researchers can assimilate a surprising amount of background knowledge about particular industrial techniques and applications. Professional interviewing skills are necessarily the most important factor – technical competence alone does not ensure effective interviewing.

It is clearly important to interview whoever is able to provide relevant and accurate information about the subject of the survey, and as discussed earlier, in many industrial buying decisions several executives from different management functions are likely to influence the source of supply. The buyer may not be able to give detailed answers to certain technical enquiries, and it may well be necessary to interview executives in both technical and commercial spheres.

The survey may, therefore, be divided into several parts. Interviewers may have to exercise considerable diplomacy to ensure that the buyer, for instance, gives them the opportunity of meeting other key executives whose opinions on technical matters may be valuable.

On the whole, industrial research is more difficult than consumer research. Fewer calls can be made during the day, and it is advisable to book appointments, as it would be unreasonable to expect executives to lay aside their duties without reasonable advance notification. They may also wish to have a little time in which to obtain specific data. In some cases, a call-back ensures that the information given is reliable.

Frequently, research organizations offer to provide respondent firms with some of the general answers are given. With some survey problems, it may be advantageous to institute continuous research at a certain agreed depth, and this could be done by forming a user panel.

Observational techniques

Industrial marketing research can also adopt observational techniques which can provide very useful information. This may involve checking types of equipment in use, or a study of the way in which certain tools are handled. Patterns of typical behaviour may be established which could prove valuable in the design of workshop equipment.

Observation may also be helpful in checking the validity of data supplied, for instance, about certain characteristics of production.

An interesting case[3] of the effective use of observation occurred when an initial assessment was being made of the market shares of glass bottles for food packaging by a company planning to build a new factory to make glass bottles. Teams of researchers visited supermarkets and noted manufacturers' identity marks on the base of bottled foods. From this observational check, all major suppliers of bottles to each food manufacturer were identified; also, the penetration of imported bottles was assessed. This observational research tactic was followed by a series of personal interviews.

Another application of observational techniques recorded by Hague[3] was connected with research into the information needs of transport and distribution managers. In response to conventional survey enquiries, they stated that they rarely used information to fulfil their duties. But from a later series of observations, it became apparent that several types of information, e.g. route planning data and pricing lists, were actually used.

As observed in Chapter 2, this technique of acquiring knowledge is prone to bias, so observers should be specially trained to maintain, as far as possible, objectivity. Recording of observed behaviour should be systematic, and to encourage this it would be advisable to have standardized report sheets.

Telephone surveys

In Chapter 5, telephone surveying techniques were seen to be growing in popularity in consumer enquiries, and new computer-based technologies have resulted in almost 'instant information'.

Industrial marketing research has also made increasing use of telephone surveys, although this approach has obvious restrictions. It cannot be used, for example, for very lengthy enquiries involving considerable detail, or where some research would be needed before answers could be given, although it may well be useful where the information sought is of a fairly rudimentary nature. In addition, as already noted, it is often used in forming sampling frames.

In a survey of the market potential for a new, small vending machine suitable only for serving between 6 and 30 employees, telephone interviews effectively filtered out suitably sized firms and institutions and information was collected from them at relatively low cost.

Before telephoning prospective respondents, some planning should be done; for example, researchers should either prepare a well-structured questionnaire so that time is used productively, or write down the main topics of investigation in a logical progression. In addition, make sure that answers can be recorded adequately, perhaps by marking off appropriate codes or entering the information given on relevant data sheets.

It is particularly important to introduce quickly and clearly the nature of the survey and its objectives, to ensure that the person answering the telephone (or those to whom the call is transferred) is knowledgeable and able to give valid information.

Computer-assisted telephone interviewing (CATI) is a method of gathering survey data through linking computer technology and telecommunications, thus eliminating paper questionnaires (see Chapter 6 for extended discussion). Various versions of CATI have been developed; they share a common basic procedure. An interviewer reads questions (displayed on a VDU) to telephoned respondents, whose responses are recorded by keyboard. The system might be applicable to fairly straightforward organizational surveys, and, as indicated in Chapter 5, is widely used in corporate image, financial, local authority, and other surveys involving matters that do not need depth investigation.

CAPI (computer-assisted personal interviewing), developed from CATI, occurs when interviewers, equipped with laptop computers, conduct face-to-face interviews and, as seen in Chapter 2, it is successfully used in European and other surveys.

Since the late 1990s, the internet has been developing as an alternative (or complementary) and relatively low-cost and speedy methodology for marketing research enquiries. As indicated in Chapter 5, this innovatory technique can be productive over a range of research topics, including those connected with professional activities, technical industries and the service sector of the economy. It is dependent on the availability and quality of specialist lists of internet users which could be used as sampling frames; such lists are more likely to relate to professional activities and the newer industries, as discussed earlier. Several market research agencies are now active in on-line research; services available include on-line focus groups, group discussions and panels.

Mail surveys

Mail surveys are frequently chosen for research in industrial markets. They are particularly valuable where the population is large and, perhaps, widely dispersed. Superficially, this method of enquiry is attractive in terms of economy, simplicity, and speed. But closer examination of the real costs involved should be made; apart from printing and postage charges, which will be relatively modest, proportionate charges for overheads and salaries should be added. These latter costs should cover the preparatory work, such as drafting the questionnaire, and the subsequent task of analysis and interpretation. Postal questionnaires are not easy to write. Since no interviewer is present to interpret the questions, they must be free from ambiguity. Several pilotings may be necessary; these obviously involve time and cost.

Another aspect to be carefully considered is the real cost of mail surveys, namely, the total cost of the operation spread over the number of effective replies received. The valid reply rate may often result in doubling or trebling the original 'crude' estimate distributed over the total number of questionnaires posted.

In addition, some attempt should be made to compare the values of different methods of survey. This entails studying not merely comparative costs, but also considering the quality of the findings of alternative methods, such as postal surveys and personal interviews. Admittedly, the initial overall costs of a postal questionnaire may be only half of those involved in a personal interview covering domestic products, and very substantially less than personal interviewing in an industrial survey. But the true costs depend on effective response rates and these vary significantly.

Various experiments have been made to assess the effects on response rates of variations in the layout and printing of questionnaires, covering letters and reply-paid facilities. In general, no clear conclusions are apparent; many factors – including sponsorship – affect the success of surveys. The physical presentation of a survey should not, of course, be neglected: it is wise – and good business practice to ensure that the recipient forms a favourable attitude to the survey from the onset, so due and detailed attention should be given to all its aspects.

Hague refers[3] to the 'interest factor' – the interest that the respondent has in the subject of the survey as affecting the response rate of a postal survey. 'A postal survey aimed at people who have just bought a new truck will generate a high response (over 30 per cent) because they are interested in the vehicle.' Whereas, he says, if the enquiry concerned the type of pen he used, 'the response rate would probably be around 5 per cent, because the subject of the survey is not so compelling'.[3] Hence, postal surveys should be confined to topics or products in which those to be sampled are believed to be personally involved and interested. Professionally relevant issues, for example those concerning health, safety and welfare, generally attract high response rates which are correlated with interest in the subjects being surveyed. Lack of identification with the topic of a particular survey is almost certain to result in a low response rate.

Since mail surveys involve self-completion questionnaires, motivating respondents to cooperate is a major factor in achieving acceptable response rates. If response rates are low, serious biases are likely to be present in the data; despite this problem, some surveys present data which, on examination, have been derived from lamentably low response rates, and the findings deserve to be treated with considerable reservations.

Non-response is a serious limitation of postal surveys. The greater the response, the more widely costs can be spread, and although this economic aspect is relatively important, the principal concern of researchers is the likelihood that non-respondents are significantly different from respondents in their attitudes towards the products under survey. The reasons for non-response are not known, and these may, in fact, be directly relative to the problem surveyed. It is advisable to make some sort of check on non-respondents, either by telephone or personal interviewing, in order to establish reasons for non-response. Data thus obtained can be compared with those secured from respondents.

Non-response may also be attributable to ambiguous questions which confuse would-be respondents who eventually discard the questionnaire. Some questionnaires may be unreasonable in the amount of information demanded, either being too lengthy or capable of being answered only after considerable reference to records.

As far as possible, survey questionnaires (with covering letters) should be addressed to those people able to deal with them effectively. This may involve patient enquiry in the course of building sampling frames, so that key personnel are identified. With some complex investigations, it may be helpful to subdivide the questionnaire into specific managerial areas of interest, so that the complete survey can be dealt with more conveniently. Direct posting of questionnaire sections can be done, or it may be possible to distribute these through the chief executive's office.

A mail survey[4] in the US involved a sample of 481 international freight forwarders, equally divided into pre-contact and no pre-contact groups; the former companies were sent a postcard about a week before the survey started indicating that they would shortly receive a mail survey and that their participation was essential for the success of the enquiry. The postcard bore the name of the sponsoring university on both sides and was signed by a senior faculty member of the research team. Of the initial sample of 481, an effective response rate of 23.6 per cent (104) was achieved. After the second mailing, the response rate for firms which had been sent a pre-contact postcard was 27.6 per cent, and for those who had not received a postcard it was 19.54 per cent. It is apparent that post-card notification of commercial organizations, such as freight forwarders, can be an effective means of improving responses to mail surveys.

Some method of following up non-respondents should be devised. Inevitably, this extends the time taken to complete the survey, and, of course, adds to the cost. Two reminder letters are customary, often at 14-day intervals. Replies received as the result of reminders should be carefully scrutinized to see if they differ significantly from early respondents. Dealing with social surveys, Moser[5] has commented that it would appear to be very reasonable to regard respondents to follow-up appeals as representative of all non-respondents rather than of initial respondents. This observation may well be borne in mind in industrial marketing research.

The popularity of postal surveys with researchers should be balanced by a clear understanding of the problems involved in using them. This appreciation will encourage better research design leading, in turn, to more reliable research findings.

Qualitative research

The valuable contributions made by qualitative research were explored in Chapter 8, and some of the principal techniques involved were described, mostly in relation to consumer products and services. However, some of these research techniques may be applied successfully in organizational market enquiries and, as proposed earlier, a multi-technique approach, involving the use of several different research methods, makes up a sound research design. Potential problems associated with one particular research method are minimized by adopting an imaginative approach which recognizes the value of combining quantitative and qualitative research techniques. An integrated research strategy is more likely to result in data that are of real value to decision-makers in industry, commerce and the public sector services. Quantitative results by themselves lack insights into perceptions, motivations and attitudes; such insights come from well-devised qualitative enquiries.

Group discussions

The technique of group discussions was referred to in Chapter 8, and it was seen to have usefulness in generating freer responses to enquiries about particular problems, often connected with household products. This qualitative research technique also has useful applications in industrial marketing investigation.

In business-to-business markets, group discussions among production engineers, marketing managers or financial specialists can result in a frank and valuable exchange of ideas and experience about particular aspects of their work, a company's product range, market performance, etc. Experts tend to react quite sharply to the views they hear expressed by fellow group members. As in well-run consumer discussion groups, the moderator should encourage participation and steer discussions so that they result in gaining insights into particular problems or opportunities. Panels of industrial users could be recruited for group discussions in order to assess, for example, their professional views on emerging trends in their industry, perhaps related to innovative production processes and new product opportunities.

Associated closely with the technique of *group discussion*, is the technique of *depth interviewing*, which is designed to collect sensitive information that may not be readily available from routine market research enquiries. In the relaxed atmosphere of a typical non-directive interview, perceptions and other behavioural influences are explored; these might relate to safety or hygiene procedures in industrial plants or commercial offices.

Continuous research

There is some evidence of panel research (see Chapter 8) in industrial markets. Some truck firms, for example, operate 'user panels', but this technique is by no means as widely used as in consumer product marketing research. There are opportunities, it would appear, for drawing systematically on the experience of customers, although the generic problems of ensuring representativeness and active participation are likely to discourage experiments.

A number of panel-type services have been developed over recent years in some specific industrial and commercial markets, such as agro-chemicals, ethical pharmaceuticals and office equipment.

Omnibus surveys

BMRB operates a monthly telephone omnibus survey of 1000 department heads over various industries. Audience Selection organizes a 'Key Directors Omnibus' survey based on a sample of 400 telephone enquiries each quarter.

KEYPOINT

Aspects of primary data

Sampling frames

Expert informants

Consumption factors

Sampling

Questionnaires

Interviewing

Observational techniques

Qualitative techniques

Group discussions

User panels

Omnibus surveys

Conclusion

As stressed in Chapter 2, it is desirable to develop a creative research strategy using a well-balanced mix of methodologies in order to achieve valid and reliable findings.

Industrial marketing research has a long way to go before it is used as extensively as consumer product research. The problems of industry are no less vital than those of manufacturers of consumer products, and in times of difficult trading it is more important than ever to assist the process of decision-making by gathering accurate information about the problem in hand.

In general, British industry has neglected marketing and has undertaken comparatively little marketing research, perhaps because of some in-built prejudice about using techniques of management which have become closely associated with supermarket trading.

Technical and industrial marketing enquiries are seldom easy; often they are demanding in their complexity and call for the highest skills in research practice. Over 30 years ago, it was said[6] that British industry suffers from a removable uncertainty – it does not pay sufficient attention to marketing research. While there are signs of a more ready interest in industrial marketing research, there is still a long way to go before there is general acceptance of its vital importance to the successful marketing of industrial and technical goods and services.

11.5 Aspects of marketing research for the service sector

In common with the industrial sector, the service sector of the economy, as a whole, was slow to adopt a marketing orientation. Still less did organizations in both the public and private services realize that marketing research techniques could help in identifying opportunities for them to serve their customers more effectively, as well as opening new opportunities for their services.

Financial services

The joint stock banks, for instance, perceived no need to market their services professionally and, because of this, no marketing research was done. In 1975, Robert Worcester, a leading market and opinion researcher, observed that the terms 'marketing' and 'banking' were considered to be mutually exclusive by British bankers.[7] Since those days the financial services have experienced unprecedented turbulence and competition.

Marketing is now widely practised by the banks, insurance companies, building societies and other service industries. Many also use marketing research to monitor their markets, including the evaluation of competitors' activities. It is almost inconceivable that about 30 years ago the general managers of the clearing banks who had responsibility for marketing (such as it was) had no effective means of detecting brand share movements, 'much less of explaining why they had occurred'.[7]

However, the picture today is very different: financial services and the public sector services are now two of the fastest growing areas of marketing research in the UK.

Notable innovations in banking services did, in fact, occur in 1989, when the Midland Bank (now HSBC) introduced telephone banking through its subsidiary FirstDirect – a bank without branches but with all transactions effected by phone. This pioneering service developed from an idea generated by a think-tank. It was realized that competitive pricing would necessitate a centralized, low-cost operation, and from research it was known that current account holders rarely had any personal contact with their bank managers. Since face-to-face relationships were no longer influential, the next best thing was the telephone. So, telebanking – FirstDirect – was developed, targeted at 22–44-year-olds, ABC1s. This financial organization now offers personal computer banking services.

In the insurance industry, DirectLine, started by an imaginative entrepreneur in 1985 and subsequently bought by the Royal Bank of Scotland, revolutionized the car insurance market. Household insurance was later added to the range of DirectLine's services. The dramatic success of this new entrant inevitably attracted competitors who opened up further telephone insurance facilities. The rapid acceptance of telephone-linked financial services has, of course, been facilitated by the significant increase in domestic telephone installations (see Chapters 3 and 5). The tele-culture was born; it was to be the prelude to the Web culture of the internet (see Chapter 5). In 1999, the first interactive TV banking service, '*Open*' was launched by BSkyB, BT, HSBC and Matsushita. Prudential also floated EGG, the first stand-alone internet banking operation, which attracted a million customers in just 18 months. The Co-operative Bank followed with Smile. In March 2000, Peter Wood, the original founder of DirectLine, returned to the UK insurance market, by linking with Halifax, the former building society which became a bank, to launch e-sure.com. This internet insurance service sells car and household insurance as well as insurance to small businesses.

The trend towards on-line banking is apparent across Europe: France's Mintel, a telephone-based interactive system, has been operating since the early 1980s, although its success 'is now proving a barrier to the take-up of internet banking'.[8] In the four Scandinavian countries internet banking is being adopted, especially in Finland. The four big German banks are all on-line, 'even if their strategies seem somewhat confused'.[8] But in some countries, such as Ireland, Spain, Greece and Italy, face-to-face banking is still generally favoured, so on-line progress is not so marked.

In 1989, the Prudential Assurance commissioned Research International[9] to undertake qualitative research concerned with branding and personal services; to no one's surprise, the conclusion was that branding was the key means of discriminating between companies, and it appeared to be under-used in the financial services sector. While 'the Pru' had, over years, built up a strong image of security, there were also negative perceptions of its being old-fashioned, staid and unexciting. A new corporate identity was designed, linked with an aggressive advertising campaign, resulting in a transformed corporate image. Various qualitative studies revealed that 'the Pru' had successfully shaken out of its 'stuck-in-the-mud' image, and was now perceived as a modern organization.

Prudential again benefited from market research when, in 1994, they wished to ensure that their marketing and sales literature, which covered a vast and diverse range of services and market segments, conveyed a consistent brand image. Dewe Rogerson research[10] and Prudential marketing and design specialists set up a series of extended focus groups and one-to-one interviews concentrating, for clarity of research, on personal pensions. All participants were prime pension prospects, as defined by Prudential. They were asked to note and evaluate particular aspects of an 'ideal' pensions brochure. Research findings from each group were communicated in a 'design workbook', which formed the basis for a design brief and guide when promotional communications concerned with other specific branded services marketed through the Prudential's international network were being developed.

Continuous tracking studies of the overall perceptions and image of Halifax's advertising include information on a range of key factors, such as awareness levels, communication of important messages, image perception, and brand values (see Chapter 10 for discussion of tracking studies).

Clerical Medical Investment Group, a relatively unknown, medium-sized life assurance company, has used market research in the development of its long-term marketing strategy and also distinctive corporate brand. This 170-year-old company traditionally sold its services through independent brokers and so had a low public profile. Like its competitors, it has only fairly recently – in the 1990s – developed full-service marketing activities.

Two challenges were faced

1. how to survive against major competitors in an overcrowded market and develop an effective brand identity; and

2. what contribution could marketing research make to solve such problems?

The research programme, undertaken by consultants, included desk research, geodemographic profiling of existing customers, telephone and postal enquiries, group discussions and depth interviews, and tracking studies. These varied activities were designed to provide information on market trends, competitors, customers, distribution, brand image perception, and communications effectiveness. From analyses of the data Clerical Medical was able to identify the most suitable strategic position to adopt, viz. a focus strategy which concentrated on only one market segment. In its case, this related to independent financial advisers (IFAs), who are particularly important sources of financial advice for professional people (defined as both 'traditional' and 'modern' professionals covering an extensive range of expertise), and also retired professionals.

A communications strategy incorporating television, and consumer and trade press advertising was launched in 1990 and carried through to early 1992. Millward Brown Insurance Tracking data revealed encouraging increases in awareness in target segments, with low levels of wastage.

Although, as Clerical Medical freely admits,[11] it is 'virtually impossible to disentangle the impact of all the factors which influence sales', the facts are that sales to 'professionals' were well ahead of the market in 1990 and 1991, and this trend was persisting. Clerical Medical's experience indicates that well-devised marketing research can provide highly valuable information to guide a specialized service firm to expand, even in increasingly competitive conditions.

KEYPOINT

Services sector: financial

Generally slow to adopt marketing orientation

Financial services now use marketing research widely

Notable innovations: telephone banking: FirstDirect; cash points; more competitive behaviour; DirectLine insurance; TV banking service 'OPEN'; Internet banking; Internet insurance: e.sure.com; Prudential (EGG Bank)

Travel and leisure research

The travel and leisure industries take an increasingly large share of consumers' expenditure in a developed country like Britain. Tourism and sport attract vast sums of money which are competed for by hotel chains, restaurateurs, air, sea, and land travel organizations, insurance companies, 'special activity' holiday centres, etc. These leisure markets are highly segmented with distinctive patterns of buying behaviour, expectations, and attitudes.

Several leading market research agencies are very active in offering tailored research facilities to tourist boards, hotel groups, motoring organizations, and the myriad other firms eager to secure a share of the growing leisure market.

Public sector services

For many generations the town halls of the UK were symbols of local power and patronage. Like the high street banks, they were built to reflect solidity and probity, as well as the aura of knowing what was best for the ratepayers. The wind of change blew past them, although society itself had undergone elemental experiences in its economic and social life. Public expectations have risen, for example, of the leisure facilities supplied by local authorities, as also of the ways in which the banking services could be made more 'user-friendly'.

At one time, the local authorities were often in a virtually monopolistic position in many of the services they provided: schools, day-nurseries, sports and recreational facilities, etc. Since the 1990s, privately-run health and fitness centres have multiplied to cater for those seeking a variety of modern facilities. These discriminating, and often affluent, participants are representative of a more critical and demanding pattern of consumption, which is now evident in other facets of consumption, such as restaurants, retailing, etc.

As seen earlier, the financial services sector has had to regenerate itself by making full use of the advances in technological communication. Competition has become more marked with the steady flow of mergers, and the restructuring of several of the large building societies and insurance companies. Marketing research is now an integral part of the financial services market.

The dynamic nature of commercial investigations has bred in market researchers a sense of urgency, allied with professional commitment to objectivity in all aspects of research activities. This blend of attitudes and experience should not be regarded as useful in industry and commerce, but really of decidedly little value in the public sector. In fact, the history of marketing research suggests otherwise, for survey practice in the UK during the first 30 years or so of the twentieth century stemmed from social investigations, stimulated mostly by pioneering social reformers who were disturbed by the distressing living conditions of the working classes.

The widening horizons of marketing research may be noted from the variety of problems which leading research agencies have been involved with over recent years. For example, the Harris Research Centre, now part of Taylor Nelson Sofres, has surveyed the problems of hypothermia among the elderly, unemployment among Black people in a London borough, and the relationships between Asian young people and their parents as they grow up in Western society. Public Attitude Surveys has undertaken many surveys related to social security and housing, and also evaluative studies of government policies and interventions. BMRB and four other leading research agencies formed a consortium to deal with large-scale research projects in the public sector.

Policy making in the public sector is frequently influenced by political creeds; the philosophies of the ruling party are dominant. Objective survey data, if collected at all, may play a limited role during discussions. Instead of seeking data to support value judgements, policy makers should use professional research in a creative way: to find out, for instance, about people's emerging needs, some of which may be matters of personal preference and decision-making which lie outside the orbit of the public sector. But there are other issues, such as the role of public libraries in this growing culture of the World Wide Web, as discussed in Chapter 5, which require very careful evaluation.

Consultation itself is not enough, and survey research should be designed not just to provide statistical data but also to give insights into the behaviour, expectations and experiences of those who use specific public services. When the National Audit commissioned MORI, a leading research firm, to examine the official services provided to families on income support, it was found that 53 per cent had no problems; 35 per cent had some; and 12 per cent had a lot. However, the survey also revealed that 36 per cent thought that their money had arrived late; 31 per cent thought that they had to wait too long to be seen; and 25 per cent thought they had been given the wrong amount of money or that their claims took too long to process. Delay, error and communication lay, therefore, at the heart of their complaints, and this extra information gave valuable guidance for improving specific aspects of the service.

For many years, the Government *Social Survey* has been responsible for conducting a very wide range of surveys covering trade, health, housing, social welfare, etc. The excellence of these reports has helped significantly to raise the general level of research standards and practices. In addition, there are official censuses and surveys carried out by various ministries dealing with demographic analyses, family expenditure patterns, employment, etc., and published by the Office for National Statistics (ONS).

Research sponsored by the Department of the Environment evaluated road safety publicity, particularly related to the use of car seat belts; a series of controlled area experiments with media advertising was continually monitored. The results showed both a direct and positive relationship between advertising exposure and the extent of seat belt wearing. Alternative advertising themes were evaluated for their influence on motorists' attitudes towards road safety practices, especially the regular use of seat belts. Of all the themes used, the catch-phrase 'clunk-click' appears to have been the most memorable and to have been effective in 'converting' non-wearers to wearers. Subsequently, legislation enforced the use of car seat belts.

Survey findings are not necessarily acted upon in ways in which the researchers might expect, as happened with the Royal Commission on Local Government some years ago. Survey findings had indicated concern about remoteness and a wish for participation in local affairs, whereas the Report subsequently recommended that greater responsibility should be given to much larger and more remote forms of local government. Another example of the apparently limited influence of survey findings occurred in the research commissioned by the Committee on the Age of Majority set up by the Labour Government of 1966–70. The findings – that young people between the ages of 18 and 21 had little interest in becoming full adults at 18 and were in no way dissatisfied with their existing legal status – were, in fact, ignored by the Committee, which recommended that the age of majority should be reduced to 18 years.

On the other hand, survey research was able to demonstrate that, contrary to the motoring organizations' representations, there was considerable public support (including a majority of motorists) for the legislation in the late 1960s which introduced the 70 mph speed limit and also the breathalyser.

Researching the arts

In advanced, prosperous communities the arts flourish, even though some manifestations of the so-called pop culture may lack universal appeal.

Marketing research can (and should) be applied in identifying patrons, their preferences, living styles, media habits, travelling arrangements, etc. Theatres, music concerts, cultural exhibitions, museums and art galleries can all benefit from specific information to guide them in developing programmes and facilities which are likely to win the favour of their customers.

In 1987 and again in 1992, the Market Research Society's journal contained special papers on marketing research applications in a wide range of artistic enterprises. It should be said that the adoption of marketing research methodologies in no way debases cultural and aesthetic standards; rather the reverse is likely. Management should be encouraged to be responsive to the needs of their patrons, and enhance the quality and diversity of their particular presentations. The Arts Council has developed a research database and has commissioned large-scale studies. With such high-level endorsement, the various arts activities in Britain should experience no distaste in finding out how marketing research can assist them in their artistic ambitions.

KEYPOINT

Public sector services need market research

Education

Health

Social services

Planning

Recreation etc.

Government Social Survey

Departmental Surveys

Royal Commission

Marketing research into community needs gives objective information to guide policy making

Summary

Business-to-business marketing research covers a very wide spectrum of economic and social activities in both the private and public sectors, and includes industrial and commercial research, the service industries of banking, insurance, leisure, etc., and the public sector services such as education, welfare, and national and local government.

Basically, the methodologies of marketing research apply across all these various sector activities, but variations will occur in, for example, sampling, technical and professional areas of questioning, and interviewing techniques.

Industrial markets have complex structures; buying behaviour is frequently complex; derived demand and end-use markets are distinctive features of industrial marketing research.

Developed communities depend significantly on the service industries. Several leading marketing research agencies offer tailor-made facilities for the service industries.

As always: before field work is considered, full value should be obtained from published data, both official and commercial.

Review and discussion questions

1. From a research standpoint, what are the principal differences in investigating industrial as opposed to consumer decision-making.

2. How would you respond to the view that qualitative rather than quantitative research instruments are more appropriate for the study of industrial DMUs?

3. Industrial marketing research often involves personal interviews with senior management. In what ways might such interviews differ from standard consumer interviews both with regard to choice of research instrument and method of administration?

4. Discuss the relative merits of telephone surveys compared to mail surveys in industrial marketing research. Your answer should address in particular the problem of minimizing non-response levels.

▶

5. An insurance company wishes to study the salesperson–client relationship in the marketing of life assurance policies. What research method and survey instrument would you recommend?

6. A bank manager claims that customer transaction records are by far the most effective, speedy, and cost-efficient means of consumer research for banks. To what extent do you agree with this sentiment?

CAMEO CASE: ATC Colours

ATC Colours, a subsidiary of a Spanish company, was founded in 1989 and is located in Cheadle, Staffordshire. The company is small, with a staff of only 10, and not unsurprisingly the Managing Director is directly involved in most aspects of the company operations. ATC Colours is a specialist manufacturer of ceramic colourings and glazes, and sells exclusively to companies in the ceramics industry. ATC produces a range of onglaze colourings, underglaze colours, glazes, and other related products; the onglaze and underglaze colours tend to be sold on a daily basis, and the glazings on a weekly basis.

ATC Colours feels that the secret of its success in the highly competitive ceramics industry lies in its flexible and rapid response to customer orders/enquiries. This is both a consequence and a determinant of its marketing/sales strategy, in which it emphasizes the development of close relationships with customers, encouraging direct customer contact and joint problem solving. Contact with both existing business and potential new customers is through the MD and a technician, emphasizing the highly technical aspects of the business, and the

company's emphasis on business relationship development.

The company operates exclusively in the domestic UK market, and over the last five years has benefited from consistent and substantial growth, with a 200 per cent increase in turnover, from £250 000 in 1994–1995, to £750 000 in 1998–1999.

ATC Colours has generally used its own personnel for marketing research, and mostly as a means of determining areas for new product development. Specific research objectives have included identifying market opportunities, and determining pricing levels. Of the four product markets in which the company operates (onglaze colour, underglaze colour, glaze, medium/covercoat), direct liaison with customers is considered the best method.

Marketing research is also used by the company to monitor the activities of its competitors: as already highlighted, close liaison with customers is the preferred means of keeping an eye on the competition, although specific objectives and the frequency of monitoring vary according to the specific product-market:

Monitoring competitor activities:
Specific objectives, means and frequency of monitoring

Product market	Specific objectives	Means of monitoring	Frequency of monitoring
Onglaze colour	Product awareness	Customer liaison	Daily/on-going basis
Underglaze colour	Pricing levels	Customer liaison	Daily/on-going basis
Glaze	Pricing levels	Customer liaison	Daily/on-going basis
Medium and covercoat	Product awareness	Customer liaison	Daily/on-going basis

▶

Questions

1. Discuss the relative advantages and disadvantages of using ATC's own personnel to carry out marketing research.

2. In view of the 200 per cent increase in turnover over the last five years, do you think that the company can continue to use its existing personnel? If so, what pressures are they increasingly likely to face in the future, assuming that growth continues at the present rate? If not, what other means of obtaining marketing intelligence should the company adopt, and why?

3. To what extent and why is it advantageous to rely heavily on existing customers when researching competitor activities?

Jonathan S. Swift

References

1. Chisnall, Peter M., *Strategic Business Marketing*, Prentice-Hall, Hemel Hempstead, 1995.
2. 'Wealth in services', *The Economist*, 21 February 1993.
3. Hague, Paul, *The Industrial Market Research Handbook*, Kogan Page, London, 1992.
4. Murphy, Paul R., James M. Daley, and Douglas R. Dalenberg, 'Exploring the effects of postcard prenotification on industrial firms' response to mail surveys', *Journal of Market Research Society*, vol. 33, no. 4, 4 October 1991.
5. Moser, C. A., and G. Kalton, *Survey Methods in Social Investigation*, Heinemann, London, 1971.
6. Carter, C. F., and B. R. Williams, 'The characteristics of technically progressive firms', *Journal of Industrial Economics*, vol. 7, no. 2, 1959.
7. Worcester, R. M., and R. Stubbs, 'Marketing research for financial services', ESOMAR, Versailles, 1975.
8. 'Smile, you're on the net', *The Economist*, vol. 353, no. 8148, 4 December 1999.
9. Churchill, David, 'Fresh face from the Pru', *The Financial Times*, 30 September 1990.
10. Lyng, Anita, 'How the man from the Pru got the message to the people', *Researchplus*, Market Research Society, March 1995.
11. Shelton, David, 'What have clerics and medics in common with market researchers and computer programmers? A study in corporate brand building in financial services', *Journal of Market Research Society*, vol. 34, no. 3, July 1992.

International marketing research

- Note specific nature of international marketing research and typical approaches

- Be aware of particular importance of desk research

- Understand value of official assistance in developing overseas business

- Discuss principal methods of research overseas and their relative effectiveness

12.1 Introduction

For many firms, marketing overseas is taken for granted: without it they could not exist. Some are large multinational or transnational organizations with years of trading experience, developed through skilful negotiation and backed by vast corporate resources. Others are small and medium-sized businesses, headed by energetic and talented entrepreneurs who, with the daring of merchant adventurers, have identified market opportunities which they have exploited successfully with specialized products and services. While the scale of their operations will clearly be different from those giants who seek to dominate their markets, the principles of marketing apply equally if they are to succeed in the highly competitive markets in which most business, home or overseas, is now transacted.

Sir John Harvey-Jones,[1] the former dynamic leader of ICI, stressed that even huge organizations faced international competition in their own home markets. ICI experienced this from subsidiaries of competitors like Dow, Du Pont, Hoechst, Badische, Bayer and Ciba-Geigy who openly challenged them. In turn, ICI companies fought for business in the US, Germany and Switzerland.

No firm, however large, is immune for long from the challenges and risks which are inevitable in competitive conditions; they have to scan the world for suitable business opportunities to which they can apply their specific sets of skills and experience. They cannot afford to adopt a random approach and hope that 'things will work out, somehow'. Today, that is asking for real trouble and a short, hard corporate life, probably ending in bankruptcy or a forced takeover.

Over the years, many reports have been published – and doubtless many more will appear – that cast withering glances at the performance of British exporters. To the understandable annoyance of some hard-working and efficient firms, these criticisms have caught the eye of commentators in the mass media who have tended to paint an unfavourable picture of Britain's exporting activities. But despite generalizations, it has to be admitted that complacency is seductive and leads to disaster; the sting of criticism can act like a spur to better performance, even from those who are already pulling more than their weight in the never-ceasing tug-of-war against foreign competition in both home and export markets.

One of the principal accusations which has been made regularly about British exporters is that they fail to recognize the crucial importance of *critical mass* in achieving success in overseas markets. Critical mass – a term borrowed from nuclear physics – refers, as Drucker has noted,[2] to the smallest fraction which is big enough to alter the nature and behaviour of the whole. A company needs to attain a minimum level of size in order to achieve critical mass, if it is to make its mark in a competitive market or sector – and these should be carefully targeted to ensure that corporate resources are efficiently focused. This strong advice was echoed in a report over 20 years ago by BETRO,[3] which was highly critical of certain aspects of British exporting performance, including the tendency to dissipate limited resources over too many countries.

This tendency to spread exporting efforts too widely was also noted in American companies. One telecommunications equipment company tried to sell its products through agents in 50 countries rather than determine precisely which countries offered the best long-term potential and were worth increased investment. Unfortunately the company persisted in its 'shot-gun' approach and never developed strongly in any of these markets.

The attraction of critical mass motivated the giant organizations ICI and Du Pont to develop 'swap deals' involving their nylon and acrylic businesses; BASF, also, secured critical mass in the European polypropylene market.

Critical mass does not necessarily have to be limited to mass markets; selective targeting enables small and medium-sized companies to build up strong competitive positions in market segments or niches, where opportunities exist which are favourable to the scale of their operations. These may relate to highly specialized technologies or knowledge-based industries, such as those which are typical of electronics and computer software applications.

Concentration on key markets, as the BETRO report[3] urged, is the key to success and is the natural partner of a critical mass policy. Competitive advantage in a whole range of industrial and commercial activity is created and developed through a sound grasp of a company's resources – manpower skills, management abilities, trading experience, core technologies, financial skills – and thorough knowledge of the comparative advantages of specific trading opportunities. Matching resources (existing and planned) to carefully selected markets lays the foundation for corporate success. Companies should realize, of course, that whatever markets they choose to enter will, if they are growing, attract competition. Further, product/service innovation is likely to put pressure on existing suppliers as well as on those who are seeking to establish themselves in a new environment. Because of the dynamic nature of many, if not most, markets today, key markets may change their characters and become less attractive to the suppliers who originally targeted them.

Hague[4] has drawn attention to the fact that although there are about 150 nation states, each offering some potential opportunities for exporters, 'only a quarter of these are of sufficient size, political disposition or state of economic development to warrant study except in special circumstances'. On the bases of GNP and percentage of population, he identified 'key countries' which deserve special investigation: *Western Europe*: 30 per cent of global GNP and 8 per cent of global population; *'Anglo-America'*: 24 per cent of global GNP and 6 per cent population; *South East Asia*: 18 per cent global GNP and 55 per cent population; *South America*: 3 per cent global GNP, 5 per cent population; *Caribbean*: 2 per cent global GNP, 3 per cent population.

It will be seen that while the first two clusters contain only 14 per cent of the world's population, they account for over half of global GNP.

Competitive advantage is a further aspect of successful business operations, as mentioned earlier. According to Porter,[5] a firm may exercise two types of competitive advantage: low relative cost, or differentiation. It could, perhaps, make a comparable product, or offer a comparable service, at lower cost; or a comparable product/service with *enhanced value* that will justify a premium price. What is necessary for success, is to provide customers/clients with greater buyer-value than competitors. Every firm, Porter says,[5] is engaged in 'value activities', which should result in products/services that are attractive to particular kinds of customers. This value-added concept is directly related, of course, to the well-articulated marketing concept of providing customers with 'benefits' – and this can only be done effectively if customers' needs have been expertly studied and assessed.

The principle of competitive advantage appears closely linked to the concept of *leverage*, which states that companies enjoying particular market advantages have developed significant strengths in one feature of their business. This places them in a distinctive competitive position that, for a time at least, enables them to build up their customer base in competitive markets. Admittedly, the factor bestowing leverage is subject to the dynamic conditions of the market, and competitors, for example, might well 'follow the leader', as far as they can, and so reduce or even eliminate the exclusive nature of leverage.

Porter admits, however, that it is difficult, 'though not impossible'[5] for a firm to be both lower-cost and differentiated relative to its competitors. Competitors – as noted – will imitate, and so the firm enjoying competitive advantage for some years will be forced to reconsider its strategy. However, another important variable alleviates threats: competitive scope or 'the breadth of the firm's target within its industry'.[5] In other words, companies must be alert to the importance of market segmentation: different market segments develop (and can be created) to serve different kinds of customers. This strategy gives rise to distinct variations of product, pricing, promotional and distribution policies. Competitive advantage can be fostered, therefore, by astute market sector positioning, ensuring that every aspect of a product, e.g. design, quality, after-sale-service, etc., adds up to total value as *perceived* by identified types of customers.

12.2 Need for marketing research

The various factors just outlined are among those which show how important it is to identify customers' needs, and to plan and offer products and services which are designed to satisfy certain of these needs as fully as possible.

To do this efficiently, it is necessary, first of all, to find out what particular kinds of people want, their buying motivations and other factors influencing demand, and then to make some estimates, in both quantitative and qualitative terms, of likely demand.

Before attempting to devise a marketing strategy – a method of approaching the market – some form of marketing research should be undertaken so that marketing opportunities can be evaluated and related to overall company policy.

It is likely that less will be known about overseas markets than the home market; there will be greater areas of uncertainty – 'grey' areas of undetermined risk which management should attempt to dissipate. Marketing research helps to clear away some of these uncertainties and provides additional information on which management decisions may be taken.

The type of marketing information required for successful overseas trading is basically similar to that needed for the home market. Often, however, it is more difficult to obtain reliable information about export markets, but the problem should be approached along very similar lines.

The key to success in any market is to understand the needs of people and of organizations; to gain sensitive insights into the ways in which these many varieties (and scale) of needs are satisfied through the ownership or use of certain kinds of products and services. Some of these needs are generic, others more specific and capable of almost infinite extension. The fulfilment of needs is largely dependent on the environment in which people live, both globally and personally. Motives and needs are inter-dependent: the former activate actions to satisfy the latter, e.g. for transport, food, entertainment, etc. Motivation is subject to personal perception of needs, which evolve from physical, psychological, socio-cultural and other factors.

Marketing research provides the means of acquiring objective knowledge about the buying habits and preferences of certain groups of people living in particular countries or regions. Consumption is often closely bound up with social, religious and other cultural norms and value systems. People are alike in many ways, but they are also different as well. Crude assumptions that what sells in the home market is bound to sell overseas deservedly leads to disaster.

KEYPOINT

Essential for successful international marketing

Customer knowledge: needs of people/organizations; motivations, attitudes, perceptions, etc.

Critical mass: size needed to achieve impact markets/segments

Concentration on key markets: natural partner of critical mass

Competitive advantage: develop products/services with low relative cost, enhanced value (value-added concept); use product/market positioning

12.3 Preliminary evaluation

Before committing themselves to overseas trading, companies would do well to pose themselves a few questions and to answer these as honestly as possible.

1. *Whether*:   Overseas markets should be entered?
2. *Where*:   What markets should be selected for development?
3. *When*:   At what time should these markets be tackled?
4. *How*:   What market strategy or strategies should be adopted?

These are certainly demanding questions and the answers may only be forthcoming after careful evaluation of the company's corporate strategy and overall trading position. For example, the first question might result in the following observations:
Why export? Is it because:

(i)   of surplus capacity?

(ii)   the home market is in a no-growth phase or is saturated?

(iii)   of the pressure of home-market competition?

(vi)   of a unique product or service which has attracted substantial business in the home market and enquiries from abroad?

(v)   of special managerial experience and abilities in overseas trading?

(vi)   the grass is always greener elsewhere?

(vii)   export market opportunities are judged to be more promising than the home market?

(viii) the managing director dreams of a worldwide empire over which he can exercise corporate and personal power?

Clearly, some of these motives are less likely than others to lead to business success. Muddled thinking springs from obscure perceptions of the strengths and weaknesses of a company, so it would be constructive to attempt a relatively fundamental corporate audit.

This audit should involve assessing the knowledge and skills of exporting that lie within the business and which are relevant to the overseas opportunities being considered. New staff may have to be recruited with specific knowledge of certain countries, including language ability. Perhaps some radical restructuring of the marketing department will be necessary to ensure that members of its staff have direct responsibility for specific overseas markets/zones. Overseas ventures are unlikely to be profitable immediately – the earning of profits tends to be a relatively long-haul task – so a very careful appraisal should be made of the costs of market entry and development. Finally, markets should be investigated in depth before committing capital and manpower: this is the responsibility of professional market research, which will be discussed more fully in this chapter.

12.4 Typical approaches

Exporting is often started accidentally: a chance enquiry lands on the desk of the managing director and, almost reluctantly, the firm is involved in overseas business. Other companies become involved through merging or associating in some way with a business that had been exporting for several years.

In other cases, companies adopt an experimental attitude, trying out, by a judicious blend of caution and verve, one or two export markets. With luck and some good judgement, their strategy might be successful, but now they are faced with bigger uncertainties as they raise their sights and aim for more difficult targets. Their fortuitous learn-as-you-go strategy will not be able to cope with the increasing complexity of the market environment.

Yet other companies scan the world, or large sectors of it, for suitable business opportunities. Particular areas are 'short-listed' for more detailed appraisal: from the macro-level to the micro-level of investigation. Research projects could be undertaken in several countries simultaneously, sequentially, or independently. However, it would be necessary to allow for seasonal factors or other special influences, such as political elections, which could distort comparative research of this nature.

These various approaches to exporting are discussed more fully elsewhere,[6] and it was noted that the purest global strategy is said to occur when an organization concentrates as many activities as possible in one country, serving the world from this home base and tightly co-ordinating those activities that must, by their nature, be performed near the buyer. This, in fact, was the strategy adopted by Toyota and many other Japanese firms in the 1960s and 1970s, although, of course, they are now tending to move from merely operating assembly plants overseas to investing in more comprehensive manufacturing and marketing facilities.

The ultimate transition from 'accidental' to full, planned commitment to exporting marks an historic stage in an organization's corporate development, and also in the whole pattern of its marketing responsibilities. Such a significant step affects not just products and distribution arrangements, it profoundly influences the whole philosophy underlying management thought and action; trading horizons become far wider than those traditionally perceived, perhaps for generations.

Increasingly, companies are adopting new and more enterprising attitudes when considering how they can grow their businesses; in some cases, direct investment in production facilities overseas or joint ventures might, as is becoming increasingly evident,[6] be feasible options.

Whatever the approach – simple or sophisticated – to overseas trading, the first and logical step is to seek some basic knowledge of the market(s) which appear to have potential value to a company. This appraisal starts with desk research.

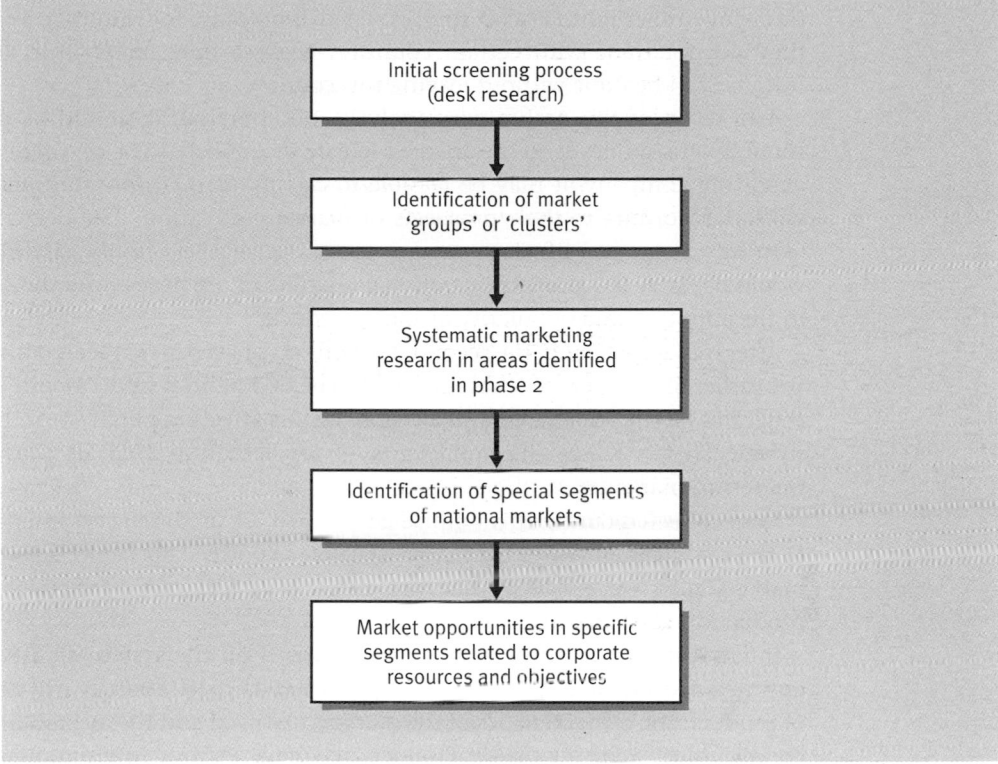

Figure 12.1 Multistage research for international markets

Multi-stage research approach

A multi-stage research operation seeks to obtain general guides and then to isolate and investigate significant market behaviour and trends. The first step, therefore, involves a macro-analysis to identify countries or areas which appear to offer potentially attractive opportunities for market development (see Figure 12.1).

This initial screening will be undertaken by means of desk research. It will entail examination of environmental factors, political and legal constraints to entry and operation, and trading blocs; broad estimates will be made of total market size, past trends and probable future developments, figures relating to per capita income, GNP and similar economic data will also be collected.

12.5 Desk research

Desk research is particularly important in export research; this type of research should be fully exploited before considering field research (see Chapter 2). It may well provide sufficient information for the particular decision which has to be made. It saves time and money, and is particularly valuable in giving an in-depth knowledge of markets. A good grasp of statistical data concerning overseas economies is essential; clearly, in some areas there is a shortage of reliable and readily available information. A great deal of desk research can be done in the UK, where extremely valuable information is freely available from governmental and other sources. There is no cause for would-be exporters to say that they do not trade with certain countries because they know little about them. Desk research can be done without leaving this country.

As a result of this preliminary analysis and appraisal, it should be possible to obtain some general guides as to the areas which are most likely to be of interest to a prospective exporting company. It may be feasible to classify market opportunities by groupings or clusters according to their prospects of market cultivation. The degree of homogeneity existing within identified clusters or groups of markets needs careful investigation. It would be naïve to assume that national boundaries are necessarily the controlling factors in the adoption and popularity of some products.

After initial screening, the second step consists of intensive research into the areas which the earlier filtering process has indicated to be of potential value. Depth knowledge will be sought of buying behaviour and all those factors affecting purchase of the products under survey. This is where the application of segmentation analysis proves to be of vital interest to marketers.

Data collected during this multistage research are analysed and interpreted and related to the resources and objectives of prospective exporters. Specialized segments of national markets may be revealed that will offer manufacturers profitable outlets for their production capacities.

International marketing strategy will be based on the systematic research programme outlined. How far it may be possible to use a standardized strategy will depend on the type of product, the characteristics of the markets involved and the availability, for instance, of comparable advertising media. Products may have a strong international appeal to certain age groups: for example, the promotion of Pepsi-Cola has deliberately fostered an international image. But it would be dangerous to assume that standardization of products and methods of presentation across world markets is the answer to successful exporting.

Government assistance

British Trade International: Export Market Information Service (EMIC)
Official reference library available to exporters on a self-service basis – there are three principal collections.

1. Statistics and Market Information Collection – comprehensive information for all countries trading with UK.
2. Directory Collection – contact information in overseas markets.
3. Multilateral Development Aid Documentation – access to potential business opportunities.

Specific services: statistical and other data available on CD-ROM; country profiles; development plans for developing countries and centrally-planned economies; dictionaries; directories (some on CD-ROM); EMIC publications catalogue; export opportunities and sales leads; internet access; mail order catalogues; market research reports; trade catalogues.

British Trade International: Trade UK
This successor to the Export Intelligence Service (EIS) originated to encourage UK businesses to have an entry on an internet database and ultimately to explore the advantages of electronic commerce through the creation of a 'virtual business park'.

In July 1998, an online database of UK exporters and an export sales lead system superseded the EIS paper-based system.

National Exporters Database (NED): available, free of charge, to any UK exporter or potential exporter with internet access.

Export Sales Leads Service (ESLS): launched in September 1998, and over 20 000 sales leads processed in 18 months. All UK companies on NED are eligible to register, and receive by e-mail, information sent directly from British embassies (and other sources) which matches their profiles. All Trade UK sales leads are stored on a database which customers can use to search for leads outside their own specific profile.

Other services

Economic surveys and reports published by the United Nations and foreign governments are available through HMSO.

Other useful publications include the *Overseas Trade Bulletin,* issued fortnightly by the Confederation of British Industries. The Overseas Directorate of the CBI is divided into special geographical areas with a network of overseas representatives and contacts.

Valuable information on export markets can also be obtained from: European Community Information Office, 8 Storey's Gate, London SW1P 3AT. Tel: 0207 222 8122; and EC/ EFTA Information Unit, Department of Trade and Industry, 1 Victoria Street, London SW1.

Export and import statistics, as summarized in the monthly overseas trade statistics of the UK, can be obtained from: Statistical Office (Bill of Entry Section), HM Customs and Excise, 27 Victoria Avenue, Southend-on-Sea, Essex.

Other sources of data

Central Office of Information (COI), Hercules Road, London SE1 (publicity unit working jointly with BOTB to promote British exports)
Foreign embassies in London
British Export Houses Association
British Standards Institution: 'Technical Help to Exporters' service.
CBI Overseas Reports issued quarterly by Confederation of British Industries.
Institute of Export (publishes *Export*)
Institute of Packaging
Institute of Directors
Chartered Institute of Marketing
Institute of Practitioners in Advertising (IPA)
London World Trade Centre, St Katherine's Dock, London E1
British joint stock banks, merchant banks, and special overseas banks with London offices (e.g. Lloyd's Economic Reports, Barclays Overseas Survey)
OECD: *Foreign Trade Statistics Bulletin*, Series A, *Overall Trade by Countries*, Series B, *Trade by Commodities Analytical Abstracts*
See Appendix 1 for extended listing.

12.6 Scope of investigations

Investigations into overseas markets should be thorough. As indicated in Fig. 12.2, three principal areas require detailed attention. These are not, of course, watertight, isolated

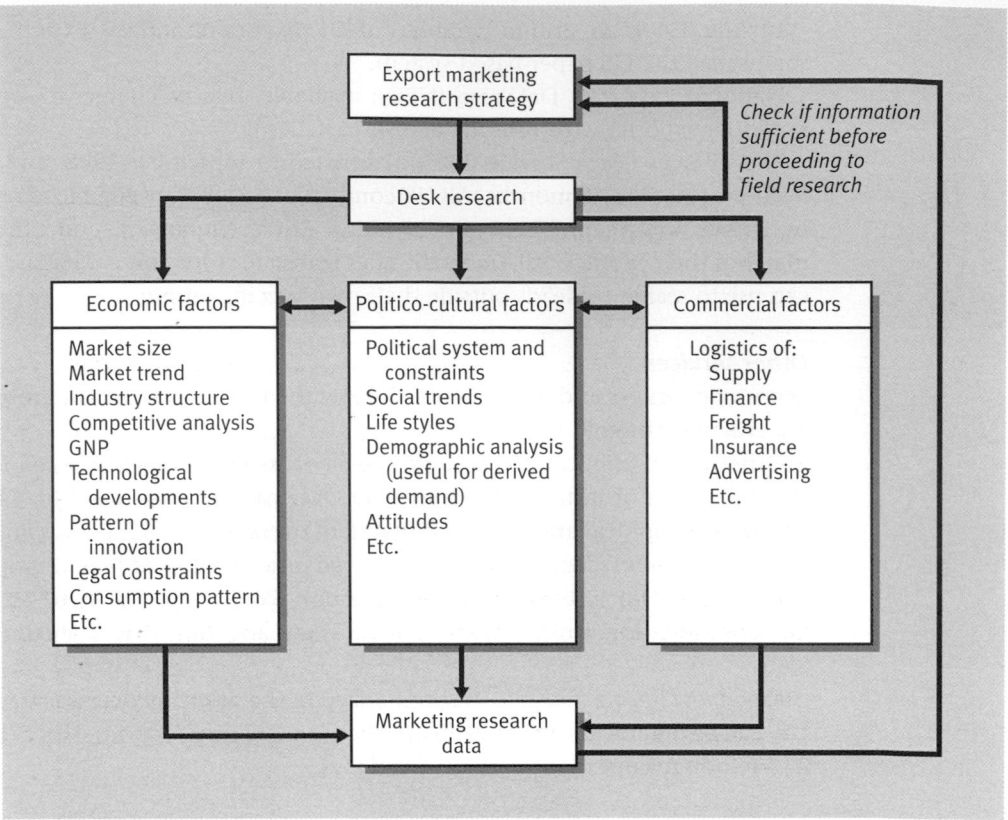

Figure 12.2 Scope of export marketing research

influences: they are interrelated and precise measurement, for example of social trends, is not always feasible or even necessary.

The theory of market segmentation applies wherever marketing is practised. In home markets, demand is popularly analysed by age, sex, social class, cultural values, personality, brand loyalty, attitudes, rate of usage of specific products and services, etc. In overseas markets, similar analyses can be effective in developing suitable marketing strategies, but it would be advisable to examine fully the socio-cultural influences affecting demand. While such factors are often taken for granted in the home market, special care should be taken to understand patterns of consumption that may be distinctly different from those which form part of the traditional culture of the exporting firm. Whirlpool, the large American white-goods corporation, has stated that in developing its European business it plans more standardization of products and marketing, but it also recognizes the importance of bearing in mind that 'globalization should not become a buzz-word . . . there are still local distinctions'.[7]

Electrolux, the Swedish multinational household appliance group is following the production strategies of the automotive and mobile telephone industries in developing a series of common basic 'platforms' or frameworks for its range of products. The first product of this new technology will be a 'euro-oven', to be made at four different plants. The Electrolux strategy follows 'an unsuccessful attempt in 1998 by US rival Whirlpool to produce a single 'world washer', which industry analysts said failed to take account of 'differing national tastes in Europe'.[8] Electrolux intended to note local market preferences.

Economic and politico-cultural factors

Economic factors will include the nature and size of market demand. Although population size is obviously of interest, it may not necessarily indicate the potential value of a market. Some smaller countries, e.g. Sweden, have high purchasing power and are particularly strong markets for certain types of products, e.g. those having a strong design element.

Enquiries would also be concerned with evaluating the nature of competition which may vary significantly over markets. Exporters sometimes overlook the fact that when they enter an overseas market, they are in competition not just with foreign-based competitors, but are also likely to face stiff competition from indigenous suppliers. Market shares should be analysed to discover what particular segments are of greatest interest. These findings should then be related to marketing proposals.

Diverse classifications have been made of the comparative economic development of countries, usually based on GNP, per capita income, and the relative distribution of sources of economic activity, from labour-intensive, agriculture-based countries to low labour density, capital-intensive mass production, and the sophisticated modern technologies of electronics, computer technology, laser applications, etc., to the dominance of the service industries which is a feature of the typical service economy of highly developed countries, such as the US, and the major European countries.

If the criterion of gross national product *per capita* is adopted, three main segments of world markets emerge: (i) industrialized countries (ICs); (ii) developing countries (DCs); (iii) less developed countries (LDCs). The DC segment accounts for 19 per cent of the population and 32 per cent of the income of the world, and because growth rates of income are outpacing those of the IC segment, it is suggested[10] that these developing economies present particularly attractive business opportunities.

Obviously countries differ in terms of economic wealth and of its distribution among the national population (GNP per capita), as various analysts have shown for many years. Another – and perhaps more revealing – evaluation is based on purchasing power parity, which takes into account price levels of similar goods in different countries. This approach reflects rather more realistically the state of the economy, e.g. inflation rates, and the nature of demand for certain kinds of products.

While country classifications are useful in market analyses, it should be borne in mind that these are likely to become outdated as industrialization spreads across the world. Modern technologies and methods of manufacture increasingly contribute to the economic development of countries once largely dependent on commodity products and agricultural produce. Largely through massive investment by the multinational corporations, these countries are rapidly acquiring new economic status in world markets. Because of the transferable nature of modern technologies, production is, in many cases, such as motor vehicles, no longer confined to the old industrialized countries. These new manufacturing centres will generate demands not only for industrial products and components, but also for a wide and growing range of consumer products and services as economies expand and incomes increase.

Politico-cultural factors, like economic factors, also cover a wide spectrum of market influences. Market researchers should endeavour to understand the social and cultural behaviour of consumers in those countries they plan to enter.

In the volatile economic, political and social conditions of the last decade of the twentieth century, countries are changing their relative economic and trading positions. Several of the less developed countries have acquired political and business skills in negotiating with international companies which seek to set up manufacturing bases or to exploit their mineral wealth.

As commented earlier, market analyses need to take account of the many factors influencing buying habits, for instance, related to food preferences, the ways in which it is prepared and the times at which it is eaten. The frequency of purchase, degree of brand awareness and loyalty, price sensitivity, and family behaviour patterns all require investigation. It is also important to check demographic trends, and the extent to which the education, health and welfare services contribute to the health and skills of particular communities. A growing community, whose standards of living are steadily rising, is likely to be interested in quality products that will add to their enjoyment of life.

The importance of understanding cultural aspects of consumption is illustrated by a *Reader's Digest* study which shows that French and German customers consume more spaghetti than Italians. This bizarre finding resulted from a survey question which asked about packaged branded spaghetti. In Italy this product is sold loose and unbranded, whereas in Germany and France it is usually sold in branded packs. The survey findings were valid but did not give the information that was needed.

Another example of misleading research occurred in a survey which indicated that *per capita* consumption of bananas in Germany was double that of the UK. Enquiries about this unusual pattern of consumption revealed the more relevant information that in terms of numbers the *per capita* consumption figures were virtually identical; the significant difference lay in the fact that bananas imported from the Caribbean into the UK tended to be much smaller than those sold to Germany.

In the US and the UK hot, milk-based drinks are marketed principally as bedtime drinks, but in much of Latin America a hot milk drink like *chocolate caliente* is a 'morning drink' or perceived as a 'nice way to start the day'. Also, the popularity of Coca-Cola as a 'morning drink' with American college students would sound appalling to a Latin American accustomed to his *café con leche* for breakfast.[9]

Market analysts should beware of broad classifications of countries or regions which may suggest that the economic, political, and social environment is practically identical. For example, it has been stated[10] that the Middle East is not a homogeneous market with similar political philosophies, economic state of development, language, and culture. 'Too often the term "Middle East" is considered to be synonymous with "Arab"', whereas 'Iran is non-Arab and has the Farsi language'. On the other hand, Arab countries penetrate deeply into Africa and now total 20 countries, such as Sudan and Somalia.

Parts of Europe are highly industrialized with large urban populations and substantial spending power. Other parts are still developing, and in some areas the level of economic activity is low. Research into such markets cannot assume that some homogeneous pattern of European buying behaviour exists; broad generalizations about national characteristics are equally misleading. The EU cannot be viewed as an entity; it is a fairly loose confederation of nearly 360 million people of several nationalities, languages, cultures, and sub-cultures.

Globalization of products already exists in some consumer markets and is increasingly evident: e.g. teenage fashions, jeans, fast-food outlets and sports equipment, but it would be naïve to assume that a 'single European market' will mean identical consumer tastes or habits. These will still need to be researched carefully:

> Shovels, even if the same sort of muck is shovelled with them, are quite differently shaped depending whether you buy them in Italy, Holland, or England. But in all these countries people use the same modern motor diggers. Meat has been butchered differently in different European countries for ages; you couldn't sell an Irish cut of meat in Germany. But the whole of Europe has embraced the Hamburger recently introduced from America.[14]

A research study for the Confederation of British Industry's 1992 information campaign[12] listed several examples of cultural differences which led to market fragmentation. 'Cultural barriers will persist long after other forms of invisible trade walls have been demolished.' Increased mobility reduces the impact of some cultural inhibitions but it does not destroy the whole intricate structure of cultural and sub-cultural preferences. How soon the French will be willing to load their washing machines from the front (like the British) or demand firmly machines that load from the top is open to speculation.

Food manufacturers, such as Nescafé, are well aware of strong regional tastes; Nescafé, for instance, markets 20 different versions of its product under the same label. A 'single market' by no means implies that a single taste will be acceptable.

A British jam manufacturer was puzzled when its initial entry into the German market was unsuccessful. Despite careful planning, it had neglected one critical factor – the product. As in the home market, this was thick and full of fruit, but it was not the sort of jam that the Germans liked, so they did not buy it.

The prospects for a pan-European culture are enthusiastically debated; satellite television networks and radio transmissions will clearly influence consumption habits, but technological innovations are not immune to social and cultural preferences. New electronic-based systems of data collection and retrieval will span the whole community of Europe, but will freezer centres become popular in Germany?

The future structure of European trade and commerce is shaping up and various, sometimes conflicting, views are being projected. Drucker[13] believes 'almost certainly' that the Europe of tomorrow 'will be both an economy of competing European businesses – in that respect it will look quite different from the "common market" of the United States. But which industry and which market will go which way?'

With the signing of the Maastricht Agreement in 1991, the *European Union* (*EU*) was established, consisting of the *European Community* (*EC*), based on a revised *Treaty of Rome* and including provisions for economic and monetary union (EMU); foreign and security policy; and justice and home affairs. One of Maastricht's central objectives is the creation of a common European citizenship with the rights to unrestricted travel across the boundaries of member states.

The unification of Germany in 1990, followed by sensational political upheavals in Eastern Europe and the dramatic disintegration of the Soviet Empire, have had far-reaching effects on European economic, political and social relationships. The industrial and political regeneration of the former East German State, and the remarkable extension of more liberal political regimes in other parts of Europe that were, for many years, Soviet satellites, have encouraged the impressive development of trade through, for example, joint ventures by large industrial groups such as Asea Brown Boveri, which has established manufacturing linkages in the Czech Republic, Hungary, Croatia, Romania, Estonia and Russia.

Europe is still in a state of flux, and although the EU has a legal existence, the populations which now come within its jurisdiction are by no means united in their buying habits. Political and economic integration may be the ambitions of Brussels-centred planners, but it would be naïve to assume that people will lightly set aside their cultural values and traditions – and these are often at the heart of their buying preferences and life-styles.

In developing countries, researchers have found that diversity is a singular characteristic: Latin America has been described[9] as a heterogeneous composite of societies, cultures, and economies, with no particular region in a country representative of that country, let alone the whole of Latin America. With a population totalling about one-tenth of the world's population, and vast stocks of mineral, agricultural, and labour resources, the Latin American markets 'have just started to unleash their enormous growth potential'.[9] Four countries: Brazil, Mexico, Argentina, and Venezuela account for about 65 per cent of Latin America's total population and 75 per cent of its total GNP. Within these communities there are two distinct socio-economic groupings: very high, and very low, with 'no appreciable middle class as yet. Marketing researchers hope to contend with not a single market but with dual markets.[9]

The size of population and its distribution are also factors to be checked in a market evaluation. Kuwait, Oman, and the United Arab Emirates, for instance, have large oil assets but small populations so that *per capita* income is extraordinarily high, though their general level of economic and cultural development is unevenly dispersed.

Cultural differences such as local holidays and other events are also likely to affect marketing research operations . . . 'virtually no productive activity transpires in Brazil three weeks before or after the carnival.'[9] Eating habits may change radically during the fasting period of Ramadan in Muslim communities.

Cultural role differences also affect the pattern of decision making as was found[18] with patent medicines in Saudi Arabia, for which the husband rather than the wife will invariably shop.

In upper-income households in Latin America, daily food purchases are bought by the maids; this fact was belatedly discovered by researchers who originally questioned affluent housewives who were found to know very little about buying food for their families.[12]

Linguistic differences influenced the brand name for household aluminium foil which was researched[6] in Germany, Belgium, and Italy for Alusuisse. Home-market brand names which, over generations, may have become virtually part of home life, are prone to being misinterpreted, exposed to ridicule or even regarded as offensive in some overseas markets. Even well known companies have made mistakes, such as when 'Irish Mist' liqueur was exported to Germany and caused some amusement, 'mist' meaning 'manure' in German. In advertising to Americans the attractions of holidaying in Britain, the British Tourist Authority replaced the word 'pub' with 'inn', because the former word had been adopted by downmarket American bars.

Switzerland has four national languages – French, Italian, German, and Romansh, a minority language probably used by about 50 000 inhabitants. However, English is widely adopted in business circles and among young people. 'Indeed, English is being used increasingly as a means of communication between Swiss whose native tongue differs.'[14]

In modern Spain there are many languages and dialects. 'Spain is not one homogeneous, single nation but a political unity created out of four distinct regions: the Basque country, Catalunya, Galicia, and the remainder'.[15] While Spanish ('Castellano', to give it its correct title) is the official language of the nation, three other languages are used, including Catalan which, after being proscribed for years by Franco, is now experiencing a rapid revival in the prosperous region of Catalunya, of which Barcelona is the thriving capital.

In developing countries, language problems may be particularly difficult, where several languages or dialects may be spoken within one country or area, as in Singapore, where Mandarin, Hokkien, Cantonese, Malay, Tamil, and English are spoken, apart from many dialects. 'India has 16 totally different languages, with 1652 known dialects.

Like Europe, Asia is not a single, homogeneous entity: it is inherently diverse and parts of it are experiencing unprecedented economic growth, as evidenced by rising disposable incomes, extensive urban developments, and industrialization.

In developing countries the extent of Westernization should be assessed, since this will give impetus to products like fashion clothing and Scotch whisky, which are perceived as reflecting sophisticated lifestyles.

Ethnic differences, as in the US, may influence patterns of consumption and present opportunities for products with specific appeal to these sub-cultural sectors of the community.

In developing countries, there are often major ethnic divisions which pose problems for researchers. For example, only just over half of the population of Malaysia is racially Malay; 35 per cent are Chinese, who are a majority in urban areas; there is also a sizeable Indian minority. Research designs would need, therefore, to take account of these strata because of significant differences in behaviour and attitudes. While Singapore has the same ethnic groups, 'the Chinese predominate to the extent that research may sometimes confine itself to this one group for reasons of cost effectiveness'.

Another important aspect of ethnic influence in research relates to interviewers who, in some cases, may have to be from the same ethnic groups as respondents in order to avoid racial or tribal antipathies. It would also be important to check that local researchers are really familiar with the consumption habits of consumers in social groups other than their own, which is likely to be superior to many of their respondents.

Education is important in influencing consumers' behaviour; growing literacy will widen the market, and tend to increase the demand for products of better design and appearance. The relative stage of educational development will suggest opportunities for products of differing levels of sophistication. Research should aim to identify the potential market in qualitative as well as quantitative terms.

As noted, cultural norms are fundamental influences in consumption habits and religious beliefs and practices which cannot be ignored by researchers in, for example, strict Muslim communities. A few years ago Singer found that in selling sewing machines in Middle Eastern countries, the husband rather than the wife had to be approached with the argument that the ownership of a sewing machine would make his wife more efficient and useful, and not merely save her personal trouble and time.[6] Ingenuity was also needed to overcome the problems of research interviewing in Saudi Arabia, where women are needed to interview women, and females are not permitted to work where they might come into contact with males. Men are protective of their womenfolk and suspicious of outsiders, so they may insist on being interviewed instead of their wives. In such circumstances, it is advisable to use the services of a local and respected research company.

Craig and Douglas[16] have drawn attention to the influence of the 'broader socio-cultural setting' on consumption behaviour, for instance, of Jewish consumers in different countries. Jewish New Yorkers' patterns of consumption reflect US culture, as well as the New York context, their level of affluence, and also country of origin. 'Similarly, consumption patterns of Jewish consumers in Paris or London are influenced by their European heritage, their urban location, as well their social-economic or occupational status'.[16]

Unspoken communication is of particular significance in negotiations with the Japanese, who are accustomed to assessing the body language of those with whom they are negotiating. Japanese negotiations typically 'involve long periods of silence, particularly where there is an impasse'.[17] Also, the gestures with which the Japanese greet visitors differ from those customary in the West, where hand-shaking is widely acceptable, whereas in Japan it is customary to bow low and shake hands or merely bow – the seller, incidentally, always bows lower than the buyer.[6]

The formality of Japanese customs was encapsulated by Tom Peters: 'The Japanese aesthetic sense is centuries old. Within the Toyota or Sony Walkman lie the modern outcroppings of the tea ceremony'.[18]

BSN, the French food group, learned the hard way that the theory of globalization of tastes needs very careful interpretation. A market survey in Japan had 'indicated that there was a vast Western-style yoghurt market waiting to be discovered in Japan.'[19] But in conducting the survey, cultural differences in responding to questions had been ignored; the Japanese are much more polite than Europeans and, if questioned, will say that they like a product even if they actually do not. It was also subsequently found that Japanese consumers of snacks, unlike Europeans, do not discriminate between different kinds of Western snacks, so they tend to switch readily from yoghurts to other sorts of snacks. BSN also discovered that consistent and heavy promotion was vital to maintain sales. As a result of the company's disappointing experiences, its marketing strategies were revised and a joint venture approach was adopted.

An experienced Japanese market researcher has admitted[20] that Japanese companies have a culture of secrecy which makes market research 'quite difficult'.

Careful examination should be made of the likely impact on trade of political developments in particular countries. (Parts of South America are particularly vulnerable.) Trade is more likely to develop where political stability is evident; this assists future planning. Economic factors are often closely linked with political decisions. Devaluation may be important: the state of the currency may be fluid; rates of exchange may fluctuate considerably, e.g. floating exchanges. The overall politico-economic situation existing in a specific market should be compared with the position in other potential markets, and the risks involved rated accordingly. The general level of trade needs attention: is the economy expanding, contracting, or static? What is the level of trade confidence and the incidence of bad debts?

Commercial factors

Research should endeavour to find out how the overall sales of a specific product or range of products are distributed. What kinds of people buy the product, and what differences exist among the products at present on sale? Is there an identifiable segmentation of the market over age and social groups, and, if so, what are the principal brands in these areas – their market shares? Do products have specific appeals to regional tastes – and how significant are these in developing sales? What is the general trend in that product market, and how is this related to the movement in special segments which may be of interest?

The development of modern methods of retail distribution, for example hypermarkets in France, has affected significantly standards of negotiation between manufacturers and retailers because of concentrated buying power. The most effective method of distribution should be identified, and costs worked out – discounts, special allowances, transport costs, etc. Speed of movement through distributing channels may be important. Related to this is the type and style of packaging. Feasibility studies of container shipments, roll on–roll off, or air freight, might be advisable. Publicity services should also be investigated. What media are available and at what cost? Commercial television, for example, is not available in every European country, and in some African countries the cinema is an influential method of publicity. France has no actual papers on the British model, while in West Germany only three papers could be classified as national. What methods of publicity are used by existing suppliers to the market? Some study should be made of the principal languages – and the relative importance of these – within specific markets. For example, Belgium, where French and Flemish are in daily use.

In South Africa, when it is necessary to use Afrikaans, the wording of research questions will be affected by the limited vocabulary of that language. It cannot be assumed that the Spanish and Portuguese spoken in the Americas, and the French and Dutch spoken in Mauritius and Indonesia are necessarily the same as is spoken in the mother country.[6] Even the common language that links the US and the UK has some distinctions in both spelling and meaning: basic roots do not eliminate diversity of cultural development.

Nigel Holden's research[21] into the relationship between language proficiency and performance in overseas markets led him to propose that firms, whose attitudes and behaviour are strongly characterized by Anglo-centric orientation towards their customers, are likely to be relatively inexpert at interpreting, and anticipating, differences in the socio-cultural environment of export markets.

Jonathan Swift[22] draws attention to the fact that, in some cases, the market language – the official language of industrial and commercial activities in a country – may not necessarily be that of the language of that country, although the two usually coincide. He instances certain areas of Africa where native languages 'may be used on a daily basis, yet English, French or Portuguese remain the national language.'[22] In many cases, countries may have more than one market language; also, 'third party' languages are noted by Swift as languages of market contact, which are acceptable means of communication between buyers and sellers, when neither speaks the language of the other. These third party languages assist negotiation between linguistically diverse groups as, for example, in Zaire, which has four native languages and French serves as the language of market contact.

Every element in marketing – price, packaging, publicity, distribution, terms of payment, etc. – should be carefully identified and analysed so that a company is in possession of the full facts. Some form of rating scale could be used as a convenient method of assessing an individual company's position relative to existing suppliers. This should be done as objectively as possible, and a company should be ready to accept that its own product may have features which are less attractive than competitive products. Systematic, objective analysis and comparison form the basic approach to evaluating marketing opportunities, wherever they may occur.

The rate of re-purchase of particular products will also be of vital interest to prospective exporters. Another critical factor is the average life-span of the product which it is proposed to market. Is it, for instance, likely to be affected by some developing technology in the next five years or so? The level of market infiltration of the particular product is also of concern, and some assessment should be made of the possibility of saturation in the next few years.

KEYPOINT

Scope of international marketing research

Economic factors

Politico-cultural factors

Commercial factors

Start with desk research

BETRO report on foreign language proficiency

The critical contribution which proficiency in foreign languages makes to export performance has been stressed over many years. Although it has been virtually impossible to isolate this factor and express it in strict statistical terms, there is sufficient evidence from industry to cause some disquiet. A survey of 200 leading British exporters, representing the main manufacturing and service industries, revealed – among several other points – that the majority did not favour language graduates for their export sales departments, because it was thought that their specific academic studies were too theoretical and literature-based. Instead, they preferred to recruit staff with business skills who could acquire a reasonable level of foreign language facility.[23]

The widespread adoption of English across the EU, and as a global commercial language has doubtless, as the BETRO Report[23] concluded, added to the general complacency which has persisted for some time. Even in the use of English, as Sir John Harvey-Jones warns, 'Perhaps the biggest area of misunderstanding [in the use of language] is in our approach to our American customers and competitors, where we are lulled into complacency by our similar language'.[1]

12.7 Research methodology

Desk research, already discussed, will have been the first step before making any other commitments. As indicated in Chapter 2, statistics from some overseas governments and other sources tend to be less reliable than others and discretion is needed when handling them. 'Of the 45 states that make up sub-Saharan Africa, barely a handful have reliable national statistics. Many of the figures about Africa are little better than guesses.'[24] The quality of statistical data varies, therefore, markedly and experienced market researchers evaluate available secondary data for validity and reliability.

It is advisable to contact the Export Market Information Service (EMIC) of British Trade International, and consult the extensive secondary data sources (see earlier details). British Trade International also offers up to 50 per cent of agreed costs to companies with fewer than 500 employees for approved marketing research projects. It also published SITPRO: advice on how to prepare export documentation, and TIHE (Technical Help to Exporters) is offered by the British Standards Institution giving information about regulations and approvals relevant to target markets. Special official schemes also give new exporters low-cost rates for visits to markets or trade fairs in Western Europe.

Sampling tends to be more complicated in overseas marketing research. It may be difficult, or even impossible, to obtain reliable sampling frames for random sampling techniques (see Chapter 3). What sampling frames there are available may not be adequate and so lead to wasted time, apart from their unreliability. Sampling methods may vary from country to country; also the meaning of 'random' is widely interpreted.

Hence, non-probability sampling is often adopted in international marketing research (see Chapter 4). This may be particularly applicable to business-to-business research, where concentration factors are active (see Chapter 11). It may be feasible to use some form of stratified sampling, like multi-stage, dividing a country or group of countries, such as Scandinavia, into geographical regions, districts, areas, cities and towns, etc. (see Chapter 4). Stratification factors may, of course, relate to ethnic or racial sub-groups, demographic analyses, business type or size, etc. Whatever factors are chosen, it is important that they are directly relevant to the usage of the product/service, and that the resultant analyses – derived from an adequate number in each stratum – will provide management with sound market knowledge. In designing the composition of a stratified sample within a country or region, the diversity of the population should be borne in mind. In cities where are likely to be several distinct sub-cultural groups based on ethnic origin and/or religious affinity. Such sub-groups may have distinct patterns of consumption. Differences in behaviour may also arise from wide variations in income, as in Latin America. Levels of education are also significant in buying preferences, and in the range of recreational and cultural interests.

Experienced judgement may have to be the basis for constructing a sample in countries where social and economic data are sparse. The accepted practice of marketing research cannot always be directly transferred to some overseas markets, and data may have to be collected by less formalized methods. Free samples, small gifts, and free lottery tickets have been used to attract co-operation in some economically under-developed countries.

The lack of reliable sampling frames in Latin America has led to the widespread adoption of quota or convenience sampling (see Chapter 2). Because quota sampling procedures vary considerably in different Latin American countries, the comparability of the data is severely affected. 'For example, a research agency in one country may select their respondents by a quota sample of housing units, while one agency in another Latin American country may use a quota sample in a shopping area'.[9]

Telephone rentals are likely to be inadequate sampling frames in many developing countries. Even in Venezuela, one of the more developed countries of Latin America, average telephone ownership is around 6 per cent of homes. Another problem is that telephone listings 'cannot even be used as an adequate sampling frame for the wealthier segments of the market because in many Latin American countries telephones are listed under the name of the owner but possessed by others.'[9] This applies particularly to Brazil, where a telephone line costs from $2000 for initial service. Hence, the relative scarcity and the investment value of these lines have resulted in a secondary market in which telephones are traded; some individuals may own up to four or five telephones. A further drawback in Latin America to telephone surveys is the high refusal rate (30–50 per cent), because of the marked suspicion of strangers. This is particularly evident with women, and this problem is also experienced in personal interviewing, particularly in affluent homes where the maid tends to act as a 'gatekeeper'. It is observed[16] that in the Middle East, where interviewers are invariably male, interviews with housewives often have to be conducted in the evenings when husbands are present.

Because of the significant problems encountered in contacting representative samples of respondents and of ensuring the consistent quality of interviews in extensive market research enquiries in Europe, an experienced researcher[25] experimented with central location telephone interviewing in Switzerland during 1981. At that time, this agency were already operating a CATI system of interviewing (see Chapter 5); the pilot scheme proved a success. As a result of this experience, the agency now routinely considers whether each assignment received by it could be carried out by telephone. The interviewers/operators are grouped in seven different teams speaking different languages, covering English, French, German, Swiss-German dialect, Italian, Dutch, Swedish, and Spanish. Interviews vary between 5 and 45 minutes. 'The quantity of information a well-trained telephone operator can collect in 10 minutes is fabulous, since there are almost no pauses in interviewing'.[25]

Primary data collection

As discussed in Chapter 2, this stage is a core part of the research activities, and the relative efficiencies of the various methods of collecting primary data have to be carefully considered.

Most marketing research involves some form of questionnaire: personal face-to-face interviewing, mail or telephone, as well as electronically based methods such as fax, e-mail, internet, bar-coding, electronic meters, etc. As with home-based marketing research, the first step is to establish the objectives of the survey, time constraints, and the suitability and relative costs of different methodologies. In addition, in overseas research, it is important to be aware of the communications infrastructure, the degree of literacy, the quality of the mail and telephone services, and the travel facilities available.

In Chapter 5, detailed consideration has been given to the various methods of asking for information, and the comparative advantages and disadvantages of these methodologies in the UK have been evaluated. In the highly developed countries across the world, the marketing research services are largely the same but not necessarily as extensive as in the USA or the UK. In other countries, particularly outside the cities and major towns, the position will vary considerably. Mailing lists and/or the mail service may be unreliable, and the telephone system erratic, although it has improved greatly over the past decade or so. This has allowed telephone surveys to develop, using computer-linked technology (see Chapter 5). The meteoric advance of the internet has added vastly to the range of marketing research techniques available, especially for business-to-business research in international surveys. As noted in Chapter 5, problems of technical comparability and competence, representative sampling frames, and adequate response rates are at present limiting factors in general.

The Harris Research Centre runs a centralized international telephone system which provides fully controlled and computerized research at a pan-European level and beyond for the leading multinationals.

Several research organizations offer continuous marketing research services in overseas markets; these tend to focus on specific groups such as air travellers in Europe and Asia, consumer financial services panel (US), wines and spirits, cosmetics, and branded confectionery. Omnibus surveys (see Chapter 8) are also conducted by several UK-based market research agencies such as Mass Observation which runs a monthly telephone omnibus of consumers and business sectors in Europe.

Gallup also offers a Europe Omnibus survey which, apart from August, is run monthly with 1000 nationally representative respondents in all European countries. Information is gathered by face-to-face interviewing or, where quick results are vital, by 500 telephone interviews each month. The Gallup service can provide tracking studies of international advertising campaigns, brand monitoring, cross-cultural consumption habits, and harmonized demographic data.

Questionnaires, as indicated in Chapter 5, need care in drafting; this is particularly so in the case of overseas surveys. Literal translation would obviously be totally wrong, and expert local knowledge in drafting questionnaires is vital to ensure that they will be acceptable and effective. In some cases, pictorial methods, e.g. the barometer, have been particularly valuable in assessing consumer response, and some ingenuity should be used in designing suitable diagrams. (Details of these methods are given in Chapter 7.)

Multi-country surveys obviously require expert attention to questionnaire construction. Gallup's London office, for example, pilots such enquiries in the UK, and the revised final questionnaire is then sent to the other interested countries for translation and further piloting if this is considered desirable. Translated questionnaires, together with any comments, are returned to London where re-translation into English takes place. These are then checked against the original questionnaire and if any divergences have occurred, corrections are made. Any changes to take account of local conditions in particular markets are made at this stage, and the translations are then agreed with clients.

The analysis required by clients is compared with the questionnaire to ensure that the correct type of data results.

Coding instructions, to agreed standards, are given by London to affiliate research companies. Punching and tabulation are also controlled by London and processing is by computer in the UK.

ACNielsen International operates its well-known research services on a global basis through a network of locally based companies in more than 90 countries spanning five continents. These cover the principal European countries, the US, Canada, Australia, New Zealand, Mexico and Korea, and in newer markets such as Hungary, Poland, Turkey, the Slovak Republic and the Czech Republic. Over 70 per cent of Nielsen's business is now outside the US – where it originated in the 1920s.

ACNielsen provide a fully harmonized service throughout Europe. Core databases are available in every country which facilitate cross country comparisons; tracking, for example, competitor performance, promotional effectiveness, price trends, trade inventory levels, and monitoring out-of-stocks and distribution. (See also panel information in Chapter 8.)

ACNielsen data help Cadbury Schweppes to evaluate local marketing efforts in 16 nations and to develop their strategic plans for multi-country brands.

In conjunction with the *Wall Street Journal Europe*, Nielsen has produced nearly 100 Marketscan columns, which appear weekly and give current and practical examples of how Nielsen databases have been used in developing a wide variety of marketing plans.

Among its wide portfolio of market research services, MBL Research conducts major surveys of automotive and related products throughout Europe, North America and the Middle East. Research operations are coordinated at the London headquarters.

BMRB International develops a master questionnaire in London, which is translated by local agencies. BMRB linguist executives visit the agencies to brief research teams and check translations. Final questionnaires are validated at pilot interviews in each country in the presence of the BMRB executive. Local agencies edit the questionnaire and code open-ended responses according to a code frame developed in London from listings drawn from a subsample of completed questionnaires in each country, thus ensuring comparability across countries while maintaining sensitivity to variations between them. Data entry may be carried out either in London or locally; final checks are carried out in London. Data are analysed in London to agreed specifications.

Qualitative research techniques (see Chapter 7) are also valuable in international marketing research, especially because of the trend towards globalization of products and brands, when knowledge of cultural values is of key importance. Although, as discussed later, consensualism, as opposed to individualism, is an important dimension of Asian cultures, as Asian consumers develop and experience some of the economic and social conflict of industrialized societies, there may be a move away from such traditional values to those of 'individualistic' capitalist values. This trend may encourage the acceptance by Eastern consumers of Western branded products. Leading household brands such as *Lux* and *Persil* are deliberately promoted with the dual attributes of tradition and modernity, so that they will appeal both to those who uphold consensualist values and those who are attracted by more individualist values.[26]

BMRB Business Solutions, a division of BMRB International, specializes in the measurement of customer satisfaction. The measures entail examination of *all* aspects of company/customer relationships, so as to identify the factors which are crucial for success. Multi-country studies are implemented through its centralized telephone facilities or via the Walker Information Global Network in more than 20 countries, including Australia, Canada, France, Germany, Italy, Japan, The Netherlands, Scandinavia, Latin America, the US and the UK.

The Harris Centre of TNSofres has developed 'Semotrie', which is based on semiotics, a branch of linguistics dealing with signs and symbols and their meanings, in order to obtain more fully cultural differences in Europe. This survey operated in the UK, Germany, France, Italy and Spain, and involved 122 000 respondents, aged 15 and over. They were asked to score a list of 210 words, which acted as stimuli to find out their values and emotions.

Semiometrie has been validated by more than 500 surveys throughout Europe. From factor analyses, the following common factors emerged:

Duty vs Pleasure
Community vs Singularity
Materialism vs Culture
Idealism vs Pragmatism.

However, beyond these common factors, 'Europe looks more like a mosaic'.[27] Between the countries surveyed, there were strong differences in the cultural values. 'National identity has as much weight as, sometimes even more than, standard demographics like sex, age and education'.[27]

Nowadays, when films, and television and radio programmes rapidly disseminate the values of advanced industrialized communities, socio-cultural changes in developing countries may result in consumers being ready earlier to buy more sophisticated versions of products than formerly. Marketers, therefore, must keep a close watch on the pace of cultural change and ensure that their products (and brands) are in tune with rapidly rising expectations and changing perceptions.

Qualitative methods in international marketing research should fit the culture of particular countries and regions; some adaptations may be necessary. 'For instance in Arab cultures the meanings of dreams are very potent and therefore the guided dream works particularly well; in India, the use of gods as an analogy for brands is effective; psychodrawings and collages are part of upbringing in Japan and work well there. . . .'[27]

In Asia, qualitative research has revealed the influence of shared cultural values, of which a key factor is 'power distance'. This refers to the general cultural willingness to accept that, for instance, certain people in authority – rulers – and even leading brands of products, are entitled to exercise dominance or power. While this cultural acceptance is not a value shared much with Europeans, it appears to be influential in Asian buying behaviour. 'Basically, big market-share brands are the kings of their brand world and consumers in Asia believe in them implicitly'.[28] 'Power brands', like Cordon Bleu, State Express 555, Coca Cola, Nescafé, San Miguel and Singha beer are so well established that 'upstart new brands' have an extremely difficult task to get attention and achieve credibility.

Another important dimension of Asian societies which was noted is that they are 'basically much more "consensual" than individualistic'.[28] Through parental upbringing and schooling, individual sets of beliefs and attitudes are 'submerged to fit with the greater good – or what is acceptable in society as a whole'.[28] This fostering of consensual or collective values influences brand selection and loyalty.

The third dimension of Asian cultural differences relates to risk, viz. 'uncertainty avoidance'. Associated with this characteristic seems to be the importance attached to social cohesion. Brands, therefore, are symbolic: 'One is not buying a watch, or even a status brand, one is buying club membership'.[28] Buying the 'acceptable brands' gives reassurance to other Asians about the personality of the buyer.

Toiletries, fragrances and cosmetics abound in Europe, and there are many brands, of which there are a few 'mega-brands', which include Pantene, ProV, Plenitude, Sure/Rexona and Nivea. These are backed by extensive promotional campaigns across Europe. TNSofres European Toiletries and Cosmetics Database continually monitors the similarities and differences in the use of a wide variety of personal care products by means of 14 000 usage diaries, collected yearly, across Britain, France, Germany, Italy and Spain. Research has indicated that 'where marketers set their minds towards pursuing multi-national brands they can succeed if their spend is high enough and the product good enough'.[29]

KEYPOINT

International marketing research primary data collection

Be aware of:
communications infrastructure; degree of literacy; quality of mail and phone services; travel facilities available; cultural norms; mailing lists (adequacy and reliability); internet availability; sampling frames (availability and reliability); computer-linked phone installations.

Pan European Survey

RSL-Research Services Ltd of Harrow, in conjunction with 16 European research companies, has conducted detailed surveys of media habits among high-status professional and business people in Europe for several years. The 1992 Pan European Survey was the fifth of its kind and was sponsored by *The Economist, The Financial Times, The International Herald Tribune, Newsweek, Scientific American,* and *Time.* The following European countries were covered: Belgium, Denmark, Finland, France, Germany, Great Britain, Greece, the Irish Republic, Italy, Luxembourg, The Netherlands, Norway, Portugal, Spain, Sweden, and Switzerland; basic readership figures for 380 publications were collected; 7789 interviews were effected; and a remarkable overall response rate of 58 per cent was achieved.

The population was defined as economically active men and women, aged 25 and over, who have achieved high status educationally or professionally, or who have a specified income (income levels were specified for each country).

A two-stage probability sample was used in each country (see Chapter 4). From a representative national sample of all eligible people, the addresses of 30–40 per cent were discarded, since they lived in areas with the lowest concentrations of eligible respondents. The residual (60–70 per cent) addresses generated the first sampling points. Respondents were screened from all men and women in consecutive addresses on a predetermined route from the starting address.

Face-to-face interviews, lasting about 45 minutes, took place in the homes of eligible respondents; trained interviewers used the mother tongue of the respondents. Questionnaires were translated for use in each country; the publications listed in questionnaires were selected from those with readership profiles of high-status individuals. The list of titles appeared in the same order on questionnaires, but the order in which groups of publications (daily, weekly, fortnightly, bi-monthly, monthly and quarterly) appeared was rotated so as to minimize the general order effects of reduced levels of claimed readership for titles near the end of lists (see Chapter 6). Income data were grouped into four broad categories as follows:

	Income code position	Approx. $US value during fieldwork
Lower	X,A,B	Up to 46 000
Medium	C	46 000–58 999
Upper	O,E	59 000–94 999
High	F,G	95 000–169 999
Highest	H,I	170 000 or over

Income was defined as 'your own personal income before tax', and expressed on a showcard in the currency of the survey country. The 10 points of the income scale (X–I) were approximately similar for all countries at the beginning of the fieldwork, allowing for rounding and exchange rate fluctuations.

The administration of this extensive survey and the British fieldwork were undertaken by RSL-Research Services Ltd, whose associated companies conducted the fieldwork in the other countries. Editing, coding, and preparation of all materials, including questionnaires, were carried out by RSL-Research Services.

Interviews were weighted on a point by point basis, corrected for differential response by sex and number of eligibles in the household, and grossed to the estimated national universe size.

Eurodemographics

Socio-economic classification in the UK has been discussed earlier, notably in Chapters 4 and 10, and it is clearly a complex matter which concerns market and social researchers, particularly when surveys are being conducted overseas.

In an attempt to clarify European demographic approaches, ESOMAR, in 1980, set up a working party[30] to deal with the harmonization of demographics; a substantial part of their time was devoted to the problem of defining, and working with, social class, which was found to have widely different meanings across the countries studied.

A second working party was organized in 1988, refined the original Social Grade matrix and developed the Economic Status scale. The working party was expanded in 1990, and further analyses were conducted over 1995–96, which resulted in a revised definition of the ESOMAR Social Grade Variable. This revised scheme is outlined below. The ESOMAR Social Grade Variable is constructed from:

(a) the occupation of the main income earner in the household;

(b) the terminal age of education of the main income earner, suitably adjusted to take note of any further education/professional training;

(c) in the case of 'non-active main income earners', the economic status of the household is based on ownership of ten selected consumer durables.

Sixteen occupational categories and five categories of terminal education are used in this classification. The ten products used in the assessment of 'non-active main income earners' are colour TV set, video recorder, video camera, two or more cars, still camera, PC or home computer, electric drill, electric deep fat fryer, a radio clock, second/holiday home/flat. This list is subject to revision in line with general trends in ownership.

Six ESOMAR Social Grades[31] result from these variables:

A, B, C1, C2, D, E

These A–E grades can be aggregated, for the purpose of everyday research, into the following four classifications:

AB   managers and professionals
C1   well educated non-manual and skilled workers
C2   unskilled workers and non-manual employees
DE   unskilled manual workers and other less well educated workers/employees

Source: ESOMAR[31]

These social grade categories are based on data collected on behalf of the European Union Commission in seven Eurobarometer surveys between September 1992 and May 1995. ESOMAR state that because of the 'generally slow rate at which socio-demographic developments take place, these data can be regarded for the European Union as a whole'.[31] The Eurobarometer surveys are based on a 'relatively large national random sample per country, with the basic sample size per wave generally being 1000'.[31] The questionnaire is currently in English, German and French.

12.8 Managing international marketing research

Research for export marketing can be undertaken in various ways, and a brief outline of the principal methods will now be considered.

1. *Using own staff or importing agents*
    (a) The first objection to this method is probably lack of objectivity; sales staff are usually incapable of giving an unbiased estimate of their products' likelihood of success.
    (b) The second objection is that the agents may have other interests which prevent them from giving an objective assessment of the market.
    (c) Research is a specialist's job which requires particular training and experience.
    (d) This method may, perhaps, be the only feasible way of researching in some 'backward' markets.

2. *Using research agencies in overseas markets*
    (a) Selection of these can be difficult and risky.
    (b) Where several markets are involved, multiple agencies may have to be used to cover the whole export programme.
    (c) A big advantage is that national research organizations should possess intimate knowledge of their own home market.

3. *Using a marketing research organization based in the UK plus the services of a locally based research firm*
    (a) This method is rather cumbersome and offers few advantages over method 2.
    (b) It could be useful where manufacturers had no trained research staff (often the case in smaller companies).

4. *Using the services of a consortium of research agencies*
   (a) Superficially attractive, but member firms may vary considerably in the quality of their services.
   (b) Closely related to this method is that of an international research organization linked with advertising agencies over principal markets. This is generally effective.

Several of the larger marketing research organizations, e.g. Gallup, BMRB via its sister company, MRBI, and IPSOS-RSL have already been quoted as active in multi-country research. These and other highly experienced companies are able to handle complex and far-ranging market investigations.

A useful checklist[32] of the necessary requirements for an international market research project include the following recommendations:

1. Obtain information from the Market Research Society on international agencies and their relevant services.

2. Select two or three which appear capable of handling the required research – this entails assessing their specific experience and expertise.

3. Brief potential suppliers thoroughly on the nature of the marketing opportunity and the types of information needed that would enable decisions to be taken within acceptable levels of risk.

4. Stipulate any budgetary or time constraints.

5. Scrutinize the resultant research proposal, assessing, in particular, the agency's understanding of the marketing issue(s), and examine carefully the proposed methodologies, provisions for controlling the research operations, and the arrangements for translation, as necessary, of survey documents, etc.

6. Determine the legal status of any contract, and establish the methods, and currency, of payment.

(These points have been discussed more fully in Chapter 2.)

Appraisal of opportunities

The markets studied in desk and field research should now be related to company resources – finance, production, labour, distribution.

Particular marketing opportunities should be isolated and their implications studied, both long and short term. Following this evaluation, a series of decisions should then be made.

These, as stated earlier, will take into account the quantitative and qualitative information which has been collected, analysed and interpreted in the marketing research operations with the objective of improved management decision making.

In reviewing opportunities abroad it would be wise for a company to spread its risks, so that it does not become too dependent on one or two large markets, which could, through political or economic circumstances, suddenly decline, e.g. the American protectionist policy of 1971 or the collapse of major industrial or commercial undertakings.

Exporting generally involves management in higher risks than confining activities to the home market. Sir John Harvey-Jones,[1] speaks of taking acceptable risks; companies that take no risks disappear while those that take unwise levels of risk also go to the wall. Risk evaluation is an inseparable part of a sound management policy; successful overseas operations, in particular, depend significantly on the development of a carefully conceived risk policy. In this important task, marketing research has a key role to play.

Organization of overseas operation

The following factors need to be carefully considered:

1. Production
   - (a) Direct export
   - (b) Licensing arrangements
   - (c) Build new factory overseas
   - (d) Joint venture with foreign company
2. Distribution
   - (a) Direct marketing
   - (b) Stockist–distributor network
   - (c) Agencies
     - (i) exclusive
     - (ii) shared

The type of product may largely determine its method of sale; capital goods requiring long negotiation and special after-sales service are obviously different from low priced 'quick-repeat' consumer products, and different methods of marketing will apply.

The type of distribution must also be decided. For example, whether sales should be exclusively through selected large stores in major cities and towns by direct selling from the manufacturer's head office, or, alternatively, whether distribution should be via the sales force of the local distributor, who may be expected to hold reasonable stocks for quick delivery. Manufacturers may prefer to set up their own sales offices in major centres and control the marketing operation in this way.

Some large international companies divide their marketing activities into 'zones', with a distribution network controlled by the 'zone' company.

The form of organization adopted will depend upon individual companies, their resources, products, objectives, and the characteristics of the market they plan to enter. As markets develop, new organizational structures may be necessary, to give flexibility to local companies operating in different environments.

Whatever system of overseas organization is adopted, rigidity should be avoided and remote control should not be allowed to frustrate marketing opportunities. Although modern travel encourages head office staff to visit overseas markets regularly, and on special missions, constant intervention will not develop in local marketing staff their personal responsibility for the success of the agreed marketing strategy in their area. Overseas staff should be selected not only for their technical knowledge but also for their commercial abilities. If the right people are appointed, they should be given the opportunity of developing management judgement in their particular sphere of operations. Tactical decisions should largely be left to them within, of course, the framework of the company's policy.

Summary   Overseas marketing research has grown in importance with the development of export markets which demand expert knowledge of commercial, industrial, economic, political, cultural, and demographic factors affecting buying behaviour, both industrial and consumer.

Exporting is often entered into accidentally; at the other extreme are those companies which deliberately scan the world for growth opportunities.

As with home market research, desk research is the starting point for finding out about overseas markets; there are many sources of information available to prospective exporters.

Research methodology at the primary level will be likely to be more complicated than in Britain; sampling frames, for example, may not be available or may be very unreliable in some countries, so random sampling may be impossible. Telephone and mail surveys obviously depend on the availability of efficient mail and telephone services; many developing countries do not have these.

Interviewing techniques may have to be modified to suit cultural inhibitions. Questionnaires need expert drafting and translation.

Various methods of organizing marketing research can be adopted: from using own staff to sophisticated systems of research agencies in consortia.

Standards of marketing research should always be kept high to ensure that the resultant data are valid and reliable for management decision making.

Review and discussion questions	1. What form of market research would you recommend to a small Scottish manufacturer of shortbread biscuits wishing to investigate possible markets for her product in France?
	2. The manufacturer of a British natural ale is considering launching his product in Hungary, Slovakia, and the Czech Republic. With the help of newspapers and magazines, suggest a number of relevant politico-cultural factors that might be profitably researched.
	3. A research agency that has administered a personal questionnaire on attitudes to green consumer products in the UK intends to use the same survey instrument for a similar survey in Germany. What modifications, if any, to the questionnaire should be considered?
	4. The management of a firm marketing white consumer goods in all EU states is undecided on whether a telephone survey administered in the UK should also be administered in English to a sample of Swedish consumers. How would you advise them?
	5. How would you respond to the view that EU consumer markets have become so homogeneous that research in one market need not be replicated in other markets? Your answer should make reference to specific products/services you have read about.
	6. To what extent is rigorous marketing research possible in developing countries?

CAMEO CASE: Elequis Ltd

Elequis Ltd (a fictitious name but a real company) is an independent manufacturer of school, home and office stationery products, such as mathematical/ drawing instruments, cash boxes, key safes, and filing accessories. It was established in 1886, and operates from premises in the West Midlands district of Lye, near Stourbridge. Employees number just over 200, and senior management consists of ten directors, who are respectively in charge of manufacturing, logistics, sales, marketing, export, and finance; each director reports to the chief executive officer. The other four directors include the CEO and three non-executive board members.

Elequis products have earned a high reputation for their innovative approach to new product

▶

development and originality. A high level of brand awareness exists amongst the general public, reflecting the quality and value for money that their products represent. They are essentially bought because of their reliability and functionality. Sales are made to retailers (50 per cent), via home market wholesalers (25 per cent), and through agents and distributors overseas (25 per cent).

Between 1994 and 1997, the ratio of domestic to overseas sales stood at 80 per cent : 20 per cent; since 1998, this has changed slightly, and exports now account for 25 per cent of total sales. About 50 per cent of export sales are to six markets: the United Arab Emirates (this is a entrepot market for school/office products, and accounts for some 16 per cent of total overseas business; Canada (mathematical instruments/school products, 10 per cent of total overseas business); Australia (school/office products, 8 per cent); France (commercial and security products, 5 per cent); Jamaica (large range of school/office products,

5 per cent); and South Africa (large range of school/office products, 5 per cent).

Company turnover has risen steadily from £14 million in 1994–1995, to £18 million in 1998–1999.

Market research is viewed by Elequis as an essential prerequisite to product development and launch both in the domestic and overseas markets. The company does not generally launch any product whatsoever without appropriate qualitative and quantitative research. One strand of research is to predict future trends (particularly in the Licensed or Fashion product markets). Intelligence is then collated, and referred to when deciding on product specifications or presentation. Many of their recent successes, such as the Licensed product range, are In the view of the Export Director '... directly attributable to in depth market research'.

The main methods by which research data is collected abroad is through the company's overseas distributors and their marketing managers; in

Monitoring competitor activities:
Specific objectives, means and frequency of monitoring

Product market	Specific objectives	Means of monitoring	Frequency of monitoring
Domestic	Observation of sales, and liaison with marketing managers	Store visits and advice from customers	Daily/on-going basis
UAE	Observation of sales, and liaison with marketing managers	Market (country) visits	At approximately six month intervals
Canada	Observation of sales, and liaison with marketing managers	Market (country) visits	At approximately six month intervals
Australia	Observation of sales, and liaison with marketing managers	Market (country) visits	At approximately six month intervals
France	Observation of sales, and liaison with marketing managers	Market (country) visits	Monthly
Jamaica	Observation of sales, and liaison with marketing managers	Market (country) visits	Annually
South Africa	Observation of sales, and liaison with marketing managers	Market (country) visits	At approximately six month intervals

▶

the domestic market, the company tends to rely on its own marketing personnel to carry out the various forms of research required.

The DTI has been of help in providing the company with some financial assistance to carry out research in the Australian market. In this market, the prime research objectives were to identify distributors and determine pricing levels prior to market entry. To this end the company undertook a large scale market survey based on third party references, combined with interviews of potential distributors.

Due to the nature of the product and in general, there has been little or no requirement for adaptation of the company's product range for export purposes, so the products sold overseas are exactly the same as those sold in the domestic market. The only changes required were in the French and Canadian markets, and these related to the packaging. In France packaging is required to be in French (in addition to any other language); in Canada, dual language (both English and French) is required by law. This did not create a problem for Elequis, as their existing packaging already includes English, French, and four other European languages.

Elequis find market research a useful means of monitoring the activities of their competitors; specifics vary from product to product, and market to market, and are summarized below.

Questions

1. What are the major advantages of Elequis relying on distributors overseas to carry out marketing research?

2. To what extent do you think that the choice of overseas markets has been influenced by cultural, linguistic, historical or geographical considerations? In general, how important is the cultural background of a market in assessing potential demand levels for the type of products that the company sells?

3. In which overseas markets would you suggest that Elequis next undertakes research, and why?

Jonathan S. Swift

References

1. Harvey-Jones, Sir John, *Making it Happen*, Collins, London, 1988.
2. Drucker, Peter F., 'Social innovation in management's new dimension', *Long Range Planning*, vol. 200, no. 6, 1987.
3. Royal Society of Arts, 'Concentration on key markets', *BETRO Report*, 1975.
4. Hague, Paul, *The Industrial Market Research Handbook*, Kogan Page, London, 1992.
5. Porter, Michael E., *The Competitive Advantage of Nations*, Macmillan, London, 1990.
6. Chisnall, Peter M., *Strategic Business Management*, Prentice-Hall, Hemel Hempstead, 1995.
7. Tait, Nikki, 'Waiting to see what comes out in the wash', *The Financial Times*, 16 December 1991.
8. Burt, Tim, 'Electrolux plan global platform', *Financial Times*, 12 February 1999.
9. Stanton, John L., Rajan Chandran, and Sigfredo A. Hernandez, 'Marketing research problems in Latin America', *Journal of Market Research Society*, vol. 24, no. 2, 1982.
10. Upshaw, Douglas N., 'Organising to sell to Middle East markets', *Conference Board Record*, vol. 13, no. 2, February 1976.
11. Van Mesdag, Martin, 'Multinational, global, international or what?', in: Seminar on International Marketing Research, ESOMAR, Amsterdam, 1988.
12. Martin, Peter, 'Why the single market is a misnomer – and the consequences', *The Financial Times*, 21 October 1988.
13. Drucker, Peter F., 'Strategies for survival in Europe in 1993', *Wall Street Journal*, 12 July 1988.
14. Baumer-Burton, Helen, Editorial, *Swiss Business*, September/October 1990.
15. Swift, J. S., 'Language as a facet of distance in UK firms' interactions with the Spanish Market', unpublished MSc Dissertation, Manchester School of Management, UMIST, 1989.
16. Craig, C. Samuel, and Susan P. Douglas, *International Marketing Research*, John Wiley, Chichester, 2000.
17. Shane, Scott, 'Language and marketing in Japan', *International Journal of Advertising*, vol. 7, no. 2, 1988.
18. Peters, Tom, *Thriving on Chaos*, Macmillan, London, 1987.

19. Wagstyl, Stefan, 'A hard lesson to learn to swallow', *The Financial Times*, 14 July 1988.
20. Miki, Yasuo, Interview report about Japanese market research practices, *Newsplus*, Market Research Society, April 1992.
21. Holden, Nigel J., 'The development of the concept of communication competence in relation to firms' interactions in overseas markets', unpublished PhD thesis, Manchester Business School, University of Manchester, January 1986.
22. Swift, Jonathan S., 'Problems with learning foreign languages for international business', *Journal of European Industrial Training*, vol. 17, no. 10, 1993.
23. BETRO Trust, 'Languages and export performance', Royal Society of Arts, September 1979.
24. Holman, Michael, 'An uncharted crisis', *The Financial Times*, 14 December 1989.
25. Robert, Paul A., 'International telephone research: An interesting *intermediate* stage between the inefficiency of large-scale personal field research, and the future direct dialogue with the consumer', in: Seminar on International Marketing Research, ESOMAR, Amsterdam, 1988.
26. Pawle, John, 'Mining the international consumer', *Journal of Market Research Society*, vol. 41, no. 1, January 1999.
27. Morrison, Valerie, 'The real values behind national stereotypes', *Researchplus*, Market Research Society, Autumn, 1998.
28. Robinson, Chris, 'Asian cultures: the marketing consequence', vol. 38, no. 1, 1996.
29. Fellowes, Carol, 'Research holds up a mirror to the grooming of a continent', *Researchplus*, Market Research Society, November 1996.
30. Røhme, Nils, and Tjarki Veldman, 'Harmonisation of demographics', ESOMAR Congress, Vienna, 1982.
31. Bates, Bryan, 'Standard Demographic Classification', in: *ESOMAR Handbook of Market and Opinion Research*, Colin McDonald, and Phyllis Vangelder (eds), ESOMAR, Amsterdam, 1998.
32. Kelly, John, 'In the kingdom of the blind . . .', *Research*, Market Research Society, December 1992.

4

Data handling and interpretation

Final stages of the survey

Learning Objectives

- Note final stages of research: editing; coding; tabulation; computer analyses

- Be aware of types of data and of data fusion and data bases

- Note structure of survey report

- Note importance of ethics in research, and impact of Data Protection Act, ICC/ESOMAR Codes and MRS Codes

13.1 Introduction

The field research has been completed and now there is the task of dealing with the wealth of data that has been collected. It is well to remember that data are only as good as the research design: a poor design will result in low quality research data. This unfortunate outcome may arise because of an unrepresentative sample, a biased questionnaire, badly conducted interviewing, or inappropriate research techniques. Data are dependent, there-fore, on the professional competence with which each element of the research has been designed and executed. These points were discussed in Chapter 2, but at this stage of the research – and after so much time, energy and cost have been expended on the design and implementation of a research survey – it is tempting, perhaps, to put forward views on a particular aspect of the research topic that could not be fully supported by the data collected during the survey. Apart from being dependent, data also have limitations and it is better to acknowledge these constraints – which may have been the result of problems in locating the planned sources of information, or because the original research scheme had to be fundamentally re-designed due to radical changes in certain economic or political conditions in specific markets.

Data are the raw materials of research findings: they need to be processed into a usable form for the purposes of analysis and interpretation.

13.2 Editing

Editing ensures that the information on questionnaire forms is complete, accurate, and consistent. This is inclined to be rather dull, repetitive work, but it is a vital task which cannot be shirked. It is a responsibility to be accepted by experienced staff who recognize the importance of this phase of research. Every question must be checked to see either that it has been answered, or, if omitted, that it is not applicable to the particular circumstances of the respondent. Where answers have been omitted, it may be possible for the researcher to deduce the correct responses from other data given, or the interviewer may be able to recollect what was told. If the missing information is vitally important, interviewers can be asked to call back and collect it. Alternatively, and certainly attractive economically, respondents may be contacted by post or telephone. In view of the likelihood of 'missing' answers, it would be advisable to check survey forms at very short intervals, so that any call-backs can be made conveniently by field staff, who would probably still be working in the same area. Guessing at answers is not good research practice, because there are several possible reasons why responses are not recorded: the interviewer may have forgotten to ask a certain question, or asked it but omitted to record it; some respondents may have objected to answering certain questions, and the interviewer may have failed to note their refusal. Even experienced interviewers lapse occasionally, so editing calls for vigilance and patience.

Accuracy is another important aspect of editing. Obvious inaccuracies in answers should be rejected; some may be facetious or extremely doubtful, and these can be checked against other sections of the questionnaire. Frequently, surveys contain 'check' questions to test the validity of other responses. Arithmetical answers should be checked; for example, 'number in family' could be compared with individual information concerning marital status, number of children, etc. Where daily consumption figures have been requested, has the respondent, by chance, given weekly consumption?

Consistency and accuracy are closely bound together. Such details as a respondent's personal qualifications for inclusion in the survey should be checked. Is he or she living in the specified district under survey? Do the occupations given seem compatible with the type of housing reported, or the income level? Inconsistent answers must be rejected or changed. If some serious doubt arises, then interviewers may have to call back to clarify apparent inconsistencies. Inconsistencies might also suggest that some interviewers have been insufficiently trained to spot such responses during the course of field enquiries, and retraining or better supervision should be considered.

Editing is, therefore, a slow, laborious task, perhaps unexciting compared with other activities in research. It must largely be done by personal scrutiny. Good organizational work helps to reduce the load by ensuring a regular flow of survey forms throughout the course of the investigation. Particular sections of the questionnaire could be audited by specialists who will be able to complete the task speedily.

13.3 Coding

When editing has been completed, the next stage is the coding of answers for analysis purposes. Coding is usually printed on questionnaire forms to enable interviewers to pre-code responses during the course of interviewing. This cuts down considerably the final coding task and speeds up the whole operation. The codes entered on questionnaires are based on work carried out at the pilot stage of the survey. The amount of detailed break-down (classification of data) is largely a matter of judgement, but as the pilot survey progresses it may well be necessary to amend certain classifications as more general data become available. Only after further testing should researchers accept coding frames for inclusion in the final survey. Investigators indicate responses by encircling or ticking the appropriate coded answers. Open questions require coding by experienced research staff who, after an examination of a representative selection of completed survey forms, draw up certain categories into which answers can be allocated and coded. It will readily be understood that the coding of answers is a delicate matter, calling for considerable attention to the needs of particular surveys. Experience at the pilot stage is reinforced by later examination of a selected number of completed surveys; this is the general practice of the Government Social Survey which takes 10 per cent of schedules in order to construct the final coding frame. In 1983, the Market Research Society published the findings[1] of a special study group on coding practice and the way in which it should be integrated into good survey operations.

> It is easy for the researcher to ignore the processes that occur between finalising a questionnaire and receiving tabulated responses. Efficient field and data processing departments encourage the researcher to think of tasks as mechanical routines. In fact, of course, they involve as much judgement and skill as the process of survey design, and they can influence profoundly the data upon which a survey report is based.[1]

In Chapter 5 it has already been noted that numerical values should be allocated to various responses of a questionnaire; these are usually ringed for easy identification; for example:

How long have you lived in your present house?

	Code
Up to one year	1
Over one year up to two years	2
Over two years up to four years	3

Over four years up to six years	4
Over six years up to ten years	5
Over ten years	6

Pre-coded questions similar to the quoted example are often referred to as 'multi-choice' or 'cafeteria' questions.

The layout of the questions should enable coding to be done easily by the interviewers, often while working in difficult conditions. Where street interviewing is concerned, the interviewer must be able to complete the questionnaire fairly quickly. Interviewing may frequently involve calling at houses in the evening. In some cases, the questionnaire may have to be filled in by the interviewer while standing on the doorstep.

Since the late 1980s, computer-based interviewing techniques have revolutionized the coding process: CAT with SDDE (simultaneous direct data entry), CAPI, the use of lap-top computers, and CASI with direct interaction with computers (see Chapter 5), as well as the development of internet surveys, are all dynamic influences in rapid data inputting.

13.4 Tabulation

After editing and coding, the next stage in processing data is tabulation, the objective of which is to prepare quantitative data so that they are readily understandable and their significance is appreciated. This entails counting the frequency of certain cases within classifications relevant to particular surveys. Tabulation can be either manual, mechanical or electronic; the method will be determined by the nature of the survey, namely size, complexity, and also speed with which the findings are needed by management. Generally speaking, a simple survey involving fewer than 500 questionnaires could be hand processed. This would also be advisable where the qualitative aspects are greater than the quantitative elements.

Hand tabulation is easy and, provided a little organizing ability is present, convenient. Summary tables are designed to show the various characteristics being measured, and simple tally marks are then entered and added together. These are often entered in sets of five tally marks thus: ‖‖, which simple device makes the process of totalling easy.

Admittedly, hand processing gets difficult when cross-tabulations become complex or lengthy. On the other hand, manual processing is flexible – there is no time wasted waiting for machine availability – and it can be done by relatively junior staff under supervision. Machine tabulation is a complex operation, particularly suited to extensive surveys where large quantities of data are to be handled or intricate analysis is required. Before this method can be used, data have to be transferred to punch cards by means of punching equipment. The Hollerith system was widely used in marketing research data processing for many years, but has now largely been replaced by mainframe and micro computers. However, this system is not entirely abandoned, and BMRB, for instance, has a full-time analysis staff of around 30, who are responsible for editing, coding, detailed response analysis, and tabulations. The preparation of the editing and coding manuals is the responsibility of research teams headed by an analysis officer. Conventional punch cards are sometimes used, and BMRB has about six in-house punch operators supported by a few selected punching agencies.

Punch cards, measuring about 7⅜ in × 3¼ in, are generally printed with 80 columns and in each column there are 12 positions. One or more columns of a card are allocated to each question, and the various answers to that question are represented by a punched hole in that column. Reference to any position on a card can easily be given by quoting column and hole numbers.

Key punch operators punch codes on to the cards direct from questionnaires, and the possibility of error is minimized, therefore, by a well-designed questionnaire. It is advisable for key punching to be checked, if possible by a different operator, to ensure accuracy at this stage of analysis.

Hence, when the cards have been punched, they are verified, i.e. if the re-punch does not agree with the original punching on the card, the verifier locks the machine and thus enables the discrepancy to be checked. The next step is to place the cards in a sorter. A particularly useful version of this machine is called a counter-sorter which is popular for the tabulation of surveys. It counts the number of cards in each answer classification and records the total on a dial. Another piece of vital equipment is the tabulator, which extracts cards with numbers punched in given columns, totals these, and prints the total on special forms. It will also reproduce, direct from the cards, the coded information.

Machine tabulation requires skilled operators and is fairly expensive. From the efficiency angle it is very attractive, but there is a danger that this may encourage researchers to accumulate an enormous amount of classified data, some of which may never be used or even read. Researchers should be guided by the agreed objectives of the survey, and resist the temptation to expand the research area unreasonably. This does not mean to say that researchers should not remain sensitive to the experiences gathered during the survey, which may sometimes lead them to discuss with management the original objectives and modifications that circumstances now suggest to be desirable.

An alternative to punch cards is specially designed paper tape which, unlike cards, can accommodate as many columns as a questionnaire may need. This flexibility is somewhat diminished by the fact that subsequent analysis is confined to computer processing. Alternatively, data may be punched directly on to magnetic tape, one reel of which (usually about 2400 feet) can contain a very considerable volume of data.

An experienced marketing researcher has commented that 'before computers, questionnaires were far more succinct (i.e. shorter!), mainly because "processing" first meant hand analysis and then Hollerith punch cards . . . Fat and flabby questionnaires became commonplace in the computer age and were only seriously reformed with the introduction of CAPI and CATI'.[2]

13.5 Computers

Computers have become so much a part of business and professional activities, and even of personal living, that, as John O'Brien says,[3] 'it is increasingly hard to imagine the days of "knitting needle" analysis', when a rod similar to a knitting needle was pushed through a card with punched holes, and then the remaining cards were manually counted.

Computers have advanced in complexity and reduced in size and cost. In the later part of the 1980s, PCs became lighter and so were more portable: lap-top computers (as noted earlier) were introduced into field surveys. User-friendly software packages have enabled researchers to conduct complex calculations, produce relevant charts, and greatly increase the value of survey findings.

The immense ease with which complex calculations can be handled by computers may itself be counter-productive for effective management. Discretion should be exercised as to the quality and the quantity of data inputs to avoid what has been popularly termed 'the GIGO syndrome' (garbage in–garbage out). Computers enable sophisticated multi-variate statistical analyses to be applied to research data – and these, unless used with skill and understanding, may merely clog up a research report with impressive but never-to-be-read data.

Data have to be organized systematically before they can be processed by computer. Computer 'software packages' enable data to be organized into 'language' which is 'understood' by the computer. In other words, a set of data is fed into the computer which is instructed to handle it in specific ways, e.g. calculating correlations.

Computer 'software packages' involve 'programs' which provide complete printed instructions on carrying out a series of operations designed to achieve certain kinds of data outputs. There are many computer programs available; the researcher should refer to the respective manuals and establish the suitability of a particular program for the survey. Researchers must satisfy themselves that a particular program is capable of producing the data analyses specified in the original brief.

Of the many programs in use, the Statistical Package for the Social Sciences (SPSS) offers marketing researchers and other analysts a very considerable and flexible means of analysing data. SPSS MR under the banner *Vision 2000*, is a radical move towards simplification in usage, and an open database.

The Economic and Social Research Council (ESRC) keeps a register of software packages applicable to market and social surveys. Specialist agencies offer data-processing services in most cities and large towns.

There are special market research packages for micros; spreadsheets of varying levels of sophistication are widely adopted. Several research firms offer specialized services related to coding and tabulation of data from clients' questionnaires. Their services can extend to multivariable analyses, if desired. Companies such as Demotab are listed in the *Market Research Society Yearbook*.

The Market Research Society[4] has published a guide to software which analyses 120 software applications created specially for marketing research. Comparative performance tables are based on a detailed e-mail survey among specialist software providers, and cover the vast majority of marketing research software titles currently in use in the UK, as well as those in widespread use throughout the world.

As seen in Chapters 5 and 6, the introduction and swift dissemination of CAPI and other computer-linked interviewing methodologies, and the adoption of these by leading research organizations, have added significantly to the trend towards the simplification of data processing. Direct data inputting, and the dynamic internet developments also contribute to this fundamental change in data capture and processing. Although, as Keller[5] observes, batch editing 'is less necessary for CAPI/CATI interviews (since all checks can often be done during the interview), most mail surveys may benefit from it'.

13.6 Use of weights

Some data derived from a sample may need to be corrected for differences in the composition of the sample and the known characteristics of the population from which it was drawn. Weights are needed, for example, when unequal probability is used in sampling (see Chapter 3: Variable sampling fraction).

In the case of a survey of buyers of sports equipment, a sample may have resulted in too many respondents in the older age groups rather than 18–30 year-olds, who are recognized to be the prime market segment, so weighting of, say, 2 might be applied to the sample data from this group of buyers.

Where too many males were sampled in a survey of the general population, weighting could be applied to male and female respondents, so that the sample data reflected the composition of the population. The sample differences may have occurred because of differing levels of response by male and female interviewees or by mere chance. The weighting factors are readily applied by computer, but they are not easily done by hand or mechanical methods.

Where weighting is used, the method must be recorded in the resultant report, as is done in the National Readership Survey (NRS), to ensure that their sample data are representative. The MRS Code of Conduct (see later discussion), and also ESOMAR's International Code require that clients should be given details of the sampling method and any weighting methods used.

KEYPOINT

Final stages of survey

Data are raw materials of research findings

They need to be processed into usable form by:

Editing

Coding

Tabulation

All these tasks must be expertly done to ensure accuracy

13.7 Data fusion ('statistical matching')

This process involves merging the results from two separate surveys with different samples into a single database. One survey is termed the 'donor' and the other, the 'recipient' survey. The data to be transferred from donor to recipient is termed the 'missing' data. For example, media data from the first survey may be taken and fused with product data in the second survey, hence resulting in the formation of 'single-source' information, which would be valuable to marketers of such products.[6] Another example might relate to one survey indicating the readership profile of a particular journal, and which could be fused with data from another survey giving the holiday travel habits of certain socio-economic groups of consumers.

Fusion techniques in marketing research in Europe were used in the early 1980s in connection with media studies in France and Germany; in Britain, as Baker notes,[6] the 'first major step was taken in 1987 with the fusion of the National Readership Survey (NRS) with NOP's Financial Research Survey (FRS)'. This aroused considerable interest and led to the experiment by the Market Research Development Fund (MRDF) in 1988, on two separate sub-samples of the Target Group Index (TGI). It was shown that there were problems in checking the results for validity.[6] Although the results overall seemed 'highly impressive', there was concern about the 'real problems which could arise from the relationship between the "real" recipient data and data fused from the donor file'.[6] The 'first major conclusion' from the MRDF experiment was that 'when looking at marginal totals of fused data and comparing them with the donor data', the fused data should be regarded as a sample of the donor data, 'albeit often a complex sample.

However, if the sample sizes are large, the fusion would appear to be very accurate indeed'.[6]

This qualified assessment is echoed in the recommendation that a 'considerable amount of thought and preparatory work must be undertaken before embarking on fusion . . . Whether or not fusion will be universally accepted is doubtful'.[6] However, it is conceded that some researchers regard well-designed fusion schemes capable of enriching data to a greater extent than would two separate surveys.

Jephcott and Bock[7] have also reflected on the credibility of data fusion, and they identify 'at least three areas of interest to marketers': media planning, general marketing research, and direct marketing. They note that there has been a 'lively dialogue', for some time, over the validity of fusion techniques, and accept that 'in the best of all worlds', the single-source survey is preferable even though the advocates of fusion argue against its practicality. The use of fusion methods is seen by them 'to be a way of avoiding the biased and misleading data' resulting from single-source surveys 'due to inappropriate data collection methods being applied in a burdensome fashion'.[7]

Among the proponents of single-source data there is, it is alleged, a sub-group who 'appear to argue that even if the sample is unrepresentative and the collection methods are flawed, the results of a single-source survey are more valid than those produced by a synthetic approach'.[7] Such zealous defence, however, seems to lack a certain professional objectivity.

Jephcott and Bock conclude that although data fusion methodologies 'do not contain much in the way of internal validity checks', and therefore the 'very real possibility' that decisions will be based on a fused database that 'does not represent reality', such methodologies will become routinely used.[7]

In line with this opinion is that of Dina Raimonde: 'originally the question was "Is fusion an appropriate technique for true research?" But more recently there has been a new wave of interest in fusion, with more demanding questions such as: "When should we use it or not?" and "How reliable is it?" '[8] She concludes that fusion and benchmarking may become more widely available because of PC technology and software advances. Nevertheless, it is admitted that 'fusion remains a mysterious and problematic technique', and that the statistical margins of error connected with fusion are 'unknown at present'.[8]

With the increasing demand for rapidly-available marketing research information, and the virtually perpetual advance of computer technology, data fusion techniques also seem destined to grow and become accepted as part of the research tool kit. But even those who support this technique have expressed certain caveats; these should be balanced against the attractions which, its advocates suggest, outweigh the inherent uncertainties.

Single-source data which, for example, incorporate information about individual buying habits, TV exposure, and specific product usage clearly avoid the problems of data fusion. Some mass media industry surveys often include limited details of product use linked with media exposure.

13.8 Database marketing

The growth in this research activity and its affinity to data fusion methodology suggest that discussion of the one should follow closely that of the other.

Basically, databases are sets of customer data stored in the files of computers and available for analyses. Over the past decade or so there has been, as Peter Mouncey observes, 'a massive growth in the availability of data to support marketers, facilitated by the application of information technology'.[9] The proliferation of such data – derived from customer information files, electronic home-based meters, panel data, etc. – has 'challenged the role and status of traditional market research'.[9] It also gives rise to concern about 'issues of reliability, representativeness and interpretation in the use of data'; the use of data as a sampling frame may also lead to biases.[9]

The trend towards customer database methodology has been particularly marked in continuous market research and in advertising media research (see Chapters 8 and 10). It is apparent that database marketing is now impinging significantly, as Peter Mouncey notes,[9] on traditional marketing research activities. In doing so, it puts at risk the diverse contributions made by the latter in providing, for instance, qualitative insights into consumer buying behaviour by substituting, instead, relatively low-cost quantitative, computerized information.

Research[10] on the interactions between database marketing and marketing research activities was based on 18 in-depth interviews with senior managers in market research firms, database marketing companies, and financial service organizations in the USA and the UK during April–July 1994. It was found that clients used database marketing techniques and sources to acquire purchasing and demographic data on their customers and prospects. Their need for attitudinal data – which was increasing – was still mostly supplied by market research companies. Another finding was that there was a need to emphasize the distinctive roles of marketing research and of database marketing, and so ensure that client companies clearly understood the characteristic ways in which these types of activities could supply their information needs and help in their long-term strategic development. Both marketing research firms and database companies felt that it was extremely important that their distinctive roles should be clearly understood by all concerned, particularly the general public.

Life-style data are not covered by the professional codes of the MRS or ESOMAR (see later discussion), but in 1995, the Professional Standards Committee of the MRS published a set of guidelines for handling databases and, as noted, to assist market researchers working with databases containing personal details of respondents, prospective respondents or respondent-identified survey data. The MRS Code of Conduct stipulates respondent confidentiality, and the guidelines provide a framework for marketing researchers working with database marketers, 'who by definition select and promote to known individuals'. Barry Leventhal[11] has described a specific approach to this problem by combining customer transactional data with market research on the same individuals in the financial services sector.

NOP Financial Research Survey (FRS) is a continuous monitor of consumer financial holdings, which is undertaken on the back of the NOP Random Omnibus Survey (see Chapter 8). The survey is conducted by in-home personal interviews by the CAPI method. Fieldwork is throughout the year; an annual sample size of 60 000 adults across Britain is achieved.

This linked approach has six stages which utilize sets of data from NOP's Research Survey (FRS) and customers' databases. Stage I segments FRS adults aged 18 and over, according to their likely use of financial services; Stage II involves mapping this segmentation (known as FRuitS) on to an organization's customer base; at Stage III, FRS variables, including FRuitS, and customer attributes are appended to the matched sample. All personal identifiers are then removed, so that the sample can only be used for statistical analyses and model development. Stage IV profiles each segment by customer variables such as demographics, product holdings (i.e. financial assets) and transactional behaviour. Predictive variables are identified. At Stage V, statistical models are developed which estimate the likelihood of a customer belonging to each segment; in the final Stage VI, the models are applied to the customer database in order to determine the most likely segment for *every* customer.

In this way, the FRS is matched with a customer database to form a 'workbench of anonymized data on customers, which is compliant with the MRS Code, the MRS Guidelines for Handling Databases, and the Data Protection Act'.[11]

Phyllis Macfarlane declares that market researchers 'must widen their brief. The internal database is no longer a joke – cumbersome and inaccurate – it is an increasingly important information source and method of collecting data, which must be integrated with the research function'.[12] She asks who, in any case, is going to analyse and make sense of all the data pouring from database marketing: 'Surely this is one of market research's core competences?'[12]

13.9 Data handling and interpretation

Classification of data

Three broad divisions of survey data may be identified as follows:

1. *Uni-variate*; where a single variable is analysed along, e.g. sample statistic such as the mean, which might refer to the age of a certain type of consumer or, independently, to the consumption of a particular kind of food.

2. *Bi-variate*: where some association is measured between two variables simultaneously, e.g. cross-classification of age group and consumption of a product. This extends the amount of information, which is severely restricted in uni-variate analysis, and allows study of the relationship between the variables, e.g. age group and product usage. These are customarily presented as two-way cross tabulations or contingency tables; these variables cannot be shown graphically. 'Cross-tabs' are usually derived from computer packages, such as SPSS MR.

3. *Multi-variate*: where simultaneous relationships between more than two variables are involved. Such analysis extends further the analyses feasible by uni-variate and bi-variate methods; most multi-variable statistical techniques require the use of a computer to calculate, for instance, factor and cluster analyses, multiple regression, etc. Such analyses might be concerned with identifying consumption habits in terms of age, sex, socio-economic group, geographical location, etc.

It will be seen that there is a dependent relationship between the intrinsic nature of the data; for instance, bi-variate, and the statistical measures which may be applied. In the vast field of data analysis there are many analytical techniques and reference should be made to a good standard textbook on statistical methods. It is also recommended that the *Research Guide to Software*, recently issued by the Market Research Society should be consulted. In addition, there is a selective list of software suppliers given in the 1998 edition of the ESOMAR Handbook (p. 415).[13]

KEYPOINT

Classification of data

Univariate: single variable

Bivariate: two variables

Multivariate: more than two variables

Analytical techniques are dependent on type of data. Tests of significance show whether specific data variations are statistically significant or occur merely by chance.

Tests of hypotheses and significance

In order to check that sampling variations are *not* responsible for variations in the consumption, for example, of a particular food product in certain selected areas of the UK, tests of significance may be applied to the data. However, it is important to remember that the findings are relevant to the particular samples taken during the survey. Other samples (of different size) may reveal data that react differently to a test of significance.[14]

This point should be clearly appreciated by researchers who should not be misled into making sweeping assertions based on tests of significance. Moser[15] has directed attention to the fact that an effect shown to be statistically significant may yet be of such small magnitude that it is of no substantive interest to researchers. These two aspects of the outcome of significance tests should be carefully borne in mind by marketing researchers.

Apart from the estimation of population parameters, sampling theory is also concerned with the testing of statistical hypotheses. Decisions have frequently to be taken on the basis of information obtained in sampling, and in the process of reaching such decisions certain assumptions have to be made about the population under survey. These tentative theories or guesses are termed 'statistical hypotheses'. They are statements about the probability distribution of the population.

Typical hypotheses could be concerned with deciding whether one method of advertising was more effective than another, or whether consumption of a particular food product was significantly different in certain selected areas of the country. On the basis of a stated hypothesis, characteristics of a population are explored and the information obtained compared with the supposition contained in the hypothesis which will then be accepted or rejected according to the probability that it is true.

Hypotheses which have a very good chance of being accepted or found true are termed 'probably true'; those with a very poor chance of acceptance are called 'probably false'. For example, the probability of getting 15 heads in 20 tosses of a fair coin would be very small, and so any hypothesis based on this event would be improbable.

Often, a statistical hypothesis is formed for the sole purpose of rejecting or nullifying it, and it is then termed a 'null hypothesis' (NH). For example, if the relative efficiency of two different mailing shots was being investigated, a null hypothesis would state that there was no real difference between them, and that any difference that did occur was merely the result of chance sampling fluctuations. In effect, the assumption in a null hypothesis is directly opposite to what it is hoped to prove.

Tests of significance enable statistical hypotheses to be accepted or rejected. They provide evidence which must then be evaluated by statisticians; they do not provide absolute or final reasons for accepting or rejecting a particular hypothesis. The fact that sample size improves the precision of sample findings means that the results of significance tests will be valid for particular samples. Moser[15] warns that although a test may produce a negative result, i.e. not statistically significant, it cannot be automatically assumed that the effect does not exist in the population under survey. The results of significance tests indicate merely that particular samples have failed to indicate a significant relationship.

Table 13.1   Types of error

	Accept hypothesis	Reject hypothesis
Hypothesis is true	Correct decision	Type 1 error
Hypothesis is false	Type 2 error	Correct decision

Two types of error may occur in dealing with hypotheses. Type 1 error occurs when a hypothesis is rejected when it should have been accepted as true. Type 2 error occurs when a hypothesis is accepted which should be rejected as false (see Table 13.1).

After the data have been tabulated, the processes of analysis and interpretation play their part in the development of the final survey.

Analysis and interpretation are closely linked and depend largely on the objectives of individual surveys. Analysis aims to organize and clarify data so that they become more comprehensible. It is influenced and largely controlled by the type of information which was sought in the objectives of the survey. This demands, therefore, thorough planning of every stage of the survey to ensure that the critical task of analysis will be supported by the right kinds of tabulation. Last-minute arrangements should be avoided; market researchers must think well ahead and work to a soundly conceived research design.

Analysis of data may cover simple statistical descriptions such as averages, percentages, distributions, and measures of dispersion, to be found in most surveys. Data are examined to detect possible relationships and their significance. It is customary, for example, to discover either a positive or negative correlation between product use and income level or social group, although these are less marked than some years ago; for example, telephones are now in nearly every UK home (96 per cent: 1999), whereas they were at one time mostly limited to the middle and upper-middle classes. Today, innovations tend to be electronically based products, such as PCs used in the home, or video recorders, which are more likely to be associated with age group and recreational interests than directly related to a particular socio-economic group.

Correlation indicates the degree of movement between two variables; it gives a measure of the association but the existence of correlation does not imply that the relationship is causal. The relationship may have occurred by chance and have nothing to do with cause and effect. In some cases, however, the relationship is causal as in the cases of the birth rate and the sale of perambulators.

An example of wrongly inferring a relationship between x and y because a set of observations on x and y gave a high measure of correlation was illustrated by a study[14] of the proportion of Church of England marriages to all marriages in England and Wales during the period 1866 to 1911 compared with the standardized mortality rate for the same period. This resulted in a correlation coefficient of 0.95. (It is generally agreed that correlations above 0.8 represent a very high degree of relationship.) To conclude from this study that the greater the proportion of marriages solemnized by the Church of England the higher the death rate would, of course, be absurd. In fact, the trend in both sets of statistics showed a steady fall over the years 1866 to 1911 for quite unconnected reasons, but because of this common movement their values over the period followed each other.

With many marketing problems, for example the volume of sales, several variables have to be considered, which involve the use of more sophisticated statistical methods such as multiple regression. A third factor might, in fact, be the cause of the association noted between two other factors. The cold weather might have been the cause of reduced sales of ice-cream in a holiday resort, although analysis of the number of visitors showed that they were increasing while sales of ice-cream were falling, and a negative correlation appeared to exist between these two variables. It would be incorrect to assume that increased numbers of visitors caused the sales of ice-cream to fall over a certain period.

It will be apparent that correlation analysis has to be handled with care and common sense. Correlation indicates that certain variables appear to be associated, but it does not state that they are connected in a cause-and-effect relationship. The task of skilled interpretation lies in studying the nature of the association and its significance. Data should be scrutinized carefully for likely relationships, though the intrusion of sampling errors must never be overlooked.

For a specified hypothesis which is being tested, the level of significance of the test refers to the maximum probability with which a Type 1 error would be an acceptable risk. In statistics, it is customary to use the Greek letters α and β (alpha and beta) to denote the probabilities of committing Type 1 and Type 2 errors respectively.

The probability value of α is often specified before the samples are drawn to avoid any possible bias which might arise when the results of the survey are known.

Although the choice of an actual level of significance is purely arbitrary, in practice the levels most commonly used are 0.05 (5 per cent) and 0.01 (1 per cent). The former means there are 5 chances in 100 that the hypothesis would be rejected when it should actually have been accepted; in other words, the confidence level of the decision is 95 per cent. In the latter case, there is only 1 chance in 100 that the hypothesis would be rejected when it should have been accepted, and the resulting confidence level of the decision is 99 per cent.

Where a sampling distribution is distributed normally with a given hypothesis that is true, it can be stated with 95 per cent confidence that the Z score of an actual sample statistic will lie between -1.96 and 1.96 (see Fig. 13.1).

If a sample statistic, e.g. $\bar{x}$, selected at random, were found to be outside the limits (± 1.96), it would be concluded that such an event would be likely to occur in only 5 per cent samples drawn from populations. It could then be stated that this statistic differed significantly from μ, and the hypothesis would be rejected at the 5 per cent (0.05) level of significance.

Other levels of significance can, of course, be used. For example, 1 per cent (0.01) could be used where more stringent testing of an estimate was thought to be desirable. In this case, the Z value would be ± 2.58 (refer to Table 3.4 on p. 78).

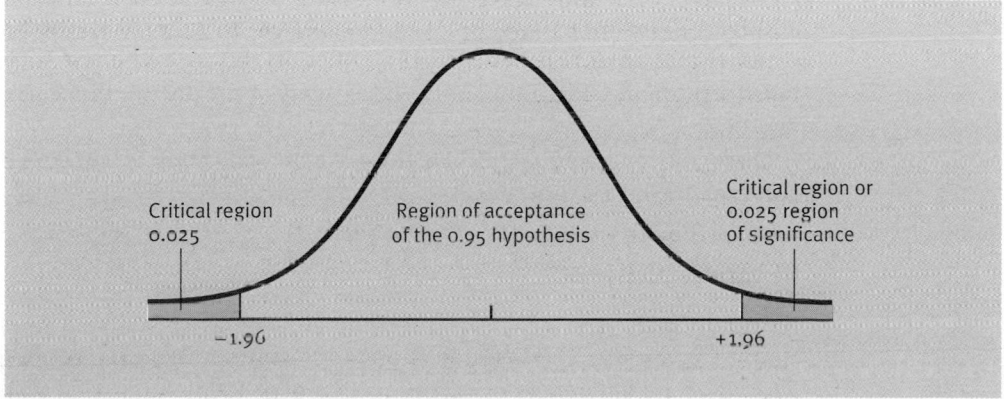

Figure 13.1 Example of 95 per cent confidence level

Table 13.2   The significant region

Significant level α	0.10	0.05	0.01	0.005	0.002
Critical region values of Z for one-tailed tests	−1.28 or 1.28	−1.645 or 1.645	−2.33 or 2.33	−2.58 or 2.58	−2.88 or 2.88
Critical region values of Z for two-tailed tests	−1.645 and 1.645	−1.96 and 1.96	−2.58 and 2.58	−2.81 and 2.81	−3.08 and 3.08

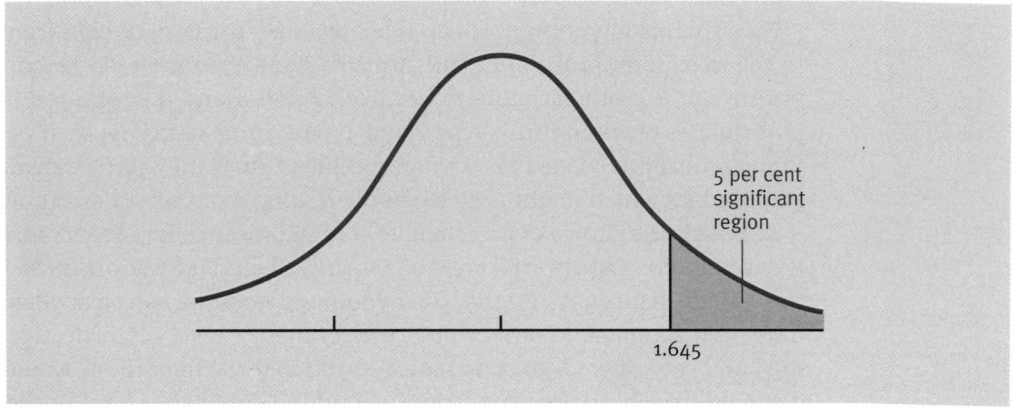

Figure 13.2   Levels of significance

As already noted, the researcher must decide beforehand at what level of significance her hypothesis will be tested. She must accept the risk that she cannot expect to make the right decision *every* time; she may accept where she should have rejected or reject where she should have accepted. Whatever level of significance is used, the researcher must eventually use her judgement based on the statistical evidence which has become available. She may, in fact, conclude that the results of experimental surveys so far achieved have not provided her with sufficiently reliable grounds on which to base some critical decision. Further research may be warranted in such cases.

So far the extreme values occurring on both sides of the mean have been considered, e.g. $\mu \pm 2.58\sigma$, and the tests of significance involved are known as two-tailed (or two-sided) tests. This concerns tests to discover whether one process (or product) is different from another. Sometimes, however, the hypothesis may be concerned only with testing whether one product is better than another. In this case, the test is referred to as a one-tailed test (or one-sided), and only one extreme of the distribution curve is considered (see Fig. 13.2).

The significant region (critical region) of a one-tailed test is based on the *total* area of the curve, as Table 13.2 indicates.

Bi-variate analysis

Bi-variate analysis uses statistical techniques such as chi-square, simple correlation and simple regression, cross-classification and analysis of variance to give insight into why there are differences or variations in a dependent variable. It will be recalled that a dependent variable is one which, as the name suggests, is dependent upon the action taken; for example, by a marketing manager. His or her activities will affect sales volume, brand preferences, etc. The independent variable is the one the marketing researcher believes may account for the observed differences or variations in the dependent variable, e.g. changes in price, packaging, methods of distribution, etc.

Changes in the independent variable are carefully studied to see in what way they influence the dependent variable. A popular method of testing the significance of sets of data is chi-square.

Chi-square

Chi-square (pronounced ki and denoted by χ^2) distribution has many applications and is particularly useful in testing whether observed frequencies in a sample distribution differ significantly from frequencies which could be expected to arise from some hypothesis. Chi-square tests are concerned with establishing whether the discrepancies between observed frequencies and expected frequencies are, in fact, statistically significant or whether they may be attributed to chance sampling errors or variations in the data.

Chi square tests are particularly useful in studying the relationship between attributes which is frequently of interest in marketing. Data can be arranged conveniently in cross-classification or matrix form. The number of frequencies in each cell should not be fewer than five – it may be necessary to combine cells in order to achieve this figure, though this may lead to some loss of precision in definition. At least 50 observations should be included in the total sample, and these must be randomly selected. Chi-square data are always stated in terms of original units and not percentages.

Basically, the χ^2 test procedure is quite simple: an hypothesis is set up – frequently a null hypothesis. Observed frequencies are then compared with data based on some assumed frequencies. The χ^2 statistic is computed from special statistical tables (found in most statistical textbooks), at some agreed level of significance, usually either 5 per cent or 1 per cent. The resultant figure is compared with that obtained from the equation involving observed and expected frequencies. The hypothesis is then accepted or rejected on the basis of this statistical evidence of probability.

The equation to compare observed and expected frequencies is:

$$\chi^2 = \sum \frac{(O_i - E_i)^2}{E_i}$$

where O_i = observed frequencies in a distribution

E_i = expected frequencies under the hypothesis that the data have a particular distribution.

The larger the value of χ^2, the greater the difference between observed and expected frequencies. Note also that since the right-hand side of the formula represents a sum of squared quantities, χ^2 is always positive.

If data are originally expressed in percentage or proportional form, they should be converted to *absolute* numbers. For example, if 40 per cent of people in a sample size of 200, is female, then computations for calculating χ^2 should be based on 80 females (and *not* on 40 per cent of a sample being female).

Multi-variate analysis

Multi-variate analysis involves complex and sophisticated statistical methods which focus upon and bring out in bold relief, the structure of *simultaneous* relationships among three or more phenomena'. Unlike simple uni-variate methods which deal with averages and variances, and bi-variate techniques which deal with pairwise relationships, multi-variate methods concentrate on the more complex relationships among several variables in a set of data. Multi-variate methods can be described as either functional or structural. The former are 'most appropriate for building predictive models and for explaining one or more phenomena based on their relationships'. Multiple regression is a widely used technique; also used are multiple discriminant analysis, multi-variate analysis of variance, canonical correlation analysis, and conjoint or trade-off analysis. The latter type is more descriptive than predictive, and includes factor analysis, cluster analysis, and multi-dimensional scaling.

Factor analysis

Factor analysis, not to be confused with factorial design (see Chapter 2), has grown in popularity, although it has also attracted criticism because certain aspects, it is alleged, lack mathematical rigour. It is a form of multi-variate analysis based on the hypothesis that buying behaviour, for example, is rarely attributable merely to one cause or influence. Therefore, enquiry should endeavour to identify the multiple factors which are influential in certain buying conditions.

In a brand image study related to consumers' life styles in America, a factor analysis program was used to identify 25 factors which were significant in establishing life styles. Beer drinkers and non-beer drinkers were compared and distinct brand loyalties emerged.

> Brand Y drinkers are Outdoorsmen, and thus more inclined to be Hard Drinkers; whereas the Brand W drinkers are more associated with the Cosmopolitan Traveller, the Dress-Conscious Man, the Well-Groomed Man, the Cocktail Drinker, and the Car-Conscious Man. Brand W drinkers seem to seek more oral satisfaction, being associated with the Candy Consumer, and the Cigar and Pipe Smoker. Among light beer drinkers, approximately the same type of pattern can be discerned, though with less extreme differences between the brands.[16]

Craig and Douglas[17] indicate that factor analysis is particularly useful in multi-country research because, for example, it allows examination of inter-relationships among a set of variables. For instance, in a comparative survey of magazine readership in the United States and France, the frequency of reading different magazines in each country was the first factor analysed, and divergent behaviour was established. In the United States, family, news, and housemaker magazines were the most frequently read groups, whereas in France, readership was more diverse; the most frequently read were those magazines focusing on women's interests, fashion, business, and television.

Factor analysis[17] was also used in a study[19] of women's lifestyle patterns in the United States, the UK, and France. Five factors were highly similar in all countries, of which four: home; social; frustration; and innovation were extracted.

Harper[18] used factor analysis techniques to study the relationships between Cheshire and Cheddar cheeses. Over a period of time, five Cheshire cheeses from each day's production at a cheese factory 'were subjected to light mechanical tests and six types of subjective assessment'. Product moment correlation coefficients were finally calculated between all pairs of variables, and it was possible to identify 'at least three dimensions' which differentiate Cheshire cheeses. Comparative tests were then made with Cheddar cheeses. 'In the study on Cheshire cheeses, firmness and springiness emerge effectively indistinguishable in spite of the fact that two forms of assessment are not perfectly correlated. In the Cheddar cheese studies, the qualitative distinction between firmness and springiness is well substantiated.'

Factor analysis was also used in a study[19] of the qualitative attributes of coffee. Fourteen attributes of coffee were developed from open discussion with a group of consumers; these attributes were rated on a 10-point semantic differential scale (see Chapter 7). Ninety-four consumers, randomly selected, rated each of the 14 attributes after drinking a cup of coffee, the brand of which was unknown to them. In fact, only one brand was tested. The data were processed by an appropriate computer program, and the findings revealed that four factors were significant influences in coffee preferences: 'comforting taste', 'heartiness of flavour', 'genuineness of product', 'freshness'. Other attributes such as 'alive taste' and 'tastes like real coffee' appeared related to the last mentioned significant factor. The researcher concluded that this could imply 'that a major factor behind coffee preference may be the distinction between pure coffee and artificial coffee'; advertisements could profitably accentuate the 'genuineness' of their product.

Doyle[20] has reported a study of eight beverages: tea-bags, coffee-instant, fruit juice, soft drinks, coffee-fresh, tea-packet, drinking chocolate, and milk, in which factor analysis techniques were successfully used.

Cluster analysis

In this analytical approach, variables are placed in sub-groups or clusters based on specific attributes, such as brand loyalty, lifestyles, etc. Cluster analysis examines people, products or brands, and attempts, often through factor analysis, to evaluate them in terms of clusters or comparative profiles. As a result of this cluster analysis, gaps may be found in the market where new products might be introduced. But one of the problems of cluster analysis has been that of definition: what determines the boundaries of clusters – 'the criterion for admission to a cluster is rather arbitrary', and clusters tend to be defined in various ways, according to the 'discipline and purpose of the researcher'. It has been suggested[21] that clusters should have two properties: external isolation (objects in a cluster should be separated from those in another cluster by well-defined 'space'); and internal cohesion (objects within the same cluster should be similar).

In other words, for clustering to be a valid and reliable method of analysis, it is of paramount importance that the objects or individuals within a cluster should be more similar to each other than to those in another cluster. In overseas research, for example, it may be possible to develop groups of countries that share significant lifestyles, stages of economic development, etc. (see Chapter 12).

Morgan and Purnell[22] designed 10 clusters in a study of electors' attitudes to political issues as follows: High Tory; Me first; Whig; Labour (little England); Meritocrat; Me first (anti-Europe); One-nation Tories; Left-wing labour; Meritocrat (pro-Europe); and right-wing Labour.

Marketing segmentation for a new drink was derived from cluster analysis,[22] from which three 'clusters' of existing drinks were apparent: hot health drinks, cold drinks, and hot non-health drinks (see Fig. 13.3).

Between these three clusters point NEW 1 was calculated, equidistant from Chocolate 1, Hot Lemon Barley, and Ideal Hot Drink. Further product suggestions resulted from reclustering until finally a total of five new products resulted. Thus, an area was highlighted 'where a product perhaps, Hot Fruit Juice: as healthy as Lemon Juice and as hot as Hot Lemon Barley might be marketed'.

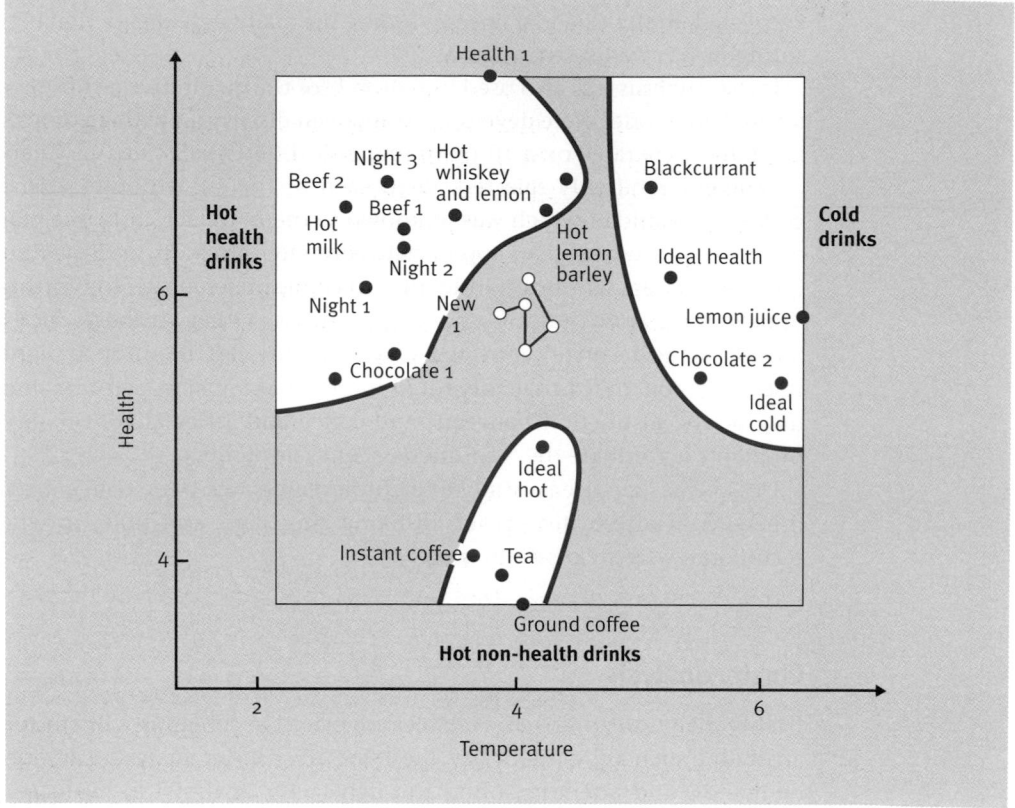

Figure 13.3   Development of a new drink (*Source*: Morgan and Purnell)

Discretion is needed in handling this method of researching new products. Market gaps might be identified which are clearly nonsensical; for example, a product cheaper than existing brands but of the highest quality. Such meaningless concepts would, of course, be eliminated immediately.

Cluster analysis, as Fitzroy[23] emphasizes, is not an analytical technique or single method, but a set of numerical methods in which there are large areas of subjectivity, so researchers should proceed cautiously. The scepticism with which the uninhibited use of cluster analysis has sometimes been greeted is also referred to in a review paper by Punj and Stewart.[24]

Conjoint analysis

This is a 'trade-off' or 'considered jointly' approach. When people buy products and services they tend to compare alternative suppliers and make some evaluation (which will vary in depth, according to the nature of the purchase) of the advantages and disadvantages which they perceive as attached to certain sources of supply and/or brands. What marketers need to have is some way of measuring and understanding the 'trade-offs' which specific people make when comparing kinds of products and eventually, perhaps, deciding on a particular brand.

A basic assumption of conjoint analysis is that products and services are made up of features or 'attributes': these may be varied according to the identified preferences of consumers. The more dominant the interest in a particular attribute of a product, the higher will be the 'utility' value given to it by actual or potential purchasers. The word 'conjoint' as Johnson[25] points out, refers to 'the fact that we can measure relative values of things considered jointly which might be unmeasurable taken one at a time. . . . The greatest strength of the procedure seems to be its ability to generate rather refined predictions from quite primitive data.'

A new paper tissue, for example, may be available in three different colours, several sizes, and various thicknesses, with some price differentials. 'The trade-off approach would not only predict the winning combination of these attributes but would also estimate how much consumers value changes in one attribute against changes in the others – in other words, to what extent they are prepared to "trade-off" size against thickness, colour against size, and all of these against price.'[26]

Green and Wind[27] refer to the difficult problem facing marketing managers when the nature of the product under consideration has several disparate qualities, each attractive to a diverse number of consumers with different interests. For example, when considering replacement radial tyres for his two-year-old car, a motorist might be faced with three options: 'Goodyear's, with a tread life of 30000 miles at $40 per tyre, and available at a store 10 minutes drive from his home; Firestone's, with a tread life of 50000 miles, at $85 per tyre, and available after 20 minutes drive; or Sears, with a tread life of 40000 miles, at $55 per tyre, and available within 10 minutes drive from home.

To tackle this kind of problem, Green and Wind[27] noted that the conjoint measurement, which starts with the consumer's overall judgement about a set of complex alternatives, can help 'in sorting out the relative importance of a product's multi-dimensional attributes'. The relative utilities of each attribute are worked out from ranked order responses by various computer programs.

With some products, such as cars, houses, or office machinery, the possible design factors are virtually unlimited and it could be expensive, if not impossible, to offer physical specimens across all possible variations. In such cases, 'the researcher usually resorts to verbalized descriptions of the principal factors of interest'.[27] A study among car owners in the United States to identify preferences for new vehicles, focused on the relative influences of mileage per gallon, price, country of manufacture, maximum speed, roominess, and length. Consumers evaluated these factor levels on a two-at-a-time basis. It was found that evaluations of attributes desired in a new car were highly associated with the type of car currently used.

Two approaches to the application of conjoint analysis have been identified[28] as: the profile or scenario approach, and the pairwise or trade-off method.

With the former, a respondent could be asked to choose between all the attributes of a product at the one time; for example, a red cubic scented soap versus a blue cubic unscented soap, and so forth. This method is often thought to reflect realistically the decisions facing buyers; the problem is that survey data covering five attributes each at three levels, result in 243 possible combinations of product (i.e. 3^5), an unmanageable number.

The alternative method – pairwise or trade-off – allows a respondent to consider possible alternatives in a simpler way; first of all, for example, trading colour against shape, and then colour against aroma, and shape against aroma. Compared with the profile or scenario approach, this method merely handles nine sets of stimuli (3^2) (see Fig. 13.4).

A respondent could give ranked preferences for the attribute combinations; or a seven-point scale, for instance, could be used to indicate reactions to photographs or sketches of the alternative versions of the product.

Aroma \ Colour	Red	Blue	Yellow
Scented			
Unscented			

Figure 13.4   Soap: aroma/colour matrix

An interesting application[29] of the 'trade-off ' approach to customer service in industrial markets in Germany and Benelux was used in a mail survey of UK exporters and their European customers who were asked to choose between a number of alternative customer service 'packages'. Utility values were calculated for each factor/level for each respondent; the results showed that exporters' perceptions differed quite significantly from prospective customers' in many cases; for example, delivery promise reliability was ranked first with UK exporters, third with German customers, but was considered of paramount importance by Benelux customers; after-sales service was ranked second by UK firms, first by German customers, and third by Benelux customers; multi-language literature was particularly important to Benelux customers, less so to German customers, but it was not thought important by UK exporters.

With the development of computer programs, the complexity of multi-variate analysis has expanded considerably. A detailed knowledge of these and other statistical methodologies should be obtained from statistical textbooks, specialist books, and professional journals.[30]

Finally, sophisticated techniques should not be applied indiscriminately. Researchers who are familiar with a particular multi-variate method may be tempted to use that technique across all research problems. They should, instead, ensure that the technique matches the specific nature of the data which have resulted from well-devised and executed research projects.

Non-metric multi-dimensional scaling (MDS) or mapping

In the 1970s, an interesting method of presenting a comparative evaluation of products and brands was introduced and adopted the rather awesome title of 'non-metric multi-dimensional scaling', or the more understandable description: 'mapping'. A 'perceptual map' is drawn of how consumers perceive comparative products along certain dimensions or attributes. A perceptual map of four brands of a given product may be shown, as in Fig. 13.5. Where products or brands are mapped close to one another, it may be presumed that they are in fairly direct competition. 'It should be emphasized, however, that . . . it is only the relative location of the points representing the stimuli that has meaning – the axes are arbitrary.'[23] To name the axes, additional information could be obtained from Kelly's Repertory Grid or, perhaps, semantic differential scales (see Chapter 7).

Basically, respondents are asked to rank order pairs of brands in terms of their perceived similarities, so that eventually some insight will be gained of people's choice criteria.

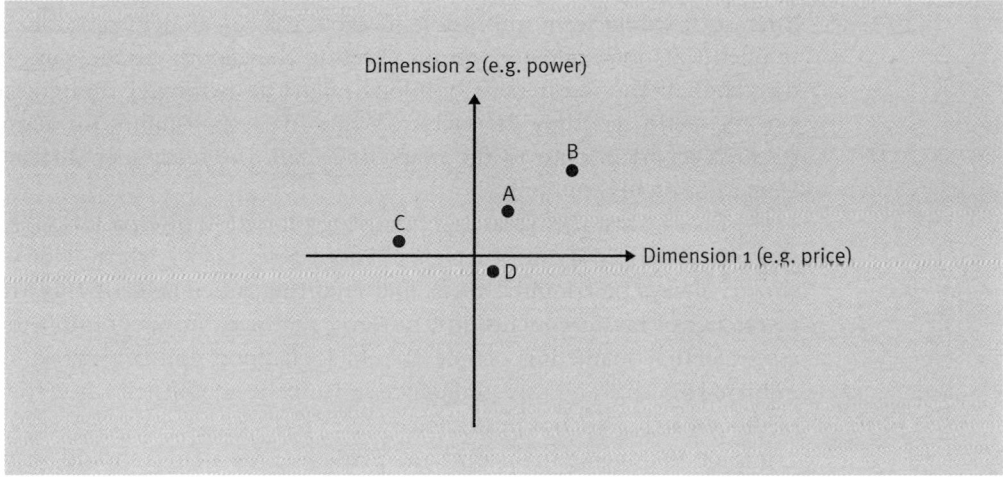

Figure 13.5   Perceptual map of four brands

Hence, ordinal data underlie this technique which has developed with specially devised computer programs. Doyle[31] has observed that the purpose of a spatial representation is to find out how brands or products in a class are perceived in comparative terms, so that strategic guides may be obtained for the development or improvement of new brands or products.

Because of the degree of subjectivity involved in this technique and its relatively limited applications, researchers need to use it with care. In multi-country research, it is important to keep in mind that 'perceptions of the same objects will often differ dramatically'.[17] In these situations, respondents can be asked to state their preferences, so that 'preference data can be combined with perceptual data to develop joint-space maps'[17] (see Chapter 9 for further discussion)

Interpretation of survey findings

Interpretation of survey findings is a matter on which experts express strongly conflicting views. Some would have researchers give their own interpretation of the findings of surveys, while others, equally dogmatic, believe that researchers should limit themselves to reporting the facts discovered through the survey. The comments of leading experts are worth careful reading; what is acceptable practice would seem to depend largely on the brief given to individual researchers.

Moser[15] states categorically that 'whatever the nature of data, the task of interpretation falls squarely on the shoulders of the researcher'. During the course of research, he will have obtained valuable experience in dealing with raw data, and 'while every reader is entitled to draw his own conclusions, the writer of the survey report should not shirk the duty of giving his own'. Furthermore, the researcher would fail to make his own full contribution to the survey if he did not include his 'own ideas and speculations, even if he cannot offer chapter and verse to substantiate them'.

This controversial view is supported by a paper by Ehrenberg[32] who feels that 'The proposition that the researcher should restrict himself in his report to "describing the facts" conflicts implicitly with his duties as a researcher'. He pleads that the proposition is impossible, or, alternatively, that it would inhibit good research and not be in the public interest. It would seem impossible to avoid the researcher's opinions and conclusions – implicitly if not explicitly – from entering the report. At the same time, there is the danger that 'the researcher's opinions might be [wrongly] thought to be as incontrovertible as his reporting of "facts"'. While the responsibility for acting on a marketing research report belongs to the marketing man, the researcher should not be precluded from offering his opinions.

The case against the researcher involving himself in interpretation of survey findings is strongly advanced by another experienced researcher[33] whose views are 'that findings should always be confined to factual reporting, unembellished by the opinions of the researcher or by his conclusions, however pertinent in his opinion these might be. It is essential that marketing people should look upon and rely upon research reports as unbiased findings and this confidence can only be established when the personal opinions of the researcher are not in evidence.'

It is felt that marketing people and marketing researchers should be encouraged to work closely together making full use of their special expertise and not attempting 'to usurp each other's functions'. In this way, good research will develop 'based on unimpeachable techniques and speedily reported in order not to lose actuality'.

Dr John Treasure[34] feels that the researcher 'must do more than report on the facts he has found'. He would prefer that recommendations should *not* be added – 'these tend to be distressingly naïve' – but he would expect questions to be put to the data and some attempt made to answer them:

For example, what are the main reasons why the repurchase rate is low? how important is the heavy user? is social class of any importance in determining consumer demand? This means asking the right questions, assembling all the data available (not necessarily all taken from the current survey) and producing coherent, reasoned, well-written answers.

Experts, such as those quoted, differ sharply in their views on the interpretation of research findings, and it is surely only reasonable to expect that they should do so. Marketing research is still developing and improving its techniques, and it is increasingly able to make a valid contribution to the marketing strategy of companies over a wide range of industries. The skill and knowledge of professional researchers should be used fully by their clients. Their professionalism ensures that the findings of surveys are the result of objective research, while, at the same time, from the wealth of their experience, they are able to indicate to clients particular developments in their markets. Skilled and sensitive handling of data brings with it valuable insight, which it would seem bad business practice to ignore.

As suggested in the introduction to this aspect of research, the question of interpretation by marketing researchers when presenting their reports rests on the brief given to them. No experienced researcher would wish to accept an assignment that contained conditions which, in his opinion, would inhibit good research practice.

13.10 The survey report

The final step in marketing research is to report the survey findings to those who authorized the investigation. Preparation of the research report deserves, therefore, special consideration. Essentially, the report must communicate to management, clearly and concisely, the findings of the research survey related to the specific marketing problems as defined in the objectives states in the research brief.

When preparing a research report, the researcher should keep in mind those who will read it. He or she should form an opinion of their needs and make sure that the report is drafted in language that will be fully understood by those particular readers. As in the preparation of any type of report, words should be carefully chosen so that they convey the findings of the survey clearly. This calls for a good command of English, but it does not mean that literary effects should be the ambition of report writers. Good, clear, grammatical English, free of jargon, and organized in a logical flow to assist readers to assimilate without difficulty the evidence collected as a result of the research, should be the aim of professional researchers.

Some years ago, a small book on the use of English for official purposes was published by the Treasury, and deservedly won the support of a much wider readership. The current, and revised, edition[35] approaches the problem of report writing with refreshing candour and helpfulness. Marketing researchers will find in this manual some very helpful guides to the art of good report writing and also questionnaire wording (see Chapter 5); they should not neglect the critical task of communication, which is an inherent part of an effective survey report. The technical skills involved in planning and executing a research programme are different from those required to write a clearly understandable report. Report writing requires a thorough knowledge of the survey, and the ability to synthesize and transmit that knowledge so that it is perfectly understood. Professional writers cannot hope to influence their readers precisely as they wish without care and practice in the use of words.

Researchers should, therefore, always bear in mind that a report is a method of *communication*. This essential process cannot be successful if too little emphasis is placed on the art and science of display and communication while too much attention is given to the elegant techniques which were involved in gathering and analysing the data. Many years ago, Edgar Allan Poe wrote scathingly of 'donkeys who bray, using inordinate language which no man has ever understood, and which any well-educated baboon would blush in being accused of understanding'.

If technical terms are used in the survey report, they should be defined to prevent possible misunderstanding. Researchers should not presume that their readers will automatically understand technical jargon, and, at first appearance, it is advisable to qualify it. Where the report is to be read exclusively by technical specialists, the general level of writing can be more specialized. In practice, most survey reports are the subject of discussion between commercial and technical management, and unless two separate editions are planned, it is advisable to write the report in a style comprehensible to both areas of management. A summary report, covering the main features of a highly technical survey, is a useful means of ensuring that commercial management knows the facts which research has established.

KEYPOINT

Survey report

Essentially is *communication*

Use clear, concise phrasing

Define technical terms

Present facts in logical order

Presentation of a survey report

On completion of the survey, a presentation of the survey findings is often made to senior management. This may be done at an agreed time after the detailed report has been submitted, so that management have the opportunity to note the findings and to consider the related issues. Such presentations should be carefully planned and well structured, so that the essence of the report is given logically and concisely. A small set of handout summaries of the main points of the presentation should be available after the meeting.

The presentation should be supported – but not dominated – by professionally-designed videos, overhead slides, tape-recordings, etc. After the main presentation, the chairman of the meeting might open a short discussion on the research findings.

Structure of the survey report

Research reports should present survey findings within a logical framework. Although particular reports will obviously cover different subjects of enquiry, the following main elements form the general construction: introduction, main body, and appendices. These will now be considered in some detail.

Title page
This gives a simple description of the research, e.g. 'National Consumer Survey into Supermarket Shopping in the UK'. It also contains the name of the client, the organization which undertook the research, and the date.

Table of contents
This is a detailed guide to the report. It should be designed to facilitate easy reference by systematically numbering sections and sub-sections of the main areas of the report. A list of appendices (covering graphs and statistical tables used in the report) should also be included.

Introduction
This describes the purpose and scope of the research, and essentially echoes the research proposal agreed between clients and researchers. Objectives, methodologies, and constraints experienced during the research should be reported succinctly.

Executive summary
This is a brief description of the salient findings of the survey, supported by references to the appropriate sections of the main report. The objectives of the research should be re-visited in light of the reported findings of the survey. If the researchers have already been invited to present recommendations on feasible strategies in light of the research findings, these should be outlined. The conclusions should be clear, succinct, and objective.

Main body
The next part of the report contains the main body which presents the survey findings in some considerable detail. The material should be presented systematically, and there should be some framework outlined beforehand to control the development of the report. The actual contents of this section of the report depend largely on the nature of the

survey. Where quantitative measures are involved, the text and statistical extracts from the main body of the report will be almost completely textual.

Data used should be relevant to the objectives of the survey and the report should present these so that they are readily understood. Major relationships should be adequately discussed and compared, where available, with published facts from other sources.

Strict standards of professional research should always be maintained, and clients should never be encouraged to read into reports more than researchers can legitimately support by their survey findings. Marketing research has limitations as well as great values, and management should not expect researchers to provide them with information outside the scope of the survey. To avoid any possible confusion at a later date, the objectives of research should, as noted earlier, always be fully discussed and agreed by both parties before the survey is undertaken.

Ehrenberg[36] has emphasized the importance of presenting numerical data in an intelligible way. He has drawn attention to the fact that numeracy has two facets – *extracting numerical information* and *presenting* it. Tabulated data should be so laid out that the overall patterns and exceptions should be 'obvious at a glance'. Simplification of data, e.g. rounding to two significant or effective digits, may get rid of a bewildering array of top-heavy data. Cluttered tables do not aid mental digestion. Spurious accuracy in the presentation of data should also be avoided.

Where market researchers have been invited to present their recommendations in the survey report, they might well consider offering these to be effective over a period of time. A phased plan of operation is more likely to attract management interest than a wholesale change of policy which could be more disruptive than beneficial. Researchers should form an opinion of the 'management climate' in which their clients are accustomed to work and design recommendations that will have a good chance of being heard favourably. If these recommendations follow a logical progression, management feels more willing to accept them.

Appendices

The last section of the report is in the form of appendices giving supplementary information, sometimes of a fairly extensive type. A detailed description of the sample design used is given; the questionnaire used in the survey is also included, and so are the instructions given to interviewers. Full statistical tables are given for reference (extracts from these will have appeared in the main body of the report). Where survey information has been drawn from official or other sources, full details of these are listed. In the case of motivation research, it is customary to include one or two typical interviews verbatim. Photographs or other illustrative material might also be included featuring, perhaps, packaging or advertising which was of interest to the survey.

In accordance with the MRS Code of Conduct, information about any weighting methods used (see earlier discussion), fieldwork response rates, precise geographical coverage of the fieldwork, etc. should be stated.

Overall contents of research report

The essential elements of a typical marketing research report are shown in Figure 13.6 .

The type of printing and binding of survey reports should be carefully considered by researchers. The method of printing the report depends largely on the number required for distribution. Wordprocessors and electronic typewriters used in conjunction with efficient

TITLE PAGE
CONTENTS PAGE
LIST OF APPENDICES
EXECUTIVE SUMMARY
TEXT OF REPORT (survey findings)
   Introduction (purpose of report)
   Methodology (outline of research)
   Details of research methodology (research design, types of data, data collection, sampling
      methodology, data analyses, etc.)

   Survey findings (text plus tables and diagrams)
      Definition of product market
      Nature of competition
      Domestic production
      Imports
      Exports
      Market trends (home; export)

   Target market size (demographic details)
   Planned market share (including market segments)
      Nature of buying behaviour
      Nature of competition (prices; promotion; distribution; packaging; after-sales service; delivery)
   Summary of survey findings
   Limitations and constraints of survey
APPENDICES
LIST OF TABLES
LIST OF DIAGRAMS
REFERENCES

Figure 13.6   Essential elements of market report

printers can produce attractive, well-presented reports. Although these modern facilities may encourage ingenuity in, for example, the use of multiple fonts, some restraint is advisable to ensure that the resultant report does not end up with an exuberant mix of typefaces and other typographical features that confuse rather than please the eye of the reader. Good-quality paper should always be used, and the binding should be serviceable. Laminated boards are particularly suitable. The research title, etc., should be entered clearly on the outside covers.

13.11 Managerial attitudes to marketing research

In the opening chapter, the role of marketing research in management decision making was recognized. It was seen that while managerial experience and judgement are vital elements of decision making – and these are particularly applicable to daily decisions which are largely of a routine nature – there are times when the existing fund of knowledge is inadequate. It is on such occasions, in particular, that marketing researchers may be called in to lend their expertise to the decision makers.

Market researchers may well encounter managers with ingrained attitudes towards marketing research. For instance, there is the so-called 'plumber' who believes that marketing research can be turned on and off like a tap; then there is the 'feudal potentate' and even the 'feudal lord', who attempt to treat market researchers like vassals, anxious to provide only reassuring information.

These portrayals may seem to be almost caricatures, but experienced marketing researchers will probably have little difficulty in recognizing some of the managerial attitudes described. The 'plumber' appears to be a 'crisis-shooter' who does not realize that a regular flow of information, in addition to ad hoc research, would help marketing decisions. The 'oriental potentate' and the 'feudal lord' suggest an authoritarian and not very intelligent use of managerial power in the naïve belief that marketing research can provide answers to problems which they have not really thought about sufficiently.

As a professional in his own right, the marketing researcher is unlikely to be either dazzled or dismayed when encountering such restrictive attitudes. He will endeavour to get to the heart of the problem and, after securing agreement, then proceed to apply his analytical skills in objective research. Uncertainty in decision making will remain, but with valid and reliable data it should be possible to reduce its level significantly.

In Mintel's opinion,[37] stress may sometimes be detected in the relationship between research and marketing specialists, the latter feeling that it is their prerogative to initiate changes to marketing strategy; marketing researchers, on the other hand, may feel that their experience and knowledge are not really being used fully by their clients.

13.12 Buying marketing research

In industry, management often has to consider the problem of whether to produce, in its own plant, specific components needed in the assembly of a final product or, alternatively, whether to buy these parts from an outside supplier, possibly more advantageously. 'Make-or-buy' decisions are largely accepted as routine administration.

With professional services, the principle of 'make or buy' may also be applied. Many companies rely on specialist advice from outside consultants in complex areas such as the law, taxation, design, and similar activities. At the same time, some of these companies may have members of their staff, qualified in these professions, acting as general practitioners. When expert knowledge is required at some depth, companies may well call in the services of specialists, who are able to contribute valuably to the quality of management decisions. To employ talent of this nature on a staff basis would generally be outside the resources and needs of most companies. However, Mintel[37] stated that almost two-thirds of market research projects in the UK are commissioned by specialist market research buyers, and most large companies involved in consumer goods and services employ professional staff for this purpose.

Marketing information, both quantitative and qualitative, is necessary in companies of all sizes. This information may be available, to some extent, inside the company or from external published sources. Whether to 'make', i.e. rely on existing company resources, or to 'buy', i.e. use the services of professional marketing research organizations, will depend on several factors. These will include assessing the present state of knowledge related to the particular decision which has to be taken. For example, what data can be obtained from company records and published sources on the present and potential market for a specific type of product? Available information may be sufficient for a decision to be taken at an acceptable level of risk. Where this is not the case, gaps in information should be identified by careful analysis of the situation, and an evaluation made of the benefits which further data would be likely to bring to the process of decision making. An estimate of the costs involved should, of course, be included in the assessment. Management must then decide what further research is justified, bearing in mind that this will inevitably delay the final decision.

Where and how to buy this extra marketing information causes concern to many companies, which are considering, perhaps for the first time, the need for more specialized research into their marketing problems. It will be a matter of company policy whether to build up research facilities within the organization or to rely entirely on outside experts: the degree of urgency of the research will need to be borne in mind.

As in other areas of professional expertise, it is advisable for companies to decide whether their research needs warrant special research appointments. Where new markets are under consideration and the organization is expanding its other resources, a staff researcher would be likely to be fully and usefully occupied. But even then, some outside assistance may be sought in connection with surveys involving, for example, psychological methods of investigation. In such cases, the staff researcher would control the research programme and collaborate closely with experts handling specific aspects of the survey.

At one time, large companies recruited specialists to undertake/manage market research projects, but the slimming-down of staff and the trend towards buying-in of specialist services is now evident; this occurred, for instance, when, as noted in Chapter 3, the BBC Audience Research Department was closed down in the 1990s, and the BBC Broadcasting Research Department now contracts out fieldwork operations such as interviewing.

Those companies preferring to buy their marketing research externally are faced with the problem of seeking the best source of supply. Buying research is admittedly more difficult than ordering tangible products, the physical characteristics of which can be fairly easily assessed.

Before the search for suitable marketing investigators commences, companies should spend some time in analysing their marketing problem, forming objectives, and specifying the type of data which they are seeking. This exercise provides a sound base for discussions with prospective research agencies.

Marketing research organizations fall into three main categories:

1. Large groups of research firms with services operating in many countries

2. Independent market research companies

3. Market research departments in advertising agencies

Independent marketing research companies tend to be of two kinds: those offering a comprehensive range of services, and those specializing by function or by type of research undertaken. The larger agencies, such as Taylor Nelson Sofres or BMRB International, are able to give clients the benefit of broadly based experience in all aspects of survey practice. Smaller agencies often specialize in providing useful services such as questionnaire construction or interviewing, and in investigations into specific markets. Large specialist agencies like Nielsen's undertake a continuous audit of selected retail outlets.

In addition to commercial research organizations, several academic institutions have been notably successful in practical research projects over a wide range of industries. Universities, colleges and business schools are usually willing to offer professional assistance with the marketing problems of companies of all sizes.

A few of the larger advertising agencies have marketing research departments. These tend to have particular expertise in advertising research techniques, though they also cover other types of research.

Professional organizations, such as the Market Research Society, ESOMAR and the Chartered Institute of Marketing, provide companies with lists of their members who are able to undertake specific types of market research assistance.

Guidance in selecting a research agency may also be forthcoming from trade associations and from business associates who have commissioned research in the past.

A short list of agencies who appear to be suitable should be drawn up and invited to submit details of their services. These should include information on the experience and qualifications of their research staff, the type of research customarily undertaken, the principal industries they have covered. A list of past and present clients is often a valuable clue to the standing of the agency. Some of these clients may be willing to offer an assessment of the capabilities of the agency they employed.

The next stage in selecting an agency consists of selecting two or three firms whose background and experience suggest they could be of particular value in solving the present marketing problem. (Refer also to Chapter 12 – checklist of research agencies offering international market research services.)

13.13 Costing marketing research

Management information costs money and involves the use of scarce resources. It is important, therefore, to check that the value of the information will be greater than the costs involved in its collection and processing.

Alternative methods of acquiring marketing research expertise have been outlined already; attention will now be given to alternative methods of evaluating expenditure on marketing research.

The ways in which this problem can be tackled range from subjective estimates to sophisticated decision theory based on Bayesian statistics.

The simplest method of deciding whether or not to enter a particular market would be to toss a coin; the chances of a correct decision would be 50:50, so on the basis of a £500 000 market launch the estimated possible loss would be £250 000.

But this simplistic approach is likely to be modified by the fund of knowledge and experience which management may already possess. This 'background knowledge' is, as observed earlier, a necessary constituent of management decision making and, in some cases, it may be adequate. The more novel the product and the more dynamic the marketing environments, the greater the risk in making decisions on this basis.

To continue the example given above and assuming that present information is judged to be sufficient for management to make a correct decision on a 60:40 basis, the estimated cost of making a wrong decision could be calculated thus: £500 000 × 40 per cent = £200 000.

Management may then consider the increased chances of a successful decision being taken if it had access to extra information about the proposed market. An estimate might be made that more information would be likely to increase the probability of success to 80:20. On the basis of a £500 000 market launch, the estimated loss could then total £100 000 if the market entry failed. In this case, the value of marketing research would be computed thus:

£200 000 (wrong decision taken   − £100 000 (wrong decision with = £100 000
        with present information)   extra information)

Hence, management could usefully spend up to £100 000 on marketing research to improve the chances of market success.

Managers who seek a more sophisticated method of evaluating expenditure on marketing research could apply formal Bayesian decision rules.

In dealing with day-to-day problems, managers may be accustomed to making three levels of estimates of the outcome of decisions: an expected, an optimistic, and a pessimistic one. They may, in a relatively informal way, attach probabilities to these projections. Bayesian decision theory offers a formal procedure for enabling management to make an efficient choice from among various alternatives.

The processes involved in the Bayesian approach are detailed in statistical textbooks. Essentially, the process makes use of the concepts of utility, subjective probabilities, and Bayes's theorem for revision of prior judgements or hypotheses.

The Bayesian decision process involves four stages: (i) definition of problem; (ii) prior analysis; (iii) posterior analysis; and (iv) preposterior analysis.

So that mathematical calculations can be projected, the problem must be defined in quantitative terms. Prior analysis refers to the existing state of knowledge relative to the problem which will enable prior probabilities to be applied. Posterior analysis occurs after the management decision has been taken and when feedback may be available about the outcome of the action. Preposterior analysis is the intermediate stage which may occur if management decides that more information is needed before a final decision can be taken. At this stage, a marketing research survey, for example, may be considered.

The following simplified example will indicate the essential nature of Bayesian analysis applied to the evaluation of marketing research.

A company wishing to expand into a new market has been told that detailed marketing research investigation would cost about £50 000.

Prior analysis of this marketing venture allows the company to estimate the probability of attaining a market share of at least 15 per cent at 0.6.

	Market share Probability	$\geqslant 15$ per cent Pay-off	Market share Probability	< 15 per cent Pay-off
Enter market	0.6	£300 000	0.4	(£50 000)
Do not enter market	0.6	0	0.4	0

Expected Monetary Value (EMV) is one of the most suitable criteria which could be adopted for evaluating this project, although there are others which might also be applied. Hence, EMV = 0.6 (£300 000) + 0.4 (−£50 000) = £160 000.

If posterior analysis is now applied, it may be assumed that this product is already on sale in another market. Information on existing sales performance indicates that earlier predictions of 75 per cent success were actually realized.

Taking this increased probability into account, the revised EMV can be calculated as follows:

$$EMV_2 = 0.75 \, (£300\,000) + 0.25 \, (-£50\,000) = £212\,500$$

The value of the additional information is calculated thus:

$$EMV_2 - EMV_1$$
$$= £212\,500 - £160\,000$$
$$= £52\,500$$

A marketing survey costing £30 000 could, therefore, be afforded. It would appear worthwhile to reduce the level of uncertainty regarding market entry, provided that research findings could be available without a long delay.

It should be borne in mind, however, that although Bayesian decision theory applies probabilities and results in fairly imposing mathematical equations, the probabilities are derived from estimates and are subjective in nature. The elegance of the theory should not be allowed to obscure its inherent fragility. So far this technique does not appear to be widely used in evaluating marketing research estimates.

With most research projects, time is a critical factor, so everything possible must be done to avoid delays at the many different stages of the survey. The whole operation should be programmed, and a continuous check kept on the progress of office staff, interviewers, printers, etc.

A distillation of the research findings may be submitted to clients if some urgent decision has to be taken within a limited period of time. Clients often find it helpful for researchers to make a formal presentation of the main findings of a survey at a meeting of senior executives. This matter should be checked with clients before the research project is accepted (see earlier discussion).

Management will be particularly concerned with the meanings and applications of the research findings; the actual process involved in the research process will be of secondary interest.

Researchers should avoid pretentious jargon and, at the same time, ensure that management are given insights into the behaviour and attitudes of those who actually use the products/services which are being researched.

The task of the market research statistician should not be confined to techniques; he or she must increasingly become a better communicator and skilled in presenting complicated technical data to a non-technical audience in language which they can understand. This is a challenging, new and expanded role for statisticians, who are often dealing today with arcane concepts and methodologies that are more likely to confuse rather than enlighten their clients. Skilful exposition should encourage management to read the report in full, and so reduce the temptation to put it to one side and probably never refer to it again.

KEYPOINT

Structure of report

Title page
Contents page
List of appendices
Executive summary
Text of report
 Introduction
 Methodology
 Findings
Limitations/constraints
Summary
General conclusions and recommendations

Appendices
List of tables
List of diagrams
References

13.14 Ethics and marketing research

For some years the conduct of business and industry in developed economies has been under searching scrutiny; the activities of certain multinational corporations have attracted the attention of 'activist' groups which, for various motives, have energetically attacked some aspects of their corporate behaviour. Priorities and values are endlessly debated in the mass media – ever eager to seize on contentious issues. But fundamental shifts in people's attitudes and expectations clearly indicate that there is growing recognition of the need for policy makers in business, industry and the public sector to be aware that their decisions affect not just their own organizations but impact also on society.

Social responsibility is being voiced in many circles: political, professional, academic, and the trade unions. Ethical behaviour in business is not an abstract notion, although cynics may attempt to dismiss the concept of business ethics as a contradiction in terms, virtually an oxymoron. In 1986, the Institute of Business Ethics was founded from an initiative by the Christian Association of Business Executives, and also supported by leaders of the Jewish and Islamic communities in the UK. Their view is 'Good ethics are good business, you don't have to choose between the two. You can get away with most behaviour in the short run, but you can't stay in business in the long term without an ethical approach to your product, your market, and your employees'.[38]

This pragmatic approach can be contrasted with that of the 'moralists': that business ethics are part of personal ethics, i.e. they are inseparable and universally applicable, as Professor Jack Mahoney S.J., first director of the Business Ethics Centre at King's College, London, declared, emphasizing that there must be a 'dialogue between the business community and the rest of society'.[39]

Ethical behaviour in business expands the responsibilities of management; decisions involving ethics permeate an organization. Most businesses do not face major ethical dilemmas, and conduct their day-to-day transactions without dramatic problems of this kind arising. But this does not mean that ethical issues do not exist – they may not be perceived or recognized. Apart from legislative constraints, many industries and sectors of commerce have acknowledged that corporate behaviour must go beyond and above what the law demands, and have developed codes of conduct which, to a greater or lesser extent, reflect their ethical sensitivities.

According to the research director of the Institute of Business Ethics, 'fair dealing and honesty can be entirely compatible with the creation of wealth'.[40] Although costs may be incurred through introducing a code of ethics, most companies have found that these have been more than worthwhile in the longer term. In 1987, 18 per cent of the 300 largest companies in Britain had adopted a code of ethics; by 1999, of the top 500 firms, 57 per cent had established ethical codes.[40]

The market research industry, through its widespread survey interviewing activities, has close links with the public, as well as serving a wide range of industrial, commercial and public sector organizations. It has always taken a pre-emptive position on ethical standards, both through its own self-regulatory professional codes, as well as by maintaining close contacts with, for example, legislators when data protection legislation in the UK was being drafted.

13.15 Codes of conduct

The first professional code of conduct for market researchers was published by the European Society for Opinion and Marketing Research (ESOMAR) in 1948. Following this initial code, several national marketing research societies developed their own codes, including the UK's Market Research Society's (MRS's) first code in 1948. In 1976, ESOMAR and the International Chamber of Commerce (ICC) agreed that it would be advantageous to have a single international code, so a joint ICC/ESOMAR Code was published in 1977. This code was revised in 1986, and a new version appeared in 1994, to take account of developments in research methodologies as well as increasing international legislation. The 1994 ICC/ESOMAR Code aims to give, clearly and concisely, the basic ethical and business principles governing market and social research practice. Acceptance of the Code is a condition of membership of ESOMAR and of all other national and international bodies which, like the MRS, have officially adopted the Code. Guidelines are published to indicate how the Code should be applied in practice; these are constantly reviewed to ensure that they maintain their relevance.

ESOMAR, which was founded in 1948, has over 4000 members in 100 countries and regards itself as European in origin and global in nature. In countries where the local code extends beyond the ICC/ESOMAR Code, such specific national requirements take precedence.

Problems which have been considered include so-called 'mystery shopping' (see Chapter 2), 'sugging' (selling under the guise of marketing research), and 'frugging' (fund-raising under the pretext of market research). The incidence of databases (see earlier discussion) and their growing association with marketing research has also concerned ESOMAR. Databases compiled from respondents who have agreed to have their names used for this purpose 'are not illegal . . . but they will increasingly be used alongside market research, and often instead of it. But they are not market research'.[41] 'If such a "survey" pretends to be confidential, it is in breach of the ICC/ESOMAR Code'.[41] Even if such activities are 'above board in this respect', it is very likely that their primary objectives will be 'incompatible with the aims of genuine research'.[41] However, it is important not to confuse such databases with 'respondent access panels', which are recruited from people who are willing to be re-interviewed for purely research purposes.[41] These types of panel may develop because of the acknowledged problems of securing co-operation in survey interviews (see Chapters 5 and 6).

MRS Code of Conduct

As already noted, this self-regulatory code has existed since 1954 and has been revised from time to time so that, with the development of new technologies, it retains its relevance and effectiveness. It is conducted in accordance with the principles of data protection laid down by the Data Protection Act of 1998. This legislation gave effect to EC Directive 95/46/EC. The MRS Code is based upon and is fully compatible with the ICC/ECOMAR International Code of Marketing and Social Research Practice, is designed to support researchers in maintaining professional standards, and applies to all quantitative and qualitative data collection methods.,

All MRS members engaged in consumer, business-to-business, social opinion or any other type of confidential survey research activities are subject to the Code. This does not, however, take precedence over national law; members engaged in international research 'shall take its provisions as a minimum requirement and fulfil any other responsibilities set down in law or by nationally agreed standards'.[42]

The current MRS Code (revised July 1999), like its predecessors, is based on the following eight principles:

1. Personal data shall be processed fairly and lawfully.

2. Personal data shall be obtained only for one or more specified and lawful purposes, and shall not be further processed in any manner incompatible with that purpose or for those purposes.

3. Personal data shall be adequate, relevant and not excessive in relation to the purpose or purposes for which they are processed.

4. Personal data shall be accurate and, where necessary, kept up-to-date.

5. Personal data processed for any purpose or purposes shall not be kept longer than is necessary for that purpose or those purposes.

6. Personal data shall be processed in accordance with the rights of data subjects under this Act (Data Protection).

7. Appropriate technical and organizational measures shall be taken against unauthorized or unlawful processing of personal data and against accidental loss or destruction of, or damage to, personal data.

8. Personal data shall not be transferred to a country or territory outside the European Economic Area, unless that country or territory ensures an adequate level of protection for the rights and freedoms of data subjects in relation to the processing of personal data.

The MRS recognizes that research is founded upon the willing co-operation of the public and of business organizations, and that their confidence in the integrity and objectivity of research operations is vital. 'It is in this spirit that the Code of Conduct has been devised'.[42]

The MRS operate 'Codeline' – free confidential answer service – for enquiries related to the code of conduct.

The 1999 revision of the MRS Code has ensured that its principles conform to EC directives and are fully compatible with the ICC/ESOMAR Code. This process of harmonization was tackled by the Professional Standards Committee of the MRS with dogged determination; the importance of developing effective contacts at the European level became evident during their negotiations.

In February 1995, the MRS distributed to members *guidelines*[43] for handling databases; these, following extensive discussions, had been drafted by three members of its Professional Standards Committee. The increasing diversity of members' activities – some of which were not covered by the Code of Conduct – were recognized by the Committee, and further guidelines were given; these were intended to complement existing legal and ethical requirements for members of the Market Research Society working with the following databases: (i) data supplied as a sampling frame for confidential survey research; (ii) data with respondents' names and addresses held for confidential research purposes only; and (iii) respondent-identified survey data which may be used for purposes other than confidential survey research.

The guidelines were issued with the knowledge and agreement of the Data Protection Registry.

Codes of Conduct cannot, of course, avoid every possible problem that might materialize in survey practice, but they do provide clients with stated standards of marketing research practice which should reassure, in particular, those who are seeking to commission marketing research surveys for the first time.

Mary and Peter Bartram[44] have reflected on the 'ethical dilemmas' facing marketing researchers in today's highly competitive conditions. They argue that there is a 'pressing need' to define the boundaries of market research which, over the past 40 years or so, have extended considerably into areas not envisaged by its early practitioners. It is, these experienced researchers state, essential that the core values of the market research industry 'should not be undermined by any temptation to accommodate the wishes of other bodies, or of individual members, with conflicting "objectives"'. These core values should be fully recognized; they embrace: (i) total respect for the respondent; (ii) professional competence in data collection and analysis; (iii) use of information for research and not directly for selling purposes; and (iv) independent objectivity in the interpretation of survey findings.

13.16 Data protection legislation

As noted, there has been increasing international legislation concerned with consumer protection and related matters, and also European directives on these issues, including, in particular, the conduct of marketing research.

Following signature by the UK of the European Convention for the Protection of Individuals with regard to Automatic Processing of Personal Data, implementation was effected by passing the Data Protection Act, which became law on 12 July 1984. Its purpose was 'to regulate the use of automatically processed information relating to individuals and the provision of services in respect of such information'.[45] Personal data referred to data related to a living person who can be identified from the information. The Act was concerned, therefore, with individuals, not corporate bodies; it did not refer to the processing of personal data by manual means. The types of equipment which might be described as 'automatic processes' were not closely defined.

The UK was comparatively late in adopting data protection legislation; such laws had existed for some time in, for example, Sweden, Germany, Austria and France. This lag was advantageous because it enabled UK legislators to benefit from the earlier experiences, and attempt to avoid the serious problems for industry in general and for marketing researchers in particular, which had arisen in certain countries, such as Germany. As mentioned, close contact with legislators during these development stages was maintained by the UK market research industry.

In accordance with an EC Directive the Data Protection Act 1998 replaced the 1984 Act and became effective in 1999. It lays down broad principles which leave many important gaps to be filled in, presumably through secondary legislation in due course.

The new Act extends the definition of data to include all manual and electronic records; research companies will be allowed specific periods of time to adjust their record-keeping arrangements. The definition of 'processing' in the new Act is far wider than the 1984 Act: 'It is a compendious definition and it is difficult to envisage any action involving data which does not amount to processing within the definition.'[45] It is apparent that audio and video recordings of group discussions are now classified as data and so fall within the Act.

The eight Data Protection Principles of the 1999 Act are not exactly the same as the 1984 Act; there is, for example, special reference to 'sensitive personal data', which consists of information on racial or ethnic origin; political opinions; religious or other similar beliefs; trade union membership; physical or mental health; sex life; criminal convictions or proceedings. Conditions are stipulated under which sensitive personal data may be lawfully processed.

The assistant data protection registrar intimated that the final details of the new Act would be unlikely to have a significant effect on market research; processing sensitive data was recognized to be of particular relevance to market research activities and was an issue for further consideration.[46]

The 1984 Act established a system of registration for all users of personal data covered by the Act; details covered the data user's name and address; a description of the personal data held; the purposes for which the personal data are held; a description of the sources from which data are derived; a description of people to whom the data may be disclosed; names or descriptions of places outside the UK to which the data may be transferred; and an address for the receipt of requests from data subjects who wish to have access to the data.

The 1998 Act introduced a new system of notification, with certain exemptions for data users already registered until the end of their registration period or, if earlier, 24 October 2001.[45]

It is illegal to hold or use data in any way inconsistent with the registered entry; any changes have to be recorded officially; registration entries are valid for specified periods.

KEYPOINT

Ethics and marketing research

General growth of interest in 'business ethics'

Institute of Business Ethics

Corporate codes of conduct

ICC/ESOMAR Code (1948)

MRS Code (1954)

EC Directive

Data Protection Act 1984 (revised 1998)

ESOMAR and MRS codes fully comply with legal requirements

Summary

Survey data have to be processed before they are useful for management decision making: the processing stages cover editing, coding, and tabulation. All these activities must be expertly done to ensure that the processed data are valid and reliable.

Computers have revolutionized the handling of data and enabled complex analyses to be made: various programs are available; it is important to remember that sophisticated computer printouts are only as good as the programs from which they are derived.

Analysis and interpretation of processed data are closely linked and depend largely on the objectives of the survey. Statistical measures may range from the relatively simple, e.g. average, to sophisticated multi-variate analyses involving, perhaps, factor analysis, cluster analysis, etc.

It is largely a matter of opinion, plus the expressed wishes of clients, whether research reports should not only present survey data but also comment on such findings and offer specific strategic recommendations. Survey reports should be carefully planned in every detail: wording, format, printing, binding, etc.

Buying marketing research may be approached on the 'make-or-buy' principle common to other professional services to management. Evaluating the costs of marketing research can range from subjective estimates to sophisticated decision-tree theory based on Bayesian statistics.

<table>
<tr><td>

Review and discussion questions

</td><td>

1. Suggest possible headings for a report on a postal survey commissioned by the Royal Society for the Protection of Cruelty to Animals on consumer attitudes towards the export of live cattle to the Continent.

2. Identify factors relating to presentation which may adversely affect the way clients view marketing research reports.

3. A small local firm providing chiropractic and homeopathic services keeps a computer database of patient records. What factors relating to the Data Protection Act should be borne in mind in maintaining and expanding this database?

4. The management of an estate agency chain is faced with a choice of three marketing research firms to investigate satisfaction levels among its customers. What factors should they bear in mind in making their choice?

5. Identify three undesirable/unproductive reasons why management might commission marketing research.

6. Compose a ten item 'closed' questionnaire to assess student attitudes towards your marketing research course. Provide possible coding options alongside each question.

</td></tr>
</table>

CAMEO CASE: Eyeline Opticians

Eyeline Opticians, founded in 1990, is a British retail optician partnership, based in Salford, Manchester, and employs 13 people. The company offers its clients a wide range of products and related services, including eye examinations, screening for conditions such as glaucoma and diabetes, and the supply of spectacles, contact lenses and sundry related items. In general, replacement spectacles are sold to clients every two years, contact lenses annually, and contact lens solution monthly. This means that, depending on the product/service required, existing customers can be serviced by either the partners (new spectacle prescriptions), or the other staff.

The company is headed by two partners who are responsible for major strategic and planning decisions, including the development of new products and services; reporting directly to them are two practice managers, who are responsible for the day-to-day running of the retail business. Under the practice managers are nine ancillary staff, who carry out general duties, such as the sale of vision-related sundry products, and making consultation appointments. Business is exclusively domestic, and in the three years 1997–2000, turnover has increased from £505 000 to £526 000.

There are two major motivatory influences on customers to purchase: to begin with there is the eminently practical need to have clear vision, and/or correct any other vision-related problems. In addition, however, eye-wear is increasingly being regarded as a fashion item by many consumers, especially in the younger age groups. According to the senior partner, Eyeline Opticians understands the need for consumers '... to appear fashionable wearing the latest styles of frames'. In order to meet the ever-changing demands of customers, the company has adopted a flexible approach to product availability. This degree of flexibility is a key to the company's success, allowing it to compete with some of the larger retail chain opticians, for which stock decisions are generally taken by head office, and which cannot be as immediately responsive to changing fashion trends at a national or regional level. The second, and equally important element of Eyeline Opticians' competitive strategy is based on good, individual service to customers from the partners and the staff, offering detailed, objective advice on the choice of products and services available, and the different pricing structures for each. Point-of-sale activities are also seen as an important element of the company's marketing strategy, and great care is taken over window displays, aimed largely at prospective customers.

Whilst the company is not heavily involved in marketing research, it does, nevertheless, monitor competitor activities, in addition to making great use of its customer database. Pricing levels and special promotional offers are the areas of competitor activity that generally receive the greatest scrutiny, and this is usually undertaken on a regular basis through examining competitor window displays, and looking at advertisements in the local press.

The company's own client database allows a high level of contact with existing customers. Some 500–600 letters are sent out each month, generally to inform patients that they are due for another eye examination. To date, response rates average some 30 per cent, with a further 12 per cent responding to the second (back up) reminder that is sent. In addition to (but separate from) the appointment reminder letters, customers can be targeted for specific purposes: the database allows the company to segment its market in terms of a variety of variables, including age, location (post-code), and previous spend. This information is vital when deciding which promotional offer to target at each group.

Questions

1. It has been suggested that consumer fashion and current trends are important considerations in the retail optician sector. Bearing this in mind, how would you propose that the company could best monitor such changes in consumer demand patterns?

2. Eyeline Opticians estimate a 30 per cent response rate to their eye examination reminder letters, with an additional 12 per cent replying to the follow-up letters: resulting in a 42 per cent overall response rate. What are the most likely reasons for the non-response by the remaining 58 per cent, and what measures would you suggest should be adopted by the company to encourage these people to respond?

3. To what extent could/should the company make use of new technology such as the internet to promote its products and services?

Jonathan S. Swift

References

1. Market Research Society, *Guide to Good Coding Practice*, July 1983.
2. Mitchell, Dawn, 'From ex-Army terrorisers to captains of industry', *Researchplus* 5, May 1996.
3. O'Brien, John, 'From the Machine came forth meaning', *Researchplus* 5, May 1996.
4. Market Research Society, *Research Guide to Software*, January 2000.
5. Keller, Wouter J., 'Trends in survey data processing', *Journal of Market Research Society*, vol. 35, no. 3, July 1993.
6. Baker, Ken, 'Data Fusion', in: *A Handbook of Market Research Techniques*, Robin Birn, Paul Hague, and Phyllis Vangelder (eds), Kogan Page, London, 1996.
7. Jephcott, Jonathan, and Timothy Bock, 'The application and validation of data fusion', *Journal of Market Research Society*, vol. 40, no. 3, July 1998.

8. Raimondi, Dina, 'Market Research', in: *ESOMAR Handbook of Market and Opinion Research*, Colin McDonald, and Phyllis Vangelder (eds), ESOMAR, Amsterdam, 1998.

9. Mouncey, Peter, 'With growing demands for data, will purity prove only theoretical?', *Researchplus* 9, May 1996.

10. Fletcher, Keith, and Linda Peters, 'Issues in information management', *Journal of Market Research Society*, vol. 38, no. 2, April 1996.

11. Leventhal, Barry, 'An approach to fusing market research with database marketing', *Journal of Market Research Society*, vol. 39, no. 4, October 1997.

12. Macfarlane, Phyllis, 'Data fusion – where does it fit in?', *MRS Scene*, September 1998.

13. Gramme, Niels, 'Data processing and analysis', in: *ESOMAR Handbook of Market and Opinion Research*, Colin McDonald, and Phyllis Valgelder (eds), ESOMAR, Amsterdam, 1998.

14. Yule, G. A., 'Why do we get sometimes nonsense correlations between time series?', *Journal of the Royal Statistical Society*, vol. 89, January 1926.

15. Moser, C. A., and G. Kalton, *Survey Methods in Social Investigation*, Heinemann, London, 1971.

16. Alpert, Lewis, and Ronal Getty, 'Product positioning by behavioural life-styles', *Journal of Marketing*, April 1969.

17. Craig, C. Samuel, and Susan P. Douglas, *International Market Research*, John Wiley, Chichester, 1999.

18. Harper, Roland, 'Factor analysis as a technique for examining complex data on foodstuffs', *Applied Statistics*, vol. 1, no. 1, March 1956.

19. Mukherjee, Bishwa Nath, 'A factor analysis of some qualitative attributes of coffee', *Journal of Advertising Research*, vol. 5, no. 1, March 1965.

20. Doyle, P. M., 'Market segmentation by factor analysis', *European Journal of Marketing*, vol. 6, no. 1, 1972.

21. Cormack, R. M., 'A review of classifications', *Journal of the Royal Statistical Society*, vol. 134, 1971.

22. Morgan, N., and J. Purnell, 'Isolating openings for new products in a multi-dimensional space', *Journal of Market Research Society*, vol. 11, no. 3, July 1969.

23. Fitzroy, Peter, *Analytical Methods for Marketing Management*, McGraw-Hill, Maidenhead, 1976.

24. Punj, Girish, and David W. Stewart, 'Cluster analysis in marketing research', *Journal of Marketing Research*, vol. 20, May 1983.

25. Johnson, Richard M., 'Trade-off analysis of consumer values', *Journal of Marketing Research*, vol. 11, May 1974.

26. Greenhalgh, Colin, 'Research for new product development', in: *Consumer Market Research Handbook*, Robert M. Worcester, and John Downham (eds), Van Nostrand Reinhold, Wokingham, 1978.

27. Green, Paul E., and Yoram Wind, 'New way to measure consumers' judgements', *Harvard Business Review*, July/August 1975.

28. Mullett, Gary M., 'Using customer references to design products', *Business*, vol. 27, October/December 1983.

29. Marr, Norman E., 'The impact of customer service in international markets', *International Marketing Review*, vol. 1, no. 4, Autumn/Winter 1984.

30. Baker, Ken, 'Multivariate analysis of survey data', in: *ESOMAR Handbook of Market and Opinion Research*, Colin McDonald, and Phyllis Vangelder (eds), ESOMAR, Amsterdam, 1998.

31. Doyle, Peter, 'Non-metric multi-dimensional scaling: A user's guide', *European Journal of Marketing*, vol. 7, no. 2, 1973.

32. Ehrenberg, A. S. C., 'What research for what problem', in: *Research in Marketing*, Market Research Society, London, 1964.

33. Nowik, Henry, 'The role of market research in a marketing orientated company', in: *Research in Marketing*, Market Research Society, London, 1964.

34. Treasure, John, 'Discussion opener', in: *Research in Marketing*, Market Research Society, London, 1964.

35. Gowers, Ernest, *The Complete Plain Words* (revised by Sir Bruce Fraser), HMSO, London, 1973.

36. Ehrenberg, A. S. C., 'Rudiments of numeracy', *Journal of the Royal Statistical Society*, vol. 140, part 3, 1977.

37. 'Market Research', Special Report, Mintel, London, 1990.

38. Benedy, Alex, 'Ethics man is good for business', *Sunday Telegraph*, 20 October 1991.

39. Lloyd, John, 'Ethics and business at loggerheads?', *Financial Times*, 10 June 1988.

40. White, David, 'Ethical policy can bear fruit', *Sunday Telegraph*, 19 March 2000.

41. McDonald, Colin, and Phyllis Vangelder, 'The changing context for research', *ESOMAR Handbook of Market and Opinion Research*, ESOMAR, Amsterdam, 1998.

42. 'Code of Conduct', Market Research Society, London, July 1999.

43. Reynolds, Joy, 'Guidelines for handling databases containing details of respondents or potential respondents and the conduct of identifies surveys', MRS Professional Standards Committee, Market Research Society, February 1995.
44. Bartram, Mary, and Peter Bartram, 'Ethical dilemmas of the market researcher: Where do we now draw the line?', *European Research*, vol. 16, no. 4, November 1988.
45. 'Data Protection Act 1998: An Introduction', the Data Protection Registrar, Wilmslow, 1998.
46. Savage, Mike, 'Balancing Act', *Research*, Marketing Research Society, London, 1999.

Appendix

Contents

- Sources of secondary data

Official information sources

Annual Abstract of Statistics: provides information on population, housing, manufactured goods, etc.

Monthly Digest of Statistics: similar to above but published at monthly intervals

Abstract of Regional Statistics: main statistics for Scotland

Digest of Welsh Statistics: main statistics for Wales

Economic Trends: monthly review of economic situation

Social Trends: collection of key social statistics covering demographic trends, income and wealth, education, employment, households and families, leisure, etc.; published yearly (ONS)

Financial Statistics: key UK monetary and financial statistics (monthly)

Digest of Energy Statistics (yearly)

Housing and Construction Statistics (quarterly)

Monthly Bulletin of Construction Statistics

Overseas Trade Statistics of the UK (monthly)

Family Expenditure Survey: annual detailed report which presents income and expenditure by type of household for the UK, and includes some regional analyses

General Household Survey: interdepartmental survey based on a continuous survey of UK households, and designed to measure household behaviour related to factors such as housing, health, employment and education (ONS)

National Food Survey: formerly the *Household Food Consumption and Expenditure Survey*; a continuous survey of UK household food consumption and expenditure; published by HMSO for the Ministry of Agriculture, Fisheries and Food (see Chapter 9).

Census of Distribution: last full census was in 1971 and census since replaced by the *Retail Inquiry*, conducted annually until 1980, and now every five years with small surveys in the intermediate years. *Retail Inquiry* provides estimates of numbers of businesses, outlets, employees, sales volume, gross margin, purchases and stocks, and capital expenditure, analysed by seven classifications of businesses

National Income and Expenditure 'Blue Book' (yearly)

Census of Production: conducted since the beginning of this century at approximately five-yearly intervals

Census of Population: full census every 10 years (ONS)

Annual Estimates of the Population of England and Wales and of Local Authority Areas (yearly)

Department of Employment Gazette (monthly)

Bill of Entry Service: Customs and Excise data

Business Monitors: detailed information about many important industries in the UK

Key Data: over 130 tables, maps and coloured charts, and range of social and economic data

Digest of Agriculture; Census Statistics UK 1992

Transport Statistics: Great Britain; published quarterly and annually

Retail Prices Index MM23 (monthly)

Population Trends (quarterly)

Key Population and Vital Statistics (annually)

Regio: describes the contents of the Statistical Office of the European Union's regional data-bank; available from the Statistical Office of the EU, L2920, Luxembourg

Europe in Figures: Eurostat; available from the Office for Official Publications of the EU, L2985, Luxembourg

Non-official sources of data

Non-official sources of data in the UK are plentiful and are published by trade associations, banks, academic institutions, the trade and professional press, and national newspapers, as well as survey reports by commercial research firms.

Sources of European Economic and Business Information, compiled by the University of Warwick Business Information Service, lists major sources of economic and statistical information by country across Europe (Gower Press). *The European Directory of Trade and Business Journals*, published by Euromonitor, is a comprehensive guide to over 2000 main business and trade journals which are useful and relevant to companies marketing goods and services in Western Europe.

Some specific sources of market data

National Press
The Economist; The Financial Times; The Times; The Daily Telegraph; Guardian; Sunday Times; Observer; etc.

Specialist publication
British Briefing replaced *British Business*, which ceased publication in September 1989. It is published by the British Chambers of Commerce and contains data covering business, travel and also DTI news.

Trade press and technical
Specialist journals cover almost every major industry and trade; some cater for highly specific segments. Typical examples are: *The Grocer; Chemist and Druggist; Packaging News; The Architect; Motor Trader; Applied Ergonomics; Footwear Weekly.* (Details can be found in *Willing's Press Guide* and *British Rate and Data Guide (BRAD)*.)

Subscription services
Mintel Market Intelligence Reports, published monthly, with useful cumulated index at end of each new issue; mostly concerned with consumer products. Mintel also publishes a quarterly *Retail Intelligence* and some special major studies of various market sectors.

ADMAP: monthly journal giving information and statistical data covering all advertising media with special thrice-yearly analyses of advertising expenditures by product categories and media.

Media Expenditure Analysis (MEAL): monitors advertising expenditure across all media and publishes detailed information related to product groups and individual advertisers.

The Economist Group, partly under the name The Economist Intelligence Unit (EIU), publishes, on a regular basis, reports on certain industrial sectors, e.g. the automotive industry, retail distribution, etc., as well as special reports on topics of current interest.

Retail Business and Marketing in Europe, published monthly, gives valuable coverage of specific aspects of markets; a series of printed indexes enable past data to be readily tracked and trends evaluated.

BLA Group publishes *Market Assessment* (bi-monthly) covering home, office and leisure market sectors in the UK, often useful for industrial market analysis.

Verdict Research publish survey-based retail reports covering, for example, mail order trading in the UK.

As a result of a management buy-out in 1984, *The Corporate Intelligence Group* was formed; this publishes ad hoc surveys for clients and an extensive range of research publications and reports.

Research publications include:

Europe's Top Retailers (2 volumes) – comprehensive profiles of 100 major European retailers (Corporate Intelligence Group-CIG).

Cross-border Retailing in Europe – comprehensive guide to the increasing internationalization of European retailing and retailers (CIG).

Europe's Top Food Retailers – profiles of the 180 leaders (CIG).

US Retailers in Europe: the New Wave (CIG).

DIY Retailing in Europe (CIG).

Specialist reports from CIG include:

Retail rankings – annual reference database of Britain's top 650 retailers with sales of £3–£8 billion.

Discount non-food retailing in the UK.

Future for factory outlet centres in the UK.

Petrol forecourt shops in the UK.

Convenience stores in the UK.

Euromonitor, established in 1972, has a business publications division for over 150 titles, and also offers research services based on a database of 500 researchers in 50 countries around the world. Its journals include:

Market Research Europe (monthly) which covers the major and secondary markets in Europe, and also amplified by special market reports;

Market Research International (monthly) covering global markets, trends and developments;

Retail Monitor International (monthly) which provides up-to-date company profiles, sector reviews, and retail fact-file;

Market Research GB (monthly) which concentrates on UK consumer markets.

Euromonitor publishes an extensive range of reference books and market direction reports covering a very wide range of specific product sectors in the UK, US, France, Germany, Italy, Spain, Latin America, Japan and South-East Asia.

Taylor Nelson Sofres publishes a range of reports with data derived from long-established activities in consumer markets, such as food, chemists, toiletries, cooking and eating, etc. Taylor Nelson Sofres was elected in 1995 as the UK member of the Gallup International Association, the network of Gallup affiliates worldwide.

The Financial Times Group includes a broadly based impartial business intelligence service covering all aspects of national and international industry and commerce.

FT Country Surveys: Basic details about a wide range of overseas countries, which have appeared regularly in *The Financial Times* are now available on disk to facilitate easy updating on the political and economic factors influencing business opportunities.

FT Information, comprising FT EXTEL, FT PROFILE and the Broadcast Monitoring Company – Lincoln Hannah (BMC), is one of the leading providers of business and specialist financial information in the world.

FT Information provides a wide range of on-line, CD-ROM and PC-based services and computer-readable data. Its financial information includes international securities and company data, financial news and taxation services, while the business information incorporates news, marketing, business opportunities, political and economic data.

FT EXTEL: Formerly Extel Financial, this long established business was acquired by *The Financial Times* Group in December 1993. It offers a comprehensive range of modern electronic financial and business information services.

Extel Market Data: FT EXTEL is the leading supplier of international market data to the fund valuation and administration operations of the global asset management community. The comprehensive range of data includes prices, dividend and interest payments, corporate announcements, market trading and settlement data, prospectus terms and conditions, classification, cross-reference and coding information. Instruments covered include equities, bonds, F/X rates, convertibles, warrants, options, futures, unit funds and indices. Data are provided in line with valuation points, from real-time through intra-day to end-of-day snapshots.

FT McCarthy: FT McCarthy, established for more than 25 years, examines over 70 international daily and weekly business publications to extract key articles on companies and industries. Sophisticated indexing systems provide rapid access to all the relevant articles on a company or industry. Access is available on-line through FT PROFILE in hard copy or on CD-ROM.

CD-ROM Publishing: Titles currently available include *The Financial Times*, *The Economist*, *The Independent*, *The Daily Telegraph*, *Quest Economics* and *FT McCarthy*. These titles can be ordered in one annual disk or with regular monthly or quarterly updates.

The Broadcast Monitoring Company – Lincoln Hannah (BMC): BMC is the UK's leading monitoring company, covering more than 700 print and broadcast sources worldwide. Company products include: a same day international press monitoring and translation service; verbatim transcripts of all news and current affairs programmes in the UK; an overnight UK press monitoring and reprint service, and full evaluation and analysis of media coverage.

For further information contact: The Broadcast Monitoring Company, 89 1/2 Worship Street, London EC2A 2BE, UK. Tel: (44) 171 247 1166; Fax: (44) 171 377 6103.

Special financial analyses

ICC Business Ratio Reports give specific information related to corporate efficiency.

Key Note Publications provide readily accessible reports on over 200 major UK markets.

Gower Press publish a valuable series of economic surveys covering several industries/markets.

Confederation of British Industries (CBI): quarterly and monthly reports covering UK manufacturing industry; also overseas reports (quarterly).

Yearbooks and directories

There are very many of these types of publication, some specializing in certain industries and others of a more general nature; some leading publications are:

Kelly's Directory of Manufacturers and Merchants (*UK Volume*)

Kompass – 4 volumes (UK) – valuable source for developing industrial samples, company profiles, etc.

Dun and Bradstreet – several directories including *Guide to Key Enterprises*, *International Market Guide*, and *British Middle Market Directory*. A major drawback is that these registers are based on companies, not establishments, so branch offices are omitted and subsidiary companies are not always recorded.

CBD Directory of UK Associations and *CBD Directory of European Associations* list under industry headings, relevant trade associations.

Times Top 1000 lists major British-based companies.

Advertisers Annual lists media, suppliers of advertising and promotional services, advertising agencies, and principal advertisers listed geographically.

Benn's Press Directory, in two volumes, gives details of printed media, e.g. regional newspapers.

BRAD (*British Rate and DATA*) (see Chapter 10).

Retail Directory (Newman) lists stores and other distributors' outlets.

Croner Publications give detailed and regularly updated business information covering commercial law, business strategy, EU data, etc.

TV audience reports

Available from individual television contractors and also specialist research agencies.

Professional institutions, etc.

The British Market Research Association (BMRA), 16 Creigton Avenue, London N10 1NU (www.brma.org.uk), is the trade association for organizations involved in providing market research services. It represents 80 per cent of all market research placed in the UK, currently around £1 billion.

Broadcasters' Audience Research Board Ltd (BARB), 18 Dering Street, London W1R 9AF (www.barb.co.uk). TV audience research co-ordinating body.

Chartered Institute of Marketing (CIM), Moor Hall, Cookham, Berkshire SL6 9QH.

ESOMAR (The European Society for Opinion and Marketing Research), Amsterdam, was founded in 1948, and has over 4000 members in 100 countries, both users and providers of research.

Institute of Practitioners in Advertising (IPA), 44 Belgrave Square, London SW1V 8QS.

National Readership Surveys Ltd, 42 Drury Lane, London WC2B 5RT (www.nrs.co.uk) is responsible for NRS surveys on press readership.

Advertising Association, Abford House, 15 Wilton Road, London SW1V 1NJ.

The Institute of Management (IM) – formerly entitled the British Institute of Management (BIM), Management House, Cottingham Road, Corby, Northants NN17 1TT.

Market Research Society, 15 Northburgh Street, London EC1V 0AH (www.marketresearch. org.uk). The MRS has over 8000 members in more than 50 countries, and is the largest international organization for researchers and others engaged in market, social and opinion research. In collaboration with NTC Publications, the MRS publish the *International Journal of Market Research* (quarterly). Other publications include *Research* (monthly), the *Researcher Buyers Guide* (annually), and other specialist publications.

Office for National Statistics (ONS), 1 Drummond Gate, London SW1V 2QQ (www. statistics.gov.uk).

Office of the Data Protection Registrar, Wycliffe House, Water Lane, Wilmslow, Cheshire SK9 5AF (www.dataprotection.gov.uk).

Association for Information Management (Aslib), 20–24 Old Street, London EC1V 9AP.

Association of British Chambers of Commerce, 4 Westwood House, Westwood Business Park, Coventry CV4 8HS.

British Standards Institution, Linford Wood, Milton Keynes MK14 6LE.

Business Statistics Office (BSO), Cardiff Road, Newport, Gwent NP9 1XG.

Central Office of Information (COI), Hercules Road, London SE1 7DU.

Commission of the European Communities Press Information Office, 8 Storey's Gate, London SW1P 3AT.

Companies House (Registrar of Companies), Crown Way, Maindy, Cardiff CF4 3UZ.

Department of Trade and Industry, 66–74 Victoria Street, London SW1E 6SW (and also regional offices).

Export Market Information Centre, 123 Victoria Street, London SW1E 6RB.

Office of Population Censuses and Surveys, St Catherine's House, Kingsway, London WC2B 6JP.

National Institute of Economic and Social Research, 2 Dean Tench Street, London SW1.

Barclays Bank Group, Economic Intelligence Unit, 54 Lombard Street, London EC3.

Lloyds Bank, Overseas Department, 5 Eastcheap, London EC3.

In addition, some of the larger Chambers of Commerce, e.g. London, Birmingham, and Manchester, may be able to provide very useful data related to specific industries. Local authorities, particularly the larger ones, may also be able to provide industrial and commercial data for their areas. Another useful source could be organizations that promote industry in specific regions, New Town Development Corporations, etc.

Companies House may also be relevant for certain types of enquiries; some leading firms of stockbrokers may have undertaken research into specific industries.

Leading commercial libraries

City Business Library, 55 Basinghall Street, London EC2V 5BX.

Science Reference Library, 25 Southampton Buildings, Chancery Lane, London WC2A 1AW.

Statistics and Market Intelligence Library, 1 Victoria Street, London SW1.

London Business School Library.

Manchester Business School Library.

Lancaster University, etc.

Civic commercial libraries.

In Chapter 12 (International Market Research), details were given of British Trade International's official services to exporters. Many of the publications listed in this appendix could be consulted in the Statistics and Market Information collection.

Overseas governments issue statistics and reports of use to marketing researchers. Some sources tend to be more reliable than others, and experienced researchers evaluate the information obtainable. Some of the larger research organizations, ACNielsen or Gallup, have overseas companies or associates which can provide accurate data in specific market areas.

Exploitation of all relevant and reliable sources of data during desk research should be the first step in marketing research. In some cases the information resulting from persistent and patient desk research, as noted earlier, may be sufficient for management's needs.

On-line services

These have grown spectacularly since the early 1980s and have revolutionized data collection by providing ready access to published information from virtually all over the world. Databases are of two types: (i) based on bibliographic sources such as reports, or abstracts, from newspapers and other journals; and (ii) numeric, consisting of statistical data on the economy, companies, international trade, etc.

Examples of the first category are: *Infoline Ltd*, which has many databases covering marketing, finance and credit checking, business intelligence and news, and British Trademarks and British Standards.

Examples of the second type are: *ICC Database* and the *Central Statistical Office* (*CSO*) which offers extensive data covering, for instance, population, manpower, and industrial products. *Datastar* is one of a number of 'host' on-line services which holds both bibliographic and numeric databases from several sources, such as *The Financial Times*.

On-line patents search is offered by the Patents Office, Newport, Gwent, covering extensive, specialized searches in patent literature at national and international levels. New product concepts can be checked against international technical trends and commercial developments. *British Standards database Standardline* contains bibliographical and subject details of all current British Standards, their amendments and drafts for comment. *Standardline* uses a basic file structure set up by ISONET (the International Organization for Standardization) – a worldwide network of national standards information centres. The most comprehensive source of standards information on-line is IHS (International Standards and Specifications) available on the host *Dialog*.

On-line searching can provide almost instant information on very many topics, but, as always, discretion should be exercised to ensure that relevant data are being accessed. Guidance is obtainable from Aslib and the *Directory of Online Databases*, published by Cuadra Associates, Inc. Another extremely useful reference guide to on-line databases is *On-line/CD-ROM Business Source Book* (eds) Pamela and Alan Foster (Headland Business Information, Headland, Cleveland).

McCarthy CD-ROM database (produced by FT Information Services) covers the full text of selected articles from *The Financial Times*, *The Economist*, *Investors' Chronicle*, *The Times*, etc. (see earlier reference under FT Information).

Kompass On-line, based on the well-known Kompass hard-copy directories, covers over 23 000 companies in Europe; it provides company name and address, telephone/telex numbers, description of business, number of employees, names of executives, and, where, feasible, sales figures.

On-line searches generally involve a computer access charge covering the time involved in the collection of specific information. To use on-line searches effectively, it would be advisable to train staff so that professional skills are acquired. While competition among on-line data suppliers has resulted in some price adjustments, the costs involved are still significant; full value should be derived through expert accessing.

Case studies

Contents

- How Tesco keeps the customer satisfied
- Music making in Britain
- Qualitative research in ethnic minority communities in Britain
- Mystery shopping's contribution to London Underground's investment decisions
- Market research and water supply
- Art sponsorship: the Tate Gallery

How Tesco keeps the customer satisfied

In the highly competitive grocery market in the UK, Tesco's reputation as shrewd marketers has risen substantially since those early days of 'pile it high and sell it cheap'. Over the past few years Tesco has developed from being generally perceived as running cut-price supermarkets to becoming a prime challenger to long-established grocery businesses, such as Sainsbury's. This remarkable metamorphosis has been effected as the result of radical changes inside the business, which were instigated by Terry Leahy, who at that time (1993) was marketing director.

This case study shows how this large grocery retailer went about the challenging task of changing its nature and direction, so that a loss of 3 per cent of their customers would be corrected and the whole business turned around. To achieve these objectives, a strategic plan, written by Terry Leahy and Tim Mason, was based on research which had earlier been conducted. They concluded that while there had been a lot done in the past to improve the over-all efficiency of the business, what was now missing was an emphasis on the customer and the benefits which they should be able to enjoy. It was decided that the company should be more responsive to the changing needs of customers. Research had indicated that customers liked businesses to be innovative and to give them 'best value'.

Tesco was faced with the demanding problem of becoming better and cheaper at the same time. Tim Mason noted that some competitors aimed to offer the best prices, others to provide the best food, whereas customers were believed to shop at Tesco 'for a lot of different reasons. Originally, it was because of a price/quality trade-off and price plus quality equals value'. However, it was now recognized that customers were 'a lot more sophisticated' and were influenced by far more variables when assessing value.

Tesco aimed to provide the 'best shopping trip'; this would be built up by paying detailed attention to a number of critical factors, such as pricing and promotional policies, product quality, store design, including location and car-parking facilities. The trading slogan was to be: 'Tesco is the best place for me to do my shopping'.

These initiatives included an analysis of 'core commodity products' and major branded lines, many of which were competitively re-priced. This was followed by certain key lines of vegetables and fruit, notably bananas, also being re-priced. About a year later – 1996 – Tesco tackled the problem of their in-store bakeries, whose products, as customers had consistently complained, were too expensive; price cuts were immediately introduced at all in-store bakeries. After these operations, a wider price-cutting exercise: 'Unbeatable value' was introduced; this involved about 600 core products, and was supported by the promise to refund twice the difference to customers if the same product could be bought elsewhere at a lower price.

Apart from planned pricing attractions, Tesco 'tried very hard to improve' the appearance of their stores, and also to reduce the costs of building them. New retailing ventures such as 'Compacts' – a bit smaller than the standard superstore and suitable for minor market towns; 'Metro', which has become familiar and very popular in high street locations, particularly in London; and 'Express' – an extremely popular convenience store and petrol station retailing format.

Tesco insist that it is always important to return to the question: 'What's in it for the customer?'; and to find out more about their customers, a programme called 'Listening to customers' was organized, and consumer panels have been in use for the past four years or so. Customers are 'recruited as they come through the checkouts' and are invited to return later to take part in panel discussions. These take place over three convenient time periods: post-lunch (for afternoon shoppers), at tea-time, and in the evening for later shoppers. Store management with one or two head office staff, invite customers to discuss openly their shopping experiences, expectations, etc. From these sessions, Tesco management are made aware of issues which are of concern to their customers; such matters may relate to in-store improvements like customer service desks or better-designed trolleys. Research revealed, for instance, that customers strongly disliked queueing but 'as long as there was only one person in front of them and they could be getting on with unloading, and they were busy, it was not a queue'. So Tesco launched the highly successful 'One in Front' initiative in 1994 to ensure that this type of service was available to their customers.

Another very successful introduction was the employment of 'customer assistants', whose function is directly to help customers in their shopping trips.

The introduction of the 'Clubcard' enabled Tesco to know more about their customers, from the database derived from around 8 million cards which have so far been issued. Customers are rewarded for their loyalty, and the scheme has been used by Tesco to 'promote and indeed defend stores', which may, for instance, have lost customers because of building activities. They have been written to regretting that they have ceased shopping at the local store, and have been invited to resume their custom now that the building problems are over. These types of close linkage with customers exemplifies Tesco's trading philosophy of thinking about customers as individuals, or at least, 'in smaller segments. There is no such thing as an average customer'.

'Clubcard plus', developed from the success of 'Clubcards', offered an 'unbeatable deal': 5 per cent on deposit, 9 per cent on borrowing and no minimum amount. Tim Mason stresses that the grocery supermarket industry is 'extremely fortunate because of its dynamics, to have data which are constantly refreshed'. It should, of course, be borne in mind that while database marketing (see Chapter 13), provides store operators with, for example, customer profiles and purchasing preferences, the information is restricted to particular stores and does not necessarily reflect what is going on in the world outside, nor does it cover the buying habits of non-card holders. However, the ways in which Tesco have developed through building close personal links with their customers, and so learned at first hand about their likes and dislikes through regular panel discussions, are clear indications of their commitment to keeping their customers satisfied.

This case study is distilled from Tim Mason, 'The best shopping trip? How Tesco keeps the customer satisfied', *Journal of the Market Research Society*, vol. 40, no. 1, January 1998, and is published with the permission of the Market Research Society.

Music making in Britain

In Chapter 11, marketing research methodologies were seen to have a valuable role in researching the arts, specifically in identifying patrons, and their living styles, media habits, travelling arrangements, etc. Theatres, concert halls, museums and other cultural centres could all benefit from relevant information about the interests and preferences of those whose patronage they wish to attract. For years, a well-known art gallery had no team room or coffee bar, while the choice of souvenirs was limited to a few postcards. These deficiencies were identified as the result of market research into the problems of declining patronage, and specific recommendations were made, which included the installation of a small bistro and a gift shop. These facilities were introduced and contributed markedly to the increasing number of visitors from a much wider age and social spectrum than formerly.

This case study focuses on another example of cultural activities, viz. music making, and describes how marketing research can effectively contribute to music education in Britain, particularly related to instrumental music tuition. Like many other specialized activities, music education has experienced radical changes over recent years. Free or unsubsidized instrumental music tuition has suffered heavily from public sector education cost-cutting exercises and radical changes in policies. Eventually, the music industry itself will feel the effects of these severe contractions in music education which, as will be seen, have an unequal social and geographic impact on school pupils in England and Wales.

For years – and until the late 1980s – local education authorities (LEAs) in England and Wales subsidized instrumental music tuition, which was generally available in almost all areas. This specialized teaching service had been provided by peripatetic tutors at no charge to the schools or, in many areas, without cost to the pupils. In the 1990s, schools and LEAs no longer had any statutory obligations to provide instrumental music education, while learning to play an instrument was not a specific part of the national curriculum.

There was a critical need for information about the nature of instrumental music education services across England and Wales; it was apparent that earlier research had concentrated on the service providers rather than the ultimate users – the child or adult who is learning to play an instrument. For almost half a century, LEA-supported music services had generally exercised a strong influence on what, how and where instruments should be featured in LEA schools. This approach was 'based on LEAs' educational ethos and knowledge that a grateful client would take advantage of what they offered'.

The Associated Board of the Royal Schools of Music (ABRSM) is the 'pre-eminent provider' of graded music examinations in the UK, as well as being a major provider of such services on a global scale. It is also a leading publisher of both examination and non-examination music.

By reason of its examination procedures, the ABRSM has ready access to information about the nature of the demand for its services related to musical instrument tuition, but it was felt that it needed to know about the *total* market for music making in the UK. It was decided that a strategic market research programme should be organized to determine the numbers and types of individuals aged 5 years and over who were involved in musical activities, what instruments they learned and played, and how many might be involved in such activities in the future. In addition, it was thought important to 'find out more about instrumental teachers: who they are, what they teach and up to what grades', as well as to identify their own particular professional needs which they considered were not being met.

These research objectives were covered in the following four studies:

1. A nationally representative survey of 1959 individuals aged 15 and over

2. A nationally representative sample of 858 children aged 5–15
   (*Both of these surveys involved face-to-face interviews*)

3. A mail survey of music teachers on ABRSM's register; this resulted in a 37 per cent response rate from 5000 sampled.

4. A series of group discussions with a cross-section of music teachers who taught different instruments.

From this well devised research – and for the first time – the total market for instrumental music in Britain was profiled. Among the findings, instrumental music making was seen to be a minority activity: only 45 per cent of all children claimed to be able to play a musical instrument; but only 26 per cent of adults were able to.

The propensity to have music tuition or to play an instrument was apparently significantly influenced by gender, social grade and geographic region, i.e. there was a distinct bias related to social status and place of residence. For instance, 56 per cent of children from AB socio-economic groups played a musical instrument, whereas only 35 per cent of the children of unskilled workers did so. The geographic variations are also marked: in the south, more than 50 per cent of children claimed to be able to play a musical instrument; in the Midlands, 46 per cent stated they could, and in the north, 38 per cent said they could. The researchers commented that these relative differences tended to persist in later life.

In addition, there was a significant gender bias: girls were one and a half times as likely as boys to have taken music lessons. Again, this bias persisted into adulthood, and women were one and a half times as likely as men to have ever had music tuition.

The report concluded that there is 'no doubt that access to both music and music lessons is directly correlated, with social status, gender and region.

A major finding of the research related to the age at which to start learning an instrument: if a child 'is not playing something by the age of eleven, the probabilities are that he or she will never learn to play'. Among child-players, five and six year olds were found to be the 'most enthusiastic to learn', but by seven years of age, the desire to play an instrument halved and the decline continued so that by 14, only 4 per cent said they were likely to start to play an instrument.

The researchers state that these survey findings have 'major policy implications'. It might, for instance, be advisable to review the current allocation of teaching resources between the primary and secondary sectors, since the present allocation of disproportionate resources to the latter may result in reinforcing the gender and social biases revealed by the research.

The research also showed that a change is occurring in the instruments played by children: the electronic keyboard is second only in popularity to the piano. Further, it not only reverses the general gender bias but also the social grade bias in music making. However, at the time of the research the ABRSM offered no graded examinations in the electronic keyboard, but this matter was later reviewed.

Analyses showed that children who play the least popular instruments are most likely to be taking music lessons, whilst the reverse applies to those playing the most popular instruments.

The researchers 'currently believe' that the electronic keyboard's popularity is principally due to two factors: the rising electronic gift market, 'where the pupil is having "fun" rather than seriously attempting to learn a musical instrument'; and the 'role of the school market where the electronic keyboard is a resource for the delivery of the national curriculum'.

There appears to be a 'potential mismatch' between what educational providers are offering and what is being played by young musicians, because at present there is a declining interest in the piano but more teachers are teaching it, while hardly any instrumental teachers are teaching electronic keyboard playing which, as noted, has grown so much in popularity.

Apart from these pragmatic views, the researchers reflected on the future prospects for music making, and they stated that market research points to a model of music making 'at variance with the current one'. Musicians of the future may create (and learn) music, at home, via their own computers and keyboards; they would be increasingly self-taught, and not be entirely dependent on traditional methods of music tuition.

Qualitative investigations during this extensive survey indicated that 'some music teachers, especially in the private sector without any specific teacher training qualifications, felt a real need for professional development'. There was also a general interest by teachers in the concept of a recognized professional qualification in music teaching. As a result of this finding, the ABRSM established the 'Professional Development Course for Instrumental and Singing Teachers' in 1995/96 at five locations in the UK, and which is a notable contribution to music education.

The market research data was also used by the Music Industries Association for political lobbying. Major sponsorship has also been provided by the ABRSM in support of the 'Music for Youth' organization.

As the market research exercise developed, the researchers admitted that rather like peeling an onion, after one layer had been removed, 'there is more and more to follow up'. Understandably, many issues remain to be investigated: trends in all aspects of music education need to be monitored, so that the needs of students, parents and teachers will be identified and recognized when policy decisions are being made.

This case study is distilled from Mike Cooke and Richard Morris, 'Music Making in Great Britain', *Journal of the Market Research Society*, vol. 38, no. 2, April 1996, and is published with the permission of the Market Research Society.

Qualitative research in ethnic minority communities in Britain

Local authorities are responsible for a wide variety of services: education, sports and cultural facilities such as libraries, and many other kinds of services. At one time, local authorities were in a virtually monopolistic situation, but increasingly alternative and commercially-motivated services have developed to meet the rising expectations of more affluent consumers. This trend is observable, for instance, in the growth of privately-run health and fitness centres.

But local authorities have largely retained responsibilities either as 'agents' for central government, or through their own direct remit, for specific and vital aspects of personal and community life within their areas. As noted in Chapter 11, marketing research has been used to investigate many problems affecting the well-being of particular groups of people, such as the elderly or those suffering from various kinds of disability. The application of marketing research to such issues is not surprising, for its survey principles and practices can be traced back to the social investigations carried out by pioneers like Booth and Rowntree, who were disturbed by the distressing working and living conditions of the working classes in Britain in those days.

Research among the ethnic communities of Britain has been undertaken by leading marketing research organizations: the Harris Research Centre at Taylor Nelson Sofres has focused on several matters of concern, for example, the incidence of unemployment among Black people in a London borough.

This case study gives guidance on the use of qualitative research when investigating ethnic minorities from diverse cultures and now resident in the London Borough of Newham.

In common with other local authorities, Newham Council provides many types of service, and it undertakes research to monitor public awareness, attitudes, and changing needs of the population in general. This task is made more complex because of the ethnic diversity within the borough. According to the 1991 Census, 42 per cent of the 212 170 population were from 'ethnic minority' communities, which form one of the highest concentrations in the UK. Complexity is compounded because Newham has no single dominant ethnic group, although 13 per cent of the total population is Indian and 7.2 per cent Black Caribbean. Hence, the range of languages spoken is extremely wide. This presented the Council with serious problems when, during their annual survey, attempts were made to identify and examine the opinions of these diverse ethnic groups. Survey data analyses are limited to a simple breakdown of White, Caribbean and Asian, so further opportunities to study in more detail the diverse ethnic population are severely limited.

However, the Council conducts a quarterly programme of qualitative research involving four focus groups, and these have been 'extremely successful' in exploring, on an area basis, matters like tenants' attitudes towards housing in advance of competitive tendering. But some problems were encountered, particularly among older ethnic people.

Focus groups (as discussed in Chapter 7), have become very popular in qualitative research, although their uninhibited adoption has led to concerns being expressed by experienced professional researchers in both the UK and the USA, and, to a lesser extent in Europe. Misgivings have been voiced, for instance, about the representativeness of the small numbers of participants involved in typical qualitative enquiries.

In this particular research project, the researchers were fully aware of the inherent problems of focus group research; these were identified as: sample design, recruitment and moderation. The sample design or composition of these focus groups was, of course, influenced by the nature of the topic being researched but it was complicated because of the many variations that existed within one specific ethnic group. For example, 'a group of young African men might include an affluent Nigerian doing postgraduate study, a recently arrived Somali refugee who speaks little English, and a mixture of Kenyan and Ugandan men with jobs as minicab drivers, who are trying to pay their way through college'. Such men are from countries with distinct cultures and histories and are geographically far apart; they have little in common except the colour of their skin. Problems may also arise from introducing into the same focus group a mixture of ethnic groups; some members may feel repressed when a topic is being discussed which is considered to be highly sensitive in their own communities.

Another salient issue is that of racism; research has shown that 'racist attitudes are not confined to any one ethnic group – respondents from any community may hold unfavourable attitudes about other ethnic groups, but are less likely to express these views in groups drawn from several ethnic origins'. It is recommended that group discussions among ethnic minorities should be separate from the white population, unless there are specific reasons to combine them.

Recruitment of focus group participants encountered difficulties with Asians for various reasons: failure to attend; arrival at meetings with their family and friends; lack of participation in group discussions, particularly by older women.

Moderation of a focus group is a skilled task; a facilitator or moderator plays a key role in encouraging individual members of a group to participate while, at the same time, diplomatically intervening if attempts are made to dominate discussions by any one member (see Chapter 7). Newham's past experience of organizing focus groups via interpreters had not been particularly successful, and moderators were, in effect, isolated from the flow of discussion. Hence they were incapable of fulfilling their vital function.

In view of the difficulties outlined, Newham Council recognized that a new approach to researching ethnic minority communities was needed. This should bear in mind that language was the primary factor in designing this type of research: the sample should be broken down into language groups rather than broader ethnic categories such as Asians or Indians. Having agreed this, the next step was to decide to focus, in depth, on a few communities rather than attempt to cover all of the local ethnic minority groups. To do so would invariably result in less depth of understanding about ethnic communities as a whole. It was also decided that, as the research progressed, other language communities, such as the Chinese, would be added.

Eventually, three ethnic groups were focused on during the initial stages of the research: Indians

(13 per cent of Newham's population), Pakistanis (5.9 per cent), and Bangladeshis (3.8 per cent). The first two groups represented long-settled communities, and in the last group were those who had recently arrived.

The next stage involved consideration of how these specific ethnic communities could be classified for research purposes. As with UK socio-economic groupings based on occupations (see Chapter 9), problems with ethnic research categories were also evident. Among South Asian populations, for instance, there are 'considerable gaps between the educational and employment backgrounds of parents and children'. Because of employment problems, social class may therefore be a less reliable indicator of the general outlook of ethnic respondents than their level of education. It was decided to recruit respondents of limited formal education, with little or no fluency in English, and in the broad age range of 25–45 (extended to 50 in one particular case), and either unemployed or manual workers. Those with total fluency were excluded, since it was feared that they would tend to 'unbalance' focus group discussions.

As noted, recruitment of participants presented some problems, but these were greatly reduced by advice from community and grass-roots workers. The Council's interpreting and translation staff also helped in the design of the sampling scheme, choice of suitable venues and the timing of the research sessions. As a result, attendance at the groups was high (80 per cent), and the levels of participation confirmed that consultation with those intimately involved in ethnic community life was very worthwhile.

Moderation of the groups has been seen to be of prime importance to the outcome of such research. The researchers consider that qualitative investigations among ethnic communities in Britain have much in common with international research (see Chapter 12), and it certainly seems that, to some degree, the problems of diverse cultures and languages are likely to complicate research activities in both cases.

In the Newham research, the role of moderator was not confined to running a group; beforehand, they had been fully briefed about the nature of the research and had suggested how the research plan could be adapted to meet the needs of particular focus group sessions. For instance, many Pakistanis prefer to speak Punjabi but have learnt to write in Urdu; this affects any written or audio-visual materials supplied.

The importance of non-verbal communication and of group dynamics was also recognized, so even though researchers might not understand what was being said, they attended some sessions in order to 'get the feel' of the discussions. These experiences helped in later reading of the transcripts.

After the fieldwork was completed, the next task was translation of the transcripts. This work was entrusted to the moderators, who were debriefed collectively, and encouraged to give their impressions of the dynamics, etc., of their groups.

The following 'methodological implications' resulted from this qualitative research among the diverse ethnic communities of Newham.

1. Such research involves more than just getting the language right;
2. Conventional demographic variables should be carefully considered before applying them to such research;
3. Community networks are more successful in recruiting suitable participants than in-street recruiting or door-knocking;
4. Mother-tongue moderators produce higher quality data than that from interpreters.

Key findings of this research are, briefly, that although language problems were evident, a far broader range of issues needed attention; such as the following.

1. Level of awareness
2. The message
3. Level of literacy
4. Language
5. Medium
6. Delivery
7. Monitoring

Mere translation of existing information leaflets, etc., into ethnic community languages is not sufficient. If effective communication with non-English speaking residents is intended, other factors should be given attention, such as the purpose and content of messages, awareness of the specific types of people who are expected to read and understand the content of such messages, the methods of communication used, and some system of monitoring the impact of these messages.

The text of such messages should be written so that it is easily understood, in whatever language is used. 'Officialese' should be avoided; the style should be appropriate for the known level of literacy.

Although translation of written material is the usual method used by public authorities to give information to non-English speaking residents, the research found that oral communication was preferred by many residents, including those who spoke English. 'Intermediaries' were often used (family, friends, community workers, etc.) in dealing with officials, such as housing officers. This particular insight led the Council to strengthen its links with community-based organizations which offer oral advice and advocacy services.

The effective distribution of official information was, as noted, an important factor in successful communication with ethnic communities. Although a great deal of effort, and considerable costs, had gone into translation and printing of leaflets, comparatively little of this printed information reached those it was intended to help. Newham Council established, therefore, 'The Network', which consisted of some 80 voluntary and community organizations who agreed to take and display official material.

The responsibilities of monitoring were projected as extending beyond checking whether specific population groups had received and read various leaflets, but should also entail the systematic study of the aspirations, behaviour and needs of ethnic groups, so as to guide Council policies and actions affecting these communities.

This case illustrates how a qualitative research technique, viz. focus groups, can be used in developing insights into the needs of ethnic minority groups in an English borough, where diversity of cultures, including several languages, added to the complexity of the research project. It showed that, despite many problems, some worthwhile findings enabled the Council to improve its level of communication with its diverse ethnic community.

This case study is distilled from Andrew Sills and Philly Desai, 'Qualitative research amongst ethnic minority communities in Britain', *Journal of the Market Research Society*, vol. 38, no. 3, July 1996, and is published with the permission of the Market Research Society.

CASE STUDY 4

Mystery shopping's contribution to London Underground's investment decisions

Over the past twenty years or so, mystery shopping (or mystery customer research) has become increasingly used, notably by the service industries, including banks, travel organizations and public transport operators. As noted in Chapter 2, around 120 research agencies in the UK were listed in the 1998/99 edition of the *Research Buyers' Guide* as offering mystery shopping services; in 1994, only 28 firms were listed. This significant increase reflects the growing importance of the service sector in people's lives, as well as in the national economy.

A brief account of London Underground's use of mystery shopping was given earlier in this text, but the discussion will be extended because of the sophisticated application of this technique in the development of large-scale investment decisions taken to improve the efficiency and levels of customer satisfaction in this major transport system.

Basically, mystery shopping is a type of participant observation which, when undertaken by trained and skilful researchers, makes a unique contribution to the total research effort. It has its roots in cultural anthropology, where a researcher interacts with those who are being observed. In the field of marketing research, interviewers, posing as shoppers or potential clients, note carefully specific aspects of their experiences when seeking, for example, information about holiday travel or hotel accommodation. By this technique, an evaluation can be made of the complete service offered to a typical client. This would involve observing the behavioural elements of the transaction, as well as the economic or factual details, such as price, location, etc. A satisfactory deal for a customer will be made up of an acceptable mix or blend of these two elements. Customer satisfaction surveys provide, of course, some useful information, but such surveys lack the evidence which an experienced mystery shopper is able to gather during a typical buying experience.

The London Underground system, part of London Transport, is responsible for managing and operating the underground public transport network in and around London. It is the oldest underground rail system in the world; the first section of the underground railway began operating in 1863.

London Transport has the following marketing objectives:

1. To increase public transport's market share by stimulating new travel, attracting travel from private motorists and retaining existing customers

2. To improve continuously the satisfaction of existing and new customers.

These objectives can only be achieved by improvements in the quality of the services offered, so that attitudes towards public transport will be favourably influenced, and public transport will be perceived as an acceptable alternative to car travel, rather than as a 'mode of last resort'.

Research by London Underground identified six key factors which influenced customers' attitudes towards the network and affected the use of the service. Briefly, these were:

1. A reliable and regular service

2. Co-ordination and integration of various public transport networks

3. An ambience or environment which projects a sense of order, structure, control and efficiency

4. Security and safety

5. Professional staff holding positive attitudes towards customers

6. Provision of timely, consistent and relevant information.

It was acknowledged that these objectives were feasible only by sustained investment and commitment. As might be expected, expenditure tended to be determined by safety and maintenance requirements, while heavy investment was also made in the extension of underground lines as well as the development of new lines, interchanges and stations.

In order to check the level and consistency of their service to passengers, London Underground adopted a 'mystery shopping' approach and trained independent customer-service auditors (i.e. mystery shoppers) acted, anonymously, as Underground passengers. Four times a year, teams of these auditors travel the network in pairs, following strictly specified routines and assessing by 26 performance factors related to trains, and 116 performance factors concerned with stations. These mystery shopping measures are as follows:

Stations
Cleanliness and environment
Lighting and brightness
Temporary and short-term information
Permanent and long-term information
Electric and electronic information
Comfort factors
Customer facilities
Ticket purchase and use
Staff
Customer mobility
Access

Trains
Cleanliness and environment
Brightness and comfort
Maps and information
Permanent and long-term information
Electric and electronic information
Public address
Staff
Safety
General impression
Personal safety

The routes followed by the mystery shoppers are carefully planned so that they result in at least seven visits to each platform of the 246 London Underground stations. Researchers are instructed in the nature of the rating scale and its usage. Some attributes can be readily verified, for example, whether information is accurate or the number of ticket machines in use. In other cases, a degree of subjectivity may, admittedly, influence judgements, such as in assessing the appearance of the station and staff, as well as the product knowledge, politeness or helpfulness of the latter. This subjectivity is minimized by relating descriptive phrases to positions on the rating scale, as shown with reference to the 'politeness of staff'.

10. Excellent – very courteous. Smiling and eye contact; conversations maintained

9. –

8. Polite manner – smiling

7. –

6. Polite manner – perhaps lacking smile/welcome

5. –

4. Polite approach, business-like, but not enough eye contact or conversation

3. –

2. Impersonal or brusque: very little eye contact or conversation

1. –

0. Abrupt or rude: no eye contact, very little conversation.

New mystery shoppers are trained by being accompanied by supervisors on 'dummy runs'; in addition, on about 8 per cent of the routes measured, spot-checks are done on shoppers or they are accompanied by a supervisor. A typical mystery shopper's route consists of six station visits with five train assessments taking place while travelling between stations. At station level, the following factors are noted: trip directions, train types, lines serving the stations/number of platforms, number of booking halls, days of week, peak vs off-peak.

The results of mystery shopping researches are weighted to take account of the number of passengers passing through a station or travelling on a line, and how long the average passenger spends in the booking hall, routeway, platform or train.

After each wave of research, the results are distributed to over 100 members of the operational management of stations and tracks, who use the mystery shopping scores to set targets for staff and contractors, as well as devising methods of improving operational efficiency in general. The data are also used by line development managers and corporate planners as inputs into proposals for capital investment.

Although the mystery shopping scores are recognized as valuable data, they are not sufficient in themselves to warrant network improvements, and other factors have to be borne in mind. For example, the availability of public telephones on Underground platforms may be given a poor shopping score because most passengers do not regard this facility as particularly important. Hence, it is not viewed by management as a matter needing further investment.

London Underground have, therefore, designed a Value Improvements Model which quantifies the benefits of potential changes and so enables priorities to be established. The three main inputs to this model are:

1. The current level of service delivery as measured by mystery shopping scores
2. Current traffic flows or passenger numbers
3. Passenger priorities measured by the values placed by passengers on improvements.

These priorities are derived from 2250 interviews with passengers and potential passengers, using trade-off analysis and conjoint analysis (see Chapter 13). By these techniques, the value of a specific improvement in each of the service attributes is calculated according to how much extra passengers would be willing to pay for such an improvement in each of these elements. For instance, some passengers might be willing to pay an extra 1p per journey for some general improvements in the cleanliness of a station, while to achieve 'reasonably clean everywhere' might be considered to be worth twice as much, i.e. 2p. But to reach a state of 'spotlessly clean everywhere' could be thought worth only a ½p more. These kinds of customer-evaluated opinions are combined with the number of journeys made on specific rail lines and result in overall improvement scores. In this way, investment proposals can be ranked from information based on relative values as perceived by passengers.

To check the reliability of the scores obtained as a result of mystery shopping research, London Underground used regression analysis to see what, if any, relationship existed between changes in mystery shopping scores and levels of customer satisfaction (see Chapter 13). The latter is measured by around 2300 face-to-face interviews, using rating scales, which are conducted every four weeks with passengers who have just completed a journey on the Underground.

Regression analysis was then applied to the data from mystery shopping research and that resulting from the 'customer-satisfaction' interviews. Results showed that for every one-point change in the overall mystery shopping score there was an increase of 0.9 in the average customer-satisfaction score. Although there was a relationship between scores on individual scores, it was weaker than that between average scores. Taken as a whole, statistical proof supported the use of mystery shopping research and indicated that changes in shopping scores feed through to variations in levels of customer satisfaction. London Underground felt that these findings confirmed the value of their specific research activities.

This case shows how a major transport undertaking has applied a mix of research techniques to obtain data to guide investment decisions. Further, they submitted the results derived from complementary methods of research to statistical testing, in order to check the legitimacy and productivity of their research activities.

This case study is distilled from Alan Wilson and Justin Gutmann, 'Public transport: the role of mystery shopping in investment decisions', *Journal of the Market Research Society*, vol. 40, no. 4, October 1998, and is published with the permission of the Market Research Society.

CASE STUDY 5

Market research and water supply

In 1989 the ten water authorities of England and Wales became public limited companies with extensive responsibilities for water supply, land drainage, sewage disposal and water recreational facilities. These undertakings are answerable to a statutory body: OFWAT, which was set up by the government to regulate the water industry. OFWAT has far-reaching powers connected with the quality of water supplies, more efficient methods of sewage treatment, as well as the development of higher standards in water conservation by better management of reservoir stocks, and also through encouraging the adoption of domestic water meters. Apart from Welsh Water, the rest of the ten major water and sewerage companies in England and Wales automatically meter new properties, and in 1997–98, 11 per cent of households in England and Wales had a water meter. Official statistics show that consumption of water (litres per head per day) is markedly lower in metered than in unmetered households, over all the ten water authorities' regions (*Social Trends* 30, ONS, 2000).

Anglian Water were concerned about public distrust of the water industry following privatization, and which appeared to persist. So in the summer of 1982, their corporate relations office decided to embark on a full-scale television advertising campaign to tackle this perceptual problem. Millward Brown, a highly regarded marketing research company, was approached and asked to provide a means of monitoring the effectiveness of the projected TV advertising campaign. As a result, and in October 1992, Anglian Water's continuous Advanced Tracking Programme (ATP) came into being (see Chapter 10). Since that date, on-going levels of customer satisfaction and corporate imagery have been monitored every four weeks among 400 Anglian Water customers (some of the critical findings are discussed later).

At around the same time, the business planning function of Anglian Water was facing another kind of problem; this involved the ceiling to be placed on projected increases in water charges for approval by OFWAT. It had already been hinted by OFWAT that

apart from 'obligatory expenditure' – to finance service improvements – the water companies were expected to draw little or no extra revenue from their customers, *unless* they could show that people were willing to pay more to meet additional investments which would result in improvements to the service provided to them.

On Millward Brown's advice, a programme of trade-off research was developed in order to evaluate the degree of customers' tolerance for price increases over and above those related to 'obligatory expenditure'. The research also sought to find out what (if any) services customers should benefit from as a result of the extra charges.

Customers' priorities were explored over five months of qualitative research to determine which of the three investment options, which had emerged from the trade-off study, was preferred. A £14 tolerance limit for bill increases was confirmed as acceptable, and there was also general agreement for their stated priorities for investment.

Following this qualitative research and a pilot quantitative study, Millward Brown, in March 1993, conducted a face-to-face consultation with 1300 Anglian Water customers. The agency worked closely with CACI to produce a stratified random sample of 130 enumeration districts (EDs) proportionate to the population spread of Anglian Water's administrative areas. Stratification was by ACORN profiles – see Chapter 10 for details of ACORN classifications – to ensure a representative spread of neighbourhood types. Within each ED, interviewers operated a quota sample, based on regional census data for each administrative area, covering age, sex, and the presence of children.

An abridged version of the original trade-off research methodology, involving a sample of 1000, was commissioned by Anglian Water in June 1994, shortly before the water companies announced their new charges. The findings showed that while customers' investment priorities remained virtually unchanged, there was a significant decrease in their overall willingness to pay for extra service improvements: viz. from an average of £14, there was a fall to about £12.50. This decline could not be attributed to the adjustments to the research methodology which had taken place, and the underlying reason was discovered from examination of Millward Brown's ATP continuous research data.

This trend data was linked with specific advertising campaigns in February–March 1993 and May–June 1993. Feedback indicated that Anglian Water's corporate image had improved significantly during the first campaign and had then levelled off. The first advertisement was a 'soft sell' approach, mentioning the quality checks the company made on drinking water supplies; the later advertisement also adopted a sensitive approach, but the topic was household waste disposal, perhaps a rather unattractive theme. The decline in favourable perceptions of Anglian Water also coincided with unfavourable press comment following their decision to pursue a policy of compulsory water-metering.

Further, the initial 'soft sell' promotion on television had been supported by other forms of publicity, such as leaflets, which were mailed to all customers separately from their water bills. However, the same high level of promotional support was not maintained with later TV advertising.

Anglian Water then decided to pursue their policy decision to enforce water-metering by arranging for a series of TV advertisements between December 1993 and June 1994. The campaign format of the earlier advertisements was used, but this latest campaign was by no means as successful. ATP data indicated that the reason for this was a dramatic decline in people's perceptions that the water company had 'customers' best interests at heart'. A serious credibility gap was caused by the proposal to make domestic water meters compulsory; this unfavourable reaction was inflamed by sustained and hostile press comment.

The net effect of the TV metering campaign was to increase public awareness but to harden attitudes against the proposal. It is instructive to note that ATP research showed that 'Don't knows' about the issue fell sharply from 23 per cent (December 1993–January 1994) to 9 per cent (February–April 1994), and most of those in this category switched to negative views: 'not a very good idea', and 'a bad idea'.

From these various research studies, Anglian Water accepted that:

(a) It is better to stick to incontrovertible messages on television

(b) Rather than occasional 'bursts' on television, a continued presence is likely to reduce vulnerability to negative PR

(c) Advertising is part of the total promotional effort, so campaigns should make use of supporting media, especially leaflets

(d) Controversial and sensitive issues like water-metering are better handled by alternative communication methods (PR, 'road shows', print, etc.) which allow such cases to be presented more fully.

With the prospect that compulsory water-metering might have to be adopted in the future, Anglian Water thought that it was important to know what were the views of actual meter users compared with those who had not had meters installed. ATP data over January–September 1994 revealed that metered customers strongly favoured the system (39 per cent 'a very good idea'; 38 per cent 'quite a good idea'). However, of non-users, who accounted for about 90 per cent of all domestic customers, 20 per cent thought meters 'a bad idea', and 18 per cent 'not a very good idea'; so water meters still suffered an image problem. Users, of course, gave opinions based on actual experience, and this reinforced their favourable perceptions. Presumably their water bills were noticeably lower.

This case study shows how a large utility company supplying vital services was able to gain insights into its customers' opinions and attitudes from the use of continuous marketing research. With Millward Brown's professional help, an effective system of monitoring its retail market was introduced, and was directly productive in providing objective data, from which valuable data were derived to guide policy making. Marketing research's portfolio of research instruments can be applied to a very wide variety of problems and markets, as this case indicates.

This case study is distilled from Graham Kerr and Edward Fox, 'Anglian Water: improving customer service: the fragility of perceptions', Research Works 3, NTC Publications Ltd, Henley-on-Thames, 1996, and is published by permission of the publishers.

Art sponsorship: the Tate Gallery

As a social and economic phenomenon sponsorship is not, of course, new: in Victorian England, for example, the brass bands of industrial towns were largely supported by the local collieries and mills, whose names they proudly featured. Later, large-scale sponsorship grew rapidly with the professionalization of sport. From the mid 1950s, when commercial television was introduced into Britain, sponsorship of sporting activities developed strongly, so that virtually every kind of sport – prestigious golf tournaments, classic horse racing, tennis tournaments, league football, and eventually even cricket – has eagerly sought sponsorship to augment revenues and provide opportunities for expansion.

In the rather less vigorous recreational interests offered by the arts, sponsorship has been sought by several organizations committed to the propagation of drama, musical concerts, museums and art galleries. Some of these cultural activities exist precariously, relying on grants from public bodies such as the Arts Council or other external sources of income. Several of them would not, however, be able to survive without the generous support of individual or corporate sponsors. Planning to attract sponsorship is now part and parcel of management responsibilities in almost all museums, art galleries and other related cultural activities.

Britain's rise to prominence as a global centre for an exceptionally wide variety of cultural life has owed much to the success with which sponsorship schemes have been pursued by the new generation of arts management. In London, in particular, the rich diversity of the arts has added greatly to its attractions to visitors from all over the world. The museums and art galleries of London are virtually household names, among which the Tate Gallery is likely to be readily recalled. It is one of the most popular tourist attractions and, according to *Social Trends* 30 (ONS, 2000), visitors to the gallery increased from 900 000 in 1981 to almost 2.5 million in 1998.

One of the leading market and opinion research firms, Market and Opinion Research (MORI), has worked closely with the Tate Gallery since 1993 on research related to arts sponsorship. Before MORI's linkages with the gallery, which resulted in on-going market research, most arts sponsors evaluated their sponsorship by the number of times it received media coverage. This relatively simplistic method gave very little insight into the many facets of arts sponsorship and its effects on audiences, visitors, etc. To stay ahead in competitive conditions (after all, visitors have many alternative attractions competing for their attention), it is vital to adopt a more sophisticated method of showing that arts sponsorship enables sponsors to reach key target audiences and to influence their perceptions and attitudes.

At the Tate Gallery, in 1990, a special Development Office was set up with a remit covering all aspects of private-sector funding for the gallery from individuals, Trusts and Foundations and corporate funding, including corporate membership.

In the autumn of 1993, and after considering several proposals, MORI was commissioned by the Tate's Development Office to undertake an on-going research programme. The following three key audiences were identified as relevant to the gallery's exhibition sponsorships.

1. Existing and potential sponsors
2. Visitors
3. Opinion leaders (MPs; captains of industry; editors of national broadcast and print media).

It was realized that the expectations and needs of these three key audiences would vary and that they would be likely to have different attitudes towards the critical issues connected with sponsorship. As in other market research fields, it was important to research these behavioural factors, so that they could be approached with sponsorship packages tailored to the needs of their organizations.

Likewise, it was vital to know about the expectations and opinions of visitors to the Tate Gallery concerning sponsorships, including details like the size of logos, and the extent to which they felt that commercial sponsorship was compatible with the type of art they had come to view. Also, they could give some indication of the effectiveness of sponsorship in making them aware of the sponsors' business activities.

Opinion leaders are influential in the formation of attitudes in general towards issues, including arts sponsorship, but these people are difficult to reach through conventional forms of advertising. However, they can often be targeted effectively through corporate hospitality events. It was considered essential that these élite audiences should be researched.

The resultant research objectives were organized in two broad groups: *market-based* and *sponsorship-oriented*.

The first category of objectives included:

Identifying variations in visitor profiles by time of year, exhibition being shown, etc.

Understanding what motivates visits to the Tate Gallery and considering how these could be influenced by marketing activities by the gallery and by sponsors

Defining key media for the Tate and its sponsors in order to target general visitors about specific exhibitions

Examining the role of exhibitions in building up the visitor base and in developing loyal and long-term commitment from visitors.

The second category of objectives included:

Examining visitor awareness of sponsors and sponsorships, and measuring opinions of sponsorship at the Tate

Examining whether the Tate is currently giving information about sponsors in suitable and effective ways

Understanding how sponsors judge sponsorship-value to enable the Tate to provide useful feedback

Gauging views of the Tate among the three key audience groups identified

Establishing attendance at Tate hospitality functions by opinion leaders, and gauging their perceptions of the Tate in that context

Examining views of sponsorship in general and its role and value in the context of the arts and, in particular, the Tate Gallery.

The methods of data collection used for each of the three key audiences were selected for their appropriateness and cost-effectiveness.

Existing and potential sponsors were researched by means of in-depth interviews at their place of business; the information sought was concerned with understanding why organizations became involved in arts sponsorship in general and, in particular, of the Tate. Transcripts of the recorded interviews were subjected to rigorous content analysis to identify salient issues and concerns facing current and potential sponsors.

Visitors to the Tate Gallery were researched in three phases during the year: each phase consisted of interviews with over 250 visitors. Information collected covered profiles, awareness of and attitudes towards sponsorship, specific sponsors, and various aspects of sponsorship such as size of logos and brand sponsoring. Interviews took place when visitors had completed their visits and had the opportunity to evaluate their experiences.

Elite audiences were surveyed by face-to-face interviews, which were linked with MORI's Corporate Communications Programme involving a number of multi-client surveys among audiences of this nature.

From this extensive and independent sponsorship research programme the following findings resulted.

Sponsors: a great deal of information was gathered to help the gallery provide a superior service for its sponsors; the Tate's image was that of an innovative, high quality and professional organization which offers opportunities to target key opinion leaders effectively. Sponsors expect to receive appropriate crediting of their sponsorship.

Opinion leaders: entertaining at the Tate is seen as a privilege which is exclusive to current sponsors and corporate members, and this policy was confirmed as acceptable. The Tate is recognized to be the most popular venue among all the major London arts organizations (not only museums and galleries) for attendance by MPs (doubtless its location close to the Houses of Parliament influenced this opinion). Among captains of industry, the Tate was ranked the third most popular corporate entertaining venue. Clearly, the Tate is regarded as one of the most prestigious art venues in London for corporate events.

Visitors: continuous surveys (as described earlier) had enabled the Tate to track a wide range of visitor information, including profiles, attitudes, etc. Visitors are upmarket and almost half are under

35 years of age; this is vital information for certain brand sponsors. Research also tracked how audiences change according to the time of year, and enabled the Tate to explore whether those issues which were regarded as important by sponsors were considered appropriate by visitors; for example, attitudes towards logos – which most visitors accepted as being about the right size – although they were strongly against product promotion in the gallery. Attitudes towards sponsoring organizations are generally favourable, and rarely less than positive. Visitors are well aware of the benefits of sponsorship to both sponsors and the Tate. While the former benefit from publicity and the enhancement of their corporate image, the latter derive financial support which includes support for exhibitions and for buying new works of art. Essentially, visitors perceive no conflict between the art and educational role of the gallery and the commercial support arising from sponsorship.

The results of this research are distributed to senior staff of the gallery, and the information is used in the various departments to improve facilities and provide appropriate services to visitors, whose expectations and needs have been thoroughly researched. The Tate also acquired accurate information about their audiences which enables them to provide targeted and highly specific information.

Finally, the cost–benefit ratio to the Tate in the financial year following this research was in the region of 1 : 20 (i.e. £20 realized for every £1 invested in the research programme).

This case study indicates how marketing research was used most effectively to produce information for the development of sponsorship at a major London art gallery which faced the challenge of finding new sponsors to support their art exhibitions. The well-devised research design contributed significantly to the success of this highly productive research.

This case study is distilled from Lynn Roseman, Andrea Nixon, and James Hudson, 'The Tate Gallery: research underpins record-breaking sponsorship', Research Works 3, NTC Publications Ltd, Henley-on-Thames, 1996, and is published with the permission of the publishers.